AN INTRODUCTION TO
W I S D O M
AND POETRY
OF THE OLD TESTAMENT

AN INTRODUCTION TO

WISDOM

AND POETRY

OF THE OLD TESTAMENT

DONALD K. BERRY

BROADMAN
&HOLMAN
PUBLISHERS

Nashville, Tennessee

0-8054-1999-3

Dewey Decimal Classification: 223.007
Subject Heading: BIBLE. O.T. WISDOM LITERATURE \ BIBLE.
O.T. POETICAL BOOKS
Library of Congress Card Catalog Number: 94-45302

Typography by TF Designs

Originally published in hardcover (1995) but no longer available.
Previously the Library of Congress has cataloged the hardcover edition as follows:

Library of Congress Cataloging-in-Publication Data
Berry, Donald K.
    Introduction to wisdom and poetry of the Old Testament / Donald K. Berry.
      p. cm.
    Includes bibliographical references and index.
    ISBN 0-8054-1547-5
    1. Wisdom literature—Criticism, interpretation, etc. 2. Wisdom—Biblical
teaching. I. Title.
    BS1455.B394   1995   94-45302
    223'.061—dc20   CIP

ISBN 0-8054-1999-3 (pbk.)

to the Memory of

Dr. Edward Beaven

Who introduced me to the study of

Hebrew wisdom

Contents

List of Abbreviations . . . . *xiii*
List of Tables . . . . *xv*

PART ONE: WISDOM

Introduction: A Preliminary Definition of Wisdom *1*

The Beginning Point
A Canonical Approach
General Characteristics of Wisdom
A Working Definition of Wisdom
Wisdom as Training for Leaders
Wisdom as a Corrective to Torah
Wisdom as Training for Children
Summary: Multiple Perspectives

1. *Overview of Wisdom* *11*
Wisdom Features in Job, Proverbs, and Ecclesiastes
Wisdom Outside the Wisdom Canon
Wisdom Themes and Vocabulary
The Sociological Setting of Wisdom
Summary: *Identification of Wisdom Materials*

2. *Ancient Near Eastern Wisdom Documents* *29*
Introduction: The International Character of
    Wisdom Documents
Egyptian Documents

Canaanite Documents
Greek Documents
The Special Character of Hebrew Wisdom
Summary: The Pervasiveness of Wisdom in Israelite Society

3. *History of Interpretation Before the Reformation* *43*
    Introduction: The Later Wisdom Tradition in Israel
    Wisdom in the Deuterocanon and Pseudepigrapha
    Early Jewish Interpretations
    Wisdom in the New Testament
    Wisdom in Patristic Literature
    Wisdom in Medieval Literature
    Summary: General Trends

4. *History of Interpretation Since the Reformation* *77*
    Introduction: The Reformation and Freedom of Interpretation
    Interpretation During the Reformation Period
    Interpretation after the Reformers
    Historical-Critical Interpretation
    Suggestions Regarding the Origins of Hebrew Wisdom
    Road to Definition
    Latest Trends in Interpretation
    Summary: A Future of Specialization

5. *Wisdom Books Outside the Wisdom Canon* *97*
    Introduction: The Search for Wisdom Outside the Wisdom Canon
    Wisdom in the Torah
    Wisdom in the Former Prophets
    Wisdom in the Latter Prophets
    Wisdom in the Writings
    Deuterocanonical Works
    Summary: The Encompassing Nature of Wisdom

6. *Wisdom in Proverbs* *117*
    Introduction to Proverbs
    Major Themes in Proverbs
    Themes in Proverbs 1–9
    Themes in Proverbs 10–31
    Summary: Proverbs as a Wisdom Anthology

7. *Wisdom in Job* *141*
    Introduction to Job
    The Structure and Meaning of Job
    Summary: The Literary Structure of Job

8. *Wisdom in Ecclesiastes* *157*
    Introduction to Ecclesiastes
    Qoheleth's Purpose and Philosophy
    Qoheleth's Findings
    Qoheleth's Special View of Wisdom
    Summary: Qoheleth's Contribution to the Wisdom Canon
    Conclusion: A Canonical Definition of Wisdom

PART TWO: POETRY

Introduction to Poetry *173*

   Distinctions Between Hebrew and Western Poetry
   Distinguishing Hebrew Poetry from Prose
   Use of Poetry in Ancient Israelite Society

9. *Overview of Poetry* *185*
    The Poetry of Psalms
    The Poetry of Lamentations
    The Poetry of the Song of Songs
    Poetry in Nonpoetic Books
    The Poetry of Deuterocanonical Wisdom
    The Nature of Hebrew Poetry
    Poetry in Israel's Life and Worship
    Types of Hebrew Poetry
    Israel's Employment of Poetry
    Summary: Poetry at the Extremes of Life

10. *Ancient Near Eastern Poetic Documents* *221*
    Poetry in Egypt
    Poetry in Canaan
    Poetry in Mesopotamia
    Summary: Israel's Loose Dependence on Other Poetry

11. *History of Interpretation Before the Reformation* *233*
    The Later Poetic Traditions in Israel
    Early Jewish Interpretation
    Poetry in Patristic Literature
    Poetry in Medieval Literature
    Summary: Scripture First, Poetry Second
    Questions for Discussion

12. *History of Interpretation Since the Reformation* *263*
     Precursors to the Reformation
     The Reformers
     Post-Reformation Interpretation
     Historical-Critical Interpretation
     Latest Trends in Interpretation
     Distinctives of Hebrew Poetry
     Summary: The Shape of the Canonical Text

13. *Poetry Outside the Poetic Canon* *299*
     Poetry in the Torah
     Poetry in the Former Prophets
     Poetry in the Latter Prophets: Major Prophets
     Poetry in the Latter Prophets: Minor Prophets
     Poetry in the Wisdom Books
     Poetry in Other Books of the Writings
     Poetry in the Deuterocanon
     Summary: Poetry Outside the Poetic Canon

14. *Poetry in the Psalms* *357*
     Introduction to Psalms
     Form Criticism and the Psalms
     Characteristics of Individual Psalms
     The Canonical Context of the Psalms
     Summary: The Role of the Psalms in the Community

15. *Poetry in the Song of Songs* *383*
     Introduction to the Song of Songs
     The Structure of the Drama
     The Song as Poetry and Wisdom
     Metathemes
     Summary: The Canonical Context of the Song of Songs

16. *The Poetry of Lamentations* *411*
     Introduction to Lamentations
     The Structure of Lamentations
     Summary: Differences and Similarities with the Psalms
     Conclusion: A Canonical Portrait of Poetry

     Glossary of Terms *423*

     Bibliography—Wisdom *431*

     Bibliography—Poetry *433*

Bibliography—History of Interpretation *436*

Bibliography—Ancient Near Eastern Literature *440*

Name Index *441*

Subject Index *443*

Scripture Index *455*

List of Abbreviations

AB	Anchor Bible
ABD	The Anchor Bible Dictionary
AEL	*Ancient Egyptian Literature,* M. Lichtheim
ANET	*Ancient Near Eastern Texts,* ed. J. B. Pritchard, 3rd ed., 1968
BDB	Francis Brown, S. R. Driver, Charles A. Briggs, *A Hebrew and English Lexicon of the Old Testament* based on the lexicon of William Gesenius, Oxford, 1907.
BZAW	Beihefte zur *Zeitschrift für die alttestamentliche Wissenschaft*
CBQ	Catholic Biblical Quarterly
CBQMS	Catholic Biblical Quarterly Monograph Series
CTA	A. Herdner, Corpus des tablettes en cunéiformes alphabé-tiques découvertes à Ras Shamra
FOTL	Forms of Old Testament Literature Commentary
Her	Hermeneia Commentary
Int	Interpretation
ITOT	*The Intellectual Tradition in the Old Testament,* Whybray, 1974
JBL	Journal of Biblical Literature
JSOTSup	Journal for the Study of the Old Testament—Supplement Series
LCC	Library of Christian Classics
LXX	Septuagint
NAC	New American Commentary
OTL	Old Testament Library

OTP	*Old Testament Parallels: Laws and Stories from the Ancient Near East*, ed. Victgor H. Matthews, Don Benjamin, 1991
RS	Ras Shamra
SBLDS	Society of Biblical Literature Dissertation Series
SBT	Studies in Biblical Theology
SIANE	*The Sage in Israel and the Ancient Near East*, ed. John G. Gammie, Leo G. Perdue, 1991
TOTC	Tyndale Old Testament Commentaries
VT	*Vetus Testamentum*
VTSup	Supplements to *Vetus Testamentum*
WBC	Word Biblical Commentary
WIANE	*Wisdom in Israel and the Ancient Near East*, Rowley Festschrift, ed. Martin Noth, D. Winton Thomas, VTSup 3, 1955
ZAW	*Zeitschrift für die alttestamentliche Wissenschaft*
ZTK	*Zeitschrift für Theologie und Kirche*

List of Tables

Table 1
Wisdom Texts in the Hebrew Bible *27*

Table 2
Rinkart and Sirach *82*

Table 3
Account of Solomon's Reign *100*

Table 4
Collections in Proverbs *120*

Table 5
Doxologies in Psalms *185*

Table 6
Poetic Texts in the Hebrew Bible *207*

Table 7
Types of Poetic Units in the Hebrew Bible *210*

Table 8
Parallelism in Proverbs and Amen-em-opet *222*

Table 9
Unusual Features of 11QPs *234*

Table 10
Types of Poetry in the Pseudepigrapha *236*

Table 11
Blessings in Genesis *300*

Table 12
    Earliest Hebrew Poetry According to Freedman *301*

Table 13
    Types of Poetic Units in the Former Prophets *323*

Table 14
    Poetic Units in Sirach *348*

Table 15
    Major Divisions of Psalms *358*

Table 16
    Speakers in the Song of Songs *385*

Table 17
    Thematic or Formal Units in the Song of Songs *386*

Table 18
    Dialogue from the Chorus in the Song of Songs *387*

Table 19
    Description of the Woman's Body in Song of Songs 4:1–5 . . . . . .*393*

Table 20
    Description of the Man's Body in Song of Songs 5:10–15 . . . . . .*394*

Table 21
    Description of the Woman in Song of Songs 7:1–5 . . . .*397*

Table 22
    Rhetorical Questions in the Song of Songs *403*

Table 23
    Garden Images in the Song of Songs *406*

Table 24
    Thematic Subgroups in the Wasfs of the Song of Songs *407*

Table 25
    Acrostic Form in Lamentations *413*

Table 26
    Types of Units in Lamentations *415*

Table 27
    "Once . . . Now" Formula in Lamentations 1 . . . .*416*

PART ONE: WISDOM

Introduction: A Preliminary Definition of Wisdom

How much better it is to get wisdom than gold!
And to get understanding is to be chosen above silver.
(Prov. 16:16, NASB)

Passages in Proverbs and Psalms place top priority on securing wisdom; this book continues the age-old quest for wisdom. The seeker of wisdom immediately faces a question that shapes all further exploration: What is wisdom?

Innumerable scholarly definitions invite consideration, but this study follows what appears to be a sounder approach to understanding biblical wisdom: seek such understanding from the contents of the Bible's wisdom books. Understanding wisdom in terms of the literature of wisdom involves many levels of study:

- Which books do we include in the scope of wisdom?

- What interests do the books of wisdom share with wisdom materials from other ancient civilizations?

- How did the wisdom sayings fit within the community of worship in ancient Israel?

- How were the books understood and interpreted in subsequent history?

- What are the unique and common features of each of the wisdom books?

- How does the combination of the books' unique features expand the general concept of wisdom?

The Beginning Point

All these issues rely on an answer to a more basic question: What is wisdom? Answers come from various quarters, reflecting the special perspectives assumed by various communities and individuals. For our purposes we will assume a beginning definition: *Wisdom is the exercise of mind as a religious pursuit.*

This definition provides a broad base from which to consider many specific definitions. More specific definitions arise from four sources. First, the biblical books of wisdom contain several depictions of wisdom. One special approach characterizes wisdom as *the ability to live well.* Accordingly, Proverbs contains advice intended to lead the novice to a successful and happy life. Artisans, kings, and other professionals display wisdom through vocational or practical skill. Ecclesiastes' attention to the philosophy of living presents a concept of wisdom based in the understanding of ultimate concepts. The Deuterocanonical works from the Septuagint (Sirach and The Wisdom of Solomon) include the basic perspective of Proverbs. These two works add more immediate historical concerns to their special concepts of wisdom. This chapter and following chapters fill in the details involved in the biblical portrait of wisdom.

Second, beyond the confines of biblical literature, wisdom carried special connotations in related Near Eastern literature. The common history Israel shared with these cultures led to overlap in their conceptions of wisdom.

Third, many current notions related to the word *wisdom* come from Jewish and Christian interpretations. These are classical, but secondary, descriptions based on the primary biblical materials.

Fourth, consistency demands special awareness that contemporary descriptions of biblical wisdom reflect the presuppositions of the present life and times. One objective of this study involves careful distinction between ancient views and contemporary interpretations.

All these ideas influence the study of biblical wisdom. This necessitates an approach marked by humility and the confession of this writer's biases. The basic presupposition that a canonical approach provides the best angle of vision on biblical materials accounts for most of the unique interests in this review of wisdom. The word *canon* stands as a near synonym for *Scripture.* A canonical approach to biblical literature reflects keen interest in the history of the books' acceptance and use as inspired works. The interpreter remains consistently aware of the ties between the content of the books and the various communities of faith which valued them.

For example, the interest of certain groups in the Song of Songs as love poetry shows one level of concern, and the interest of others in the Song of Songs as an allegory of God's love shows another. Both views fall within a long, varied tradition affirming the ultimate worth of the book as an inspired document. Both views provide insight into the nature of the interpreting communities as well as insight into the nature of the biblical book.

A Canonical Approach

Wisdom vocabulary and themes appear in a broad range of biblical literature. A canonical view involves a commitment to investigate specific wisdom units in light of the entire scope of biblical wisdom. The slightest indication of wisdom concern qualifies a brief biblical passage for inclusion. At times these smaller passages indicate a need to expand the general definition of wisdom. In this way, the content of the briefer passages influences the description of the general collection. Admittedly, the checks and balances resulting from this method lead to inconclusiveness. It is difficult to say what wisdom is when the definition continually contracts and expands.

For example, we can take the often-repeated maxim, "The fear of the LORD is the begnning of wisdom" and understand it as a reference to wisdom as religious devotion. This conception proves too small to allow for the anger of Job or the skepticism of Ecclesiastes. If we are to affirm their wisdom nature, we must admit that these books express ideas and emotions inconsistent with Proverbs' ideal of religious devotion. A canonical approach offers full description of the contents of wisdom books rather than absolute characterizations of wisdom. Such absolute characterizations cannot account for opposing trends. This suits biblical wisdom on its own terms. According to its perspective on human action, "Every matter has its time and way" (Eccles. 8:6).

So, what is appropriate in one context is out of place in another. The secret of wisdom is to know when and how. It involves the ability to match activities with the proper circumstances. Similarly, canonical criticism seeks to match ideas with their proponents rather than assuming a single audience or context for biblical wisdom. The Bible is a complex document spanning many centuries and types of social structure. Consequently, it is more inclusive than uniform in its entirety.

One of the by-products of the broad canonical approach relates to the content of the canon itself. Throughout this study, I refer to the books commonly known as Apocrypha as Deuterocanon. This includes all the biblical books included in the Roman Catholic and Eastern Orthodox canons. All other early Jewish and Christian works which claim special authority for themselves are referred to with the conventional term, *Pseudepigrapha*, with the exception of Talmud and other Jewish writings, which bear their own designations.

The early Christian communities accepted many, if not all, the works of Deuterocanon as scriptural in authority. A few early thinkers, such as Jerome, questioned their value. However, only in the sixteenth century, shortly before Luther's Reformation, did Christian thinkers first distinguish the Deuterocanon as less valid than other works of Scripture. The original King James Version included the works. Many of their teachings (such as those on hell, angels, and wisdom) play important roles in Protestant biblical interpretation, though these ideas are not often recognized as deuterocanonical. (The reader may refer to the discussion of Sirach in chapter 3 for a few examples.) The term *Apocrypha* has been used to designate these books as invalid resources, but the less extreme view of Martin Luther is assumed here. Namely, these books contain valuable information, though not fully scriptural in terms of inspiration. For some communities of faith, the Deuterocanon assumes full scriptural status. In this work, we adopt sensitive terminology, but presume a narrower definition of Scripture.

General Characteristics of Wisdom

Interpreters agree on the general characteristics of biblical wisdom. This consensus includes such themes as (1) the doctrine of divine reward for good or evil conduct, (2) the choice of living responsibly or recklessly, (3) creation, and (4) citizenship. The consensus also involves the use of the form known as "proverb" in all wisdom books. The feature of biblical wisdom that receives the most attention in practically all studies of wisdom is the practical side of wisdom, which addresses issues relating to everyday decisions and conduct. In style as well as content, wisdom focuses on the ins and outs of daily living—business, love and marriage, morals, child rearing, and so forth. Wide agreement exists on such basic concerns.

As the definition grows narrower, however, each specialist limits the field of wisdom because each scholar assigns priority to different materials in the canon. A preference for Ecclesiastes leads to a more speculative, quasi-philosophical description. An opposing perspective based on Proverbs highlights a practical focus, including a utilitarianism consistent with the theology of the Deuteronomist. This more practical perspective, also present in a few psalms, stands at odds with the calculated denial of meaning that marks Ecclesiastes.

The wisdom books themselves provide the basis for the depiction of wisdom in this study. This approach raises the basic question, "Where does the canon of Israel's wisdom begin and end?" Job, Proverbs, and Ecclesiastes appear in all studies of biblical wisdom. Including the Song of Songs in Israel's wisdom canon greatly increases the scope of *wisdom literature*. This book contains no sages, few if any proverbs, and no discussion of wisdom as a theme. It consists entirely of love poetry. Two features commend its inclusion: its ascription to Solomon, and the practical nature of its discourse. In other respects, the Song of Songs bears less resemblance to Job, Proverbs, and Ecclesiastes than do Sirach and the Wisdom of Solomon. Yet these two later works lie outside the Protestant canon.

Segments of Hosea, Amos, Isaiah, and Jeremiah exhibit numerous wisdom themes and forms. The narratives relating to Joseph and the court history of David also show traits common to Israel's wisdom. All these texts support the definition and discussion of wisdom, but are not "wisdom literature" in the full sense. Some scholars claim wisdom personnel shaped specific portions of the Bible not typically regarded as wisdom. They find wisdom's traits in the Decalogue,[1] the succession narrative (2 Sam. 9–20, 1 Kings 1–2)[2] and Deuteronomy.[3] Assuredly, "the interests of scholarly investigation are not served by the application of the word 'wisdom' to every manifestation of brains in ancient Israel."[4] One could counter with the claim that since wisdom's origins are so ambiguous, study must begin with the elements of wisdom as they appear in the broad spectrum of Israel's literature.

All material containing wisdom themes, vocabulary, and literary forms must be included in the early course of this study. Since they indicate the huge proportion of wisdom influence on Israel's sacred literature, the materials outside the wisdom canon supply valuable information concerning the scope and diversity of the wisdom corpus, leading to a more refined sense of context. This prevents excessive dependence on conceptions of wisdom too narrow to account for its diversity. It also shows the necessity for a complex definition.

A Working Definition of Wisdom

Our study begins with a broad definition of wisdom drawn from and applied to Proverbs, Job, Ecclesiastes, Song of Songs, Wisdom of Solomon, and Sirach. For Proverbs, Job, and Ecclesiastes the chief end is *ḥokmâ* (חָכְמָה).[5] The simplistic translation, "wisdom," can lead to confusion. The confusion arises as contemporary notions of wisdom replace the natural breadth in meaning of the Hebrew term. The Hebrew concept embodies all the ethical and social abilities that distinguish the wise person from the fool or the unrighteous—skill, discretion, education, morality, and faith. In the Hebrew Bible *wisdom* refers to predominantly practical activities. Action and thinking are inseparable. To possess wisdom is to excel at pragmatic activity rather than to participate in sustained reflection. Wisdom indicates skill or ability: to perform manual labor like spinning (Exod. 35:25), to discern good and evil (Job 28:28), to solve riddles (Prov. 1:6) or, generally, to know how to live well. *Ḥokmâ* is knowing in the Aristotelian as distinguished from

---

1. See J. J. Stamm, *The Ten Commandments in Recent Research*, trans. M. E. Andrew (London: SCM Press Ltd., 1967), 71–72.

2. Gerhard von Rad, *Old Testament Theology*, vol. 1, trans. D. M. G. Stalker (New York: Harper & Row, 1962), 56.

3. See Joseph Blenkinsopp, *Wisdom and Law in the Old Testament* (Oxford: Oxford University Press, 1983).

4. R. N. Whybray, *The Intellectual Tradition in the Old Testament*, BZAW 135 (New York: Walter deGruyter, 1974), 3.

5. Although the vocabulary of wisdom contains a wealth of related words, themes, and ideas, this universal concept can serve as a minimal foundation. Additional vocabulary is introduced and discussed as more specific matters are treated in the chapters which follow. The reader should not conclude that the oversimplification here in any way approximates the breadth and depth of Hebrew wisdom. Included in this preliminary discussion are only those issues that apply to all of or most of the obviously wisdom books of the Hebrew Bible and its Deuterocanon.

the Platonic sense: If unused, knowledge remains unrecognized. If it were possible to know the good without doing it, such a thinker would nonetheless be identified as a fool. Since wisdom was inseparably bound to conduct, anyone who could do a thing well was considered "wise" in regard to the field of specialization.

Hebrew wisdom displays a dynamic element that aims for excellence in every area of living. Israel's wisdom was not offered in support of the status quo. Wisdom books model an approach to life that challenges the reader/hearer to reach beyond typical behavior patterns to a lifestyle exemplary in its discretion. The wise person possesses a heightened sensitivity. This leads to more careful and thorough decision making. In various distinct ways the wise excel at the business of living! Because of their extraordinary success at living, the figures Job and Solomon carry strong authorial voices in the books of Job and Ecclesiastes. Select passages in Proverbs and Sirach reflect a similar call to distinction. The Greek author of the Wisdom of Solomon exploited this feature of wisdom. He used Solomon as a foil through which to present wisdom concerns relating to his historical situation. This involved the reader's commitment to a biblical lifestyle rather than concessions to Greek culture.

This call to discretion as well as other practical orientations that relate wisdom to living makes the scope of wisdom difficult to limit. Wisdom includes all of human conduct. Later books such as Sirach and the Wisdom of Solomon can be discussed under this broad rubric. The Song of Songs exhibits only one specific feature named in the previous discussion (practical concerns related to daily affairs). Still, the Song easily fits within the scope of wisdom when wisdom incorporates all of human action and existence.

This broad perspective offers the most general context indicated by the designation, "wisdom literature": *Wisdom literature consists of those biblical documents preoccupied with human responses to God and the world.* To the degree that books or passages display an interest in the whole philosophy of living according to the discussion above, those books or passages are at least wisdom-influenced or related, if not wisdom themselves. Due to the special interests of this study, the term *wisdom literature* includes only Proverbs, Job, and Ecclesiastes in the Hebrew canon and Sirach and The Wisdom of Solomon in the Deuterocanon.

Wisdom as Training for Leaders

A careful study of biblical wisdom demands more specific descriptions of its nature; therefore each modern interpreter limits the scope of wisdom in order to study it meaningfully. The scholar refines the domain indicated by wisdom literature by concentrating on a specific view of wisdom's origins and aims.

The narrower viewpoint necessarily limits the relevance of the designation wisdom literature to the full wisdom canon. Three examples are sufficient. First, some critics note that instruction in wisdom was necessary for the training of the king and his advisers as well as the maintenance of the authority of the monarch. They stress the clear connections between sage and kingdom in Egypt and elsewhere in the ancient Near East. They conceive Israel's wisdom as borrowed from neighboring centralized states (principally Egypt) and codified at the birth of Israel's monarchy.[6] According to this view, the sages functioned as advisers and were perhaps the major literate group during the monarchical period. Those who hold this view tend to take the biblical references to Solomon as the patron of wisdom seriously.[7]

This rendering receives support in a number of units in Ecclesiastes (especially 8:2–5) and Proverbs (for example, 25:1–15) that enjoin faithfulness to the king. Some passages seem to advise members of the court in the proper conduct of their business (for example, Eccles. 4:13–14). Certain sections of Job imply Job's connection with the royal court.[8]

In spite of such evidence, this point of view is to some degree an argument from silence. Nowhere in the Hebrew Bible are wisdom officials in the court specifically identified as the recorders of Israel's wisdom traditions or the writers of the wisdom books. Only David and Solomon among all the kings of Israel are described as wise.

Wisdom as a Corrective to Torah

Second, a completely different methodology and body of information lead some scholars to view wisdom as a corrective to what they see as the stifling legalism of the Torah.[9] A related view considers certain theological expressions in wisdom as reactions against superficial worship. Such ideas express the conception of wisdom as an innovative movement. According to this view, wisdom challenged current expressions of faith. Wisdom encouraged its adherents to question commonly accepted social traditions.

The Books of Job and Ecclesiastes offer clear support for this conception. Job challenges the belief that reward and punishment come as direct results of obedience and disobedience to God (see 21:7–34). The conventional view, affirming the connection of obedience and reward, occurs in

---

6. A clear expression of this view is presented in R. B. Y. Scott, *The Way of Wisdom in the Old Testament* (New York: Collier Books, Macmillan Publishing Co., 1971), 12–16, 105–8.

7. First Kings 4:32 attests Solomon's authorship of three thousand proverbs. The opening lines of Song of Songs, Proverbs, and Ecclesiastes identify Solomon as author. The Greek work, Wisdom of Solomon, also contains an ascription to Solomon, but the date of the book allows no connection with Solomon.

8. "In the poetry Job is presented in the guise of an ancient king (chaps. 29–31) who, like many of his Mesopotamian counterparts, has experienced an inexplicable fall from status and power . . . ." Leo G. Perdue, "Cosmology and Social Order in the Wisdom Tradition" in *The Sage in Israel and the Ancient Near East*, eds. John G. Gammie and Leo G. Perdue (Winona Lake, Wis.: Eisenbrauns, 1990), 475.

9. Stamm, 72. He understood wisdom as a means for emphasizing the role of context in ethical decision-making. As such, wisdom reacted against the rigid application of the limited number of laws contained in the Torah. The wisdom teachers assumed the authority of Torah. They provided a corrective which enabled a person to judge conduct in a host of specific situations.

Part One

the Torah, especially Deuteronomy, in a number of Proverbs, and in the history of Joshua through Kings. Exceeding Job's challenge, Ecclesiastes protests the idea that God blesses his people. Ecclesiastes questions the existence of any direct "good" in the course of life (see 1:12–14). In other portions of the Hebrew canon, God confers his blessing by bestowing favor on humans through creation, providing care for the Hebrews, and offering redemption of various natures. The first chapter of Genesis leaves no doubt that the world is "good." In keeping with such conventional expressions, Proverbs supports rather than challenges social conceptions, while Sirach and Wisdom of Solomon equate the keeping of Torah with wisdom.

Direct support for the notion that wisdom conveys reactions against conventional theology occurs in relatively few cases. No doubt, the special perspectives of wisdom led to social change at times, but viewing wisdom as a movement with a social agenda distorts the long and varied history connected with Israel's wisdom.

Wisdom as Training for Children

Third, one fundamental portrait of wisdom emphasizes the role of the family in the development and transmission of wisdom materials. This view, like the first suggestion, concentrates on the origins of wisdom. Proponents argue that the origins of Israel's wisdom are predominantly in the family. Wisdom schools related to the court, such as those in Egypt, are unattested in biblical literature. Consequently, according to this view, court use of wisdom, legal use of wisdom, and wisdom in formal education are secondary to forms related to parental instruction.[10] The role of royalty in preserving and promoting wisdom is not denied, but wisdom began on the tribal level as oral instruction which served as a cohesive influence for the family and early society.

The fairly mundane instructions in Proverbs fit this description well. However, extended discourses like Job do not conform to the proposal of family settings. Furthermore, the literature of Job and Ecclesiastes is unabashedly "adult" in its expression and themes. Wisdom forms which present specific directions regarding day-to-day conduct (for example, Eccles. 5:1–9) certainly fit the familial context, but more complex forms, such as the lengthy dialogues in Job, seem to have originated elsewhere.[11]

Summary: Multiple Perspectives

These three examples are selected almost arbitrarily as representative positions. They offer minimal suggestions for wisdom's nature, among

10. Roland E. Murphy, *The Tree of Life: An Exploration of Biblical Wisdom Literature* (New York: Doubleday, 1990), 4–5.
11. James L. Crenshaw, "The Sage in Proverbs" in *SIANE*, 205, argued that three primary contexts for wisdom literature (family, royal court, formal education) produced representative forms of proverbs.

other suggestions. All present important depictions of wisdom's traits, but none is large enough to include the entire scope of biblical wisdom.

The merger of the views could account for three independent facets of Israel's complex wisdom traditions. In support of this, wisdom clearly shows connections to the monarchy, a corrective nature, and ties to the family. When combined, even these basic perspectives complicate the study due to the numerous possibilities for discussion they create. As a result, wisdom appears as several different subjects rather than as a single entity. When the definition of wisdom accounts for all the biblical literature, the multiple perspectives present materials too independent to provide a backdrop for the discussion of a particular book or segment of the wisdom material. When the definition is narrowed sufficiently to allow for cogent discussion, the definition fits a single book or perspective but cannot account for others.

The difficulty lies not in the wisdom materials themselves but in the various shades of meaning common to the word *wisdom*. On one hand this leads to assumptions that all biblical materials described by the word *wisdom* display more similarities than differences. On the other hand this leads some interpreters to presume that once they propose a single origin or description for wisdom, it applies to all portions of the wisdom canon. These tendencies fail to account for three factors: (1) the long and varied history of Israel's wisdom traditions, (2) the several distinct contexts in which wisdom flourished, and (3) the tendency of the contemporary interpreter to impose rigid theological consistency on biblical materials. Based on these factors, this study resorts to the wisdom books themselves to discover the unique features in individual books and the features common to the entire collection of biblical wisdom.

Questions for Discussion

1. What beginning definition of wisdom is offered here? How would you define or modify this definition?

2. What effect does a canonical perspective have on a definition of wisdom?

3. What factors make the definition of wisdom so complex? Why?

4. What elements must be included in a comprehensive definition of wisdom? Does any definition fit all wisdom literature? Why?

Chapter One

Overview of Wisdom

Wisdom Features in Job, Proverbs, and Ecclesiastes

Having set forth a preliminary definition of wisdom, the next step is to turn to the principal collections of wisdom in the Hebrew Bible and establish the nature of wisdom based on their contents. The principal collections are Job, Proverbs, and Ecclesiastes, plus wisdom passages from other books in the Hebrew canon. The Song of Songs is omitted due to its lack of an explicit concern for wisdom. (The book contains no mention of the word *wisdom.*) The three basic wisdom works exhibit the features identified at the beginning of this study: They express concern for wisdom as the exercise of mind as a religious pursuit. They each describe as wisdom: (1) the ability to live well, (2) vocational or practical skill, and (3) ultimate concepts. Two deuterocanonical books, Sirach and Wisdom of Solomon, mirror certain aspects of Hebrew wisdom. They provide some helpful comparisons to mark the transition from Hebrew wisdom to its early interpretation. Before approaching interpretation; however, this chapter will explore wisdom's themes and vocabulary as well as its social settings.

Wisdom in Job

The approach to wisdom in Job resides in the shadows of Job's struggle with his problem. Job's identification as a righteous, pious person (1:1; 42:7) links him to wise conduct so often praised or commended by a vast array of biblical proverbs. His fundamental identity, however, is not expressed in terms of wisdom. Job is not described as wise, and his struggle is not introduced as a struggle for wisdom. The prologue (chaps. 1–2) and epilogue (42:7–17) conspicuously omit references to wisdom, presenting integrity as the central issue. In the poetic section, Job wrestles with God's refusal to explain the suffering of the righteous as understood in Job's own religious tradition. As a spokesman for wisdom, Job expresses the indignation of those who express consistent devotion to God, but experience difficulty equal to or greater than the difficulty the wicked or brutish encounter. The question itself, "Is God unjust?" exhibits no special appeal to wisdom; but Job's explorations, indeed, even his need for an answer, fall within the parameter of wisdom.

Job serves as the best example of our first unwieldy definition of wisdom—*the exercise of mind as a religious pursuit.* Wisdom expresses the human struggle for understanding of ultimate issues, though in Job's case no "answer" is given. The prologue and epilogue include more direct involvement of God in the struggle for understanding. They place the poetry (chaps. 3–41) in the framework of a divine test. A series of catastrophes test Job's loyalty to God. Can the intervention of God in human affairs also be understood as a wisdom feature? Since the story contains a super-worldly explanation for the contest (1:6–12; 2:1–7), the test lacks the preoccupation with the human struggle toward understanding already identified as key to wisdom.

Wisdom normally concentrates on the human response to God rather than on God's personal activity. However, elsewhere in Job, God's revelation of himself (chaps. 38–42) brings Job to the point of understanding. For Job, wisdom comes not so much through human device or natural revelation as through an act of God (special revelation). In some respect, God satisfies Job with the thundering speeches which conclude the test. This divine communication, like the test of the prologue, places emphasis on divine activity rather than human activity. Wisdom involves not only the human struggle for religious discernment, but also the intervention of God, providing answers and silencing complaints. The degree of emphasis on this facet of wisdom is unique to Job, but concern for God's sovereignty and the notice of his wisdom in the created order appear in all the wisdom literature.

The previous consideration of wisdom in Job relates to Job's setting and conclusion. The approach to wisdom fostered in the bulk of Job arises from a series of relatively lengthy wisdom speeches by Job and his friends. In form as well as theme, the book is distinct. More than in any of the other wisdom literature books, Job presents wisdom in terms of a literary enterprise. The bulk of Job comprises a mini-epic poem with all the stateliness and attention to form that the term *epic* implies. Its cyclical format makes it one of the most carefully patterned books in the Hebrew Bible. By comparison Ecclesiastes appears chaotic; Proverbs, disorganized.

The unique form complicates the issue of wisdom's origins, resembling the work of no known officials in Israel's monarchy. Of the origins for wisdom proposed in the previous section, only formal education holds promise: the arrangement of Job into debate-style speeches indicates instructional use. Job may be the product of a literary elite, but no external evidence exists for such literary enterprises. An attractive (though illegitimate) option is to designate the book under the title "corrective literature." Such a proposal reveals the critic's level of discomfort with the unusual understanding of wisdom Job promotes. To describe Job as corrective literature is to say little more than that its contents cannot fit under the rubric "wisdom" according to the interpreter's definition. The canonical approach leads to a wholesale acceptance of its wisdom character on the basis of its longstanding acceptance as wisdom by Jewish and Christian communities of faith. Assuming this conventional view, the book offers normative wisdom based on Job's special perspective. This moderates the attempt to force it into some more attractive (that is, more easily recognized) category. This cautious approach involves few specific conclusions at this point. Instead, it presents the preference for general description rather than specific hypotheses.

Wisdom in Proverbs

For many readers, Proverbs serves as the guideline for determining whether other forms and themes throughout the Bible conform to the category, "wisdom." Perhaps the lack of a clear original context for its statements makes it an attractive point of reference. Proverbs implies no single origin for wisdom and encompasses many of its themes. These features identify Proverbs as a loose starting point for an understanding of wisdom. If Proverbs serves as the ultimate model for wisdom, the works of Ecclesiastes and Job appear abnormal. Using any particular book in this fashion opens the critic to the accusation of circularity: "All wisdom is like Proverbs; and what is wisdom? Material that looks like Proverbs."

Wisdom in Ecclesiastes

Ecclesiastes exhibits peculiar features, whether viewed in the context of wisdom literature or in the context of the entire Hebrew canon. The book displays a unique literary form, but the skeptical tone provides the book's most glaring distinction. In a rather random collection of proverbs, personal recollections, and admonitions the book supports the contention that "all is emptiness" (vanity). Ecclesiastes also includes brief encouragements to enjoy life. The keyword *hebel* (הֶבֶל) means vapor or breath and represents in Ecclesiastes the transience of human life: Life is mist, an almost imperceptible flow of wind that is gone as soon as it is noticed.[1]

Ecclesiastes presents itself as the perceptions of an elderly man based upon the course of a rich and full life. The speaker in the text laments the vanity of common human goals and encourages the reader to simply fear God (live piously) and enjoy work. Job and Ecclesiastes both indicate a predisposition to challenge the status quo. Though Ecclesiastes does not directly challenge God himself, it questions the value of the experience of his created beings, creating tension with the affirmation of Genesis 1:31: "Everything . . . was very good."

The type of argument assumed in Ecclesiastes reduces human activity to its barest elements. The narrator searches for basic principles to describe human experience. The rules discovered offer guidelines for conduct on a

---

1. This interpretation was suggested by Robert Gordis, *Koheleth—The Man and His World: A Study of Ecclesiastes*, 3rd ed. (New York: Schocken Books, 1968), 204–5.

wide scale. A process of elimination finally leads to the simple conclusion
that life is vanity. In response, the reader receives encouragement to enjoy
life while it lasts. The following passage shows the progression from basic
principles to suggested conduct: "What do mortals get from all the toil and
strain with which they toil under the sun? For all their days are full of pain,
and their work is a vexation; even at night their minds do not rest. This also
is vanity. There is nothing better for mortals than to eat and drink, and find
enjoyment in their toil" (Eccles. 2:22–24).

As in Job, wisdom searches for answers to disturbing propositions, but
Ecclesiastes includes no climax and denouement. The glum phrase, "all is
emptiness (vanity)," opens and closes the work. The positive contributions
of Ecclesiastes consist of numerous pieces of advice on well-considered conduct. Poetic passages in 1:2–11; 3:1–8; and 12:1–8 elaborate on the theme
of meaninglessness with ironic eloquence—beautiful treatments of a dread-
ful theme. The negative conclusions of the book make it unsuitable to serve
as a model for wisdom; however, its clear wisdom terminology and themes
effectively force the reader of biblical wisdom to stretch the category "wisdom." Proverbs presents sayings of two-sentence length. They convey a
simple yet broad understanding of wisdom. Job's complicated dialogues
stand at the opposite extreme. They represent attempts to exhaust specific
claims to truth. Ecclesiastes provides a bridge between the sentence literature in Proverbs and the propositional dialogues in Job—Ecclesiastes contains a measure of both.

Summary: Using Job, Proverbs, and Ecclesiastes as Markers

The three books explicitly labeled "wisdom" provide the backdrop for a
consideration of wisdom themes occurring throughout the Hebrew canon.
Themes, forms, and vocabulary common to these books qualify as markers of
wisdom materials. Such markers lead to the identification of other segments
of the Hebrew Bible as wisdom. These additional wisdom segments may also
expand or clarify the nature of the wisdom writings themselves. The three
books of the wisdom canon offer primary indicators of wisdom, but not all-
inclusive limits. Each portion of text outside the wisdom canon may include
a general portrait of wisdom, but interest lies in the special perspective on
wisdom each text presents. Rather than providing a full account of all the
wisdom features in each passage, only those features which contribute special
understandings of wisdom demand attention. This approach prevents passages outside the wisdom canon from exercising too great a role in the definition of wisdom. The following passages form a strong sample of a far wider
list of wisdom-related texts based on the above suggestions for identifying wisdom. These texts do not fall under the rubric "wisdom literature." This designation formally applies only to Job, Proverbs, Ecclesiastes, Wisdom of
Solomon, Sirach, and in a limited respect, the Song of Songs.[2]

---

2. An excellent study of wisdom themes throughout the Hebrew Bible is contained in
Donn Morgan, *Wisdom in the Old Testament Traditions* (Atlanta: John Knox, 1981).

Wisdom Outside the Wisdom Canon

Wisdom in the Torah

Wisdom themes, vocabulary, and concerns are not limited to the basic wisdom canon of Job, Proverbs, and Ecclesiastes. They appear here and there throughout the Bible and beyond. In the first five books of the Bible, wisdom concerns predominate only in the story of Joseph (Gen. 37–50) and the work of Deuteronomy. Joseph served as counselor and judge in Egypt, the nation Israel often considered the superlative source of wisdom activity.[3] Joseph's wisdom possessed a distinctive nature. It originated as pure gift from God (see Gen. 41:38–39). His sojourn in Egypt, his ability to interpret dreams, and his ability to save Egypt from the famine are all attributed to divine intervention. Joseph possessed the "spirit of God" (Gen. 41:38) and introduced himself to his estranged brothers as one who feared God (Gen. 42:18). The later emphasis on the "fear of the LORD" in Proverbs indicates that this theme serves as a distinguishing mark of Israel's wisdom tradition. It also supports the notion that wisdom relied primarily on God's gift. The designation "fear of the LORD" includes much more than mere reference to wisdom as divine gift. The phrase indicates that in spite of the practical emphases of wisdom, its roots existed beyond the realm of human control.[4]

Deuteronomy blends wisdom forms and terminology with prophetic forms and terminology to support the view that prosperity is linked to obedience.[5] The Shema (6:4–5) carries the force of blessing or curse dependent upon the response to the laws it assumes. Passages such as 11:8–17 threaten disaster or blessing dependent on behavior. Proverbs promises similar threat or blessing to the wicked or righteous, as illustrated in Proverbs 2:31–33, "Therefore walk in the way of the good, and keep to the paths of the just. For the upright will abide in the land, and the innocent will remain in it; but the wicked will be cut off from the land, and the treacherous will be rooted out of it."

The two-sided blessing-curse continuum applies to wisdom as well as Torah. The ability to make choices which lead to blessing distinguishes the wise from the foolish. In much of the wisdom literature a very fine line separates wisdom as the source of right living and wisdom as equal to right living. Deuteronomy identifies keeping the Torah with wisdom, and merges obedience and discernment: "You must observe them diligently, for this will show your wisdom and discernment to the peoples, who, when they hear all

---

3. Support for Joseph's association with Israel's wisdom traditions comes from Gerhard von Rad, "The Joseph Narrative and Ancient Wisdom" in *The Problem of the Hexateuch and Other Essays*, trans. E. W. Trueman Dicken (London: SCM Press, 1966). Originally published in German in 1953.

4. In other respects, Joseph's abilities matched those associated with wisdom by the Egyptians. His ability to interpret dreams differed in degree, but not in substance, from the same ability among Egyptian sages (Gen. 41:8).

5. For further connections between law and wisdom, see Joseph Blenkinsopp, *Wisdom and Law in the Old Testament* (Oxford: Oxford University Press, 1983).

these statutes, will say, 'Surely this great nation is a wise and discerning people!'" (4:6).

Seemingly, wisdom (expressed in terms of the choice between obedience and disobedience) appeared inherently in the Torah itself. The sense of moral responsibility Deuteronomy fostered related directly to the human activity of choosing obedience (righteousness). This is not a radical departure from the approach of other wisdom books, since all assume or imply that wisdom's source is God and the human component consists of tuning the life and intellect to his frequency.

Wisdom in the Former Prophets

In the Former Prophets the claims regarding Solomon's wisdom far outweigh other traces of wisdom themes. Deuteronomy's linkage between wisdom and obedience continues in these books. For example, Joshua reviews Israel's history in Joshua 23:14–16 in terms of punishment or reward based on obedience. The absence of the word *wisdom* does not remove this passage from consideration. Emphasis on the divine blessing or curse itself occurs frequently in wisdom literature as well as the Former Prophets. Solomon gained his unrivaled wisdom in response to God's offer to grant one request (1 Kings 3:5–14; 2 Chron. 1:7–12). His wisdom included at least three aspects: (1) skill to rule with distinction, (2) skill to perform as a judge in deciding right and wrong, and (3) precocious depth and breadth of intelligence, particularly associated with the natural order. [6]

First Kings 4; 5; and 10 also laud Solomon for his legendary wisdom. The king's wisdom conforms to the model of wisdom at court; however, he is also credited with the composition of proverbs and songs and with classifications of living things (1 Kings 4:32–33). First Kings 4:29–33 (Heb. 5:11–14) describes Solomon as wiser than other figures who apparently served as models for supreme wisdom. The identification of Solomon as the consummate wise king leads to a natural association of wisdom materials with him. In the wisdom literature, only Job and Sirach lack a direct association with Solomon. Several of the activities related to Solomon's wisdom indicate intellectual activity that can only be indirectly linked to the performance of his duties as king. Perhaps wisdom suited the monarch better than other professionals. More than any other citizen of Israel, the king needed wisdom to accomplish his ends. The wisdom granted Solomon far exceeded the political and social interests necessary for his royal duties. In this case wisdom consists of much more than skill to perform special tasks. Solomon's general intellectual ability identified him as "wise."

---

6. R. B. Y. Scott, "Solomon and the Beginnings of Wisdom in Israel" in *Wisdom in Israel*, VTSup vol. 3, presented to H. H. Rowley, eds. Martin Noth and D. Winton Thomas (Leiden: Brill, 1955), 270–71.

Wisdom in the Latter Prophets

The Latter Prophets contribute minimally to the further understanding of wisdom. They borrow wisdom forms and themes but do not conceive wisdom according to any special pattern.[7] Isaiah (especially 1–39) seems most acutely aware of wisdom traditions. Wisdom serves as the subject of several direct statements (for example, 19:11–15; 28:23–29, and 40:13–14). The same is true of Jeremiah (8:8–9; 9:12, and 23). Ezekiel, rather than referring directly to wisdom, employs wisdom forms to convey the prophetic message. Ezekiel 16:44 and 18:2, for example, open with introductions as *mĕsālîm* (proverbs). Amos presents a series of rhetorical questions in 3:3–8 similar to those occuring in Proverbs 6:27–28 and elsewhere. Other units resemble the depiction of God in Job 38–41 (Amos 5:8–15; 9:2–6). Habakkuk deals with the theodicy question at length. Theodicy explains apparent injustices in a world controlled by God. The use of wisdom language and forms in the prophetic literature indicates merely that prophets drew from existing wisdom material for their oracles. It is less likely that both wisdom and prophecy made common use of materials from a separate context accessible to both, since the wisdom forms are so widely attested in the ancient Near East prior to the appearance of the eighth-century prophets.

Wisdom in the Psalms

Psalms associates wisdom with fidelity to the Torah (19 and 119). Depictions of the righteous and the wicked abound (Ps. 1, for instance) in what is the closest approximation to Deuteronomy's view in the Hebrew canon. Like Deuteronomy, Psalms makes use of wisdom themes to support a retributive theology. This viewpoint consistently defends God's just compensation for the goodness or wickedness practiced by each individual. Psalm 73 raises the theodicy issue, a view of divine compensation settling the issue: "Those who are far from you perish" (v. 27). Job and Ecclesiastes contain challenges to this view. Wisdom writings patterned after the nature of Job or Ecclesiastes were apparently deemed unsuitable as backgrounds for psalms. The function of wisdom as employed by the Psalms was to reinforce the divine blessing upon the righteous and curse upon the wicked.

Wisdom in the Deuterocanon

The Septuagint (the Greek version of the Old Testament) includes two additional books of wisdom, Sirach and The Wisdom of Solomon. Sirach faithfully reproduces the *mĕsālîm* forms presented in Proverbs as well as the traditional teachings of prosperity for the righteous and adversity for the wicked.

---

7. An excellent early overview of wisdom concerns in the prophets is available in Johannes Lindblom, "Wisdom in the Old Testament Prophets" in Noth and Thomas, *Wisdom in Israel*, 192–204.

Wisdom in Sirach

Sirach innovates by linking wisdom with Torah and with cultic ritual in a way unparalleled in the Hebrew canon. In Deuteronomy, where obedience shows wisdom, the focus centers upon the response to God's election: Wisdom grew out of relationship with the deity. Sirach goes well beyond this by practically equating Torah and wisdom. A hymn praises wisdom: "All this [wisdom] is the book of the covenant of the Most High God, the law which Moses commanded us" (24:23).

Wisdom becomes less an operation of reflection and more a matter of doing one's duty in the community of faith. Commitment to temple ritual and doctrine replaces the more dynamic personal response to the Torah's demands.

Sirach places emphasis on the Torah as an end in itself. The religious instructions of Sirach display a strong authoritarian tone. Jesus son of Sirach speaks, whereas the language of common wisdom in Proverbs presumes no named speaker. Sirach presents a different approach to wisdom by tying it more closely to the faith and culture of Judaism. The son of Sirach apparently understood wisdom as that which enabled later Israel to live out its distinctiveness. The references to Israel's history (especially in chaps. 44–50 of Sirach), unprecedented in wisdom literature, confirm this. This approach associates wisdom with the specific forms of Israel's faith. Earlier wisdom literature associated wisdom with sound decisions possible for persons in almost any historical situation. Faith in Yahweh comprised one such decision, but wisdom included activities in other arenas. Sirach's identification of wisdom with Torah makes religious identity the key element in wisdom.

Wisdom in Wisdom of Solomon

The Wisdom of Solomon presents further departures from Israel's oldest wisdom tradition. The opening verse and 6:1–11 are ostensibly addressed to rulers, though clearly Wisdom assumes a larger audience. The book stresses the sovereignty of God (Yahweh) in contrast to Greek rational religion. The Wisdom of Solomon at times equates wisdom with God's personal transcendence. His work in (1) creation, (2) the history of Israel, and (3) the future end of the world serve as illustrations of his transcendence. The Wisdom of Solomon acts as a vehicle for a larger theological message to the believing community, one of hope and encouragement grounded in the nature of God. Wisdom becomes a tool beneficial for the defense of faith in Israel's God, rather than for guidance in daily affairs (as in the three books of the Hebrew canon).

Summary: An Expanding Definition

Much more could be said regarding the perspectives toward wisdom inherent in the individual wisdom books as well as the implications of the entire collection. Both issues are addressed as the books are discussed and conclusions are drawn.

The previous discussion attempts a "definition" of biblical wisdom on the basis of wisdom themes and vocabulary throughout the Bible. The so-called "working definition"[8] provides a loose framework for further discussion. The brief reviews given above of the contents of wisdom passages offer a preliminary sense of the character of biblical wisdom. The findings stop far short of final definition. Presuming the wisdom nature of Job, Proverbs, Ecclesiastes, Sirach, and The Wisdom of Solomon shifts the emphasis from hypothetical definitions to the actual content of the works. Our canonical approach sees all their contents related to wisdom. Only clear canonical evidence to the contrary changes this assessment. This preference for the works of wisdom themselves places the interpretation of the works at the apex of study.

Other issues affecting the view of wisdom command attention. These include the comparative study of wisdom literature in the ancient Near East and the history of the interpretation of wisdom books, along with a more thorough review of the themes and vocabulary distinct to wisdom. In the review above, features arose from individual wisdom passages. By contrast, the following themes and vocabulary appear widely in all the wisdom books. These concepts support the subsequent comparative study and the overview of the history of interpretation.

Wisdom Themes and Vocabulary

Israel's wisdom teachers were first and foremost students of the universe. They studied Yahweh's creation to determine order and commend human conduct which would sustain that order socially and cosmologically. They were not philosophers, since their interest was in the world as it existed and not in speculations on origins or cosmic significance. They assumed rather than questioned the world's origin as God's creation (considered an act of wisdom in Job 28). Even in Ecclesiastes, speculations are limited to human conduct and thought. Within this impossibly-broad range the wisdom teachers pursued a number of more modest aims. The following list presents the principal goals of the wisdom thinker:

(1)   to reduce broad truth to a simple statement or image;

(2)   to establish priorities that distinguish the wise, and so, to define wisdom;

(3)   to identify and discuss key philosophical questions or problematic issues;

(4)   to persuade the foolish and the ignorant to search for life's truths and in other ways pursue conscientious living;

(5)   to mark the impasses (God's sovereignty, mysteries of nature, etc.);

---

8. See above, pp. 5–8.

(6)   to share proven insights on practical matters;

(7)   to warn against excesses and foster temperance (e.g., alcohol, food, sexual conduct, anger);

(8)   to define virtue and vice;

(9)   to teach *joie de vivre* (French for "joy in living");

(10)   to extol wisdom as the greatest good; and

(11)   to complement conventional theology by increasing personal awareness of propriety.

The list remains open in two ways: (1) it represents a partial overview with no claim to be complete, (2) it presents aims perceived eclectically from throughout the wisdom corpus, rather than features exhibited within any one wisdom book.

The Fear of the LORD and Wisdom

A few broad themes and characteristics can be traced through the wisdom books. One overarching concern is the close association of "the fear of the LORD" with wisdom. The two are intimately related in at least five passages from wisdom literature: Proverbs 1:7; 9:10; 15:33; Psalm 111:10; and Job 28:28. Typically, the statement assumes the form: "The fear of the LORD is the beginning of wisdom." The maxim carries no self-evident meaning. It vaguely designates religion (one equivalent of "fear of the LORD") as the starting point for wisdom. It may imply that wisdom is impossible without the fear of Yahweh, but to ask whether or not it is possible to possess wisdom without the fear of Yahweh is to ask the wrong question.

The Hebrews identified religious devotion as a component of wisdom, but did not equate religious devotion with wisdom. Most of the truths of Hebrew wisdom maintain their relevance whether applied to religious contexts or not. At least three possibilities exist for the meaning of the phrase, "the fear of the LORD is the beginning of wisdom." First, this statement expresses the positive claim: "One who has reverence for God already possesses a chief part of wisdom." One who recognizes the obligation owed to God displays a recognizable advantage over those who wish to be wise and have not made the same recognition. It represents an extremely significant head start.

Second, the phrase probably addresses the hearer's lifestyle. One who lives honestly, justly, and reverently exercises the fear of the LORD. This effectively identifies the fear of the LORD with wisdom. After all, to live in such a way not only shows regard for God, but also shows the ability to make good choices. Such discretion serves as the basic component of wisdom.

Third, the phrase reminds the reader that wisdom's field of interest was shrouded in mystery like the name and character of Yahweh himself.[9]

---

9. Gerhard von Rad, *Wisdom in Israel* (Nashville: Abingdon, 1972), 108–9.

The name "Yahweh" carries connotations of mystery and transcendence. If wisdom resides in the fear of Yahweh (translated, "LORD"), then it remains in some measure beyond the reach of humans. Humans may possess and exercise wisdom, but its origins lie with the creator.

This last understanding of the meaning of "the fear of the LORD is the beginning of wisdom" offers an appealing concept of wisdom. However, the phrase "fear of the LORD" normally refers to human response to God, rather than alluding to the nature of the deity. To fear the LORD involves pious living more than recognition of God's special character. Consequently, the first two explanations appear plausible: The phrase embraces piety as a part of wisdom and identifies the righteous person as fundamentally wise. The last explanation remains suspect.

Prosperity and Suffering

Issues relating to prosperity and suffering provide a second major theme of wisdom. In Proverbs the theology of retribution offers a pat answer to almost all questions of human fortunes. The wicked suffer; the righteous prosper. The Wisdom of Solomon and Sirach adopt the same answer. Yet two wisdom books challenge the doctrine of fair retribution in major fashion—Job and, in somewhat lesser degree, Ecclesiastes, claimed their personal experiences contradicted the common philosophy of retribution. Job's three companions expressed the conventional view: His suffering showed God's displeasure with his life. Job maintained his innocence throughout the ordeal: "If I have walked with falsehood, and my foot has hurried to deceit—let me be weighed in a just balance, and let God know my integrity!" (31:5-6).

Ecclesiastes contains this blunt assertion: "There are righteous people who perish in their righteousness, and there are wicked people who prolong their life in their evil-doing" (7:15). These challenges in Job and Ecclesiastes represent a major distinction among wisdom books. When the entire collection of wisdom comes under discussion, attention centers on this difference. Perhaps the greatest challenge in developing a concept of Hebrew wisdom lies in the reconciliation of Proverb's positivism with the skepticism found in Job and Ecclesiastes. The wisdom of Proverbs focuses on the hope of God's reward and punishment. In Job and Ecclesiastes wisdom includes acceptance that good and evil sometimes come without identifiable cause. In spite of such willingness to challenge conventional notions, Israel's sages refused to speculate on the source of evil. Job's question, "Shall we receive the good at the hand of God, and not receive the bad?" (2:10b) places all human fortunes in God's hands. All experience (good and evil) was relegated to God in the sense that all events were attributed to his pleasure to act or not to act. Thus, Hebrew theology emphasized God's sovereignty and self-determination and deemphasized human ability to control (sometimes even to understand) the divine will.

The Best and Worst of Human Conduct

A third major theme involves human action. Israelite wisdom emphasized the extremes. The sages did not condone mediocrity—Job was completely blameless; Solomon, preeminently wise; the wise person, meticulously scrupulous (the fool, equally incompetent). The subject matter for the wise comprises the best, most pertinent, unquestionably proven guidelines for human activity. A mediating viewpoint placed a corresponding value on temperance, lest the superlative become a platform for extremism. One must not value wealth too highly, or seek too much pleasure, or become too wise (for example, Eccles. 7:15–18).

Vocabulary: "Wisdom"

The special vocabulary which describes biblical wisdom both conveys its distinct themes and complements the themes discussed above. *Hokmâ* (חָכְמָה) occurs as the basic term for the wisdom enterprise. It designates both the exercise of reason and the reception of the divine will. As mentioned above, Solomon received *hokmâ* as a gift from God. The development of personal discernment and trade skills fall into the semantic range of *hokmâ* and *hākhām* (adjective, "wise") as well. The words may refer, on one extreme, to a proponent of wisdom who speaks and acts with absolute discretion. Solomon's method of determining the mother of the infant in 1 Kings 3:23–38 provides an example of wisdom. On the other extreme, wisdom refers to a skilled laborer or expert in a specific field. The artisans who worked on the Tabernacle exercised wisdom in this regard (for example, Exod. 28:3). The Hebrew Bible shows no preference for one of these ranges of meaning above the other: They are equally legitimate manifestations of wisdom.

Two other words approach the meaning of *hokmâ* — *dăʿăt* and *ʿēṣâ*. *Dăʿăt* (דַּעַת) is derived from the verb *yādăʿ* (יָדַע) and is widely used in the Hebrew Bible with the meaning "knowledge." In Proverbs 10:14 it applies to the distinction between the wise and the fool: "The wise lay up *knowledge*, but the babbling of a fool brings ruin near" (italics added). When the word appears in wisdom literature, it takes on a special connotation of intellectual discernment.

The word *ʿēṣa* (עֵצָה) originated from the verb *yāʿaṣ* (יָעַץ) translated, "to advise or counsel." *ʿēṣa* commonly refers to the recommendation a professional adviser offered to a king and appears frequently throughout the entire Hebrew canon. In Job 29:21 *ʿēṣa* describes Job's status before his illness. "They listened to me, and waited, and kept silence for my *counsel*" (italics added).

Its usage in the wisdom books provides a piece of evidence for wisdom's connection to the court.[10] It also identifies wisdom as primarily verbal, a perspective maintained throughout the wisdom literature. No matter

---

10. This does not indicate that the palace was necessarily the primary locus for Israel's wisdom activity. See Whybray, *The Intellectual Tradition*.

what additional auxiliary traits are attributed to wisdom, wisdom comes through the presentation of advice. The tone of Proverbs and the tone of collections of such sayings in other books reveal a "this is what you should do" approach. This contrasts with approaches in which wisdom primarily designates individual introspection. The introspective approach presents meditation or reflection as the avenue to wisdom. Psalm 49 (a wisdom psalm) encourages the reader to find hope through reflecting on the idea that death cancels the advantage of the oppressing rich. The Hebrew Bible seldom displays such a meditative approach to wisdom.

Vocabulary: Related Words

The verb *śākal* (שָׂכַל to be prudent) and the related noun *śēkel* (שֶׂכֶל) (prudence, insight, understanding) occur frequently in Job, Proverbs, Deuteronomy, and the work of the Chronicler. In 1 Samuel 25:3 the noun distinguishes Abigail from her mean-spirited husband. The verb conveys a wide spectrum of meanings—to live circumspectly, to listen, to teach, to prosper. In general usage, the word is often linked to the notion of prosperity, even when defined otherwise. Proverbs 10:5 shows this connection between diligence and prosperity: "A child who gathers in summer is *prudent,* but a child who sleeps in harvest brings shame"(italics added). This word, more than any other single word, unites thought and practice in an indication that the distinction between the two was subtle or nonexistent for the sage.

The content of the sages' advice is at times described as *leqaḥ* (לֶקַח instruction or teaching), a word based on the extremely common verb, *lāqaḥ* (לָקַח to take). The noun indicates *ideas offered for willful reception.* Proverbs uses it to designate teaching either by word or example, as in 1:5a: "Let the wise also hear and gain in learning."

The word, *taḥbūlâ* (תַּחְבֻּלָה direction or counsel) also describes the content of the sages' instruction. It typically refers to the *direction given by professional advisers,* as in Proverbs 20:18: "Plans are established by taking advice; wage war by following *wise guidance*" (italics added). The root may indicate ropes used for steering a ship.[11] The noun occurs only in the plural and appears only in Job and Proverbs.

The word *mūsār* (מוּסָר discipline or correction), often used of corporal punishment, indicates an element of severity accompanying instruction in wisdom. It also refers to the self-discipline required to master wisdom. The wicked "die for lack of *discipline,* and because of their great folly they are lost," according to Proverbs 5:23 (italics added). The primary connotation is of painful rigors, as indicated in the verb (to discipline or admonish). The word is common in the Prophets as well as the wisdom books.

---

11. Suggested in תַּחְבֻּלָה, *BDB*, 287.

Vocabulary: Characteristics of the Wise

The remaining wisdom vocabulary relates to the characteristics which mark the wise person or faithful student of wisdom. The synonyms *bînâ* (בִּינָה) and *tĕbûnâ* (תְּבוּנָה) are derived from *bîn* (בֵּן), to understand). They designate discernment or understanding and appear extensively in Job and Proverbs. They apply to God's acts in creation and his maintenance of the world (for example, Job 26:12 and Prov. 3:19). They also apply to the goal of the human quest for wisdom: "Understanding" describes the ultimate aim of the student of wisdom (for example, Prov. 2:3 and Job 28:12). The terms imply the ability to distinguish one thing from another. This activity applies to the work of judges who must distinguish right from wrong or truth from lies. For the wisdom teacher the distinctions often relate to choices that determine the quality of life: The wise person can discriminate between folly and wisdom or wickedness and righteousness. In Job 39:26 and elsewhere *bînâ* carries the general meaning "wisdom": "Is it by your *wisdom* that the hawk soars and spreads its wings toward the south?" The two words refer to such wisdom in general more often than they refer to specific characteristics of wisdom. In these contexts, they designate abilities close to or identical to the abilities implied by *ḥokmâ*.

יָשֵׁר (*yošer*) describes the teacher or student as "upright." The common verb יָשַׁר (*yāšār*) denotes the righteous as distinct from the wicked. In the wisdom canon, the adjective almost always refers to proper moral conduct. A related noun, מֵישָׁר (*mêšār*), appears in its plural form in Proverbs and the Psalms with the meaning "equity."

The final important wisdom term is the adjective, עָרוּם (*ʿārûm*, crafty, shrewd, or sensible). In Genesis 3:1, the word applies to the serpent as one of the most wily of God's creatures. As indicated in the verb עָרֹם (*ʿārōm*) it designates "one exhibiting crafty, shrewd, or sensible behavior." In Proverbs the word carries positive overtones. Even in Genesis 3, it does not necessarily carry connotations of wicked intent, though the serpent's actions could not be considered "sensible" according to wisdom's standards of morality.

The Sociological Setting of Wisdom

Understanding Hebrew wisdom requires placing its themes and vocabulary in a plausible social setting. Support for the connection of the wisdom books, Proverbs and Ecclesiastes, to Solomon would greatly simplify this task. Unfortunately, these works offer no extended passages providing definite confirmation of the connection.

Connections with Solomon

Scant evidence exists in Proverbs, connecting only a few of the sayings with the court. Ecclesiastes includes more significant biographical statements (for example, 1:12 and 2:9) and mentions of kingship and royal settings (for example, 4:13 and 9:13–15). In other cases, the author of

Ecclesiastes assumes the role of one who lives under the command of the king (8:2–5). In short, our evidence consists mainly of the opening lines of the books. Proverbs begins, "The proverbs of Solomon son of David, king of Israel." Ecclesiastes opens with, "The words of the Teacher, the son of David, king in Jerusalem." First Kings 4:29–34 notes that Solomon authored proverbs and songs, but mentions no book. The lack of evidence allows for a wide range of suggestions from the claim that Solomon's connection with wisdom was "royal propaganda"[12] to the assertion that "it is *sociologically probable* [author's italics] that Solomon was a patron of . . . wisdom."[13]

A strong connection between Solomon and the study of wisdom in a formal system of some type seems likely. It is difficult to imagine that the biblical authors or editors contrived the relationship as pure fiction. It is equally improbable that Solomon himself served as author or editor of a substantial portion of Israel's wisdom canon. He may indeed have "authored" much of the contents of the books, but probably produced no finished work as the modern use of the term "author" implies. As our subsequent study of ancient Near Eastern wisdom indicates, much of the court-type wisdom originated in Mesopotamian or Egyptian sources. Solomon's international contacts make him a likely editor of such wisdom, though the final forms of Proverbs and Ecclesiastes date much later than his reign. The later date of Proverbs receives confirmation from 25:1: "These are other proverbs of Solomon that the officials of King Hezekiah of Judah copied." Proverbs appeared no earlier than Hezekiah's reign (715–687 B.C.E.).

With respect to Solomonic authorship and many other issues, the origins of Israel's wisdom remain too complex a problem to solve with a single hypothesis. The present study focuses on the canonical materials. It emphasizes the perspective of each book rather than the history of the development of wisdom in Israel. This special perspective makes unnecessary a tedious review of all possible origins for Hebrew wisdom. Instead, the origins suggested by various forms and features of each book set the stage for discussion. A canonical approach reflects to a certain degree the lack of such historical concerns in the Hebrew Bible itself. Assuming their scriptural character (the canonical approach) shifts attention to their contents rather than their origins.

Whatever the earliest sources of the material, the books as we have them come to us from communities who accepted their ultimate worth. These communities affirmed the content of the collection without resorting to a single explanation of wisdom's setting. In the Hebrew Bible the wisdom writings appear without such a setting. Wisdom traits occur throughout the Scriptures, but seem to originate in no single location.

---

12. Glendon E. Bryce, *A Legacy of Wisdom* (Lewisburg: Bucknell University Press, 1979), 170.
13. Walter A. Brueggeman, "The Social Significance of Solomon as Patron of Wisdom" in *SIANE*, 131.

International Influences

Wisdom forms may have entered Israel by way of Canaanite culture at large. The nation and its professionals then accepted them as part of the common heritage shared with neighboring ethnic groups. To the degree this is the case, the prebiblical origins of Israel's wisdom remain lost to the Bible student, except as the study of wisdom in adjacent civilizations reveals its origin. Israel's wisdom reveals some traces of class influence in its forms, but in the main wisdom did not belong to the sophisticates, nor was it clearly connected to the lower class family which represented the bulk of Israel's population. Wisdom pervaded all aspects of the culture and left its influence throughout the Hebrew Bible. If Israel's wisdom possessed a clear line of development, surely a strong imprint of the social class responsible would remain on much of the literature.

Relation of Wisdom to Hebrew Society

Given the classless nature of the material, how did the teachings of wisdom relate to the society as a whole? Leo Perdue finds two paradigms: "Order and conflict." Ecclesiastes, with its encouragements to submit to God and the king, followed the model of order, as did Proverbs, with its emphasis on righteousness and discipline. By contrast, Job presented God's creative forces in struggle with nihilistic forces.[14] A larger issue seems to divide the social setting of these books along different lines. Proverbs, Psalms, Sirach, and The Wisdom of Solomon endorse ideas of prosperity for the righteous and punishment for the wicked. This represents orthodox wisdom. Both Job and Ecclesiastes deny such common assumptions regarding the basis for divine reward and punishment and so question human capability to predict or induce God's favor. The intriguing question thus arises: Did wisdom teachings primarily enforce or challenge prevailing cultural-religious attitudes? Interpreters remain divided on the issue. Central to the question is the interpreter's choice of Proverbs or Job/Ecclesiastes as normative wisdom. The direct opposition of the claims (the righteous do/do not suffer; the wicked do/do not prosper) makes such divisions inevitable.

Another perspective on the social setting of wisdom analyzes the literature in terms of ethics. Ecclesiastes shows little of the concern for the poor presented in Job. Rather than encouraging compassion, Ecclesiastes suggests a few relatively rigid patterns for behavior in what approximates a "least resistance" philosophy. The book advises the reader to find a measure of enjoyment amid life's confusion. Proverbs mixes concern for following rules and showing humane concern. In the Deuteronomistic literature a certain ethical component (obedience to God) is the core of wisdom. This perspective is common to Sirach and The Wisdom of Solomon as well. Again, the implications are too diverse for a single theory of wisdom's point of view on the issue. All of the possible responses share a pragmatic view that

---

14. "Cosmology and the Social Order in the Wisdom Tradition" in *SIANE*, 459–60.

tailored wisdom according to the responses demanded for specific cultural settings. Wisdom served as a tool which could be used either to reinforce or challenge the consensus depending on the perspective of the thinker and the situation of the community.

Summary: Identification of Wisdom Materials

This dual usage for wisdom manifests itself in the wide array of wisdom-related texts in the Hebrew Bible. The list below includes passages "influenced by" wisdom and passages "addressing" wisdom. Those "influenced by" wisdom display wisdom themes, forms, or vocabulary (for example, wisdom psalms and wisdom in the Torah). Those "addressing" wisdom use the word *wisdom* or related vocabulary to discuss aspects of wisdom itself (for example, descriptions of the wisdom of Solomon in 1 Kings, Joseph in Genesis, and Daniel in the Book of Daniel). This study reserves the term *wisdom literature* for Job, Proverbs, Ecclesiastes, Sirach, and The Wisdom of Solomon. All other wisdom-related materials fall under the two designations above.

"Wisdom" itself comprises the most important element of vocabulary leading to inclusion of materials in the following list. Thematic concerns identified as wisdom include a number of topics: (1) Texts addressing the acts of *ruling and judging*, such as Jethro's suggestions of judicial organization to Moses (Exod. 18:13–27), show wisdom influence. (2) *Advice offered in the court* like that offered Rehoboam (1 Kings 12:1–15) bears relation to wisdom. (3) A few of the passages deal with *cunning activity* (for example, the serpent in Gen. 3:1–7). (4) *Theophanic passages* (those involving an appearance of God) included in the list (Hab. 3; Amos 9:2–6) are those that emphasize God's uniqueness comparable to the theophany at the conclusion of Job (chaps. 38–41). (5) The theme of *divine reward and retribution*, such as that displayed throughout Deuteronomy, is not accounted wisdom unless the passage revealed *other wisdom traits*. For example, the introduction to the Song of Moses (Deut. 32) identifies it as a unit of teaching (also Hos. 14:9). (6) A number of *proverbs* (Hos. 4:11; Jer. 5:26–27), *riddles* (Ezek. 17:2–10), and similar forms such as the *allegories* of Ezekiel (15:2–8; 20:49) or the *rhetorical questions* of Amos 3:3–8 are easily identified as wisdom. (7) Beyond themes and forms, certain texts display a perspective which can be characterized as *didactic intent*. Not all apparently "teaching" texts may be described as wisdom, but as a criterion complementary to form and theme it provides an additonal helpful guideline.

Table 1
Wisdom Texts in the Hebrew Bible

Genesis	3:1–7; 37–50
Exodus	1:8–2:14; 7:11; 18:13–27; 28:3; 31:3; 35:31–39:31
Deuteronomy	1:13,15; 6:1–25; 32:1–47
Joshua	1:8
1 Samuel	25:2–42

Table 1 (Continued)
Wisdom Texts in the Hebrew Bible

2 Samuel	9–20
1 Kings	1–2; 3:1–12:15
Isaiah	1:2–3, 26; 3:2–3; 5:20–21, 24; 8:9–10; 10:13–15; 19:11–15; 26; 28:23–29; 29:13–16; 32:5–8; 40:12–41:1; 42:5; 44:9–20; 44:24–26; 45:9–23; 46; 48:13; 53:11; 61:11; 65:6–7
Jeremiah	4:22; 5:3, 20–29; 7:28; 8:4–9; 9:12, 23–24; 10:1–16, 23–24; 12:1–4; 13:12–14; 17:5–11,23; 18:18–23; 20:7–18; 23:18–22; 31:35–37; 49:7; 50:35–36
Ezekiel	12:21–25; 15:2–8; 16:44–63; 17:2–10; 18:2–30; 20:49; 28:2–19
Hosea	4:11, 14; 9:7; 14:9 (14:10 Hebrew)
Amos	3:3–8; 5:8–15; 9:2–6
Obadiah	8
Habakkuk	1:1–2:5; 3
Malachi	1:6; 2:6–9
Psalms	1; 9:1–10:18; 14 and 53; 19:7–13; 36; 37; 49; 73; 112; 119; 127; 128; 144:3–4
Job	(entirety)
Proverbs	(entirety)
Ecclesiastes	(entirety)
Lamentations	3:37–45
Esther	1:13–20
Daniel	1:3–5,17,20; 2:12,20–23,25–30; 9:22; 12:3
2 Chronicles	1:10–12; 9:1–9,22–23
Sirach*	(entirety)
The Wisdom of Solomon*	(entirety)

* Deuterocanon works

Questions for Discussion

1. What are the basic concerns of Old Testament wisdom? How did such concerns fit into the life and worship of Israel?

2. Identify the books in the wisdom canon and the distinct contribution each makes to the meaning of wisdom.

3. What wisdom concerns appear in books outside the wisdom canon?

Chapter 2

Ancient Near Eastern
Wisdom Documents

Introduction:
The International Character of Wisdom Documents

Israel's wisdom did not develop in isolation from their ancient Near Eastern neighbors, nor did it originate within the nation Israel itself. The inclusion of major portions of the Instruction of Amenemopet in Proverbs 22:17–24:34 demonstrates that Israel borrowed a portion of its proverbial wisdom from Egypt. Mesopotamia also provides examples of the pattern for wisdom in the royal court.[1] From the semi-nomadic and patriarchal groupings of Canaan and Mesopotamia came the familial instruction which plays such a prominent role in Proverbs and Ecclesiastes.[2] From the later Greek culture the deuterocanonical wisdom books, Sirach and especially The Wisdom of Solomon, gain Hellenistic viewpoints.[3]

Each of these neighboring regions deserves detailed attention, but first, the reasons for such wide-ranging influence on Israel's wisdom demand at least hypothetical explanation. Signs of influence from earlier cultures exist for practically all the literature of the Hebrew Bible. The history of Israel, as presented in the Bible, provides a basis for this. The Hebrews assumed their cultural identity in Egypt under Moses. The land they later possessed provided a home for numerous other Canaanite cultures,

---

1. Egyptian sources include "The Instruction of Prince Hardjedef," "The Instruction of Ptahhotep," and "The Instruction to King Merikare." The Assyrian story, "Ahiqar," exemplifies court wisdom from Mesopotamia.
2. Support for this view comes from Job's association with Uz (not a Hebrew town) and the passages indicating Edom as a wisdom center (Job 1:1; Jer. 49:7; Obad. 8).
3. The Wisdom of Solomon's hypostatization of wisdom and the strong didactic tone of Sirach are examples.

influenced by older Mesopotamian cultures. In fact, the Hebrews themselves lived among these Canaanites before their bondage in Egypt.[4] The Hebrews expressed their devotion to Yahweh in the literary forms common to their heritage. They became heirs not only to Canaanite houses and lands, but also to Canaanite language and literature. Israel's unique contributions to theology and culture arise from the special themes of the biblical literature. Its forms show parallels to all the surrounding cultures.[5]

The distinction Israel brought to these forms resided in her special monotheistic theology. The lack of emphasis on monotheism in Hebrew wisdom serves as a first clue to the international character of wisdom. Wisdom addressed the pragmatic concerns of daily conduct. Such guidelines for daily living did not depend on exclusive monotheism for their validity. The need for such things as discipline, hard work, and marital fidelity remained constant in all cultures and religions. Hebrew wisdom conveys this spirit. If wisdom downplayed Israel's exclusive claims for Yahweh, it also blunted the extreme polytheism of other nations. In Egypt, for example, wisdom documents often address "God" (the Creator) instead of naming one of the deities of the pantheon. From Israel's standpoint the "orthodox" understanding of God-and-Israel-in-tandem was surely assumed by wisdom teachers. God directed the fortunes of his people, and those who exhibited wisdom and morality especially benefited from his providence. The proponents of Israel's wisdom assuredly presupposed the necessity of personal faith. This explains the recurrence of "the fear of the LORD" in Job, Ecclesiastes, and Proverbs. Whether the sages acted as professionals or family members, they presumed their hearers worshiped Yahweh. Yet the sages were open to sound advice from any quarter since experience in living yielded self-justifying truths. When proverbs and lengthier reflections were recognized as valid (by community or individual), they were also "canonized" as the will of Yahweh for Israel.

These wisdom materials, oral and written, came from many quarters (ancient family traditions, travelers' tales, court libraries, prophecy, experience, or individual creativity). However, Israel made little attempt to cover the alien origins of wisdom literature. For instance, a portion of Proverbs (31:1) opens with the name of a non-Israelite king. Also, Job lived in Uz,

---

4. Joshua 24:2 says of Terah, Abraham's father, "[He] lived beyond the Euphrates and served other gods." In 24:14–15 Joshua asked the people to choose loyalty for (1) the gods of Mesopotamia, (2) the gods of Egypt, (3) the gods of the Amorites (Canaanites), or (4) Yahweh. Such frank discussions illustrate the great influence these neighboring cultures exercised for Israel.

5. Psalmic literature existed throughout Palestine well before Israel's entry as seen in the vast number of Assyrian and Babylonian hymns. Prophetic oracles guaranteeing the deity's blessing or curse issued from several civilizations. The activity of the prophet Balaam in Numbers 22–24 indicates the Moabites used blessings and curses in forms similar to those Israel used. Legal materials such as the ancient Babylonian Code of Hammurabi (eighteenth century B.C.E.) convey an instructional tone like that of the Torah. The sacred history of the Epic of Gilgamesh depicts the origins of the world through the use of a few images common to Genesis (for example, the distinction between oceans and fresh water and the separation of creation into several distinct acts).

rather than in Israel. The proverbs copied from Amenemopet provide further evidence of wisdom's international base.

The sages allowed themselves more freedom to directly employ foreign literary forms than Israel's sacred historians and prophets. This openness to outside influence resulted from the differences in the intentions of the literature. The Law and the Prophets relate moral obligations conveyed directly by God. They also encourage worship based on these obligations. So, the Law and the Prophets supported Israel's nationhood in a way that wisdom did not. Wisdom's role in the canon seems to be one of support. While wisdom's facets belong to the members of Yahweh's community, engagement in wise conduct does not in itself identify a person as a member of Israel. Wisdom eventually became a further means to accomplish the moral and religious ends common to God's people. Wisdom without religious devotion remained incomplete. God spoke through wisdom.

Egyptian Documents

Israel's history shows Egypt exerted primary influence on early Israelite wisdom.[6] Accordingly, the literature of Egypt attracts earliest attention in this study. However, the biblical materials provide little indication of direct dependence on the written documents known to Egyptian wisdom. The basic Egyptian word for wisdom, *ma'at*, evokes the notion of a divinely ordered creation ("cosmos"). Even though the earliest wisdom influence on Israel came from Egypt, Israel did not share the basic concept that wisdom existed as a latent force in the natural order. This view seems better suited to fertility religions than the distinct monotheism reflected in the Hebrew canon.

Egypt's commitment to wisdom activity began long before the time of Joseph. Hieroglyphic writing originated around 3000 B.C.E. With the birth of writing, a class of literary scholars arose. Didactic materials authored for the training of these scribes constitutes the earliest Egyptian wisdom.[7] Schools for instruction in writing and training in general wisdom became common among the aristocracy in Egypt. To support these institutions, libraries developed.

Written between 2500 and 2100 B.C.E., "The Instruction of Prince Hardjedef," "The Instruction of Kagemni," and "The Instruction of Ptahhotep"[8] contained proverbs scarcely distinguishable from those in the Hebrew canon. The opening lines of "Kagemni" offer the following proverb:

---

6. The biblical accounts of the life of Joseph and the Exodus indicate strong ties with Egypt during the formative years of Hebraic culture. Egyptian wise men appear as early as Genesis 41:8, in connection with dream interpretation. "Magicians" are mentioned with indications that this office is subsidiary to wisdom in general. Joseph's value to the kingdom lay in his ability to interpret dreams, forecast the future, and devise plans to insure the prosperity of the kingdom.

7. Ronald J. Williams, "The Sage in Egyptian Literature" in *SIANE*, 19.

8. Miriam Lichtheim, *Ancient Egyptian Literature: A Book of Readings*, vol. 1 (Berkeley: University of California Press, 1973); "Hardjedef," 58–59; "Kagemni," 59–61; "Ptahhotep," 61–80.

The respectful man prospers,
Praised is the modest one,
The tent is open to the silent,
The seat of the quiet is spacious.
Do not chatter![9]

"Ptahhotep" is far more significant due to its length. The introduction of the work spells out the disadvantages of age, reminiscent of Ecclesiastes 12. Lines in "Ptahhotep" similar to the form and content of Proverbs, include the following:

Do not be greedy in the division,
Do not covet more than your share;
Do not be greedy toward your kin,
The mild has a greater share than the harsh (strophe 20a).[10]

Passages throughout the document relay its intended use for the training of Egyptian officials in a manner far more pronounced than in the biblical Proverbs.

"The Instruction to King Merikare"[11] (about 1350 B.C.E.) contained similar maxims, but displayed stylistic unity within longer sections. Short proverbs are consistently linked within strophes. The Book of Proverbs and earlier Egyptian examples do not display such unity.

Not all Egyptian wisdom related to the court. "The Instruction of Ani"[12] (about 1000 B.C.E.) recorded the teachings of a father to his son. Although the form of its contents tends to be more complex and free-flowing than the Book of Proverbs, the didactic tone of the two works shows a close correspondence.

Two further examples of Egyptian didactic literature parallel biblical material. First, a clear connection between "The Instruction of Amenemopet"[13] and "The Sayings of the Wise" in Proverbs 22:17–24:22 was demonstrated by Adolf Erman in the 1920s.[14] The Egyptian work dates to about 1150 B.C.E. or earlier. Numerous duplicated proverbs indicate direct dependence by the later author of the passage in Proverbs. Second, a lesser connection exists between Hebraic lists of the components of the created order and Egyptian onomastica.[15]

An onomasticon attempts to list comprehensively all natural phenomena or a more specialized group of things under generic headings. One

9. Lichtheim, *AEL* 1, 59.

10. Ibid.

11. Ibid., 97–109.

12. Trans. and ed. John A. Wilson, James B. Pritchard, *Ancient Near Eastern Texts Relating to the Old Testament*, 3rd ed. with supplement (Princeton: Princeton University Press, 1969), 420–21.

13. Victor H. Matthews and Don C. Benjamin, *Old Testament Parallels: Laws and Stories from the Ancient Near East* (New York: Paulist Press, 1991), 189–98. Wilson and Pritchard, 421–25.

14. "Eine Ägyptische Quelle der Sprüche Salamos" in *Sitzungsberichte der preussischen Akademie der Wissenschaften*, Philosophisch-historische Klasse 15,16 (May 1924).

15. For representative onomastica, see A. H. Gardiner, *Ancient Egyptian Onomastica*, 2 vols. (Oxford: Oxford University Press, 1947).

plausible reading of 1 Kings 4:33 (Heb. 5:13)—"He [Solomon] would speak of trees, from the cedar that is in the Lebanon to the hyssop that grows in the wall; he would speak of animals, and birds, and reptiles, and fish"— attributes the categories mentioned to nature lists (onomastica). The list of the wonders of the natural world in Job 38–39, though not as comprehensive, shows similarities to the Egyptian list of Amenope. Sirach 43 also displays parallels to Amenope.[16]

Egypt's so-called "pessimistic literature" reproduces Ecclesiastes' questioning of meaning or Job's challenge to the fairness of life. Among these works is "A Dispute over Suicide," also known as "The Sufferer and His *Ba*/ Soul"[17] (about 2000 B.C.E.). This work presents a person in dialogue with his eternal self over the propriety of suicide. The work contains parallels to Job 3. In "Admonitions of Ipuwer"[18] (about 2000 B.C.E.), the speaker, like Job, communicates dissatisfaction to the deity regarding social and cosmic injustice. "The Song of the Harper" inscribed on the tomb of Intef[19] (about 1250 B.C.E.) offers encouragements to enjoy life because of the inevitability of death, a theme repeated in Ecclesiastes.

Canaanite Documents

Excavations at Ugarit (in ancient Syria) from 1929–1976 discovered numerous documents, including several didactic texts. For Ugarit as well as Israel, the traditions arising in Sumer, Babylon, and Assyria laid the foundation for later wisdom. Ugaritic poetic texts employed parallel word pairs, some of which are identical to the parallel terms of Hebrew poetry. At times these parallel word pairs consist of wisdom vocabulary and are used in contexts which approximate the form of the biblical *māšāl* (proverb). Ugaritic texts also contain challenges to traditional, orthodox teaching regarding suffering such as those present in Job. Though the date of its origins can only be guessed, the tablets contain a story of a righteous sufferer who survived the destruction of Ugarit just after 1200 B.C.E.[20]

This story, in an even older version, may have served as the basis for the prose framework of Job.[21] Its appearance in the Akkadian language rather than Ugaritic indicates its antiquity. A later version exists in the Babylonian, "The Poem of the Righteous Sufferer." Other Ugaritic wisdom texts present proverbial or pessimistic content.

Evidence for wisdom among Israel's immediate neighbors comes from biblical references to wisdom in Edom, which bordered Israel on the

16. The date of Amenope's work approximates the date of "The Instruction of Amenemopet," earlier than its earliest known biblical counterpart.

17. Wilson, *ANET*, 405–7. Matthews and Benjamin, 206–11.

18. Lichtheim, *AEL* 1, 149–63. Wilson, *ANET*, 441–44.

19. Lichtheim, *AEL* 1, 194–97. Wilson, *ANET*, 467.

20. RS 25.460 published in Jean Nougayrol, Emmanuel Laroche, Charles Virolleaud, and C. F. A. Schaeffer, *Ugaritica V*, Mission de Ras Shamra 16 (Paris: Imprimerie Nationale, 1968), 265–73. The translation is in French.

21. Leo Perdue, *Wisdom and Cult* (Missoula, Mont.: Scholors Press, 1977), 166.

southwest. Perhaps Job's homeland, Uz (1:1), was Edom. Both Obadiah and Jeremiah 49:7 indicate an important emphasis on wisdom in Edom, but no Edomite wisdom texts exist to confirm such an emphasis.

Mesopotamian Documents

Three distinct yet related civilizations in Mesopotamia also produced wisdom documents. The earliest was Sumer, which yielded wisdom texts dating to approximately 2500 B.C.E. Among these are proverbs classified in two major groupings: those relating to practical matters and those dealing with contradictions or ironies of existence. Here, in miniature, are the two major aspects of Hebrew wisdom as shown in Proverbs and Ecclesiastes, respectively.[22] A Sumerian account of the Job motif bears the title, "Man and His God."[23] In this work a completely just person suffers and continually cries to his deity until the deity responds and replaces his suffering with joy. To some extent the text simply affirms the theology of retribution, but it also contains questions and doubts much like Job's. Babylon, according to the evidence, possessed the richest tradition of wisdom in the ancient Near East. The Babylonian words for wisdom, however, refer to abilities in divination and worship rites.[24] One document, "The Poem of the Righteous Sufferer"[25] (1500–1200 B.C.E.) shows some affinities with and some differences from Job. Like Job, the sufferer embodies complete righteousness, endures extensive suffering, and describes his bodily suffering using common terms (including loss of appetite, dreams, and other features explicitly given in Job). Unlike Job, his suffering is more directly attributed to the wrath of the deity, with less overt theodicy. Also, the Babylonian document mentions incantations (especially their lack of effect).[26]

Around 1000 B.C.E., a document known as "Theodicy"[27] presented alternating speeches of a sufferer and his friend. The sufferer maintains the gods are punishing him for nothing, while the friend cautions that he is angering the deity and should be patient and wait for ultimate rewards. The parallel to the story of Job is astounding. "Counsels of Wisdom"[28] (1500–1200 B.C.E.) presents multiple two-line proverbs which read much like biblical proverbs and relate identical themes. The brief units seem to be gathered into loosely connected thematic units similar to those in Proverbs. Enuma Elish[29] described the Babylonian god, Ea, as wise, omniscient, know-

22. Samuel Noah Kramer, "The Sage in Sumerian Literature" in *SIANE*, 33.
23. Trans. S. N. Kramer, ANET, 589–91.
24. W. G. Lambert, *Babylonian Wisdom Literature* (London: Oxford University Press, 1960), 1.
25. Ibid., 21–62. The poem may also bear the title, "I Will Praise the Lord of Wisdom," based on the first line.
26. Ibid., 32–36.
27. Lambert, 63–91. Matthews and Benjamin, 219–24. Trans. R. D. Biggs, *ANET*, 601–4.
28. Lambert, 96–107. Lambert included numerous additional proverbs, 222–82. R. H. Pfeiffer, *ANET*, 425–27 translated various brief collections of Akkadian proverbs dating between the eighteenth and fourteenth centuries B.C.E. Each saying functioned in isolation from the preceding and following, similar to portions of Proverbs. The units are mostly 1–2 lines.
29. E. A. Speiser, *ANET*, 60–72.

ing all wisdom, and embracing all through his knowledge. This is reminiscent of the repeated, "The fear of the LORD is the beginning of wisdom" in Proverbs, as well as Job's descriptions of God's superior wisdom at the conclusion of the poetry of the book.

Didactic literature arose from two contexts in Assyria: the court (nobility and advisers) and the tablet house (scribes). Just before 700 B.C.E., "wise" especially designated the Assyrian king. A document from a later period, known as "Ahiqar"[30] is written as a tale rather than as a wisdom document; but as Ahiqar (the protagonist) defended himself, he offered proverbs and metaphors. Ahiqar acted as counselor to Sennacherib (704–681) and to his son Esarhaddon (680–669). Esarhaddon sought to kill Ahiqar out of fear that he would use his wisdom skills to incite the populace against the king.

The association of wisdom with the monarch involved both the king's office and his activity. Sargon spoke of his own wisdom. The attribution of wisdom to Sennacherib resulted from his building programs. Biblical accounts imply that Solomon's achievements result from his wisdom. His most obvious achievements were his building campaigns (palace, stables, temple). Merodach-baladan II (Babylonian usurper of the Assyrian throne, 721–710) also gains the designation "wise" in Assyrian literature.[31]

A further parallel with Hebrew wisdom concerns vocabulary: The Assyrian noun, nēmequ (wisdom), denotes among other things, possession of skill for the performance of an occupation. In this respect, it echoes the Hebrew ḥŏkmâ (חָכְמָה). The later perspectives of Assyria provide evidence of views held in common with Israel. Such shared outlooks came as the result of universal cultural development, common influences, and the influence of Assyria as Israel's suzerain.

Greek Documents

Vocabulary also provides an example of the corollaries between Hebrew and Greek wisdom. Direct influence of Greek ideology on Hebrew wisdom materials can only be maintained for the two latest wisdom books—Sirach and The Wisdom of Solomon. Israel's wisdom, however, exercised strong influence on Greek wisdom documents, as indicated by the nearly identical semantic ranges of mētis (Gk. μῆτις, wisdom). Greek literature contains numerous examples of philosophical reflections on good and evil like those found in Job. Greek Stoicism and Skepticism provided even more examples of pessimistic literature like Ecclesiastes. In Greek wisdom, however, the element of personal theology (the sovereign direction of the creator God) is replaced by specific systems of rational speculation. This makes comparisons difficult to draw. The wise among the Greeks did not engage

---

30. Trans. H. L. Ginsberg, ANET, 427–30.
31. Ronald F. G. Sweet, "The Sage in Akkadian Literature," in SIANE, 52–54. On the connection of wisdom with temple-building, see 57.

in the production of sentences and couplets like those found in Proverbs. At least such activity did not comprise a major portion of their activity. Indications of Greek influence on Sirach and The Wisdom of Solomon are integral to the interpretations of the books, and these issues are reserved for the chapter which offers brief interpretations.

The Special Character of Hebrew Wisdom

The larger themes approached in Israel's wisdom books occur repeatedly in cognate literatures. In some cases, the common facets emanate from the Near Eastern milieu, but in others, features recur which manifest universal interest. The Job motif, like the story of the primeval flood, appears in many civilizations around the globe, and the doctrine of deserved retribution, which Job's experience challenged, displays an equally wide distribution. While this observation will not enable the student to identify the unique characteristics of Israel's wisdom tradition, it offers caution against the tendency to view Israel's literature as isolated or unique. The story of Job did not originate in Israel, as indicated in Job 1:1. The existence of literature nearly identical to Job which predates Israel and its patriarchs further identifies the Book of Job as an accomplished retelling of an older story. In spite of such heavy interchange, Israel offered distinct contributions to the wisdom enterprise in the Near East. Israel's writings are so distinctive that some scholars object to the use of the term *wisdom literature* in reference to non-Israelite wisdom, preferring the nonaligned description *didactic literature.*[32]

Israel's wisdom presented in Proverbs, Job, and Ecclesiastes concerns informed observations regarding life and its challenges, rather than formal instruction by scribes or others. Hebrew wisdom encourages readers not to study, but to practice discretion. This leads to equating wisdom with righteousness and (later in the development of wisdom) with religiosity. These strictly practical, plebian concerns play only a minor role in the wisdom of companion cultures. Other civilizations developed schools. They associated the investigations of the sage with the office of scribe. They mixed reflections on the art of living with general education. Israel borrowed themes from international wisdom, but used them in a less regimented fashion. Their adaptations suited the literature for Hebrew culture. In distinction from its neighbors, Israel's religious literature (1) granted less priority to the privileged class, (2) remembered familial obligations in connection with its tribal roots, and (3) understood itself in terms of Yahweh's demands. This idealistic portrait of Hebrew culture reflects the perspective assumed by the canonical literature. Their special attitude toward their nation as anti-oligarchic, orally literate, and radically monotheistic left its mark upon wisdom materials. Eventually (perhaps at the time of the captivity or at the time

---

32. First proposed by Lambert, 1; and reiterated by Fisher, "The Didactic Literature of Ugarit" in *SIANE*, 74.

when Assyrian dominance made self-governance impossible), Israel's interests in wisdom turned from international interdependence. This resulted in the view of wisdom as the product of Yahweh's inspiration alone. This accounts for the difference in tone in Proverbs 1–9 as compared to the remainder of the book. Even later in Israel's history, wisdom finds its definition in the personality of the deity. This view, known as hypostasis, occurs in fully-developed form only in The Wisdom of Solomon (see chaps. 6–9). Israel's commerce in wisdom had narrowed to the point of cultural isolation, though the borrowing continued (Greek forms and Greek rhetoric).

The international perspective allows us to position Israel's literature among that of their neighbors. Having done that we must ask more specific questions. How was wisdom put to use? For what audience was wisdom intended? At least six answers are possible, and none of the suggestions are exclusive. Wisdom was preserved for (1) the upper class (a general audience), (2) royalty and governmental leaders, (3) judges, (4) business professionals, (5) wisdom professionals, and (6) children (in a family setting).[33]

Wisdom as Literature of the Upper Class

The contention that wisdom served the higher social stratum in Israel presumes the existence of academies for the training of the elite class.[34] This view must overcome a large gap in evidence. Prerabbinic Israel left neither indications of schools nor any intimation of a significant upper class (except those associated with palace and temple). Texts such as Ecclesiastes 12:12 do encourage the study of wisdom for wisdom's sake, but the notion that such study belonged only to the social elite reflects a much later view of education. The earliest mention of a school for wisdom is Sirach 51:23. The date of this work (shortly after 200 B.C.E.) reveals that such institutions assumed no integral role in the development of classical wisdom. The proposal of some type of training system for the wise in ancient Israel contains merit. The contention that this machinery served broad public interests appears unlikely. The strong popular tone of the wisdom books offers the most convincing evidence against the view. Specialized segments of society propagated wisdom in so far as formal training was concerned.

Wisdom as Literature for the Training of Royalty

The use of wisdom by members of the royal court and official governmental personnel remains incontestable. The three figures—Daniel, Joseph, and Solomon—stand out. Daniel 1:4 provides evidence that Daniel

---

33. For recent studies on the social setting of the wise or sages, see R. N. Whybray, "The Social World of the Wisdom Writers," in *The World of Ancient Israel*, ed. R. E. Clements (New York: Cambridge University Press, 1989), 227–50; R. E. Clements, *Wisdom in Theology* (Grand Rapids: Eerdmans, 1992); John G. Gammie and Leo G. Perdue, eds. *The Sage in Israel and the Ancient Near East* (Winona Lake: Eisenbrauns, 1990); Duane A. Garrett, *Proverbs, Ecclesiastes, Song of Songs*, New American Commentary 14 (Nashville: Broadman Press, 1993), 23–26.

34. See James L. Crenshaw, "Education in Ancient Israel," *JBL* 104 (1985), 601–15; Andre Lemaire, "The Sage in School and Temple, *SIANE*, 165–81.

exhibited capabilities associated with wisdom which made him valuable to the king. These abilities also suited him for further education. The relatively late date of Daniel and its setting in a foreign court decrease its value in indicating the nature of classical wisdom. Earlier texts, however, provide views of court wisdom similar to those in Daniel. Genesis 39:2–6 attributes Joseph's wisdom to natural ability and divine gift. The Joseph narrative includes no indication of instruction either before or after his entry into Pharaoh's court. It does relate his wisdom to his prosperity, which indicated God's presence. It also reckons his service to the kingdom as "wise" precisely because of the financial success he brought to Pharaoh. Israel's literature contends that what our society attributes to business savvy and common sense actually reveals gifts of God and signs of his nearness. This holds true for Daniel, Joseph, and Solomon.

Solomon's wisdom showed itself in the skills which enabled him to rule well. The recognition that training in wisdom could improve the monarch's abilities lies only one step beyond such appreciation of wisdom's benefit. Solomon's propagation of wisdom instruction through Proverbs and Ecclesiastes rests on a secure foundation. The reader must also reckon with the suggestion that the attribution of wisdom to court life came late in the development of the court history. The model for royal wisdom could have been adapted from the Assyrians or Babylonians and applied to Solomon retroactively. This would explain the lack of court sages and the lack of mention of court study of wisdom before Daniel. Perhaps for the entire population of Israel, emphasis on the formal study of wisdom came only in the exile. With the appearance of the synagogues, rabbinic thinkers projected speculations similar to their own into the past. Under such influence, the idealization of Israel's former monarchy made its figures likely sources of later wisdom. The formative influence of the exilic and postexilic periods must be recognized, but it remains unlikely that Israel's commitment to wisdom instruction fell so far behind the position of nearby civilizations.

Wisdom as Literature for the Training of Judges

Less direct evidence exists to support the claim that wisdom served as preparation and continued training for judges. The account of Jethro's reform of Moses' judgeship in Exodus 18:13–27 fails to mention wisdom. However, for the author of Kings, Solomon's ability to decide the case between the two prostitutes (1 Kings 3:16–28) provides proof of his wisdom (v. 28). If Jethro's suggestions fall into the domain of wisdom, the context for judicial wisdom could be projected to Israel's tribal roots. This suggests familial and popular roots for wisdom prior to its adoption by the monarchy. This so-called clan wisdom serves as an illusory subject for study. Such wisdom survived through oral transmission. This means the clues to its operation exist in the transmission of tribal traditions rather than in written records.

Within this perspective, the origins of the Book of Job may rest in a tribal "test case." Such a view depicts the story of Job as a dramatic retelling of the fortunes of one who experienced the extreme limits of divine retribution and questioned its justice. The supposed setting for the tribal retelling of Job's story relates to the meeting of elders at the city gate, a council named *sōdh* (סוֹד) in Hebrew. This council of elders decided on local judicial cases. During such a meeting, it is supposed, the character Job offered his arguments, which disparaged conventional theology.[35] The format of the book provides further support for this view: Its dialogues may be construed as three cycles of "testimony."

Wisdom as the Literature of Traders

Scattered throughout the wisdom canon, evidence exists for the assertion that wisdom supported trade guilds. This offers a ready explanation for the international scope of wisdom. When any sort of international affiliation occurs, trade usually forms its earliest basis. The emphasis upon diligence in Proverbs and Ecclesiastes fits within this pattern. The wide experience assumed by the speaker in Ecclesiastes matches the circumstances of a successful businessman engaged in world travel. The lack of any reference to training schools for merchants disappoints the critic who places heavy emphasis on this social setting.

Wisdom as Literature for the Training of Sages

Numerous references to the wise and wisdom in the Hebrew Bible lead to the hypothesis that the wisdom writings served an office of wisdom professionals. Jeremiah 18:18, Ezekiel 7:26, and comparable passages attest to the existence of the wisdom teacher, or sage. The previous generation of scholarship assumed the presence of such wisdom officials. Beginning in the 1970s, the basis for the recognition of a distinguishable social office for the sage came into question. The place of the wisdom professional in Israel's wisdom tradition currently attracts attention as one of the most hotly contested issues in wisdom studies. Wisdom possessed specialized vocabulary and used words with general application in contexts demanding specialized ideas, which supports a professional understanding of Hebrew wisdom. Contrary to the identification of "sage" as a professional office, Jeremiah 18:18 may merely refer to the king's advisors, whose duty it was to give *ʿēṣā* (עֵצָה counsel).

The passage in Jeremiah mentions the office of sage along with that of priest and prophet. Despite obvious indications that sages functioned as independent professionals in Egypt and elsewhere, the title "sage," interpreted as "wisdom teacher," must be used cautiously when referring to Israel's earlier wisdom traditions.[36]

---

35. Whybray, *Intellectual Tradition*, 65 or more briefly with literature in "The Social World of the Wisdom Writers," 229–34.
36. See the articles in *SIANE*.

Wisdom as Literature for Family Training

The claim that Israel's wisdom supported the training of children cannot be questioned. Several references to "my son" in Proverbs offer evidence for this social setting. Such instruction took place in the home rather than in a formal setting. The literature concentrates on child rearing, though it includes other family concerns such as marriage, work, and religion. Beyond this, much of the wisdom addressed to the youth may be directed toward the young as a community resource rather than issued from parent to child. On the other hand, the archetypal tribal wisdom likely consisted of guidelines for living relayed from generation to generation, many of which were later adopted by wisdom proponents.[37] The use of the noun *children* does not imply pre-teens. Instructions on sexual behavior in Proverbs 1–9 and the admonitions to enjoy life before senility in Ecclesiastes 12:1ff are hardly addressed to younger children. The simplistic nature of many proverbs accords with the parental tone of Proverbs and portions of Ecclesiastes. Parenting occurs as a common theme, but this seems to relate to the origins of the sayings rather than their current canonical context. The bitterness expressed in Ecclesiastes provides evidence against the association of wisdom literature with children: This harsh message is better suited for adults with some breadth of experience. Likewise, the lesson of Job appeals to those who have engaged in enough social intercourse to be stripped of excessive idealism.

Summary: The Pervasiveness of Wisdom in Israelite Society

The foregoing account of social contexts directs attention to specific groups of individuals who benefited from wisdom. Proverbs 1:2–6 implies, however, that sagacity consists of a general orientation toward life. This text indicates no targeting of select social groups. In a corollary fashion, Sirach and The Wisdom of Solomon direct their sayings to the community at large rather than specialized societies. These documents function much like sermons for which the wisdom teacher plays the role of rhetorician. The words issue from key individuals who possess the authority necessary to address the Jewish community. Such wisdom teachings promoted social solidarity in the face of challenges to the community.

Wisdom appears to have come from nowhere, because of its primacy everywhere. The accessibility of wisdom to the prophets, most notably Isaiah, Jeremiah, and Ezekiel, relates to this issue. Are we to attribute the prophets' predispositions toward wisdom themes and forms to some other common office? For example, could the major prophets' ties to the priesthood (only Jeremiah was not a priest, and he was a priest's son) indicate the temple or other sanctuary as the locus of wisdom? Perhaps some other standard curriculum in prophetic training provided a link with wisdom. Perhaps the prophets' connections with the royal court offer the answer.

---

37. For the adoption of family terms into wisdom texts, see Carole R. Fontaine, "The Sage in Family and Tribe," *SIANE*, 155–64.

Perhaps the resolution lies in the availability of wisdom literature to the general public, making wisdom forms and themes attractive vehicles for prophetic images.

By using wisdom themes and vocabulary, prophetic speakers chose common metaphors, not professionalized forms. If wisdom existed as widely used oral literature, it appealed to many segments of society. They regarded it as a self-justifying popular form of truth. In certain times and places, its tenets may have been as much a model for speaking and acting in ancient Israel as those standards which current Western societies term "logic" and "reason."

All the previous suggestions of settings for wisdom in Israel's life assume a didactic role for wisdom. Wisdom (written, oral, or experiential) existed for training. Specialists agree on several broad goals this training attempted to achieve—morality, success at vocation, realistic theology. The most divisive issue among current students of Israel's wisdom is the question of provenance: Who kept Israel's wisdom? For what audience was it intended? Who benefited most from its propagation? These questions remain unanswered; rather, they are answered in manifold ways. A final solution appears unlikely, though the following chapter provides an overview of the attempts of previous thinkers to understand Israel's wisdom traditions.

Despite these uncertainties, a broad outline of wisdom's social setting can be traced. The royalty and aristocracy sponsored Israel's wisdom writings during the first temple period (960–586 B.C.E.). The early wisdom writings of the Hebrew canon (Proverbs, Job, and Ecclesiastes) reveal an international scope. Their connection with the monarchy remains inexplicit, but later connections with the temple and synagogue receive more support. The change in the base of authority from national institutions to religious ones occurred during the era of the second temple (515 B.C.E.–70 C.E.). The collapse of the state of Judah and its exile in Babylon forced the people to reevaluate their hope for an empire. This separated current wisdom interests from the political realm. Ironically, wisdom literature, now in the hands of religious professionals called scribes, fostered more intense national interests after the end of the monarchy than before.

With the loss of the monarchy, the survival of Israel's heritage depended upon its attention to religious traditions. Examination of the nation's wisdom literature led the scribes to increasingly Torah-centered and nationalistic interests. All the community's energies were mustered to consolidate the otherwise loose union and to offer apology for the state's continued existence. The belief that Israel alone, among all the nations, possessed "wisdom" represents the ultimate effect of this religious nationalism on wisdom.[38]

---

38. See John G. Gammie, "From Prudentialism to Apocalyptic" in *SIANE*, 490.

Questions for Discussion

1. Discuss the international character of wisdom. How was Israel's wisdom related to interntional wisdom? How does God's work of inspiration relate to Israel's experience with international wisdom?

2. What special characteristics does Israel's wisdom possess?

3. In what settings did Israel's wisdom originate and develop? Of what importance is it for you to understand the sociological settings of wisdom?

Chapter 3

History of Interpretation
Before the Reformation

Introduction: The Later Wisdom Tradition in Israel

Interpretation of Israel's wisdom literature began almost as soon as it was written. The first two chapters showed us the nature of wisdom and its shift from a political base to a religious one, especially after the rebuilding of the temple in 515 B.C.E. Political necessity provided the major impetus for these changes, but the bridge between the law and wisdom existed in Israel's earlier literature. Passages such as Deuteronomy 29:29, "The secret things belong to the LORD our God, but the revealed things belong to us and to our children forever, to observe all the words of this torah" (law or teaching), served as the basis for equating wisdom and law.[1] The verse relates wisdom and law in that both are "things revealed" and distinct from the "secret things" known only to God. Later wisdom centered its attention on this equation and assumed its task was to meditate on the Torah and wisdom which has been revealed.

Greek influence which grew after Alexander's invasion in 332 B.C.E. led to major cultural adaptations especially apparent in the literature of the Judaic community. The pervasiveness of Greek culture led to hellenized literary forms and genres. The most notable influence was the style of interpretation known as allegory. Allegorical interpretations of texts originated with the Greeks, who had developed the method well by 600 B.C.E. Its direct influence on recognized Jewish documents is not apparent before 400 B.C.E. Allegorical interpretations enabled the Diaspora community to renew ancient oral and written traditions by adding a contemporary relevance to

---

1. Joseph Blenkinsopp, *Wisdom and Law in the Old Testament* (Oxford: Oxford University Press, 1983), 131.

problematic or exhausted texts. Philo and later Christians used the method extensively.

Wisdom in the Deuterocanon and Pseudepigrapha

Our entry into later Jewish wisdom comes from the Deuterocanon. Examining each book that reflects wisdom interests will help us see the continuing influence and development of wisdom thinking in the Jewish community.

Tobit

The Book of Tobit (about 200 B.C.E.) offers an example of secondary wisdom. The protagonist whose name provides the title of the work serves as a Diaspora embodiment of Job. He illustrated righteousness, kindness to the needy, dedication to religious ritual, undeserved suffering, and ultimate reward.[2] Tobit also contains proverbs quoted from or influenced by similar maxims in the Book of Proverbs. The idea "almsgiving delivers from death" in Tobit 4:10 closely reflects the encouragements to proper financial conduct in Proverbs 10:2 and 11:4.

Sirach

The deuterocanonical book entitled the Wisdom of Jesus Son of Sirach (or Ecclesiasticus) provides a snapshot of Jewish wisdom around 180 B.C.E. Since the entire book was conceived as a book of wisdom, it yields information regarding continuity and discontinuity with the wisdom traditions associated with Solomon. Sirach's wisdom serves as the keystone in many, if not most, of the arguments detailing the "degeneration" of classic wisdom. No other book offers such a useful comparison to Proverbs, Job, and Ecclesiastes. Ben Sirach employed citations from Proverbs to support encouragements to faithful worship and living in accordance with the teachings of the Pentateuch. He apparently intended to protect the Jewish community from assimilation into Hellenism.[3]

To some degree, Sirach equates the practice of traditional Jewish piety with wisdom. Sirach's wisdom narrows the scope of wisdom to the nation Israel for the first time, effectively eliminating its international character.[4] Contemporary interpreters of Israel's wisdom commonly portray this

---

2. Devorah Dimant lists nine points of similarity between Job and Tobit in "Use and Interpretation of Mikra in the Apocrypha and Pseudepigrapha" in *Mikra: Text, Translation, Reading, and Interpretation of the Hebrew Bible in Ancient Judaism and Early Christianity,* ed. Martin Jan Mulder (Philadelphia: Fortress Press, 1988), 418.

3. This idea is supported by Teresa Brown, "Ben Sira's 'In Praise of Israel's Ancestors': An Example of Intra-Biblical Midrash" (M.A. thesis, Mobile College, 1992).

4. See Coert Rylaarsdam, *Revelation in Jewish Wisdom Literature* (Chicago: University of Chicago Press, 1946), 27. In the chapter entitled "The Nationalization of Wisdom" Rylaarsdam claimed a noticeable increase in the use of Israel's own religious traditions beginning with Sirach.

parochial emphasis and related changes apparent in Sirach as a weakening of the more valuable ideas in Proverbs, Job, and Ecclesiastes. The argument, in simplified form, builds as follows: Wisdom began as a system which reveled in the divine moral order as illustrated in Proverbs. The pursuit of such knowledge entailed the study and application of "natural" principles. This pristine quest for practical information related to, but did not equal, Israel's understanding of God. As Israel incorporated its specially revealed understanding of Yahweh into this search for order, the study of Torah became a substitute for the findings yielded by observation of the world and human conduct. Wisdom degenerated into an apology for Israel's election, leading to emphasis upon simple obedience to the demands of Torah.[5]

Such an ordering of the facts reveals strong Western biases toward scientific observation, intercultural interchange, and natural law. The greatest difficulty resides in the manner of reporting the change which is itself obvious. The transition can be clarified by tracing the redirection of the meaning of the word *tōrâ* (תּוֹרָה).

In the following passage the Book of Sirach relates wisdom to a specific body of knowledge.

> He seeks out the wisdom of all the ancients, and is concerned with prophecies; He preserves the sayings of the famous and penetrates the subtleties of parables; He seeks out the hidden meanings of proverbs and is at home with the obscurities of parables. He serves among the great and appears before rulers; he travels in foreign lands and learns what is good and evil in the human lot. He sets his heart to rise early to seek the Lord who made him, and to petition the most high; he opens his mouth in prayer and asks pardon for his sins. If the great Lord is willing, he will be filled with the spirit of understanding; he will pour forth words of wisdom of his own and give thanks to the Lord in prayer. The Lord will direct his counsel and knowledge, as he meditates on his mysteries. He will show the wisdom of what he has learned, and will glory in the law of the Lord's covenant. (Sirach 39:1–8)

This indicates the canonical turning point at which the Torah was identified with wisdom. Previously even the word *Torah* possessed an indefinite meaning (teaching or instruction as well as law), but the word increasingly came to designate the first five books of the canon as embodying all the demands of God. When the concept of wisdom was subordinated to Torah, the Law became the exclusive locus of wisdom. Increasingly the discipline lent itself to legalistic interpretations. Consequently, the scribe achieved status as the wisest of the wise. For Ben Sira wisdom and Torah merged into near equivalence.

---

5. For a classic statement of this view, see James Crenshaw, "Wisdom Literature" in *The Hebrew Bible and Its Modern Interpreters*, eds. Douglas A. Knight and Gene M. Tucker (Chico, Calif.: Scholars Press, 1985), 373. Rylaarsdam related this development to the changing concept of revelation in *Revelation in Jewish Wisdom Literature*.

In 38:24–39:11 Ben Sira gives evidence of the high social status of the scribe who needed free time to develop wisdom. Sirach recognized other careers as essential, but assigned priority to the scribal profession since the duty of contemplating the wisdom of the ages was unequaled. The ascendancy of the scribe led to Ben Sira's own wide reputation as Torah scholar and wisdom teacher.

Testaments of the Twelve Patriarchs

In its earliest form, the Testaments of the Twelve Patriarchs was contemporary with the Book of Sirach. Although its contents do not reflect the classic two-line form of the biblical *māshāl*, its existence confirms the continued use of proverb-like sayings. Its closest resemblance to biblical proverbs rests in its strong didactic emphasis, including addresses to children as students. It also contains narratives, prophecy, and apocalypticism. Christian interpolations later adapted the work for direct application to the church. This shows the ongoing preference for the simplistic didactic unit of the proverb. These worshiping communities apparently found that the proverb served as an effective vehicle for ecclesiastical instruction. By contrast, Job and Ecclesiastes were apparently little used.

The Wisdom of Solomon and 1 Enoch

Although Sirach was more widely accepted by the Christian community, it exercised considerable influence among Jews as well. Another Jewish work, The Wisdom of Solomon (100 B.C.E.) depicted wisdom in terms common to Greek philosophy but clearly addressed a Hebrew audience. It left little impression on the Jews but was widely accepted by Christians. Its distinctly Hebraic approach contrasts Greek religious thought, such as idolatry, to the wisdom of Israel. Repeated presentations regard Egypt as a symbolic title for the Hellenistic world.

The primary importance of Wisdom for this study rests in its attestation to the vitality of the ascription of wisdom to Solomon. The idea of wisdom existing as a separate manifestation of the deity related to the belief that the person of God inhabited the individual specially endowed with wisdom. This conception began as early as the time of Solomon.[6] The Wisdom of Solomon exceeds the trend toward hypostatization in Sirach by regarding wisdom as including prophetic knowledge (7:18, 21, 27). "[She] passes into holy souls and makes them friends of God and prophets" (7:27). The Wisdom of Solomon presents full-blown hypostasis in contrast to mere personification in Proverbs 8:1–21: "The Lord created me at the beginning of his work, the first of his acts of long ago. Ages ago I was set up, at the first, before the beginning of the earth. . . . When he marked out the foundations of the earth, then I was beside him, like a master worker, and I was daily his delight, rejoicing before him always" (Prov. 8:22–23, 29–30).

---

6. E. Earle Ellis, "Biblical Interpretation in the New Testament Church" in *Mikra*, 718.

This passage does not equate wisdom with God, but grants wisdom ascendancy over everything else God created. Sirach portrays wisdom as a more freestanding entity, having wisdom speak:

> Wisdom praises herself, and tells of her glory in the midst of her people. In the assembly of the Most High she opens her mouth, and in the presence of his hosts she tells of her glory: "I came forth from the mouth of the Most High, and covered the earth like a mist. Among all these I sought a resting place; in whose territory should I abide? Then the Creator of all things gave me a command, and my Creator chose the place for my tent: He said, 'Make your dwelling in Jacob, and in Israel receive your inheritance.'" (Sirach 24:1–8)

After Wisdom finishes her speech, the comment is added: "All this is the book of the covenant of the Most High God, the law that Moses commanded us" (24:23).

The Torah represents the seat of wisdom, but subsequent verses show that Ben Sira intended no simplistic equivalence of the Law and wisdom. Wisdom remained mysterious (Sirach 24:28–29). Greek influence led to definite hypostatization in the Wisdom of Solomon. The Wisdom of Solomon magnified Sirach's transcendent view of wisdom, making wisdom a member of the Godhead:

> I learned both what is secret and what is manifest, for wisdom, the fashioner of things, taught me. There is in her a spirit that is intelligent, holy, unique, manifold, subtle, mobile, clear, unpolluted, distinct, invulnerable, loving the good, keen, irresistable, beneficient, humane, steadfast, sure, free from anxiety, all-powerful, overseeing all, and penetrating through all spirits that are intelligent, pure, and altogether subtle, for wisdom is more mobile than any motion; because of her pureness, she pervades and penetrates all things. For she is a breath of the power of God, and a pure emanation of the glory of the Almighty; therefore nothing defiled gains entrance into her. For she is a reflection of eternal light, a spotless mirror of the working of God, and an image of his goodness. Although she is but one, she can do all things, and while remaining in herself, she renews all things; in every generation she passes into holy souls and makes them friends of God, and prophets; She reaches mightily from one end of the earth to the other, and she orders all things well. (Wisdom of Solomon 7:21-27; 8:1)

Wisdom performs the acts of God. A further example of praise to wisdom occurs in the pseudepigraphical Book of 1 Enoch (about 300 B.C.E.). In 42:1–2; 83:3; and 94:5 the work hypostatizes wisdom:

> Wisdom could not find a place in which she could dwell; but a place was found [for her] in the heavens. Then Wisdom went out to dwell with the children of the people, but she found no dwelling place. [So] Wisdom returned to her place, and she settled permanently among the angels. Then Iniquity went out of her rooms, and found whom she did

not expect. And she dwelt with them, like rain in a desert, like dew on a thirsty land. (1 Enoch 42:1–3)[7]

First Enoch presents a more pronounced portrait of wisdom as an independent being than Sirach. Even if Sirach were read as identifying Torah with wisdom, this would present a dependent entity rather than the self-determining agent of Wisdom 7–8 or 1 Enoch 42:1–2. Wisdom takes on a distinct personality as though a person of the Godhead or a deity in itself. Such presentations seem to have two major bases. First the Book of Proverbs personifies wisdom as a beautiful woman. In Proverbs the image functions on a purely literary basis with no intent to make wisdom a separate entity, but later writers saw Proverbs as a warrant to give "dame wisdom" a personality. Second, hypostatization occurs in Greek religious thought, where the world teems with spiritual essences and powers which enliven the physical world and reflect human experiences. A portion of these spiritual forces relate to human virtues, including wisdom.

Jewish authors probably did not intend to invoke a special deity or even a spiritual life force. The hypostasis assumes its place as an attribute of Yahweh, a lesser divine being under his control, or simply a vivid image to encourage devotion to wisdom. The implications of this development for the social setting of wisdom remain less than obvious. One may hazard the proposal that the vocational emphasis on wisdom fostered by the sage and later by the scribe dissipated into the identification of wisdom with God. This could result from the replacement of the professional interests of the sage with the more secretarian interests of the scribe (or other religious leader). Such a leader might produce a simplistic theology useful in consolidating a community. This describes one of the aims of apocalyptic literature, like 1 Enoch. In 1 Enoch, "wisdom" most often refers to the message of Enoch himself. Its meaning approximates the understanding of the prophets that their message had its source in the "Spirit of God" or his "word." The resultant theology in Enoch and elsewhere provided for a merger of competing or conflicting notions of revelation. The early church, or later Judaism sought a union among concepts of wisdom in (1) the Hebrew Bible, (2) rabbinic thought, and (3) Greek thought.[8]

Wisdom entered the Godhead in the guise of the Spirit as one byproduct of this merger of theologies. This, in turn, enabled the later proponents of biblical wisdom to present a compact authoritative portrait of the existent wisdom canon (including Hebrew, Jewish, and Greek works). They directed such effort toward the specific aim of solidifying a given group of wisdom's adherents. Contemporary interpreters often depict earlier wisdom as secular in comparison to later religious concepts. More correctly expressed, early wisdom embraced a wider ranging system of thought

---

7. Unless otherwise noted, quotations of the Pseudepigrapha are taken from James Charlesworth, *The Old Testament Pseudepigrapha*, 2 vols. (Garden City, N.Y.: Doubleday & Company, Inc., 1983). First Enoch, translated by E. Isaac, 1: 33.

8. As will be seen, Christians also identified wisdom as the preexistent Christ.

(expansive wisdom). Later wisdom molded its concepts to fit into a narrower theological scheme (reductive wisdom).

Psalms of Solomon

The Psalms of Solomon (about 50 B.C.E.) attempt to vest a later document with authority due Solomon based on his wisdom. The Psalms does not display the characteristics of Hebrew wisdom. The desire to claim Solomonic authority led to the incorporation of allusions to and quotations from Proverbs and other canonical materials without citation.

Psalm 154

In another pseudepigraphical writing, Psalm 154 (about 100 B.C.E.), the identification of Torah and wisdom reaches new heights. The "word" of Torah students coincides with the "word" of Wisdom (vv. 14–15):

> In a great voice glorify God: in the congregation of the many ones proclaim his glory. And in the multitude of the upright ones glorify his excellence; and with the faithful ones narrate his gloriousness. Associate yourselves with the good ones; and with the innocent ones to glorify the Most High. Gather together to announce his power; and do not neglect to declare his salvation, and his glory to all children. So that the honor of the Lord shall be made known, wisdom has been given. And to narrate his works, she has made known to humanity: To announce to children his power, and to explain to those lacking understanding his gloriousness, Those who are far from her entrances, and are dispersed from her gate. Because the Most High is the Lord of Jacob, and his pride is over all his works. And a person who glorifies the Most High, he accepts as one who offers a meal offering. And as one who offers he-goats and baby bulls; and as he who anoints the altar with many burnt offerings; and as sweet-smelling fragrance from the hand of the righteous ones. From the gates of the just ones is heard her voice; and from the voice of the just ones her admonition. And concerning their food fullness [is] in truth; and concerning their feast their portions [are] together. Their discussions [are] on the Law of the Most High; and their word is to announce his power. How far from the wicked ones [is] her word; and from all evil ones her understanding. (Ps. 154)[9]

Wisdom, personified as in Proverbs, enjoins righteousness and praise to God as the highest form of service. In a rather strong echo of the canonical voice of Wisdom, she calls for those who lack understanding to learn from her. Attendance to the temple and its ritual measures, at least in part, is the response to wisdom (vv. 1–4, 8, 10–13).

---

9. This text comes from Charlesworth's translation of the Syriac version, II, 620–21 5ApocSyrPs 2 rather than the incomplete Hebrew version from Qumran (1Qps154)II, 618–19.

The earliest portions of the Deuterocanon and Pseudepigrapha give evidence for a depreciation of wisdom literature beginning with the restoration community (after 539 B.C.E., but especially beginnining with Ezra, about 400 B.C.E.). The emphasis upon Torah, such as that displayed later by the Alexandrian Jew, Philo, contributed to this neglect. As will be seen, the intense preoccupation with allegorical readings by Christians and Jews tended to de-emphasize the themes of classical wisdom. Further, when early Christians read beyond the Torah of the Hebrew Bible, they most often turned to the prophets out of a desire to support their messianic claims for Jesus of Nazareth.

Early Jewish Interpretations

Apart from the Deuterocanon and the Pseudepigrapha, Jewish interpretations of wisdom literature follow their own course in writings ranging from the Septuagint version of the Hebrew Bible to Philo, and, of course, the Talmud. Sometime after the return from Babylon just before 500 B.C.E., a transition took place: the activity of the scribes, who guarded the sacred text, shifted to the activity of Torah scholars, who produced the Talmud.[10] This shifted emphasis away from wisdom and wisdom forms to the Law and its corollary traditions.

Rabbinic reflections on the doctrine of the "two ways" led to a combination of Decalogue prohibitions and exhortations from Proverbs. Similar mergers of the Decalogue and proverbial instruction appear in the Didache (chap. 2), Barnabas (chap. 19), and *Doctrina Apostolorum (Apostle's Doctrine)* —all Christian works.[11] In the first-century document, the *Shepherd of Hermes*, Ecclesiastes 12:13 ("Fear the Lord, and keep his commandments") appeared as the opening of the seventh mandate from the shepherd.[12] While these tendencies fall short of claiming equivalence for wisdom and Torah, they show the tendency to conflate law and wisdom. Such a practice may represent an intermediate stage between the identification of law and wisdom as somewhat separate concerns and the achievement of wisdom through faithfulness to Torah.

Wisdom in the Septuagint

Several modifications of the Hebrew texts of wisdom books in the Septuagint (the Greek version of the Hebrew Scriptures) give evidence of the interpretive tendencies of its translators. For example, the translators identified Job as a contemporary of the patriarchs by adding an explanation of Job's identity to the conclusion of the book. According to this epilogue,

---

10. See Michael Fishbane, "From Scribalism to Rabbinism: Perspectives on the Emergence of Classical Judaism" in *SIANE*, 440.

11. Suggested by William Horbury, "Old Testament Interpretation" in *Mikra*, 737.

12. William Jardine, ed., *Shepherd of Hermes: The Gentile Apocalypse* (Redwood City, Calif.: Proteus Publishing, 1992), 58.

Job is the Edomite king Jobab indentified in the genealogy of Edomite kings in Genesis 36:33–34. Some early Jewish interpreters dated Job to the time of Moses. The tendency to connect Job with the descendants of Abraham or the cultural milieu of the exodus provides an indirect indication of the subserviency of the writings to the epic narratives of the Pentateuch. These attempts to increase the relative significance of Job's experience are telltale signs that at least some in the Jewish community saw the authority of the book weakened by Job's Edomite origin or his "distance" from Israel's sacred history.

Several Septuagint renderings are expanded or modified to explain, clarify, or give application to the slightly different or briefer Hebrew originals. A relatively lengthy addition occurs in Proverbs 13:15. "Good sense wins favor" becomes "sound discretion gives favour, and to know the law is the part of a sound understanding." Such expansion may serve to add "religious color to secular descriptions."[13] In Ecclesiastes 11:9b the modification apparently issues not so much from religious motives but from an intention to provide direct moral instruction for the young. "Follow the inclination of your heart and the desire of your eyes," appears as "walk in the ways of your heart blameless, but not in the sight of your eyes." The original piece of advice doubtless appeared dangerous. Consequently, the community read it in conformity to group mores rather than literally.

Perhaps doctrinal orthodoxy prompted the addition to Ecclesiastes (Hebrew, Qoheleth) 2:15 which claimed that his wisdom led to emptiness (vanity) since his fate (death) was the same as the fool's. The Septuagint added a more specific explanation of the vanity—"because the fool speaks of his abundance." Evidently, the translator rejected the notion that Qoheleth's end matched the fate of the fool, deducing rather that Qoheleth's property (gained by wisdom) served as subject of the passage. If conscious intention motivated such a change, it first of all denied that the quest for wisdom leads to emptiness. Beyond this, the translator affirmed the existence of an afterlife (which is not assumed in Ecclesiastes). It also offered the hope of eternal reward for the wise.

The Septuagint version of Proverbs 13:10 expresses a specific definition of wisdom. The Hebrew text reads, "By insolence the heedless make strife, but with those who take advice is wisdom." The Greek version changes this to, "A bad man does evil with insolence, but they that are judges of themselves are wise." The special reading manifests interpretive sophistication: whether insolent or heedless, the opposing mindset encourages self-reflection to lead to well-considered behavior. The predisposition toward introspection recurs as a frequent theme in Proverbs, though often overlooked by contemporary as well as ancient Jewish interpreters. The adaptations and expansions of statements within wisdom literature in the Septuagint indicate the vitality of wisdom teaching during the development of the Septuagint. The translation of the wisdom writings probably took

---

13. Emmanuel Tov, "The Septuagint" in *Mikra*, 177.

place shortly before 100 B.C.E. The development of these translations may have continued until about 100 C.E. The special readings noted above may be either early or late; their provenance may be either Jewish or Christian. Still, they faithfully reflect the type of wisdom exegesis characteristic of scribes and rabbis during the early period of Septuagint production. For a slightly later and more incautious approach, attention turns to the noted Alexandrian allegorist, Philo, a contemporary of Jesus.

Wisdom in Philo

For Philo's distinctive thought, the wisdom literature served a more important role than the Law or Prophets. He typically employed wisdom forms and themes in an allegorical approach aimed at emphasizing the relevance of Hebraic traditions for the Hellenized Jews at Alexandria. In Philo *logos* (λόγος translated "word" in John 1) occurs as the principal word for wisdom. תּוֹרָה (*tōrâ*), and חָכְמָה (*hŏkmâ*) appear as synonyms. According to Philo, God had intercourse with his knowledge and begat a created being: "Thus wisdom is represented by one of the divine chorus as speaking of herself in this manner: 'God obtained me first of all his works and founded me before the ages'" (Prov. 8:22).[14]

For Philo, the *Logos,* or divine word, mediated wisdom as identified in Proverbs 8:22. Wisdom could bear many names. A further allusion to Proverbs 8:22 appears in *On the Virtues*: "Now wisdom is older not only than my generation but even the whole world, and it is not right that anyone should judge her except God himself."[15]

Sarah, wife of Abraham, presented one embodiment of divine wisdom. Due to her lack of female genealogy in the biblical text, Philo considered Sarah begotten of God. Philo also noted she turned the serious concerns of men to laughter as wisdom can do for those who rely on her.[16] Here, he referred to Genesis 18:11–15 and Sarah's laughter at the suggestion she would bear Abraham's heir, and perhaps to the name Isaac ("he laughs," Gen. 21:2–12). The interpretive freeplay of allegory enabled Philo to build bridges between Greek philosophy and traditional Hebraic motifs. His interest in wisdom provided a blend of Hebraic convention and the Greek concept of the *Logos*. In a similar manner, the church employed allegory to support christological readings of the Hebrew Bible, and the concept of *Logos* was an important point of entry.

Wisdom in the Talmud

Philo's allegorical readings of wisdom relate the ideas of a single prominent thinker whose suggestions offered opportunity for innovations

---

14. *Die Ebrietate* 30–31, trans. David Winston, *Philo of Alexandria: The Contemplative Life, The Giants, and Selections* (New York: Paulist, 1981), 102.

15. 62, trans. Ronald Williamson, *Jews in the Hellenistic World: Philo* (New York: Cambridge, 1989), 222.

16. *De Ebrietate* 56–62, trans. David Winston, *Philo,* 258. All of Philo's association of Sarah and wisdom relates to the personification of wisdom as a woman in Proverbs 1–9. The reader may refer to the discussion of Proverbs in chapter 6 for more information.

among a wide community in Alexandria. The Mishnah offers more immediate, exclusively rabbinic concerns. The Mishnah presents the most pronounced identification of Torah with wisdom yet encountered in this study. Abot 3:14[17] stresses, "Do not forsake my *Torah*" (see Prov. 4:2), clearly interpreted as a reference to the Pentateuch. According to Qinnim 3:6 AA.-BB., ordinary persons grow senile in old age (Job 12:20—God deprives the elders of their discernment), but sages of the Torah grow wiser (Job 12:12—wisdom is shown in "length of days."). The preoccupation with Torah resulted in some rather narrow interpretations of wisdom, such as the use of Ecclesiastes 1:15, the "crooked cannot be made straight," to indicate that missed meals during the Passover cannot be made up (Sukkah 2:6). The same principle applies to festal offerings in Haggai 1:6.

The Mishnah shows great interest in areas other than laws and regulations, but the rabbis avoided every appearance of subjugating Torah to wisdom. A primary concern involved conduct for the good of the community and in conformity to scriptural stipulations. To support this, the Mishnah quotes Proverbs more often than any non-Torah book other than Psalms. Proverbs serve to reinforce community morals and laws in much the same way that the early Christian community used wisdom for *parenesis* (instructions for daily conduct). For example, in Abot 2:9 the "straight path" stands in contrast to the "bad road." This "two ways" approach to ethics certainly stems from the text of Proverbs. Abot 4:1 warns against passion's ascent over judgment by citing Proverbs 16:32: "Who is strong? He who overcomes his desire, as it is said, 'He who is slow to anger is better than the mighty and he who rules his spirit than he who takes a city.'"

The rabbis kept the original meaning of Proverbs as guides to human conduct rather than using them as allegories to convey a message on another level. In some cases wisdom is reduced in the Mishnah to the equivalent of proper conduct. Abot 3:9 records the words of Rabbi Haninah ben Dosa: "For anyone whose fear of sin takes precedence over his wisdom, his wisdom will endure. And for anyone whose wisdom takes precedence over his fear of sin, his wisdom will not endure. . . . Anyone whose deeds are more than his wisdom—his wisdom will endure. And anyone whose wisdom is more than his deeds—his wisdom will not endure."

When the Torah assumed its place as the center of the canon, other perspectives were read as competing claims. In the collection of the Hebrew canon, the presence of several varied perspectives (for example, Proverbs and Ecclesiastes) reflect the relatively equal value placed on complementary perspectives. The collection appears to value the materials' general support of Yahwism rather than any single religious viewpoint. Proverbs valued the efforts of human reason as a legitimate means of perceiving order in the natural and social worlds. The Torah scholars accepted such an enterprise with skepticism. They feared the compromise of the priority of the Law.

---

17. The following citations of the Mishnah are from the translation by Jacob Neusner, *The Mishnah: A New Translation* (New Haven: Yale University Press, 1988) unless otherwise noted.

Consequently, they showed reluctance to present the Law as in any way subject to human reflection.

The modes of interpretation fostered by the Talmud are more fluid and unpredictable than those employed by the early Christians. The type of exegesis known as midrash led Torah scholars to locate truths applicable to then current audiences in minute or hidden clues sometimes limited to a single word. For example, in the Palestinian Talmud, the proverb, "She is like the ships of the merchant, she brings her food from far away" (Prov. 31:14), conveyed the truth, "Words of Tora may be sparse in one place and plentiful in another."[18] Such free-flowing connections commonly place the cited text in subservience to the intended message of the rabbis. Though citations of biblical wisdom appear infrequently, the rabbis at times indicated a preference for its approach: Baba Bathra 12 described the wise man as greater than the prophet.[19]

A slightly different rendering of the Hebrew of Psalm 90:20 enabled Amemar to cite it as proof of the sage's superiority. נָבֵא (nābi') "we gain," was rendered נָבִיא (nābi'), "a prophet" to yield the phrase "a prophet has a heart of wisdom" (Baba Bathra 12a). The same work in 18c presents prophecy itself as having passed from the prophets to the wise. Verse 12a contains this citation: "R. Abdimi from Haifa said: Since the day when the Temple was destroyed, prophecy has been taken from the prophets and given to the wise. Is then the wise not also a prophet?" So, the prophets lost the gift of prophecy, but not the wise, who possessed it simultaneously. Such a perspective holds open the possiblity for continued revelation through human mediums. This practically equates wisdom with rabbinic study, but certainly the idea is related to canonical wisdom as well. Wisdom here exhibits strong differences from the notion of wisdom in the Hebrew Bible. There wisdom belonged to every person (even every living creature) that showed special ability. For Rabbi Abdimi, wisdom receives official status related to divine sanction. An even higher picture of wisdom implied that the saying of the wise person was simply a reiteration of wisdom once given to Moses at Sinai (Baba Bathra 12b). Aboth 2:7 virtually equated the study of Torah with wisdom. The elevation of the Torah also relates to authorship of the wisdom canon. Baba Bathra suggested Moses wrote Job (14b) and Hezekiah and his men wrote Proverbs and Ecclesiastes (15a).[20] M. Sanhedrin 8:2 used Proverbs 23:20 to aid in the interpretation of Deuteronomy 21:20—"a glutton and a drunkard." Sanhedrin presents the text as a description of the seriousness of the child's rebellion.

---

18. Rosh Hashana 3:5:16, 58d attributed to Rabbi Nehemia in *The Talmud of the Land of Israel*, vol. 16, trans. Edward A. Goldman (Chicago: University of Chicago Press, 1988).

19. All following references to the Talmud, unless otherwise noted, are based on *The Babylonian Talmud*, Seder Nezikin, trans. I. Epstein (London: Soncino, 1935).

20. The Proverbs of 25:1–29:27 begin with the note that officials of Hezekiah copied the collection. Hezekiah's time (727–698 B.C.E.) approximates the actual date of the canonical form of the book. The tendency to connect Hezekiah and Ecclesiastes relates to two features of the book: First, Ecclesiastes emphasizes rulers and submission to rulers (for example, Eccles. 8:2–8). Second, the book identifies the author as a wise king in 2:9–12.

A very inventive rabbi quoted the proverb, "Be not among winebib-bers or among gluttonous eaters of meat" to show, "He cannot be called a stubborn and rebellious son until he eats meat and drinks wine" (70*a*–71*a*). This interpretation would not allow the stoning of a rebellious child before adolescence. This presents an otherwise unfamiliar use of wisdom materials to set standard interpretations for legal materials. It provides further evidence of the overwhelming importance of the Torah for talmudic thinkers. Baba Bathra 15–16 contains a lengthy exposition of Job. One portion cited a tradition which understood the Book of Job as a parable comparable to Nathan's story of the lamb in 2 Samuel 12:1–6. The Talmud refuted this manner of reading Job with the question, "Why is his name and the name of his town mentioned?"[21] Readers do not expect parables to include such biographical information.

The following passage lauds the blamelessness of Job: "Greater praise is accorded to Job than to Abraham. For of Abraham it is written, 'For now I know that thou fearest God;' whereas of Job it is written, 'That man was perfect and upright and one that feared God and eschewed evil'" (Baba Bathra 15*b*). Job is further described as a "heathen" though pious. The narrators of Baba Bathra disagreed, claiming Job was from Israel (15*b*). Rabbah presented the most charming interpretation from Job. He claimed Job said, "A tempest has passed before thee [i.e. before God] and caused thee to confuse *'iyob* [Heb. אִיּוֹב Job] and *'oyeb* [אוֹיֵב, enemy]." Rabbah surmised God answered Job from a tempest giving him examples of his meticulous discriminations which illustrated he could not possibly confuse *'iyob* and *'oyeb* (16*a*–*b*). In Job 13:24 Job actually asks God, "Why do you treat me as your enemy?" God's response comes in the voice from the whirlwind (tempest) in 38:1–42:34. The suggestion of the wordplay provides an important angle on the story of Job. The ancient reader/hearer could not have overlooked the similarity between the words. According to the stringent view of retribution, Job in fact appeared the enemy of Yahweh.

Shabbath interprets Ecclesiastes: "Whoever breaks through a wall will be bitten by a snake" (Eccles. 10:8) appears as a warning against departing from rabbinic interpretations of the Law. The clues offered for interpretation are: the words of the wise are a hedge to the Law and the bite of a serpent is incurable (110*a*). Those who depart from official interpretations face grave consequences. Shabbath 30b notes contradictions between verses 7:3 and 2:2 as well as verses 8:15 and 2:2 of Ecclesiastes. "Anger is better than play" (7:3) contrasts with "I said of laughter, it is to be praised" (2:2) and "then I commended joy" (8:15) contrasts with, "and of joy I said, 'What doeth it?'" (2:2).[22]

In spite of these contradictions, Shabbath affirmed Ecclesiastes because its beginning (1:3) and its end (12:13) are "words of Torah"

---

21. *The Talmud: Selected Writings*, trans. Ben Zion Bokser (New York: Paulist, 1989).

22. Proverbs 26:4 and 26:5 are also noted as contradictions: Answer/do not answer a fool according to his folly (Shabbath 30*b*).

(Shabbath 30*b*). Due to this feature, the sages who "wished to hide it" (that is, remove it from circulation) did not. The interpretations of wisdom in the Talmud and other Jewish sources present the most wide-reaching and vital perspectives on wisdom. A portion of this dynamic relates to the Jewish communities' continued interest in wisdom as their living canon. By contrast, the Christian interpreters felt a compulsion to reconcile the teachings of wisdom to a somewhat independent ongoing tradition. The rabbis displayed freedom to read from past or present perspectives. Certainly, the changes in the fortunes of Jews in several areas led to changes in interpretation. Christian communities experienced this as well. However, changes such as the shift from wisdom as living with discretion to wisdom as Torah involved little change. Changes such as the identification of personified wisdom as Christ or Spirit involved greater change. In addition, the continued Jewish interest in wisdom spawned both the most creative suggestions and the interpretations most directly related to the books of wisdom themselves. This direct interest in wisdom helped to promote attention to wisdom in subsequent centuries. During the Middle Ages, Jewish interpretation of wisdom flourished while Christian comment on wisdom during the same period scarcely existed.

Wisdom in the New Testament

In early Christianity (as well as Judaism of the same period) wisdom literature served as the basis for catechesis (basic instruction in religious practice). The large number of Greek translations of wisdom books confirms this.[23] The appearence of wisdom materials in the New Testament shows the heavy dependence of the early church on biblical wisdom. Citations of and allusions to wisdom commonly appear in the teachings of Jesus. Paul's writings indicate more extensive dependence upon wisdom than that revealed at first reading. The strongest instance of direct dependence occurs in James. This book provides a lucid model of the catechetical interest in wisdom mentioned above.

The New Testament only occasionally offers a direct citation of a wisdom book. Christian thinkers tended to use the wisdom materials in a derivative manner. Wisdom provided veiled references to Christ and more direct references to the lifestyle he taught. The early church clearly considered the works canonical, but accepted this as an underlying assumption rather than an issue requiring comment. For this reason, the New Testament provides no direct evidence that the early church attributed Proverbs and Ecclesiastes to Solomon. It does not, however, diminish the likelihood that early Christians affirmed such views. No record exists of dissenting voices.

---

23. This is the assessment of William Horbury, "Old Testament Interpretation in the Writings of the Church Fathers" in *Mikra*, 737, note 4.

The biblical writers' chief interest lay in the stability of the fledgling community. Wisdom literature offered directly applicable moral principles. Polytheism or skepticism provided the groundwork for much of the Greek instruction. The early church avoided such bases for its moral instruction. Ideas drawn from Judaism offered ready acceptance with little adaptation. The church considered Jewish heritage as its own history. Maxims from Job, Proverbs, Ecclesiastes, Sirach, and The Wisdom of Solomon typically reveal the Christian writer's own formula for achieving distinctive Christian identity.

The Gospels

As might be expected, Jesus' use of wisdom as recorded in the Gospels does not fit the pattern according to which the early church employed wisdom parenetically. Three examples show Jesus' familiarity with Sirach. In Sirach 51:23–27 Ben Sirach lauds wisdom as a pleasant yet rewarding task:

> Draw near to me, you who are uneducated, and lodge in the house of instruction. . . . Put your neck under her yoke, and let your souls receive instruction; it is to be found close by. . . . See with your own eyes that I have labored but little and found for myself much serenity. (Sirach 51:23–27)

Compare this to Jesus' encouragement for his hearers to accept his instruction:

> Come to me, all you that are weary and are carrying heavy burdens, and I will give you rest. Take my yoke upon you, and learn from me; for I am gentle and humble in heart, and you will find rest for your souls. For my yoke is easy, and my burden is light. (Matt. 11:28–30)

The passage in Matthew manifests an awareness of Sirach 51. Analysis should stop short of suggesting that Jesus intended to depict himself as wisdom incarnate. As one facet of his self-interpretation, Matthew 11:28–30 expresses his priority of announcing the kingdom era. References to Jesus as "wisdom" function metaphorically rather than metonymically: wisdom represents the person of Jesus rather than naming him as its embodiment. The Gospel writer depicts Jesus speaking of his teaching as an extension of Hebrew wisdom, indicating high regard for wisdom's tenets.

The evidence for an allusion to Sirach 24:21 in John 6:35 appears less convincing, though plausible. Jesus described himself as the bread of life in John, saying, "Whoever comes to me will never be hungry, and whoever believes in me will never be thirsty." Sirach 24:21, "Those who eat of me will hunger for more and those who drink of me will thirst for more," may serve as a basis for the interpretation which claims Christ's superiority over all previous wisdom. According to this presentation, wisdom in Sirach's poem of praise produces an insatiable appetite for more, but the bread of life (as ultimate wisdom?) satisfies the appetite ultimately. The distinction remains fluid, since the satisfaction implied in John most likely intends continued association with Jesus as the Christ rather than a one-time "taste."

The text of Sirach 11:18–19 contains reference to a rich presumptious person very much like the "barn builder" of Luke 12:16–21: "One becomes rich through diligence and self-denial, and the reward allotted to him is this: when he says, 'I have found rest and now I shall feast on my goods!' he does not know how long it will be until he leaves them to others and dies" (Sirach 11:18–19). The parable in Luke displays a thematic connection to Sirach 11:18-19 stronger than that attributable to coincidence.

Proverbs 25:6–7 recalls Jesus' advice, recorded in Luke 14:8–10, to take the lower seat when invited to a feast: "Do not put yourself forward in the king's presence or stand in the place of the great; for it is better to be told, 'Come up here,' than to be put lower in the presence of a noble."

In similar fashion, Matthew 23:12 reflects Proverbs 29:23 in form and content without the marks of direct citation:

> A person's pride will bring humiliation, but one who is lowly in spirit will obtain honor. (Prov. 29:23)

> All who exalt themselves will be humbled, and all who humble themselves will be exalted. (Matt. 23:12)

The examples given in Luke 14 and Matthew 23 provide evidence that wisdom's influence on Jesus and his followers consisted of more than simple reference. Historians of Jesus suggest the concept "sage" identifies one facet of Jesus' role. At the conclusion of the Sermon on the Mount, Jesus described those who heed or do not heed his teachings as wise or foolish, respectively (Matt. 7:24–27; Luke 6:46–49). Similarly, the illustration of the wide and narrow gates or doors reflects the "two ways" theology of wisdom literature (Matt. 7:13–14; Luke 13:23–24). One interpreter understood the wide way to refer to the way of conventional wisdom and the narrow way to refer to Jesus' more radical presentation of wisdom.[24] In partial confirmation of this view, Jesus' orientation toward wisdom certainly owes more to the questioning of Job and Ecclesiastes than the emphases on "two ways" and retribution which characterized the Proverbs.

The Gospels of Matthew and Luke contain some emphasis on wisdom which again operates on a level beyond quotation of wisdom documents. Matthew records Jesus' counsel that his disciples be "wise as serpents and harmless as doves" in the fulfillment of their mission (10:16). This emphasizes self-protection in the face of certain persecution. In defense of his free lifestyle Jesus replied, "Wisdom is vindicated by her deeds/children" (11:19; also Luke 7:35). This reiterates the common and practical nature of wisdom. On other occasions Jesus pointed to his actions to indicate the soundness of his proclamation and advised his followers to judge others and seek

---

24. Marcus J. Borg, *Jesus, A New Vision: Spirit, Culture, and the Life of Discipleship* (Harper, San Francisco, 1987), 97–124. Borg's portrait of Jesus as sage stems from an attempt to reconsider Jesus of Nazareth in light of his own culture and tradition.

to be judged themselves according to their personal conduct. The call to pragmatism (rather than dogma or ritual) shows some dependence on wisdom traditions. Matthew attributes wisdom to Jesus in at least two passages. Jesus compared his teaching to the wisdom of King Solomon (12:42). Citizens of Jesus' hometown noted his wisdom, even though exhibiting suspicion due to his common origins (13:54).

The parable of the wise and foolish bridesmaids in Matthew 25:1–13 presents the clearest dependence on wisdom in Matthew. The passage applies the doctrine of the two ways to followers of Jesus. The wise disciple brings extra oil and thus remains prepared for the bridegroom's delay. Most likely this relates to the delay of the parousia: Matthew encouraged the church to remain faithful to the kingdom lifestyle even though the expected return of Christ was delayed. Another attribution of wisdom to those prepared for the return occurs in 24:45. The association of preparedness with wisdom appears commonly in Proverbs, Job, and Ecclesiastes. Loyalty to God (and the ruler as his representative) in spite of delays in justice also serves as an important theme. In Matthew the doctrine of the two ways receives special application to the diligent and the lax followers of Christ. The description of lack of preparedness as folly implies the course of these disciples was set, since folly was not typically a condition from which one was expected to recover.

The few mentions of wisdom in Matthew do not indicate the willingness of its writer to depict wisdom as the highest goal or the best description of the gospel movement. On the contrary, Jesus' prayer, "I thank you Father . . . because you have hidden these things from the wise and the intelligent and have revealed them to infants" (11:25), suggests that commitment to the kingdom involves an affront to conventional notions of wisdom. The term remains fluid in that it can describe the wisdom that impedes faith as well as the wisdom involved in and gained by faith. Luke also records Jesus' statement on the hiddenness of God's revelation to the wise (10:21). The single statement identifying one prepared for the delayed dawn of the kingdom as wise also appears in Luke (12:42). Beyond these similarities, the Gospel of Luke shows more willingness to use the term wisdom to describe the person and activity of Jesus. For Luke "wisdom" apparently held close connections with justice. Luke displays interest in fairness and humane treatment, especially toward the disadvantaged. The direct influence of the wisdom canon in this regard appears slight. Proverbs does emphasize kindness toward the needy. Both benevolence and fair dealing appear as major components in the wisdom of Job.

The first citation of the Hebrew Bible in Luke reveals these special interests through Luke's use of Malachi 4:5–6: "With the spirit and power of Elijah he will go before him, to turn the hearts of parents to their children, and the disobedient to the wisdom of the righteous, to make ready a people prepared for the Lord" (Luke 1:17). These words to Zechariah (father of John the Baptizer) include the phrase, "wisdom of the righteous," not included in Malachi. The emphasis in Malachi seems to be on religious instruction and fidelity to the Torah. Perhaps the Gospel of Luke equates this with "wisdom of the righteous." Biblical wisdom typically includes moral conduct as an essential element.

Luke 2:40, 52 depict Jesus' maturing with wisdom. The Gospel apparently identified this as the characteristic which marked Jesus' distinction among humans. Jesus himself quoted "Wisdom" in 11:49, introducing a quotation with, "the Wisdom of God said. . . ." The reference quotes an unknown book or refers to wisdom as hypostasis or near hypostasis. Here, Jesus indicated the Pharisees and scribes rejected wisdom by continuing the trend of persecution of God's messengers. By contrast, when Jesus warned the disciples of the persecution they would face, he promised a gift of wisdom that would overcome their enemies (21:15). Luke does not display signs of a methodical treatment of wisdom integral to the gospel, but the random references reveal the author had some commitment to key facets of canonical wisdom.

Jesus did not assume the role of priest or scribe. This in itself compels the critic to look for other descriptions of his role. He regularly taught, and some accepted his authority apart from his identification with God. Perhaps the crowds principally admired his wisdom. Certainly, his teaching in parables owed much to the proverbial form, though the opening, "The kingdom of God is like . . ." is much more explicit than we find in Proverbs. At the same time, parables are like *měšālîm* in that they encourage reflection on human activity.

Infrequently, Jesus performed the role of arbitrator by deciding cases and solving problems for his acquaintances (for example, Luke 12:13–21). His refusal to do so on occasion holds less importance for the issue than the peoples' presumption of his qualification to do so. In the Hebrew Bible, both Solomon and clan leaders exercised wisdom in such a fashion. Jesus' emphasis upon preparedness furthers his association with wisdom. This includes his advice to prospective followers to consider the cost of discipleship and his warnings regarding its dangers. Jesus affirmed the shrewd actions of the unjust steward in Luke 16:1–9 in spite of his dishonesty. Jesus also shares with canonical wisdom a commitment to the basic authority of the Law and the Prophets which serves as a platform for determining prudent conduct.

In spite of Jesus' commitment to classical tenets of wisdom, it is not appropriate to use "sage" as the definitive description of his role. Jesus' unwillingness to identify himself as priest or prophet provides only an argument from silence for his self-understanding as wisdom teacher. Many of his teachings and actions did not conform to this model. Sages committed themselves to conventional wisdom, while Jesus' proclamation of the gospel era was an all-encompassing and radically new program. Jesus' concern for the kingdom conditioned all of his teachings. Consequently, Jesus showed no special commitment to the distinct attributes characteristic of Hebrew wisdom. In addition, miracles and wonders, so important to the Gospel narratives, formed no part of the sage's repertoire.

In some cases, Jesus literally reversed the tendencies of wisdom: (1) he taught the first would be last; (2) he claimed a child would lead all to God; (3) he contended leaders must first of all be servants against wisdom's implicit approval of social stratifications; (4) he called his followers to a lifestyle of suffering and molded his ministry after the suffering servant motif of Isaiah 40–55; and (5) he warned his followers the gospel would create enmity within families. This certainly represented a new variety of wisdom for his Jewish contemporaries. Contrary to the strong work ethic of the sages, Jesus advised disciples not to worry about necessities in Luke 12:22–31 and Matthew 6:24–33. Jesus' sayings reveal in most respects a more sermonic tone than that of Proverbs, Job, and Ecclesiastes. He advised behavior based upon surprising standards rather than commending conventionally approved standards as the wisdom books do. His theory of retribution and basis for the doctrine of the two ways were predominantly otherworldly. The Hebrew canon scarcely anticipates this. Jesus' preference for the poor and his contact with sinners also challenged the conventional portrait of wisdom.

The most convincing evidence against identification of Jesus as a wisdom teacher appears, or rather, fails to appear at the conclusion of the Gospel accounts. The accounts of the passion and crucifixion contain no mention of wisdom. Since the identity of Jesus is central to these narratives, they determine the issue. In retrospect, Jesus relied on the wisdom tradition and borrowed or received influence from its forms, but Jesus' identity in the Gospels as Messiah and Son of God preclude other more limiting concepts of his official status. Jesus' attitude toward wisdom, like his attitude toward Law, led him to fulfill it by transcendending it rather than reviving its classic form. In terms of direct dependence, Jesus owed much more to the more current wisdom Book of Sirach than to the canonical works. Similarly, his orientation toward his own work as wisdom depended more on contemporary conditioning than the wisdom canon. Jesus certainly held the Hebrew wisdom canon in authority, but he evidently chose to employ wisdom in the most practical and readily applicable formats.

Paul

Paul at times used scriptural maxims to support general moral directions. Elsewhere, Paul discussed wisdom, typically contrasting Greek intellectualism with God's wisdom. In one instance, Christology serves as the theme. Expanding the claims of Proverbs 8:22, Paul equated Christ with wisdom (1 Cor. 1:24).

Three primary examples show the employment of proverbs to reinforce ethical advice. First, Romans 3:15–17 echoes the thought of Proverbs 1:16, depicting the human predisposition to do wrong. Second, in Romans 9:21 the concept of God as the potter apparently comes from The Wisdom of Solomon 15:7: "A potter kneads the soft earth and laboriously molds each vessel for our service, fashioning out of the same clay both the vessels that serve clean uses and those for contrary uses, making all alike; but which shall be the use of each of them the worker in clay decides."

Paul portrayed God as the potter. He claimed humans had no right to question his choices. Both Romans and The Wisdom of Solomon lay emphasis on the potter's privilege to decide the use of his products. The focus on clean and unclean uses for the product, so prominent in Paul's employment of the image, does not occur in related prophetic passages (Jer. 18:1–11; Isa. 29:16; 45:9; 64:8). Third, in the realm of human interaction, Romans 12:20 reproduces Proverbs 25:21–22 nearly verbatim: "If your enemies are hungry, give them bread to eat; and if they are thirsty, give them water to drink; for you will heap coals of fire on their heads, and the Lord will reward you" (vv. 21–22). Wisdom texts served as an important source for moral instruction for Paul, though he found textual support in many other quarters as well.

In at least two passages, quotations from wisdom literature appear in discussions of wisdom. In 1 Corinthians 3:18–21 Paul contrasted the wisdom of faith in Christ (apparent folly) with the wisdom "of this world": "Do not deceive yourselves. If you think that you are wise in this age, you should become fools so that you may become wise. For the wisdom of this world is foolishness with God. For it is written, 'He catches the wise in their craftiness,' and again, 'The Lord knows the thoughts of the wise, that they are futile.' So let no one boast about human leaders."

Job 15:13a is cited in 1 Corinthians 3:19b, an ironic use of wisdom materials to counter wisdom. Romans 1:20–31 relates wisdom to revelation by depicting those who reject what they know about God from nature as fools. Among these fools, idolatry led to immorality, which resulted in complete abandonment by the creator. This represents ultimate folly, characterized by uncontrolled passions. Three ideas from Wisdom of Solomon 12:24–14:24 are reflected in Romans: (1) humans can recognize God through nature; (2) humans rejected God for lifeless idols; and (3) this idolatry led to gross immorality.[25]

Again, human wisdom led to foolishness resulting in immorality and ruin. For Paul, wisdom issued only from God, and the human role consisted of submitting to divine wisdom. The view of revelation presented in Romans 1 offered some hope that divine wisdom could be recognized through natural means of perception. In most cases, however, Paul's bleak view of human moral responsibility practically denied wisdom to those who engaged in a direct quest for it. This constitutes a redirection of Hebrew wisdom in which openness to the world could meet the sage's goals.

Paul's impetus to reconceive the nature of wisdom doubtlessly issued from his view of the transformation achieved by Christ's incarnation, sacri-

---

25. Bruce Metzger, *Introduction to the Apocrypha* (Oxford: Oxford University Press, 1957), 160. This work also presents the parallel passages in side-by-side columns (p. 159) illustrating definite dependence.

fice, and resurrection. Colossians 1:15–18 expresses radical commitment to the Christ event as determinative for theology:

> He is the image of the invisible God, the firstborn of all creation; for in him all things in heaven and on earth were created, things visible and invisible, whether thrones or dominions or rulers or powers—all things have been created through him and for him. He himself is before all things, and in him all things hold together. He is the head of the body, the church; he is the beginning, the firstborn from the dead, so that he might come to have first place in everything.

It is likely that this passage is a christological interpretation of Proverbs 8:22–31:

> The LORD created me at the beginning of his work, the first of his acts of long ago. Ages ago I was set up, at the first, before the beginning of the earth. When there were no depths I was brought forth, when there were no springs abounding with water. Before the mountains had been shaped, before the hills, I was brought forth—when he had not yet made earth and fields, or the world's first bits of soil. When he established the heavens, I was there, when he drew a circle on the face of the deep, when he made firm the skies above, when he established the fountains of the deep, when he assigned to the sea its limit, so that the waters might not transgress his command, when he marked out the foundations of the earth, then I was beside him, like a master worker; and I was daily his delight, rejoicing before him always, rejoicing in his inhabited world and delighting in the human race. (Prov. 8:22–31)

This single wisdom text recurs most frequently in early Christian interpretation. In nearly every instance the writers understood it as an allegorical reference to Christ—the Logos, Eternal Wisdom. The commitment to Christ as ultimate wisdom forced Christian interpreters to view wisdom as experiential. Those properly related to God through Christ possessed wisdom. Consequently, Paul and others downplayed the part of the intellect. They substituted the mysterious participation of the believer in divine wisdom through Christ. While their Jewish contemporaries perceived the fulfillment of wisdom in Torah, Christians found the fulfillment of wisdom in Christ. Each community tended to "decode" canonical wisdom according to their respective commitments.

The General Letters

The approach to wisdom nurtured in the Book of James, itself a wisdom book, reveals a utilitarian approach to wisdom rather than a philosophical one. Interest in wisdom focuses upon the behavior of humans in community. The Septuagint version of Proverbs 3:3–4: "The Lord resists the proud; but he gives grace to the humble," appears in James 4:6 (also 1 Pet. 5:5). James also contains a reference to Job's "patience" (James 5:11), a common expression of Job's significance during the first and second centuries. James 3 presents an overview of the entire book's approach to wisdom. It involves (1) self-control, (2) careful speech, and (3) pious, compassionate living. Three present pivotal ideas appear in verses 13–18:

> Who is wise and understanding among you? Show by your good life that your works are done with gentleness born of wisdom. But if you have bitter envy and selfish ambition in your hearts, do not be boastful and false to the truth. Such wisdom does not come down from above, but is earthly, unspiritual, devilish. For where there is envy and selfish ambition, there will also be disorder and wickedness of every kind. But the wisdom from above is first pure, then peaceable, gentle, willing to yield, full of mercy and good fruits, without a trace of partiality or hypocrisy. And a harvest of righteousness is sown in peace for those who make peace.

The Book of James stands as testimony to a continuing wisdom tradition. Encouragements to wholesome living bear strong resemblance to the suggestions in Proverbs and portions of Job. This New Testament version of proverbial wisdom sets such behavior in the Christian context. It presents wisdom as the natural outcome of a transforming relationship to God in Christ.

Additional references to wisdom in the New Testament include Hebrews' citation of the stipulation of Proverbs 3:7 that God chastens those whom he loves (Heb. 12:5–6). Revelation 3:14 refers to Jesus as the beginning of creation, recalling Proverbs 8:22–31. First Peter's claim, "Love covers a multitude of sins" (4:8), seems dependent on Proverbs 10:12*b*, "Love covers all offenses." A few other quotations occur, but add little to the New Testament protrait of wisdom.

Ecclesiastes played almost no role in the New Testament conception of wisdom. The book, certainly known to the authors, typically served the Christian community by providing a negative example—a presentation of the vanity of life without Christ.[26]

Wisdom in Patristic Literature

Patristic literature frequently reflects interests in wisdom similar or identical to the New Testament. Proverbs and Job typically illustrate the sovereignty of God and provide platforms for instruction in discipline and Christian living. To the end of the first century, writers displayed no emphasis on wisdom as an attempt to explore life's mysteries or its inconclusiveness. The early church placed greater emphasis on order and discipline than research and creativity. However, one innovation clarifies the Christian movement's commitment to Scripture and illustrates the church's dynamic approach to wisdom texts. The interest in the Hebrew Bible

---

26. See James L. Crenshaw, "The Wisdom Literature" in *The Hebrew Bible and Its Modern Interpreters*, eds. Douglas A. Knight and Gene M. Tucker (Chico, Calif.: Scholars Press, 1985), 380.

expressed by early Christian thinkers showed overwhelming preoccupation with messianic prediction. In dealing with wisdom texts that on the literal level display intentions not readily reconcilable to the Christian message, the early church turned to allegory. When "allegory" is used for the primitive church's reading of canon, "christological interpretation" could, in most cases, serve in its place.

Allegorical readings enabled the church to continue its commitment to segments of the Hebrew Bible with marginal significance for their conception of revelation in Christ. Without such methods, the community remained open to "Marcionite" claims that the old covenant was irrelevant to Christianity. Secular notions, Jewish elements, and cryptic passages were sifted through the sieve of "Christ as ultimate revelation." The church transformed these into object lessons and models. They even understood some as designating the very substance of Christ. The church's allegorical interpretations of wisdom expressed dual concerns. First, the church affirmed the relevance of biblical literature. Second, they confirmed Jesus' divine origins and messianic identity. Alternately, biblical personalities provided universal models of good or bad behavior when texts were read literally rather than allegorically. Job presented the example of patience. Instructive literature such as Proverbs or the Wisdom of Solomon provided an entire program for positive living.

The Odes of Solomon, *Doctrina Apostolorum*, the Didache, Barnabas, and 1 Clement

Odes of Solomon (about 100 C.E.) relied on the authority of Solomon to solidify the theology of the early Christian community. The book contains hymns with theological similarities to John's gospel. Its language recalls the Song of Songs in that Christ assumes the title, "Beloved." Indirectly, the book favors the notion that Solomon's familiarity with the Son substantiated his claim to wisdom. This illustrates the radical priority of revelation in Christ for the first-century community.

Other first-century works reveal more plausible connections with canonical wisdom. The *Doctrina Apostolorum*, the Didache, Barnabas, and 1 Clement all show some interest in the conventional "fear of the LORD" promoted in each book of Hebrew wisdom. The patristic literature defined the designation in terms of moral conduct and discipline for the young. The *Doctrina Apostolorum* and the Didache also elaborate on the "two ways" concept which stems from Hebrew wisdom. Neither work may be precisely designated "wisdom," but both include moral and cultic instruction. The doctrine of the two ways later influenced fourth-century documents such as the Apostolic Church Ordinances, the Summary of Doctrine, *Fides Nicaena*, and the Life of Schnudi.

The *Doctrina Apostolorum*, the Didache, Barnabas, and 1 Clement quote and allude to the Wisdom of Solomon more than any other wisdom book. The Greek concept of wisdom contained in the Wisdom of Solomon may contribute to its popularity. The equation of Torah and wisdom in the Wisdom of Solomon exercised appeal as well. The fathers understood moral discipline as the epitome of Hebrew wisdom. This preference for the Wisdom of Solomon dissipated after the first century. Select passages from 1 Clement reveal interests in wisdom related to canonical wisdom. The prayer begun in 1 Clement 59:1–60:4 connects God's wisdom in creation to the moral wisdom of believers. God's own beneficence in creating a good world acts as incentive for Christians to live with kindness. In previous chapters the book of 1 Clement offered quotations from Job and Proverbs to encourage moral conduct.

Job 5:17–26 appears in 1 Clement 56:6–15, following an appeal to believers to pray that the disobedient among them will accept God's discipline. Job 5:17ff celebrates the benefit of God's discipline. A reference to those "who laid the foundation of disorder" (57:1) follows the quotation in 1 Clement. The work encourages the rebellious to accept the judgment of the elders and Proverbs 1:23–33 (1 Clement 57:3–7). In both quotations, wisdom texts reinforce efforts to maintain moral and punitive discipline in the church. First Clement uses biblical proverbs throughout to encourage right living. In chapters 20 and 26, 1 Clement's language resembles Job 28's catalog of the works of God in creation. Additional themes which 1 Clement shares with biblical wisdom include the impropriety of human questioning of God's activity, importance of proper training in the family, God's transcendence, limits of human activity, God's omniscience, respect for rulers, and death and resurrection as a divine prerogative. First Clement manifests the strongest commitment to the wisdom canon present in the early patristic period.

Justin Martyr and Irenaeus

Justin Martyr's *Dialog with Trypho* assumes importance due to its concentration on a particular passage from Proverbs. In *Dialog* 60–61, Proverbs 8:1–36 provides support for comments on Christ's preexistence. Arians later used this passage to foster their Christology. (Arianism is the view that Christ was created rather than coeternal with God the Father.) According to *Dialog* 61, "a certain rational power" appeared as the first of created beings. The father created Jesus as one fire lights another. Justin continued, "My statement will now be confirmed by none other than the Word of Wisdom, who is the God begotten from the Universal Father, and who is the Word and Wisdom and Power and Glory of Him who begot him."[27] With these words Justin Martyr introduced Proverbs 8:1–36 as the words of Jesus.

Irenaeus, as well, identified wisdom at creation in Proverbs 8 with Christ as "Word."[28] The text of Proverbs 3:19–20 presents a similar

---

27. Justin Martyr, *Dialogue with Trypho* in *Saint Justin Martyr*, trans. Thomas B. Falls, The Fathers of the Church, vol. 6 (New York: Christian Heritage, Inc., 1948), 139–368.

28. Irenaeus, *Against Heresies* 4:20.3–4 in *The Writings of Irenaeus*, trans. W. H. Rambaut, vol. 1 (Edinburgh: T&T Clark, 1868).

conception of wisdom's origins: "The LORD by wisdom founded the earth; by understanding he established the heavens; by his knowledge the deeps broke open, and the clouds drop down the dew." Here, the church's emphasis fell upon Jesus' work as co-creator, rather than his own origin. This manner of reading Proverbs 8 and related texts continued for centuries as the Christian mode for the hypostatization of wisdom. In a similar vein, Irenaeus equated the Spirit with wisdom in *Against Heresies* 4:20.4, a common, though less frequent, conception.

The Apostolic Constitutions

Between 100 and 300 C.E. the Apostolic Constitutions made extensive use of Proverbs. In Book 1 the majority of Proverbs employed were applied to men's relations with women and women's behavior. Proverbs 31 (a section which outlines the activity of the ideal wife) appears as the lengthiest quotation, indicating proper conduct for wives and women (Constitutions 2:7–3:10). Much of the content of Book 1 concerns the same subject, as though the writer compiled all such passages from Proverbs. The writer then applied these passages to difficulties with disreputable women as well as the discipline of women and wives. Apostolic Constitutions also contains continual references to God's work of creation. These take the form of prayers, possibly adapted by the church from earlier synagogue prayers.[29]

One rather distinct unit reveals an approach toward wisdom uncommon in rabbinic and Christian literature:

(5) Thereafter were prepared races of differing living creatures; those found on dry land, those living in water, those traversing the air, [and] amphibians. And by the skilled Wisdom of your forethought is given to each one the appropriate providence. For just as she was not exhausted in bringing forth differing races, neither has she neglected to make for each one a different providence. (6) And the goal of the creative work—the rational living creature, the world citizen—having given order by your Wisdom, you created, saying, Let us make man according to our image and likeness; having declared him a [micro-]cosm of the cosmos, having formed for him the body out of the four elements; and having prepared for him the soul out of non-being, and having given to him fivefold perception, and having placed over him the perception and mind, the holder of the reins of the soul. (Apostolic Constitutions 3:15–21 [7:34.5–6])

The unit presents the creation of humans in itself as the supreme act of wisdom in creation. Prior to this unit, the work identifies wisdom with Christ. Hellenistic influence issues in the Greek "scientific" depictions.

29. D. A. Fiensy, "Introduction to Hellenistic Synagogal Prayers" in Charlesworth, *Old Testament Pseudepigrapha*, 1:671–72.

Gregory Thaumaturgos

Gregory Thaumaturgos (213–270) provided a paraphrase of Ecclesi-astes in an attempt to make the work more palatable for Christians. He tried to smooth theological trouble spots.[30] Origen had written a commentary on Ecclesiastes which influenced Gregory, but the paraphrase was the first sys-tematic treatment of the wisdom book. Gregory modified (1) any implica-tion that the cause of evil in the world is other than human sin, (2) encouragements to eat and drink by reading them as behaviors to avoid, (3) the Hebraic view of death by reading into Ecclesiastes the hope of an after-life, and (4) any question of fair retribution, proposing "good" as the nec-essary and guaranteed reward for proper conduct.[31] Effectively, Gregory's paraphrase brought Ecclesiastes into line with Proverbs' portrait of wisdom. This met the church's need for practical instruction. To accomplish these aims, Gregory negated Qoheleth's skepticism.

Athanasius

Creation forms the backdrop for Athanasius' interest in wisdom. He led the church in fighting Arian theology. Arius (280–336 C.E.) and his later fol-lowers promoted the idea that Christ was a created being. As such, Christ could not equal the Father in divinity. In *Against the Arians,* Athanasius (296–373 C.E.) defended at length Christ's character as uncreated. He used terms that clearly invoke Proverbs 9:1 and 8:22ff (*Against the Arians,* 8:41–44). Else-where, in the same work, rather lengthy expositions of Proverbs 8:22–30 apply the text specifically to Christ (23:206–223; 17:1–23:223). The controversy forced the Christian community to produce a clearer portrait of the origins of Christ intimated in the texts of Proverbs. This Christology led Athanasius to interpret the statement, "Wisdom had built her house . . ." (Prov. 9:1) as a reference to the human body and Christ's indwelling (*Against the Arians,* 20:162). By virtue of Christ's indwelling, the human body becomes wisdom's house. Christ acts as the divine agent at work rather than a passive recipient of the Father's activity.

Cyprian

The wisdom literature served a central role in Cyprian's writings, because Cyprian was deeply interested in Christian conduct. Cyprian, a con-temporary of Athanasius, was fascinated with Job. He used Job's experi-ences to illustrate the inevitability of just suffering, the inscrutability of divine sovereignty, and the virtue of faithful service. In his own words: "Who was more diligent in good works than Job, stronger in temptation, more patient in suffering, more submissive in fear, more true in faith?"[32] Cyprian

---

30. *Gregory Thaumaturgos' Paraphrase of Ecclesiastes,* trans. John Jarick (Atlanta: Scholars Press, 1990), 315–16.

31. Ibid., 311–12.

32. In *Saint Cyprian: Treatises,* trans. Roy J. Deferrari, The Fathers of the Church, vol. 36 (New York: The Fathers of the Church, Inc.,1958), 55–88.

used this description to support his view that God was not obligated to answer the prayers of the righteous, since even Job suffered without answer. In "Works and Almsgiving" Cyprian presented Job as the example of a diligent father (chap. 18). "On the Advantages of Patience" used Job as the model of patience: Job's patience in extreme suffering is presented as the height of virtue. Cyprian's attraction to Job evidently arose from the conviction that Christians must suffer more than others ("On the Morality" par. 10). Job served as prime example of this principle. Several of Cyprian's treatises quote numerous Proverbs in a moralistic fashion.

Ambrose

Ambrose (339–397 C.E.) expressed a similar interest in Job in "The Prayer of Job and David." He compared Job's frustration in trouble to that expressed by David in the Psalms. Ambrose admitted the suffering of the righteous. He promised a happy end for those who remained faithful. In letter 20 to Marcellina (his sister), Ambrose compared the pressure on his congregation to yield their building to Arians to the temptations that Satan placed on Job. He recounted the sermon he preached on the day the church was stormed, claiming his parishioners behaved like "Jobs." Ambrose (and Origen, over one hundred years earlier) called for the reading of Job in worship during the passion week.

Jerome

Jerome (342–420) contributed some distinct interpretations of wisdom indicative of the special interests of the time. In his letter to Nepotianus (no. 52) he identified the Shunammite woman who warmed David in his old age with wisdom presented in Proverbs 4:5–9. He introduced the text in this way, "Let Solomon, wisest of men, tell us of his father's favorite."[33] Such statements added a level of significance to texts which, like 1 Kings 1:1–4, caused offense when taken literally. Like most early Christian interpreters, Jerome read Proverbs 8:22 and other references to wisdom's beginnings as references to Christ. His approach to Proverbs 22:20 appears most unusual to the contemporary reader. The Septuagint reads, "And do thou too repeatedly [three times] record them for thyself on the table of thine heart, for counsel and knowledge." Jerome used this verse as a proof text for the interpretive approach that favored a threefold sense of Scripture. The methodology began with Origen, who claimed a literal, moral, and mystic sense for Scripture. This tripartite approach probably arose from the platonic division of human existence into body, soul, and spirit.

Cyril of Jerusalem

Cyril of Jerusalem (315–386) showed interest in the Book of Job in Lecture 11, "On the Son of God or true God, only begotten before all ages, by whom all things were made." He used the following proof texts: (1) Job

---

33. Jerome, "Letter to Nepotianus" in *Early Latin Theology*, ed. and trans. Stanley Lawrence Greenslade, Library of Christian Classics, vol. 5 (Philadelphia: Westminster, 1956), 316.

9:8 depicted Jesus walking on the sea; (2) Job 38:4 presented Jesus as the fashioner of humans; and (3) Job 38:17 told of Jesus' descent to hell. These verses, as well as others, proved that Christ is the "Maker of the world."[34]

Theodore of Mopsuestia

Theodore of Mopsuestia (345–407) fostered an opposing interest in Job. He supposed the original figure Job possessed pagan origins. Theodore presented several pieces of "evidence:" (1) the irreverent content of Job's early speeches, (2) Job's Edomite hometown (Uz), and (3) the name of his third daughter in 42:14, "Qeren Happuk." The name *Qeren Happuk* resembled the name of the goat horn which nourished Zeus in Greek mythology.[35] The fifth Council of the church (553) accused Theodore of claiming Job and Ecclesiastes were written from human experience and intellect rather than divine inspiration.[36] The charge accurately described Theodore's view, but Theodore did not question the sacred value of the works. His view of the authorship of Job also fell outside the norm. He disagreed with the view held by Baba Bathra and the Christian interpreter John Chrysostom (347–407) that Moses wrote Job. Theodore suggested an Israelite recorded a written version of the already common folk story sometime after the return from Babylon (539 B.C.E.).[37]

Augustine

Augustine's use of Job's example appears somewhat less skeptical than Theodore's ideas. In his conflicts with Pelagians, Augustine (354–430) used wisdom literature for apologetics. In paragraph 29 of his treatise, "On Man's Perfection in Righteousness," Augustine suggested that "my heart does not reproach me for any of my days" (Job 27:6) indicated Job's awareness of sin though he was protected from its peril.[38] Augustine understood this as the condition of all believers under the protection of God's grace. On several occasions Augustine referred to Job to indicate the pervasiveness of sin. If sin were present in even the most righteous (Job), all humans must engage in sin. Wisdom also provided the basis for some of Augustine's views of free will. He used Proverbs' exhortations to proper conduct to show the biblical regard for human choice: Proverbs advises all persons to follow certain patterns of conduct. Fairness demanded these individuals possess a real choice in determining behavior.[39]

---

34. Cyril of Jerusalem, "Lecture 11" in *Cyril of Jerusalem and Nemesius of Emesa*, ed. and trans. William Telfar, The Library of Christian Classics, vol. 4 (Philadelphia: Westminster, 1955), 146.

35. "Fragmenta in Vetus Testamentum" in *Patrologiae Graecae*, ed. Jacques P. Migne (Turnholt: Brepols, 1967), vol. 66, 698.

36. Dimitri Z. Zaharopoulos, *Theodore of Mopsuestia on the Bible: A Study of His Old Testament Exegesis* (New York: Paulist, 1989), 33, 46. The record of the council is available only in Latin: Acts of the Fifth General Council.

37. Ibid., 46–47.

38. *A Select Library of Nicene and Post-Nicene Fathers of the Christian Church*, vol. 5, trans. Peter Holmes and Robert Wallis (Grand Rapids: Eerdmans, 1887), 168.

39. "On Grace and Free Will" in *A Select Library*, vol. 5, 445.

Gregory the Great

Gregory the Great (540–604) addressed the authorship of Job in his commentary on Job entitled *Moralia in Job*.[40] Gregory declared the human authorship of Job indeterminate and irrelevant. God, who dictated it, was the only author of concern. Aquinas (1225–1274) employed the same approach. Gregory and a few earlier interpreters such as Theodore of Mopsuestia and Pseudo-Chrysostom reacted against the extremes of allegorical interpretation. In his letter of dedication prefacing *Moralia*, Gregory warned against extreme literal readings and allegorical readings which ignored obvious moral teachings present in Job.

Wisdom in Medieval Literature

After the patristic period mainstream interpreters largely ignored the Hebrew Bible until the Reformation.[41] Allegorical and literal interpretation of wisdom books became standardized so that spokespersons for the church were left to address more timely applications of Scripture to experience. Only after 1200 did interest in wisdom literature (especially The Wisdom of Solomon) blossom in the universities. This development, though widely noted, left scant impression on the surviving documents of the period. Although this assessment proves useful to the Christian interpreter, it manifests a grave deficiency in that Jewish interest in the wisdom books never waned. A detailed overview of Jewish readings of the Job motif from 1 C.E. to 1600 C.E. by Nahum Glatzer illustrates the continued interest in wisdom. Summarizing over twenty works, he characterized the presentations of Job in several categories, including Job as a saint, a rebel, a person confused regarding providence, an imperfect human, a person who misunderstood evil, and a scapegoat. A few interpreters recognized knowledge as a central theme in Job. Among them, Maimonides (1135–1204) and Saadia understood the Book of Job on its own terms, according to Glatzer. All the commentators rejected God's lack of concern for humans implied by the book. All viewed the speeches of Elihu and God as either correcting Job in minor points or transforming him in a fantastic enlightenment. All ignored Job's relative ignorance and powerlessness revealed in the theophany.[42]

Midrashim and Targums

Ecclesiastes Rabbah (seventh century C.E.) incorporated numerous stories in its explanation of the wisdom texts. It also tended to compile various interpretations from several dates and places. In tone, it displays interest in

---

40. *Magna moralia in Job* in Patrologia Latina, ed. J. P. Migne, vols. 75–79 (Paris: Apud Garnier Fratres Editores, 1849–1878).

41. Edward M. Gray, *Old Testament Criticism: Its Rise and Progress* (New York: Harper & Brothers, 1923), 50.

42. Nahum N. Glatzer, "The Book of Job and Its Interpreters," in *Biblical Motifs: Origins and Transformations*, ed. Alexander Altmann (Cambridge: Harvard University Press, 1966), 197–220; conclusions on p. 220.

the study of the book of Ecclesiastes itself. This involves the exclusion of moralisms and thematic summaries which would limit the scope of comments. Its editors valued inclusiveness above consistency and directive communication. A single example illustrates its more freeflowing comments: To elucidate the phrase, "vanity of vanities," the text described a person who sets seven pots atop one another on a fire. The steam from the top pot "has no substance in it [and such is man]."[43]

Showing the same style of exegesis, the Jewish Targums translated בְּרֵאשִׁית (bĕrē'šît) in Genesis 1:1 "In wisdom" rather than "in the beginning." Rēšit (Beginning) serves as the name of wisdom in Proverbs 8:22. Through this operation, wisdom becomes the agent of creation in Genesis 1:1![44] From about 800 C.E. a midrash on Proverbs quoted each proverb in turn. After each quotation, the midrash provided explanations approximately equal in length to the length of each proverb. The explications tended to employ (1) wordplay, (2) quotations of Rabbis, (3) explanations which relate the saying to current conduct, and (4) occasional stories offered in illustration of the truths involved. The midrash equates personified wisdom with Torah throughout.[45]

Gaon's The Book of Beliefs and Opinions

The tenth-century Babylonian, Saadia Gaon, left record of his interest in Hebrew wisdom in The Book of Beliefs and Opinions. Disagreeing with the Genesis Rabbah, he rejected the portrayal of wisdom as hypostasis. Instead, he presented a description of wisdom in philosophical terms.[46] He found in Proverbs and Ecclesiastes the key to enjoyment and benefit in life.[47] According to Saadia, to use the mind to bring "appetites and impulses" under control amounted to wisdom (Prov. 1:7; and 7:22; 15:33 cited).[48] His distinctive view of Ecclesiastes saw that for Solomon, the pursuit of wisdom led to vanity. Such vanity results when the seeker of wisdom takes the search to the excess of denying other human pleasures and needs. Extreme devotion to wisdom as the only center of attention caused the despair Solomon voiced in Ecclesiastes. Gaion understood Ecclesiastes itself to commend a more balanced approach.[49]

43. *Midrash Rabbah Ecclesiastes*, trans. A. Cohen, vol. 8, Ruth and Ecclesiastes, series eds. H. Freedman and Maurice Simon (London: Soncino, 1939), 4–5.

44. John Bowker, ed., *The Targums and Rabbinic Literature: An Introduction to Jewish Interpretations of Scripture* (Cambridge: Cambridge University Press, 1969). The interpretation comes from a fragmentary Targum on p. 98. Editorial explanation appears on p. 100.

45. *The Midrash on Proverbs*, trans. Burton L. Visotzky (New Haven: Yale University Press, 1992).

46. *The Book of Beliefs and Opinions*, trans. Samuel Rosenblatt (New Haven: Yale University Press, 1948), 55.

47. Saadia Gaon also authored *The Book of Theodicy* which contained a version of Job and commentary on the book.

48. *Beliefs*, 361.

49. Ibid., 362.

Maimonides' *Guide to the Perplexed*

Slightly later, Moses ben Maimonides (1135–1204) offered comments on each of the three books of the wisdom canon in *The Guide to the Perplexed*. In his exposition of Job he proposed that the writing illustrated the difference between the human idea of the world's order and the divine ideal.[50] A distinct shift in perspective enabled Maimonides to investigate the character of the document. Earlier interpreters concentrated on Job, the person. A specific Talmudic view of Job, common throughout the Middle Ages, probably encouraged such an impartial approach. The Talmud suggested the reading of the Book of Job as a parable rather than a historical account.[51] From this perspective, the divine truth communicated through the work no longer depends on the authority of the character. Job (the person) becomes the investigator of divine truth instead of the source of that truth. Maimonides globalized Proverbs' warnings against contact with the adulterous woman in 7:6–21. He read it as an allegory warning humans not to yield to their lower nature, which is enticed by all things material.[52] He contended that Ecclesiastes demanded a figurative interpretation, since otherwise its contents would contradict Torah.[53]

Kimhi's *Commentary on the Book of Job*

Maimonides' contemporary, Moses Kimhi, authored a commentary on Job in 1184. He affirmed the traditional Jewish view of Mosaic authorship and interpreted the book in light of Proverbs 3:12: "For the LORD reproves the one he loves, as a father the son in whom he delights." According to Kimhi, Job's troubles showed God's approval of Job.[54] This attitude toward Job effectively begs the question of the difficult content of the book. The view remains true to the book's canonical form by locating the source of Job's suffering in God. Kimhi's perspective implies Job needed discipline, perhaps on account of pride. One further feature distinguishes Kimhi's approach. Rather than allegorizing, he read the narrative of Job straightforwardly, as a story of the experience of an individual.

---

50. Moses ben Maimonides, *The Guide to the Perplexed*, trans. Shlomo Pines (Chicago: University of Chicago Press, 1963), 497.

51. At the end of the thirteenth century, a proponent of the views of Maimonides clarified the argument that Job was a parable rather than a historical figure. He cited, among other evidence: (1) Baba Bathra 15a (2) a connection between Uz and עֵצָה (*ʿēṣâ*, counsel) which indicated the place name should not be taken literally, (3) wordplay between אוֹיֵב (*ʾōyēb*), "enemy" and אִיּוֹב (*ʾiyōb*) "Job," as further evidence of its nonliteral nature, and (4) the logical conclusion Satan could not manipulate God in the way the book records. Moshe Greenberg, "Appendix: Zeraya of Barcelona's Commentary to Job (Rome, 1291)" in *"Sh'arei Talmon": Studies in the Bible, Qumran, and the Ancient Near East Presented to Shemaryahu Talmon*, eds. Michael Fishbane and Emmanuel Tov (Winona Lake, Ind.: Eisenbrauns,1992), 9–11; summary on p. 9.

52. *Perplexed*, 13.

53. Ibid., 334.

54. *Commentary on the Book of Job*, ed. Herbert Basser and Barry D. Walfish (Atlanta: Scholars Press, 1992), xviii.

Francis of Assisi's "A Salutation of Virtues"

The contemplative lifestyle of Francis of Assisi (1182–1226) made wisdom an important attribute. Accordingly, Francis listed wisdom first in "A Salutation of the Virtues."[55] Wisdom receives the title, "Queen of the Virtues." Further, in line 9 of the same work, wisdom offered the benefit of defeat to false wisdom: "Holy Wisdom destroys Satan and all his subtlety." The opening address of the poem shows Francis' view of wisdom closely allied to his views on poverty and solitude: "Hail, Queen Wisdom, may the Lord protect you with your sister, holy pure Simplicity." One cannot know the degree of influence the wisdom literature exercised on Francis. Such high praise for wisdom would surely owe something to the five books under discussion (especially The Wisdom of Solomon).

Summary: General Trends

Bishop Longland in a sermon at Oxford in 1525 explained "wisdom has set her table" (Prov. 9:2) in terms of four "courses": history, tropology, anagogy, and allegory, each of the four specifying a specific method in the exposition of Scripture.[56] The rebirth of interest in creative biblical exposition on the verge of the reformation signaled the renewal of wisdom studies. Longland's remark coordinated both the interest in exegesis and the interest in wisdom studies. The tone of his sermon evokes the more objective (according to scientific bias, more "responsible") stance toward interpretation implemented by the reformers.

During the patristic period and slightly before, wisdom served as the embodiment of Torah and Scripture, or Christ as ultimate revelation. Allegory became the normative means for explication. Of course, the goal for the church lay in the propagation of a lifestyle reflecting the indwelling of Christ (Wisdom). The emphasis upon wisdom as a means for achieving fitting Christian conduct did not disappear in the medieval period. At the same time, the monastic movement created a mystic elite. They modeled a spirituality which blunted the edge of wisdom's claims on the populace. The monks and scholars perceived truths of Scripture known only to them. They veiled wisdom in mystery. Allegory not only substantiated Christ's identity, but also validated the interpreters' own scriptural strategies. This led the way for defensive readings of Scripture with spurious connections to the biblical context.

Jewish exegesis used midrashic methods to apply wisdom to contemporary ethical and philosophical issues. It also struggled to show wisdom's consistency with other parts of canon, especially Torah.

---

55. In Regis J. Armstrong and Ignatius C. Brady, trans., *Francis and Clare: The Complete Works* (New York: Paulist, 1982), 151–52.

56. Frederic W. Farrar, *History of Interpretation* (New York: E. P. Dutton, 1886), 295–96.

Questions for Discussion

1. Trace the history of interpretation that led to the identification of wisdom and Torah. What theological significance does this have?

2. How did wisdom become identified as part of the Godhead? What effect did this have on New Testament writers?

3. What ethical concerns did early Jewish and Christian writers find in wisdom?

Chapter 4

History of Interpretation
Since the Reformation

Introduction: The Reformation and Freedom of Interpretation

Irresponsible modes of exegesis both gave impetus to and were used to support the Reformation's call to the popularization of Scripture. According to most reformers, biblical wisdom remained open to all. These interpreters accepted their interpretive findings as significant in themselves. Consequently, wisdom materials received greater attention, whether or not the materials yielded results acceptable to orthodoxy. In the new climate, many scholars expressed their freedom by rejecting allegory altogether.

Before the end of the first century, Judaism limited its canon by excluding all books displaying heavy Greek influence or signs of Christian redaction. Christian communities made differing choices regarding the precise content of the canon. Curiously, Jerome presented the first argument for distinction between the Hebrew canon and later books (the Deuterocanon). Jerome included the deuterocanonical books in the Vulgate in spite of his opinion of their secondary status. Protestants expressed a reticence to regard the works as fully canonical. Wyclif's introduction to the Deuterocanon in his English translation (about 1400) indicates this reticence. He denied the works' scriptural authority, but included them in his translation. Carlstadt, in 1520, described the Wisdom of Solomon, Sirach, and Tobit as holy, but far inferior to Scripture. The English Puritans excluded these and other books from their Bibles, considering them unfit for publication with canonical materials. Protestantism remains divided on the status of these works, between the extremes of outright rejection and modified acceptance of a few of the works (for example, Sirach) as scriptural in authority. The Roman Catholic Church responded to Carlstadt and others at the Council of Trent (1546). They declared the books named above and other deuterocanonical works to be fully canonical. Over a century later, the Synod of Jersualem (1672) declared Tobit, Sirach, and the Wisdom of Solomon to be unquestionably canonical for the Eastern Church (Greek Orthodox).

Protestant rejection of the Wisdom of Solomon, Sirach, and Tobit results in some lack of scholarly interest in these works and leaves a five-century gap between Hebrew wisdom and its New Testament counterparts. The wisdom of the New Testament, and so, the canonical interest in Hebrew wisdom expressed by the current church, developed through the mediacy of Hellenism and Judaism. Many additional rabbinical, deuterocanonical, and apocryphal sources indicate the Christian interpretation of wisdom did not emerge full blown in the first century. It developed among the various communities of intertestamental Judaism. For this reason, the study of the wisdom literature of the deuterocanonical period assumes importance for present wisdom scholarship.

Interpretation During the Reformation Period

The intellectual, institutional, and sociological ferment between 1450 and 1550 gave rise to new interest in education, new concern for a holistic view of life, and thus a new look at the meaning and purpose of the church. Study of wisdom literature played a significant role that has not always been recognized or appreciated.

Erasmus' *Enchiridion*

Erasmus (1469–1536), like Bishop Longland, operated in the medial period between medieval and Reformation interpretation. *The Enchiridion* (1515) elaborated on the text, "wisdom conquers malice" (Wisdom of Solomon 7:30) by ascribing the mentioned conquest to Jesus Christ, "the Author of wisdom, and himself wisdom."[1] Erasmus' expression offers a curious personification which verges on apocalypticism. The dynamic quality of this exposition lies in its emphasis upon the work of Christ. The usual focus fell upon his divinity and preexistence. Erasmus also presented a strikingly realistic portrait of Job: "Job (that veteran, undefeated soldier) testifies that the life of mortals is nothing else than a sort of perpetual warfare" (Job 7:1).[2]

Erasmus used this statement to introduce the need for a life like Job's. Eschewing the moralistic oversimplifications of his predecessors, he presumed Job's questioning of life's fairness was a legitimate response.

---

1. Erasmus, "The Enchiridion" in *Advocates of Reform: From Wyclif to Erasmus,* ed. Matthew Spinka, The Library of Christian Classics, vol. 14 (Philadelphia: Westminster, 1953), 309.
2. Ibid., 296.

Bucer's *Common Places*

Martin Bucer (1491–1551), like Augustine, used Job as an example of human sinfulness. He interpreted "Who can make a clean thing out of an unclean?" (14:4) as Job's reference to his own uncleanness.[3] Bucer revised the typical translation of Ecclesiastes 9:1 as well: "Whether love or hate" is rendered "both love and hatred alike man does not know."[4] "Bucer's translation protected God from the ambivalence which seems intentional to the Book of Job. In his "Refutation to Zwingli," John Eck (1486–1543) rendered Ecclesiastes 9:1: "Man knoweth not whether he be worthy of love or hatred." With this translation Eck showed his acceptance of the wording of the Vulgate.[5]

Zwingli's *Commentary on True and False Religion*

Ulrich Zwingli (1484–1531) offered a passionate defense of God's wisdom and providence. He resorted to Proverbs for support: "Solomon, Prov. 8:22–36, has a fine description in praise of wisdom, commending it first for its antiquity, in that it was with the Lord Himself before He began to create the universe; and then because afterwards through it the poles of the world were hung in place, and all things put together."[6] Zwingli stopped short of the identification of wisdom as a member of the Trinity (whether Christ or Spirit).

Luther

According to Martin Luther (1483–1546), all the Bible tells of Christ. It should be understood that way unless another message was unavoidable. This represents a basic hermeneutical principle and does not imply that allegory was his preferred approach. In his *Notes on Ecclesiastes* he avoided allegorical and Christological interpretations. Instead, he provided an original circumstance for the work. He suggested that Ecclesiastes constituted a public address delivered by Solomon at table after an evening meal. The address summed up Solomon's long reflection on human affairs and conveyed the dissatisfaction common to humans. In this way Luther accounted for the skeptical tone of Ecclesiastes, refusing to gloss its pessimism. Luther blamed the rise of the monastic movement on Jerome's poor interpretation of Ecclesiastes which fostered "the contempt of the world."[7]

Apparently, as Luther saw it, Jerome applied Ecclesiastes' "vanity" to all human experience. By contrast, Luther affirmed such experience as a gift of

---

3. "Original Sin" in *Common Places of Martin Bucer*, trans. and ed. D. F. Wright (Appleford, Eng.: The Sutton Courtenay Press, 1972), 127 and elsewhere.

4. "Faith" in *Common Places*, 180.

5. John Eck, "Refutation to Zwingli" in *Zwingli: On Providence and Other Essays*, ed. and trans. William John Hinke (Durham, N.C.: The Labyrinth Press, 1922), 77.

6. *Commentary on True and False Religion*, eds. Samuel Macauley Jackson and Clarence Nevin Heller, trans. Samuel Macauley Jackson (Durham, N.C.: The Labryinth Press, 1981), 68.

7. "Notes on Ecclesiastes" in *Luther's Works*, gen. ed. and trans. Jaroslav Pelikan (Saint Louis: Concordia, 1972), 4.

God. In marked opposition to Jerome's view, Luther supposed Solomon expressed a positive aim in Ecclesiastes: Solomon attempted to make persons more content with life in all its vanity, advising the opposite of monastic withdrawal. What Solomon condemned as vain was the "depraved desire" of humans. This made persons unsatisfied with a good world.[8] Luther contended that the conviction that good deeds are always rewarded resulted in "speculative theology." Luther bluntly claimed such theology "belongs to the devil in hell." In response to the simplistic theology of retribution, Luther quoted Sirach 1:13: "Whoso feareth the Lord, it shall go well with him at the last." Luther distinguished this promise from promise of rewards.[9]

In the "Table Talks," wisdom literature occasionally provides the basis for arguments in defense of God's self-determination. This emphasis on God's sovereignty counters human pride of intellect. Such a mode of interpretation shares more with contemporary readings of Job and Ecclesiastes than with the bulk of Reformation readings.

Grebel's Letters

Conrad Grebel (1498–1526) used a wisdom text to support his doctrine that children receive God's grace even before the moment of conversion. Wisdom of Solomon mentions children (vv. 5, 19, 21, 24–25). The passages generally assure the chance for repentance to the rebellious as revealed in the following: "Through such works you have taught your people that the righteous must be kind, and you have filled your children with good hope, because you give repentance for sins" (v. 19). This reminder of God's patience and mercy assured Grebel that God's wrath would not be spent upon children. The limit of this mercy, according to Grebel, was the point at which a child learned to distinguish good from evil.[10]

Meno Simons

Meno Simons (1496-1561) showed the same tendency toward proof texts from the wisdom books of Sirach and Wisdom of Solomon, but with less adeptness than Grebel. His works lack citations from the wisdom of the Hebrew canon. He offered no words of interpretation, but used wisdom aphorisms he reckoned to agree with his own positions. He used Sirach and Wisdom to support his own theology. He also used similar quotations to refute his opponents. The statements offered, void of their context, provided flimsy reinforcement.[11]

---

8. Ibid., 7–8.
9. "Table Talk" in *Luther's Works*, vol. 54, ed. and trans. Theodore G. Tappert, gen. ed. Helmut Lehmann (Philadelphia: Fortress, 1967), 22.
10. *Conrad Grebel's Programmatic Letters of 1524*, trans. John C. Wenger (Scottsdale, Pa.: Herald Press, 1970), 31.
11. *The Complete Works of Meno Simons c. 1496–1561*, trans. Leonard Verduin, ed. John Christian Wenger (Scottsdale, Pa.: Herald Press, 1956).

Calvin

John Calvin (1509–1564) relied on the experience of Job to reinforce his predestinarian concepts. Most often he used the wisdom writings to provide proof texts for his theology, notably to buttress God's sovereignty. Calvin carefully portrayed God as the instigator of Job's troubles. To question such divine designs was the height of human ignorance and the ultimate impropriety, as Job learned. Calvin used this defense of divine freedom to sanction his entire theological system. Based on this mode of reading Job, Calvin favored the speeches of Job's antagonists above the speeches of Job. Job 26:14 contended God's ways (that is, his wisdom) were hidden from humans: "These are indeed but the outskirts of his ways; and how small a whisper do we hear of him! But the thunder of his power who can understand?" In response Calvin chose not to encourage the quest for knowledge, advising fatalistic trust instead. He read "the fear of the LORD is wisdom" (Job 28:28) as equivalent to the verse above. Humans could properly respond to divine mystery only with unquestioning subservience.[12]

Calvin cautiously used Job 19:25–27 ("I know that my Redeemer lives") to defend Job's belief in immortality. He admitted Job did not present a full-blown concept of resurrection, but saw his expression as a hope beyond this life.[13] Calvin glossed Job's dissatisfaction with life's retribution, refusing to reckon his doubt as central to the argument: "Job maintaining a good case pleads it poorly, and the others bringing a poor case plead it well."[14] Job's "good case" rested in his contention evil was not always caused by sin. Job "pled his case poorly" in that he exaggerated the cases and expressed anger toward God. Calvin apparently valued the orthodoxy of Job's comforters in the same amount he valued Job's argument, an approach which helped to reconcile Job to the tamer wisdom of Proverbs. Calvin considered Job's brutal honesty out of bounds for the Christian, though affirming the basic sense of his claims.

Interpretation after the Reformers

Spinoza's *Theologico-Political Treatise*

Benedict de Spinoza (1569–1630) promoted a theory of special revelation based on wisdom. His ideas directly connect Christ with wisdom as personified in Proverbs. Spinoza ascribed supernatural wisdom to Jesus.[15] Spinoza mentioned rabbis who wished to exclude Proverbs and Ecclesiastes from the canon. He claimed they would have succeeded except for scant

---

12. John Calvin, *Institutes of the Christian Religion*, Book One 17:2, trans. Ford Lewis Battles, ed. John T. McNeill, Library of Christian Classics, vol. 20 (Philadelphia: Westminster, 1960), 213.
13. *Institutes*, Book Two 10:19, Library of Christian Classics, vol. 21, p. 445.
14. *Sermons from Job*, trans. Leroy Nixon (Grand Rapids: Eerdmans, 1952), 5.
15. Benedict de Spinoza, *A Theologico-Political Treatise* in *A Theologico-Political Treatise and a Political Treatise*, trans. R. H. M. Elwes (New York: Dover Publications, 1951), 19.

mentions of the Torah in these books.[16] His own willingness to defend the presence of these books in the Hebrew canon shows his commitment to wisdom. Spinoza also discussed rabbinic views on Job's authorship, notably its ascription to Moses and connection with the patriarchs. Spinoza himself considered Job a foreigner. He described the book as a translation from a language other than Hebrew.[17]

Martin Rinkart

In 1636 Martin Rinkart wrote the words to the hymn, "*Nun danket alle Gott*" (Now thank we all our God) based on Sirach 50:22–24.[18] Such direct literary influence reveals little regarding interpretive methods, but shows high regard for the Deuterocanon.

Table 2
Rinkart and Sirach

Rinkart	Sirach
Now thank we all our God	Now therefore bless ye the God of all
With heart and hands and voices,	
Who wondrous things hath done,	who only doeth wondrous things every where
In whom His world rejoices;	
Who, from our mother's arms,	which exalteth our days from the womb,
Hath blessed us on our way	and dealeth with us according to his mercy
With countless gifts of love,	
And still is ours today.	
O may this bounteous God,	May he grant us
Through all our life be near us,	
With ever joyfull hearts	joyfulness of heart,
And blessed peace to cheer us;	and that peace may be in our days in Israel forever:
And keep us in His grace,	that he would confirm his mercy with us;
And guide us when perplexed,	

---

16. Ibid., 155.
17. Ibid., 149.
18. This comparison appears in Bruce Metzger, *Introduction to the Apocrypha* (Oxford: Oxford University Press, 1957), 213–14.

Table 2 (Continued)
Rinkart and Sirach

And free us from all ills	
In this world and the next.	and deliver us at his time! (KJV)

Historical-Critical Interpretation

Freed by the Reformation from the strictures imposed by the church's control of Scripture, new generations of biblical scholars developed new methods of research and new types of questions as they searched God's Word for God's truth.

Hobbes' "Christian Commonwealth"

Discussion of the most recent era of interpretation begins with Thomas Hobbes. He fostered a comparative approach toward Job. He claimed the poetry of Job followed a common form for "ancient moral philosophy."[19] Hobbes' interest in Job remained apart from Christology and Christian interest. This represents a shift toward interpreting Hebrew Bible materials in their own right. With similar detachment, he suggested Ecclesiastes and Song of Solomon took Solomon's name out of concern not only for the Torah, but also for the characters (Solomon) contained in it.[20]

Form Criticism

Shortly after 1800, critical scholarship developed theories that found wisdom late and dependent upon the prophets. Form critical studies refuted these ideas in part by showing the literary uniqueness of wisdom's genres. Such forms showed invention rather than simple borrowing of older materials. Form criticism also pointed to discoveries of Near Eastern parallels with forms similar to those in canonical wisdom that predate the prophets. Slightly before 1900, several scholars assigned an extremely late date to Proverbs (late postexilic). This assessment arose from the presumption that Proverb's view of divine retribution was postexilic. The so-called "secular" character of the Proverbs also promoted this view. In spite of the emphasis upon divine reward and punishment based on behavior, wisdom appeared more secular (at the least, less Yahwistic) than other segments of the Hebrew canon. Its pragmatic character seemed to indicate a less-than-orthodox theology. Interpreters understood this secular character to reflect the thought of later Judaism rather than ancient Israel.

The discovery of wisdom traditions in neighboring cultures showed themes present in Israel's wisdom appeared at various times and places. On

---

19. Thomas Hobbes, *Leviathan*, Book Three, "Of a Christian Commonwealth" in Great Books of the Western World, vol. 23 (Chicago: Encyclopedia Britannica, Inc., 1952), 169.
20. Ibid.

this basis, the secular themes rendered Israel's wisdom neither early nor late. In part, the unusual forms, themes, and styles led to assessments, such as dating, which attributed a different milieu to wisdom. Form criticism helped prove that wisdom constituted an independent phenomenon rather than a late derivative movement. As a result, the special approach of wisdom writings captured the attention of interpreters who previously devalued them. When Hermann Gunkel analyzed wisdom according to the form critical program, its unique didactic forms led him to suggest an international group of wisdom teachers as its originators. The contents of the books did not provide warrant for connections with priests, prophets, or other Israelite professionals. This assessment continues to suit most wisdom scholars. Wide disagreements continue on the degree of international cooperation as well as the precise provenance of Israel's wisdom. The role of the typical wisdom teacher remains something of a mystery. Gunkel claimed that the basic form of wisdom teaching, the מָשָׁל (māšāl), was later expanded into more complex forms. As the following discussion indicates, this finding remains central to much current study. Gunkel's claims for sage and proverb notwithstanding, "the discovery of forms did not seem to provide a bridge to a provenance [Sitz im Leben] in the same way the method had done with the narrative and prophetic material."[21]

In other words, though form criticism provided likely identifications of wisdom's genres and personnel, even these remained conjectural. Scholars lacked definite cultural settings for the practice of the sages.

The Theology of Wisdom

The lack of clarity for wisdom's settings combined with the distinctiveness of its contents resulted in a depreciation of wisdom materials among theologians. The lack of attention seems less a deliberate choice than a result of lack of understanding of the place of wisdom in Israel's history. Eichrodt relegated wisdom to approximately ten pages in his *Theology of the Old Testament*. He described wisdom as the cosmic power of God and affirmed hypostatization as a normative Israelite approach to wisdom. Curiously, he neglected the humanistic nature of wisdom. He also offered little place for the sages' role in shaping Israel's traditions. In a lengthy discussion of Israel's leaders in volume two, he omitted the sage from consideration. He gave minimal attention to the office elsewhere.[22] During the same period Johannes Fichtner made explicit the close connections between wisdom's maxims and the commandments of the Torah. This laid the groundwork for later discussions of wisdom and law which considered wisdom integral to Israel's religious history.[23]

---

21. Gerald T. Sheppard, *Wisdom as a Hermeneutical Construct: A Study in the Sapientializing of the Old Testament* (Berlin: Walter deGruyter, 1980), 5.
22. Walther Eichrodt, *Old Testament Theology*, 2 vols., trans. J. A. Baker (Philadelphia: Westminster, 1967), 2:80–92. Originally published in German in 1933.
23. Johannes Fichtner, *Die altorientalische Weisheit in ihrer israelitisch-jüdischen Ausprägung: Eine Studie zur Nationalisierung der Weisheit in Israel*, BZAW 62 (Giessen: Töpelmann, 1933).

Walther Zimmerli effectively denied such interchange in 1935, when he proposed that theology of wisdom literature differed substantially from conventional theology. Zimmerli claimed sages limited God's activity according to preconceived patterns, such as retribution. By contrast, God remained free to act self-determinatively elsewhere in the Hebrew canon, including in Ecclesiastes. According to Zimmerli, Ecclesiastes' emphasis on divine freedom and the limits of human understanding make it distinct among wisdom books.[24] The positions of Eichrodt and Zimmerli give indication that before World War II critics and theologians reserved little or no place for wisdom literature in the development of Israelite theology.[25]

Rylaarsdam's View of Revelation in Wisdom

In 1946 Coert Rylaarsdam took a new approach to Hebrew wisdom which both illustrated the then current improved status of wisdom in criticism and laid a foundation for further developments. The mainstream of wisdom scholars, following Gunkel's work, understood the earliest and most basic wisdom forms as completely secular. Rylaarsdam did not understand the distinction between earlier gnomic (proverbial) wisdom and later forms in terms of the sacred or secular nature of the material. Instead, the difference between earlier and later forms of wisdom rested upon the basis for revelation. The theology of earlier proverbial forms depended upon a natural basis of revelation, and later forms (like most of the Hebrew Bible) relied on special revelation.[26] Rather than promoting a secular outlook, they espoused a monotheism exhibiting less of the distinctive character of specifically Israelite theology. Rylaarsdam's study of wisdom focused upon the dynamic interchange between the divine and the human which lay behind its development. This provided an avenue for the consideration of the unique emphases of wisdom. Other studies equated the differences between wisdom literature and other portions of canon as "aberration." The rather lengthy quotation that follows summarizes Rylaarsdam's purpose and findings:

> The debate opens with an advocacy of personal freedom and an employment of the natural human endowment of mind and reason as the sufficient resources to attain an understanding of life. It closes with assertations that this understanding of life which is the attainment of widom is not made possible by the unfettered human mind but by God's special gift. This special gift is wisdom, the Law of the Jews, or, as in the Wisdom of Solomon, the divine spirit. It is granted only to some—that is, in classical theological terms the movement begins with

---

24. Walther Zimmerli and Helmut Ringren, *Sprüche/Prediger*, Das Alte Testament Deutsch xvi/I (Göttingen: Vandenhoeck and Ruprecht, 1980).

25. Hayes and Prussner examine Sellin's contribution in this regard. John Hayes and Frederick Prussner, *Old Testament Theology: Its History and Development* (Atlanta: John Knox, 1985), 186.

26. J. Coert Rylaarsdam, *Revelation in Jewish Wisdom Literature* (Chicago: University of Chicago Press, 1946), 67–73.

an emphasis upon the sufficiency of nature, reason, creation, and it ends with an assertion of the necessity of grace, faith, and redemption. It opens in a spirit of indifference toward the national cult, including the Law; it closes in glorification of the cult and absorption by it.

Yet the transition from one extreme to the other is a very gradual process. Neither "side" of the debate ever wholly denies the other. They oppose each other but are held in tension by the awareness that both rest on a common foundation. The side emphatic about personal freedom and reason is aware of its creaturehood and recognizes its natural powers as gifts of God; and the side emphatic about special divine initiative never discounts the place of human reason. There is wisdom in God and there is wisdom in man. Both have spirit. The Hebrew wisdom movement throughout has a place for the divine image in which man was created, albeit not always equally spacious.[27]

Expansion of Interest in Wisdom in Recent Study

In other respects as well, the study of wisdom broadened in the postwar period. In 1953 Ludwig Köhler interpreted the Book of Job as a סוֹד (sōd).[28] This represents a turn away from the connection of Job with proverbial forms. The sōd was a discussion among elders which took place in the gate of the city. Sages developed and studied proverbs as "literary" professionals. The present form of the Book of Job shows careful literary effort. If the Book of Job began as or was modeled after the sōd, it originated from less elitist surroundings. This indicates a more pragmatic, juridical form of Job preceded the current literary form. In addition to such novel investigations of works long accepted as wisdom, the scope of wisdom study expanded to include narratives not previously included under the designation "wisdom." Von Rad's consideration of the Joseph saga as a "didactic wisdom story" began a trend which continues in less extreme forms.[29]

Study of wisdom's links to other literature flourished. Johannes Lindblom's article, "Wisdom in the Old Testament Prophets," continues to serve as an adequate, if cautious, introduction to the basic concerns involved.[30] The study of wisdom in the prophets centered on (1) wisdom vocabulary, (2) forms such as proverbs, parables and allegories, and (3) apparent invectives against wisdom in the prophetic literature.[31] Subsequent studies in the prophets have raised claims of direct connections between individual prophets (Amos and Jeremiah, for example) and wisdom settings. Albright

---

27. *Revelation*, ix–x.
28. Ludwig Köhler, *Hebrew Man*, trans. Peter Ackroyd (Nashville: Abingdon, 1957), 127–50 (Appendix).
29. Gerhard von Rad, "The Joseph Narrative and Ancient Wisdom" in *The Problem of the Hexateuch and Other Essays*, trans. E. W. Trueman Dicken (London: SCM Press, 1966). Originally published in German in 1953.
30. In *Wisdom in the Old Testament and in the Ancient Near East*, VTSup 3 (Leiden: E. J. Brill, 1955), 192–204.
31. For a recent summary, see Raymond C. Van Leeuwen, "The Sage in the Prophetic Literature," *SIANE*, 295–306.

reversed the earlier trend by assigning all of Proverbs a preexilic date and postulating a "Solomonic nucleus."[32] Von Rad compared Job to Egyptian wisdom literature.[33] Albright and others linked the discovery of parallel word pairs in Ugaritic texts to wisdom vocabulary.[34]

These and similar studies led to a new respect for the age and pervasiveness of wisdom. Cross-cultural studies provided a new basis for portraits of wisdom. The new approach showed an integral relationship between Hebrew wisdom and the ancient-Near-Eastern-thought world. When scholars surrendered notions regarding wisdom as late and derivative, the search began for aspects linking biblical narratives and figures to the wisdom tradition.

Suggestions Regarding the Origins of Hebrew Wisdom

Von Rad

Gerhard von Rad presented a creative, epoch-making study of wisdom. His suggestions set the course for wisdom study during the following twenty years. He suggested wisdom literature understood creation as the "basis for faith." Wisdom proponents espoused this creation theology without the addition of religious elements in the interpretation of creation. Considering this and other clues, von Rad accounted it likely that Genesis 1 served as a wisdom document of some sort. He proposed that wisdom tradents produced the succession narrative (2 Samuel 9; 1 Kings 2). For the first time, von Rad connected apocalyptic to wisdom rather than prophecy (see Dan. 5:11, 14). He used Proverbs as the paradigm for understanding Hebrew wisdom. The proverb changed shape in each of three stages: (1) in its pristine form, the proverb contained observations that enabled higher living (Prov. 10–29); (2) later proverbs rested on a rational basis which lended support to the aristocratic concern to consolidate the monarchy under Solomon (Prov. 10–29); and (3) postexilic proverbs broadened to eventually include all of Israel's "theological thinking" (Prov. 1–9). Von Rad avoided the designation "hypostatization" in reference to Proverbs' characterization of wisdom. He viewed Ecclesiastes as anti-wisdom in that it challenged the wisdom tradition itself.[35]

Assigning "revelation in history" the central place in the development of Old Testament theology leaves creation theology in a marginal position, as von Rad himself noted. Later figures such as Ernest Wright and Claus

---

32. William F. Albright, "Canaanite-Phoenician Sources of Hebrew Wisdom" in *WIANE*, 13.

33. "Job xxxviii and Ancient Egyptian Wisdom" in *The Problem of the Hexateuch*. Originally published in German in 1955.

34. "Canaanite," 7.

35. Gerhard von Rad, *Old Testament Theology*, vol. 1, trans. D. M. G. Stalker (New York: Harper & Row, 1962); creation, p. 139; Genesis, p. 143; succession narrative, p. 56; apocalyptic, p. 102; paradigm, pp. 418–53; hypostasis, pp. 447–48; Ecclesiastes, pp. 453–59. See also his *Wisdom in Israel*, trans. James D. Martin (London: SCM Press, 1972)—basically a supplement to von Rad's two-volume theology, giving more attention to wisdom.

Westermann also gave evidence of problems in appropriating wisdom literature due to their emphasis on historical revelation. A minority of scholars in the same decade laid the foundation for understanding Israel's wisdom based on a general concept of divine order rather than a detailed study of Proverbs. Hartmut Gese related the Hebrew concept of wisdom to Egyptian *ma'at.* This suggested a particular view of divine order rather than a series of programmatic (often nonreligious) aphorisms.[36] Such a view can lead to a link between law and wisdom, as well as an alternative to an historical approach and the acceptance of hypostatization.

The narrative of the Hebrew Bible yields little evidence of such a view of divine order. The Hebrews related to God as a person rather than a life force. Yahweh presented himself as the sovereign of world order rather than identifying with the natural world. In spite of difficulties, a modified view of wisdom, by which it embodied divinely-ordered ethical behavior rather than the universal *ma'at,* probably complemented Israel's view of the God who acts in history. Choices relating to human activity could support or damage the moral fabric inherent in the world as God created it. However, the Hebrews could not imagine human conduct (good or evil) limiting or prescribing the conduct of the deity. God himself stood outside the scope of such ordered systems.[37]

Eissfeldt

Eissfeldt's coverage of wisdom in his monumental introduction encompassed less than ten pages. He depicted the authorship of wisdom forms as primarily a literary enterprise. He described them as "artistic." Such forms originated in some sort of school, as Gunkel had indicated. In an assessment typical of earlier studies, Eissfeldt dated all three wisdom books in the postexilic period.[38] The persistence of views from the turn of the century resulted from the lack of verifiable evidence for dating within the works of the wisdom canon. Resistance toward the data yielded in comparative studies rarely occurs in contemporary studies.[39]

Gerstenberger

One of the most provocative suggestions of recent scholarship commends the connection of laws with wisdom forms. The hypothesis chal-

---

36. Hartmut Gese, *Lehre und Wirklichkeit in der alten Weisheit* (Tübingen: J. C. B. Mohr [Paul Siebeck], 1958); compare H. H. Schmid, *Gerechtigkeit als Weltordnung* (Tübingen: Mohr, 1968) and "Schöpfung, Gerechtigkeit, und Heil: Schöpfungstheologie als Gesamthorizont biblischer Theologie," ZTK 70 (1973), 1–19.

37. Joseph Blenkinsopp, *Wisdom and Law in the Old Testament* (Oxford: Oxford University Press, 1983), 139, found only a single concept in Hebrew wisdom in support of Gese's view: The idea that *ma'at* was Re's favorite child parallels the relationship between God and wisdom in Proverbs 8:22–31, where wisdom stands beside God at creation.

38. Otto Eissfeldt, *The Old Testament: An Introduction,* trans. Peter Ackroyd (New York: Harper & Row, 1965), 81–87.

39. The study of Gerald T. Sheppard, *Wisdom as a Hermeneutical Construct,* serves as an exemplary model of current openness to comparative data.

lenges the previous assumption that the roots of wisdom lay in a covenant formula. Erhard Gerstenberger cited Proverbs 3:27–30 as an example of the wisdom commandment:

> Do not withhold good from those to whom it is due, when it is in your power to do it. Do not say to your neighbor, "Go, and come again, tomorrow I will give it"—when you have it with you. Do not plan harm against your neighbor who lives trustingly beside you. Do not quarrel with anyone without cause, when no harm has been done to you.

Rather than unique "apodictic laws" (such as Albrecht Alt observed), the Decalogue contains "the expression of moral precepts in collections of commandments and prohibitions. These help preserve basic social institutions. The father or clan leader held the primary responsibility for passing these teachings on within the family group."[40]

This proposal shows no signs of forming the basis for Torah studies. It serves as a reminder of the fluidity of interchange between Israelite traditions (law and wisdom). It advises caution to those who isolate law and wisdom into distinctive categories. Contemporary critics show more reluctance to make extreme claims regarding the lack of dependence of law on wisdom or vice versa.

Whybray

Whybray developed von Rad's proposal on wisdom influence in the succession narrative. Much of his argument depends on the humanistic perspective of 2 Samuel 9–20 and 1 Kings 1–2. The succession narrative traces David's lineage with primary interest on court intrigues. The special humanistic perspective of the succession narrative, combined with its scant reference to Israel's sacred history, provides evidence of the need for a more detailed study of its origins. Whybray proposed the succession narrative presented "a dramatization of Hebrew wisdom."[41]

Whybray's challenge to conventional scholarship concerned the identity of wisdom teachers. He contested the notion of a class of professional sages. Instead, he proposed a diverse group of well-educated (literate) Israelites without professional affiliation.[42] Whybray's contention, like the conventional idea it challenges, is not easily confirmed. It is representative of a number of suggestions which moderate the over-specific claims of previous scholarship. The division of offices in Israel cannot become so clear-cut as to deny the interaction of professionals. Perhaps the differing traditions in Israel whose legacies are identified with Torah, prophecy, and wisdom worked to check and balance one another.[43]

---

40. Erhard Gerstenberger, "Covenant and Commandment," *JBL* 84 (1965), 50–51.

41. Roger N. Whybray, *The Succession Narrative: A Study of 2 Samuel 9–20; 1 Kings 1 and 2*, Studies in Biblical Theology 2/9 (London: SCM Press , 1968), 78 and more recently, "The Sage in the Israelite Royal Court," *SIANE*, 133–39.

42. Roger N. Whybray, *Intellectual Tradition*, 221, note 6.

43. According to Donn F. Morgan, *Wisdom in the Old Testament Traditions* (Philadelphia: John Knox, 1981), 152, each of the mainstream traditions periodically rose to challenge the extremism of another.

Crenshaw

The burgeoning of influence studies prompted James Crenshaw to write "Method in Determining Wisdom Influence upon 'Historical Literature.'"[44] He intended to urge caution because the rapid rise of studies on the subject threatened to trivialize key issues by dilution. He presented five considerations for review of wisdom influence: (1) the definition of wisdom, (2) assessment of style and theme on the basis of wisdom literature (Proverbs, Job, Ecclesiastes), (3) the context in which the wisdom vocabulary or theme resided, (4) an accounting of the strand of tradition which depicted wisdom as contrary to dependence on Yahweh, and (5) the history of wisdom (insofar as it is traceable).[45] Using these criteria, he questioned von Rad's thesis on the Joseph narrative, Whybray's suggestion regarding the succession narrative, and Talmon's view of Esther as wisdom,[46] among many others. To read Crenshaw's sugggestions as the last word in influence studies would be the ironical equivalent of the excess in influence claims themselves. On the other hand, the mere presence of wisdom terminology serves as poor support for the claim of dependence. The scholar needs to be sensitive to the shades of distinction between supposition and proof.

Crenshaw's reticence to accommodate claims of influence now appears extreme, but his writing supplied a crucial sense of balance which may have checked the flood of rash claims. Much of the enthusiasm for the prospect of a relationship between wisdom and other traditions resulted from a consensus that wisdom exemplified by Proverbs predated the postexilic period. Perhaps von Rad's evolutionary theory of the development of Proverbs, mentioned above, influenced this view.[47]

Wolff

Early challenges to postexilic dating come from Christa Bauer-Kayatz[48] and William McKane.[49] Later scholars no longer presented wisdom as a late evolution of prior traditions. Wisdom possessed its own line of development concurrent with Israel's earliest national documents. One of the most pervasive assertions of influence appeared in the early 1970s, when Hans Walter Wolff proposed an interconnection between law and wisdom by way of tribal society. The early connection between law and wisdom dated to the period of Amos' ministry. Such tribal or clan wisdom took form as understandings of Yahweh's demands circulated among semi-nomads.[50]

---

44. *JBL* 88 (1969), 129–42.

45. "Method," 130–35.

46. Shemaryahu Talmon, "'Wisdom' in the Book of Esther," *VT* 13 (1963), 419–55.

47. John A. Emerton, "Wisdom" in *Tradition and Interpretation*, ed. George W. Anderson (Oxford: Clarendon, 1979), 229–30, suggested the dependence of dating practices on Von Rad's ideas.

48. *Studien zu Proverbien 1–9*, Wissenschaftliche Monographien zum Alten und Neuen Testament, vol. 22 (Neukirchen-Vluyn: Neukirchener Verlag, 1966).

49. *Prophets and Wisemen*, SBT 44 (Napierville, Ill.: Alec R. Allenson, 1965); compare his *Proverbs: A New Approach*, OTL (Philadelphia: Westminster Press, 1970).

50. Hans Walter Wolff, *Amos the Prophet: The Man and His Background*, trans. Foster R. McCurley (Philadelphia: Fortress Press, 1973); compare his *Joel and Amos*, Her (Philadelphia: Fortress Press, 1977).

According to this view, such forms of teaching as didactic questions, numerical sayings, and comparisons of human activity with natural phenomena show the influence of clan wisdom on Amos.

Wolff stopped short of claiming Amos acted as a wisdom teacher rather than a prophet. The proposal remains attractive. Unfortunately, the suggestions remain untestable because clan wisdom by its very nature produced no writing.[51] Ronald Clements noted that the high ethical standards of the prophets predated them as did wisdom. Earlier documents such as Amenemopet prove this.[52] On this basis, interpreters adjusted notions of the priority of Torah and Prophets over wisdom. Future reconstructions of Israel's tribal origins must account for a nascent clan wisdom. At the least, studies of wisdom must justify their omission of clan wisdom.[53] In the absence of such a theory, wisdom, as typified by Amos and other early figures, remains without identifiable roots.

Road to Definition

Its differences with the legal and prophetic strands of thought help to define wisdom. Those qualities (social standing, training, worldview) which characterize its major proponents provide the platform for such definitions. Using the corrective nature of wisdom to guide its definition, wisdom existed to challenge contemporary adherents of the biblical canon to account for diverse perspectives. According to such a view, neither the sages nor the wisdom movement in general may be characterized as secular rather than sacred. Responses to outside stimuli determine the religious character of wisdom rather than internal characteristics (such as a secular approach). Nor can wisdom be characterized as predominantly early or late, since the corrective of wisdom shows itself present in earliest traditions. Thus, the Hebrew Bible presents no clear evolutionary development of wisdom. Our brief schematization appears hopelessly speculative, but remains preferable to a simplified portrait which cannot account for the bulk of wisdom writings and influence. The interactive nature of wisdom satisfies the need for a theological center to bridge the two testaments, according to Samuel Terrien. Wisdom serves a mediating role between Law and Prophets, and "through wisdom the *deus absconditus* [God concealed] still remains the *deus praesens* [God present]."[54] In solving the dialectic between the Law

---

51. The same lack of evidence plagues other theories of wisdom's origins such as the theory relating the wisdom tradition to schools. Roger N. Whybray shows how scant the evidence for this theory is in *The Intellectual Tradition in the Old Testament*, BZAW 135 (New York: de Gruyter, 1974), 31ff. Such schools would be expected to produce physical evidence of their existence.

52. Ronald Clements, *100 Years of Old Testament Interpretation* (Philadelphia: Westminster, 1976), 106.

53. It is remarkable that Norman Gottwald's *The Tribes of Yahweh* (Maryknoll, N.Y.: Orbis, 1979) practically omitted wisdom from consideration. Gottwald understood wisdom as a late influence on Israel's development and dealt only with the earliest period (1250–1050). Surely the structures noted by Wolff belong to Israel's earliest organization.

54. Samuel Terrien, "The Play of Wisdom: Turning Point in Biblical Theology," *Horizons in Biblical Theology* 3 (1981), 137.

and Prophets, wisdom associates the deity of uncompromising holiness with Wisdom who "communicates in play the presence of God to mankind."[55] For Terrien this provides a mediating theology of God's presence between that presented in the Prophets and that presented in the Torah. The prophetic understanding involves direct relations with God. The Torah involves communion with God through worship and ritual. Wisdom involves something between the two. An identification of the *Logos* of John 1 with Wisdom relates this divine presence to Jesus of Nazareth and provides a pivotal point between the Hebrew Bible and Christian Scriptures.

Latest Trends in Interpretation

Some of the most recent claims regarding Proverbs originated in William McKane's commentary. Since proverbs occur without a context, they must be studied according to broad classes. Three are identified: Class A proverbs lead individuals to a successful lifestyle; Class B proverbs are community-oriented and tend to negatively portray behavior detrimental to the community; and Class C proverbs are religious proverbs that contain theological language including references to God.[56] In another innovation McKane defined a *māšāl* as an originally popular saying which became recognized as a representation of other phenomena of the same sort. A single proverb could be employed in a variety of diverse settings and its interpretation would depend upon the context.[57]

Editorial Composition of Proverbs

In "Thoughts on the Composition of Proverbs 10–29," R. N. Whybray's interest lay in the connection of individual proverbs within the book. He cautiously affirmed signs of editorial connections between individual proverbs and groups of proverbs.[58] This presents a relatively new direction in Proverbs study. Though largely unproven, it may provide a new vista on the collection as a whole. Such an approach complements the isolated study of individual units such as that fostered by McKane.

The Theory of Retribution

James Crenshaw offered a suggestion pertinent to Proverbs and wisdom study in general. He called for recognition that the theory of retribution belonged to the Hebrew Bible as a whole, not simply to portions showing wisdom influence. The theme of divine reward and punishment necessarily occurs in wisdom due to wisdom's preoccupation with the

---

55. Ibid., 134.
56. McKane, *Proverbs*, 10–11.
57. Ibid., 31.
58. Roger N. Whybray, "Thoughts on the Composition of Proverbs 10–29" in *Priests, Prophets, and Scribes: Essays on the Formation and Heritage of Second Temple Judaism in Honour of Joseph Blenkinsopp*, ed. Eugene Ulrich et. al., JSOTSup vol. 149 (Sheffield: Sheffield Academic Press, 1992).

human condition. The theme commonly occurs in all ancient Near Eastern societies and in various types of literature. Suggesting that the question of divine retribution rested in the domain of wisdom exaggerates the importance of this strand of thought for the sage.[59] While retribution theology commonly appears throughout the Hebrew Bible, this cannot lessen its importance for wisdom. All the wisdom books deal with the issue. Each mention of retribution does not indicate a direct tie to wisdom traditions. Instead, views of reward and punishment, shared by all canonical traditions, assume special merit for the sage because of the sages' interests in moral issues, understanding divine behavior, and prescribing human behavior. While the recognition of the doctrine of retribution does not prove wisdom connections, it does indicate related strands of thought.

Job as Cosmological Struggle

Recent studies which employ literary or canonical approaches offer promise for a more balanced (if less straightforward) assessment of wisdom's origins and domain. Among the more provocative of these is Leo Perdue's reading of Job's experience as the account of a cosmological struggle.[60] The dependence on creation theology in the wisdom canon leads to Job's struggle. Job struggles, according to an archetypal understanding, with chaos itself. The crisis of meaning Job experienced called into question God's rule of the elements. Current wisdom interpreters can expect a number of similar comparative studies of books in the wisdom canon in the future.

Clan Wisdom

Claudia Camp identified the wise women mentioned in 2 Samuel as proponents of clan wisdom. Her study reflects the type of gender-influenced studies currently pursued. Her contributions relate to other issues as well as feminist concerns.[61] Such studies challenge the attribution of wisdom to a single stratum of Israelite society. Camp reminds critics of texts which indicate Israel's wisdom developed in its own way. Aside from such evidence, researchers tend to conclude Israel's wisdom developed in a manner identical to the development of wisdom in one or more neighboring civilizations.

Mead's *Pseudonymity and Canon*

David Mead challenged both the traditional view of Solomonic authorship and the understanding of pseudonymity as a spurious bid for

---

59. "The Wisdom Literature," *The Hebrew Bible and Its Modern Interpreters,* ed. Douglas Knight and Gene M. Tucker (Philadelphia: Fortress Press, 1985).

60. *Wisdom in Revolt: A Metaphorical Theology in the Book of Job,* JSOTSup vol. 112 (Sheffield: Almond Press, 1991).

61. Claudia V. Camp, "The Wise Women of 2 Samuel: A Role Model for Women in Early Israel," *CBQ* 43 (1981): 14–29.

attention. Instead, he proposed Solomon's "signature" functioned as an endorsement of the works' authoritative tradition. Mead did not read the title as an indication of authorship. Nor did he understand it as an attempt to capitalize on Solomon's reputation furtively. Often, a false choice between "authenticity" and "pseudonymity" restricts decisions related to authorship to a yes-or-no dichotomy. Caution dictates that other more legitimate motivations for ascriptions be considered. Before the compilation of the biblical canon, the name *Solomon* may have marked a work as important to the community. The title expressed the community's confidence in the book. In effect, the title earmarked the volume as a worthwhile (scriptural?) work. This distinguished it from works which never achieved a comparable seal of approval.[62] In this case, the warning against simplistic characterizations relates to the canonical process rather than the theology or origins of wisdom. But the trend toward the rejection of earlier simplistic understandings continues in this area and many other areas.

Comparative Studies of Proverbial Literature

More basic trends in wisdom study include recurring assessment of the relationship of Hebrew proverbs to ancient Near Eastern parallels. At present, Sumerian and Babylonian proverbs appear quite different from Israelite, while Egyptian parallels appear more acute.[63] Unfortunately, identifiably Hebrew non-biblical texts which could confirm close connections between Israelite and Egyptian wisdom do not exist. This makes close, unbiased observation of parallels even more necessary. Similarities in theme and form have served as confirmation of interchange in the past. These similarities do not necessarily indicate dependence or influence.

Renewed Interest in Intertestamental Literature

Current study pays close attention to the interrelationship of wisdom concerns in the Hebrew Bible, documents from the post-restoration Jewish community (600 B.C.E. to 100 C.E.), and the New Testament. The three perspectives may be studied independently, but important points of transition attract the focus. Contemporary scholars seem to concentrate on the period beginning immediately preceding the church and ending immediately following its rapid expansion. During this period, Judaism disassociated itself from Greek and Christian influences.[64] This period of transition represents an effectively "lost" history essential to the placement of the New Testament materials in their proper canonical perspective.

---

62. David G. Meade, *Pseudonymity and Canon: An Investigation of the Relationship of Authorship and Authority in Jewish and Christian Tradition* (Grand Rapids: Eerdmans, 1986). See chapter 3— "Authorship, Revelation and Canon in the Wisdom Tradition."

63. According to Crenshaw, *Hebrew Bible*, 376.

64. See Blenkinsopp, *Wisdom and Law*, 130–58. In the final chapter he treated later wisdom showing contacts between ancient Israel, Judaism, and early Christianity.

Dates of the Wisdom Books

The relatively late dates assigned to Proverbs by an earlier generation of historical critics have undergone significant revision. Most interpreters date chapters 1–9 no later than 400 B.C.E. Few wisdom specialists doubt chapters 1–9 come from a later period than the core of the collection.[65] The presence of several collections in chapters 10–31 complicates the issue of date. Some of the proverbs in all the sections of the book predate Solomon. The bulk of the book's contents cannot precede the time of Hezekiah (about 700 B.C.E.; see Prov. 25:1). Final redaction of Proverbs in the third century remains a possibility. Currently, scholars simply assess each of the various units of the book on its own terms, but this presents challenges of its own.

By contrast, the relatively late date of Ecclesiastes (around 300 B.C.E.) remains the scholarly consensus.[66] However, the strong support for direct Hellenistic influence on Ecclesiastes has abated. Instead, current studies more cautiously compare the contents of various Greek texts with the content of Ecclesiastes.[67] Its presence in the canon indicates its existence no later than 200 B.C.E. As with other wisdom books, the absence of historical content leaves uncertainty regarding date.

Job may come from originals dating to the patriarchal period. Similar stories exist at this time and before. The form of the biblical book appears postexilic, due to its philosophical debate style. The book contains no reliable historical markers. Moreso than even Proverbs or Ecclesiastes, Job is undatable. Distinctions between the prose framework and the poetry provide no help for dating. To provide some sense of direction, we can think of Job existing in brief form in Israel's earliest history. The biblical book comprises a more literary form probably produced by second temple Judaism (no earlier than 520 B.C.E.).[68]

---

65. R. N. Whybray suggested chapters 1–9 present an inseparable mixture of early and late material. *The Composition of the Book of Proverbs*, JSOTS 168 (Sheffield: Sheffield Academic Press, 1994), 56–61. Duane A. Garrett, *Proverbs, Ecclesiastes, Song of Songs*, NAC 14 (Nashville: Broadman Press, 1993), 39–52 presents recent comparative and redactional studies and concludes the "the majority of Proverbs, particularly the Book of Solomon (chapters 1–24), may be confidently ascribed to the early monarchy on the basis of the evidence of the text itself and structural considerations. The other collections—Hezekiah, Agur, and Lemuel—are later but probably preexilic. No hard evidence supports the common assertion that Proverbs 1–9 is late." (Quote is from p. 52).

66. Garrett, NAC 14, pp. 244–67 surveys the evidence and comparative materials, concluding (p. 266) that "tradition ascribes Ecclesiastes to Solomon, and this evidence supports the reasonableness of that view. Furthermore, Scripture presents Solomon as one who had access to the wealth of Egyptian and Babylonian literature and who was renowned for wide literary and intellectual interests. It is much less likely that someone in the postexilic period would have had acquaintance with these texts."

67. Crenshaw, *Hebrew Bible*, 380.

68. Robert Alden, *Job* NAC 11 (Nashville: Broadman and Holman Publishers, 1993), 25–29 discusses the evidence and shows the impossibility of dating the book or determining its author.

Summary: A Future of Specialization

As research continues, increasing distinction shows itself among fields of specialization within Hebrew wisdom studies. Definitions of Hebrew wisdom demand increasing qualification. Wisdom, more than law or prophecy, evades simplistic description. The word itself carries a wide application in biblical literature. Its references range between the extremes of designating a specialized skill and that of denoting adeptness in behavior which amounts to nothing less than "excelling at the art of human conduct." Beyond this, of course, wisdom belongs to any living creature especially suited for success. When the scope of wisdom expands to include clan wisdom, prophetic wisdom, and other specialized groups, the understanding of wisdom itself must broaden and diversify to fit these domains. Contemporary scholars consider the status of wisdom in the Hebrew canon as equal to the Law or Prophets. If wisdom exerted the persuasive influence on the Law, and especially the Prophets, that current trends indicate, then the problem is complicated by the breadth of influence rather than its shallowness. A further inhibiting factor is the lack of internal evidence—clear, definite records to prove reliance on wisdom traditions and professionals. This forces wisdom study into a somewhat isolated program. Further evidence to confirm the centrality of wisdom appears unlikely. The study of wisdom will remain a study of influences of *definite* importance though equally *indefinite* in shape.

Questions for Discussion

1. What are some key features of the interpretation of wisdom in medieval literature? During the Reformation?

2. Select some concerns of historical critical interpreters and compare them with the concerns of earlier interpreters.

3. Outline the latest trends in wisdom research.

Chapter 5

Wisdom Books Outside the Wisdom Canon

Introduction: The Search for Wisdom Outside the Wisdom Canon

Understanding wisdom requires reading the literature. Before considering the works typically included in the wisdom canon (Proverbs, Job, Ecclesiastes), a study of wisdom themes, vocabulary, and interests within the broader Hebrew canon and the later Deuterocanon (limited here to Sirach and the Wisdom of Solomon) provides a helpful foundation for the consideration of wisdom books as wisdom. Discussion of each unit emphasizes elements which may confirm or deny the identification as "wisdom." The identified wisdom elements supply one pole of the dialectic, and the discovery of trends more properly associated with other canonical traditions supplies the equally important contrast. Complementing this dialectical approach, an overview of the content of the passages provides a more generalized portrait of wisdom literature.

Wisdom in the Torah

Genesis[1]

Explicit wisdom concerns appear as early as Eve's dialogue with the serpent in Genesis 3:1–7. The vocabulary and philosophical bent of the dialogue confirm sapiential connections. The serpent presents self as the proponent of anti-wisdom, threatening the world order maintained by prudent conduct. Identifying the serpent as a mere equivalent of the devil obscures the philosophic overtones of the text. Such a moralistic reading robs the text of the irony involved in the identification of the creature as a part of

---

1. See Tikva Frymer-Kensky, "The Sage in the Pentateuch: Soundings," *SIANE*, 275–87.

the natural order God recently created. The knowledge of good and evil may be less an evil end in itself than an intrusion into a domain that belonged properly only to God. In the instant of transgression the individuals become less aware of the divine (by implication) and more aware of their corporeal appearance (their nakedness). The tree of life in sProverbs (and Psalm 1) provides an archetypal contrast to the tree of knowledge: the tree of life leads to permanence and security while the serpent's tree leads to shame and vulnerability. Such isolated tales or sagas may well have circulated as tribal wisdom.

While the Joseph story displays wisdom interests throughout, it does not contain such philosophical dialogues as Genesis 3. Perhaps later storytellers supplied the wisdom interests in Genesis 37–50, long after the story developed. If so, the wisdom interests bring an extra element, generated at a distance from the original story. From another perspective, perhaps the wisdom elements belonged to an earlier form of the story. In this case, the latest recorders of the story considered the wisdom elements secondary to their more historical interests. In either case, the direct allusions to wise conduct remain scant. This holds in spite of Joseph's prodigious wisdom gained as the consequence of his election. Joseph's first revelations to his family of his prescience indicate an immature response to the gift of wisdom (dreams in 37:5–11). His abilities remain dormant until discovered in Egypt. Joseph's wisdom in fleeing Potiphar's wife reflects the warnings against adultery in Proverbs 1–9. The warnings in Proverbs come from a much later period. Joseph's response certainly provides a patriarchal model of behavior later recommended in Proverbs 1–9. Joseph's phenomenal success in Egypt affirms his reception of a wisdom so great it spilled beyond him to affect the fortunes of future Israel. The promise of blessing and riches to the wise occupies a central place in each of the five wisdom books. Beyond this, Joseph's craft in contriving mock indictments against his brothers further illustrates his wisdom. In Jacob's blessing Joseph is named "a fruitful bough" (49:22). A flourishing plant serves as a conventional image of the wise (Ps. 1, for instance).

Exodus

Exodus contains a few indefinite allusions to wise conduct scattered through the book. Exodus 1:8–2:14 presents three instances of crafty behavior. First, Pharaoh devised a scheme to destroy Hebrew males and later showed himself astute in his confrontation of wills with Moses. Second, the midwives outstripped Pharaoh by improvising excuses for their noncompliance to his order to kill males. Third, Moses' mother succeeded in disobeying Pharaoh's command. Jethro outshone Moses in 18:13–27 by solving Moses' scheduling problems with reasoned simplicity. In this case, tribal wisdom proves superior to understanding Moses may have gained in his training at Pharaoh's court. Jethro's role fits the pattern of the clan sage.

Wisdom connections with the Decalogue are less clear and cannot be confirmed or denied in this study.[2]

The last example of wisdom in Exodus is more clear. In Exodus 35:31–39:31, חָכְמָה (hokmâ) is attributed to Bezalel, who with Oholiab taught metallurgy, woodwork, carving, and other construction skills. This enabled fellow Hebrews to assist in the building of the tabernacle and the ark. One primary conception of Hebrew wisdom connects it with the vocational savvy of the artisan or professional. Vocational wisdom enables a person to accomplish anything the average (unskilled) person cannot do.

Deuteronomy

An entirely different aspect of wisdom presents itself in Deuteronomy 6:1–25. This passage displays moral connections with wisdom. Its moral tone shows similarities to the direct instructions in Proverbs 1–9 as does reference to the "fear of the LORD." This phrase plays a prominent role in Proverbs 1–9, though common throughout the Hebrew Scriptures. The blessing (6:3) promised for proper conduct appears similar to the emphases of Psalm 1 (a wisdom psalm) and certain proverbs. This feature appears commonly in deuteronomic literature as well as wisdom literature. This indicates shared interests rather than direct dependence on wisdom traditions or dependence on deuteronomistic theology by wisdom writers. In Deuteronomy 11:8–21, a passage partially parallel to Deuteronomy 6:1–25, additional emphasis is placed upon the retribution meted out to those who heed or do not heed the call to religious obligation.[3]

Wisdom in the Former Prophets

Samuel

The retribution upon Nabal in 1 Samuel 25:2–42, first threatened by David, eventually comes from Yahweh himself. The insightfulness (שֵׂכֶל, sékel) of Abigail stands in contrast to the shallow intolerance of Nabal, whose name (נָבָל) means "folly" or "shamelessness." David would have reacted with harsh retaliation for Nabal's refusal to offer aid to his protectors. Abigail interceded to save David from bloodguilt. Nabal symbolizes the epitome of folly through his lack of concern for others and ignorance of

---

2. J. J. Stamm and M. E. Andrew in *The Ten Commandments in Recent Research*, SBT 2nd ser. 2 (London: SCM Press 1962), 43 propose a dependence on Egyptian wisdom writings for the Decalogue, based on the presence of numerous "prohibitions and commands" in Egyptian wisdom. See also p. 89 in this book.

3. See Moshe Weinfeld, *Deuteronomy and the Deuteronomic School* (Oxford: Clarendon Press, 1971), especially 58–162 and *Deuteronomy 1–11*, AB 5 (New York: Doubleday, 1991), 62–65. He concludes: "Would it be legitimate to suppose that the scribes of the courts of Hezekiah and Josiah are responsible for this transition from a book for the king to a book for the whole people?" (p. 57). Patrick D. Miller, *Deuteronomy*, Int (Louisville: John Knox Press, 1990), 5–17, appears to share this view with Weinfeld. Eugene H. Merrill, *Deuteronomy*, NAC 4 (Nashville: Broadman and Holman Publishers, 1994) presents the case for the traditional authorship and influences on Deuteronomy.

religious obligations. Abigail offered to bear the guilt for Nabal's offense, making her his opposite. Grace provided her motivation, while her husband reacted with brutal hardness. Abigail also showed a nearly prophetic awareness of God's future blessing of David. The passage invites comparisons of the ultimate fortunes of the three. These outcomes show the effect of their actions and intentions. In this way, the story serves as an illustration of retribution.

The succession narrative,[4] 2 Samuel 9–20 and 1 Kings 1–2, presents a patchwork of admirable and illicit behavior. It mixes fools and faulty decision making with calculated wisdom and revenge. The accounts display a tone which often seems more literary-philosophical than salvation-historical. Absalom employs mechanical rationalism to achieve his selfish goals. David's role appears more passive. Concern for his family members seems to cloud his reason. Only the wisdom of others enables David to regain his throne. The counselor Hushai outsmarts Absalom by a careful argument in 2 Samuel 17. The role of personal activity takes priority over the divine plan in the entire succession narrative. The narrator appears a secular moralist, emphasizing human control of divine destinies. The interest in the human drama marks the account as distinct within the deuteronomistic history. This feature reflects concerns related to the preoccupation with wise and foolish conduct in Proverbs and Ecclesiastes.

Kings

The account of Solomon's reign in 1 Kings 3–12 presents a less vital connection with the humanism of wisdom. It describes the rule of Solomon through the use of wisdom terminology. The following passages relate to Solomon's wisdom:

Table 3
Account of Solomon's Reign

3:5–12	Divine gift equips him for rule
3:16–28	Wise judgment regarding prostitute's child
4:29–31	Wisdom above all in known world
4:32–33	Proverbs, songs, "science" (trees, animals)
5–8	Organization and implementation of work on palace and temple

4. See suggestions of Whybray discussed on p. 89; P. Kyle McCarter, Jr, *II Samuel*, AB 9 (New York: Doubleday, 1984), 10–11, argues that "Whybray seems to have gone too far. Apart from generalized thematic parallels, there is nothing in the succession narrative of a stylistic or ideological nature to link it peculiarly to wisdom. The points of contact with Proverbs noted by Whybray are most useful in defining the cultural and intellectual horizons of the author, and in this respect we should note the more modest claims of Hermisson who speaks of wisdom as one factor, among others, that comes into play in the conception of history found in the succession narrative."

Table 3 (Continued)
Account of Solomon's Reign

10:1–3	Queen of Sheba's test questions
10:4–5	Abundance of food, richness of clothes, organization of court
10:6–29	Receipts of gold, imports, ivory throne, fleet, chariot trade, etc.

The portrait of Solomon reverses from positive to negative with the mention of sins in 1 Kings 11. After this the narrative contains no further reference to wisdom.[5] The absence of wisdom terminology in chapter 11 and following remains mysterious. The absence of an expected moral tone in 1 Kings 3–10 may indicate the interests of a special wisdom group. This group concentrated on the achievements of Solomon rather than defense of the interests of conventional wisdom. They promoted Solomon's successes as validation of his wisdom and ceased to refer to wisdom when he ceased to exercise it (as shown in his worship of other deities). The writer of 3–10 wished only to account for the economic success of Solomon through some obvious means. From this viewpoint, the wisdom previously given was forfeited (like God's spirit from King Saul) when Solomon departed from Torah. Second Chronicles 1–9 focuses upon Solomon's wisdom with special attention to his success. Chronicles fails to mention Solomon's errors. Chronicles more consistently presents Solomon's success as attributable to his wisdom and avoids the discussion of Solomon's folly.

In the twelfth chapter, Rehoboam instantly showed his lack of discretion by attempting to gain control of people through scaring them into submission. The previous chapters indicate Solomon's immunity to such poor advice. Rehoboam's stupidity supplied the key event fulfilling the previous prophecy (1 Kings 11:26–39) of the separation of David's dynasty. This implies God's intervention in either Hushai's advice or Rehoboam's decision to follow it. The text leaves this conclusion to the reader.

Wisdom in the Latter Prophets

Isaiah[6]

Vocabulary, forms, and content show Isaiah's relationship to wisdom. After promising to punish the king of Assyria, Isaiah pictured wisdom enabling God to enact his role as the judge of nations:

---

5. In spite of the lack of corroborating history, Solomon's connection with wisdom in 1 Kings 4:20–28 is *sociologically* probable, considering his new state could use wisdom to legitimate itself and solidify its claims to power, according to Walter Brueggemann, "The Social Significance of Solomon as Patron of Wisdom" in *SIANE*, 117–32.

6. See Raymond C. Van Leeuwen, "The Sage in the Prophetic Literature," *SIANE*, 295–306. For Isaiah, see especially, J. W. Whedbee, *Isaiah and Wisdom* (Nashville: Abingdon, 1971).

By the strength of my hand I have done it, and by my wisdom, for I have understanding; I have removed the boundaries of peoples, and have plundered their treasures; like a bull I have brought down those who sat on thrones. My hand has found, like a nest, the wealth of the peoples; and as one gathers eggs that have been forsaken, so I have gathered all the earth; and there was none that moved a wing, or opened its mouth, or chirped. Shall the ax vaunt itself over the one who wields it, or the saw magnify itself against the one who handles it? As if a rod should raise the one who lifts it up, or as if a staff should lift the one who is not wood! (Isa. 10:13–15)

Such a self-presentation of the deity recalls the final chapters of Job. Much of the poetry with wisdom features in the Prophets and the Psalms shows similarities with Job 38–41. In Isaiah 10, wisdom describes the perfect match between God's identity (or vocation) and his ability. He manifests wisdom in his perfect suitability for his job and his unique abilities to perform it. The poem employs specific imagery relating to judgment. Yet God acts out of his role as creator and sustainer of the world, a common theme of wisdom theology. Isaiah 26:7–15 more directly portrays God's judgment as the factor which separates the fortunes of the righteous from the fortunes of the wicked. It also includes more pronounced emphasis on retribution based on human choices.

Isaiah presents a poetic unit with proverbial form and content:

Listen, and hear my voice; Pay attention, and hear my speech. Do those who plow for sowing plow continually? Do they continually open and harrow their ground? When they have leveled its surface, do they not scatter dill, sow cummin, and plant wheat in rows and barley in its proper place, and spelt as the border? For they are well instructed; their God teaches them. Dill is not threshed with a threshing sledge, nor is a cart wheel rolled over cummin; but dill is beaten out with a stick, and cummin with a rod. Grain is crushed for bread, but one does not thresh it forever; one drives the cart wheel and horses over it, but does not pulverize it. This also comes from the LORD of hosts; he is wonderful in counsel, and excellent in wisdom. (Isa. 28:23–29)

When judgment accomplished its end, it would cease and leave in its wake a more useful product. Farming skills provide a metaphor for wisdom. Wisdom receives double meaning, referring to agricultural skill as well as divine knowledge. The overview covers the complete planting cycle from plowing to harvest. A correlation also exists with the avoidance of extremes (here, extreme judgment) as a mark of wisdom, a theme repeated in Ecclesiastes.

When wisdom describes human conduct in Isaiah 32:5–8, it signifies care for the hungry, thirsty, and needy. No direct link with the demands of the Torah appears. Isaiah 32 simply presents general moral concern. Leaders who act in a manner contrary to this humane wisdom find no place in the messianic age (v. 5). Throughout the first thirty-nine chapters of Isaiah most references to wisdom are brief, isolated series of lines. These units function as proverbs and wise sayings known to and quoted by the prophet. The same description could also fit the longer units covered in the foregoing discussion. The second portion of the Book of Isaiah (chaps. 40–55, with special interest in the period of the captivity) sets all direct references to God's wisdom against the background of creation theology. Typically, God's unique creative abilities challenge the presumption of humans. One of the units above (10:13–15) contains similar themes.[7]

Isaiah 40:12–41:1 relates God's incomparable wisdom, knowledge, and power to human limits. This passage shows affinity to the speeches of God to Job in Job 38–41. One of the most appealing sections in Isaiah ridicules idols. They receive scorn for their nature as materialistic products of humans. The description in Isaiah 44:9–20 deftly omits the opposing connotations of God's infiniteness and sovereignty (44:9–20). Uncharacteristically, folly (idolatry) achieves predominant treatment. The "fear of the LORD" serves as contrast only by implication. This intentional gap in the discussion leaves such an impression that divine wisdom can hardly be said to be "absent" at all. Similarly, Isaiah 40–55 implies the wisdom of the suffering servant. For example, 53:11 presents righteousness (wisdom?) as an attribute gained through the suffering of the righteous one. The emphasis on knowledge in the verse lends credence to the connection between righteousness and wisdom. Only one faint echo of the theme of wisdom occurs in chapters 56–66 (distinguished by its interest in the period of restoration after the captivity). In 66:1, God's possession of the created order illustrates the relative insignificance of the temple as a monument to him. These chapters present little else of interest to the student of wisdom.

Jeremiah[8]

In a certain respect, the wisdom concerns of Jeremiah are far more theocentric (centered on God, rather than humans) than those of Isaiah. In the following passage, wisdom takes second place to relational knowledge of God, a relationship we see as integral to Israel's view of wisdom: "Thus says the LORD: Do not let the wise boast in their wisdom, do not let the mighty boast in their might, do not let the wealthy boast in their wealth; but let those who boast boast in this, that they understand and know me, that I am the LORD; I act with steadfast love, justice, and righteousness in the earth, for in these things I delight, says the LORD" (Jer. 9:23–24).

Some discrepancy exists between the content of this passage and the general view that religious activity equals wisdom. This indicates the special perspective of the Book of Jeremiah. The book characteristically subsumes all other concerns to the priority of restoring Israel's failed relationship to Yahweh.

---

7. See Isaiah 42:5; 44:24–26; 45:9–23; 46; and 48:13.
8. See Van Leeuwen, *SIANE*, 303–5.

The four proverbs in Jeremiah 17:5–11 provide an example of wisdom forms and terms employed to accomplish reconciliation of Israel to God. The four proverbs offer the following comparisons: (1) those who trust in humans are like a shrub in the desert; (2) those who trust in the LORD are like a tree planted by water (compare Ps. 1); (3) no one except God can understand and judge the human mind and heart (quoted in Rom. 7:18–19); and (4) unjust wealth will leave its owner bereft, like a partridge who sat on another bird's eggs.

Jeremiah 10:1–16 contains creation theology like that observed in Isaiah 40–55 and Job. The section in 31:35–37 presents another example of creation theology. It includes a claim that as long as the universe remains, God will not reject Judah.[9] Jeremiah also contains an important reference to wisdom in Edom: "Concerning Edom. Thus says the LORD of hosts: Is there no longer wisdom in Teman? Has counsel perished from the prudent? Has their wisdom vanished?" (Jer. 49:7). Judgment begins with the denial of Edom's most prominent trait. Sarcastic questions mock the territory's wisdom. The fall of Edom at Yahweh's hands serves notice of the ineffective nature of their wisdom. Mention of Edom's wisdom in Obadiah 8 lends confirmation to the popular association of wisdom with Edom.[10] Jeremiah's indictment against Judah includes the notion that the people's sin and subsequent alienation from God resulted from their lack of wisdom (5:20–29). Their primary sins include social injustice and the worship of other gods.

Ezekiel

In Ezekiel wisdom forms serve as vehicles for the prophetic message. Ezekiel shows special interest in riddles and allegories. Ezekiel 12:21–25 presents the proverb, "The days are prolonged, and every vision comes to nothing" (v. 22). The prophet counters the proverb with a competing proverb: "The days are near and the fulfillment of every vision" (v. 23). Multiple proverbs in the biblical collection put forward contradictory claims. Skill in the use of proverbs lay in their application to appropriate situations. Ezekiel charges that the people wrongly quoted the former proverb in a context to which the latter proverb actually applied. The prophet similarly rejected the pertinency of the "sour grapes" proverb in 18:2–30. His contemporaries used it to disclaim personal responsibility for Judah's condition. In both cases, Judah's understanding of its situation stands exactly opposite to the reality! The interplay of such dialectic claims serves a central role in the pro-

---

9. Amos 5:8–9 compares to this passage. God, portrayed as the maker of Pleiades and Orion, sends destruction. Creation theology does not necessarily indicate wisdom concerns. The presentation of God's power, skill, and infinitude always falls under the rubric of wisdom in a more general sense.

10. In similar fashion, the Book of Ezekiel refers to Tyre's wisdom in 28:2–19, also an oracle of judgment. Tyre's wisdom was evident in its riches won through trade, but the gain was ill-gotten and so incurred God's wrath. In both Jeremiah and Ezekiel foreign wisdom brought power, but their wisdom was mentioned ironically as nations faced divine judgment.

verbial branch of wisdom, as will be noted in the discussion of Proverbs. Ezekiel 17:2–10 contains a lengthier wisdom form—allegory. Allegory may certainly be construed as a wisdom form. Achieving understanding of the riddles of the wise appears in Proverbs 1:6 as one of the purposes for the collection. The riddle or allegory depicts the king of Babylon as an eagle who plucked the top branch (Judah's king and officials) from a cedar (Judah). Used as a reference to Judah's impending exile, the unit contains no direct reference to wisdom by vocabulary or theme.

Additional proverbs in Ezekiel occur with explanations. In 15:2–8 an extended proverb likens exilic Judah to a wild grapevine which was good for nothing *before* being half burned in the fire. Ezekiel 16:44–63 contains the proverb, "like mother, like daughter" (v. 44). Following comments describe Judah's mother as a Hittite. Judah behaved even more wickedly than her mother. The Book of Ezekiel uses such proverbs to full effect, with unmistakable applications and messages which could scarcely be stronger. In this respect prophetic use of wisdom material seems uniform: Nearly every example employs recognizable forms and sayings to force the hearer to reckon with an unanticipated or unwelcome message.

Hosea

Hosea shows its connection with wisdom more through its tone than its theme or vocabulary. Many of the prophetic images deal with behavior construed as "like" something else, but Hosea contains few true proverbs. Although Hosea makes use of few, if any, distinct wisdom forms, 4:11,14; and 14:9 (Heb. 14:10) present Israel's problem as "lack of understanding." The Hebrew verb *bîn* (בִּין understand) denotes perception or proper insight. Thus, "a people without understanding" (4:14) lacks moral perception. This lack of understanding seems to derive from their ignorance of God's love which motivated their election. The conclusion of the book underscores the importance of this theme for the prophetic work:

> O Ephraim, what have I to do with idols? It is I who answer and look after you. I am like an evergreen cypress; your faithfulness comes from me. Those who are wise understand these things; those who are discerning know them. For the ways of the LORD are right, and the upright walk in them, but transgressors stumble in them.
> (Hosea 14:8–9; see Heb. 14:9–10)

God's retribution occurs in some measure as a natural outcome of their rebellion. The people can choose the way of wisdom or lack of understanding.[11] Some interpreters consider these verses a later addition to the book due to their similarity to statements within wisdom books.

---

11. See C. L. Seow, "Hosea, Book of," *The Anchor Bible Dictionary*, ed. David Noel Freedman (New York: Doubleday, 1992), 3:293, for a cautious approach.

Amos

Many of Amos' rhetorical devices possibly originated as wisdom sayings. Since the themes of the units show no interest in wisdom per se, this remains conjectural pending a broader investigation.[12] The rhetorical questions in Amos 3:3–8 present one example of sayings with possible wisdom connections: "Do two walk together unless they have made an appointment?" The subsequent questions expect negative answers. The obvious connections they reveal herald a fearful inevitability: "The lion [Yahweh] has roared; who will not fear?" (v. 8).[13] The variation in the pattern beginning in verse 7 leads the reader to make the transition from protasis to apodosis ("if . . . then"). If this pattern occurs in Hebrew wisdom, it appears only rarely.[14] Questions expecting negative answers occur repeatedly in Ecclesiastes. In both Amos and Ecclesiastes, these questions apply to negative or skeptical situations. When wisdom themes do occur in Amos, they reinforce the theme of God's delivery of a terrible judgment. His transcendence, typically presented through creation theology, serves the purpose of warning. For example, Amos 9:2–6 contends the guilty cannot escape his wrath in Sheol, at the bottom of the sea, or in exile.

Habakkuk

Habakkuk also employs wisdom themes against the backdrop of broader theological issues. The interest in theodicy in 1:1–2:5 combines questioning of God's administration of justice with other issues relating to God's nature. Included are his use of incredibly powerful nations and his otherness (he will not die). The psalm in Habakkuk 3 presents God as the controlling force behind irrepressible natural phenomena. In every sense God remains superior to these elements of nature. This power provides reason for the psalmist's trust in God despite apparent loss of hope. As in Job, the questioning ends when God's transcendence falls under consideration.[15]

---

12. The possible importance of Tekoa as a center for wisdom activity adds to the import of the book for wisdom study. In addition to Amos' own origin there (1:1), the wise woman who speaks to David on behalf of Absalom hailed from Tekoa (2 Sam. 14:2). The town was located less than ten miles nearly due south from Jerusalem and may have been a center for clan wisdom. See Claudia V. Camp, "The Wise Women of 2 Samuel: A Role Model for Women in Early Israel?" *CBQ* 43 (1981), 14–29. For a treatment of wisdom concerns relating to Amos, see H. W. Wolff, *Joel and Amos*, Her (Philadelphia: Fortress, 1977). For further bibliography see Van Leeuwen, *SIANE*, p. 298, n. 15, especially J. L. Crenshaw, "The Influence of the Wise upon Amos," ZAW 79 (1967), 42–52.

13. Rhetorical questions in Jeremiah serve as an identical device. They indicate Judah's incredible rebellion.

14. Some similarity to this exists in Job 38–41. With the appearance of God in Job 38 and following, Job is questioned with the recurring pattern, "Can you?" which leads to the conclusion that he should cease questioning God.

15. See D. E. Gowan, "Habakkuk and Wisdom," *Perspective* 9 (1968). 157–166; and G. A. Tuttle, "Wisdom and Habakkuk," *Studia Biblica et Theologica* 3 (1973), 3–14.

Wisdom in the Writings

Psalms

Wisdom psalms demand a more organized approach. In spite of differences in theme and form, psalms with wisdom interests can be remarkably similar (especially with regard to formal aspects). Sigmund Mowinckel claimed "learned writers" who collected and recorded all the psalms themselves authored the wisdom psalms.[16] These figures served as temple personnel, the predecessors of the scribes, according to Mowinckel. Given the practically untraceable roots of wisdom, it seems impossible to so specifically identify the authors of wisdom psalms.

The following discussion categorizes wisdom psalms primarily in terms of perspective, governed by two central questions: (1) to whom is the psalm directed? and (2) in what perspective is the language cast (first, second, or third person)? By perspective, a psalm may be *hymnic* (usually third person praise of God), *didactic* (overt or implied instructions to the reader), *directive* or *nondirective* (indicated by the authority assumed by the psalmist's voice), or *proverbial*.[17]

The description of a wisdom psalm's perspective entails the shading of these elements. In spite of their uniqueness, regular features appear in wisdom psalms. Such psalms tend to present moral instruction in a didactic framework, employ the אַשְׁרֵי (*ʾašrē*) "happy" or "blessed" formula, be preoccupied with the righteous and wicked, and deal with theodicy. Psalm 1 expresses a didactic tone, but in a nondirective style. It consistently presents a third person perspective. Its nondirective nature rests in its aim to inform and encourage, rather than prescribe specific behavior. The אַשְׁרֵי (*ʾašrē*, "happy are . . .") formula provides one example of this nondirective style.[18] The word carries connotations of well being and success. Since the verb אָשַׁר (*ʾāšar*) means "to advance," the noun may imply that good fortune rests in the future. Unlike certain other units in the Psalms, successive lines do not repeat the word, *ʾašrē*. This makes the statements appear as wisdom sayings imported to the Psalms texts rather than as cultic elements integral to the service of worship.

The opening of the Psalms with a text so undeniably influenced by wisdom illustrates the predominance of such thinking. It also indicates the pervasiveness of wisdom in Israel's worship. Overall, this psalm outlines the

---

16. Sigmund Mowinckel, "Psalms and Wisdom" in *Wisdom in Israel*, VTSup, vol. 3, presented to H. H. Rowley, eds. Martin Noth and D. Winton Thomas (Leiden: Brill, 1955), 207; compare "The Learned Psalmography," ch. XVI of *The Psalms in Israel's Worship*, trans. D. R. Ap-Thomas (Nashville: Abingdon Press, 1962), 2:176–92.

17. Leo Perdue distinguished wisdom psalms (produced by sages for cultic use) from didactic psalms (his general term for all psalms with wisdom forms and vocabulary). The relationship between cult and wisdom is beyond the scope of this study. See *Wisdom and Cult*, SBLDS 30 (Missoula, Mont.: Scholar's Press, 1977), 261, and note 1, p. 325.

18. אַשְׁרֵי (*ʾašrē*) forms also occur in Psalms 112:1; 119:1–2; 127:5; 128:1, elsewhere in Psalms and Proverbs (for example, Prov. 8:34; 20:7), and in Job 5:17. Compare the Beatitudes (Matt. 5:3–12; Luke 6:20–23).

behavior which pleases Israel's God. Its moral content takes shape in language common to wisdom. This shows awareness of the role of human choice in religious and ethical determinations. Torah represents the primary means to achieve a lifestyle leading to happiness and reward.

According to outward form Psalms 9:1–10:18 directs comments to God. The unrestrained evil of those at counter purposes to the devout psalmist occasions bitter complaint. Yet the words express philosophical concerns. A second person perspective identifies the poem as something of a prayer, but observations occur in third person form. The unit presents no prescriptions for conduct. Its identity as a complaint directed to God probably precludes such moral directives. The psalmist also voices trust that justice will reign through God's intervention.

Psalm 14 differs from its parallel (Psalm 53) mainly in the use of "Yahweh" rather than "Elohim." It displays a general didactic perspective in third person, containing observations regarding the attitude of the person who does not consider the divine consequences of action. One line (v. 6) directly addresses this audience: "You would confound the plans of the poor, but the LORD is their refuge." Perhaps "the poor" functions as a metonym for the entire congregation of Israel. Their national enemies would comprise the opposing group as implied by the reference to national deliverance in verse 7.

Psalm 19:7–13 presents classical wisdom concerns in terms of God's demands. It also commends corresponding personal morality:

> The law of the LORD is perfect, reviving the soul; the decrees of the LORD are sure, making wise the simple; the precepts of the LORD are right, rejoicing the heart; the commandment of the LORD is clear, enlightening the eyes; the fear of the LORD is pure, enduring forever; the ordinances of the LORD are true and righteous altogether. More to be desired are they than gold, even much fine gold; sweeter also than honey, and drippings of the honeycomb. Moreover by them is your servant warned; in keeping them there is great reward. But who can detect their errors? Clear me from hidden faults. Keep back your servant from [proud thoughts]; do not let them have dominion over me. Then I shall be blameless, and innocent of great transgression. (Ps. 19:7–13)

Psalm 19:7–13 follows creation theology in verses 1–6. Torah-centered wisdom attracts attention as the focal point of this unit. Verses 1–6 are hymnic and 7–10 strictly didactic, proclaiming the universal good of the Torah. Verses 11–13 address Yahweh directly. The transition from didactic tone to petition progresses until direct requests appear in verse 13. Verses 7–9 show similarities in content to the multiple sections of Psalm 119, the extended hymn to Torah. Verses 11–13 imply a private reflective moment, but 7–10 stand in dialectic tension by projecting a tone of instruction at large.

Psalm 36 presents a hymnic celebration of God's חֶסֶד (hesed, steadfast love or mercy). A description of the behavior of the wicked precedes the hymn. A request for protection from the wicked follows the hymn. The entire chapter ends with a postscript describing their downfall. The prologue conveys information to the hearer, enabling the hearer to identify wickedness. The central section conveys praise. Its direct address to God contrasts with the didactic tone of the previous section. Divine mercy offers the alternative to wicked hubris. Discipline and obedience serve secondary roles. This increases the appeal of the way of knowledge of God (implying personal relationship).

Though Psalm 49 appears didactic throughout, it employs philosophical rather than moralistic language. A first-person perspective predominates in the psalm, but third-person reports comment on the inevitability of death (death cancels the advantage of the wicked rich). Advice begins with verse 16, "Do not be afraid when some become rich . . .," but this simply introduces explanations which appear in a third-person format. Actually, clues to perspective tend to introduce strophes as in verse 1 (third person), verses 5 and 10 (first person), and verse 16 (second person).

A first-person narrator governs the perspective of Psalm 73. The speaker addresses God with statements expressing trust. The psalmist expects vindication in response to the arrogance of the wicked. The narrator expresses inability to understand or change this injustice. The psalm contains more pathos than other didactic poems with similar themes. The typical approach to retribution provides the framework for this theodicy.

A third-person perspective marks Psalm 112 throughout. The psalm serves as a standard affirmation of the benefits of the fear of the LORD. Expressions of justice and generosity distinguish those who fear the LORD. It prescribes (or suggests) specific conduct through the description of exemplary activity. It displays a proverbial character. The psalm follows an acrostic organization (successive lines begin with succeeding letters of the alphabet).

Psalm 119 presents an extended first-person recounting of the greatness of the Torah.[19] The psalm includes repeated testimonials by the narrator indicating commitment to God's demands. It appears the writer consciously developed an individualized response to the Shema (Deut. 6:1–25). Perhaps this lengthy psalm originated as a Torah catechism. If so, it does not seem to be directed to a specific audience, as expected. The opening, conclusion, and scattered references fix it as a lament. Perhaps it served as a liturgy which ensured God's response based on the traditional view of retribution. Psalm 119 exhibits numerous wisdom elements, including: (1) the righteous-wicked dichotomy, (2) the view of divine retribution for proper action and wickedness, (3) mention of the young (v. 9), as in Proverbs, (4) emphasis on God's teaching of the psalmist, (5) use of the verb חָכַם (ḥākam) in verse 98 and the noun בִּין (bîn) repeatedly, and (6) the theme of the eternity of God's decrees.

---

19. This psalm employs references to the written law in lines of praise and thanks offered directly to God by previous psalmists. In other words, the psalmist praises God's commandments rather than God himself. See Michael Fishbane, "From Scribalism to Rabbinism: Perspectives on the Emergence of Classical Judaism" in *SIANE*, 446.

The form of Psalm 127 sets it apart as the most unique of the wisdom psalms. It contains a series of five third-person proverbs. The first two encourage trust in God rather than anxiety due to overdependence on self. The last three celebrate sons as an affirmation of God's acceptance and a source of happiness.

Form criticism identifies Psalm 128 as a song of ascent. After an ʾašrê introduction in third person ("Happy are those who fear the LORD"), the psalm offers a brief list of benefits and a concluding blessing on the worshiper, Jerusalem, and Israel. The affirmation of reward for upright behavior stands out as the most notable wisdom characteristic.

Daniel

The consideration of wisdom material outside the wisdom canon concludes with two passages from the Book of Daniel.[20] In Daniel 2:20–23 a hymn offers praise for God's wisdom. The timbre of this context presents a striking difference from previous presentations of wisdom. In this case, Daniel thanks God for revelation of a mystery. Daniel devotes a hymn to God's wisdom in thanks for the share of wisdom which enabled him to interpret the dream. The song shows similarities to celebrations of wisdom in Sirach and the Wisdom of Solomon. Daniel offers the praise more directly to God rather than to his attribute, wisdom.

Daniel operates as a wise interpreter of prophetic material according to 9:2. This connects the content of chapters 9–12 with Jeremiah's prophecy of a seventy-year domination by Babylon (Jer. 25:9–11). Daniel's apocalyptic message neither comes to him nor issues from him in typical prophetic oracles. Daniel's wisdom is the medium for divine communication of this apocalyptic message. The writing of Daniel conveys the message. According to Daniel 12:3–4, the Book of Daniel hides wisdom. Daniel makes clear that other means of revelation are not kept from the wise and the righteous. The idea that wisdom waits fuller revelation certainly influences Revelation. Perhaps Jesus himself believed that the revelation of God's wisdom awaited the proper moment. He taught in parables and kept his divinity secret until his "hour" had come.

The wisdom materials in Daniel appear to be late derivative employments of sapiential concerns, if based on older wisdom at all. Daniel's identity as a sage likewise gives the appearance of a later interpretation of the prophet/apocalyptic hero. The attribution of wisdom elements to apocalyptic resembles the blanket attribution of canonical materials to Solomon. Both Daniel and Solomon imply a special interpretation of wisdom as well as a special characterization of the figure involved.

Common ethics or common traditions could account for most of the traces of wisdom noted in nonwisdom books. Direct contact from wisdom

---

20. For further consideration of the broader application of the term "wisdom" in the Hebrew Bible, see Donn F. Morgan, *Wisdom in the Old Testament Traditions* (Atlanta: John Knox, 1981).

sources presents the other major option. Whichever the case, the presence of wisdom themes and vocabulary nonetheless underscores wisdom's pervasiveness. Whether through formal categories or through nondescript influences, wisdom themes receive much attention in the Hebrew Bible. The more diverse this influence, the more far-reaching the importance of wisdom traditions in the development of the Hebrew canon.

Deuterocanonical Works

The Wisdom of Solomon

The Wisdom of Solomon, dating somewhere between late 225 to 10 B.C.E., presents wisdom as an agent active in its own right. Proverbs presented the fear of the Lord as the foundation for wisdom. The Wisdom of Solomon identified wisdom as the Spirit of God himself, but always describing wisdom as feminine (for example, 1:6–7). Like Woman Wisdom in Proverbs 1–9, Wisdom seeks adherents (6:16). Unlike Proverbs, hypostatized wisdom in the Wisdom of Solomon 1–9 actually performs activity directly attributable only to God.

In keeping with the pseudonymous title of the work, the first two sections address rulers and kings (1:1; 6:1–11, 21). References to pharaohs and Canaanite leaders throughout Wisdom indicate the address intends non-Israelite rulers. Considering the late date of the writing, Greek or Roman rulers provide the key to the hermeneutic. In spite of the direct address to others, the work clearly speaks to Jews rather than any other cultural group. Each of the three main sections of the book describes the plight of believers in Yahweh. The work contrasts this with the fate of sinners, either among the ranks of Israel or her oppressors.

In the first section (chaps. 1–5) the view of retribution embraces the afterlife. There the righteous (the wise) attain immortality, and the wicked are destroyed. Various themes from the Book of Proverbs appear; for example, the wicked lie in wait for the righteous; persons' lifestyles determine the fortunes of their progeny; and immoral conduct leads to death. Chapters 1–5 present a scene beyond time. The wicked realize their mistake in the face of God's eternal vindication of the righteous. The chapters even contain a scene in which the righteous dead return to judge the wicked who remain (4:16–5:13).

The second section (chaps. 6–9) assumes the form of a speech by Solomon emphasizing the importance of wisdom. Solomon speaks to the rulers of other nations. Solomon's description of himself in 7:1–4 interrupts the discussion of wisdom, yet it presents a key discussion on the common experience of all humans. Solomon remains nameless, even though the description in 7:1–7 leaves no doubt of his identity. The Wisdom of Solomon exhibits the unusual feature of a complete lack of proper names, as if the work presented a lengthy riddle or apocalyptic puzzle. This anonymity figures even more prominently in the final section. If the work came from Alexandria, as some suggest, the disguised treatment of the exodus protected readers from persecution or less serious reprisals. By content, chapters 6–9 possess the tone of an ode to wisdom rather than that of practical instruction to rulers which the introduction claims. Characteristic attention to wisdom appears in the following: "I will tell you what wisdom is and how she came to be, and I will hide no secrets from you, but I will trace her course from the beginning of creation, and make knowledge of her clear, and I will not pass by truth" (The Wisdom of Solomon 6:22).

Chapters 10–19 compare the fortunes of Israel to those of the nations: Wisdom protected Israel. The segment begins (10:1–11:1) with allusions to various leaders of Israel who remain nameless though easily identified (Adam, Cain, Noah, Abraham, Lot, Jacob, Joseph). All are, of course, prior to Solomon, but more importantly their history led to the captivity in and deliverance from Egypt. 11:2–20 presents wisdom as the agent of the miracles and divine judgment performed in the wilderness. Throughout the section an underlying motif appears, expressed in 11:16: "One is punished by the very things by which one sins." A more specific irony occurs in God's benefit to Israel by use of animals and materials similar to those under which the Egyptians suffered during the plagues. Chapter 12 establishes God's mercy, revealed in his gradual judgment of the Canaanites. Chapters 13–15 elaborate on the folly of idolatry. The next three chapters commemorate events related to the deliverance from Egypt and wilderness period: (1) the deliverance of the righteous and destruction of the wicked in the wilderness (chap. 16), (2) the plague of darkness (chap. 17), and (3) the death of the firstborn (chap. 18). The deliverance from Egypt itself receives attention in 19:1–12, but the remainder of the chapter reverts to the time of the judgment of the inhabitants of Sodom (vv. 13–17). According to the author, God reverses natural phenomena (for example, the darkness/blindness placed on the Sodomites) as he pursues his purpose of providing aid to his people. The closing verse makes this divine purpose explicit: "For in everything, O Lord, you have exalted and glorified your people, and you have not neglected to help them at all times and in all places" (19:22). Previously, at the occasion of the deliverance from Egypt, the narrator described God's willingness to refashion the world for the sake of his people: "For the whole creation in its nature was fashioned anew, complying with your commands, so that your children might be kept unharmed" (19:6).

Direct interest in wisdom dissipates in the third section of the book until wisdom themes scarcely appear at all. Wisdom vocabulary ends with the discussion of the "foolish" who worship false gods and idols (13:1; 15:14). Actually, even before this section, wisdom no longer comprises a central concern. The less convincing wisdom elements of 16–19 are (1) the folly of those who oppose God, (2) retribution (a pronounced theme throughout the book), and (3) the consideration of God's transcendent activity. In this half of the book, the term *Wisdom* in the title takes on the special connotations related to God's care of his righteous people. According to this section, the ascription of the book to Solomon may relate more to his ascendancy over the nation of Egypt than to his wisdom.

Sirach

The only remaining deuterocanonical work with distinct ties to wisdom assumes several titles. The name Ecclesiasticus designates the work as a church document. Other titles include the more proper title, the Wisdom of Jesus ben (son of) Sira, or Sirach. The work can be reliably dated between 200 and 180 B.C.E.   The prologue was written by the original author's grandson fifty to sixty years after the original writing. The prologue describes the grandson's purposes and concerns in the translation of Sirach from Hebrew to Greek. The length of the work and its nonsequential arrangement make it difficult to summarize. For this reason analysis involves descriptions of the types of smaller units it contains. The study of its canonical counterpart, Proverbs, exhibits the same difficulty.

Without attempting comprehensiveness, and recognizing overlapping categories, Sirach presents at least eight different types of literary units. All of these directly relate to the book's instructional aims. First, one type of literature voices *songs in praise of God and his wisdom.* A conventional hymn in 1:1-10 unites with a passage praising the fear of the Lord as humans' access to wisdom (1:11-21). The following section adds instructions advising specific behavior which shows fear of the Lord (1:22-30). Much like Proverbs, yet through different literary forms, the intention of the book revealed in its introductory lines manifests definite wisdom interests. Additional songs praising wisdom appear in 24:3-22; 39:12-35; and 42:15-43:33. One of the verses amid those of the final unit sums up the global attributions of greatness which are identified with God's wisdom: "We could say more but could never say enough; let the final word be: 'He is the all'" (Sirach 43:27).

A second type of literature offers *advice in the format of the instruction of a parent to children.* In 3:1-4:10 repeated references to children make the section intensely didactic. Infrequent references to children ("my child") occur through the twenty-third chapter, and less frequently to the end of the book. This reference to the addressees cannot be considered a literary form in itself. Yet some sections, like the passage in 38:16-23 concerning the proper expression and measure of grief, seem consciously designed to fit the tone of parental instruction.

Two-line or longer sayings comprise the third type of literature. The sayings proceed from various perspectives. They display a form generally indistinguishable from similar genres in Proverbs. Subject headings introduce two groups of sayings (that is, 30:1-13 "Concerning Children" and 30:18-25 "Concerning Food"). Transitions seldom mark units clearly, but some small anthologies of proverbs in Sirach typically display more thematic unity than Proverbs 10-29. In this respect, much of the book resembles Proverbs 1-9 in regard to the strength of connections. Sirach 36:23-37:31 contains

numerous sayings of this third type. Though thematic associations determine the placement of groups of sayings more than in Proverbs 10–29, the
arrangement of individual sayings themselves can vary a great deal. The
proverb in 37:3 offers this homiletic comment: "O inclination to evil, why
were you formed to cover the land with deceit?" Such a sermonic tone
clearly distinguishes between the collections of sayings in Proverbs and
those in Sirach. In 41:14–42:1a is a unique list of things causing shame. A
following list presents things which should not occasion shame (42:1b–8).
The special forms in which parenetic material appears generates much of
the wide respect accorded ben Sirach's instruction.

Lengthier units carefully molded around a given theme constitute the fourth
type of literature. These units join several proverbs or pieces of instruction
relating to a specific theme. No comparable units occur in Proverbs, but the
forms nearly reproduce Job's speeches or Qoheleth's reflections. Promises
of God's retribution for good and evil unify the section in 35:13–26. The
righteous receive encouragement through a litany of promises in verses
21–26. They assure the reader God will not rest before the complete
destruction of the disobedient. Each of four lines begins with the formula
"until he . . ." followed by a verb indicating retribution to faithful and rebellious alike. A segment similar in size in 38:1–15 expresses an entirely different focus: The passage encourages Sirach's students to honor physicians,
who at times achieved God's healing as surely as prayers. The theme of
38:24–39:11 clearly shows the personal bias of Sirach. This section contends
for the superiority of the scribe to other professionals. The unit identifies
the scribe with the sage. Thus, Ben Sirach makes it clear that he intends his
students to assume the superlative career of the savant. Sirach 40:1–13
serves as the final example of this form. It describes the human condition
as characterized by hard work, necessary for the common and the great.
Death comes to all, but belongs "seven times more" (v. 8) to the wicked. Ben
Sirach, like the Proverbs, remains unwilling to admit the apparent inconsistencies of retribution.

The most distinct section of Sirach, the *hymn in praise of Israel's ancestors*
in 44:1–50:21, comprises a fifth type of literature. Interpreters usually
describe this section as Hellenistic historiography, encomium (Greek praise
of individuals for heroic deeds or Jewish midrash). The biblical basis for the
section and Sirach's Jewish interests led one interpreter to view it as a
midrash on portions of the sacred history.[21] The poem celebrates the
exploits of various individuals from Enoch to Zerubbabel. Sirach's contemporary, Simon, receives last mention in chapter 50. Chapter 50 shows breaks
in style from the main body of the poem.[22] The poem shows only indirect
ties to Hebrew wisdom.

---

21. Teresa Brown, "Ben Sira's 'In Praise of Israel's Ancestors': An Example of Intra-Biblical
Midrash" (M.A. thesis, Mobile College, 1992).
22. Brown suggested the addition of Simon was the culmination of the unit, displaying ben
Sira's intent to connect the authority of the current priest to the standing of Israel's legendary
leaders. See "Ben Sira's 'In Praise of Israel's Ancestors,'" 61–62, 71.

At least two examples of *psalmic material* appear in Sirach. These constitute the sixth type of literature evident in the book. The appeal to God for justice in 36:1–22 functions as a prayer. The prayer omits some of the formal elements that mark 51:1–12 as a psalm of lament. The prayer in 36:1–22 requests intervention yet does not assume it will occur, whereas laments characteristically express confidence in God's deliverance. Both passages deal with retribution. Chapter 36 expresses some of Ben Sirach's doubt concerning the inevitability of reward and punishment, though this doubt is relatively slight. Most critics consider the entire content of the chapter as secondary. Each of the three units in the chapter could conceivably have a different origin. The mention of a school ("house of instruction") in 51:23 does not offer incontrovertible proof that the book supported formal education. Even the prologue includes no allusion to such a context.

The last two types of literature relate only to the closing chapter of the book. One ancient manuscript adds an *antiphon* very much like Psalm 136. The refrain, "for his mercy endures forever" occurs after each mention of God's work. Sirach ends with an *acrostic poem* (similar in style to Prov. 31:10–31) recounting Sirach's devotion to wisdom and offering the benefits of wisdom to the uneducated. 50:27–29 seems the most plausible original ending to the book:

> Instruction in understanding and knowledge I have written in this book, Jesus son of Eleazar son of Sirach of Jerusalem, whose mind poured forth wisdom. Happy are those who concern themselves with these things, and those who lay them to heart will become wise. For if they put them into practice, they will be equal to anything, for the fear of the Lord is their path.

Summary: The Encompassing Nature of Wisdom

Wisdom forms, themes, and arguments appear throughout Israel's literature—from Genesis to the Deuterocanon. A wisdom framework helps narrators, poets, prophets, and apocalyptists examine Israel's life under God in categories that teach Israel a heightened perspective on life with Yahweh. Wisdom guides Israel on the path to life and equips Israel to walk that path.

Questions for Discussion

1. How do you identify wisdom materials and influences in books outside the wisdom canon?

2. Compare and contrast how wisdom is used in Torah, Former Prophets, Latter Prophets, and in the Writings.

3. What new elements appear in the Deuterocanon wisdom? What importance do these have for later Christian theology?

Chapter 6

Wisdom in Proverbs

Introduction to Proverbs

Proverbs features classic wisdom vocabulary, the *māšāl* form, emphasis on common sense activity, and a tone which is neither distinctly parenetic (rules providing specific directives to fit specific situations) nor directly linked to the ethical demands of Torah. In this way Proverbs takes on a different flavor than Torah or prophetic literature, even when these segments of canon contain advice regarding conduct. Proverbs displays a pronounced lack of conventional narrative: the book contains only poetic stories and didactic units (in a formalistic sense). On the other hand, Proverbs does not contain liturgical poetry, though psalms are otherwise widely distributed among diverse biblical materials.

Mišlê (מִשְׁלֵי) is the abbreviated title of the work, designating the book, "proverbs of [Solomon]." The Hebrew *māšāl* (מָשָׁל)[1] names a literary unit of varying size which may be either wisdom sayings or a unit of teaching from a wide variety of wisdom and nonwisdom contexts. The Book of Proverbs, with some exceptions in the first nine chapters and the final two chapters, favors the pithy, two-line variety. This basic proverb shows a penchant for simplistic and often ironic expressions of truths intended to guide the practice of the reader. Most often, "proverb," denotes a poetic two-line saying such as: "It is honorable to refrain from strife, but every fool is quick to quarrel" (20:3). In function, proverbs are usually comparisons or parables as indicated in the etymology of the word, most literally a "representation" or "likeness."

Expansions of the simple two-line comparative pattern led to the longer units. In their longer forms, *mešālîm* become much more than

---

1. The word, *māšāl*, is used in the Hebrew Bible to describe all types of poetry, with the exceptions of psalms and love poetry. Balaam's prophetic oracles (Num. 23–24) bear the term as well as the persons known as "ballad singers" (NRSV translation of the plural of *māšāl*, "poets?") in Numbers 21:27. *BDB* connects the word with parallelism.

simple comparisons as seen in the lengthier narratives on the avoidance of unhealthy sexual relations in chapters 1–9. The groups of sayings arranged around themes or numerical schemata in Proverbs 30 and 31 also comprise proverbs.

Ezekiel 17:3–10 contains a longer saying with this title (so named in v. 2). This *māšāl* presents a prophetic allegory used as a prophetic oracle. Similarly, the initial verse of Job 27 attaches the designation to a lengthy discourse (23 verses). The great differences in the type of unit designated in Ezekiel 17:1 and Proverbs 1:1 illustrates the wide application of the term, *māšāl*.

The *māšāl* stands out as the most notable formal feature of the Book of Proverbs. The *mešalîm* themselves always display a didactic nature. They communicate pictorally and playfully through images, even when they present grave themes. Some interpreters claim that with proverbs everything undergoes transformation to the suprapersonal level, to the level of general validity.[2] The predominance of third-person forms may lead to such a conclusion. Applicability to a wide variety of situations does demand indirectness, but each application surely made the proverbs personal and related them to a specific context.

Types of Proverbs

The Proverbs typically appear in two-line units described as *parallel terms*. This poetic form receives fuller description in chapter 10 of this work. Sets of double lines normally comprise one verse as well as one proverb. The nature of the *māšāl* depends in part on the balance between lines provided by parallelism. Unlike most popular aphorisms the *māšāl* contains two interdependent phrases: "A false balance is an abomination to the LORD, but an accurate weight is his delight" (Prov. 11:1). Such sayings foster reflection by encouraging comparative reading of the two lines. The lines, like the majority in the Book of Proverbs, are patterned in an antithetic relationship: One line seems to describe the description directly opposed to the other. Such an observation does not in itself do justice either to the complexity of the interplay between the lines or to the precise intent of the opposing phrases. The Proverbs illustrate that parallelism works not so much through its metrical arrangement as through the semantics (meanings) of its content. The designation "thought rhyme" describes its operation. The sense units "false balance" and "abomination" invite contrast with the following: "accurate weight" and "delight."

Proverbs contains two doublets which show a synonymous relationship:

Do not fret because of evildoers. Do not envy the wicked; for the evil have no future; the lamp of the wicked will go out. (Prov. 24:19–20)

Rather than conventional wise sayings, the first verse offers a double admonition, and the second verse complements the admonitions with

2. Von Rad, *Wisdom*, 32.

observations. These observations provide the rationale which serves as the basis for the courage of the righteous. The unit appears to possess design as a four-line saying rather than as the conjunction of two formerly independent units.

The first few lines of the unit in 23:29–30 contain *questions*: "Who has woe? Who has sorrow? Who has strife? Who has complaining? Who has wounds without cause? Who has redness of eyes? Those who linger late over wine, those who keep trying mixed wines" (Prov. 23:29–30). The combination of questions represents a form of communication entirely different from the counterposed lines of parallelism. At least for the duration of the single verse, the queries represent a riddle with multiple clues. This proverb reinforces acceptable conduct quite subtly. It merely reproduces experiences common to heavy drinkers. More direct advice comes in later verses (31–35).

A *māšāl* may also take the form of comparison as illustrated in 16:8: "Better is a little with righteousness than large income with injustice." Normally a known evil (here poverty) stands in contrast to a greater evil or to a good situation complicated by negative factors. Comparisons of items such as money with the nonmaterial values of the sage reinforce the reordering of priorities necessary to a life devoted to wisdom.

Passages like 25:14 may be termed *juxtapositions*: "Like clouds and wind without rain is one who boasts of a gift never given." This example compares one frustration to another. The proverb leaves it unclear whether the gift giver described habitually makes false promises or continues to promise a single gift. The proverb applies equally to either situation.

Other proverbs follow a *numerical formula*: "Under three things the earth trembles; under four it cannot bear up; a slave when he becomes king, and a fool when glutted with food; an unloved woman when she gets a husband, and a maid when she succeeds her mistress" (Prov. 30:21–23). The form resembles the "three transgressions and four" in Amos 1–2. Numerical formulas exhibit a looser connection between form and message than in other proverbial schemata. The four things introduced could bear any number of relationships to one another. All the lines in this example refer to an inferior who assumes a status higher than the one to which the person is accustomed. The line that does not fit as well may stand out purposefully so that the listener will connect the well-fed fool with more obvious potential abusers of power.

One type of wisdom form, better known from Ecclesiastes than Proverbs, issues from a *personal perspective*. The following passage displays this *autobiographical* point of view:

> I passed by the field of one who was lazy, by the vineyard of a stupid person; and see, it was all overgrown with thorns; the ground was covered with nettles, and its stone wall was broken down. Then I saw and considered it; I looked and received instruction. A little sleep, a little slumber, a little folding of the hands to rest, and poverty will come upon you like a robber, and want, like an armed warrior. (Prov. 24:30–34)

The autobiographic introduction provides an imaginary framework which associates images of dilapidation with lack of industry. Much like a prophetic vision, the optical "seeing" leads to a perception unrelated to the five senses. Autobiographical forms assume many differing images. They usually emphasize "seeing," especially in Ecclesiastes.

Collections in Proverbs

In its present form, the Book of Proverbs appears as seven collections of proverbs and sayings.

Table 4
Collections in Proverbs

Title	Chapters
Proverbs of Solomon	1–9
Proverbs of Solomon	10:1–22:16
Proverbs of Solomon copied by Hezekiah's men	25–29
Words of the Wise	22:17–24:22
Sayings of the Wise	24:23–34
Words of Agur	30
Words of Lemuel	31

The units lack clear marks of a beginning and end. They also lack thematic development. Chapters 1–9 constitute something of an exception to this. These chapters show unity with regard to theme. Otherwise, the headings which indicate collections simply serve as markers like the five books of the Psalms. Perhaps the collections existed as individually developed units, but little evidence supports or denies this conclusion.

The special qualities which distinguish chapters 1–9 as a unit to itself include (1) frequent reference to the child (probably "student" is intended), (2) lengthier rhetorical units, (3) extended exhortations to follow wisdom and avoid immoral women as sexual partners, and (4) groupings of sayings closely related to a single theme. These features lead current critics to identify the unit as a late addition to the other collections. According to this view, the addition, like the title in 1:1, provided the work its desired canonical or precanonical form.[3]

---

3. Patrick Skehan, "The Seven Columns of Wisdom's House in Proverbs 1–9" in *Studies in Israelite Poetry and Wisdom*, ed. Patrick Skehan (Washington: The Catholic Biblical Association of America, 1971), 9–14. Skehan presented a fanciful portrait of the unit's construction as seven wisdom poems of equal size in chapters 2–7. He understood the "seven pillars of wisdom" in 9:1 to refer to the seven poems. Proverbs provides a literary representation of the preexilic temple with various facades (back, front, side) paralleled in the arrangement of lines by section ("Wisdom's House," 27–45).

Most critical interpreters identify the postexilic or restoration period as the date of the present book. Some of the individual sayings occurring even in the latest portions of the book predate all the biblical materials. The portions of the collections attributed to Solomon cannot be dated with certainty. Solomon possibly served as the collector rather than the author of the oldest segments of the book, since some of the sayings were known before the time of Solomon. In contrast to this, some consider the authorship by Solomon an invention of a later period, with no historical basis. One less extreme view substitutes the figure Hezekiah (note chaps. 25–29) as the regent who introduced professional wisdom to Israel.[4] It served Hezekiah's interest to strengthen an already existing notion that Solomon fathered the wisdom tradition. This option exercises strong appeal since Deuteronomistic editing may have begun in Hezekiah's times. Hezekiah's own court historians possibly reinforced Solomon's role in wisdom as presented in the text of 2 Kings. A collection of Solomonic proverbs would add a great deal of impetus to the effort.

"The Sayings of the Wise" in 22:17–24:22 displays strong connections with an earlier book of Egyptian wisdom, *Amenemopet*, described in chapter 2. The segment displays clear signs of its identity as a separate collection. Notable features include (1) the grouping of proverbs around a single theme, (2) frequent identification of the hearer as "my child," and (3) several nonproverbial lines of instruction uncharacteristic or rare in other portions of Proverbs. This section also contains numerous proverbs on the themes of kingship and subjection to the king. This feature leads some interpreters to associate the unit with the training of cabinet officials and others in service to the king.[5] The court setting presents a likely possibility for *Amenemopet*, but Hebrew collections of proverbs cannot be incontestably connected with court education. Also, many of the proverbs within these units show no association with court life.

Major Themes in Proverbs

Most of the literary units in Proverbs fit into one or more of the forms given above. The subsequent discussion of the general themes of Proverbs (including fear of the LORD) provides some sense of the overall nature of the work. Beyond this, the study of the book's distinct themes and their special application provides a better basis for understanding the collection as a unified document. These themes seldom find extensive development. Proverbs contains byte-sized truisms with occasional runs of four to eight lines. Longer units are exceptional.

Certain themes in Proverbs appear almost exclusively in the wisdom books. These include paired themes such as industry and laziness; wisdom

4. R. B. Y. Scott, "Solomon and the Beginnings of Wisdom in Israel" in *WIANE*, 279; consult also Duane A. Garrett, NAC 14, 48–52 on authorship and dating issues.
5. See Glendon E. Bryce, *A Legacy of Wisdom* (Lewisburg, Pa.: Buchnell University Press, 1979), 148–54; who included the twenty-fifth chapter in this court document.

and folly. Some of the single themes common to wisdom include the nagging wife, avoiding excess, and accepting correction. Proverbs displays an intense preoccupation with speech, a common theme throughout the Hebrew Bible. Proverbs emphasizes the regulation of personal speech with such force that it represents a new variety of the theme.

Doctrine of the Two Ways

Two recurring themes constitute the most distinctive feature of Proverbs and provide much of its character as a unique book, undergirding and serving as vehicles for lesser themes. They deserve the designation "meta-theme." The so-called *doctrine of the two ways* serves as a dialectical foil for many of the observations regarding good and evil. The related concept of *retribution* for good and evil appears even more often and seems an indispensable element of proverbial wisdom. The doctrine of the two ways is a part of the doctrine of retribution, providing a form in which to express the universally applicable doctrine of retribution. The choice of a "one or the other" mode of conduct is the premise for nearly all the ethical content of the book.

Well over one-fourth of the contents of Proverbs deals directly with the theme of retribution. Even though Job presents an extended case history involving an exception to this theology, few verses in Proverbs (for example, 17:8; 18:11) admit exceptions. The doctrine of the two ways finds clear expression in 15:9: "The way of the wicked is an abomination to the LORD, but he loves the one who pursues righteousness." Both individuals alluded to in 15:9 proceed on certain courses, and the ends of the two courses are in direct opposition. One displeases God and ends with destruction, while the other pleases God and ends with benefit. In the original context, the destinies do not correspond to the heaven/hell dichotomy of later Christianity. They relate to temporal pains or pleasures for the moral agent and progeny.

Most statements of the two ways do not spell out both sides of the equation as the previous example does. Instead, they focus on the blessing due the wise, righteous, and industrious or on the misery due the fool, wicked, and lazy. The dualistic concept appears simple, but the reader is warned: "There is a way that seems right to a person, but its end is the way of death" (14:12). The concept conveys moral training through a philosophy which contains both negative and positive elements. Right behavior can be achieved by rejecting the "other" way. Such a stance becomes in itself a choice to do well, since Proverbs identifies no middle ground between proper and improper conduct. Whether for the purpose of direct instruction (Proverbs) or as the predisposition of a protagonist who chooses the better course (Job and Ecclesiastes), this doctrine remains essential to Hebrew wisdom.

The term *retribution* most often describes God's punishment in consequence of offense or disobedience, but retribution can also describe the positive consequences of proper conduct. The theology of Proverbs affirms both poles of retribution, supporting the convictions that the righteous prosper and the wicked suffer. The possible expressions of retribution are endless, so the examples which follow provide a thin representation of the whole:

> Treasures gained by wickedness do not profit, but righteousness delivers from death. (Prov. 10:2)

> When the ways of people please the LORD, he causes even their enemies to be at peace with them. (Prov. 16:7)

> A slave who deals wisely will rule over a child who acts shamefully, and will share the inheritance as one of the family. (Prov. 17:2)

> Whoever digs a pit will fall into it, and a stone will come back on the one who starts it rolling. (Prov. 26:27)

The first of these proverbs leaves the enforcer of the principle unnamed, and the second names Yahweh as the one who gives the reward. At times it remains unclear whether the consequence of an action occurs as a natural outcome or a result of divine intervention. It seems likely Hebrew sages identified God as the agent behind all retribution. His power drove all the natural order. In other cases, such as the third example, the individual displaying wisdom or folly assumes responsibility for the result: either slave or child can subvert expected outcomes to be honored or shamed. Likewise, the fourth example makes it clear that the forces of retribution are under human control, though once initiated the outcomes appear inevitable. This unit reduces the doctrine to its bare logic and makes it appear atheological. The following passage, however, expresses the metatheme in unambiguous theological terms: "The LORD's curse is on the house of the wicked, but he blesses the abode of the righteous. Toward the scorners he is scornful, but to the humble he shows favor. The wise will inherit honor, but stubborn fools, disgrace" (Prov. 3:33–35).

Proverbs 19:23 promises retribution to those who fear the LORD in the form of the greatest positive rewards: "The fear of the LORD is life indeed; filled with it one rests secure and suffers no harm." Other expressions of classic retribution, notable for their clarity, appear in Proverbs 10:1–17.

Other biblical books feature the consequences of human action. The prophets speak on the theme in forms that look more or less like the proverbs. Deuteronomistic literature (Deuteronomy, Joshua, Judges, Samuel, and Kings) presents the most striking similarity to the retribution of Proverbs.[6] The two works contain the identical theological concept. Evidence indicates more than a related concept or a development from one book to another. The implications of the doctrine for religious identity provide the basis of the deuteronomistic history. The moral logic of the doctrine pro-

---

6. For consideration of other similarities between Deuteronomy and Proverbs, see Donn Morgan, *Wisdom in the Old Testament Traditions* (Philadelphia: John Knox, 1981).

vides the basis of Proverbs. The Deuteronomist uses the philosophy to point out Israel's mistakes, which led to its troubled history. Proverbs employs the doctrine to support the moral claim, "All acts bear consequences," playing on this idea from nearly every possible perspective. This characteristic alone lends Proverbs its own "wisdom" distinct from Deuteronomy's similar use of retribution.

Theme does not distinguish Proverbs from the rest of canon. Much of the book reverbrates with the ethical demands of Torah (avoidance of adultery, sins of speech, obedience to parents, etc.). In addition, Proverbs contains emphasis on social injustices forbidden in Law and condemned by the eighth-century prophets. These concerns include the use of false balances (11:1; 16:11), care for the poor (22:9, 22; 31:20), and the preference of justice over sacrificial ritual (21:3).

The Fear of the LORD

The fear of the LORD appears as one of the distinctly Israelite themes of Proverbs. The editor of Proverbs showed the theme's importance by placing it as the first statement following the introduction of 1:2–6.[7] This phrase serves an important theological function. The vast majority of proverbs do not independently show direct theological connections and might be seen as part of the international wisdom literature common to Egypt, Mesopotamia, and Canaan. Israel's sages needed a method to demonstrate wisdom as the unique property of the Hebrews. Defining knowledge as "fear of Yahweh" gave this unique theological method.

Proper understanding of the term "fear of God" indicates how the editors of Proverbs viewed the collection as religious literature. Perhaps the pair of parallel lines from Job explain the phrase:[8] "But you are doing away with the fear of God, and hindering meditation before God" (Job 15:4). The term translated "meditation" is שִׂיחָה (síhâ) which contains overtones of deep thought or study. Eliphaz emphasizes that Job should do more listening and less speaking. If the line stands in synonymous relation to the previous line, the fear of the LORD corresponds to contemplation of the religious demands contained in and implied by the Torah.[9] In this case, the phrase means "sincere Yahwistic faith," not unlike our usage of the term belief. It often carries the connotation of mystical commitment. This mystical element leads some scholars to think of the phrase, "the fear of the LORD is wisdom," as a statement regarding the transcendent quality of wisdom. It represents an attempt to identify wisdom as something ultimately beyond the limit of human understanding. So the phrase may refer to wisdom as divine. On the other extreme the phrase may refer to "religion" conceived in a simpler and less intellectual sense than described above.

7. The phrases "fear of the LORD" and "fear the LORD" occur in 1:7; 2:5; 3:7; 8:13; 9:10; 10:27; 14:2, 27; 19:23; 31:30.

8. Suggested in the Brown, Driver, Briggs edition of William Gesenius' *A Hebrew and English Lexicon of the Old Testament* (Oxford: Clarendon, 1953), 432.

9. See the Shema in Deuteronomy 6:4–9, a context also referring to "fear of the LORD."

The phrase occurs more often in Proverbs than elsewhere in the Hebrew Bible. The meaning of the fear of the LORD may become clearer by investigating the term most often opposed to it: "The fool says in his heart 'There is no God'" (Ps. 14:1). "Folly is practical atheism."[10] The fool's reluctance to "do the right thing" reveals the unbelief in the depth of the person's consciousness. To act foolishly involves the denial of one's own religious impulse and vice versa. The phrase "The fear of the LORD is the beginning of wisdom" directly relates ethical dispositions to religious belief and commitment. This reflects knowledge in the Aristotelian sense, as reflected in the statement "to know the good is to do the good."

Reflective Tone

The special perspective on wisdom entailed in Proverbs' approach at first glance seems directive or legalistic. Though the proverbs are directive by intent, the tone of the teachings encourages reflection rather than blind obedience. The reader who shares the point of view of the sages perceives truth beyond morality and rationality, responding with a sympathetic, "Aha!" The following proverb elicits a host of mental images, reinforcing proper conduct without a direct moral imperative: "Better to be poor and walk in integrity than to be crooked in one's ways even though rich" (28:6).

A number of proverbs do indeed contain simple moral commands: "Do not be a witness against your neighbor without cause, and do not deceive with your lips. Do not say, 'I will do to others as they have done to me; I will pay them back for what they have done'" (24:28–29).

The "do not" sayings in 24:1, 15, 17, 19, 28–29 are far less common than those with less demanding tones like 28:6. The commands appear more like the legalistic sections of the Torah than do other proverbs.

Wisdom

To understand this reflective, less-demanding tone of Proverbs requires examination of themes that provide its structure and focus. Wisdom appears as the most prominent theme (however expressed). Several passages emphasize the value of wisdom, comparing it to currency or precious metals (16:16) and presenting it as a commodity for "purchase" and hoarding (23:23). Proverbs 24:3–4 describes its value in more poetic terms: "By wisdom a house is built, and by understanding it is established; by knowledge the rooms are filled with all precious and pleasant riches" (Prov. 24:3–4). This extended metaphor describes the reorientation involved in a life devoted to wisdom. It presents wisdom as a desirable characteristic. The proverb uses a concrete image to describe an abstract concept, wisdom. This reminds the reader that wisdom involved decisive actions, each equivalent to a piece of the house.

---

10. Von Rad, *Wisdom*, 65.

Understanding the working of the human mind belongs to wisdom: "The purposes of the human mind are like deep water, but the intelligent will draw them out" (Prov. 20:5). This goes beyond the themes of awareness of right and wrong behavior so typical of Proverbs. The relation of thinking and wisdom illustrates the less concrete aspects of the Proverbs.

Given the preeminent value of wisdom, the Proverbs have much to say regarding wisdom's benefits. The wise know where they are going, but fools are led according to their folly (14:8). Consequently, to obtain wisdom shows love for oneself in that it leads to an understanding of what activity actually benefits the self (19:8). Wisdom provides a future and hope (24:14). This implies those without wisdom act only to meet immediate needs.

Based on a reasoned judgment of the evidence, wisdom involves reflection on the meaning of life. The wise person determines which course of action leads to long-term rewards. Proverbs associates wisdom with several concomitant pursuits. These include discipline, understanding, righteousness, and humility, among others. Discipline sometimes involves corporal punishment. For example, Proverbs 29:15 advises the rod as a means to avoid later disgrace resulting from poor parenting. Physical punishment benefits not only children, but also fools (10:13). Beatings serve to communicate where reason fails. Since the punishment serves the best interests of the recipient, it shows kindness rather than brutality.

"Understanding" designates wisdom itself at times and at other times, an attitude which serves wisdom interests. If one's mind possesses understanding, wisdom can reside there (14:33). Understanding enables a person to pursue wisdom rather than filling the mind with random thoughts (17:24). In short, understanding makes wisdom an achievable goal. The righteous person exudes wisdom (10:31), as evident in speech and acts. Wisdom and righteousness each confirm the presence of the other. Wisdom bears a stronger relationship to righteousness than to any other descriptive noun in Proverbs.

Wisdom and Folly

The following *māšāl* equates right conduct with wisdom by equating improper conduct with folly: "Doing wrong is like sport to a fool, but wise conduct is a pleasure to a person of understanding" (10:23). Wise conduct directly correlates with moral activity. Humility and its paired word, pride, represent the positive and negative poles of the wise person's self-understanding. Pride leads to disgrace, but humility shows wisdom (11:2). Those who possess wisdom accept advice (13:10). The very acknowledgment of God requires humility and leads to his instruction in wisdom (15:33).

Proverbs occasionally expresses a certain ambivalence regarding the human capacity for wisdom. This occurs more frequently in Ecclesiastes and Job. Proverbs such as 30:3 convey extreme doubt regarding the wisdom proponent's achievements: "I have not learned wisdom, nor have I knowledge of the holy ones." This passage presents Agur's lack of understanding of God and his works. (The last two words may also be rendered "Holy One.") The sage's humility develops into honest skepticism regarding all personal judgments.

Wise persons recognize their own limits. "No wisdom, no understanding, no counsel can avail against the LORD" (Prov. 21:30). These lines suggest the following paraphrase: "No amount of human understanding or planning can frustrate God's plans." This relates not so much to God's omnipotence as to the determinism of his control. This does not render the sage's task any less important. It places wisdom as humans' greatest accomplishment in its proper perspective, relative to the divine will.

Fools experience subordination to the wise of slightly less degree than the wise experience subordination to God. Wisdom lies beyond the reach of fools. They experience confusion when placed among sages (24:7). As a complement to this idea, the wise should keep silent in the presence of a fool, since that person will not recognize or respect profound judgment (23:9). Whatever the possible achievements of wisdom, it can in no way benefit those who resist its truth. Wisdom can prevail over other causes of lack of discretion, such as immaturity or indolence. The fool remains without hope of progress and this by definition. Fools live incorrigibly.

Themes in Proverbs 1–9

A thematic study of Proverbs must separate chapters 1–9 as a distinct and determinative unit. Three factors demand this: (1) its placement at the beginning of the book, (2) its special didactic flavor, and (3) its polished style and forms. The character of the book as a whole depends to a large extent on the nature of wisdom and its themes as introduced in these chapters. Chapters 1–9 set wisdom within a religious-philosophical system not apparent in the remainder of the book. The reader's understanding of the book in terms of its religious message and didactic ends arises from these chapters. They prevent, in part, understanding of chapters 10–31 as a loose collection of isolated units. The reader learns from 1–9 what to expect of the book. Further reading tends to place subsequent passages within this framework.

Forms in Proverbs 1–9

In this section synonymous or synthetic relationships appear as the most frequent formulas for parallel lines. In synthetic (also known as "incomplete") parallelism the second line builds on the first without the sense of balance communicated by synonymous or opposing semantic units. The sentence, "Do not withhold good from those to whom it is due, when it is in your power to do it" (Prov. 3:27), shows little dependence on a poetic two-line form. Prose could provide an equally expressive format for the saying. Semantically, the second line completes the thought of the first:

they exhibit parallelism only in a metrical sense. They do not conform to the designation of parallelism as "thought rhyme." This feature indicates a preoccupation with the communication of content (rather than form). The writer used pseudo-parallelism to communicate a more systemic program for wisdom. In addition to parallel form, the special perspective of Proverbs 1–9 shows itself through the tone of its instruction. Rather than originating from "nowhere" or from "everywhere" (as universal wisdom, which is nearly instinctual), these proverbs come from "somewhere." They tend to express the approach of a specific individual (identified in the prologue as Solomon) toward the tenets of wisdom.

The common use of longer units which display parallel relationships on the level of multiple lines further expresses this tendency. A single theme (made explicit in vv. 15 and 19) dominates 1:10–19. Other individual verses present and represent related themes. Some of the two-line units show a synonymous relationship; others, synthetic. All work together as a single *māšāl* rather than a series of independent proverbs. This seems more a result of literary creation than remembered aphorisms.

The suppression of irony (irony frequently appears in chaps. 10–31) stands out as another pronounced feature of chapters 1–9. An example is: "'Bad, bad,'" says the buyer, then goes away and boasts" (Prov. 20:14). The tone of 20:14 seems more humorous than serious and does not supply an application of the saying to the desired behavior of the student of wisdom. Should the student identify with the buyer? If we presume that the buyer made the purchase, should we interpret the purchase as misconduct? Is his boasting an acquired right or foolish conduct? The message seems integral to the irony itself—that one should complain and boast about the same item. Whether the item actually possesses value worthy of the boasting, the reader does not know. The sober tone of the early chapters of Proverbs will not allow such an inconclusive observation. The implied author of chapters 1–9 shows dissatisfaction with such untidy didacticism. The narrator of chapters 1–9 prefers premeditated moral instruction most often expressed in encouragements to fear Yahweh and honor the moral code of the Torah. Wisdom equals the fear of God. The religious impulse provides access to wisdom. After chapter 9, Proverbs concentrates on behavior, politics, and common sense. The early chapters predominantly contain religious instruction.

Themes in Proverbs 1–9

Verses 2–6 of the first chapter convey the themes which determine the special nature of chapters 1–9:

> For learning about wisdom and instruction, for understanding words of insight, for gaining instruction in wise dealing, righteousness, justice, and equity; to teach shrewdness to the simple, knowledge and prudence to the young— Let the wise also hear and gain in learning, and

the discerning acquire skill, to understand a proverb and a figure, the words of the wise and their riddles. (Prov. 1:2–6)

The unit expresses some intent to provide reference material for those seeking an understanding of wisdom in general or of specific sayings. Verse 3 identifies the practical aims of the collection. This may comprise the central purpose of Proverbs from the limited perspective of chapters 1–9— *to convey to the reader "how to" live wisely.* Verse 4 shows the rather specific audience intended: The work targets those who are young in terms of age, experience, or lack of submission to the principles of wisdom. Stated more positively, the work would lead its reader or student toward maturity. However, verse 5 broadens the focus of the work to include those already wise who can benefit from a sharpening of their wisdom skills. Verse 6 presents the most basic aim of all: *Study of this work leads to a more sophisticated understanding of wisdom sayings and their proponents.* This indicates the intent of a reference work. By continued exposure, the reader would increase proficiency toward the unattainable goal of perfect wisdom.

The words *my child* and related addresses occur frequently in 1–9. This identifies the chapters as intended for instructional purposes in the narrow sense of parenesis. At the very least, the addresses encourage reflection focused on moral behavior. This does not mean that the chapters served as textbook in a formal educational system. This thesis would fit chapters 1–9 better than the remainder of the book. If Proverbs 1–9 did not support an educational institution, it displays no less formal demands on its students. The direct guidelines given provide for straightforward evaluations of individual "students." The following chapters present no such organized program. The isolated units they contain assume varied contexts. The address to "my child" would not fit all the proverbs in chapters 10–31, either in the familial or the educational sense of the expression!

Wisdom and Folly as Women

The employment of feminine characters to represent wisdom and folly presents a further distinctive of chapters 1–9. Images of the foolish woman bear messages relating to sexual misconduct. Wisdom represents the chaste and faithful lifestyle. Throughout the chapters wisdom assumes other layers of meaning. For example, the adulterous woman, in addition to her role as a symbol of sexual misconduct, also represents the waste and danger of a life without wisdom. Part of the basis for the portrayal of wisdom and folly as women lies in the feminine gender of the noun for wisdom (חָכְמָה, *hokmâ*). More important than this, the youth and inexperience of the male students presumed by chapters 1–9 called for such images.

The theme of the seductive woman occurs more frequently than any other common theme in chapters 1–9.[11] The passages generally portray her

---

11. Pleas to avoid the adulteress along with vignettes describing her wiles occur in 2:16–19; 5:3–20; 6:23–35; 7:6–27; 9:13–18.

as an unfaithful wife. She resembles a common prostitute in her appeals to the wisdom student. The first passage sets the tone for subsequent depictions (2:16–19): She uses speech persuasively; denies the one to whom she was earlier betrothed; and leads the unsuspecting to their doom. Perhaps a Hebrew prostitute who ran from an impending marriage or was disowned by her husband served as the model for this woman. The loss of the security of membership in her husband's family forced her to make her own way with limited opportunities for socially acceptable work. The woman portrayed in Proverbs shows some skill at finding clients and finds perverse enjoyment in her work. Chapter 5:3–20 advises the student to maintain enough distance from her to ensure he will not be tempted by her offers. Otherwise, he will end up without wealth and reputation. An attractive description of the wisdom of sexual fidelity occurs in 5:15–17: "Drink water from your own cistern, flowing water from your own well. Should your springs be scattered abroad, streams of water in the streets? Let them be for yourself alone, and not for sharing with strangers." The passage continues with an encouragement to sexual devotion to "the wife of your youth" (v. 18). Chapter 6:23–35 describes the woman as the current wife of another. Her beauty ironically tempts the young man to accept her invitation and risk death at the hands of her husband: "Can fire be carried in the bosom without burning one's clothes?" (6:27).

The understandable jealousy and fury of the offended husband makes adultery the most foolish conduct imaginable (6:32). Chapter 7:6–27 presents the "wayward woman" and "young man without sense" through dramatic means. The account begins as the sage-storyteller recounts looking out his window as the woman encountered her prey. She used several lines of argument to persuade him. First, she kissed him and told her offering sacrifices earlier in the day. Perhaps this assured the youth plenty of food lay in store. She had prepared the bed with colorful coverings and spices. She promised her husband would not return for some time. Melodramatic images describe the youth's consent. Three separate images relate the killing of animals by humans—the ox at slaughter, the stag killed by an arrow, and the bird caught in a snare. All who engage in similar sexual misconduct, like the young man, willingly bring on their own deaths.[12]

The final unit, 9:13–18, contains only a vague allusion to sexual misconduct: "Stolen water is sweet, and bread eaten in secret is pleasant" (9:17). "The foolish woman" speaks these lines. This character serves as a metaphor for the destructive lifestyle of the fool. Illicit sexual conduct with its danger and consequences makes the immoral woman a logical choice for the image of Folly. As will be seen, Wisdom plays a much clearer role in this

---

12. In response to the view that this woman worked as a fertility prostitute, one critic suggested her alleged need to repay a vow was used to incite the pity of her partner. According to this view, mention of her husband's traveling with money relates to her own need of funds to make a temple payment she promised. Karel van der Toorn, "Cultic Prostitution," *ABD*, vol. 5, 511.

regard. In the depiction of Wisdom, the sexual overtones emphasized in regard to Folly receive less attention.

Passages which personify wisdom include 3:3–18; 4:5–9; 7:4; 1:20–33; 8:1–36, and 9:1–6. In 3:3–18 wisdom offers a future opposite to that promised by the seductress. Her benefits—long life, wealth, and honor (v. 16)—constitute exactly those things the adultress denies. The phrase, "tree of life," connotes, as well, all the benefits of wisdom.[13] Chapter 4:5–9 suggests those who give wisdom a place receive from her a victor's wreath. Whereas folly offered self-destruction, wisdom offers self-benefit. Wisdom becomes a lifelong companion. A faithful wife offers the nearest corollary in common experience. She benefits her husband in proportion to the honor he accords her. The portrayal in 7:4 seems to turn from the image of wisdom as wife: "Say to wisdom, 'You are my sister,' and call insight your intimate friend" (Prov. 7:4). Actually, the designation "sister" legitimately applies to marital relationships (compare Song of Sol. 4:9–12) which ideally transcend the customary physical aspects. So, the term *sister* serves as a nonliteral signification for a deep mutual respect. In its own way, this level of personification communicates as deeply as the portrayal of wisdom speaking. Wisdom responds in kind toward those who attend to her.

When Wisdom calls to the uninitiated in 1:20–33, she directs her appeals toward fools. The summons emphasizes the consequences of rejecting wisdom. The foolish audience makes hers a futile appeal for converts. Her lack of success indicates she intends, in spite of appearances, to appeal to the inexperienced devotee of wisdom rather than the fool. "Because I have called and you refused . . . I also will laugh at your calamity" (vv. 24a and 26a), she says. She does not fully identify the calamity in the remaining verses. Nonetheless, the warning receives emphasis to the end of the passage. Wisdom warns of the regret the fool will experience when he needs help and receives no response.

Invitation to Wisdom

A four-section invitation to wisdom appears in 8:1–21, 22–31, 32–36; 9:1–6. In 8:1–31, Wisdom describes herself as the source of truth, righteousness, understanding, knowledge, prudence, discretion, humility, good advice, wealth, honor, and justice. In 8:22–31 she identifies herself as the source of the created order. This passage reads as if a sage composed a hymn intended to include all the positive traits of and rewards for wisdom. In comprehensiveness it compares to the description of the purposes of the Book of Proverbs in chapter 1 (vv. 2–6). Wisdom's invitation includes an appeal to the learner to heed her (vv. 32–36). It also incorporates a report concerning her feast, to which she invites the inexperienced (9:1–6). In

---

13. The centrality of this image to biblical wisdom as well as to Psalms led to its use as a title for a significant introduction to wisdom: Roland E. Murphy, *The Tree of Life: An Exploration of Biblical Wisdom Literature*, Anchor Bible Reference Library (New York: Doubleday, 1990).

many ways, the hymnlike description of Wisdom's role in creation (chap. 8) presents the most striking portion of the unit:

> The LORD created me at the beginning of his work, the first of his acts of long ago. Ages ago I was set up, at the first, before the beginning of the earth. When there were no depths I was brought forth, when there were no springs abounding with water. Before the mountains had been shaped, before the hills, I was brought forth—when he had not yet made earth and fields, or the world's first bits of soil. When he established the heavens, I was there, when he drew a circle on the face of the deep, when he made firm the skies above, when he established the fountains of the deep, when he assigned to the sea its limit, so that the waters might not transgress his command, when he marked out the foundations of the earth, then I was beside him, like a master worker; and I was daily his delight, rejoicing before him always, rejoicing in his inhabited world and delighting in the human race. (Prov. 8:22–31)

The placement of Wisdom's creation prior to the world's creation emphasizes Wisdom's close affinity with God as well as her primacy as a human concern.[14] Undergirding home, family, property, and basic necessities, Wisdom plays a fundamental role

The concept of Wisdom as first creation provides the foundation for later views of wisdom as hypostatization and its subsequent identification with Christ and the *Logos* of John 1 (see chap. 3 of this study). Wisdom appears not only as the first creation but also serves as an agent of creation depicted in the image of an assistant, or a child affirming the creation with play (8:30–31). Some interpreters connect this figure with the creative spirit of God himself. In terms of Christian theology, the Holy Spirit as a source of God's power offers the closest counterpart to Wisdom at creation.[15]

The rejoicing of Wisdom as indicated in verses 30 and 31 paints a positive picture of the human potential for enjoyment of the physical creation: "Then I was beside him, like a master worker [or 'little child']; and I was daily his delight, rejoicing before him always, rejoicing in his inhabited world and delighting in the human race." Wisdom becomes a lively sprite, reveling in the goodness of creation and so urging humans to the same joy.

Verses 32–36, which emphasize the blessing of wisdom with two אַשְׁרֵי (ʾašrê) forms, naturally follow this celebration of creation. They recommend wisdom as a happy course and equate folly with death. The wise gain full benefit from humanity and the creation at large. By contrast, the fool

---

14. A few critics understand Wisdom's personification as an identification with a goddess of wisdom. See, for example, Leo G. Perdue, *Wisdom and Cult*, 153.

15. The ancient worldview commonly associated such forces with deities such as the Mesopotamian goddess Nisaba. She possessed intelligence as her defining characteristic. She served as the patron deity of the scribes and offered divine guidance to those who engaged in writing. See Rivkah Harris, "The Feminine Sage in Mesopotamian Literature" in *SIANE*, 3–17. Though the Hebrew,"Wisdom" seems more a metaphor than a deity, she may serve as similar a role as possible, given Israel's monotheism.

effectively denies self the enjoyment of life. Subsequently, the fool faces the natural end, death.

Similarly, Wisdom's festival in 9:1–6 remains available only to those who accept wisdom—in effect, the ticket to the party. The benefits of food, drink, and companionship with Wisdom and her servant girls represent the "goods" available to those who seek her insight. Here, as elsewhere, Wisdom herself utters the appeal. This active call seems to indicate that the opportunity for understanding always presents itself. This augments the depiction of her rejectors as dull oafs too stupid to heed a summons clearly heard.

Ideal Wife

A figure appears in the final chapter who may well represent wisdom, though she plays the role of the ideal wife. This woman, recommended by Lemuel's mother (31:1), leaves little work for her husband. She adds financial affairs, day labor, benevolence, weaving, and "wisdom" to her domestic duties. She performs all her work with excessive quality. Primarily, the passage (31:10–41) imagines the perfect mate who reaches almost impossibly high standards. Secondarily, the wise wife in her most perfect form appears more than coincidentally similar to Wisdom herself. Rather than prescribing certain conduct for Hebrew women, the unit supplies Hebrew men with a "mock up" of the ideal wife. The amazingly high standards reflect a mother's (31:1) or a teacher's caution to make a careful choice. This includes advice which could apply to those who arrange marriages as well as the person who chooses a mate. Perhaps the passage attempts to list all the desirable characteristics so that the person can recognize one or a number of them in a potential partner.

As this ideal figure identifies wisdom, the strange woman or adulteress identifies folly. When a passage describing the immoral woman (for example, 9:13–18) appears next to a lengthy description of Wisdom (for example, 9:1–12), the conjunction of the two descriptions implies that the immoral woman is the personification of folly. The ideas behind the portrait of the immoral woman remain smaller, that is, less universal, than the personification of wisdom elsewhere.

Industry and Laziness

Other themes besides the striking portrayals of women in chapters 1–9 appear in units longer than the usual two lines. A comparison of the industry of the ant with the sloth of a lazy person serves as the vehicle for 6:6–11:

> Go to the ant, you lazybones; consider its ways and be wise. Without having any chief or officer or ruler it prepares its food in summer, and gathers its sustenance in harvest. How long will you lie there, O lazybones? When will you rise from your sleep? A little sleep, a little slumber, a little folding of the hands to rest, and poverty will come upon you like a robber, and want, like an armed warrior. (Prov. 6:6–11)

Thematically, the proverb speaks for itself: Even an ant possesses enough sense to prepare for the future. This unit can illustrate the means by which individual proverbs adhere to one another throughout the book. There are three sets of descriptions in this larger *māšal* which could stand on their own: (1) the ant, (2) the lazybones, and (3) sleep and poverty. These cohere in loose fashion like individual pearls on a string. The same loose connections appear throughout the thirty-one chapters of Proverbs. Often, the mere mention of a single word provides a strange transition to a new subject. A more compact thematic organization appears in 6:12–15:

> A scoundrel and a villain goes around with crooked speech, winking the eyes, shuffling the feet, pointing the fingers, with perverted mind devising evil, continually sowing discord; on such a one calamity will descend suddenly; in a moment, damage beyond repair.

The passage contains variations on a single thought—the conduct of a troublemaker. As such, it stretches the convention of the two-line *māšal*. Narrative lists present the nearest parallels to this formal arrangement in chapters 10–29. The sayings present the rehearsed answer to an imaginary question: "How do you recognize the divisive person?"

Extended proverbs appearing in the form of lists show the same potential for recitation: An authority figure asks such questions as, "What are the seven things abominable to God?" 6:16–19 records one answer:

> There are six things that the LORD hates, seven that are an abomination to him: haughty eyes, a lying tongue, and hands that shed innocent blood, a heart that devises wicked plans, feet that hurry to run to evil, a lying witness who testifies falsely, and one who sows discord in a family.

The unit functions as a simple mnemonic device. This enables the speaker to include any number of loosely related items. However, the introduction to the list takes an imperialistic tone indicating this as the list of things God hates. In this particular list, mentions of body parts act as a controlling set of images (eyes, tongue, hands, heart, and feet). While not as sophisticated as the rhetorical structure of classical narrative or prophetic oracles, such units reveal careful literary design.[16] In all three of the examples given, the concern to offer rules for conduct outweighs the concern for formal literary shaping.

---

16. A related and most significant question presents itself, "Is this basic thematic pattern a sign of oral rather than written development?" Any suggestion proves conjectural, but the movement from one theme to another of some relation could indicate mental links important for oral composition. Against this suggestion, perhaps the proverbs function as literary compositions *designed* for rather than *arising* from oral performance.

Themes in Proverbs 10–31

In chapters 10–31 as well as chapters 1–9, the units show no literary shaping beyond the two-line structure of the *māšāl.* The majority of proverbs possess more than a single theme. The additional theme can serve as the vehicle for the metaphor. If the relationship between the lines is antithetic, the second theme serves as an opposing idea which provides balance. A simple proverb such as 26:9 presents two ideas for comparison: "Like a thornbush brandished by the hand of a drunkard is a proverb in the mouth of a fool." The pictoral image, in this case a comical one, stands in direct comparision to the pragmatic truth: fools misuse proverbs.

In 17:22, the interpreter cannot identify one image as the literary tool and another as the message conveyed: "A cheerful heart is a good medicine, but a downcast spirit dries up the bones." This proverb does not operate (as the previous example) through the presentation of an undesirable action which parrots the truth of a more subtle message regarding wisdom. Instead, both elements, attitude and health, bear equal importance for the potential sage. One further example presents a host of insinuations in a very basic statement regarding wealth and friendship: "Wealth brings many friends, but the poor are left friendless" (19:4). Is the comparison intended historically (that is as an observation on human nature) rather than as moral advice? Other proverbs unambiguously attack greed and unjust wealth. Perhaps the saying advises against poverty. If so, it also contains an ironic twist. It conveys cynicism by means of sarcastic notice of the feigned admiration so often expressed toward the rich. Ultimately, the current reader cannot make clear determinations of the subtle intentions of such a proverb.

Studying the various types of relationships between themes in proverbs can lead one to recognize some sophisticated patterns and nuances. This allows the student to see plausible thematic interconnections not apparent in a surface-level reading. Even with their simplistic appearance, the scant images of a single proverb can generate a great deal of confusion, indirection, and creativity in the mind of the hearer or reader. All the literary associations and moral connections occur in the most basic literary forms imaginable—phrases or sentences which could be described as "truth statements."

Controlling Themes in Chapters 10–31

The atomistic presentation of themes in single units does not preclude far-reaching claims regarding the general themes of the book. Several larger interests constitute controlling themes which shape the contents of the entire collection in 10–31. The two most important received attention above—retribution and the two ways. Others overlap these, yet appear in discreet form as well. These include life and death, health, moderation, God's "loves" and "hates," security, and a few others.

"Explicit themes" designates those interests communicated in the wording of individual proverbs. These themes exercise little control over the organiztion of Proverbs. This study need name only a few: speech, divine determinism, discord, anger, honesty, friendship. Explicit themes in chapters 10–31 appear randomly. Tracing their appearance through the chapters provides a more accurate conception of the theme as viewed from the perspective of sapiential literature. Three such themes provide examples—discipline, family, and king.

The wise welcome *discipline* in the form of rebuke or beatings as a valuable thing (25:12; 20:30). Acceptance or rejection of discipline determines the successful or unsuccessful course of one's life (15:10; 19:25; 10:17). Resisting correction epitomizes the stubbornness characteristic to the fool. For this reason the fool deserves severe discipline and will ultimately receive retribution for continued resistance (29:1; 26:3). Proverbs recommends corporal punishment for children and servants as a means to help them avoid a harsher fate (22:15; 29:15; 23:13–14; 29:19). Those who enforce discipline through verbal rebuke receive benefits for their trouble. This may come in the form of divine reward or appreciation from the one corrected (24:25; 28:23).

Proverbs often addresses *family* relationships. The content warns the reader about the pitfalls of marriage to a quarreling wife (19:13; 21:19; 27:15–16; 25:24). A wise woman insures the success of her household, but a foolish one insures its downfall (14:1). A good wife serves as a sign of God's favor and a gift from him (18:22; 19:14). Most of the proverbs concerning the family relate to relationships between parents and children. Righteous parents leave happy circumstances to their children (20:7). Relationships between parents and children constitute one of life's greatest goods (17:6). Children give indication of their nature in their activity. If properly trained, they exhibit good conduct throughout their lives (20:11; 22:6). One of the lengthiest units in the collection urges children to heed parental instruction:

> Listen to your father who begot you, and do not despise your mother when she is old. Buy truth, and do not sell it; buy wisdom, instruction, and understanding. The father of the righteous will greatly rejoice; he who begets a wise son will be glad in him. Let your father and mother be glad; let her who bore you rejoice. (Prov. 23:22–25)

Several Proverbs consider disobedience to parents a serious offense with severe consequences (20:20; 28:4; 30:17; 17:2). Consequences also fall to the parents, whether deserved or not (17:21, 25; 19:26). Parallel lines which compare the fortunes and benefits of a wise child to those of a foolish one occur frequently (10:1; 15:20; 10:5; 13:1; 29:3). Failure to discipline children shows lack of parental love (13:24). In addition, the parent, by living rightly, guarantees that children will enjoy a full inheritance (13:22). Some units encourage parents to discipline children while they are young, for this will secure the future happiness of the parents (19:18; 29:17).

Proverbs regarding the king fall into two general categories of relatively equal importance—those directed to his subjects and those directed to the king himself. Subjects should appease the king in order to bring favor and avoid his anger (16:14, 15; 19:12; 20:2). Those who overtly seek a place of importance face possible embarrassment (25:6–7). Fear of the consequences that rebellion can bring motivate obedience both to God and to king (24:21–22). Wise and righteous conduct both please the king and provide his success (14:35; 16:13; 20:28; 22:11). After all, how can a king reign without a group to rule (14:28)? An unassuming rather than direct approach most effectively persuades the king (25:15). Many people want the favor of the king, but the LORD alone provides justice (29:26). The divine will governs the decisions of the king himself, so his decisions allow no questioning (16:10; 21:1). An intelligent ruler quells rebellion and judges with fairness. In this way he provides a future for his reign (28:2; 29:14). The king roots out evil and must not heed evil advice (20:8; 20:26; 29:12). If the ruler himself acts wickedly or oppresses his subjects, he faces a brief reign, misery, or assassination (16:12; 28:3; 28:15; 28:16; 29:4).

Word Pairs

From another perspective, word pairs provide a means for the study of the themes of Proverbs 10–31. The wise contrast with the foolish. The righteous contrast with the wicked. Wealth plays against poverty. The fortunes of the industrious show the folly of laziness. Life and death each provide meaning to the other. Gladness and sorrow assume their respective roles. Pride and humility serve as both goals and ends. Many others exist. The absence of the corresponding word or variation in the word pair also carries an effect: "The evil do not understand justice, but those who seek the LORD understand it completely" (28:5). The word *righteous*, which would parallel *evil*, does not appear. This leaves the reader to connect "those who seek the LORD" with the opposing term. This special definition of "righteous" provides insight into the attitude toward religion assumed in Proverbs.

Function of Proverbs

Various forms of proverbs appear in the previous discussions. A more poetic approach to their employment can yield a sense of their artistry. At times, they carry a sarcastic tone:

> The wealth of the rich is their strong city; in their imagination it is like a high wall. (18:11)

> A bribe is like a magic stone in the eyes of those who give it; wherever they turn they prosper. (17:8)

In other cases, the strength or effect of the images captures the imagination. Chapter 15:21 presents an image of wisdom "walking." The pervasiveness of discord compares to the effect of a leak in a watercourse (17:14), and 18:9 suggests little difference exists between the repercussions of laziness and vandalism. The following provides a list of four things never satisfied: "Three things are never satisfied; four never say, 'Enough': Sheol, the barren womb, the earth ever thirsty for water, and the fire that never says, 'Enough'" (Prov. 30:15b–16). The passion of a fool for folly resembles the protection of a bear for her cubs (17:2). Wisdom supplies its benefits like an artesian well (18:4).

Other proverbs convey truth abstractly. "Desire without knowledge is not good, and one who moves too hurriedly misses the way" (Prov. 19:2). This proverb applies to any situation in which haste threatens detriment. Beneath the outward expression of truth, 20:27 provides an indication of the inward dynamic expressed in proverbial wisdom: "The human spirit is the lamp of the LORD, searching every innermost part." Likewise, 30:18–19 presents a series of mysteries which lie beyond the purview of the wise: "Three things are too wonderful for me; four I do not understand; the way of an eagle in the sky, the way of a snake on a rock, the way of a ship on the high seas, and the way of a man with a girl" (30:18–19).

A number of proverbs in chapters 10–31 anticipate questions. The truth behind 18:13—"If one gives answer before hearing, it is folly and shame"—lies in the reason (why?). The answer: One cannot render proper judgment or advice without full knowledge. In a similar fashion, "A fool's lips bring strife, and a fool's mouth invites a flogging" (18:6) begs the question by not referring to speech itself. The content of the unsignified speech brings on the punishment. The reader asks, "How?"

At times the anticipated question relates to the relationship of differentiated lines:

One who loves transgression loves strife; one who builds a high threshhold invites broken bones. (17:19)

Do not forsake your friend or the friend of your parent; do not go to the house of your kindred in the day of your calamity. Better is a neighbor who is nearby than kindred who are far away. (27:10)

In each instance, the reader answers the question, "How are the two related?" in order to make sense of the units. 20:12 leaves in doubt the very significance of the proverbial lines: "The hearing ear and the seeing eye— the LORD has made them both."

In some cases the reader must deliberate regarding the result of an activity: "It is like binding a stone in a sling to give honor to a fool" (26:8; compare 26:9 above). "Like somebody who takes a passing dog by the ears is one who meddles in the quarrel of another" (26:17). Those sayings which appear to operate straightforwardly contrast with the preceding deliberative style of proverb: "To watch over mouth and tongue is to keep out of trouble" (21:23).

The recognition of *rhetorical patterns* reveals the dynamics employed to carry an infinite variety of messages. When the lines are duplicate in form as in 21:5, often two things mentioned in the first line compare to two things mentioned in the second: "The plans of the diligent lead surely to abundance, but everyone who is hasty comes only to want." 21:1 presents two things (the vehicle and tenor of the metaphor) controlled by one: "The king's heart is a stream of water in the hand of the LORD; he turns it wherever he will." The king's heart, as surely as the stream, falls under God's control.

Comparative proverbs encourage associations between two complete sentences rather than nominal units. 15:11 follows the "two compared to two" pattern, but the proverb omits the last unit as obvious: "Sheol and Abaddon lie open before the LORD, how much more human hearts!" In a few examples, an adjectival modifier provides a key to the relationship. "Anyone who tills the land will have plenty of bread, but one who follows worthless pursuits will have plenty of poverty" (28:19). This manner of understanding proverbs leads to the identification of countless types of relationships.

Transitions Among Proverbs

Distinguishing and describing the multi-layered relationships among ideas in a single proverb presents a relatively easy task. Detailing the transitions between proverbs and small groups of proverbs presents difficult or impossible challenges. Rather than identifying loose associations of questionable value, the approach followed here recognizes some clearer associations within brief sections. In 16:1–4 each of the sayings relates to the purposes of God. 18:6–8 contains a collection of proverbs regarding the speech of the foolish and the wicked. 18:10–12 displays an organic unity uncharacteristic of the book as a whole: "The name of the LORD is a strong tower; the righteous run into it and are safe. The wealth of the rich is their strong city; in their imagination it is like a high wall. Before destruction one's heart is haughty, but humility goes before honor." The connections between the strength of the tower and the city lead to the image of destruction due to pride. The proverbs in 25:11–14 and 25:18–20 form a string of metaphors (actually similes) which certainly appear together due to their similarity in form. Similar forms appear together in 22:22–27, a series of three double proverbs that take on the appearance of four–line proverbs. The *mešālîm* in 27:19–21 appear as puzzles or riddles with explanations included. Finally, 26:20–22 repeats the same proverb in three varying versions.

Summary: Proverbs as a Wisdom Anthology

Such features provide clear indication that Proverbs displays the character of a wisdom anthology. The book contains tidbits of wisdom more or less carefully arranged, possessing an intensely directive tone. The book compels the reader to assume a student's mode and accept its tenets as ultimately authoritative. The pronounced didacticism of chapters 1–9 encourages a passive receptivity on the part of its presumably immature readership. Within this air of authority, ambiguous expressions of truth demand reflection on the part of the audience. This reflection depends on the presumption that each individual statement communicates unquestionable truth. The subordination of the pupil forces the reader to search for contextual validation for seemingly ambiguous aphorisms. The truth of the proverbs themselves allows no question when the student yields to the authority of the text. In this respect, the work validates itself for those committed to the scriptural canon. This does not indicate any sort of scientific or logical proof. Instead, the positivism resounding through all its statements pulls the serious reader into a respectful submission to its truth.

In theme, Proverbs warns about the consequences of negative behavior and promises reward as the consequence of positive behavior. The prologue (1:2–6) identifies wisdom as the central concern of the book. Proverbs consistently identifies the knowledge of consequences and adjustment of behavior to achieve reward as wisdom. This makes Proverbs the book most undebatably characterized as "wisdom." In some respects, Job and Ecclesiastes fail to show such strong affiliation with the wisdom movement.

Questions for Discussion

1. What distinguishes Proverbs from other parts of the Old Testament?

2. What different literary types do you find in Proverbs?

3. What distinctive theological themes does Proverbs offer? What importance do these have for your theology and ethics?

4. In what way is Proverbs authoritative for your life? How does this authority compare with that of Torah? of Prophets?

Chapter 7

Wisdom in Job

Introduction to Job

The current form of the Book of Job displays undeniable wisdom associations. First, the work presents Job's blamelessness as an affirmation of his wisdom. Second, his questions to God and friends reflect philosophical questions which go beyond the personal crisis he faces. Third, his reasoned arguments and those of his friends show a reflective approach to life. Fourth, the tone of the book which distinguishes it from Proverbs marks it as a wisdom source: Job engages in the extended questioning of theology rather than blind acceptance. The pessimistic attitude of the book's poetry reveals a philosophical bent in direct contrast to the positivistic tone of Proverbs. On the other hand, Job's three friends reiterate the conventional view of retribution presented in Proverbs. One can interpret the conflicting themes of Job as evidence that wisdom is a balance between questioning and orthodoxy.

Fifth, the book is preoccupied with the human condition and its inevitabilities. From Job's perspective, this knowledge belongs only to God. Sixth, several proverbs appear, especially from Job's friends. Job's less orthodox perspective leads him to question God's fairness rather than quoting proverbs. Sixth, theodicy and God's justice appear as prominent themes. Though mentioned in other books, these themes receive elaborate attention only in the wisdom canon. Seventh, references to the "gate" provide some evidence of the Hebrew social setting. The court of elders, at times identified as sages, met near the gate of the city or village. These elders may have served as the official spokespersons for clan wisdom. All these clues attest to the wisdom associations of Job.

The Distinctiveness of Job

Similarities to the story of Job appear in the patriarchial narratives (Gen. 12–50) and portions of the history of kingship (Samuel and Kings).

141

In these units, however, nothing resembles the extended poetic form of Job's dialogues. Non-Israelite literature contains more parallels to Job's dialogues than biblical literature. These non-Israelite documents come from backgrounds which usually involve wisdom elements. Representative documents receive attention in chapter 2 of this study.

The moral optimism and theological simplicity of Proverbs probably represented the norm for wisdom during much of Israel's history. In the biblical canon, only Ecclesiastes contains many of the distinctive features—such as questioning of human existence—identified here as determinants of wisdom. Our canonical perspective must include the pessimism and questioning of Job and Ecclesiastes as definitive for biblical wisdom. In part, the interpreter seeks a balance between the conformity assumed in Proverbs and the challenges raised by Job.

Job also utilizes various speech forms that lay outside the purview of wisdom. Job's speeches reveal a deep psalmic appeal for divine consideration. The spirit of these complaints resembles the mood of certain laments in Psalms. Job's statements of innocence also resemble those in the Psalms. The entire book assumes the form of a "lived" psalm of lament, including deliverance! Even the substance of God's answer to Job (38–41) appears similar to the hymns of the psalter: God uses natural wonders to show His incomparable power.

Job carries his complaint to an extreme not recognized in the Psalms. He calls for a meeting with God, rather than stopping at the request for and expectation of divine vindication. Essentially, Job expects vindication which does not come. This leads him to challenge God's sovereignty and request God to join him in the debate of his guilt or innocence (for example, Job 23:1–7). Partly because of this special perspective, the speeches of Job appear as first-person dialogue rather than the second- and third-person didacticism typical of Proverbs. In this respect as well, Job resembles Ecclesiastes.

Unlike other wisdom books, Job expresses the fear that his challenges will result in destruction at God's hands. Job joined only a handful of biblical characters in testing God, a very fearful enterprise. From another angle, the prologue and epilogue present the ordeal as God's test of Job.[1] In all the biblical canon, only Job contains this mutual "testing." When God does enter the action in response to Job's test, he acts directly. Only in God's appearance to Elijah does he show similar deference to an individual.

The relationship of the prose sections of Job (chaps. 1–2 and 42) to the bulk of the book (the poetic section in 3–41) comprises one of the central issues in the study of the book. The so-called "prose framework" contains information which appears to weaken the substance of Job's poetic complaint. The planning of Job's trouble in the heavenly court (1:6–2:7) seems to supply the reason for Job's suffering, and the rewards to Job in the

---

1. Outside of Job, God tests the Israelites by complicating their possession of Canaan in the Deuteronomistic introduction to Judges.

final chapter (42:10–17) make his suffering atypical of humans in general. If the prose explanations receive overriding weight, Job's statements appear off the mark, like those of his three companions. To reach beyond the impasse of the conflicting interests of the book requires some sort of dual hermeneutic.[2]

The prose and the poetry each present one key issue. In the prologue, the accuser's question, "Does Job fear God for nothing (1:9)?" introduces a storyline investigating the possibility of disinterested human service to God. The divine affirmation of Job in the epilogue indicates a positive answer to Satan's question. In the poetry Job attempts to discover whether righteous persons suffer. Since his own experience confirms his suspicions, he expends most of his energy in a search for the reasons for this seeming aberration.

Identity of the Character of Job

Perfect Person. The character of Job presents nine distinct functions. Some of these functions apparently exclude the possibility of others. Some complement others. First, 1:1–2 and following verses present Job as the perfect person: "There was once a man in the land of Uz whose name was Job. That man was blameless and upright, one who feared God and turned away from evil. There were born to him seven sons and three daughters" (1:1–2). The narrator does not intend to present Job as morally flawless or as a singularly exceptional individual. Job shows his blamelessness by careful atonement for all of his mistakes. Job shows such meticulous care in this regard that he offers sacrifice in behalf of his family based on the unlikely chance they had sinned unintentionally (1:5). This foundation identifies Job as a figure least likely to deserve trouble and prevents a reader from linking Job's suffering to any moral impropriety. Even the number and proportion of Job's sons and daughters illustrate Job's flawless circumstances.

Pampered Servant. The accuser offers the second assessment of Job's character: He explained Job's righteousness as a natural response to divine favor understood as a "payoff" (1:6–12): "Then Satan answered the LORD, 'Does Job fear God for nothing? Have you not put a fence around him and his house and all that he has, on every side? You have blessed the work of his hands, and his possessions have increased in the land. But stretch out your hand now, and touch all that he has, and he will curse you to your face'" (1:9–11). The accuser depicted Job as a pampered servant who owed his uprightness to God's protection. The satan strikes a deal with Yahweh to test Job by denying him all the benefits of family and wealth.[3]

---

2. One understanding of the Book of Job observes that the book manifests multipurpose functions. In its prose the reader identifies the purpose of the divine will. In its poetry the reader identifies with the ignorance and innocence of Job. Brevard Childs espoused this view in *Introduction to the Old Testament* (Philadelphia: Fortress, 1979), 533–34.

3. The name *Satan* later applies to the devil as the embodiment of all the evil forces which oppose God. Here and in Zechariah 3:1–2 the common noun applies to a member of the Divine Council. The accuser bore the responsibility of testing God's people to prove their devotion. Perhaps the common view of Satan provides the basis for the later reference in 1 Chronicles 21:1.

Disinterested Believer. Job's response to his loss of property and family reveals a third perspective on his identity (1:20–22): "Then Job arose, tore his robe, shaved his head, and fell on the ground and worshiped. He said, 'Naked I came from my mother's womb, and naked shall I return there; the LORD gave, and the LORD has taken away; blessed be the name of the LORD.' In all this Job did not sin or charge God with wrong-doing." Job's reaction to initial suffering seems to answer the accuser's question, "Does Job fear God for nothing?" (1:9) in the affirmative. Job appears a disinterested believer committed to God though the relationship offers him no profit of any kind.

Self-Centered Observer. This leads to the accuser's claim identifying Job as simply a self-centered person who cares about nothing but his own life: "Then Satan answered the LORD, 'Skin for skin! All that people have they will give to save their lives. But stretch out your hand now and touch his bone and his flesh, and he will curse you to your face'" (2:4–5). This fourth view of Job interprets Job's faithful response to loss as the lackadaisical attitude of one who did not care for others to begin with. The accuser correctly claimed Job's bodily suffering would affect him more than his losses. Job never issues the curse.

God's Guinea Pig. The prose conclusion of Job consistently depicts the figure Job as the subject of God's experiment (42:10–11a): "And the LORD restored the fortunes of Job when he had prayed for his friends; and the LORD gave Job twice as much as he had before. Then there came to him all his brothers and sisters and all who had known him before, and they ate bread with him in his house." This fifth portrait of the man details God's restoration of Job's family and property, at the same time confirming Job has been a mere guinea pig. This depiction of Job attests the validity of the Deuteronomistic view of retribution. It also distances Job's experience from the common human experience of suffering which may or may not end happily. Hebrew theology necessitated such a conclusion, because as shown in the prologue all human good and evil originated with the divine will. The five previous views of the character all arise in the prose of the book.

The expression of Job's grief in the poetic chapters more nearly matches contemporary notions. In the poetry Job interprets his suffering as circumstantial or happenstance. This observation creates confusion for one who formerly understood all human fortunes as rewards or punishments. The experience forces Job to challenge God's justice.

Universal Sufferer. The early chapters of the poetry provide alternate views which continue throughout Job's speeches. When, in chapter 3, Job curses his birthday and wishes for death, he speaks as a general sufferer and not as a person responding to unique circumstances: "After this Job opened his mouth and cursed the day of his birth. Job said: 'Let the day perish in which I was born, and the night that said, "A man-child is conceived." Let that day be darkness! May God above not seek it, or light shine on it'" (3:1–4). This sixth view of Job, Job as universal sufferer, elicits the most global and poetic interpretation of the book. All human beings can identify with this figure during the low points of life. "Why is light given to one in misery, and life to the bitter in soul?" (3:20). The question functions philosophically. It serves as an expression of grief rather than a quest for explanation. 3:23 describes the sufferer as one "whom God has fenced in," presenting an ironic contrast to the "fence" of God's protection to Job in 1:10. In both cases, God constructed the fence. The pun in 3:23 implies the radical notion of removal of both God's protection and his affliction. Such godforsakenness for the ancient Hebrew can only represent death. Job may seem to express agnostic ideas, but his world of thought could not allow such an option.

Patient Sufferer. The seventh portrayal of Job combines his patient experience of suffering with a tendency to speak as an indignant spokesperson for justice. According to this perspective, Job honestly expresses the depth of his struggle without a direct challenge to God. Job's willingness to endure pain without "rash words" (at times) provides a basis for the common expression, "the patience of Job." Those who read the book of Job tropologically (for moral instruction) use it to encourage patience during oppression. Most often the sufferer saw the oppression as originating at the hands of humans rather than God. Job's challenge questions the ultimate justice of God's retribution. Persons of faith seldom voice this challenge. Job remained patient through the loss of goods and kin as well as during a seven-day period of mourning (2:13). He lost patience when he perceived his troubles as a careless act of God. Consequently, Job rarely made reasoned statements like 1:21 and 2:10 in his soliloquies. His words to friends and God seethe with anger:

> Then Job answered: "O that my vexation were weighed, and all my calamity laid in the balances! For then it would be heavier than the sand of the sea; therefore my words have been rash. For the arrows of the Almighty are in me; my spirit drinks their poison; the terrors of God are arrayed against me." (Job 6:1–4)

Blind Sinner. From the standpoint of his three comforters and Elihu, Job appears a sinner blind to grave personal faults:

> Then Zophar the Naamathite answered: "Should a multitude of words go unanswered, and should one full of talk be vindicated? Should your babble put others to silence, and when you mock, shall no one shame you? For you say, 'My conduct is pure, and I am clean in God's sight.' But oh, that God would speak, and open his lips to you, and that he would tell you the secrets of wisdom! For wisdom is many-sided. Know then that God exacts of you less than your guilt deserves." (Job 11:1–6)

This eighth perspective on Job occurs throughout their speeches. It appears in the first reply of each individual (Eliphaz, chaps. 4–5; Bildad, chap. 8; and Zophar, chap. 11). Job himself expresses the view in the negative during his reply to Eliphaz (6:24–30): "'But now, be pleased to look at me; for I will not lie to your face. Turn, I pray, let no wrong be done. Turn now, my vindication is at stake. Is there any wrong on my tongue? Cannot my taste discern calamity?'" (6:28-30). Job maintains his innocence. His requests for God to show him his errors typically indicate defiance rather than openness to accusation.

All the characters except Job express reluctance to question the straightforward view of retribution. Yet when God appears to Job, he does not accuse him of error as the root of his suffering. God's judgment against Job centers on Job's arrogance in questioning God. Nothing in the book conflicts with the presentation of Job's ordeal in chapter 1 as a test rather than punishment. Only the human characters assail Job's reputation. From the perspective of the deity Job remains the flawless character of 1:1, except that he overreached his own authority. He overstated his innocence by mounting an attack on divine justice. Only God's special prerogatives prevent complete absolution on the basis that Job's innocent suffering provoked his harsh words.

In short, if Job's human accusers correctly assess Job's error, Job's suffering loses the special, exceptional character which enables the reader to identify with Job. Humans rarely consider themselves deserving of suffering. Job suggests, in some cases at least, they are right.

Investigator of Good and Evil. The ninth and final presentation of Job's identity occurs in chapter 7:

> "Do not human beings have a hard service on earth, and are not their days like the days of a laborer? Like a slave who longs for the shadow, and like laborers who look for their wages, so I am allotted months of emptiness, and nights of misery are apportioned to me. When I lie down I say, 'When shall I rise?' But the night is long, and I am full of tossing until dawn. My flesh is clothed with worms and dirt; my skin hardens, then breaks out again. My days are swifter than a weaver's shuttle, and come to their end without hope." (Job 7:1–6)

Here Job serves as the investigator of good and evil in God's world. He reports pessimistic findings, but also assumes a normative "good life" as an archetype opposed to his personal experience. Except for the specifics of his condition, Job's words again express the discomfort and frustration of any individual facing irresolvable torment: "What are human beings that you make so much of them, that you set your mind on them, visit them every morning, test them every moment?" (7:17–18). Clearly, the physical torture affected Job's mental state so that Job viewed existence itself antagonistically. A bias against the "torture" of life characterizes the investigator's perspective. The reader cannot accept this as the final comment on experience in the world. The sufferer, on the other hand, readily identifies with Job's anger and frustration. Often, God appears equally cruel to the disoriented victim of pain.

A review of these perspectives on the character Job reveals some inconsistency and inaccuracy. From the standpoint of the contemporary sufferer, the "guinea pig" model contains least appeal. The more we rely on this model of Job, the more we remove his ordeal from our perceptions of lived experience. The view of Job as a sinner receiving due retribution possesses the same flaw. In both cases, God "selects" a target and heaps abuse on that person. An individual's theology may lead that person to understand God as the source for suffering. Most persons do not perceive a test or punishment as the cause of suffering. Perhaps the broadest portrait of Job results from a consideration of the character as universal sufferer. In every respect, Job responds to his difficulty in human fashion. In spite of his high standards of conduct, he never appears stronger or wiser than is common to humans in general. Like all sufferers, Job's experience led him toward philosophical outlooks and theological answers (or at least questions). Like all subjects of distress, Job remained unable to achieve a single clear understanding of the cause or the meaning of his illness.

The Structure and Meaning of Job

In general outline, the Book of Job displays recognizable, if not uniform, patterns of organization. Thematically, the book contains little sequential movement, though Job's experience manifests a beginning, middle, and end. The prose prologue and epilogue provide a historical framework for the poetic body of the book. Otherwise the book shows an arrangement that is philosophical and repetitive rather than sequential. The only "historical" developments within the poetry enter with the appearance of God. This includes the displacement of Zophar's third speech with Elihu's speech (32:6–37:24), the theophany (38:1–41:34), and Job's responses to God's appearance (40:3–5; 42:1–6). In spite of the lack of historical development in the poetry, the book as a whole shows significant literary development.

The prose opening introduces the reader to the divine experiment concocted as a test of Job's character. The narrative moves to Job's complaint, which begins after seven days of silence (2:13), possibly a means of indicating the conventional period of mourning. Job's grief continues to build, and his friends' replies are in part an attempt to silence Job's extended complaint. Their concern for propriety outweighs their sympathy for Job. When Job describes them as "miserable comforters" (16:2), the reader tends to agree. God's appearance (chaps. 38–41) ends Job's ordeal, but without final answers. The ending represents more of a literary climax than a solution to Job's crisis and questions. By contrast, the prose which ends the work (chap. 42) leaves no sense of the mystery or riddle which Job's philosophical and theological probings introduced. Instead, the test begun in the introductory prose concludes with a neat, tidy finish, interpreting Job's history in comedic fashion. The prose conclusion scarcely deals with the issues raised by Job's radical challenge. It confirms the orthodox view of retribution which the sufferer Job cannot accept. If this were intended as the resolution of the matter (a "happily ever after" interpretation), one would expect the affirmation of the doctrine of retribution to originate with God's direct reply to Job. In fact the theory of retribution remains conspicuous by its absence in the report of God's words to Job.[4]

Job's Comforters

Since the bulk of the message of Job comes from the poetry in 3:2–42:6, attention centers on the content of these chapters. Before considering the statements of Job himself, the specific reactions of Eliphaz, Bildad, and Zophar demand attention. The three characters do not seem to evince separate, distinct personalities.[5] The content of their two or three speeches appears such that without the introduction to their orations the reader could not determine the identity of the speaker.

Eliphaz begins by politely requesting the opportunity to answer Job. He resorts to his personal religious experience as confirmation of the doctrine of retribution. He challenges Job to accept God's reproof as a beneficial thing (chaps 4–5). In chapter 15, Eliphaz bluntly accuses Job of blasphemous talk, identifying Job as primarily a sinner. In chapter 23 he issues a strong appeal to Job to repent. The speech employs reasoned rhetoric rather than harsh judgmentalism.

Bildad initiates his response with a warning to Job to watch his words (8:2). He expresses some hope that Job's end may yet be quite prosperous (8:7). To receive such a resolution, Job must patiently accept his lot. In his second reply Bildad issues direct accusations: only the wicked suffer. A reference to skin disease (18:13) implies Job lives among their number. Bildad issues the briefest speech of the book in his third speech (chap. 25). It also contains the most philosophical argument: Job's goodness notwithstanding, how can a mortal appear righteous to God? This represents a slight variation of the retribution motif: Human distance from the omnipotence of the Almighty makes humans evil by comparison. This takes the emphasis off the specific conduct (good or evil) of Job. So, Job's difficulties relate to the human condition rather than Job's transgressions. Even a perfect person like Job remains imperfect before God. Based on this theology, God rests under no obligation to reveal his decisions to humans, as Job requests.

Zophar observes that Job knows nothing about the subject he discusses (11:2–3). Zophar suggests a mysterious principle of wisdom by which God regulates the suffering of humans according to their deserts. Zophar's

---

4. Several scholars "historicized" the person of Job. They viewed him as a prince or king who lost his power as a result of some socio-political change. See, for example, Leo G. Perdue, "Cosmology and the Social Order in the Wisdom Tradition" in *SIANE*, 475–78. Strong support for this interpretation occurs in Job's final defense (chaps. 29–31). Despite the reference to princes and nobles in 29:9–10, nothing in the unit necessitates this interpretation. Job's sense of indignance and his perception of limited futility would relate equally well to his identity as a noted patriarch or as a recognized practitioner of clan wisdom. Mention of Job's place among the elders at the city gate (29:7) allows several explanations for his influence. These suggestions do not identify the historical figure, Job. Instead, they interpret his characterization by the author or editor of the written work.

5. For attempts to characterize the friends, see Robert Gordis, *The Book of God and Man: A Study of Job* (Chicago: The University of Chicago Press, 1965), 76–92, 286–87.

attempts to speak provocatively regarding the essence of wisdom actually appear silly. In chapter 11 he uses wisdom as a catchall category which accounts for human ignorance through an appeal to divine mystery. Such a view ignored Job's undeniable conflict. Zophar's second and final discourse (chap. 20) concerns the fate of the wicked. It also bears little direct relationship to Job's struggle. Again, Zophar remains notoriously blind to the injustice Job perceives. Zophar implies Job's suffering will be shown to be deserved in the end.

Job's Speeches

Job's defense runs in two directions: replies to the responses of his friends, and words toward God. Simply put, Job holds a low opinion of the suggestions and theology of his comforters. In effect, Job's comforters add to his misery. He replies sarcastically in 12:2–3a: "'No doubt you are the people, and wisdom will die with you. But I have understanding as well as you; I am not inferior to you.'" Job observes workings of God just as his friends do. Job's request of God in chapter 13 relies on his understanding that all human fortunes come from God. In 13:1–7 he refers to his friends' arguments as "lies." Job names them "miserable comforters" in 16:2. He accuses them of offering meaningless comfort which ignores his suffering. Job's words drip with irony in his reply to Bildad in 26:2–4: "'How you have helped one who has no power! How you have assisted the arm that has no strength! How you have counseled one who has no wisdom, and given much good advice! With whose help have you uttered words, and whose spirit has come forth from you?'"

Not much of Job's speech concerns the three men. By far, the bulk of Job's dialogue in the poetry consists of treatises regarding God's activity offered for the friends' consideration. When Job alluded to the comforters in his orations, he spoke to them as a group rather than responding specifically to the previous speaker. He primarily responds to the ideas they present rather than attempting to satisfy their arguments. The reply to Bildad in 26:2–4 presents the only exception and may mark a turning point or key section of the book. His associates form an audience for Job's complaint and philosophy as well as providing an interchange of ideas.

Before this audience, Job addresses a few challenges directly to God. In general, Job speaks of God from a third person perspective. Job challenges the fairness of God's treatment. He asks for an audience with God so he can defend his innocence (13:20–24). Such direct contact with God requires special license (13:20–21), lest God destroy Job at his appearance. Further questioning appears in the form of a hymn to mortality (chap. 14). The poem mixes lament for the finality of death with a brief speculation on immortality or resurrection (vv. 14–17). Job's direct address to God (v. 3) forms the backdrop by raising the issue of why God would level judgment against such a frail and transitory creature. His claim, "there is no justice" (19:7), serves as an assault on God's rule. He clearly believes the doctrine of

retribution is not borne out in his own experience or in the fortunes of the
wicked (21:7–34). His strongest statement in this regard comes in 24:21–22
when he claims those who abuse power do so by divine sanction. Weak sentiment for just retribution follows (24:24–25), but in the form of the necessity of time which limits good works as well: "'They are exalted a little while,
and then are gone; they wither and fade like the mallow; they are cut off like
the heads of grain'" (v. 24). This view of time's limitation shows similarity to
one of the frequent observations in Ecclesiastes.[6]

The hymn to wisdom in chapter 28 stands out as the most unique unit
of the book. It interrupts the speeches of Job which precede and follow it
and appears more liturgical than the remainder of the book. The philosophical interest of the poem, the nature of wisdom, receives little treatment elsewhere in Job.[7] The book does assume the truth of the poem's
conclusion, "The fear of the Lord is wisdom." The hymn appears between
Job's most enthusiastic defense of the eventual punishment of the wicked
(chap. 27) and Job's reminiscence of his former reputation (chap. 29). The
hymn presents the basic premise that wisdom resides with God, remaining
mysterious and somewhat inaccessible to humans. The movement of the
poem attracts attention as the most notable rhetorical feature. The speaker
searched high and low for wisdom. In the course of the search the speaker
explored nature's wonders—beauty, mystery, wealth—but wisdom did not
reside in any of these. Such investigations form a significant branch of the
activity of the wise person: the quest itself falls under the rubric of wisdom.
The essence of wisdom, however, resides beyond the scope of human
inquiry. Humans gain access by relationship to God evidenced in proper
behavior (another referent of "wisdom"): "And he said to humankind,
'Truly, the fear of the Lord, that is wisdom; and to depart from evil is understanding'" (28:28).

Portions of Job's discourse are "personal complaints," expressing his
most personal concerns. He laments his estrangement from friends and
family due to his physical appearance and their unexplained contempt.
Chapter 29 expressed his longing for his former status. Job presents this
desire in nostalgic terms and in strong contrast to his pitiful, present experience. The reader here encounters one of the most moving accounts of
the book. Even the disreputable spurn Job (30:3–10). This viewpoint on
Job's experience illustrates his dramatic fall from prominence in his community. Another portion of Job's speeches expresses his innocence in the
interest of self-defense. His high theology remains a liability throughout his
ordeal. For example, in 9:1–20, he details his reluctance to question God in
spite of his innocence. The figure leaves the impression of one whose

---

6. See the review of that book below.
7. For this reason, as well as its special style and vocabulary, critical scholars generally consider it a late addition to the previously completed story of Job. See the discussion by John E.
Hartley, *The Book of Job*, NICOT (Grand Rapids: Eerdmans, 1988), 26–27. Compare the discussion of the composition of Job by Francis I. Andersen, *Job*, TOTC (Leicester: Inter-Varsity Press,
1976), 41–55.

intense suffering pushes him beyond the bounds of proper theology. From another perspective, when faced with the choice to suffer as a sinner or to sin by attacking God, Job chooses the latter. Job's crisis of faith appears in simple terms in 10:2–13:

> "I will say to God, Do not condemn me; let me know why you contend against me. Does it seem good to you to oppress, to despise the work of your hands and favor the schemes of the wicked? Do you have eyes of flesh? Do you see as humans see? Are your days like the days of mortals, or your years like human years, that you seek out my iniquity and search for my sin, although you know that I am not guilty, and there is no one to deliver out of your hand? Your hands fashioned and made me; and now you turn and destroy me. Remember that you fashioned me like clay; and will you turn me to dust again? Did you not pour me out like milk and curdle me like cheese? You clothed me with skin and flesh, and knit me together with bones and sinews. You have granted me life and steadfast love, and your care has preserved my spirit. Yet these things you hid in your heart; I know that this was your purpose."

Recognizing that God directs his fortunes, Job understands his present situation as the divine will. He also sees himself unworthy of such treatment. Why would Yahweh turn against his own creation (vv. 3, 8)?

Job prepares his case in 13:13–18:

> "Let me have silence, and I will speak, and let come on me what may. I will take my flesh in my teeth, and put my life in my hand. See, he will kill me; I have no hope; but I will defend my ways to his face. This will be my salvation, that the godless shall not come before him. Listen carefully to my words, and let my declaration be in your ears. I have indeed prepared my case; know that I shall be vindicated."

Job expected his moral lifestyle, the expression of his commitment to God, to protect him from divine wrath (v. 16). No matter how miserable his situation, he intended to speak with integrity (27:1–6). This included both honest defense of his innocence and the communication of his true feelings to God. In other words, he would not feign guilt in order to escape further torture! Chapter 31 records his final defense of his righteousness. The entire chapter reflects an "if . . . then" curse formula. The curses form an oath of loyalty to Yahweh. After the final apodosis, verse 40 records the following conclusion: "The words of Job are ended."

Throughout his speeches Job offers a limited number of arguments. Primarily, he maintains his innocence and integrity. This premise makes his suffering unexplainable. Consequently, he asks the question most common to sufferers, "Why?" Beyond this, Job's own feelings trouble him. This crisis of confidence compounds his disorientation. He engages in behavior (speech) which he previously condemned as sacrilegious. Words remain the only outlet for Job's anger, frustration, and sense of injustice. He repeatedly directs strong appeals to God, notably (1) "kill me," (2) "leave me alone," (3) "tell me my sin," and (4) "grant me a hearing." As seen in the following, God's reaction falls under the final appeal. God's response offers less than the hearing and more than the judgment Job requested.

Elihu

God's appearance to Job contains a prologue in the speech of Elihu (chaps. 32–37). Elihu is angry because Job spent his efforts defending himself rather than God's justice (32:2). He expresses a piety that demands the defense of God at the expense of absolute denial of personal experience. Elihu's youth reveals itself in the enthusiasm and extremism of the speech. The editor or author of the book presents Elihu's words as a serious advance of the argument. His name, "He is my God," leads to a special identification of the character with God. The names of Eliphaz, Bildad, and Zophar express no such associations. Elihu maintained God had spoken through Job's suffering. Job refused the divine communication indicating he had sinned (33:12–28). Elihu presented a rather enigmatic picture of a redeemer who paid a ransom to deliver such a sufferer as Job from death (33:23). Elihu imagined that the sufferer redeemed in this way responds with repentance and joy at his undeserved rescue (33:26–27). Elihu also claimed that God remains detached from human activity (35:3–8). According to Elihu, Job's quest for justice became an unhealthy obsession (36:15–23). He warned against several pitfalls of this intense preoccupation with fairness. Instead, Elihu suggested Job consider the creation to gain a sense of proper perspective (36:24–37:24). The description of God's activity leads into the emphasis on the created world in the following theophany. Job took a similar tone when he contemplated his challenge of God's justice in 9:5–13. The storyteller has carefully woven the account of Elihu's intervention into the storyline of Job's experience. Elihu's speech performs two important functions. First, it serves as a fitting conclusion to the debate between Job and his friends. Second, it supplies a transition to God's appearance, anticipating the content of God's rebuke of Job.[8]

The Theophany of Chapters 38–41

Reading the appearance of God (chaps. 38–41) as the resolution of the book rests on three principal factors. First of all, in this section, God speaks. The book repeatedly accords the highest respect to his authority. Second, through his appearance God responds to Job's request for a hearing. Third, the appearance effectively ends the book.

The theophany employs images of natural phenomena, maintaining the book's interest in human experience. The blunt interrogation of Job—

---

8. Many commentators consider the Elihu speeches as a secondary literary addition to the book. The absence of mention of Elihu in the epilogue (42:7–9) presents the strongest evidence for the secondary nature of the Elihu account. Most likely, the compiler, whether early or late, intended to depict Elihu's statements as typologically equivalent to those of the deity (38:1–41:34). For this reason the editor offered no further comment on Elihu. See the discussion of Hartley, *The Book of Job*, 28–30.

"Can you do what God can do?"—provides the format for a review of the wonders of creation and the natural elements. Chapter 38 considers the layout of the cosmos itself. 38:39–39:30 concentrates on animals, including lions, mountain goats, wild asses, wild oxen, ostriches, horses, hawks, and eagles. Job's first reply appears in the form of a pitiful apology (40:3–5) in which Job admits he overstepped his authority. When God again spoke "out of the whirlwind" (38:1; 40:6), he turned the tables on Job. Job no longer questioned God regarding things he did not understand. Instead, God questioned Job. Through his questions he proved Job's inferior status. His inferiority to God allowed him no basis for challenges. The divine speech portrays God's personal activity:

> See, the Lord GOD comes with might, and his arm rules for him; his reward is with him, and his recompense before him. He will feed his flock like a shepherd; he will gather the lambs in his arms and carry them in his bosom, and gently lead the mother sheep. Who has measured the waters in the hollow of his hand and marked off the heavens with a span, enclosed the dust of the earth in a measure, and weighed the mountains in scales and the hills in a balance? Who has directed the spirit of the LORD, or as his counselor has instructed him? Whom did he consult for his enlightenment, and who taught him the path of justice? Who taught him knowledge, and showed him the way of understanding? (Isa. 40:10–14)

Job recognized God's transcendence and the inscrutability of his acts. He confessed his ignorance, recognizing that he responded to situations beyond his limited understanding. In 42:3–4 Job mimicked God's rebuke while offering contrition. Verse 5 presents both the resolution to the book and Job's advantage over his three friends: "'I had heard of you by the hearing of the ear, but now my eye sees you" (v. 5). The difference between "hearing" and "seeing" corresponds to the difference between theology and revelation, or encounter. Perhaps "seeing" describes experience. From his experience (both the suffering and God's appearance) Job gained the illusive quality—wisdom. At this point in the narrative Job achieves a degree of satisfaction. He receives no answer to his questions. God does not vindicate his righteousness. God does grant Job an answer to one of his requests—he gains a direct audience with God. We can judge Job satisfied in that he ceases to challenge God and affirms the truth of God's claims. Admittedly, at this point a limited number of options remain open to Job. Yet Job's answers to God indicate passive submission rather than subjection under pressure. In other words, Job chose to end his rebellion. His repentance implied support for God's position, expressed in the theophany.

Structure and Meaning

The Book of Job interests us as a story of human struggle with which we can all identify. It also gives theological insights into those human struggles that help us through life's difficulties. No descriptive understanding of suffering offers help to Job. To the contrary, Job's experience created unsolved problems. In this respect, the content of the Book of Job shows a more realistic tone (less idealistic) than the content of the Book of Proverbs. Proverbs presents an entirely predictable view of God. Such tidy theology involves a small degree of manipulation: God must   reward righteousness and punish evil. The view of God presented in Job grants priority to God's self–determinism. God possesses an unquestionable right to pursue his plans without making them understandable according to human logic. Job reached peace with his experience through a transcendent encounter with the deity. God did not satisfy Job's reason. In this way the book emphasizes human experience above theological answer-making. Job recognizes silent endurance as the way through certain problems (such as suffering). No immediate explanation makes suffering understandable. Perhaps sufferers show more awareness of the existence and operations of God because of such uncertainty.

Job's words end with repentance (42:6). Only the poetic portion of the book includes Job's repentance. Yet the narrative of the prose epilogue affirms Job's statements as "right" (42:7). The reader expects such conventional responses as contrition in the more orthodox prose sections. The poetry elsewhere challenges the theology of retribution. Reading the prose and poetic conclusions together, a related discrepancy appears. If Job has "spoken rightly" (42:7), why should he also repent (42:6) in this brief span of verses? Perhaps the phrases relate to two different referents: Job repented of his challenges to God but correctly challenged the traditional view of retribution. Two factors deny this interpretation. First, Job's own experience in 42:10–17 confirms the doctrine of retribution. This experience, like the affirmation of 42:7, appears in the prose. Second, the passage does not include or imply any discrimination between the causes for the affirmation and the repentance. This suggests Job receives rebuke and affirmation for the same speech. Job does "right" by relating to the deity on the basis of honesty and directness. He overstepped the limits of his createdness by boldly accusing God of wrong. In spite of Job's angry tone, the reader perceives Job's experience as worth the risk. In contrast, the three friends spout traditional views. To the reader they appear no more authentic than pull-string dolls. Job's urgent personal experience led him to challenge his inherited religious traditions.

Job expressed a special understanding of the randomness of human fortunes. Combined with views of the inscrutability of God's actions, this understanding promoted an innovative theology. In part, Job dissolves the taboo regarding anger toward the deity. Job would not curse God, but spoke to him with force and directness. His speeches to God expressed everything short of the denial of God's authority. Job's words raise challenges to conventional theology. He presents an effective argument for readers to ponder. The reader of Job learns to challenge conventional theology when personal experience denies its truth.

Summary: The Literary Structure of Job[9]

The Book of Job displays the character of a wisdom tale. The more philosophical dialogues of the poetry fit within the narrative account of Job's life. They provide a more detailed account of a portion of Job's experience. The book's programmatic arrangement reveals an intense preoccupation with its themes. The book presents its truths, "just so." Unlike other wisdom books, Job contains no breaks in synchronicity from beginning to end. The recorders of both the prose and the drama maintained consistency by presenting the issues with no breaks from the storyline.

The exchange of speeches exhibits the most polished debate style in the Hebrew Bible. Whether or not Israel's sages commonly employed this mode of reasoned argument, it closely conforms to the current understanding of wisdom dialogue. A literary presentation of such a philosophical debate designed according to contemporary conventions would exhibit some differences. Current expectations would favor a progressive development of the argument, reserving Job's strongest challenges, harshest words, and most skeptical conclusions for the climax or end of the debate. The Book of Job evidences much more concern for formal order than for order of content.

This characteristic applies to the bulk of biblical wisdom. Previous discussion in this chapter reviewed most of the thematic clues to the identity of Job as wisdom. Job challenges then current wisdom understandings, resulting in a new manner of understanding. From this perspective the critique of the conventional view of retribution serves as a paradigm. Job compares other views of reality to this one, based on the evidence of human experience. In Job, human experience takes priority over theological defenses of God's justice. Biblical wisdom developed such a view subsequent to the emphasis on proverbial instruction. Job presents an anti-theme rather than a theme. Job challenged wisdom. He concurrently added to it. The theophany, which presents the resolution of the book, adds little to the revelation of wisdom. Instead, it repeats the age-old theme of creation as the capstone of God's wisdom. Through this theme it emphasizes human resignation in the face of the mystery of creation. To counter Job's doubt, the work resorts to a timeless and unquestionable certainty. Job's "new" questions receive an ancient, if inconclusive, answer.

Job's canonical shape reveals limited clues regarding its status as wisdom. The themes contained in the prose and those contained in the poetry show much interdependence. For this reason, the critic cannot successfully interpret one as the canonical shaping of the other. The addition of the wisdom poem of chapter 28 would give evidence a later reader or group of readers understood wisdom as an integral theme of the work. Chapter 28 yields equally strong evidence for the wisdom connections of the book when

---

9. See the commentary and outline by Robert L. Alden, *Job*, NAC 11 (Nashville: Broadman and Holman Publishers, 1993); compare Hartley, *The Book of Job*, 35–43.

considered as original to the tale. Contemporary readers of Job show a preference for the ordered prose story in isolation from the more subjective poetry. This results from a tendency to interpret the story in accord with a more simplistic view of the relation between wisdom and retribution. Ironically, such a view reproduces the preference for a straightforward theology of reward and punishment which Job's experience calls into doubt. Such responses arise because, according to most standards, Job's recognition of the unpredictable nature of human fortunes does not provide a helpful model for moral instruction. Accordingly, popular memory of Job associates him with "patience" or his eventual reward rather than his anger and doubts. From either angle, the figure Job maintains a definite affiliation with wisdom and challenges the too-easy traditional assumptions of each generation.

Questions for Discussion

1. Describe the character of Job from nine distinct viewpoints. Which one do you think best describes Job? Why?

2. Compare and contrast the understanding of retribution in Job and in Proverbs. Describe your own understanding of why and how God rewards and punishes you.

3. What role does repentance play in Job? What distinctive traits does this add to your understanding of the relationship between you and God?

4. What role does the theophany play in the structure of the Book of Job. What role do Job's comforters play in the structure of the book?

Chapter 8

Wisdom in Ecclesiastes

Introduction to Ecclesiastes

Ecclesiastes' wisdom features include the identification of its author as Solomon (1:1), the wise king (2:12). The nature of the investigation—the study of all human activity—also belongs to wisdom and reflects wisdom's intense preoccupation with human conduct and its ironic twists. The repeated emphasis upon the wisdom of the speaker and the interest displayed in the discovery of wisdom offer the strongest evidence of the book's wisdom connections. This involves vocabulary common to wisdom. It also incorporates wisdom's inherent goal of "finding things out."

Even a casual reading of Ecclesiastes reveals numerous proverbs and proverbial formulae. These indicate that the document addresses an audience familiar with proverbial instruction. Along with this, much of the message of the book parallels perspectives advanced in the Book of Proverbs. These include: (1) the embracing of opposing truths, (2) leaving outcomes to God, (3) the limitations of human thinking, (4) the fear of God, (5) a humanistic perspective, and (5) the doctrine of retribution. Advice for the king and his subjects, a common theme in Ecclesiastes, also gains some attention in Proverbs. Ecclesiastes' preoccupation with the ironies of human existence and behavior appears in Proverbs as well. The repeated suggestion that the speaker engaged in a quest for wisdom itself represents Ecclesiastes' most immediate contact with wisdom material.

Ecclesiastes, like Job, questions the justice of life's retribution. Such discussions seem as much a part of the wisdom pursuit as the corresponding endorsement of the rigid view of retribution in Proverbs. The book presents two opposing approaches to life. These exhibit no obvious connection with other Hebrew wisdom. Other wisdom books assume life's meaningfulness. The Hebrew author of Ecclesiastes called Qoheleth (קֹהֶלֶת), "the teacher" or "preacher," sees things from a different perspective. Qoheleth's claim that life is empty (for example, 1:2–11) apparently runs counter to the

157

book's advice to fear God and enjoy life (for example, 2:24–25). The themes themselves offer less difficulty than the apparent contradiction. Wisdom occasionally offers opposing truths, but it does so with proper acknowledgment and consistent advice.

Thematically, biblical wisdom literature shows no parallel to Ecclesiastes' tendency toward hedonism. Wisdom literature more characteristically advises denial of the appetite. Futility, emptiness, and skepticism characterize Qoheleth's approach. These seem irreconcilable with conventional wisdom concerns. The psalms of lament present the nearest parallel to this in biblical literature; yet the psalms of lament always contain a statement of hope or trust. Ecclesiastes substitutes skepticism for this trust.

The first chapter includes a description of the subject and end of Qoheleth's quest (1:12–13a): "I, the Teacher, when king over Israel in Jerusalem, applied my mind to seek and to search out by wisdom all that is done under heaven." The contention that "what a wisdom document looks like when it takes the question of salvation itself as the subject of its investigation can be seen in Ecclesiastes"[1] bears only limited truth. In Ecclesiastes "salvation" involves the expression of all human relations with God. Ecclesiastes addresses questions relating to God's involvement and interest in human affairs. This contrasts with the more specific issues of human standing with God. Qoheleth engaged in the explicitly theological task of discovering the meaning of all the activity on earth. His investigations, as recorded in Ecclesiastes, do not exhaust the subject. He expressed intent to "see what was good for mortals to do under heaven during the few days of their life" (2:3b). His findings remain inconclusive. They assume the form of reductionistic guidelines rather than final answers.

Moral reasoning in Qoheleth is grounded in the desire for "well-being (tôb) in human existence." "Good" for Qoheleth is not a virtue, a successful outcome, or a social sphere of well-being. Rather the only "good" to human beings is joy (simhâ), which may derive from three sources: festive occasions ("eating and drinking"), the intimate relationships with family and friends, and human labor.[2]

Qoheleth's Purpose and Philosophy

The following interpretation of Qoheleth draws distinctions between his purpose (investigation), his philosophy (skepticism), and his ultimate findings (essentialism). His investigation contained several elements. He sought to know wisdom, madness, and folly (1:16–17a; 2:12); he tested pleasure (2:1, 4–10); and he studied justice and wickedness (3:16–17). At points too numerous to mention, he supported his investigations with proverbs (for example, 1:15, 18; 2:14; 4:5–6). The doctrine of retribution appears in

---

1. Gerhard Von Rad, *Old Testament Theology*, trans. D. M. G. Stalker, vol. 1 (New York: Harper & Row, 1962), 435.
2. Leo G. Perdue, "Cosmology and the Social Order in the Wisdom Tradition" in *SIANE*, 472.

1:26 (and elsewhere): "For to the one who pleases him God gives wisdom and knowledge and joy; but to the sinner he gives the work of gathering and heaping, only to give to one who pleases God. This also is vanity and a chasing after wind."

Did Qoheleth intend to "test" this doctrine? Perhaps the closing sentence ("vanity") indicates the knowledge and control of such things lies beyond humans. The verse implies that "pleasing God" results from divine choice rather than human initiative. The previous verse (1:25) interprets the enjoyment of life as a gift of God. This suggests divine favor cannot be courted or ensured. Qoheleth tested the doctrine of retribution and advised the enjoyment of food and work. In effect, he offered the advice, "Enjoy life and don't worry about such things beyond your control."

Qoheleth's Investigations

Qoheleth's investigations result in multiple findings which evade simple description or characterization. Several of his conclusions relate generally to life and death. He concluded that human existence was an "unhappy business" (1:13). In spite of admonitions to enjoy life, he interpreted laughter as madness, and pleasure as useless (2:2). The inevitability of death preoccupied the speaker (2:14b). This involves recognition that the same fate awaits all the living (3:19–20). Consequently, only those who remain alive have hope (9:4–5).

The same work that serves as the outlet for life's enjoyment brings pain and vexation. Qoheleth listed various components of life's unfairness: the oppressed go without comfort (4:1); the poor are forgotten (9:15–16); and persons are honored or humbled inappropriately (10:6–7). This rather unhappy view of life heightens the importance of cooperation: "Two are better than one, because they have a good reward for their toil. For if they fall, one will lift up the other; but woe to one who is alone and falls and does not have another to help. Again, if two lie together, they keep warm; but how can one keep warm alone? And though one might prevail against another, two will withstand one. A threefold cord is not quickly broken" (4:9–12). In addition to cooperation, association with another provides consolation.

The investigations of Ecclesiastes also display a concern for appropriateness, especially with regard to timing. God made everything suitable for its time (3:1). He gave humans a sense of the past and the future (3:11b). The statements regarding time in 3:1–15 culminate in the vague proclamation of verse 15: "That which is, already has been; that which is to be, already is; and God seeks out what has gone by." God's interest in the past may convey the responsibility of persons for their actions. In any case, time and its significance reside with Yahweh rather than humans. The lack of understanding of time and lack of understanding of God's activity serve as components of a marked enigma. Chapter 3 implies the lack of understanding. Chapter 8:6–8 mentions this lack of understanding explicitly. From Qoheleth's perspective most events lie beyond human control. The problem leads to a pronounced theological crisis: "then I saw all the work of God, that no one can find out what is happening under the sun. However much they may toil in seeking, they will not find it out; even though those who are wise claim to know, they cannot find it out" (Eccles. 8:17).

One surprising report from Qoheleth relates to wisdom in terms of the anxiety its pursuit engenders. Wisdom brings "vexation," a word denoting anger or grief (כַּעַס, kā'as): "For in much wisdom is much vexation, and those who increase knowledge increase sorrow" (1:18). This describes one of the repetitive cycles which lead to the conclusion life is empty. The seeker of wisdom repeatedly searches for unattainable answers, which provides the negative effect of increasing distress. Wisdom, the highest goal for humans, yields misery. More common pursuits become more futile by comparison. Qoheleth remains able to affirm, "Wisdom excels folly as light excels darkness" (2:13). The discussion of wisdom in 2:26 implies wisdom pleases God. God grants it as a gift "to the one who pleases him." Wisdom offers decided benefits. Qoheleth communicated these benefits in vague terms with many qualifications. Such reservations regarding wisdom's benefits compounded his sense of frustration.

Qoheleth's study yields inconclusive findings at best (7:23–24). This directs emphasis toward the quest itself rather than any product obtained in the process. One of the conclusions reached communicates an uncompromisable truth underpinning all his findings: "God will bring every deed into judgment, including every secret thing, whether good or evil" (Eccles. 12:14). The pervasiveness of God's judgment relegates Qoheleth's investigations to a relatively minor importance. This leaves the reader in doubt concerning the writer's motivation for the complicated inquiries undertaken. Some readers of Ecclesiastes accept such contradictions as evidence that a later author softened the book's nihilistic tone.[3] A few imaginative critics read the alternating pessimism and hedonism as manifestations of Qoheleth's emotional instability.[4]

Perhaps the author intended to propose a dialectic philosophy. Such a philosophy offered a balance between the poles of sensate experience and abstract reflection on the meaning of human existence. 3:1–8 ("for everything there is a season . . .") may express this view. The direct statement of 3:1–8 involves timeliness or inevitability of certain actions. The poem contains elements of both engagement and reflection in every line. It can be accepted as an encouragement to activity or passivity as the occasion demands.

To provide a well-defined set of the conclusions which Qoheleth drew, the reader must manipulate the text. Honesty demands the recognition that his findings were overwhelmingly negative or inconclusive. A simple restatement of some of his claims illustrates this: Life is empty; human

---

3. For a discussion of the unity of the book, see Duane A. Garrett, *Proverbs, Ecclesiastes, Song of Songs*, NAC 14 (Nashville: Broadman Press, 1993), 267–70.

4. Frank Zimmerman, *The Inner World of Qohelet* (New York: KTAV Publishing House, Inc., 1973), for example, interprets the shifts in mood as neurotic behavior.

understanding is limited; just retribution is not guaranteed; and people must be content with work, pleasure, and faith. The scattered positive statements and scarce allusions to happiness cannot outweigh the skepticism of the book. Those who interpret Ecclesiastes more positively read the invitations to enjoy life as "the last word" of the book. Qoheleth's conclusions run in two directions: (1) he observes the emptiness of life; and (2) he recommends enjoyment as the only plausible course for his readers. Whether the advice to pursue pleasure presents a happy resolution or the last resort of a desperately unhappy person, Ecclesiastes leaves to the discretion of the reader.

Qoheleth's Skepticism

"Skepticism" best designates Qoheleth's philosophy.[5] The speaker's concern with the emptiness of life, more commonly referred to as "vanity," serves as a basis for a complaint regarding the illusive "substance" of life. Following the superscription, the speaker described life as vapor. The unit containing this description of life (1:1–11) introduces all the themes of the work with the exception of injustice. Life not only appears insubstantial, but the Hebrew superlative—"vapor of vapors"—effectively designates the whole of human experience as the least substantial thing imaginable. The reader cannot blunt the nihilism of this expression. The recognition of life's emptiness forms the starting point (and conclusion, 12:8) for all the reflections on life the book contains. Lessening Qoheleth's skepticism constitutes a refusal to enter the argument at the point proposed by the narrator.

Life as Empty. Qoheleth employed the word הֶבֶל (*hebel*) to designate the emptiness of life. The word literally applies to "wind" or "breath." "Vanity" or "vapor" serve as standard translations. The term stands in stark contrast to another word for breath, נֶפֶשׁ (*nepeš*), which constitutes the life of all beings. *Nepeš* issued from God's spirit (or again, "breath") according to Genesis 2:7. To the jaundiced eye of Qoheleth, that which to others seemed invested with God's own life appeared empty or at the least, profitless (v. 3). Ecclesiastes elaborated on the fragile vapor in 1:14: "All is vanity and a chasing after wind." The meaning stands clearer than the precise image. Perhaps the subject of the chase attempts to grasp the morning mist. The image also appears in Hosea 12:1 to indicate the futility of relying on treaties rather than upon Yahweh's help. This provides little indication of its meaning in Ecclesiastes, though both applications emphasize futility. In Ecclesiastes, desperation characterizes all the deeds of humans. Chapter 3 illustrates the emptiness of repetition (vv. 1–8). Qoheleth mentions the lack of innovation as an evil as early as chapter 1 (vv. 4–11). Kings face the predicament that all their innovations exist as variations of a past king's policies (2:12). God consigns such harsh patterns to humans: "I know that whatever God does endures forever; nothing can be added to it, nor anything taken

---

5. Compare Garrett, NAC 14:272.

from it; God has done this, so that all should stand in awe before him. That which is, already has been; that which is to be, already is; and God seeks out what has gone by" (3:14–15).

In all the emphasis on vain repetition the focus rests on human destiny as determined by God. Human determinations bear little impact on life's chain of events. In death humans, as far as they know, meet the same fate as other animals despite claims to the contrary (3:18–21). This observation carries the double-edged effect of devaluing human contributions to the world and increasing the importance of enjoying life's experience.

Three Crises of Meaning. Qoheleth's skepticism stemmed from at least three crises of meaning. First, his ignorance of the ultimate frustrated him. Second, his sense of life's injustice left him puzzling over its implications. Third, his perceived lack of gain generated a good deal of uncertainty regarding the proper course. The trouble with ignorance of the ultimate appears as much more than a flawed personal perspective. What Qoheleth does not know, no human knows, and what's more, God has fixed it that way:

> When I applied my mind to know wisdom, and to see the business that is done on earth, how one's eyes see sleep neither day nor night, then I saw all the work of God, that no one can find out what is happening under the sun. However much they may toil in seeking, they will not find it out; even though those who are wise claim to know, they cannot find it out. All this I laid to heart, examining it all, how the righteous and the wise and their deeds are in the hand of God; whether it is love or hate one does not know. (Eccles. 8:16–9:1)

This contains at least a suggestion that God's purposes in withholding such information are less than beneficial (9:1). The key concept remains— "We do not know."

Humans manifest a similar ignorance of time as indicated in the comments following the poem of 3:2–8: "He has made everything suitable for its time; moreover he has put a sense of past and future into their minds, yet they cannot find out what God has done from the beginning to the end" (3:11). Similarly, 6:10–12 and 8:7–8 indicate that humans possess a sense of past and future, but no elemental understanding of time. "Just as you do not know how the breath comes to the bones in a mother's womb, so you do not know the work of God, who makes everything," Qoheleth claims in 11:5. Ignorance of time represents the larger ignorance regarding all of God's purposes. According to 7:23–29, Qoheleth discovered the truth about women, even a limited truth regarding human behavior (v. 29), but finally wisdom remained "far off, and deep, very deep" (v. 24). Ultimately, he could identify folly (v. 25), but the avoidance of folly stood as the only achievement approximating wisdom. Time served as a fitting symbol of the slippery grasp for meaning. Like the concept "God's will," it existed as a constant which persons must accept but can never manipulate or define.

Qoheleth's sense of injustice reveals a commitment to an ideal of freedom from oppression and injustice for all persons. When authority makes way for injury (8:9), Qoheleth must admit that the king does what pleases him (8:3). Wickedness encroaches upon territory which properly belongs to justice and right (3:16). In addition to this unjust legal system, the speaker noted the frequency of oppression. In spite of God's demands to the contrary, no one comforts the oppressed (4:1). His sense of injustice also accounted for unpredictable loss which leaves children destitute. He implied that such an end faces everyone at death (5:13-17).

Qoheleth affirmed the conventional view of retribution in 8:11-13. He understood the delay of reward or punishment as a significant contributor to injustices of humans to humans. He did not question God's control of retribution, but expressed dismay at apparent inequities. The tendency to question God's existence or control of experience which appears so commonly in current response to evil and suffering never occurs to Ecclesiastes.

The lack of gain Qoheleth perceives provides one clear example of the intent of the word *vanity*. When he considered the work expended in the pursuit of wisdom, it appeared wasted (2:11), and pleasure, like work, seemed a useless investment (2:2). He accepts these negative results as indicative of the human condition (1:3; 3:9). In these verses he asks the question, "What gain . . . ?" The word יִתְרוֹן (*yitrōn*) applies to the profit made in business ventures. In these verses it refers to existential economics rather than finance. If no "good" comes from persons' attempts to better themselves, how can humans consider any activity meaningful?

Fatalism. Behind all of Qoheleth's pessimism rested a fatalism that read life's ambiguity as divinely predetermined. "God has done this," he claims, "so that all should stand in awe before him" (3:14). The pitiful human cannot tell whether "it is love or hate" (9:1). All persons return to the dust (3:20). Ultimately all forget even the most grand individual achievements (9:15). The good and and the evil alike face the annihilation of death (9:2-3). "Again I saw that under the sun the race is not to the swift, nor the battle to the strong, nor bread to the wise, nor riches to the intelligent, nor favor to the skillful; but time and chance happen to them all. For no one can anticipate the time of disaster. Like fish taken in a cruel net, and like birds caught in a snare, so mortals are snared at a time of calamity, when it suddenly falls upon them" (9:11-12). Such perceptions doubtlessly led to Qoheleth's confession, "So I hated life" (2:17). Like Job, he surmised that the dead or unborn enjoy a happier fortune than the living because of the evils they must face (4:2-3). This despondency also provided the motivation for the encouragement to enjoy life while young (11:9-12:7). As with every facet of the book's cynical probings, the reader searches in vain for a summary resolution of any type, least of all a comedic one.

Irony of Divine Order. The skeptical tone of the narrator is commonly expressed through ironical *mĕšalim* and aphorisms. Irony characteristically occurs throughout the Book of Proverbs. In Proverbs the irony normally relates to the quizzical behavior of persons. In Ecclesiastes the irony at times

refers to life's inevitabilities. Qoheleth finds irony both directly and indirectly in the divine order. The notice of irony threatens the integrity of
Qoheleth's entire enterprise. Even wisdom, the basis of his experiment,
remains open to irony's ridicule: "For in much wisdom is much vexation,
and those who increase knowledge increase sorrow" (1:18). Preceding paragraphs of this work discuss the absurdity of death as the common fate of all
(as in 2:14–23). In addition, the human perception of time bears an ironic
relation to humans' inability to achieve final understandings of the past and
future (3:11, 15).

Qoheleth disappoints the reader expecting more positive statements
regarding morality. Envy motivates the person who works conscientiously
and successfully (4:4). The populace denies the regard due a just king when
that king is young and poor (4:13–15). Other explicitly ironic statements
include:

5:10   The lover of money is never satisfied with money.

5:11   Consumers increase in proportion to increase in wealth.

5:12   The laborer's sleep is sweet.

6:7–9   The appetite is never satisfied.

8:10   The wicked are praised at death.

8:14   The righteous are treated as wicked and vice versa.

10:5–7 Folly appears in high places.

Qoheleth's Findings

The foregoing discussion of Qoheleth's purpose and philosophy by
necessity emphasizes the skeptical nature of his task. The analysis of his ultimate findings reveals some amazingly optimistic and somewhat epicurean
suggestions. Qoheleth does not act as a hedonist or a *bon vivant.* His interest
lies in discovering the minimal response to an unpredictable world.
Qoheleth earns the label, "essentialist." His recommendations for life
answer the question: When one strips life of all sham and notes its mysteries
and inconsistencies, what is left? The Book of Ecclesiastes answers the question with some intermediate suggestions. These represent temporary
responses rather than solutions. The vanity of life makes death a blessing
(4:2–3), but one course for the living involves temperance in all vocations:
"Do not be too righteous, and do not act too wise; why should you destroy
yourself? Do not be too wicked, and do not be a fool; why should you die
before your time? It is good that you should take hold of the one, without
letting go of the other; for the one who fears God shall succeed with both"
(7:16–18).

Enjoy Life

The advice to enjoy youth (11:9–12:7) also serves as a medial response to the ambiguity of life. Qoheleth surely finds some comfort in the knowledge that fools as well as the wise face vanity. Perhaps the fool encounters even greater vanity (2:26). Qoheleth's advice on behavior in the presence of the king reflects a basic premise of his entire program: "Calmness will undo great offenses" (10:4).

In spite of the vanity of life, Qoheleth urges readers to live with discretion. He presents some things as "better than" others. This common proverbial formula recurs in 7:1–5:

> A good name is better than precious ointment, and the day of death, than the day of birth. It is better to go to the house of mourning than to go to the house of feasting; for this is the end of everyone, and the living will lay it to heart. Sorrow is better than laughter, for by sadness of countenance the heart is made glad. The heart of the wise is in the house of mourning; but the heart of fools is in the house of mirth. It is better to hear the rebuke of the wise than to hear the song of fools.

The rather morbid propositions communicate unexpected results not unlike the Beatitudes (Matt. 5:3–12). Other comparatives suggest: two are better than one (4:9–12); a poor wise youth is better than an old foolish king (4:13); sincere listening is better than the sacrifice of fools (5:1); not to vow is better than not to fulfil a vow (5:5); looking is better than desiring (6:9); patience is better than rashness (7:8); a living dog is better than a dead lion (9:4); and one handful with quietness is better than two handfuls with worry.

In spite of suggestions like the above which fit so well within the pattern of traditional wisdom, Qoheleth's suspicion casts doubts on the entire enterprise: "The more words, the more vanity, so how is one the better? For who knows what is good for mortals while they live the few days of their vain life, which they pass like a shadow? For who can tell them what will be after them under the sun?" (6:11–12). Amid all uncertainties the narrator remained soundly committed to three "goods." First, he affirmed the religious impulse, never questioning the admonition to "fear God." Second, in spite of rare challenges, the book maintains confidence in wisdom. Wisdom alone offers promise for the achievement of meaningful experience. Third, the admission of life's emptiness leads to periodic encouragements to eat, drink, and find enjoyment in work.

Retribution

Despite the relentless challenge to the doctrine of just retribution, 8:12–13 offers a classic restatement of the dogma: "Though sinners do evil a hundred times and prolong their lives, yet I know that it will be well with those who fear God, because they stand in fear before him, but it will not be well with the wicked, neither will they prolong their days like a shadow, because they do not stand in fear before God." Much like the speeches of Job's comforters, this passage considers the prosperity of the wicked as mere appearance. Their eventual downfall will negate their supposed advantage. Improved fortunes will vindicate the righteous. For Qoheleth, "fear of the Lord" also implied submission to the inevitabilities which God mysteriously controls. In itself, this belongs in a wisdom document. In view of the fatalism of the speaker in Ecclesiastes, however, submission to God's control assumed the harshness of the protestant doctrine of double predestination. The conclusion of the book issues a statement consistent with the stern view of the divine will: "The end of the matter; all has been heard. Fear God, and keep his commandments; for that is the whole duty of everyone. For God will bring every deed into judgment, including every secret thing, whether good or evil" (12:13–14).

At times it seems Qoheleth saw little benefit in fearing God. Life's absurdity applied even to the wisest and most righteous. Yet for Qoheleth the rejection of God consistently poses a greater threat. If a devotee of Yahweh possesses little hope for achievement, the fool possesses no hope.

Conclusion

The most disputed passage of Ecclesiastes occurs at the end of the book (12:9–14).[6] Even if later than much of the work, the verses make explicit the patterns of inconsistency so vital to the entire argument of the sage. Qoheleth never counseled dereliction to religious duty though convinced its effects were less than beneficial. The contemporary interpreter who edits the work in pursuit of consistency runs the risk of homogenizing the book's enigmatic variations. These puzzles prompted Qoheleth's quest for meaning. Interpretation demands restraint. Such restraint prevents the reader from discarding objectionable verses of the canonical form of the book. The same restraint militates against privileging the concluding verses so that they become the focus for our understanding of the book. With Ecclesiastes, as with Job, no summary conclusion can capture the message of the book. Its message lies in the pursuit which it relays rather than its findings.[7]

In light of this proposal the fear of the Lord appears as the traditional attitude Qoheleth assumes (though it conflicts with his experience). The fear of the LORD also provides a necessary response to irresolvable perplexi-

---

6. Since the early application of historical critical methodology, its proponents have typically assigned this passage to a later editor. As Murphy points out in his discussion of the unit's date, nearly all critics continue to consider the verses the work of a later epilogist. See Roland Murphy, *Ecclesiastes*, WBC 23A (Dallas: Word, 1992), 126–30. They tend to date it even later than they date other late verses which seem to confirm traditional tenets of Yahwism. Garrett, NAC 14, 262–67 prefers to see one editor using the structural device of a "frame-narrator" employing three levels of discourse.

7. The book itself suggests this in 7:18 by advising a balanced approach to wisdom which incorporates traits usually thought hostile to its attainment: "It is good that you should take hold of the one, without letting go of the other; for the one who fears God will succeed with both" [righteousness and wickedness, wisdom and folly].

ties regarding human behavior. Wisdom serves as one constant in Qoheleth's limited arsenal of answers. Wisdom functions like a sharp edge on an axe in that it makes the task of living less strenuous (10:10). Though contrasted in the following lines to the vanity of wisdom, the positive assessment of 2:13–14a underpins all the investigations and truisms of the book: "Wisdom excels folly as light excels darkness. The wise have eyes in their head, but fools walk in darkness."

The denial of wisdom's benefits in 2:14b–17 cannot fully negate the commitment to wisdom evident throughout the work. The protection of wisdom resembles the protection of inherited money (7:11–12). The strength it yields enables the wise to outstrip ten monarchs in strength (7:19). The expression of 8:1 praises wisdom for its subjective (spiritual?) benefits: "Who is like the wise man? And who knows the interpretation of a thing? Wisdom makes one's face shine, and the hardness of one's countenance is changed." The change in appearance signals the happiness or peace of the recipient of wisdom. 9:16–18 employs three "better than" sayings to laud wisdom, as well as three antithetical lines to denigrate foolish behavior.

Qoheleth's Special View of Wisdom

The name *Qoheleth* itself likely designates a wisdom teacher. The teacher first investigates wisdom (1:12–18). Wisdom remains a prominent theme throughout the second chapter. Numerous passages recommend wisdom to the reader. The presence of wisdom forms (proverbs and others) attest to the prominence of wisdom for the teacher. Finally, the conclusion of the book (12:9–12) reiterates the teacher's wisdom and underscores the advantages of wisdom. The literary concern to investigate such questions as the meaning of life falls under the aegis of "wisdom" in ancient Near Eastern cultures. Another "good" in Ecclesiastes appears sporadically, but convincingly, beginning with 2:24–25: "There is nothing better for mortals than to eat and drink, and find enjoyment in their toil. This also, I saw, is from the hand of God; for apart from him who can eat or who can have enjoyment?" Such a liberal attitude seems inconsistent with the repeated denials of meaning elsewhere. It could be that rather than contradictions, the opposed truths are intended contextually. Similarly, contrasting sayings from the Book of Proverbs assume their truth in dissimilar situations. Stated explicitly, "Enjoy yourself to the fullest whenever you have the chance, for no one can tell when trouble will come." This approach adds meaning to the concept that enjoyment comes "from the hand of God." God doles out enjoyment as one of life's temporary fortunes. Humans accept this enjoyment as a gift, though God shows himself under no obligation to continue or repeat such beneficence.

In slightly varying expressions, the theme recurs in 3:12–13, 22; 8:15. Ecclesiastes urges those who enjoy wealth and success to make the most of it. In this way their enjoyment of the goods of life will keep them preoccupied so that they cannot dwell on life's frustrations (5:18–20). The threat of misfortune always looms over prosperity. Qoheleth argues that this makes good fortune more valuable: "In the day of prosperity be joyful, and in the day of adversity consider; God has made the one as well as the other, so that mortals may not find out anything that will come after them" (7:14). The teacher longs for predictability, but in its absence sees the necessity for fullest appreciation of present experience. The following unit contains the same advice given with more specificity:

> Go, eat your bread with enjoyment, and drink your wine with a merry heart; for God has long ago approved what you do. Let your garments always be white; do not let oil be lacking on your head. Enjoy life with the wife whom you love, all the days of your vain life that are given you under the sun, because that is your portion in life and in your toil at which you toil under the sun. Whatever your hand finds to do, do with your might; for there is no work or thought or knowledge or wisdom in Sheol, to which you are going. (9:7–10)

In at least one instance, Qoheleth's invitation to enjoy life leads to a festive mood producing a proverb for the *bon vivant*: "Feasts are made for laughter; wine gladdens life, and money meets every need" (10:19). A related series of comments urges the reader to action (as opposed to passivity) due to the unpredictable nature of things (11:1–4, 6): "In the morning sow your seed, and at evening do not let your hands be idle; for you do not know which will prosper, this or that, or whether both alike will be good" (v. 6). Though at times the teacher's findings led him to despondency, he does not recommend this response to the reader. Instead, Qoheleth recommends the employment of life's three "goods"—religion, intellect, and work—as essential to a relatively meaningful lifestyle.

Ecclesiastes possesses a negative viewpoint uncharacteristic of other biblical materials. In an effort to reconcile Ecclesiastes to other canonical materials and Christian doctrine, some critics suggest Qoheleth espoused an entirely secular perspective. This implies the sum of his doubts, pessimism, and dissatisfaction issue from a faulty (that is, a non-religious) basis for investigation. To the contrary, this study presumes Qoheleth's uncertainties arise precisely because of his religion. He, like Job, sees Yahweh as directly responsible for life's inequities. He possesses a theology of fatalism. It does not serve his purpose to defend God's justice. Instead, he recommends submission and limited activism in as much as human decisions can determine outcomes. We, like Qoheleth, engage in a search for happiness which, though illusive, looms as in many respects our highest goal. It also makes up a vital part of God's intention for us. Not many persons have looked "into the lion's mouth" with Qoheleth and encountered the void of death, confessed doubt about life, and confronted the full force of their own insecurities and anxiety. Far from secular, these theological issues thrill us with their reckless challenge of conventional beliefs. They threaten us with the prospect of what has been called "nonbeing." The teacher totters on the precipice which may seem more as a slippery slope leading to complete disillusionment. In spite of the danger, our guide remains remarkably surefooted, never sacrificing on the one hand his commitment to God or on the other hand his quest to succeed.

Summary: Qoheleth's Contribution to the Wisdom Canon

Of the three wisdom works of the Hebrew canon, Ecclesiastes displays the least direct relation to conventional wisdom. Whereas Proverbs contains a collection of wise sayings and Job a wisdom tale, Ecclesiastes assumes the form of a report of a sage's experience. The first-person perspective encourages the reader to see the entire work as the quest of a single sage. For this reason, its approach appears much more individualistic and personal in other ways as well. The subjective nature of the book contrasts strongly with the authoritative tone of Proverbs, making readers of Ecclesiastes less reluctant to question its findings. Since the inclinations of Qoheleth lead him to offer competing suggestions, the reader affords him less privilege. Ecclesiastes shows little uniformity in arrangement or style and presents no special sequence. This lack of organization is disappointing in a work devoted to philosophical questions, but the disorder appears consistent with the disorientation of the thinker.

In style, the remarks are presented as reports based on the results of long experience. As such, they assume an air of finality, and the reader relates to the narrator as student to teacher. The relationship involves more distance, and the narrator remains more aloof than in Proverbs. The reader receives encouragement to take up Qoheleth's quest for answers as though relatively equal with the narrator in status (with a few exceptions). In his accounts of his quest for meaning, the teacher assumed the reader would accept his negative conclusions as the final answers. Accordingly, Qoheleth's claims to wisdom are featured prominently in the opening and conclusion of the work. The entire program presents itself as a search for wisdom, even though certain conclusions run counter to common understandings of wisdom.

Thematic issues present the problems with regard to Ecclesiastes' wisdom status. Periodic injunctions to fear God are the most prominent of the infrequent themes of traditional wisdom; this feature alone cannot prove wisdom connections. It is generally assumed that the canonical shaping of Ecclesiastes blunted its skepticism. By this measure, later proponents of wisdom added many of its positive statements and affirmations of retribution. Their interest lay in shaping the work for more effective use in training the wisdom initiate for proper conduct. This represents a specialized use for wisdom materials. Other portions of the canon such as law and poetry possess limited usefulness as tools for instruction in daily conduct. If sages intended Ecclesiastes for such use, admonitions to fear God and work toward divine rewards became the authoritative conclusion to Qoheleth's indirection and doubt. The indirection and doubt would not support parenesis. These concerns make it preferable to maintain equal emphasis on doubt and faith as integral to the canonical shape of the work. Reading these dual themes in terms of their balance and contextual applicability offers some reconciliation of their contrasts.

✦

Conclusion:
A Canonical Definition of Wisdom

When the three works—Proverbs, Job, and Ecclesiastes—are viewed as a whole, several wisdom features stand out as shared by all. The themes of retribution and fear of the LORD receive prominence in each book. Also in each, inconclusive comments regarding wisdom attest to an ongoing struggle toward wisdom. Proverbs serves a larger purpose than mere factual reports of truth. It leads the reader to expend effort toward understanding. The inconclusiveness of Job relates to retribution and that of Ecclesiastes to the meaning of life itself. Job and Ecclesiastes heighten the struggle by making doubts more central to the issue. All the wisdom materials emphasize irony in relatively equal proportion. Finally, the import of *context* toward the determination of the wise course assumes far more importance than previously noted. This theme holds promise for the resolution of many of wisdom's apparent inconsistencies.

From the canonical perspective, all three books have been attributed to Solomon. With Proverbs and Ecclesiastes the attribution predates the oldest Hebrew texts. For this reason, the books bear his name. Job and Ecclesiastes also reveal additions and/or interpretations which bear the marks of readers' dissatisfaction with challenges to the conventional view of retribution. These readers attempted to weigh the books in favor of deuteronomistic theology. Up to the present, wisdom assumes a more unilateral shape in terms of reward and punishment than appears at points in Job and Ecclesiastes. These books continue to challenge the notion that limits wisdom to the expression of decisiveness. They offer a portrait of wisdom as reflection which often ends in enigma.

Questions for Discussion

1. How does Ecclesiastes resemble other wisdom materials?

2. What distinctive characteristics does Ecclesiastes give to wisdom?

3. What role does skepticism play in biblical theology?

4. What does Qoheleth attempt to discover? Summarize his findings.

5.   What special view of wisdom appears in Ecclesiastes, and what does this special view contribute to the understanding of Hebrew wisdom?

6.   Write your definition of wisdom, providing criteria for including or excluding materials as "wisdom."

PART TWO: POETRY

Introduction to Poetry

Changing topics from wisdom to poetry involves a giant leap rather than a smooth transition. In the Writings, the third division of the Hebrew canon, the reader encounters a miscellany of history and literature. These varied forms in the Writings are conveniently subdivided for study into wisdom, poetry, and history. The poetry books include Psalms, Song of Songs, and Lamentations, but the identification depends on several arbitrary decisions. As problematic as the term *wisdom* appears, the term *poetry* presents even greater difficulty. Wisdom designates materials identified on the basis of thematic concerns, but the identification of poetry only tenuously depends on theme. Formal traits assume chief interest for the reader in search of poetry. On this basis books as diverse as Genesis, Ruth, Proverbs, even portions of the deuteronomistic history, appear poetic. All three of the canonical wisdom books exhibit poetic features, as do most of the prophetic books.

Using other features such as high style or symbolic language as indicators of poetry leads to the identification of all the material in the Hebrew Bible as "poetry." The term *books of poetry* typically designates books exhibiting poetic features when those books do not fall within another division, namely Law, Prophets (including the Former Prophets or History Books), or Wisdom. Poetry remains a secondary manner of designation. From this common perspective, the divisions remain clear. This study, however, investigates the nature of biblical poetry itself, seeking to generate interest in every significant poetic unit within the canon and an appreciation for the nature of ancient Hebrew poetry.

Distinctions Between Hebrew and Western Poetry

Just as the poetic books of the Hebrew canon assume the designation on the basis of elimination, so English literary conventions also define poetry in the negative: it does not exhibit the paragraph structure of prose. Originally, Western concepts of poetry related to the ancient Greek concept of *poesis.* This word designated any artful use of language and thus identifies all literature as poetry. Going to the other extreme, a narrow definition of poetry simply distinguishes verse (poetry) from prose on the basis of lineation. Using this criterion to identify poetry in the Bible leaves English readers completely dependent on the designations left by translators. Students of the Bible should recognize that the metrical structure and lineation of the Hebrew Bible (even in the Hebrew language) represents a reconstruction at best. Verse may be intended even though current translators fail to find recognizable patterns.

A medial approach to poetry attempts to identify the type of language the word *poetry* designates. Poetry "says more and says it more intensely than does ordinary language."[1] Poetic language elucidates experience. It accomplishes this aim through condensed and concentrated expression. Virtually all theorists recognize the distinction between poetry and prose as one of degree. This leads to the suggestion that "good readers" must learn to recognize poetry.[2]

The recognition of good and bad in poetry assumes meaning only in a single culture with a standard set of conventions for literature. The contemporary reader cannot recover ancient Hebrew standards for informed reading. We may question whether such intellectual distinctions raised important issues for poets and readers in such a radically different society. Even the more specific features especially characteristic in the Western notion of poetry, when present in Hebrew poetry, may arise from the poetic genius as second nature rather than by conscious design. One list of poetic features includes denotation and connotation, imagery, figurative language (metaphor, personification, metonymy, symbol, allegory, paradox, overstatement, understatement, and irony), allusion, meaning and idea, tone, musical devices, rhythm and meter, sound and meaning, and pattern.[3] More recent theorists would suggest the identification of poetry depends upon the presuppositions of the individual reader rather than the content of the literary units. Such concepts notwithstanding, the elucidation of the poetic features named above serves a most important function in the selection of and interpretation of poetic units throughout the Hebrew Bible.

The gulf separating contemporary poetic interpretation and the use and concept of poetry in the ancient Near East always affects the work of the biblical interpreter. Our culture's notion of poetry as a pleasant diversion

---

1. Laurence Perrine, *Sound and Sense: An Introduction to Poetry,* 7th ed. (San Diego: Harcourt Brace Jovanovich, Inc., 1987), 3.
2. Ibid., 9.
3. These terms appear in Perrine's chapter titles.

makes it difficult to read sympathetically Hebrew poetry which communicates and reinforces the order of life. Every line of interpretation deserves the disclaimer: We certainly do not understand this verse as the Hebrews did. This problem relates more to hermeneutics in general than to the interpretation of poetry. A few samples of the special perspectives involved in ancient Hebrew poetry may illustrate the need for reorientation if a modern reader is to grasp as fully as possible the meaning of poetry in the Hebrew context.[4] At this early stage, three observations suffice: (1) the Hebrews sang their poetry; (2) canonical poetry exhibits a close relationship to speech; and (3) the Hebrews conceived their poetic literature orally rather than in written form.

Singing surely indicates the import of the public performance of poetry. The contexts varied as widely as the interests of the community itself. These included worship, prophecy, instruction, community meetings, weddings, festivals, work, royal ceremonies, and many more settings. The performance of poetry involved dance, ritual actions, and perhaps other unknown elements. In general, the action assumed much more significance than current folk songs (our nearest equivalent genre) even when current folk singing accompanies cultural festivals. Perhaps singing constituted a more significant means of communication than normal speech. Prophets probably sang their oracles.[5] Music certainly accompanied Psalms. This includes the five complaint songs which make up Lamentations. The high florid style of the Song of Songs indicates musical performance. In Western culture melody relates to poetry incidentally. In ancient Israel they were two parts of the same phenomenon.

When poetic units appear in narrative in the Hebrew Bible, these units typically form the speech of an identified individual.[6] The close association of speech and poetry relates to the basic Hebrew belief system. For them poetry as prophecy or liturgy arose as the creative effort of an inspired person. In the Bible, prose is the language of humans, while poetry indicates a divine message. Third person narrative voices the recounting of history but will not suffice for the direct verbal action of characters. Poetry especially expresses praise for or the wishes of the deity. Western poetry typically presents a more subdued narrative voice: the speaker need not be identified. When poems do identify the speaker, that speaker may function more as a dramatic character than the presumed voice of the composer. Poetic speeches in Exodus, Deuteronomy, or Samuel present lines composed on the spot by an actor in the narrative.

---

4. A fuller description appears in chapter 9.
5. The noun *wisdom* was especially applied to singers according to Robert Gordis, *Poets, Prophets, and Sages* (Bloomington: Indiana University Press, 1971), 32.
6. William Whallon, "Biblical Poetry and Homeric Epic" in J. R. Maier and B. L. Tollers eds., *The Bible in Its Literary Milieu* (Grand Rapids: Eerdmans, 1979), 325. Whallon claimed this feature, more than any other, determined the difference between prose and poetry in the Hebrew Bible.

The most far-reaching distinctive of Hebrew poetry relates to its oral composition. Western society exhibits few characteristics of oral culture. Even the literary stage of cultural development now lies in the Western world's past. The current technological age fosters communication through written forms and various media. This makes oral forms difficult to understand. Identifying oral forms in the Hebrew Bible also presents a challenge. The Bible, as we have it, assumes the shape of a written document. We possess only the literary vestiges of oral poetry in the Hebrew Bible. Interpreters cannot know how much of the artistry of Hebrew verse arose from desk work and how much arose from the inspiration and invention of the oral poet. This complicates the task of recapturing the spirit of Israel's oral poetry. [7]

Ancient persons considered the verbal abilities (that is, poetic composition) of the poet the result of special divine contact. The special status of the prophet and other key figures such as Moses, David, and Solomon illustrate this. They achieved recognition as communicators of divine truth. Canonical tradition attributes the Torah to Moses, the Psalms to David, and Proverbs to Solomon. Such composers received special standing among their contemporaries due to their reception of revelation. As far as is known, Israel's writers saw prose and poetry as distinct forms from the earliest history of Israel's literature. No evidence exists of an evolution of early Hebrew literature from poetry to prose.[8] The understanding of Hebrew poetry shared by contemporary exegetes likely displays wide differences from the ancient Near Eastern concepts of poetry. Still the existence and design of certain units as poetry remain unquestioned.

When the interpreter compares the criteria for understanding poetry in contemporary Western and ancient Near Eastern contexts, a major difference in orientation presents itself. The contemporary reader responds to poetry analytically, especially in critical circles. As far as is known, ancient writers chose not to study and explicate their poetic devices. Poetry's efficacy rather than its design took central place. As divergent as the modern Western and ancient Near Eastern approaches appear, together they provide complementary interests. They promote the exploration of the multidimensional layers of art and meaning comprising Hebrew poetry. Our introductory overview of Hebrew poetry studies Hebrew poetry, book by book, as *a world-ordering phenomenon* (the ancient perspective) and as a *literary phenomenon* (the current perspective). The first owes its basis to *form criticism*, a reconstruction of the ancient view of poetry. The second owes its basis to a *representative* contemporary view of poetry.

---

7. For an effective summary of oral poetry and the Hebrew Bible, see Wilfred G. E. Watson, *Classical Hebrew Poetry: A Guide to Its Techniques,* JSOTSup 25 (Sheffield: University of Sheffield Press, 1986), 66–82.

8. David Noel Freedman, "Pottery, Poetry, and Prophecy: An Essay on Biblical Poetry" in J. R. Maier and V. L. Tollers eds., *The Bible in Its Literary Milieu* (Grand Rapids: Eerdmans, 1979), 79.

Distinguishing Hebrew Poetry from Prose

How can the poetry and prose of the Hebrew be distinguished? The preceding discussion alluded to one rather novel approach. According to this view the difference between prose and poetry rests on the simple distinction between narrative description and elevated speech.[9] Can this criterion apply not only to poetry framed within narrative but also to poetic books in their entirety? Without question, the Song of Songs speaks in dramatic message. The Psalms as well presume a cultic voice. Lamentations also presumes the corporate voice of worship, for its units are psalmic. This distinction could also apply to Proverbs, since the tone of its teachings implies an authoritative voice. Extended units of highly significant speech tend to be poetic in form and style, but is this observation helpful in the exposition of poetry? It offers limited value because: (1) it relies on deductions made after the identification of poetry; (2) according to Western presuppositions, speech and poetry possess no unbreakable relationship; and (3) the casting of speech as poetry in the final form of the Hebrew text does not necessarily confirm a one-to-one relationship between poetry and speech throughout ancient Hebrew culture.

Poetry as Speech

In spite of limitations, the notation of poetry as speech provides a helpful guideline, among others. It offers some help in identifying poetry, especially in narrative. From the perspective of the Hebrew originators this speech exists not to identify poetry. They cast the units in elevated, poetic speech to mark them as works directed to God.

One of the more straightforward proposals for distinguishing poetry and prose in the Hebrew Bible follows the frequency of the occurrence of three words—*ʾet* (אֵת), *ʾăšer* (אֲשֶׁר), and *ha* (ה). The first marks the direct object; the second is a relative pronoun (who, which, or that); and the third is the definite article. These three words occur six to eight times more frequently in Hebrew prose than in poetry.[10] Freedman's suggestions added immeasurably to the discussion of Hebrew poetry. Such a mathematically confirmed criterion provides a balance to more subjective linguistic criteria. The system also provides an alternative to determinations based on conjectural metrical systems. Since the Masoretic text marks lines with practically the same notation system throughout, the provision for clues readily visible to a Hebrew reader clarifies the matter considerably. The complexities of translation, however, make it impossible for the English reader to note these differences. On the other hand, even a first semester Hebrew student could note the presence or absence of these words in a text. Psalm 23, for example, does not contain a single occurence of the words, while Genesis 1:1–5 contains fourteen occurrences.

---

9. Whallon, 325.
10. Freedman, 79.

Poetic Features

The most common means for distinguishing Hebrew prose and poetry relies on the notice of basic features which mark poetic units. These basic features appear throughout the Hebrew Bible, in prose as well as poetry. In poetry, however, these features display a pronounced character. Interpreters commonly include parallelism, meter, and strophic structure[11] as the features marking poetry. Parallelism denotes the grouping of lines similar in form or content, usually in pairs, but often in units of three or four. Meter typically refers to a patterned series of stresses, syllable counts, or word counts. Strophic structure designates larger blocks containing several sets of parallel lines. Other less determinative feaures include *ring composition* (the pairing of individual lines from top to bottom with those ascending from bottom to top in a longer unit) and *inclusio,* the tendency to begin and end units with an identical or similar line or set of parallel lines.[12] The three formal structures, like the system described in the previous paragraph, involve uncomplicated observations. English translations can indicate parallelism and strophic structure. In slightly awkward style, translations can also outline metrical patterns. This involves stress marks or translated words joined by hyphens to indicate a stress-bearing word group. The following example illustrates the latter procedure. The parallel lines exhibit a 2 + 2 pattern of stress:

> What-is-your-beloved / more-than-another-beloved,
> O-fairest / among-women?
> What-is-your-beloved / more-than-another-beloved,
> that-you-thus / adjure-us?
> (Song of Songs 5:9)

With meter, critics face the challenge of rediscovering relatively obscure rules for its employment. Contemporary interpreters of the Hebrew Bible cannot hope to recover the precise systems. Basic patterns of two to four stresses or words per line are undeniable.

Of the three features characterizing poetry, strophic structure presents the most illusive patterns. At times the units show clear divisions. In other cases, transitions make it impossible to mark units unambiguously. In the most effective Hebrew poetry, units overlap one another. They produce isolated segments which fit either at the end or the beginning of connected units. These three techniques characterizing ancient Hebrew poetry serve as the nucleus for most discussions of the subject.

The characterization of such traits differs slightly among specialists. For example, one overview described the traits of canonical poetry as paral-

---

11. This study refers to a Hebrew poetic unit as a "strophe" (pronounced strōfĕ) rather than a stanza. "Stanza" generally indicates sections of similar measure and style. Such precision rarely appears in Hebrew poetry.

12. Fuller consideration of these techinques appears in the explication of poetry on pages 272–296.

lelism, rhythm, and sound.[13] The term *rhythm* substitutes for *meter* because of the latter term's association with the precise Greek patterns (iambic pentameter, among others). The notice of sound reminds the interpreter of the oral qualities the text possessed. Hebrew poetry shows the characteristics of literature constructed for listening and written for public reading. Sound patterns including onomatopoeia, alliteration, and wordplay served as central devices to improve the sense and aesthetic quality of communication. Again, each of these and similar aural qualities occur in prose, but their importance and frequency are augmented in poetry.

The preceding proposals for identifying poetry rely almost exclusively on formal features. Omitted are the designations of poetry as artful or sublime language. Longinus' *On the Sublime*[14] and similar works elaborate on such concepts. The previous mention of the rationale for this exclusion bears repeating: Such an artistic definition of poetry encompasses all the biblical materials. In response, the proposed means for identifying poetry depend on verse structure. This verse structure involves: (1) pronounced parallelism and rhythm, (2) compressed syntax, (3) complex repetitive patterns, perhaps even (4) abstractness of theme.

Judges 4 and 5

Examining comparable prose and poetic accounts can illustrate the usefulness of the several facets employed in the measure of the prose-poetry continuum. The prose and poetry accounts of Deborah's activities provides an attractive point of entry. The rule of Deborah appears in prose in Judges 4. The account of the battle of Israel with King Jabin's forces appears in an ancient poem in chapter 5. The first criterion listed, the casting of poetic units as speech, appears in 5:1, which introduces the poem's singers—Deborah (a prophet) and Barak (the commander of Israel's forces). The speech of chapter 4, in contrast, appears less formulaic and more like common discourse. Judges 4 does not contain the periodic invitations to speech present in Judges 5:10, 12, 23. The allusions to speech mark Judges 5 as a liturgical text. Judges 5 reports the speech in the third person rather than quoting it. Chapter 4 quotes the speakers (especially 4:18–20).

In this respect, the poetry presents more of a passioned remembrance, while the prose tends toward historical report. The poetry emphasizes the outcome and God's part in it. The prose relates the events in a more straighforward fashion. The poetry actually assumes the form of personal reaction (hence speech) to divine intervention. An investigation based upon the three words characteristic to prose (according to Freedman's study)[15] yields positive results as well. Approximately sixty occurrences of the three words

13. Benjamin Hrushovski, "Prosody, Hebrew" in *Encyclopedia Judaica* (Jerusalem: Keter Publishing House Jerusalem Ltd., 1972), 1201–2.

14. Hazard Adams ed., *Critical Theory Since Plato* (San Diego: Harcourt, Brace, Jovanovich, 1971).

15. David Noel Freedman, "Pottery, Poetry, and Prophecy: An Essay on Biblical Poetry."

in the prose of chapter 4 compare to less than twenty occurrences in chapter 5. The direct object marker occurs nowhere in the song of chapter 5. The three-to-one margin suggests a high degree of correlation between the presence of the words and identification of the passage as prose.

Notice of the formal elements involves a more complex analysis. Parallelism operates through repetition. The prose in chapter 4 lacks any significant thematic repetition from one line to the next. The request of Jael that Sisera enter her tent presents the only exception: "Turn aside, my lord, turn aside to me; have no fear" (v. 18). Otherwise, the relationship of one line to the next displays steady progression rather than repetition. In the song, the verses which lack repetition change scenes or offer other poetic features, but do not mark progression. For example, verses 2 and 9 show little parallelism, but they share words which mark the beginning and end of a unit, namely, "offer themselves willingly." The last line of verse 11 also lacks parallelistic structure. It serves as a transition designating a change in action: "Then down to the gates marched the people of the LORD." The unit beginning in 15*b* and continuing through 18 stands out as the most prominent absence of parallelism. All these verses (15*b*–18) relate to the failure of certain tribes to present themselves in the battle. Their refusal to fight represented a serious crime. Its mention in ritual poetry brought a shameful loss of face. The lines do contain a rather small degree of parallelism (perhaps merely repetition) in that they appear as similar questions with similar content. All other lines in the poem of chapter 5 contain classic parallelism. Verses 26–27 present the most prominent example:

> She put her hand to the tent peg
> and her right hand to the workmen's mallet;
> she struck Sisera a blow,
> she crushed his head,
> she shattered and pierced his temple.
> He sank, he fell,
> he lay still at her feet;
> at her feet he sank, he fell;
> where he sank, there he fell dead.

Parallelism reinforces the irony and brutality of Jael's act. Sisera's death and fall mimics in its repetition the thorough defeat of his army. The prose account is noteworthy for its blunt, matter-of-fact style: "Jael wife of Heber took a tent peg, and took a hammer in her hand, and went softly to him and drove the peg into his temple, until it went down into the ground—he was lying fast asleep from weariness—and he died" (Judg. 4:21). The reader of Judges can scarcely imagine a sharper contrast than that between the simple report "and he died" and the repetitive style of 5:27.

Though not demonstrable in English, a significant difference exists in the metrical arrangement of the two chapters. The lines of Judges 5 tend to be more evenly measured so that individual lines are relatively equal in length. The prose, by contrast, contains lines with great differences in length.

The third formal determinant of poetry, strophic structure, further identifies Judges 5 as poetic. The paragraph structure of chapter 4 contains few clear transitions. Thematic structure rather than formal clues provides the basis for these transitions. The units indicated by the masoretic notes do not conform to the paragraph structure which contemporary versions follow. Masoretic paragraphs end after verses 3, 12, and 24, yet the NRSV ends paragraphs at 4:3, 10, 11, 16, 22, and 24. The relatively clear changes of theme from the Western perspective do not serve as guidelines for the Masoretes. The earliest Hebrew form of chapter 4 likely included only the conjunction between sentences as a key to blocks of text.

Several individual verses and brief units appear in chapter 5. Even in translation, decisions based on repetition, perspective, and change of mood identify several clear strophes. Other poems, in the prophecy of Isaiah for example, contain lengthier and more balanced strophes. The English of the poetry in chapter 5 provides several indications of divisions. Changes of person and perspective are important clues. The text varies from third-person report in 5:2 to second-person address in 5:3, to second person address directed toward Yahweh in 5:4. The poem returns to the third person in 5:4*b*. The longer unit in 5:6–9 ends with an appeal to others to tell the story. Previous discussion alluded to the *inclusio* designating verses 2 through 9 as a unit. Chapter 5 also reveals *sound patterns,* most of them related to the repetitions of parallelism. Verse 22 contains the most celebrated example of onomatopoeia in the Hebrew Bible. The words מִדַּהֲרוֹת דַּהֲרוֹת (*middahărōt dahărōh*) sound like what they describe, the "galloping galloping" of horses. Other sound patterns occur. The prose of chapter 4 offers few of these compared to the number in the poetry of chapter 5.

Use of Poetry in Ancient Israelite Society

Before giving a preliminary overview of the poetic units of the Hebrew Bible and the Deuterocanon, we need to draw finer distinctions between ancient and contemporary views of poetry. We will make three proposals based on perceptions revealed in the literary forms of the current Hebrew text. As such these proposals do not account for later second temple poetry (as that in the Deuterocanon).

First and most obviously, Hebrew poetry was used in *liturgical enactment.* Poetry provided the medium for sacred ritual. Its song and stylized forms approached the significance of divine communication. As such poetry found application in situations beyond, or on the fringe of, human control. The sounds and movements associated with poetry pleased the deity and so helped maintain the human link with the divine.

Second, inasmuch as poetry formed Israel's self-understanding, it served as *active remembrance of the community's origins under God.* The record included rebellion as well as election. Poetic remembrance reminded Israel of its practical identity (marked by imperfection and rebellion) and ideal identity (as a community chosen by God). In poetry, time converged as past, present, and future met. The hearer of Hebrew poetry interpreted each in light of the other. National suffering reminded Israel of sin; deliverance reminded Israel of its part in God's plans; and all other events took on meaning in light of past experiences and present hope. Prose could serve as the language of summary, but poetry provided the bridge between past and future. The medium of poetry carried the language of identity building, decision making, and responses to sudden changes in fortunes.

Third, in all cases, *poetry provided the means for emotional expression*. The more extreme the response, the more radical the distinction from ordinary language. The lamentation, for example, expressed completely uncommon themes and employed a halting metrical form. In every respect, the expression of poetry differed from the common responses of daily life. Even in worship ceremonies, the performance of poetry involved emotional displays. "The people did not sit peacefully in pews, as we do; they jumped and danced, they were jubilant, they shouted, with intoxicating music."[16] The animated involvement of the worshiper existed as a component of the poetry. The performer added body movements and other emotional expression to singing. These elements served as an essential part of poetry's performance. They formed the natural components of responses to and enactments of the most extreme emotional experiences—religion, death, and love.

The poetry of the Hebrew Bible falls into three broad categories: *psalms, prophecy,* and *love poetry*. Psalms include all forms similar to or built upon the forms within the Book of Psalms. Older poems in the historical narratives present psalmic units such as songs of victory and thanks or hymns. The previously-discussed Song of Deborah (Judg. 5) follows the pattern of a psalmic victory song. The Book of Lamentations contains laments (also called complaint songs) built on a pattern often found in Psalms.

Prophecy contains psalmic units as well, but the prophetic oracle constitutes a larger type of its own. Several subgenres within this category receive some attention in this study.[17] Prophecy incorporates no less poetic expression than other poetic forms. The forms of psalms and prophecy account for as much as 80 percent of canonical poetry. *Love poetry* occurs only in the Song of Songs and brief incidental passages in Proverbs.[18]

Numerous individual units of other types exist but account for only a small portion of the poetry in the Hebrew Bible. *Proverbs* exhibit two pro-

---

16. Hermann Gunkel, *The Psalms: A Form-Critical Introduction,* trans. Thomas M. Horner (Philadelphia: Fortress, 1967; German original, 1930), 6, note n.

17. In general, the study of prophecy incorporates too many detailed concerns for an exhaustive overview. More detailed study is available in Gary V. Smith, *The Prophets as Preachers* (Broadman & Holman Publishers, 1994) and in D. Brent Sandy and Ronald L. Giese, Jr., eds., *Cracking Old Testament Codes: A Guide to Interpreting Old Testament Literary Forms* (Nashville: Broadman & Holman Publishers, 1995).

18. The prophetic application of the love song in Isaiah 5:1–2 makes it scarcely recognizable as love poetry.

nounced features of poetry: parallelism and formulaic style. Yet the term *sentence literature*[19] describes proverbs better than the term *poetry*. The units present brief and aphoristic language. They serve to pass along traditions rather than acting as the vehicle for divine-human communication. Indeed, the theme of the *mešālîm* (proverbs) determines the issue. The literature displays subject matter far more utilitarian than divine-human themes of Hebrew poetry.

A review of the nature of the poetic passages in the Hebrew Bible provides a general understanding of its use of poetry. This general information sets the stage for later interpretations of many of the passages identified as poetry. The three books most often identified as poetry (Psalms, the Song of Songs, and Lamentations) help to form a core understanding of Hebrew poetry. On the basis of their contents, the poetic nature of other books and units takes shape.

Questions for Discussion

1. What differences can you name between biblical poetry and western poetry?

2. What are the major features of ancient Hebrew poetry?

---

19. William McKane used this term in the description of his classification system. See *Proverbs: A New Approach*, OTL (Philadelphia: Westminster, 1970), 10–22.

Chapter Nine

Overview of Poetry

The Poetry of Psalms

Commentators sometimes describe the Book of Psalms as the hymn-book of the second temple. Such generalizations achieve little more than a depiction of a single perspective on a varied and vastly influential body of literature. In its Hebrew form, the book contains a collection of five smaller groups of psalms. Each so-called "book" begins with a heading. Each ends with statements of praise (doxologies) added to the text of the final psalm. The following list marks the chapter divisions of the five units and the verses of their doxologies (verses indicated in parentheses):

Table 5
Doxologies in Psalms

Book	Chapters	Doxology
Book 1	1–41	(41:13)
Book 2	42–72	(72:18–20)
Book 3	73–89	(89:52)
Book 4	90–106	(106:48)
Book 5	107–150	no doxology added, perhaps the entirety of Psalm 150

The individual books show no central organizational tendencies or uniform themes, although the collections tend to contain several psalms of related themes.[1]

---

1. Gerald H. Wilson, "The Shape of the Book of Psalms," *Int* 46 (1992), 129–42 and literature cited there represent recent attempts to describe a literary and theological structure in the Book of Psalms. Compare Leslie C. Allen, *Psalms*, Word Biblical Themes (Waco: Word Books), 1987.

Psalm 6

The general features of poetry in the Psalms can be sketched with reference to a single psalm from each book. Psalm 6 begins with direct address to God, a common opening for psalms. The psalm relates an experience of an undetermined kind. Verses 2–3 allude to illness, but the mention of weeping (v. 6) implies emotional distress of another kind. Perhaps the enemies of verses 8–10 capitalize on the worshiper's illness or cause it. The enemies of the psalms often play the role oppposite God's role.[2] God delivers the psalmist: The enemies cause or aggravate the suffering. Scholars express differing opinions on whether or not the enemies exist as literal persons. The lack of clear mention of the nature of distress yields a universal applicability for the psalm. It can apply to any trouble of any type. The psalmist expresses the threat of death in clearer terms in verse 5. This limits the applicability of the poem to life-threatening situations. Otherwise, the nondescript nature of the distresses places heavy responsibility on the reader to supply or imagine the difficulty.

The speaker's outpouring of grief produces a series of related actions. The moaning of verse 6 leads to a reference to tears and eyes. The imagery turns from sound to sight and back to sound. Mentions of rebuke (v. 1), praise (v. 5), and prayer (v. 9) reiterate the import of sound, notably speech, throughout the psalm. A strong hyperbole in verse 6—"I flood my bed with tears"—places emphasis on the deep grief of the poet. The psalm contains no historical allusions, as the speaker remains preoccupied with personal troubles. Accordingly, the unit conveys a pessimistic or negative tone, while expressing hope for divine help. The sufferer's mood runs between the two extremes of viewing the trouble as God's wrath (v. 1) and envisioning God's hearing and deliverance (vv. 9–10).

The Hebrew composer of Psalm 6 included a semantic pattern broken with verse 3: "My soul also is struck with terror, while you, O LORD— how long?" The interrupting question conveys the speaker's sense of grief with the effect of words interrupted by crying. This represents only one aspect of the divine-human interchange in this psalm. The "me . . . you" pattern of verse 1 first expressed this interchange. The tension between the worshiper and the deity serves as the vehicle for much of the effect of verses 1–5. In the course of the psalm, the terror of the speaker (v. 2) falls to the enemies (v. 10). The enemies also replace Yahweh as the designees of the adversarial "you." In spite of this, the psalm primarily addresses the deity and expresses confidence in divine help.

The psalm presents itself as originating from an individual speaker, but its stylized nature reveals an intention toward public performance.[3] Lines 8b and 9a read together imply that the supplication itself serves as a

---

2. On enemies in the Psalms see Hans-Joachim Kraus, *Theology of the Psalms,* trans. Keith Crim (Minneapolis: Augsburg Publishing House, 1986; German original 1979), 125–36.
3. See Gerald T. Sheppard's comments on "Prayers as overheard by friends and enemies" in "Theology and the Book of Psalms," Int 46 (1992), 145–47.

formal instrument for grief. The literary tears evoke the sympathy of the deity. For the general hearers of the liturgy, the psalm serves as instruction regarding the activity of Yahweh.[4] It illustrates his pity and willingness to intercede. Obviously, the psalmist identifies an inseparable connection between God's attitude toward the worshiper and the worshiper's fortunes: God's anger is seen as a threat (v. 1). In addition, the speaker places heavy emphasis on God's hearing. God "hears" the worshiper's expression of agony though the psalm. God's response, enacted within the poem, shows Hebrew poetry not only describes reality but also constructs reality for the worshiper.

Psalm 60

Psalm 60 provides a less specific description of the trouble. The reader easily identifies the threat as military, due to the mention of Edom and other territories. Images of an earthquake (v. 2) and drunken staggering (v. 3) communicate the terror of defeat in warfare. The images of instability contrast with the fortified city (v. 9) which opponents of Edom must storm. Verses 4 and 5 appear anomalous since each stands out as an isolated unit with unusually positive themes:

> You have set up a banner for those who fear you, to rally to it out of bowshot. Give victory with your right hand, and answer us, so that those whom you love may be rescued.

The second of these two sentences expresses the intent of the entire psalm. The most notable use of literary language occurs in verses 6 and 7: various regions serve as implements belonging to Yahweh, the warrior. The anthropomorphic depiction of God stretches the literal meaning of the terms *helmet, scepter, washbasin,* and *shoe.* The image indicates tremendous size, not unlike the expression "the earth is my footstool." The menial roles of Moab, Edom, and Philistia contrast with the depiction of Israelite territories as prize possessions. The allusion to Edom, implying Manasseh (vv. 6–7) lost territory to Edom (v. 9), supplies some historical background for the psalm. The singular "me" occurs only in verse 9. It remains unclear whether this speaker speaks with the voice of the nation, its king, or a representative soldier.

The content of this notice of defeat includes a description of Israel as Yahweh's special possession (vv. 6–8). The worshiper would not consider the defeat a sign of ultimate rejection. In fact, the psalm narrates such diverse perceptions as rejection, protection, promise, and victory, all attributed to the deity. The vacillation between dejection and hope mimics the indecisiveness expected of individuals or a community shocked by disaster. The community, individually and corporately, stands between the extremes of resolve and crippling depression. The psalm enables trust in divine election to play the deciding role in the critical decision making. The impulse

---

4. See J. Clinton McCann, Jr., "The Psalms as Instruction," *Int* 46 (1992), 117–28.

of faith renews hope when without it a self-determined response offers no clear advantage. Such units relate to the dangers of an ambiguous future.

Capitulation to hopelessness threatened the end of national identity. On this precipice a song encouraging solidarity looks amazingly similar to one expecting dissolution. The willingness to express doubt mixed with trust kept the psalmist rooted in the harsh realities of life. The frankness of the description of the worshipers' struggle played the same role. Such realism and honesty were essential components in the eventual acceptance of castastrophe and the healing of the community. The double mention of rejection (vv. 1 and 10) prevents the reader from glossing over the pain by selective reading. As in Psalm 6, the fortunes of the psalmist result from the direct act of God. The psalmist's defeat illustrates God's rejection.

Theologically, this raises objections from current readers. If interpretation accounts for the ancient context, integrity demands an open appraisal of such views. Following the request for a victory, God himself voices the reply, promising to reclaim lost territory and embarrass Israel's opponents (vv. 6–8). Consistent with the accusation of divine rejection, God serves as agent for deliverance as well. Verses 9–10 use questions to express a mock search for a savior, but the identity of the redeemer is never in question.

Psalm 75

Psalm 75 opens with a statement of thanks, but the psalm presents at least three perspectives on the divine role in events. After the call to thanks, verses 2–5 and 10 contain the deity's statement of his control. Verses 6–9 celebrate his intervention. The psalm conveys a celebrative tone which calls for public recognition and involvement. It lends itself less to a mode of prayer. Consequently, only verse 1 contains an address to God. Semantically, the song elaborates on the themes of status lost and gained. Images of lifting up and putting down refer to human pride and fortunes in light of divine activity. The horn in verses 4 and 10 serves as the prominent symbol for pride (and perhaps presumption as well). The horn embodies attempts to assert dominance and exercise human control over the situations of others. God steadies the pillars (foundations) of the earth (v. 3). This sole mention of the deity's universal activity attracts attention due to its understated nature. The relation of this cosmic activity to the moral dimension of the psalm affects both contemporary and ancient perspectives. For the contemporary reader, the mention exemplifies the blending of nonliteral and literal language to convey God's control. Ancient Israel may have linked God's stabilization of the earth's pillars with the moral activity of humans. God's control of justice held the universe together. The beauty of the natural world received its complement in the beauty of the ethical order imposed by Israel's just King. Yahweh induces the tottering of the earth when he forces the wicked to drink the wine of his anger (v. 8). All the images converge in the general statement of verses 6 and 7: "For not from the east or from the west and not from the wilderness comes lifting up; but

it is God who executes judgment, putting down one and lifting up another."
These verses serve as the thematic center of the song by expressing the
cause for thanks. From a contemporary literary perspective, the strong symbols of pride and judgment attract attention (horn and wine) as the focal
centers.

The degree to which the psalmist's thanks controls the action of God
remains unclear. Can thanks determine the outcome of events? Can outcomes be equally received as acts of God without liturgical thanks? Part of
this lack of clarity comes from the overwhelming emphasis on rejoicing in
such psalms. The psalms do not necessarily fulfil the worshipers' obligation
to praise God based on his deliverance. They may simply serve as "spontaneous" choruses of joy. Some operation of the divine wrath on the wicked
clearly led to the expression of joy. The song reinforces the principle of
retribution. The evidence of deserved reward or punishment provides the
motivation for the celebration. Challenges to the doctrine of retribution,
especially undeserved suffering, provoked strong responses. Accordingly,
confirmations of divine justice occasioned festivity. God's role, from the
perspective of Psalm 75, involves his punishment of the evildoer more than
his reward to the righteous. The psalm celebrates not an event of human
making, but God's work illustrating his favor and protection.

Psalm 93

Psalm 93 employs high expressions of God's kingship to render praise.
Examples include an explicit reference to God as king, mention of a royal
robe, and references to his kingdom and reign. The robe expresses God's
majesty and strength (v. 1). His throne (v. 2) serves as a metonym for his
reign. His reign extends from the beginning of the world into the limitless
future. The kingdom, of course, consists of the world or universe. In addition to the language of kingship, the psalm's structure involves three clear
units: (1) verses 1 and 2 laud God's rule; (2) verses 3 and 4 describe his relationship to the "floods"; and (3) verse 5 comments upon the perfection of
his rule.

The psalm shows the actions of two characters: Yahweh and the water
(vv. 3–4). The voice of the floods, at first notice, could offer either praise or
challenge. The double sense could be intentional, but the reference to such
water usually depicts a threat to divine control which Yahweh easily man-
ages. In these verses the chaotic waters which normally oppose God issue
praise. The grandeur of the language and the breadth of its themes bring
attention to the emotion of the poem more than its content. The majesty of
God appears as the most frequently occurring theme. Verse 5 presents the
only statement not assuming the perspective of third-person narrative. This
final address to God rather than about God closes the poem with an appeal
to notice the quality of divine rule.

In the Hebrew context the closing line "holiness befits your house"
possibly indicated a call to worship of some sort. Since the language of the

hymn expresses such broad statements of God's control, the performance fits a public context of worship. The psalm includes no specific mentions of external strains on or excessive joys from the community. The absence of specific deeds clears way for the praise of God for his very identity. The heavy repetition of parallel lines presents evidence of liturgical use. The psalm assumes the character of a group document which employs redundancy to emphasize the special significance of God's control. In verse 3, for instance, the three lines add little progressive meaning, but each includes some form of the phrase "floods lift up." To repeat the phrase offers conviction of its truth. The repetition also strengthens the community's commitment to the proposition that the natural world offers praise to God. Certainly humans should do likewise. The report of God's deeds, however nondescript, also generates wonder in the mind of the worshiping Israelite, a further inducement to praise. The establishment of the world, mentioned in 1*b*, stands out as the only clear action of God in the psalm. In an indirect sense, creation serves as theme for the entire psalm. God as creator and ruler receives praise from the natural world. Presumably, he receives praise from humankind as well—the very function of the psalm.

Psalm 122

Psalm 122 opens and closes with references to the "house of the LORD." This phrase most specifically identifies the temple. Two main units render tribute to the holy city, Jerusalem. In comparison with the previously considered psalms, geographical concerns mark the song as special. Verses 3–5 note the historical importance of Jerusalem as a gathering place for the Hebrews. Verses 6–9 contain a litany for the peace of the city. One important image of Jerusalem's preeminence occurs with the words "bound firmly" in verse 3. This compact phrase refers: (1) to the walls surrounding the city, (2) to the city's importance as a refuge for surrounding villagers, and (3) to the unity of the people the city represents. Although the city was a refuge, outlying settlers lived at the mercy of the foes which the city repelled. Within the same unit, pseudo-historical allusions to the building, tribal significance, and political centralization of the city offer some specific positive features to associate with the worshiper's love for Jerusalem. Only these verses (3–5) contain the historical third-person form. Others emphasize speech and present action.

The psalm as a whole displays a logical sequence of development. Verse 2 announces the speaker's arrival at Jerusalem; verses 3–5 comment upon the importance of Jerusalem as a gathering place; and verses 6–9 voice the worshiper's prayer for the prosperity of the city. The "thrones for judgment" mentioned in verse 5 seem to refer to the divine choice of places for judicial action, indicating some historical importance for the city. Apparently, the pilgrim's visit relates to a religious festival rather than judicial matters. At the pilgrim's arrival thankfulness for a successful journey lends considerable cause to the praise for the city. In a more general sense, the city and God's "house" serve as symbols for God's presence. Their designation as symbols does not fully account for their significance to the Hebrew worshiper. The attention centered on Jerusalem stands in prominence against the slight mention of the journey (v. 1) and a hint of the return home (v. 9*b*).

Jerusalem and its temple claim exclusive place as the worship center of Israel. These locations claim a vital connection with the deity's presence. Given this foundation, the wishes of peace express much more than desire for the absence of war. The closing phrase of the psalm sums up the intent: wishing Jerusalem peace involves seeking its good. These blessings extend to God as well, due to his vital connections with Zion.

The parallel units of the song convey resolute assurance. With the exception of the first two lines, the psalm displays balanced and predictable repetitions. Once again, form suits content. The public show of devotion to the city solidifies the community, its government, and its religion.

Characteristics of Poetry

The rich language and tones of the Psalms make general characterizations difficult. The difficulty runs less in the direction of items wrongly perceived than in the direction of essential qualities omitted. Without presuming comprehension, the poems reviewed are considered in two loose categories. Psalms 6 and 60 express *distress,* and the other three voice *thanks* and *joy.* The psalms of distress convey remarkable depth of feeling as well as authenticity on an emotional level. The expressions of distress conveyed emotions consistent with the psychology of grief. On the literary level, the laments sacrifice a degree of order for expressiveness. They express contradictory hope and discouragement, and their statements of grief and trust come in erratic patterns though they are ultimately positive. The development that the laments demonstrate shows periodic gaps and redirection. One of the most prominent figures in the two examples discussed is the figure of God as adversary.

The remaining examples consist of fantastic depictions of God's action or God's ability to act. The psalms of thanks and praise reveal more order and more consistency in theme and development. The songs of praise also more clearly define units within the songs. These psalms show signs of careful reflection rather than the apparently emotional responses of the distress songs. The reason for praise remains unclear. The body of the psalm contains elaborate metaphors rather than historical descriptions.

These praises communicate, like the distress psalms, with emotional presentations. They include clearer semantics in descriptions and more fully developed images than the laments. They contain repeated affirmations of God's creation, influence, and control. Both general types use highly sophisticated imagery with complex levels of interrelationships. The psalms of praise and thanks exhibit more of this style. Virtually all psalms voice appeals, but the implied hearers of the two basic categories are different. Psalms of distress tend to direct appeals to God. Psalms of thanks and joy tend to direct appeals to humans. These encourage fellow worshipers to join the praise. In all the psalms a continuum exists among God, his acts, his people, and his land. Similarly interrelated are references to the opponents of Israel and to the opponents of Yahweh. These gatherings of persons, places, and things form networks from which the singer can choose any number of metaphors to refer to God and that which belongs to God.

The Poetry of Lamentations

The collection and organization of the units of Lamentations commands more attention than its poetic style and themes. In form the poems display all the emotional and the formal unevenness of psalms of distress, but the very existence of the poetry presents intriguing issues. First, how can we account for the survival of such poetry when catastrophe dismantled all Israel's centers of worship, government, and community life? Second, how do we explain the careful construction of these poems in acrostic patterns? Do these units, unlike most cultic poetry, come to us from the hand of a single author? Third, how can we understand the purpose for the performance of such a bleak rehearsal of misfortune?

Painful Events Remembered

The medium of poetry offers the ideal format for the remembrance of the painful events. The Hebrew title *ʾēkâ* (אֵיכָה) introduces the first, second, and fourth acrostics. The meaning, "how," relates the message of the book as an emotional record of how (and why) Israel suffers. Numerous statements contrast Israel's former glory with the present state of affairs, especially in chapter 1. The nation lies bereft of every vestige of nobility and honor. This forces the conclusion that God punishes Israel for rebellion. The theme of God's rejection stands paramount. High literary language also expresses pleas for God's help. The addition of remembrances of better times and infrequent imprecations against Israel's enemies compounds the pathos of the elegy. A brief selection of representative verses can grant a sense of the content of the collection:

> How lonely sits the city that once was full of people!
> How like a widow she has become,
>   she that was great among the nations!
> She that was a princess among the provinces has become a vassal. (1:1)

> Jerusalem sinned grievously, so she has become a mockery;
> all who honored her despise her, for they have seen her nakedness;
>   she herself groans, and turns her face away. (1:8)

> Is it nothing to you, all you who pass by?
> Look and see if there is any sorrow like my sorrow,
>   which was brought upon me,
> which the LORD inflicted on the day of his fierce anger. (1:12)

The Lord has become like an enemy; he has destroyed Israel;
He has destroyed all its palaces, laid in ruins its strongholds,
and multiplied in daughter Judah mourning and lamentation. (2:5)

Look, O LORD, and consider! To whom have you done this?
Should women eat their offspring, the children they have borne?
Should priest and prophet be killed in the sanctuary of the Lord? (2:20)

Let us test and examine our ways, and return to the LORD.
Let us lift up our hearts as well as our hands to God in heaven.
We have transgressed and rebelled, and you have not forgiven. (3:40–42)

The refinement of the poetic language usually takes place on the level of the triple sets of parallel lines. The book shows little development from chapter to chapter. Still, in a most important respect chapter 3 serves as an organizational center. The predominant first-person perspective and the confessions of personal suffering heighten the differentiation between chapter 3 and the remainder of the book. The triple acrostic form in chapter 3 clues the reader to look at the chapter as a special unit. Both the expression of grief and the appeals for divine deliverance assume their strongest forms here.

Repeated Themes

The shape of the book as a whole makes it impossible to follow threads of unity from beginning to end. Instead, the book gains its unity through the repetition of a number of themes. As they occur again and again the depth of need is augmented. Shreds of trust in divine vindication let the reader surmise that Israel's hope survives. The existence of the book attests to the vitality of Israel's hope for its lost institutions. In spite of Israel's loss, the strong sense of national identity survived in the least stable, least permanent thing imaginable—poetry. Israel's song replayed the hardships for the benefit of citizens. They also replayed the events for God: As long as Israel could address the diety, hope survived. In exile, Israel turned to a remembrance of the diety's mercy which took, of course, the shape of poetry. The pathetic complaints reminded Israel of sin in typical deuteronomistic fashion. The complaints also prompted divine intervention. No matter how devastating God's anger, they professed ultimate trust in his response to the hardships of the nation. For the contemporary reader, the message of Lamentations more likely relates to the inevitability of human suffering, the human response to suffering, and the dependability of God to respond to our difficult circumstances. Perhaps one reason Lamentations receives comparatively little attention from readers and exegetes relates to the book's theology. It places responsibility for the psalmist's struggles on God. As indicated, the divine role in human struggles provided a basis for liturgical poetry. The poetry intended to provoke a change in his attitude—from anger to kindness. In light of the contemporary worldview, including the teaching of Jesus recorded in the Gospels, these references to divine punishment appear more literary than real. Whether facing a personal or a corporate tragedy, sufferers do not typically think of themselves as "under the rod of God's wrath," "objects of his destruction," or "rejected by God." Even in the most metaphorical of contemporary poetry, such images rarely occur. Such descriptions lie at the center of biblical poetry. Perception of divine punishment, appeals for repentance, and appeals for God's intervention are the topics integral to Lamentations.

For this reason, Lamentations is the most poetic book of the Hebrew canon in terms of its concentration on the divine-human interchange. This interchange influenced the action of humans and deity alike. By contrast, contemporary poetry focuses upon description of human experience. Current readers emphasize many of the incidental stereotyped features of ancient poetry. These held little value for the ancient reader interested in dynamic interaction with the deity, especially the possibility of influencing benevolent action on the part of the deity. In Lamentations God originally acted through punishment. The human response aimed to incite his more positive action. Other types of poetry aimed to incite continued positive action in response to better fortunes than those found in Lamentations.

The Poetry of the Song of Songs

The Song of Songs expresses more of a celebrative intent than a liturgical intent. This feature makes the Song completely distinct in theme and form. Select psalms which offer praise to God for the wonders of creation present the canon's nearest counterparts to the Song of Songs. The joyful songs of the book celebrate the wonders of human love with similar awe. Beyond this generality more specialized readings of the book risk inaccuracy. The book relates the desire of a woman and a man and their pleasure when together. Such a description of the work leads to a false understanding that the book constitutes an organized love lyric, describing how a couple's relationship begins, develops, and is consummated. Actually, the poetic units of the work exhibit only the loosest connections, communicating the attraction between two individuals through dreamlike scenes. Detailed systems of metaphors describing the beauty of the lovers' bodies complement these accounts. How does such poetry construct reality, as in the previous discussion? Certainly, it cannot do so in the religious sense. The work does not intend to bring a response from the deity. However, the seriousness and intenseness of the human experience remains consistent with the emotional level of religious poetry.

The level of devotion between the two singers leads to the contention "love is strong as death" (8:6). To expand on the title, this poetry comprises the love song of love songs. It expresses passionate commitment on the ultimate level. To the question, "What is your beloved more than another beloved, O fairest among women?" (5:9), the lover answers, "My beloved is all radiant and ruddy, distinguished among ten thousand" (5:10). In a song about the most attractive, most appealing, and most committed couple, the language becomes paradigmatic for all human love. The exaltation of love reinforces its own truth and multiplies its effect. When praised with such high poetry, the individuals become even more desirable. The more often repeated, the more convinced the hearer becomes. This language reveals design for effect. In response to the scenes of the Song, the reader or hearer reacts with the embarrassment of an observed voyeur. Love as well as grief demands an intensity of expression which cannot be matched by the precision of prose.

Adding the Song of Songs to the list of Hebrew poetry significantly expands its scope. Apparently, even though usage provides the impetus for poetry, other factors also determine its worth. Hebrew and Western poetry share a similar interest in human experience. In Western poetry creative personal descriptions show this concern. In Hebrew poetry the effect comes by way of dramatic dialogue. Various speakers or a single speaker from multiple perspectives convey intense feelings through metaphorical language. The Song of Songs depicts speech and action which bring the couple's love to life.

Metaphor appears in all poetry. In Hebrew poetry, through the medium of parallelism, the display of metaphors accounts for most of the poet's language. The Song consists of a riot of images. Most of the images describe the individuals involved. To sum up, poetry seems especially suited for the communication of intense experiences. This includes religous performance and experiences which involve the same depth of feeling as religious expression.

Poetry in Nonpoetic Books

The Poetry of the Torah

The category "poetry" further expands when the study considers poetic content of other books in the Hebrew canon. In the Torah, poetry commonly occurs in units of speech, and almost all speech can be considered poetry. This applies to indirect as well as direct speech. In Genesis the speech of various subjects conveys God's decrees regarding the human role in the world and society. Blessings appear among other brief aphoristic units. The only exception to the appearance of poetry in brief units of speech comes in the lengthier blessings of Jacob in Genesis 49.

Exodus follows a similar pattern, with at least two exceptions. The Song of the Sea in chapter 15 presents a psalmic unit as a ceremony of deliverance. The account of the regulations for the community dictated to Moses by the deity in 20:1–23:22 reveals poetic balance. Repetitions appear poetic in spite of the infrequency of typical parallel structures. Due to thematic differences, the truths affirmed by the small poetic units in Exodus tend to be less global than those in Genesis.

The legal language of Leviticus contains few traces of poetic form, but Numbers contains numerous poetic units. The book contains blessings of various types, cultic chants, and a divine affirmation of Moses' special status

(Num. 12: 3–5). A formal description of Yahweh appears in Numbers 14:18: "The LORD is slow to anger, and abounding in steadfast love, forgiving iniquity and transgression, but by no means clearing the guilty, visiting the iniquity of the parents upon the children to the third and the fourth generation." Such brief examples of stylized cultic forms commonly occur in Numbers. All of them, or nearly all, take the shape of speech. The words of dialogue shared between Moses and rebels evinces traits of poetic composition, as does the grumbling of the people in 20:3–5. The woe oracle of 21:27–30 looks intensely poetic. A proverb introduces the oracle.

The Book of Deuteronomy presents a special case. The entire work, with a few exceptions, relays the speech of Moses. This general literary device seems not to identify the entire book as poetic.[5] Most of this speech conveys a storytelling tone with a concomitant use of language. However, when Deuteronomy quotes individuals in the course of the speech, it casts their speech in poetry. Beyond this, certain legal units exhibit the patterns of sound and measure expected of poetry. The Decalogue (5:6–21) presents one example. Unlike its form in Exodus 20, the regulations which follow the ten do not display similar poetic features. As expected, the Shema and verses following (6:4–25) give indication of careful poetic arrangement. Other legal matter shows similar poetic form (19:1–26:11; 28:16–19; and perhaps others). Curses and blessings (notably 27:15–26 and 28:1–6, respectively) occur in lengthier, perhaps more liturgical, forms. Chapters 32 and 33 each contain lengthy poetic units pronounced by Moses. The first speech offers a condemning salvation history song. The second pronounces a blessing on Israel's tribes. The legal materials described as poetic in form actually express a medial form, stylized speech or the like. The patterns of sound and calculated repetition of phrases reveal a more calculated arrangement than most prose. Prose simply links sentences and paragraphs of historical accounts with the conjunction. Admittedly, Hebrew narrative shows careful artistry, but its literary structures tend to find expression in the larger context rather than the measure of the line. The difference between legal poetry or stylized speech and narrative would likely appear as clear to the Hebrew listener as the difference between story form and rhyme appears to contemporary hearers. The poetry sounds a metrical rhythm absent in narrative readings.

The Poetry of the Former Prophets

Joshua and Judges, in spite of other similarities with Deuteronomy, contain little poetic dialogue and no poetic legal materials. Judges incorporates several poetic units of interest. The Song of Deborah (chap. 5) receives due attention elsewhere in this study.[6] It presents a psalmic celebra-

---

5. Duane L. Christensen, *Deuteronomy 1–11*, WBC 6A (Dallas: Word Books, 1991) has argued for poetic form in Deuteronomy, saying (p. xli): "In its essential nature the book of Deuteronomy is itself a work of literary art in poetic form, subject to the restraints of the musical media to which it was originally composed in ancient Israel." Such a conclusion may stretch the bounds of poetry too far for definition.

6. See pages 177–179 above under "Distinguishing Hebrew Poetry from Prose."

tion of victory sung by the prophet-judge Deborah and her chosen general—Barak. Judges also includes a fable (9:8–15), perhaps the rarest form of poetry in the Hebrew Bible. Samson's riddle and its answer provide the impetus for action resulting in Samson's aphorism: "With the jawbone of a donkey, heaps upon heaps, with the jawbone of a donkey I have slain a thousand men" (Judg. 15:16). The brief statements comprising the verbal duel between Samson and Delilah in chapter 16 also appear poetic. They consist of Delilah's questioning regarding the source of Samson's strength and Samson's answers. Samson presents an especially beautiful account of his vow, though the translation loses the special sound pattern: "A razor has never come upon my head; for I have been a nazirite to God from my mother's womb. If my head were shaved, then my strength would leave me; I would become weak, and be like anyone else" (Judg. 16:17). The interchange between Samson and Delilah involves several such riddles or gnomic sayings which provide structure for their battle of wits.

The Books of Samuel contain little poetic material, like the other books of the former prophets. Hannah's thanksgiving song responded to Samuel's birth as an answer to prayer (1 Sam. 2). Even less speech appears in the form of poetry: a few of Samuel's pronouncements, all the speech connected with the David and Goliath showdown (1 Sam. 17), and especially David's final words to Goliath preceding the contest (vv. 45–47). One of the briefest poetic sentences provides cause for Saul's hatred of David: "Saul has killed his thousands, and David his ten thousands" (1 Sam. 18:7; 21:11). At the death of Saul and Jonathan David voices a lament (2 Sam. 1:19–27) which concentrates more on the exploits of the heroes than do the laments in Psalms and Lamentations. In verse 18, the narrator cites the book of Jashar (apparently a collection of poems of historical interest) as a source for the song. The narrator attributes a hymn identical to Psalm 18 to David in chapter 22. The psalm even repeats the title from the Book of Psalms. The context for the victory celebration of Psalm 18 shows little connection with the events associated with David's deliverance from "the hand of Saul" (v. 1). It serves as a strong poetic epilogue to David's life, like those uttered by Moses in Deuteronomy 32 and 33. The following chapter presents a hymn (2 Sam. 23:1–7) described as the last words of David. This poem also resembles the psalms, but it expresses general praise by affirming God's fair retribution for acceptance or rejection of the king. It manifests a stronger tone in this regard than most royal songs.

Poetry appears in certain critical passages in the Books of Kings. The blessing and prayer Solomon offers at the dedication of the temple reveal liturgical ordering. Solomon's remembrance of God's choice to dwell in mystery begins the poetic expression: "The LORD has said that he would dwell in thick darkness. I have built you an exalted house, a place for you to dwell in forever" (1 Kings 8:12–13).

In 1 Kings 10:6–9 the queen of Sheba uses slightly awkward poetry to praise Solomon's wisdom as a gift from God. A summary statement of his wealth (10:23–25) demonstrates the same halting poetry. It contains just enough repetition to lend formality to the list. After Solomon's death, the dialogue between Rehoboam, his counselors, and his subjects take on the polished form of brief prophetic oracles (chap. 12). Poetic diction highlights (1) the emotional plea of the people, (2) the well-considered advice of the cabinet, and (3) the determined ruthlessness of Rehoboam. No wonder the interchange culminates with the response, "What share do we have in David? We have no inheritance in the son of Jesse. To your tents, O Israel! Look now to your own house, O David" (v. 16*b*). These stylized responses especially suit dramatic portrayals, where dialogue, as in all ancient drama, comes in the form of poetry.

In 2 Kings 3:16–19, the playing of musicians prompted Elisha's prophecy, which surely fit within a melody. Jehu's pretended call to solemn assembly of all Baal devotees sounded like a legitimate liturgical summons (2 Kings 10:19). Another brief poetic unit occurs with Elisha's pronouncement of victory over Aram: "The LORD's arrow of victory, the arrow of victory over Aram! For you shall fight the Arameans in Aphek until you have made an end of them" (2 Kings 13:17). The shooting of an arrow accompanied this saying as an active sign of future events. Challenges from Assyria begin a three-part poetic interchange. First, when the representative of Assyria taunts the Israelites at the wall of Judah, he employs poetic language (2 Kings 18:19–35). Second, Hezekiah's responding prayer for God's help also employs poetic language (2 Kings 19:15–19). Third, when the prophet Isaiah voices the divine answer to Hezekiah's prayer, it assumes poetic form. Isaiah's prophetic word maintains a first-person perspective throughout (2 Kings 19:21–28). The divine message condemns Assyria for challenging God's people and promises defeat and repulsion for the attacking armies. Speech from the mouth of God also occurs in 20:17–18. The condemnation of Manasseh, a rather indirect citiation of prophecy, contains little poetic sound and rhythm (2 Kings 21:11–15).

Most of the poetry in the Former Prophets appears as poetry amid prose. This especially applies to units influenced by poetic portions of the Hebrew canon like the prophecy of 2 Kings 19:21–28 (Isa. 10:13–19) and 2 Samuel 22 (Ps. 18). One would expect many more of these citations than the few which actually occur. Brief poetic quotations (like Samson's riddles) offer a further example of this tendency. The Former Prophets do not include a single work with poetry as primary content. However, the Former Prophets contain a few examples of a special poetic form. The dialogues of Samson with his opponents, David and Goliath, and Rehoboam with the people form dramatic scenes. These dialogues involve: (1) a major character and that character's antagonist(s), (2) emphasis on the speech of major actors, and (3) a violent or emotional conclusion. Such appearance of climactic dramas in the narrative of the Former Prophets shows special reliance on poetry at points of emphasis.

The Poetry of the Latter Prophets: Major Prophets

The latter prophetic books differ from law and former prophets in that poetry does not simply support and reinforce narrative in these books. Instead, poetry serves as the basic medium. Historical explanations underpin poetic oracles. Prophecy consists of the communication of divine messages gained by means of the prophet's special link with the deity. These messages assume the forms of poetic expression known as prophetic oracles. Discussion of the manifold types and situations of oracles belongs to studies specifically devoted to the subject.[7]

Isaiah. Intense interest centers on the dependence of the prophets on poetic expression not integral to the prophetic message itself. When Isaiah describes Yahweh's displeaure with Judah by means of a love song (5:1–10), for instance, notable overlap occurs between prophetic study proper and the subject of this investigation. When prophetic units appear psalmic, as they often do, the issue of dependence or interdependence between prophet and temple singer arises. Temple liturgy clearly influenced the prophets. Dependence on prophecy by temple poets and singers presents equally fruitful avenues for research. In spite of the segmentation of the study of prophets and psalmists, the two interests show more contact than a previous generation of scholars admitted.[8]

Isaiah contains some of the most carefully crafted poetry of the Bible. One example appears in 61:1–3*a*:

> The spirit of the Lord GOD is upon me,
> because the LORD has anointed me;
> he has sent me to bring good news to the oppressed,
> to bind up the brokenhearted,
> to proclaim liberty to the captives,
> and release to the prisoners;
> to proclaim the year of the LORD's favor,
> and the day of vengeance of our God;
> to comfort all who mourn;
> to provide for those who mourn in Zion—
> to give them a garland instead of ashes,

7. See D. Brent Sandy and Ronald L. Giese, Jr., eds. *Cracking Old Testament Codes: A Guide to Interpreting Old Testament Literary Forms* (Nashville: Broadman & Holman Publishers, 1995); Gary V. Smith, *The Prophets as Preachers: An Introduction to the Hebrew Prophets* (Nashville: Broadman & Holman Publishers, 1994); Gene M. Tucker, "Prophecy and the Prophetic Literature," *The Hebrew Bible and Its Modern Interpreters,* ed. Douglas A. Knight and Gene M. Tucker (Philadelphia: Fortress Press, 1985), 325–68; C. Hassell Bullock, *An Introduction to the Old Testament Prophetic Books* (Chicago: Moody Press), 1986; and Willem A. Vangemeren, *Interpreting the Prophetic Word* (Grand Rapids: Zondervan, 1990). For recent form critical terminology in prophecy, see Ronald M. Hals, *Ezekiel,* FOTL 19 (Grand Rapids: Eerdmans, 1989). Examples of earlier works include Klaus Koch, *The Prophets: The Assyrian Period* (Philadelphia: Fortress, 1982); Klaus Koch, *The Prophets: The Babylonian and Persian Periods* (Philadelphia: Fortress, 1982); and Claus Westermann, *Basic Forms of Prophetic Speech,* trans. Hugh Clayton White (Louisville: Westminster/John Knox, 1967; rev. 1991).

8. See, for example, David Noel Freedman, *Pottery, Poetry, and Prophecy: Studies in Early Hebrew Poetry* (Winona Lake, Ind.: Eisenbraun's, 1980), 7–11.

> the oil of gladness instead of mourning,
> the mantle of praise instead of a faint spirit.

The poetic tone of the three sections of Isaiah follows the themes their contents address: In 1–39 the poetry expresses divine displeasure against rebellious Judah and national neighbors; in 40–55 the tenor of comfort and hope to the nation in exile emanates from almost every oracle; and in 56–66 a mixture of judgment and promise conveys the ups and downs of morals and morale for the exiles returned to the land.

The sense of desperation common to Isaiah 1–39 pervades the record of divine commissioning in 6:9–13:

> "'Keep listening, but do not comprehend;
> keep looking, but do not understand.'
> Make the mind of this people dull,
> and stop their ears, and shut their eyes,
> so that they may not look with their eyes,
> and listen with their ears,
> and comprehend with their minds, and turn and be healed."
> Then I said, "How long, O Lord?" And he said:
> "Until cities lie waste without inhabitant,
> and houses without people, and the land is utterly desolate;
> until the Lord sends everyone far away,
> and vast is the emptiness in the midst of the land.
> Even if a tenth part remain in it, it will be burned again,
> like a terebinth or an oak whose stump remains standing
> when it is felled."
> The holy seed is its stump.

The four servant songs comprise one of the distinct features of Isaiah 40–55. The following quotation comes from the first song:

> Here is my servant, whom I uphold,
> my chosen, in whom my soul delights;
> I have put my spirit upon him;
> he will bring forth justice to the nations.
> He will not cry or lift up his voice,
> or make it heard in the street;
> a bruised reed he will not break,
> and a dimly burning wick he will not quench;
> he will faithfully bring forth justice.
> He will not grow faint or be crushed
> until he has established justice in the earth;
> and the coastlands wait for his teaching. (Isa. 42:1–4)

The poetry of Isaiah is among the best biblical poetry in terms of literariness, complexity of structure, and sensitive development of images. Little, if any, of the book exhibits prose structure.

Jeremiah. Jeremiah includes scattered prose passages interspersed with poetic oracles. Several of the oracles of Jeremiah appear in prose, but only chapters 32–44 lack poetry. These chapters do not contain oracles. Jeremiah's poetry possesses general characteristics which distinguish it from Isaiah's: (1) its vocabulary and development of images are simpler; (2) the content displays more historical and active interests, a less reflective mood; (3) the oracles confront problems more directly and are almost entirely judgment oracles against Judah and other nations; (4) its message maintains a more direct connection with the lived experience of the prophet; and (5) the individual units bear less relationship to the structure of the book as a whole.

The strength of Jeremiah's poetry lies in the deftness with which it portrays suffering of all varieties. The prominence of this theme, along with the well-documented suffering of the prophet himself, surely contributed to the association of Lamentations with Jeremiah.

Ezekiel. In contradistinction to Isaiah and Jeremiah, Ezekiel employs more prose than poetry. More likely, Ezekiel's oracles consist of measured prose or lined prose with slightly looser formal structure than that previously termed "stylized prose." For example, the "prose" of 6:3–4 and following verses exhibit several poetic features:

> You mountains of Israel, hear the work of the Lord GOD! Thus says the Lord GOD to the mountains and the hills, to the ravines and the valleys; I, I myself will bring a sword upon you, and I will destroy your high places. Your altars shall become desolate, and your incense stands shall be broken; and I will throw down your slain in front of your idols.

These lines show parallel form and sound patterns. Two double pairs of words with similar stress and endings occur in verse 4. The brief passage serves as a small sample among dozens of similarly structured oracles.

The more conspicuously poetic oracles display a thoroughness in the elaboration of images more characteristic of prose. The careful development of the messages, even through allegory, leaves little room for ambiguity or misunderstanding. Such analytic precision surprises the reader familiar with the prophet Ezekiel's eccentricity and sometime instability. Allegorical images occur in 19:1–14 (the lioness and the vine); 15:1–8 (the worthless vine); 23:1–49 (Oholah and Oholibah); and 31:2–18 (the cedar). The allegories show identical style, yet were clearly developed as isolated units. All bear the message of God's displeasure and punishment after a mocking review of history punctuated by pride. Ezekiel's development of the lamentation over city or nation shows a unique prophetic style. These remembrances of the greatness of the population centers emphasizes their futures. Ezekiel moves forward in time to witness the promised devastation. Ancient Near Eastern peoples commonly used lamentations for cities, as the book which bears the name attests. Ezekiel reconceived them as oracles of doom. He used them to predict collapse as the result of divine judgment.

When the visions of Ezekiel 36–48 peer into the distant future, they reveal similar original poetic design. The prophetic work measures the language carefully. Even the vision of the temple and redivision of the land reflect the measured prose style. In its larger organization, as well as the structure of smaller units, Ezekiel shows profound attention to the development of its message. The author placed the oracles in precise chronological order with few exceptions.

The Poetry of the Latter Prophets: Minor Prophets

In the minor prophets, poetic forms and usage parallel those present in the major prophets. Each of the minor prophets manifests distinctives, and all the minor prophets include poetry. Haggai and Malachi contain the least convincing units. Hosea and Amos present lawsuit formulas also present in the major prophets. In Hosea this takes the form of the covenant lawsuit.[9] Hosea's covenant lawsuits present Israel's obligation to Yahweh in terms of a marriage contract (see especially 4:1–6). Hosea's poetry depicts Israel's rebellion as tragic infidelity to God's proven love. The presentation of this theme exhibits a special pathos.

Amos emphasizes the voice of divine judgment. God speaks clearly and strongly of certain punishment. Amos opens with woe oracles written in a special style. These oracles convey judgment against six neighboring peoples, Judah, and last and most elaborately, Israel. Each of the oracles begins with the phrase: "For three transgressions of . . . and for four, I will not revoke the punishment." The four prophetic visions of chapters 7 and 8 exemplify Amos' vivid imagery. In each case, an apparition communicates God's intended retribution.

The poetry of Joel appears much later than that of Hosea and Amos. Joel shares with Zephaniah prophetic poetry of a special type, known as apocalyptic. This literature looks to the future and God's ultimate plans for the world. It is marked by vivid images of destruction, and occasionally, idyllic scenes of peace. Both Zephaniah and Joel employ this language in description of the expected Day of the Lord. Events associated with this day of restitution parallel those implied by the current phrase, "judgment day."

Other minor prophets emphasize God's dissatisfaction with neighboring peoples. Obadiah assumes the form of a poetic oracle against Edom, looking forward to its final destruction. Nahum portrays a similar end for Nineveh, capital of Assyria. In both Obadiah and Nahum the judgment and Israel's benefit assume the grandiose proportions of the Day of the Lord.

Micah expresses a more positive tone. Its smaller poems and formal organization distinguish Micah among the minor prophets. The book opens with judgment oracles and a rehearsal of the social ills of eighth-century Judah. Beginning with the fourth chapter, Micah envisions a bright future to follow judgment. Mentions of rebellion continue, yet the forecast of the future merciful leadership of God displaces the negative tone.

Habakkuk's approach to national woes constitutes a different reaction for later times. This poetry questions the justice of divine guidance of

---

9. See Douglas Stuart, *Hosea-Jonah*, WBC 31 (Waco: Word Books, 1987), 69–87; Trent C. Butler, "Announcements of Judgment," *Cracking Old Testament Codes*, Sandy and Giese, eds.; and the bibliography cited in each of these.

events, much as Job did. The closing chapter, introduced as a prayer, assumes the form of a hymn. Musical directions conclude Habakkuk (3:19*b*). The psalm emphasizes the sovereignty and power of God so that its relation to the previous chapters of Habakkuk is obvious. It affirms God's ability to intervene and defends the trustworthiness of his prerogative to decide when and where.

Jonah contains a single unit of poetry: the song of thanksgiving in chapter 2. Jonah sings from the belly of the fish. In all outward respects the song resembles the songs of thanks in the Psalter.

The night visions of Zechariah contain poetic themes and forms. The organization of all the poetry of Zechariah shows apocalyptic concerns. Many of the oracles in Zechariah 9–14 show signs that they existed as independent poetic units loosely strung together.

The Poetry of Wisdom Books

The first part of this work surveys general themes and content of wisdom literature. Accordingly, the interest at this point centers on basic poetic trends within the wisdom books and poetic trends common to the wisdom collection. The truisms of Proverbs assume a loose poetic form. Hymns to wisdom (for example, Prov. 8:1–36) and similar units comprise the book's most "poetic" sections. The warnings against sexual misconduct probably appeared in poetic lines. They look more like narrative in their current form. Rhythm seems more important than semantics in *mĕšālîm* (proverbs). The heavy beat that falls on the last word of the half line does not necessarily mark the most important element of the unit. Yet such structure surely influenced the understanding of the proverb. The American proverb, "a stitch in time, saves nine," though actually only a half line in length, shows similar emphasis on the last word of each phrase.

Job contains measured prose throughout, with the exception of the prologue and epilogue, which reveal no poetic form. Units such as the hymn to wisdom in chapter 28 contain slightly more poetic parallelism and rhythmic speech than other portions of Job. The content of the book fits the designation, "poetry of oration," in that it appears more dramatic than melodic. Other Hebrew poetry almost always involves musical performance.

Of the three wisdom books, Ecclesiastes shows the least poetic connections in its overall form. The interpreter cannot definitely characterize Ecclesiastes as either prose or poetry. Its choppy composition causes this difficulty. The book uses poetic stresses erratically. Ecclesiastes strings together many minute poetic sayings that exhibit very consistent forms. These units continue for only a few lines. Otherwise, the book reveals only a loose thematic organization. Longer poetic passages include the "time to" poem of 3:1–9 and collections of proverbs in chapters 7, 10, and 11. Qoheleth communicated in a disturbed form, perhaps because of the crisis of meaning he experienced.

The Poetry of the Writings Other Than Wisdom

Among the other books of the Writings, Ruth and Esther display similar prose forms. In Ruth, only two brief units are poetic: Ruth's "entreat me not to leave you . . ." (1:16–17, NKJV) and Naomi's "call me no longer Naomi" (1:20–21). The longest units of speech in Ruth occur during the account of Boaz's redemption of the family property. His speeches appear in stylized prose which approaches poetry.

By contrast, Esther narrates its story in storyteller's language throughout. This makes Esther the most consistently prose work in the Hebrew Bible. Even the examples of speech within Esther, though conveying more sound patterns than the narrative, appear decidedly as prose.

Ezra, Nehemiah, and Chronicles together make up the literature of the Chronicler and contain little poetry. Ezra includes only a brief song of praise to Yahweh in 3:11: "For he is good, for his steadfast love endures forever toward Israel." Identical and similar units occur in 2 Chronicles 5:13; 7:3; and 20:21. Psalm 118 and other psalms repeat the same phrase. This indicates the nature of the refrain as a liturgical formula known to the Chronicler.

Nehemiah includes a confession of Israel's sin in 9:6–37. Although it shows little parallelism, it includes repetitive sounds and evidence of lineation. It appears to be a creedlike form of Israel's history of rebellion. The confession mirrors deuteronomistic theology in its association of loss of freedom with misconduct.

Chronicles consists of repeated history from 2 Samuel and Kings. For this reason, significant differences in the form and use of poetry in Chronicles assume importance. First Chronicles adds only a brief prophecy (12:18) and a composite psalm (16:8–36). The psalm draws content from several psalms in the Psalter. The Chronicler attributes the psalm to David. According to the Chronicler, David instituted the singing of psalms (1 Chron. 16:7). Other than repeated material from Kings in chapters 6 and 10, Second Chronicles offers only one poetic unit. The message of Hanani the prophet to Asa in 16:7–9 displays conventional poetic features. In many respects it appears less aural in composition than older prophetic oracles. The key difference revolves around the relatively random arrangement of its sound patterns. In general, throughout the Chronicler's work speech less frequently assumes the form of poetry. On the other hand, the Chronicler always presents prophecy as poetry. The work commonly quotes liturgical material. Compositions original to the Chronicler or his times appear hastily or derivatively composed. These poetic units lack the metrical balance and aural rhythms of previous poetry.

Daniel presents numerous poetic compositions. In 2:20–23 Daniel gives thanks for God's interpretation of a dream. In 3:4–6 Nebuchadnezzar's proclamation demanding worship of the statue assumes poetic form. The account of Nebuchadnezzar's dream (Dan. 4:10–17; [Heb.4:7–14]) reveals poetic form, perhaps due to its allegorical nature. Daniel's interpretation of the dream exhibits a similar, if less consistent line structure (Dan. 4:20–27; [Heb. 4:17–24]). Not surprisingly, Nebuchadnezzar's praise of Daniel's God also takes on poetic form (Dan. 4:34–35, 37; [Heb. 4:31–32, 34]). Some difference in poetic treatment begins with chapter 5. Verses 17–28 contain carefully designed oratory interpreting the apparition Belshazzar saw. Beginning with this florid poetic passage, all remaining visions and interpretations reveal much more poetic structure than in earlier chapters. These passages account for most of the speech in chapters 5–12.

Chapters 7–12 contain apocalyptic visions. These show a preference for alliteration rather than rhythmic forms common to earlier poetry. Perhaps they sounded like incantation. Most certainly the repeated consonants reinforced the mysterious nature of the coded language. Much difference exists between this type of poetry and public psalmic forms. Apocalyptic units appear as spoken poetry rather than sung poetry. Perhaps their effectiveness depended on isolated strings of sounds like cadences rather than metrical purity.

As seen in this overview, poetry pervades the Hebrew Bible, accounting for as much as one half of its contents. The earliest prophetic message and the latest cultic response to divine demands are alike cast in poetry.

The Poetry of Deuterocanonical Wisdom

Poetry continues its preeminence in the deuterocanonical materials.[10] All this poetry derives from liturgical materials. For this reason it bears only a partial resemblance to ancient Hebrew poetry. The poetry of the deuterocanonical books accords with the poetry of the Psalms. It offers few points of contact with other segments of the Hebrew canon.

The poetry of deuterocanonical wisdom shows strong ties to the earlier wisdom books of the Hebrew canon. However, in some respects, the deuterocanonical wisdom books provide evidence of more detailed attention to poetic form. Sirach shows careful poetic organization within its several lengthier units. Its lineation mimics that of Proverbs in most respects. Sirach almost always makes use of synonymous parallelism. By contrast, Proverbs prefers antithetic parallelism. The hymn to wisdom in Sirach 24:1–22 praises wisdom with expansive, lavish language and calculated parallelism. The hymn to the ancestors (Sirach 44–50) contains a mixture of synonymous parallelism and narrative parallelism.

The Wisdom of Solomon uses both synonymous and narrative parallelism to a degree uncommon in the Hebrew Bible. The celebration of immortality in The Wisdom of Solomon 1–5 comprises the most extended unit of consistent parallelism in the greater wisdom canon. The parallel lines combine to form a carefully developed document, unique for this extended employment of synonymous units. The remainder of The

---

10. The poetry of Tobit, Baruch, Azariah and the Song of the Three Jews, the Prayer of Manasseh, and Psalm 151 receive attention pages 346–354.

Wisdom of Solomon contrasts sharply with this description due to its narrative form. Clear lineation without repetition in successive lines characterizes
the parallelism. The Wisdom of Solomon 6–19 tends to center on thematic
progression rather than larger poetic structures. The lines, like those of Sirach's narrative parallelism, show careful measure and division, but exhibit
no further poetic features.

The Nature of Hebrew Poetry

Preceding discussions observed that Hebrew poetry involved three
special activities in ancient Israel: (1) liturgical enactment, (2) active
remembrance of history and identity, and (3) intense emotional expression. Discussions also suggested canonical poetry falls into three main
rubrics: psalms, prophecy, and love poetry. Following the review above,
these basic observations need further expansion. In use and type, as well as
in formal recognition, the differences between psalms and prophecy or
prophecy and love poetry represent many shades of intent, illustrating various degrees of similarity. If degree of contrast or similarity marks the distinction between poetry and prose, degree also marks the distinctives of the
general contexts and types of poetry itself.

As Israel's poetry developed, the three activities related to poetry
listed above tended to fuse into psalmic forms. Psalmic forms expressed
emotions and emphasized historical continuity concurrently. Psalms did
not necessarily emerge as the latest forms of poetry. They did assume primary importance for later worshiping communities. The blessing and curse
comprise the earliest forms of prophetic poetry, appearing as they do, in the
earliest accounts of Israel's history. It is likely that blessings and curses
appeared quite early in the psalms of the worshiping community, along with
cultic chants and legal forms (such as the Decalogue). Psalms, proper, offer
a challenge with regard to date. The antiquity of examples like the Song of
Deborah (Judg. 5) commends an early dating for these forms as well,
although the final shaping of the Psalter would take place several centuries
later.

Early poetic units tended toward brevity. They provided in condensed
form strong incitements to solidarity. Sentence-length confessions of belief
in Yahweh and two-line curses and blessings dependent on accordance with
his purposes reveal a simplistic character. Such simplistic poetic conceptions enabled Israel to present its history against this backdrop. Both the
Deuteronomist and the Chronicler patterned history in accord with Israel's
rejection of known goods. They built this framework for history upon the
blessing, the curse, and the confession of God's trustworthiness. Accounts
of trust or rebellion could occur in prose form. Calls to faith occurred
almost exclusively in poetry. The performance of cultic ritual in the temple
took its place at the center of Israel's history. In this way Psalms fell under
the rubric of such calls to confession. Psalms promoted faithfulness to
Israel's history through passionate portrayals of Israel's identity in relation-

ship with the deity. The brief affirmations which occur so frequently within Torah and Psalms even appear in the work of the Chronicler.

The prayers of the canon, such as those offered by Jonah (2:1–9), Solomon (1 Kings 8: 22–53), and the Deuterocanon (for example, Sirach 24:1–22) also appear psalmic, that is, as liturgical compositions rather than individual compositions. Other material possesses original form. This includes various fables, parables, and allegories. The dialogical speech from Job and elsewhere compares to no known liturgical form in Israel. The visions of Daniel, though intended as prophecy of a certain sort, display a style of their own. In theme, they are like the oracles of hope of the latter prophets. In their style, the visions of Daniel appear to be literary compositions rather than oral messages. This same feature applies to the Hebrew wisdom materials. There, liturgical profession is the exception rather than the rule.

Because of the centrality of psalmic confession, one might consider the Song of Songs as the conversion to love poetry of a number of psalmic confessions. Instead, a number of Egyptian parallels attest to its original composition as love poetry. Other than a few contacts with love poetry such as Isaiah 5:1–5 (Vineyard Song) and Hosea, the Song remains unique. It manifests an entirely unclear relationship to other biblical poetry. Thematically, it bears closer resemblance to wisdom books than poetry books.

This survey makes possible the listing of all the poetry of the Hebrew Bible. The criteria for selection include: (1) appearance as verse in *Biblia Hebraica Stuttgartensia,* (2) comparatively equal length of lines based on Masoretic accents, (3) heightened alliteration and other sound patterns, (4) semantic parallelism, and (5) melodic rhythm. Of all these features, sound takes preeminence. At times sound patterns consist of repetitions or similarities in vowel and consonant sounds. At times they consist of similar metrical patterns in successive lines. At other times they consist of similarities in opening or closing words in half lines, lines, or doublets. The following list omits several single-line units and incorporates some units not previously recognized as poetry.

Table 6
Poetic Texts in the Hebrew Bible

Genesis	2:23; 3:14–19; 4:23–24; 8:22; 9:6–7, 25–27; 14:19–20; 16:11–12; 24:60; 25:23; 27:27–29, 39–40; 48:15–16, 20; 49:2–27
Exodus	3:14–15; 15:1–18, 21; 20:1–23:22; 32:18; 34:6–7
Leviticus	10:3
Numbers	6:24–26; 10:35–36; 12:6–8; 14:18; 16:3–30; 20:3–5; 21:17–18, 27–30; 23:7–10, 18–24; 24:3–9, 15–24
Deuteronomy	5:6–21; 6:4–25; 19:1–26:11; 27:15–26; 28:1–6, 15–19; 32:1–43; 33:2–29

Table 6 (Continued)
Poetic Texts in the Hebrew Bible

Joshua	6:26; 10:12–13
Judges	5:2–31; 9:8–15; 14:14, 18; 15:16; 16:6–17, 23–24
1 Samuel	2:1–10; 15:22–23, 33; 17:24–47; 18:7; 21:11; 29:5
2 Samuel	1:19–27; 3:33–34; 20:1; 22:2–51; 23:1–7
1 Kings	8:12–61; 10:6–9, 23–25; 12:4–16; 19:14
2 Kings	3:16–19; 7:1; 10:19; 18:19–35; 19:15–19, 21–28; 20:17–18; 22:13, 16–20
Isaiah	(largely poetry)
Jeremiah	(scattered poetry except for prose of 32–35)
Ezekiel	(measured prose or lined prose in oracles)
Hosea	(all poetry except for personal history of 1–3)
Joel	(all poetry except for 2:30–3:8)
Amos	(largely poetry)
Obadiah	(all poetry)
Jonah	(2:2–9)
Micah	(all poetry)
Nahum	(all poetry)
Habakkuk	(all poetry)
Zephaniah	(all poetry)
Haggai	1:4–11; 2:3–9, 14–19, 21–23
Zechariah	(largely poetry)
Malachi	(largely poetry)
Job	(3:2–42:6)
Psalms	(all poetry)
Proverbs	(all poetry)
Ecclesiastes	(small units of poetry throughout)
Song of Songs	(all poetry)
Lamentations	(all poetry)
Ruth	1:16–17, 20–21
Ezra	3:11

Table 6 (Continued)
Poetic Texts in the Hebrew Bible

Nehemiah	9:6–37
1 Chronicles	12:18; 16:8–36
2 Chronicles	5:13; 6:1–42; 7:3; 10:4–14, 16; 20:21
Daniel	2:20–23; 3:4–6; 4:3 (Heb. 3:33); 4:10–17 (Heb. 4:7–14); 4:20–27 (Heb. 4:17–24) 4:34–35 (Heb. 4:31–32); 4:37 (Heb. 4:34); 5:17–28; 6:26–27 (Heb. 27–28); chapters 7–12 (poetry throughout)

Poetry in Israel's Life and Worship

Questions regarding Israel's own view of its poetry begin with form critical interests. Israel used poetry in such diverse manners, the plural "poetries" may better apply. Poetry served multiple social functions. Its settings vary according to their setting in time as well. Biblical poetry existed at least as early as about 1300 B.C.E. and continued until about 100 B.C.E. In spite of all these variables, the genres of form criticism provide a ready means to categorize the vast literature. Our consideration of poetry in terms of canonical books places the more specific division of form criticism into broad categories. First, cultic poetry consists of the Psalms and similar liturgical material, including the lament as a major subcategory. Second, prophetic poetry accounts mostly for oracles, since much of the remaining prophetic poetry is cultic in nature. Third, love poetry focuses almost exclusively on the Song of Songs. Fourth, wisdom poetry consists of proverbs and lengthier didactic forms. Finally, a miscellaneous category is not necessarily less important. These include the measured prose of the Torah, the stylized lines of Ezekiel, and the dramatic poetry of Job and the former prophets. Indeed, in other surveys of poetry one or more of the major classifications above could legitimately be described as miscellany.

Gunkel listed three features which guided the identification of a genre: (1) a common setting in life, (2) common emotions and themes, and (3) common literary forms.[11] The first of these features eludes ready characterization. Social settings depend on the critic's educated guess as well as detailed information. Each commentator on each book of Hebrew poetry produces or borrows his own list of genres. The list below relies on the study of poetic materials in part two of this work. The list presumes no claims of comprehensiveness or originality. The genres of the list remain somewhat tentative. More thorough treatments of life settings would settle many questions. This introductory survey of poetry cannot fully explore such issues.[12]

---

11. Hermann Gunkel, *The Psalms: A Form-Critical Introduction*, trans. Thomas M. Horner (Philadelphia: Fortress Press, 1967), 10.

12. For further study, see Erhard S. Gerstenberger, *Psalms: Part 1 with an Introduction to Cultic Poetry*, FOTL 14 (Grand Rapids: Eerdmans, 1988); Sandy and Giese, eds., *Cracking Old Testament Codes*.

Table 7
Types of Poetic Units in the Hebrew Bible

Cultic Poetry	
Affirmation of Leadership	Numbers 21:17–18
Battle Blessing	Psalm 20
Blessing	Genesis 9:26–27; 14:19–20; 24:60; 27:27–29; 48:15–16, 20; Numbers 6:24–26; 23:7–10, 18–24; 24:3–9; Deuteronomy 28:1–6
Call to Fidelity	Deuteronomy 6:4–25
Call to Worship	2 Kings 10; 19; Psalms 15; 24; 122
Ceremonial Naming	Genesis 16:1–12
Cultic Disputation	Numbers 16:3–30; 20:3–5; 1 Kings 12:4–15; 2 Chronicles 10:4–14
Curse	Genesis 9:25; 27:39–40; Deuteronomy 27:15–26; 28:16–19; Joshua 6:26; 1 Samuel 15:33; Psalm 58
Divine Warrior Hymn	Habakkuk 3:2–19; Psalm 29
Etiology	Genesis 2:23; 3:14–19; 8:22
Explanation of Divine Name	Exodus 3:14–15; 34:6–7; Numbers 14:18
Holiness Pronouncement	Leviticus 10:3
Hymn	Psalms 8; 19; 33; 66; 68; 96; 97; 98; 100; 104; 111; 115; 117; 134; 135; 145; 146; 147; 148; 149; 150; 1 Chronicles 16:8–36; Daniel 4:3 (3:33); 4:34–35 (4:31–32); 37 (34); 6:26–27 (6:27–28)
Investment with Divine Authority	Numbers 12:6–8
Kingship Psalm	2 Samuel 23:1–7; Psalms 2; 47; 72; 89; 93; 95; 110; 132

Table 7 (Continued)
Types of Poetic Units in the Hebrew Bible

Lament	2 Samuel 1:19–27; 3:33–34; 1 Kings 19:14; 2 Kings 19:15–19; Lamentations 1–5; Joel 1:2–2:2; Habakkuk 1:2–2:5; Job; Psalms 3; 4; 5; 6; 7; 9; 10; 12; 13; 14; 17; 22; 25; 26; 28; 31; 35; 38; 39; 41; 42; 43; 44; 51; 52; 53; 54; 55; 56; 57; 59; 60; 61; 64; 69; 70; 71; 74; 77; 79; 80; 83; 85; 86; 88; 90; 94; 102; 108; 109; 120; 123; 126; 129; 130; 137; 139; 140; 141; 142; 143; 144; Ruth 1:20–21; Isaiah 23:1–7; 47:1–15; Jeremiah 7:29; 14:2–10, 17–22; Ezekiel 19:1–14; 27:1–36; 32:2–16
Legal Prohibition	Exodus 20:1–26; Deuteronomy 5:6–21; 22:1–12
Mercy Song	1 Kings 8:12–61
Miracle Formula	Joshua 10:12–13
Penalty Decree	Genesis 9:6
Pronouncement of Tribal Status	Genesis 49:2–27; Deuteronomy 33:1–29
Ritual Invocation	Numbers 10:35–36; 2 Chronicles 7:3
Salvation History Hymn	Deuteronomy 32:1–43; Psalms 78; 81; 105; 106; Nehemiah 9:6–37
Song of Trust	Psalms 16; 23; 27; 46; 62; 63; 121; 131
Thanksgiving/Victory Song	Exodus 15:1–18, 21; Judges 5:1–31; 16:23–24; 1 Samuel 2:1–10; 2 Samuel 22:2–51; Jonah 2:2–9; Psalms 18; 21; 30; 34; 40; 65; 67; 75; 76; 92; 103; 107; 116; 118; 124; 136; 138; Ezra 3:11; 2 Chronicles 5:13; 20:21; Daniel 2:20–23
Torah Hymn	Psalm 119
Vengeance Song	Genesis 4:23–24
Wisdom Psalm	Psalms 1; 11; 36; 37; 49; 50; 73; 82; 91; 101; 112; 125; 127; 128; 133
Zion Song	Psalms 48; 84; 87

Table 7 (Continued)
Types of Poetic Units in the Hebrew Bible

Prophetic Poetry[a]	
Account of Prophetic Suffering	Jeremiah 11:18–12:4; 15:2–21; 17:14–18; 18:19–23; 20:7–13, 14–18
Allegory	Ezekiel 15:1–8; 18:1–11; 19:1–14; 23:1–49; 32:2–18
Apocalyptic Oracle	Zephaniah 1:2–18; 3:6–20; Zechariah 1:8–6:15; 11:4–14:21; Daniel 7–12[b]
Apparition	Daniel 5:17–28
Birth Oracle	Genesis 25:23
Call to Justice	Isaiah 1:10–17; 59:1–19; Amos 5:14–15; and others
Divine Lawsuit	Hosea 4:1–11a; Isaiah 1:2–31; 40:1–29; Jeremiah 2:2–37
Dramatic Ridicule of Idols	Isaiah 40:18–20; 46:1–4; Jeremiah 10:2–16
Dramatization	Hosea 1–3; Ezekiel 4:1–17; 5:1–12; 12:1–20
Dream Account	Daniel 4:10–17 (4:7–14); 4:20–27 (4:17–24)
Judgment Oracle	1 Samuel 15:22–23; 2 Kings 22:16–20; Isaiah 22:1–14; Jeremiah 14:2–10; Ezekiel 6:1–7; and others
Messianic Oracle	Isaiah 11:1–9, 10–16; Jeremiah 23:1–8; 33:14–26
Oath Pledging Loyalty to King	1 Chronicles 12:18
Oracle Against False Prophets/Priests	Malachi 1:6–2:9; Jeremiah 23:9–15; Ezekiel 13:1–23
Oracle of Hope	for example: Isaiah 2:2–4; 25:6–10; 40:1–31; 54:1–17; 61:1–11; Ezekiel 47:13–48:35
Oracle Prophesying Defeat of Enemies	Numbers 24:15–24; 2 Kings 3:18–19; Isaiah 13:2–22; Jeremiah 46–51

Table 7 (Continued)
Types of Poetic Units in the Hebrew Bible

Parable	Isaiah 28:23–29
Profession of Divine Love	Hosea 11:1–4, 8–9
Prophecy of Dynastic Doom	2 Kings 20:17–18
Salvation Oracle	2 Kings 3:16–17; 7:1; 19:21–28; and others
Servant Song	Isaiah 42:1–4; 49:1–6; 50:4–11; 52:13–53:12
Vision Account	Amos 7:1–9; 8:1–3; Jeremiah 24:1–10; Ezekiel 1:4–28; 8:2–10:22; 37:1–14; 40:2–44:8; 46:19–47:12
Woe Oracle	Numbers 21:27–30; Habakkuk 2:6–17
Love Poetry[c]	
Love Song	Jeremiah 2:1–3; Song of Songs
Love Song/Oracle	Isaiah 5:1–7
Wedding Song	Psalm 45
Wisdom Poetry[d]	
Creation Challenge	Job 38–41
Fable	Judges 9:8–15
Dialogue	Job
Hymn to Wisdom	Job 28:1–28
Moral Instruction	Proverbs 1–9; 30:1–31:31
Pronouncement of Wisdom/Prosperity	1 Kings 10:23–25
Proverb	Exodus 32:18; Amos 3:3–8; Proverbs; Ecclesiastes
Riddle	Judges 14:14, 18;
Vanity Song	Job (various units); Ecclesiastes 1:1–11; 3:1–8

Table 7 (Continued)
Types of Poetic Units in the Hebrew Bible

Miscellaneous	
Battle Boast	Judges 15:15; 1 Samuel 18:7; 21:11; 29:5
Case Law	Exodus 21:1–23:22; Deuteronomy 19:1–21:23; 22:13–26:11
Dramatic Dialogue	Judges 16:6–17; 1 Samuel 17:24–47; 2 Kings 18:19–35; 22:13
Fealty Oath	Ruth 1:16–17
Praise Song to King	1 Kings 10:6–9
Royal Decree	Daniel 3:4–6
Summons to Withdraw	2 Samuel 20:1; 1 Kings 12:16; 2 Chronicles 10:16

a. See Ronald M. Hals, *Ezekiel*, FOTL 19 (Grand Rapids: Eerdmans, 1989); Claus Westermann, *Prophetic Oracles of Salvation in the Old Testament* (Louisville: Westminster/John Knox Press, 1991; German original 1987).
b. See John J. Collins, *Daniel: with an Introduction to Apocalyptic Literature,* FOTL 20 (Grand Rapids: Eerdmans, 1984).
c. See Roland E. Murphy, *Wisdom Literature: Job, Proverbs, Ruth, Canticles, Ecclesiastes, and Esther,* FOTL 13 (Grand Rapids: Eerdmans, 1981), 97–124.
d. Ibid., 1–82, 125–50.

Types of Hebrew Poetry

The categories of Hebrew poetry are based on themes and literary contexts.[13] Many of the above units reflect well-established form critical genres. Others remain quite tentative or rely on the special interests of specific prophets. Some titles name broad types which encompass other more specific units.

Cultic Poetry

The division named "cultic poetry" encompasses so many forms and contexts that the designation loses some significance. Such breadth suggests the division of forms into (1) early cultic use, (2) Solomonic temple

13. For the form-critical specialist, the themes and contexts of the present forms of biblical units offer guidelines but not final determinations of genre. Definite determination of genre demands a vast amount of information from archaeology, anthropology, and comparative literatures. The naming of precise form-critical genres awaits the reconstruction of the passages' conventional and unique applications in the community. Representative applications appear in subsequent chapters.

period, (3) second temple period, and (4) later use not connected with temple liturgy. Unfortunately, psalmic materials do not yield enough clues to their origins to allow absolute placement of most individual poems within this general dating scheme. The early cultic uses include materials developed during the tribal period, with simplistic rituals involving individuals and groups within the extended family. This accounts for the etiology, vengeance songs, curses and blessings, various naming rituals, some legal material, explanations of the divine name, battle cries, pronouncements of tribal status, and perhaps early songs of thanks, lament, and salvation history.

The monarchy produced the earlier material of the Psalter with new emphasis on temple ritual, kingship, and more liturgical legal forms. The second temple era produced the final form of most cultic poetry as it appears in the Hebrew Bible. Legal materials, cultic disputations, salvation history hymns, laments, wisdom psalms, Zion songs, and Torah hymns were preserved or developed during or shortly after the Babylonian exile (587–539 B.C.E.). Later nonliturgical use refers to a few forms (for example, individual laments, naming ceremonies, and songs of trust) unconnected with the priestly office and the festival calendar.

Prophetic Poetry

Prophetic poetry displays a broad range of settings and styles as well. All these settings and styles relate to the urgent divine message charged to the prophets. The most basic distinction among prophetic genres relates to the differences between oracles addressed to other nations and those addressed to Israel and Judah. Woe oracles and oracles of judgment apply at times to Israel as well as other nations. However, the demand for justice which evokes this judgment assumes primary importance in oracles against Israel. The divine choice of the Hebrews places them in a role of greater responsibility. This responsibility increases incrementally throughout the history chronicled in the prophetic books. The oracles serve as eloquent reminders of Israel's neglected privileged identity.

Prophetic poetry, like cultic poetry, presents different faces at different stages in the development of Hebrew culture. Early prophets (or seers) used brief oracles to condemn or commend the leadership of key figures. These oracles appear as shorter forms of the standard types of later prophetic oracles. They display interests common to the kingship psalms. The bulk of prophetic poetry originates in Israel's monarchical history. Historical situations forged oracles which fit those situations (for example, oracles of hope or lament). These types of oracles come from the same period of monarchical history to which they apply, unless applied to earlier history in retrospective fashion.

A small amount of prophetic poetry approaches history from a radically different perspective: apocalyptic materials place judgment and salvation on the fringe of history. Events occur at the point of God's radical intervention to finalize history. These oracles relate negatively to the historical times which produced them. They offer hope for final resolution emerging from times of absolute national frustration and disillusionment. All oracles of hope bear similarities to later apocalyptic themes, but without the special apocalyptic view of history. Poetry such as the allegories of Ezekiel furnishes the fodder for apocalyptic prophets, who employ strongly symbolic images. Apocalyptic oracles contain all the elements of former prophetic visions, yet their communications form the ultimate vision rather than a single timely message. The relaxed attitude toward everyday events makes the apocalyptic oracles of Zephaniah, Zechariah, and Daniel the most poetic of Hebrew poetry. Their construction of a future world led to abstractions which stood in stark contrast to the sometimes brutal realism of earlier prophets.

Love Poetry

The Song of Songs represents the only pure love poetry of the Hebrew Bible. Given the revelatory nature of the canon, the very appearance of secular love poetry surprises the reader. One does not expect such themes within the biblical canon. Single units related to love poetry occur in Isaiah 5:1–7 and Jeremiah 2:1–3. Psalm 45, a wedding song, shares a few of the features of the Song of Songs. Beyond this, generic equivalents and related forms do not exist in the Hebrew Bible. The thematic content of the Song rather than its poetic form provides the basis for considering it as wisdom. With the exception of a few proverbs which approach issues related to love, no wisdom genres occur in the Song. All these points of originality underscore the book's differentiation. Similar materials that might indicate its precise employment in Israel's life do not appear.

We should not suppose that the presence of only a single work indicates the rarity of love songs. Rather, the presence of secular forms in the sacred canon provides indication of their pervasiveness. The paucity of surviving forms probably replicates the comparably meager samples of cultic and prophetic poetry held in the biblical canon. We must assume the existent works of all sections of the Hebrew Bible represent thousands of texts lost to the current interpreter.

Wisdom Poetry

The proverbial form dominates the wisdom materials in terms of its frequency. Furthermore, proverbs occur in all books of the wisdom canon and in many nonwisdom books. In contrast, the poetic dialogues of Job present a relatively unique category within the canon. Compared to Job, other poetic dialogue (largely in the monarchical history accounts) show less polish and contain briefer units of speech. Each of the speeches in Job forms a composition in its own right. The debate style appears more dramatic than didactic, and serves the need of wisdom proponents to address theological questions with lengthy discussions. By comparison, the diatribes of Qoheleth form briefer units, show more prosaic style, and present settled conclusions rather than live questions.

The miscellaneous genres could just as easily fall under the cultic designation. All the forms except case law reveal connections to the monarchical period. They show few indications of temple associations, but perhaps they lost these clues in their later development. They possess no single common characteristic and so remain completely miscellaneous.

Israel's Employment of Poetry

Four avenues for the employment of poetry among the Hebrews suggest themselves. First, poetry serves as a *means for personal confession*. Second, poetry contributed to the *unity and stability of the community*. Third, poetry provided a *medium for instruction*. Fourth, poetry *accomplished real changes in the lives of its celebrants*.

Personal Confession

As an avenue for personal confession, poetry expressed the individual's disappointments and hopes. In such interests, it offered a more effective medium than common speech. For this and all the means of employment mentioned, the melody accompanying the poetry added to its significance. Indeed, the Hebrew listener recognized the presence or absence of musical accompaniment as the determinative feature distinguishing poetry from prose. These worshipers shared cultural impressions governing which religious activities belonged in a musical presentation. Poetic forms served as ritually-proven expressions meeting the needs of the individual. Hannah's song (1 Sam. 2:1–10) presents a classic example. It appears more formal than expected of an impromptu thanksgiving. Such a document provides a beautiful example of a widely accepted praise form. The community understood the form to fit the freer, spontaneous praise of the pregnant woman (Hannah and subsequently others), previously barren. They further associated such praise with any celebration of divine favor granted to a devout person of low status. Even if intended for public performance in tribal gatherings or temple assembly, the thanks issued from the experience of an individual. For this reason, the historian considered it personal confession—the very words of Hannah. Other examples of such use include Jeremiah's accounts of prophetic suffering.

Community Unity and Stability

Closer to the central significance of Hebrew poetry, its employment to strengthen the unity and stability of the community accounts for much of its religious significance. Hebrew poetry owes its survival to the needs of the worshiping population of Israel. The performance of poetry involved diverse types of ritual performances. The worshiping community invested the documents associated with these performances with the same depth of significance common to poetic forms associated with individuals. Interest now turns to the social significance of these performances. The body of historical and cultic materials shared by the religious community provided a common source for worship activity and theology. Within this array of literature, typical expressions (for example, "Yahweh, he is God") comprised a communal syntax for religious activity. The infinite variety of such simplistic expressions and the continual repetition of meaningful units appears strange to the current reader. Joint worship and social identity depended on standard forms and phrases rather than creative compositions and free expression.

Hebrew worship, thoughout its history, displayed a cyclical nature: "In this instance we do or say this, and God is pleased and responds." But Hebrew poetry involves more than attempts to please God. Israel found comfort in the respected traditions especially when its history was anything but predictable. In contemporary Christian liturgy, the value of repetition resides in the recovery of primitive forms of worship order. Israel's commitment to repeated forms and phrases probably went much deeper, approaching the status of timeless significance. Poetic ritual emphasized the bridge between everyday experience and the divine. Poetic performance offered the possibility of a repair of any breach in the stability of the community. Poetic ritual atoned for crime or sin. Poetic forms welcomed newborns as well as young adults to the community. Marriage and divorce certainly involved sung commitments. In every way, private and public performance sealed, maintained, and repaired commitments to divine expectations. This does not distinguish Israel from its neighbors, who possessed a similar commitment to poetic ritual. It does emphasize poetry as a key source for our understanding of Hebrew society in its several biblical periods.

Medium for Instruction and Instrument for Change

The view of poetry as instruction appears prominently in the wisdom materials. Based upon the content of the previous paragraph, all poetic forms involved some didacticism. Legal materials and guidelines for community living stand out as teaching forms. The materials formed Israel's Magna Charta. Prophetic materials teach through the divine voice. When God speaks to later generations through the prophetic books, his messages assume the tone of warning. The Song of the Sea (Exod. 15:1–18) and the Song of Deborah (Judg. 5:1–31) teach history as God's work for his people. They record events related to divine providence as in the salvation history psalms (for example, Ps. 78). Poetry recounts the acts of God benefiting Israel. It explicitly or implicity calls for individual and public commitments to the divine will. Poetic materials served as dramatic recollections of the identity of the children of Abraham and promoted participation in that identity by successive generations of Hebrews. More than a vehicle for literature, poetry served as a point of entry into divine power. In this way, poetry actually constituted reality.

Summary: Poetry at the Extremes of Life

The earliest poetic forms expressed blessings or curses which bore power (through the use of the divine name) to accomplish their ends. The loss of this effectiveness makes Esau's loss of Isaac's blessing so tragic. Such words were invocations for Yahweh's involvement in human affairs. For effectiveness, their speaker required a certain office of authority—patriarch, father, priest, prophet, or devout worshiper. Among many other benefits this power enabled Israel to defeat enemies in battle, to destroy the evildoer, to maintain the link between people and deity, to obtain healing, to insure agricultural success, to guarantee prosperity and progeny, and to experience divine comfort in distress.

Poetry enabled the believer to tap into divine ability and authority. With this end in mind, those on the extremes of the Hebrew society—the ruler and the powerless, the influential and the poor, the sinner and the abused, depended most on the power of poetry. Interestingly, poetry itself emanates from the extremes of Israel's history. Victories, defeats, rebellion, consolidation, even sexual passion provide the bases for canonical poetry. All its forms were collected and finalized in the crucible of exile. Poetry existed to serve human needs. The more elevated and otherworldly its praise of God, the more the worshiper needed and desired the poem's effect.

Questions for Discussion

1. What are the characteristics of Hebrew poetry? Do different characteristics appear in different poetic books?

2. Where does poetry occur in the Hebrew Bible outside the poetic books? How does poetry function outside the poetic books?

3. What kinds of activities does Hebrew poetry involve? How does understanding of these activities help you understand a passage of biblical poetry?

Chapter 10

Ancient Near Eastern Poetic Documents

The poetic forms of the Hebrew Bible come from the wider milieu of the ancient Near East. The following review of poetic material from other cultures shows that none of Israel's poetry existed without parallels in companion cultures. In most respects Israel employed existing forms. In many cases, the Hebrews added unique styles and interests stemming from their unique theology and traditions.

Poetry in Egypt

Egyptian documents include so many poetic materials, the interpreter cannot possibly trace all the parallels with Psalms and Hebrew poetry. The form which represents the key feature of Hebrew poetry—parallelism—appears in Egypt before 2000 B.C.E. in "A Dispute over Suicide": "To whom can I speak today? Men are plundering; Every man seizes his fellow's (goods)."[1]

Instruction of Amen-em-opet

In the triplets of each stanza the lead line stays the same. The second and third lines complement the first. The well-developed form predates biblical parallelism by as much as two thousand years. This indicates parallelism did not develop within Hebrew poetry. Israel borrowed this integral poetic trait from Egypt and perhaps other cultures. An intriguing related issue concerns the presence of parallelism in early wisdom texts. Could parallelism's earliest forms be associated with wisdom? Does this inform the theory that Psalms redactors were sages?[2]

---

1. Trans. John A Wilson, *ANET*, 405–07.
2. The view that Psalms editors were sages came from Sigmund Mowinckel, "Psalms and Wisdom" in *WIANE*, 207.

The "Instruction of Amen-em-opet" dates from after 1200 B.C.E. It consists entirely of parallel lines.[3] Parallel passages in Proverbs prove beyond a doubt that Israel's wisdom tradents knew the work of Amen-em-opet:[4]

Table 8
Parallelism in Proverbs and Amen-em-opet

Proverbs 22:17–18a (NASB)	Amen-em-opet ch. 1, 11. 9–11
Incline your ear and hear the words of the wise,	Give thy ears, hear what is said,
And apply your mind to my knowledge;	Give thy heart to understand them;
For it will be pleasant if you keep them within you.	To put them in thy heart is worthwhile.[a]

a. *ANET*, p. 421. Wilson's notes show other parallel passages.

Its parallelism predates Proverbs by several hundred years, coinciding with the earliest known Hebrew poetry.

Egyptian Hymns

Egyptian hymns from several periods also present forms similar to Hebrew poetry. The "Hymn to Amon-Re" praises the Egyptian god for his creation and sustenance of life.[5] Lines show precise parallelism. Thematically, the work groups units of two to five lines. The hymn differs from Hebrew poetry in the didactic means of playing one line off another. Its parallelism operates more like prose, in a style known as synthetic or incomplete parallelism. Components are carried forward, but without evoking the tension or sense of balance characteristic to the synonymous and antithetic forms of most Hebrew parallelism. Synthetic parallelism occurs frequently in biblical poetry, but in isolated lines rather than polished units. The praise of the Egyptian hymn centers more on the identity and deeds of the god than on his acts in behalf of humans as in Psalms. In the bulk of Egyptian hymns, the praise expresses specific appreciation for the particular contribution to life attributed to a single deity of the pantheon. In this respect they differ greatly from biblical hymns.

The closest parallels with biblical hymns occur in hymns to creator-gods such as the "Great Hymn to Khnum" dated sometime in the Roman period.[6] The hymn celebrates the forming of various body parts by the creator of bodies. Contacts with the Psalms and the creation in Genesis include: (1) allusions to the deity as fashioner of gods and men, (2) references to the flow of blood and forming of bones[7] as the deity's operation,

3. Trans. John A. Wilson, *ANET*, 3rd ed., 421–24.
4. For a brief presentation of views, see Garrett, NAC 14, p. 193 with note 414.
5. Trans. John A. Wilson, *ANET*, 3rd ed., 365–67.
6. Miriam Lichtheim, *AEL*: 3, 112–15.
7. Compare Job 10:11.

(3) his giving of the "breath of life" (as in Gen. 2:7), (4) thanks issuing from all creatures, and (5) his moulding of people on a wheel (as a potter, again like Gen. 2:7). The content consists entirely of praise until the final line: "May your fair face be kind to *Pharaoh ever living!*" [Lichtheim's italics] The conclusion calls to mind the connection of Yahweh's praise to the anointed (king) in kingship psalms. It also recalls the use of psalms to ensure divine blessing on the king's reign. The late date of the "Hymn to Khnum" makes it less applicable to this study. During the Roman period, Genesis and Psalms could have influenced the "Hymn to Khnum."

Similar to this hymn, the "Hymn to Amon as Creator" (approximately 650 B.C.E.) offers what Psalms' critics call descriptive praise to the deity.[8] One specific theological feature shared with the Hebrew Bible occurs in the special reliance on the "name of" Amon which repeats in four lines. Such theological similarities appear commonly in Egypt's poetry, even when forms do not appear similar. Two broad differences illustrate the significant innovations which the Hebrews brought to the literature of praise. First, Egyptian poetry couched praise in an indicative tone, fostering a "contemplative attitude." Hebrew psalmists issue an imperative tone, inviting "calls to praise" as part of the debt humans owe to God.[9] The link between human and divine being operates on a more vital and dynamic level in Hebrew poetry, resulting in poems which are more experiential and less intellectual. Second, Egyptian hymns offer less detail regarding the relation of the acts of the deity to human affairs.[10] They contain praise to the deity no less lavish than that of Hebrew hymns. Yet Psalms portray God intervening for Israel or the individual. His activity intrudes into the realm of human history, encompassing past acts of redemption and future acts of restoration. The Hebrew poet approaches God as a much more accessible figure whose domain includes the world of human activity as well as the world of divine beings. Official Egyptian accounts of the defeats of enemies bear relationships to the poetry of Nahum, Habakkuk, and Obadiah. The "Stela of Amenhotep III" (about 1350 B.C.E.) includes these lines:

> Woe to the Libyans, they have ceased to live
> In the good manner of roaming the field;
> In a single day their stand was halted,
> In a single year were the Tjehenu burned.[11]

The few lines reproduced above show more regular parallel structure than the rest of the stela. The Hebrew prophetic works consist of carefully styled lines. A more significant divergence in orientation resides in the chronological setting. The Egyptian text and others like it voice praise

---

8. Lichtheim, *AEL,* 3:30–31.
9. Claus Westermann, *Praise and Lament in the Psalms,* trans. Keith R. Crim and Richard N. Soulen (Atlanta: John Knox, 1981), 50.
10. Lichtheim, *AEL,* 1:193–209.
11. Lichtheim, *AEL,* 2:75.

after the downfall of enemies. Each of the prophets mentioned looking forward to the doom of the peoples in the future, as payment for their treatment of Israel. Celebrations of the destruction of enemies do occur in Hebrew poetry (as the Song of Deborah), but the tone taken typically emphasizes thanksgiving to God, rather than revelling in the enemy's fate. Imprecations (wishes of violence upon enemies) also occur in the psalms. These imprecations, like other wishes for destruction of enemies, envisioned such events in the future.

Egyptian Love Poetry

The most notable parallels between Egyptian literature and the Hebrew Bible come in the domain of love poetry.[12] Several Egyptian texts exist. One text appears remarkably similar to the Song of Songs in content, expression, and tone. It shows so many parallels that likenesses of other texts fade into insignificance. The Papyrus Chester Beatty I, dated approximately 1200–1150 B.C.E., begins with a love song in seven strophes. The following provides a full text and citation. Common features include: (1) the theme of seeking the one loved, (2) the request not to disturb love, (3) divisions into unconnected units (anthological), (4) separation of the lovers, (5) lovesickness, (6) gazelle and horse representing the speed and sureness of the male's arrival, and (7) threats to love (for example, a crocodile). Michael Fox's work[13] convincingly associated the Song of Songs almost entirely with Egyptian love poems. He suggested the following points of contact between all the Egyptian literature and the Song of Songs: (1) references to the female as sister, (2) the image of the doorlatch, (3) descriptions of the body, and (4) the interplay of desire and frustration. Many more similarities exist. Readers can identify several on their own in the Chester Beatty papyrus:

First Stanza

Beginning of the sayings of the great happiness
The One, the sister without peer,
the handsomest of all!
She looks like the rising morning star
At the start of a happy year.
Shining bright, fair of skin,
Lovely the look of her eyes,
Sweet the speech of her lips,
She has not a word too much.
Upright neck, shining breast,
Hair true lapis lazuli;
Arms surpassing gold,
Fingers like lotus buds.
Heavy thighs, narrow waist,

---

12. Michael B. Fox devoted an entire volume to the study of simlarities: *The Song of Songs and the Ancient Egyptian Love Songs* (Madison: University of Wisconsin Press, 1985). This volume presently serves as the best single source for the study of these interests. See also, John Wilson, trans., "Egyptian Secular Love Songs and Poems," *ANET*, 3rd ed., 467–71.
13. Fox, *The Song of Songs*.

Her legs parade her beauty;
With graceful step she treads the ground,
Captures my heart by her movements.
She causes all men's necks to turn about to see her;
Joy has he whom she embraces,
He is like the first of men!
When she steps outside she seems
Like that other One!

Second Stanza

My brother torments my heart with his voice,
He makes sickness take hold of me;
He is neighbor to my mother's house,
And I cannot go to him!
Mother is right in charging him thus;
"Give up seeing her!"
It pains my heart to think of him,
I am possessed by love of him.
Truly, he is a foolish one,
But I resemble him;
He knows not my wish to embrace him,
Or he would write to my mother.
Brother, I am promised to you
By the Gold of women!
Come to me that I see your beauty,
Father, Mother will rejoice!
My people will hail you all together,
They will hail you, O my brother!

Third Stanza

My heart devised to see her beauty
While sitting down in her house;
On the way I met Mehy on his chariot,
With him were his young men.
I knew not how to avoid him:
Should I stride on to pass him?
But the river was the road,
I knew no place for my feet.
My heart, you are very foolish,
Why accost Mehy?
If I pass before him,
I tell him my movements;
Here, I'm yours, I say to him,
Then he will shout my name,
And assign me to the first . . .
Among his followers.

Fourth Stanza

My heart flutters hastily,
When I think of my love of you;

It lets me not act sensibly,
It leaps from its place.
It lets me not put on a dress,
Nor wrap my scarf around me;
I put no paint upon my eyes,
I'm even not anointed.
"Don't wait, go there," says it to me,
As often as I think of him;
My heart, don't act so stupidly,
Why do you play the fool?
Sit still, the brother comes to you,
And many eyes as well!
Let not the people say of me:
"A woman fallen through love!;
Be steady when you think of him,
My heart, do not flutter!

Fifth Stanza

I praise the Golden,
I worship her majesty,
I extol the Lady of Heaven;
I give adoration to Hathor,
Laudations to my Mistress!
I called to her, she heard my plea,
She sent my mistress to me;
She came by herself to see me,
O great wonder that happened to me!
I was joyful, exulting, elated,
When they said: "See, she is here!"
As she came, the young men bowed,
Out of great love for her.
I make devotions to my goddess,
That she grant me my sister as gift;
Three days now that I pray to her name,
Five days since she went from me!

Sixth Stanza

I passed before his house,
I found his door ajar;
My brother stood by his mother,
And all his brothers with him,
Love of him captures the heart
Of all who tread the path;
Splendid youth who has no peer,
Brother outstanding in virtues!
He looked at me as I passed by,
And I, by myself, rejoiced;
How my heart exulted in gladness,
My brother, at your sight!
If only the mother knew my heart,

She would have understood by now;
O Golden, put it in her heart,
Then will I hurry to my brother!
I will kiss him before his companions,
I would not weep before them;
I would rejoice at their understanding
That you acknowledge me!
I will make a feast for my goddess,
My heart leaps to go;
To let me see my brother tonight,
O happiness in passing!

Seventh Stanza

Seven days since I saw my sister,
And sickness invaded me;
I am heavy in all my limbs,
My body has forsaken me.
When the physicians come to me,
My heart rejects their remedies;
The magicians are quite helpless,
My sickness is not discerned.
To tell me "She is here" would revive me!
Her name would make me rise;
Her messenger's coming and going.
That would revive my heart!
My sister is better than all prescriptions,
She does more for me than all medicines;
Her coming to me is my amulet,
The sight of her makes me well!
When she opens her eyes my body is young,
Her speaking makes me strong;
Embracing her expels my malady—
Seven days since she went from me![14]

Adolf Erman published a number of samples of Egyptian love poetry. One discourse between lovers came from the time of Sethos I (1300 B.C.E.). The phrase, "Hasten to see thy sister, as a horse . . ." recalls the depiction of the male of the Song as a deer (Song of Songs 2:8–9 and elsewhere). Mentions of lovesickness and apples appear in the document. Both images merge in Song of Songs 2:5: "Refresh me with apples, for I am faint with love."[15] Another poem in the same papyrus compares the body of the woman to a garden: "I am thy first sister. I am unto thee like a garden, which I have planted with flowers and with all manner of sweet smelling herbs. Pleasant is the channel in it . . ."[16] (compare to Song of Songs 4:12–15).

---

14. Lichtheim, *AEL*, 2:182–85.
15. Papyrus Harris, 500, trans. Aylward M. Blackman, in *The Ancient Egyptians: A Sourcebook of their Writings*, ed. Adolf Erman (New York: Harper & Row, Publishers, 1966), 244–45.
16. Papyrus Harris, 500, trans. Aylward M. Blackman, in *Ancient Egyptians*, 248–49. Other examples in pages 244–51 closely resemble garden imagery from the Song.

Poetry in Canaan

In Ugaritic texts the frequent occurrence of word pairs indicates an awareness of parallelism. Many of these pairs of words appear in Akkadian texts as well. The pairs often appear together (for example, sun and rain in English). The splitting of the pairs into separate lines of poetry provides the earliest basis for parallel expressions. Many of the Ugaritic word pairs also occur in Hebrew poetry. Ugaritic Baal myths show affiliation with divine warrior poetry of Habakkuk 3 and Deuteronomy 32, along with other Hebrew poems. The account of the fight between Baal and Yam provides a clear example. Baal's prowess with the battle ax compares to Yahweh's wielding of the bow.[17]

The distinguishing terminology portrays divine involvement in human affairs. So, war, judgment, or protection among humans takes form through images of the deity as an active warrior. Implements of war identify Baal as the deity controlling the weather. War club or ax and arrows represent thunder and lightning, respectively. Yahweh's intervention commonly takes the form of these elements as weapons. His battles, like those of Baal, create flashes of fire and other strong reactions. Clearly, much of the terminology originated in the context of Canaanite religion. The lines of the Ugaritic texts are not parallel to the same degree as Hebrew lines. They do, however, show arrangement in groups of two or three.[18] These texts along with most other known Ugaritic texts date between 1350 and 1200 B.C.E.

Few Ugaritic love songs exist, but one unit manifests close similarities to the Song of Songs. Text 603, lines 5 through 8 reads:

His head is wonderful.
Dew is between his eyes.
Of hostility speaks his leg (even) [his] horns
which are upon [him].
His head is descending from the heave[ns],
[From the ten]t of the bull.
There is his mouth like two cloud[s].[19]

Compare to these lines the following statements from the Song of Songs 5:10–16:

v. 11   His head is gold
v. 12   His eyes are like doves
v. 15   His legs are pillars of alabaster
v. 16   His mouth is sweetness

---

17. *CTA* 2.I–II, IV in Walter Beyerlin, ed., *Near Eastern Texts Relating to the Old Testament*, OTL (Philadelphia: Westminster, 1978), 203–6.
18. For additional representative texts, see H. L. Ginsberg, "Ugaritic Myths, Epics, and Legends," *ANET*, 3rd ed., 129–55.
19. Loren R. Fisher, ed. *Ras Shamra Parallels: The Texts from Ugarit and the Hebrew Bible*, vol. 2 (Rome: Pontificum Institutum Biblicum, 1975), 134.

The passages share little imagery, but the attention to parts of the body shows likenesses between the love poetry of Ugarit and Israel. Text 603 probably presented a love song about Baal sung by Anat (his companion deity). It provides some evidence for the contention that the praises of the Song of Songs come from the songs of deities or songs devoted to deities. The current form of the Song contains no such connections. This conjunction of enthronement ceremony and love song does not occur in the Hebrew Bible. It occurs, as expected, in Canaanite fertility religions.[20] According to some interpreters, the Song of Songs originated as a hymn to a fertility deity. These interpreters claim that most popular poetry of monarchical Israel carried the themes of fertility worship.

Fertility religions receive thorough condemnation in the biblical materials. Could the Song of Solomon represent an attempt to keep popular poetry alive while divesting it of its association with fertility deities? Assuming so, the producer of the Song of Songs extensively edited a common hymn to Baal. After the editing, the "hymn" affirmed normal sexual relations rather than the power of fertility ritual. Such supposition offers no assistance in the identification of poetry. The known popularity of fertility worship in spite of prophetic condemnation (especially Hosea and Amos) makes such contacts probable. The address to a male "Beloved" also represents a minor similarity between Ugaritic and Hebrew poetry. Ancient Near Eastern texts rarely used the designation.[21] Egyptian love songs typically refer to the male as "brother," rather than "beloved."

Poetry in Mesopotamia

Mesopotamian literature shows distinct points of contact with the poetry of Lamentations. The Lamentation over the Destruction of Ur (before 1500 B.C.E.) views the destruction of Ur as the work of the deity (Anu or Enlil) as in Lamentations.[22] The lament contains eleven sections. The descriptions of conditions and calls for lamentation appear similar to the Book of Lamentations. The Sumerian source looks much more like liturgy, with frequent repetition, including antiphons. In tone it tends toward emotive description rather than historical description as in Lamentations.

The Lamentation over the Destruction of Sumer and Ur dates to the same period.[23] The text contains five sections (as Lamentations) of unequal length. The first portion of the book laments the fall of other major cities. The last portion specifically laments the fall of Ur. Like the previous document it includes antiphons, but it closes in its own way with a blessing which incorporates curses on the enemies of Sumer.

Sumer exercised no direct influence on Lamentations. The common interest in suffering and in the plight of those within the cities

---

20. Ibid., 138.
21. Ibid., 135.
22. Trans. Samuel N. Kramer, *ANET*, 3rd ed., 455–63.
23. Ibid., 611–19.

presents strong evidence of cultural connections. the indication that the deity caused the suffering presents further evidence. One major theological difference between Sumerian and Hebrew lamentations exists: The Hebrews directly appealed to God for help in the bleak situation. The Sumerian laments contain no such appeal. Instead, they relate their circumstance in third person reports of a fate accepted as unchangeable. One Akkadian psalm appeared in both the Akkadian and Sumerian languages. The psalm of penance dates to sometime before 1000 B.C.E., perhaps as early as 1500. It compares to Psalms 6; 32; 38; 51; 102; and 143:

Who is there who has not sinned against his god,
who has constantly obeyed the commandments?
Every man who lives is sinful.
I, your servant, have committed every kind of sin.
Indeed I served you, but in untruthfulness,
I spoke lies and thought little of my sins,
I spoke unseemly words—you know it all.
I trespassed against the god who made me,
acted abominably, constantly committing sins.
I looked at your broad possessions,
I lusted after your precious silver.
I raised my hand and defiled what was untouchable,
I went into the temple in a state of uncleanness.
I constantly practised shameful dishonour against you,
I transgressed your commandments in every way that displeased you.
In the frenzy of my heart I blasphemed your divinity.
I constantly committed shameful acts, aware and unaware,
acted completely as I pleased, slipped back into wickedness.
Enough, my god! Let your heart be still,
may the goddess, who was angry, be utterly soothed.
Desist from the anger which has risen so high in your heart!
May your . . . by which I swore be completely reconciled with me.
Though my transgressions are many—free me of my guilt!
Though my misdeeds are seven—let your heart be still!
Though my sins be countless—show mercy and heal (me)!
(My god), I am exhausted, hold my hand.[24]

The repetition of the lines duplicates the form of much biblical parallelism. Except for the lack of a divine name, the unit looks very much like the penitential laments of the Psalms.

A hymn to Bel (also known as Marduk) from Babylon appears much like the descriptive praise of the Psalms:

Powerful master of the Igigi gods, exalted among the great gods,
Lord of the world, king of the gods, divine Marduk, who establishes the plan,

. . . .

---

24. "Akkadian invocation to an anonymous god," Beyerlin, 108–9.

Who ...s heaven, heaps up earth,
Who measures the waters of the sea, cultivates the fields,
Who dwells in the temple Eudul; lord of Babylon, exalted Marduk.[25]

The tablets date to the Seleucid period (between 300 and 100 B.C.E.), but the texts appear much older. In spite of the similarities to Psalms in tone and content, the Babylonian documents lack parallelism.

Earlier Babylonian psalms offer praise similar to biblical psalms. Again, the psalms praise the god's attributes and place in the pantheon. In Israel's praise, the role of God resides in Israel's own history.[26] Babylonian psalms share with biblical psalms the five components of hymns: (1) the address, (2) opening praise, (3) some lament, (4) a petition for hearing or help, and (5) a vow of praise.[27]

One minor similarity exists between the Song of Songs and Mesopotamian literature. An Old Babylonian "Hymn to Ishtar" offers praise to the goddess which matches the praise of the Beloved in the Song of Songs.[28] It also exceeds the imagery of human love by extolling her works as a goddess: "She is clothed with pleasure and love. She is laden with vitality, charm, and voluptuousness. Ishtar is clothed with pleasure and love." This hymn from before 1600 B.C.E. provides several indications of the unsuitability of the claim that the Song of Songs originated with religious texts. Unlike the Song of Songs, a third party (the narrative voice of the hymn) identifies Anum as the lover god. In the Song of Songs, the individuals express their love directly to each other. The Babylonian psalm offers thanks to Anum for the status he granted to the king of Babylon at Ishtar's request. Such religious interests share little with the simple celebration of love in the Song.

A number of Sumerian marriage poems exist, but they bear scant relationship to the more earthy Song of Songs.[29] Deities and kings typically serve as the subjects of the Sumerian songs. Further, none of these texts contain a *wasf* (description of the parts of the lovers' bodies) like those in the Song of Songs and Egyptian parallels.

Summary: Israel's Loose Dependence on Other Poetry

These similarities and many others indicate a great deal of contact between ancient cultures. Similarities to Egyptian literature stand out. First, Egypt employed parallelism long before the development of Hebrew poetry. Second, Egyptian hymns appear strikingly similar to Hebrew hymns. Wide differences in theology accent these similarities. Egypt worshiped many gods. Israel's poetry offers exclusive worship to the single deity, Yahweh. Differences in theology notwithstanding, Egyptian hymns

---

25. Trans. A. Sachs, "Temple Program for the New Years Festivals at Babylon," *ANET*, 3rd ed., 331–38. Quotation from p. 332.
26. Westermann, *Praise and Lament*, 42.
27. Ibid., 36–37, 152.
28. Trans. Ferris J. Stephens, "Hymn to Ishtar," *ANET*, 3rd ed., 383.
29. See Trans. Samuel N. Kramer, "Sumerian Sacred Marriage Texts," *ANET*, 637–45.

share the same tone as Hebrew hymns. They also share several specific idioms (for example, the "name of" Amun). Third, Egyptian love poetry like the Chester Beatty I papyrus offers the most convincing parallels. This document, or another like it, could have exercised direct influence on the Song. The Song of Songs' carefully designed dramatic style provides the only major difference between the two. Similarities include the lavish descriptions, romantic style, and specific images related to love. Fourth, Egyptian celebrations of enemies' defeat (victory psalms, imprecations) also share points in common with prophetic woe oracles.

Ugaritic and Mesopotamian literature also provide parallels. Hebrew poets certainly matched word pairs like those discovered in Ugarit. Also, Ugaritic depictions of Baal as god of the storm share features (here content more than form) with Hebrew hymns. From Mesopotamia, the lamentations over cities provide the closest ancient Near Eastern counterpart to Lamentations. Other similarities relate to material in Psalms. The Akkadian psalm of penance expresses attitudes often considered unique to Israel. The components of Babylonian psalms reveal themes recognizable to form critics as common in biblical hymns.

These points of contact indicate the strong influence of earlier ancient Near Eastern forms on Hebrew poetry. They do not prove any sort of direct borrowing of materials. Instead, these cultures possess the worldview from which Hebrew society sprang. Necessarily, Israel valued the forms of expression common to the ancient Near East. Their Bible represents a few of the culture's genres of material which fit into their special monotheistic faith. With the possible exception of the Song of Songs, such common forms show the distinct stamp of Israel's religion and culture. We cannot say Israel's poetry "came from" Egypt, or Ugarit, or Babylon, but Israel "based its poetry" on the content and usage of its milieu. From another perspective, Israel based its poetry on the expressions of its ancestors, but these ancestors were not yet Hebrews.

Questions for Discussion

1. What other ancient Near Eastern cultures produced poetry similar to biblical poetry? Identify a few of the major parallels.

2. What does it mean historically and theologically to conclude that Israel based its poetry on the content and usage of its milieu?

3. What differentiates Israel's poetry from the poetry of Israel's neighbors?

Chapter 11

History of Interpretation Before the Reformation

The Later Poetic Traditions in Israel

The canon does not contain all Israel's poetry. Passages such as Joshua 10:10–13 and Numbers 21:14–15 point to older poetic collections not included in Scripture. Qumran and other Jewish documents preserve later poetry. The development of such poetry was accompanied by continued interpretation of biblical poetry, interpretations often concerned with poetic qualities in its search for theological meaning and application.

Qumran

The history of interpretation of Hebrew poetry begins with post-canonical materials. The Qumran texts offer one of the earliest indications of Psalms use in a worshiping community. The biblical Psalms certainly influenced much of the community's literature. A collection of thanksgiving hymns (1QH, undatable between 200 B.C.E. and 50 C.E.) repeats the praise and images of the Psalms without the typical form of canonical thanksgiving. In addition to composing original psalms, the community responsible for the Dead Sea Scrolls also left an interpretation of Psalm 37 (4Q171). Psalm 37 takes the shape of a wisdom psalm which promised God's judgment upon the wicked. The Qumran scroll interpreted the text prophetically; the promises to the righteous in the psalm applied to the religious community of Qumran. In one case, the commentary interprets the Teacher of Righteousness (a leader of the Qumran community during the Maccabean Age, 167-63 B.C.E.) as "the righteous": "The wicked watch for the righteous, and seek to kill them. The LORD will not abandon them to their power, or let them be condemned when they are brought to trial" (Ps. 37:32–33). The scroll relates "the wicked" to a persecuting priest. According to the interpretation, the Teacher receives the promise in verse 33.[1]

---

1. Geza Vermes, *The Dead Sea Scrolls in English*, 3rd ed. (London: Penguin Books, 1987), 292.

The partial Psalms manuscript (11QPs) presents the most telling connection of Qumran literature to the Psalms. The Psalms scroll merits much attention since it dates before 200 B.C.E.[2] and contains six psalms which do not appear in the Hebrew canon. The Syriac version of the Psalter contains four of the six. Another, Psalm 151, appears in the Septuagint (Greek) Psalter.[3] Psalms 152–155 present various themes. Both 152 and 153 display titles connecting the psalms with David's deliverance from a lion and a wolf. Psalm 154 lauds wisdom and manners of behavior which reflect it. Psalm 155 lists David's request of the deity for (1) training in the Torah, (2) forgiveness, and (3) healing. This last psalm presents a rather complete list of petitions. It reveals an intent to review many of the requests common throughout the Psalms. It ends with thanks for personal deliverance and a plea for the deliverance of Israel.

The date of writing of each of these psalms is unknown, but their presence at Qumran indicates a date probably slightly before 200 B.C.E. If the date is accurate, Psalm 155 is the earliest interpretation of the Psalms available to us. The repetition of content common in the Psalter indicates their nature as summary psalms (that is, psalms later added to conclude the canonical collection). In other ways as well, the Psalms scroll presents remarkable differences from the Masoretic text. The scroll also differs from the Septuagint text of the Psalms which dates to the same general period of time as the Qumran psalms. The most notable difference contained among the Psalms themselves relates to the titles or ascriptions which begin the psalms. Other than the additions discussed above and the changes in titles, the scroll displays few differences from the biblical collection. Differences in ascription and other additions appear in the table below:

Table 9
Unusual Features of 11QPs

LOCATION	
Psalm 144	ascription to David missing though present in Septuagint
Psalm 133	ascription to David missing though present in Septuagint
Psalm 104	ascription to David added in Fragment E1, present in Septuagint
2 Samuel 23:1–7	included as a Psalm, not in Septuagint
Psalm 123	added, not in Septuagint

Sanders listed forty-eight variants from the Masoretic text and twenty-two additions to the Masoretic text in 11QPs.[4] He described the scroll as a

---

2. Ibid., 208.
3. Psalm 151 receives consideration later in this study.
4. James A. Sanders, *The Dead Sea Psalms Scroll* (Ithaca, N.Y.: Cornell University Press, 1967), variants pp. 15–16; additions p. 20.

"radical departure from any recension of the biblical Psalter heretofore known."[5] The table highlights the import of Davidic authorship for the Qumran community, in spite of the single ascription to David missing in Psalm 144. It shows the continuing life of canonical books and confirms to some extent the mainstream identity of the Septuagint.

The scroll also adds an *apocryphon* near its end: "And David, the son of Jesse, was wise, and a light like the light of the sun, and literate, and discerning and perfect in all his ways before God and men. And the LORD gave him a discerning and enlightened spirit. And he wrote 3600 psalms; and songs to sing before the altar over the whole-burnt perpetual offering every day . . . And the total was 4050. All these he composed through prophecy which was given him from before the Most High."[6] The content of the apocryphon indicates the depth of commitment expressed in the literature of the Psalms. The addition does not comprise a historical report. It does show the strong emphasis the producer and community placed on Davidic authorship of the Psalms. In part, the emotions of the Psalms provide the basis for the understanding of David the apocryphon reveals.

As indicated, other Psalters (for example, the Septuagint) vary much less from our current Hebrew text. The differences within the Dead Sea Psalms scroll indicate a freedom to manipulate the titles and content of the collection. Such changes do not appear in other Qumran biblical scrolls. This evidence suggests liturgical poetry exhibits more changes than other biblical forms as adapted by specific worshiping groups. Longer and shorter versions of Psalms served as honored collections including minor variations due to slightly different traditional forms of the book. The Qumran materials also include fragments of a lamentation (4Q179) built on the canonical pattern for Lamentations (though not acrostic): "How solitary lies the city, the princess of all peoples is desolate like a forsaken woman."[7] The lament carries out the image of Jerusalem as a bereaved widow through all its extant lines. The content cited above appears a slight variation of Lamentations 1:1: "How lonely sits the city that once was full of people! How like a widow she has become, she that was great among the nations! She that was a princess among the provinces has become a vassal."

Poetry in the Pseudepigrapha

In spite of several adaptations governed by the special interests of the Qumran community, the Qumran poetry shows a great deal of continuity with the poetry of the Hebrew Bible. This assessment holds less truth for later poetry. The table below shows the various types of poetic units in

5. Ibid., vii.
6. The translation comes from Sanders. Sanders suggested a date of 30–50 C.E., pp. 86–87. The traditional view the apocryphon expresses may be centuries older than the document itself.
7. Vermes, 215.

pseudepigrapha.[8] Some of these receive treatment in the following paragraphs..

Table 10
Types of Poetry in the Pseudepigrapha

Psalms of Thanksgiving	Joseph and Aseneth, Song of Hannah in Pseudo-Philo
Hymns	1 Enoch, Apocalypse of Abraham, Apostolic Constitutions, Ladder of Jacob
General Psalms	Psalms of Solomon
Prayer	2 Baruch
Woes	1 Enoch
Apocalyptic Oracles	1 Enoch
Blessings and Curses	Jubilees
"Epic" Poetry	Sybylline Oracles

Joseph and Aseneth. Joseph and Aseneth[9] 8:10–11 is a hymn: "Lord God of my father Israel, the Most High, the Powerful One of Jacob, who gave life to all [things] and called [them] from the darkness to the light, and from the error to the truth, and from the death to the life; you, Lord, bless this virgin" (8:10). The translator dates the work sometime between 100 B.C.E. and 135 C.E.[10] The current text exists in Greek, but shows itself a Jewish work. A verse that calls for God's blessing on Aseneth follows the text above. This makes the praise formula above appear an introduction to a more specific request. As such, it does not show the characteristics of a standard form, like the hymns of Psalms. Instead, it functions as a personal prayer highlighting a single petition.

Aseneth also voices several prayers. The quotation below comes from a lengthy prayer in 12:1–13:15:

Lord God of the ages,
who created all [things] and gave life [to them],
who gave breath of life to your whole creation,
who brought the invisible [things] out into the light,
who made the [things that] are and the [ones that] have an appear-

---

8. Several wisdom forms such as proverbs and dialogues also appear, but these are aptly covered in previous chapters.

9. Asenath [the difference in spelling reflects the difference between the Hebrew and Greek sources] names the Egyptian wife of Joseph in Genesis 41:45 and 41:50. The late Jewish interpreter(s) responsible for Joseph and Aseneth took the name from Genesis and developed or recorded legendary stories. Genesis provides practically no information on Asenath other than the name.

10. Trans. with introduction by C. Burchard in James Charlesworth, ed., *The Old Testament Pseudepigrapha*, vol. 2 (Garden City, N.Y.: Doubleday, 1983), 177–247; text cited is from p. 213.

ance from the non-appearing and non-being,
who lifted up the heaven . . .
with you I take refuge, Lord,
and to you I will shout, Lord,
to you I will pour out my supplication,
to you I will confess my sins. (12:1–3) [11]

A lengthy plea for protection and forgiveness follows, ending with an expression of love for Joseph.

In 21:11–21 Aseneth's "psalm" appears. It contains much repetition. The line, "I have sinned, Lord, I have sinned; before you I have sinned much,"[12] appears eleven times. Double lines of confession typically follow these words. The lines display parallelism. This poem, though introduced as a prayer of thanks, contains only a trace of thanksgiving at its end. The book's use of poetry shows a derivative employment of the Psalms. Many of the forms parallel those of the Psalms; yet the context for the units shows a radically different use.

2 Baruch. The context of the lamentation of 2 Baruch 10:6–19 appears quite similar to that for the laments of the Psalms. Baruch changes the form of expression rather than its context. Its negative tone makes it unlike biblical laments. It also lacks the psalms' statements of hope and trust. It directs its complaint exclusively to humans rather than to God. This indicates the importance of preaching or teaching to its originator. In other words, it manifests an overtly didactic tone. Laments in the Psalms tend to be expressive, emphasizing the emotions of the lamenter. They remain relatively unaware of an audience (other than God). Baruch's lament expresses absolute hopelessness, viewing captivity in Babylon as payment for sins. The poetry recaptures the despair of Babylonian captivity as an expression of the then current disaster—the fall of Jerusalem in 70 C.E. So, canonical poetry provides continuity between the experience of the existing community and the experience of ancient Israel. This approach appears quite a substantial basis for much of the poetry of the pseudepigrapha.

Apocalypse of Abraham. The Apocalypse of Abraham contains a hymn with some connection to the hymns of the Psalter. Its introduction as a "song" in 17:4 and its description as a prayer in 17:19 reveals some inattention to form. Abraham receives the direction: "Recite the song which I taught you" (17:4),[13] and the hymn follows:

8   Eternal One, Mighty One, Holy El, God autocrat
9   self-originate, incorruptible, immaculate,
     unbegotten, spotless, immortal,
10 self-perfected, self-devised,
     without mother, without father, ungenerated,
11 exalted, fiery,

11. Ibid., 220.
12. Ibid., 236–37.
13. Trans. R. Rubinkiewicz in Charlesworth, 1, 697.

12 just, lover of men, benevolent, compassionate, bountiful,
    jealous over me, patient one, most merciful.
13 Eli, eternal, mighty one, holy, Sabaoth,
    most glorious El, El, El, El, Iaoel,
14 you are he my soul has loved, my protector.
15 Eternal, fiery, shining,
    light-giving, thunder-voiced, lightning-visioned, many-eyed,
16 receiving the petitions of those who honor you
    and turning away from the petitions of those who restrain you
    by the restraint of their provocations,
17 redeemer of those who dwell in the midst of the wicked ones,
    of those who are dispersed among the just of the world,
    in the corruptible age.
18 Showing forth the age of the just,
    you make the light shine
    before the morning light upon your creation
    from your face
    to spend the day on the earth,
19 and in your heavenly dwelling palace
    [there is] an inexhaustible light of an invincible dawning
    from the light of your face.
20 Accept my prayer and delight in it,
    and [accept] also the sacrifice which you yourself made
    to yourself through me as I searched for you.
21 Receive me favorably,
    teach me, show me, and make known to your servant
    what you have promised me.
        (Apocalypse of Abraham 17) [14]

The unit shows much repetition. It contains a staccato pace with no parallelism. The vocabulary and style show attention to doctrine. It rehearses the nature of God in verses 8–15. In verse 16 it makes a transition from theology to his willingness to answer prayer. The psalm links God's majesty to his ability to answer prayer. Other requests for a hearing do not show such a partisan tone. The book dates to some time after the fall of Jerusalem (70 C.E.).

Odes of Solomon. At about the same time, the Odes of Solomon appeared (about 100 C.E.). The book received much influence from the Psalms, though it rarely quotes the Psalms. The book intends to present songs composed by Solomon, but many of its themes belong to the Christian community. It shows points of contact with gnosticism and the Gospel of John.[15] Among all the Pseudepigrapha, this work stands out on account of its positive tone. The themes of the work evade simple characterization due to their diversity. They bear little in common with the Psalms, and contain parallelism of inconsistent form. At times the correspondence of the

14. Ibid.
15. Trans. with introduction by J. H. Charlesworth, in 2:727–28.

lines equals that of the Hebrew Bible. At other times, it employs double-lined narrative without parallelism.

Psalms of Solomon. The first-century Jewish community produced the Psalms of Solomon at about the same time as the Odes. They offered a response to the loss of the temple and the Roman domination which followed. They copy some of the genres of the Psalms: individual and group laments, wisdom psalms, victory songs, hymns, and royal psalms. The parallel lines show less balance than ancient poetry in Psalms and elsewhere in the Hebrew Bible. Successive lines tend to add meaning to the preceding in the same way narrative lines do.

1 Enoch. The hymn of 1 Enoch appears contemporary with or slightly earlier than the works attributed to Solomon. The hymn reads:

> Blessed are you, O Great King,
> You are mighty in your greatness,
> O Lord of all the creation of heaven,
> King of kings and God of the whole world,
> Your authority and kingdom abide forever and ever;
> and your dominion throughout all the generations of generations;
> all the heavens are your throne forever,
> and the whole earth is your footstool forever and ever and ever.
> For you have created [all], and all things you rule.
>   (1 Enoch 84:2–3a)[16]

The hymn extends through the fourth verse of 1 Enoch 84. The lines quoted resemble a kingship psalm; however, the unit designates no earthly ruler. The likeness relates only to the description of God as king. The parallelism of the unit, like that of the previous samples from the pseudepigrapha, shows less careful development than that of the Psalms.

Pseudo-Philo. The book Pseudo-Philo rewrites the Bible's history from Adam to David. A Jew before 100 C.E. authored the work in Hebrew. In Pseudo-Philo 51:3–6, Hannah offers a prayer of thanks. In the prayer she celebrates the end of her infertility. Even more importantly she sings of the honor she will gain as the mother of the prophet Samuel. Special privilege applies to Samuel as the predecessor of David—God's anointed one.

Apostolic Constitutions. The Apostolic Constitutions contain a doctrinal hymn in 8.5:1–4.[17] Theological descriptions of the deity serve as praise in this hymn written between 150 and 300 C.E. In this respect it mirrors the unit previously described from the Apocalypse of Abraham. The entire work exhibits parallelism similar to that of the Psalms. It contains a string of hymns celebrating God's deeds (1) in creation, (2) in Israel's history, and (3) in current history. The text as it now exists emphasizes the preeminence of the work of Christ.

---

16. Trans. E. Isaac in Charlesworth, 1:62.
17. The translators D. A. Fiensy and D. R. Darnell, Charlesworth 2:687–88, present this unit as the ninth example of Hellenistic synagogal prayers.

Ladder of Jacob. The Ladder of Jacob cannot be accurately dated. Manuscripts do not appear before 900 C.E., but the material may date as early as 100 C.E.[18] In the book, Jacob offers a song of praise (2:6–22) after his dream (Gen. 28:12–15). The song quotes the vision of the angels from Isaiah 6:2 as well as "holy, holy, holy" from the same setting. The song ends with a request for the interpretation of the dream. Following the song, the Ladder of Jacob provides an eschatological interpretation of Jacob's dream experience. Following the prayer, God provides a direct answer through words of prophecy. It displays the common pattern of prayer-answer with the prayer worded as poetry. The direct praise of God in such hymns signals the activity of the deity. This activity of God does not always show poetic form.

Use of Canonical Poetry in the Pseudepigrapha

Two features relating to the special use of canonical poetry in the Pseudepigrapha stand out. First, the poetic units tend to emulate the Psalms. This indicates that the Psalms were the most familiar and widely-used biblical poetic materials at the time. The relevance of the Psalms endured through times when court history or prophecy offered little consolation. For that matter, the Song of Songs and Lamentations offered much more limited applicability than the Psalms. Their themes applied to the specific situations of expressive love and corporate suffering. The Psalms communicated the direct link between humans and God in both negative and positive historical situations. For these reasons the reproduction of psalms offered hope through recognition of God's presence. God could communicate displeasure with sin, identify with the sufferer, or punish enemies through psalms without the evidence of a human mediator (as in prophecy and priestly pronouncements). Accordingly, at times the Psalms comprised hymns actually embodying messages drawn from the latter prophets.

Second, most of the hymns espouse creation theology. God assumes the role of the maker and ruler of all that exists. This perspective increases in relevance when national hopes lie dashed. Like the deuteronomistic historian before them, the producers of the Pseudepigrapha could interpret even their subjugation as the act of the God of all nations. The worldwide picture of God's actions also provided support for the views of universal rule envisioned in prophetic works (for example, Isa. 40–66). The authors of pseudepigrapha did not place themselves in the idyllic era of restoration. Their sense of God's control of all human events provided a platform from which to look forward to universal dominion.

---

18. See H. G. Lunt in Charlesworth, 2, 404–05, and James H. Charlesworth, "Jacob, Ladder of," *ABD* 3, 609.

Early Jewish Interpretation

Poetry in the Septuagint

The principal issues regarding the poetic books in the Septuagint relate to the notable differences in the Psalms. The Septuagint's translation of the Hebrew Psalms into Greek dates to about 200 B.C.E.[19] The translators reveal a desire to preserve the "meter" in preference to the literal sense.[20] They avoided anthropomorphic presentations of God where possible. In style of presentation the Septuagint tends to provide interpretive readings. For example, a common metaphor applied to God in the Psalms is *ṣûr* (צוּר), "Rock," but the Septuagint renders *theos* (θέος "God") or words describing strength, in 18:31, 46; 28:1; 31:3; 61:2, and elsewhere.[21] Other metaphoric names for God receive similar treatment. The interpretations of the titles show an intent to decipher metaphors for the reader, perhaps to avoid more literal, and thus, irreverent interpretations.

As serious as this difference seems, the greatest discrepancy relates to the titles of the Psalms. The Septuagint includes more, and often, longer titles than those in the Hebrew text. No title precedes Psalm 71 in the Masoretic text, but the Septuagint presents this title: "By David of the sons of Jonadab, and the first that were taken captive."[22] The expansions of titles at times indicate the day of the week for the psalm's reading, as in Psalm 38: "A Psalm of David for remembrance concerning the Sabbath day."[23] The numbering of the chapters of Psalms in the Septuagint differs in many cases by a margin of one. This results from the combination of Psalms 9 and 10 into a single psalm. The Septuagint also combines Psalms 114 and 115. The number of total psalms remains 150 because Psalms 116 and 147 form two psalms each. Scholars generally accept the Septuagint psalter as among the least reliable of Septuagint translations. They measure this in terms of its correspondence to the Masoretic text. Not only so, but also two of the three major Greek manuscripts of the Psalms show omissions: Sinaiticus is complete; Vaticanus lacks 105:27–137:6; and Alexandrinus lacks 49:20–79:13. Previous discussion relates the peculiarities of the Qumran Psalms scroll.

Difficulties with Psalms scrolls relate to the nature of the Psalms as living literature. More Greek and Latin versions of Psalms exist than for any other book of the Hebrew Bible. Individuals or communities commonly

---

19. C. A. Briggs and E. G. Briggs, *A Critical and Exegetical Commentary on the Book of Psalms*, ICC (Edinburgh: T & T Clark, 1901), xxxiii. Compare A. A. Anderson, *Psalms*, New Century Bible (London: Oliphants, 1972), 28–29; James Limburg, "Psalms, Book of," *ABD* 5:523–24.

20. Briggs, xxv.

21. Staffan Olofsson, *God Is My Rock: A Study of Translation Technique and Theological Exegesis in the Septuagint*, Coniectanea Biblica OT Series 31 (Stockholm: Almqvist & Wiksell International, 1990), 35.

22. Quotations from the Septuagint are based on *The Septuagint Version of the Old Testament and Apocrypha with an English Translation* (London: Samuel Bagster and Sons Limited, 1870).

23. A detailed list of words and titles preceding psalms in the Septuagint and differing from the Masoretic text can be found in Henry Barclay Swete, *An Introduction to the Old Testament in Greek* (New York: KTAV, 1968), 250–51.

possessed idiosyncratic readings. Various Greek-speaking communities who adapted the Psalms to their situations adopted these readings. Perhaps these communities felt similar freedom in their adaptation of titles and division of units. They felt less freedom to change the body of psalm texts and to add new psalms. Psalm 151 appears as the last psalm, yet without numeration in the Septuagint:

> This Psalm is a genuine one of David, though supernumerary, composed when he fought in single combat with Goliad.

> I was small among my brethren, and youngest in my father's house; I tended my father's sheep. My hands formed a musical instrument, and my fingers tuned a psaltery. And who shall tell my Lord? The Lord himself, he himself hears. He sent forth his angel, and took me from my father's sheep, and he anointed me with the oil of his anointing. My brothers were handsome and tall: but the Lord did not take pleasure in them. I went forth to meet the Philistine; and he cursed me by his idols. But I drew his own sword, and beheaded him, and removed reproach from the children of Israel. (Ps. 151:1–7)

The Septuagint influenced the placement of Lamentations after Jeremiah in English Bibles. In the Hebrew canon, Lamentations appears with the Writings. The Septuagint tradition promotes the association of Lamentations with the prophet. Neither the text of Jeremiah nor the text of Lamentations confirms this. The Masoretic text begins abruptly with the first acrostic immediately following the title. The Septuagint includes the following setting before the first line of the acrostic: "And it came to pass, after Israel was taken captive, and Jerusalem made desolate, that Jeremiah sat weeping, and lamented with this lamentation over Jerusalem, and said . . ."[24]

Poetry in Josephus

Just prior to 100 C.E., Josephus read the Bible in conformity to the Greek view of poetry. He considered Moses' Song of the Sea (Exod. 15:1–18) an example of hexameter verse.[25] He also claimed David composed psalms and hymns in trimeters and pentameters.[26] No recognizable signs exist in the Masoretic text or the Septuagint that the translators and copyists of the Hebrew Bible recognized these Greek forms in Hebrew poetry.

24. Pp. 412–413 provide a few of the reasons for this association of Jeremiah with Lamentations.

25. *Antiquities* 2.16.4 and 4.8.44 in *Josephus' Complete Works*, trans. William Whiston (Grand Rapids: Kregel Publications, 1960), 64, 102.

26. *Antiquities*, 7.12.3, *Complete Works*, p. 164. The terms refer to the number of stresses per line (hexameter—six stresses, trimeter—three stresses, pentameter—five stresses). The forms appear commonly in many examples of English poetry. Translators of Psalms employ these regular meters only when translating the psalms loosely in order to set them to music.

Poetry in the Midrashim

Further insight on the ancient interpretation of poetry comes from the midrashim (ancient Jewish "commentaries" on biblical books). The midrash on Psalms presents a collection of observations on the Psalms compiled between 800 and 900 C.E. The interpretations date to the early centuries C.E. The work contains sections which begin with a quotation from a psalm and interpret it by citing another portion of Scripture presented as relating to it. For example, Psalm 1:1, "Blessed is the man that . . . sitteth not in the seat of the scornful" matches 2 Samuel 7:18, "Then David the king went in, and sat before the LORD." The midrash considers the passage an injunction against sitting in the temple court. The passage presents the possibility the king may stand as a single exception to the rule. Finally, the commentary forbids standing, even for David.[27]

The midrash shows tendencies toward the same free associations common throughout talmudic and midrashic literature. The text offers narrow interpretations—in this case limited to the behavior of Jews in the temple. Yet in the original context, Psalm 1:1 applied to all human associations. Another midrash, dating between 300 and 400 C.E., interprets Lamentations. Thirty-four lengthy proems show the importance of Lamentations to the celebrations of the feast of Ab, a festival commemorating the fall of Jerusalem. The rabbinic perspective of the midrash reflects much of the spirit of Lamentations. Rabbi Simeon ben Laish, in proem II, likened God to an angry father who beat each of his two sons (Israel and Judah) to death. The merciless father then issued a call to mourning.[28] Such comments convey the strong emotions of the mourner. The preoccupied sufferer concentrates on communicating the depth of suffering rather than speaking with propriety.

Several of the units relate to Jeremiah. This confirms that some members of the rabbinic community affirmed Jeremiah's association with Lamentations. The midrash remarks that Lamentations conforms to an acrostic form because all Israel had sinned against the Law from *aleph* to *tav* (equivalent to, "from a to z").[29] The midrash attributes the fall and captivity of the nation to Israel's sin. This feature also parallels the content of Lamentations. Apparently, successive generations regarded the poetry of Lamentations as the appropriate form for expressing their national mourning and penitence.

Interpreters remain uncertain regarding the date of the midrash on the Song of Songs in *Midrash Rabbah*. The commentary gives verse-by-verse explanation. Two examples suffice to show the outlook of the midrash. The text applies "Let him kiss me . . ." (1:2) to the giving of the Torah to Moses. The rabbis relate the "kisses" to the words dictated from the mountain

---

27. *The Midrash on Psalms*, trans. William G. Braude, vol. 1 (New Haven: Yale University Press, 1959), 3–4.

28. "Lamentations" in *Midrash Rabbah*, trans. A. Cohen, eds. H. Freedman and Maurice Simon (London: Soncino, 1961), 5.

29. R. Judah, *Midrash Rabbah*, 87.

(Exod. 20:1–23:33). In this way the love of the Song becomes love of God and his instruction. "Black but comely" (1:5) follows the same allegorical principle, explaining the blackness as sin and the comeliness as the works of ancestors. In the midrash, all sexual imagery applies to God, Israel, or the prophets. The work takes none of it literally. Parts of the body become symbols. Clearly this midrashist did not consider marital love an appropriate subject for a biblical work. The reason need not be a prudish sense of values. Perhaps the interpreter simply considered human love a lower priority than divine love. Whether taken literally or allegorically, the poetic form of the book remains unchanged. The poetic cast of the book actually aided the allegorist, since poetry lends itself to fanciful thought and free associations. In other senses as well, all three examples of midrashim show that the utility of poetic form helps to span the gap between the older community and the current community.

The frequency of Psalms use in later communities make them excellent vehicles for reinforcing commitment to Torah. As they were recited in worship, rabbinic interpretations gave the faithful some ideas to contemplate as they listened or spoke the Psalms. The later communities used Lamentations to express their misery because the content and form so suited all experiences of human suffering. On the surface, Lamentations contains a response to a historical event. At a deeper level the work voices the doubt, guilt, challenges, and frustrations of those who feel life has been unjustifiably harsh. Poetry remains an outlet for these kinds of self-searching.

Poetry in the New Testament

The New Testament materials reveal a deep respect for the Psalms. Paul quoted Psalm 14:1–2 and other portions of Psalms as well to defend his view of the sinfulness of all humanity:

> as it is written:
>   "There is no one who is righteous, not even one;
>   there is no one who has understanding.
>   there is no one who seeks God,
> All have turned aside, together they have become worthless;
>   there is no one who shows kindness,
>   there is not even one."
> "Their throats are opened graves;
>   they use their tongues to deceive."
>   "The venom of vipers is under their lips."
>   "Their mouths are full of cursing and bitterness."
> "Their feet are swift to shed blood;
>   ruin and misery are in their paths,
>   and the way of peace they have not known."
> "There is no fear of God before their eyes."
>   (Rom. 3:10–18)

The unit appears a compilation of brief units intended to support a theological stance. The Septuagint expands Psalm 14:3. Romans 3:13–18 includes much of this expansion. This series of statements originated in Psalms 53:1–2; 5:9; 140:3; 10:7; and 36:1 (Septuagint version).[30]

Psalm 110:1, 4 ranked among the most frequently quoted Scripture passages of early Christianity:[31]

> The LORD says to my lord,
> "Sit at my right hand
> until I make your enemies your footstool."

> The LORD has sworn and will not
> change his mind,
> "You are priest forever
> according to the order of Melchizedek."

Ephesians 1:20; Hebrews 1:13; 10:12–13; and Acts 2:34–35 cite verse one. The quotation comes from the mouth of Jesus himself in Luke 20:41–44:

> Then he said to them, "How can they say that the Messiah is David's son?
> For David himself says in the book of Psalms,
> 'The lord said to my Lord,
> "Sit at my right hand,
> until I make your enemies your footstool."'
> David thus calls him Lord; so how can he be his son?"[32]

In each case, the royal nature of the psalm takes second place to its reading as a messianic prediction. Hebrews 7:11–17 similarly applies 110:4 to Jesus. The psalm offers support for such an interpretation. Its theme relates not only to the rule of the king but also to the Day of the LORD (vv. 5–6). The union of these two themes made its use as a psalm confirming Christ's identity most attractive.

The example above presents direct allusion to the Psalms. An example from Lamentations shows a more literary usage of Hebrew poetry. Lamentations 3:19–42 encourages the sufferer to bear through all pains and wait for God's deliverance. The following passages indicate the tone:

> The LORD is good to those who wait for him,
> to the soul that seeks him.
> It is good that one should wait quietly
> for the salvation of the LORD.

---

30. Alternatively, Septuagint translators inserted the string of quotations from Romans. Swete, 252.

31. David M. Hay, *Glory at the Right Hand: Psalm 110 in Early Christianity* (Nashville: Abingdon, 1973), 15.

32. Mark 12:35-37 presents a parallel passage.

> It is good for one to bear
> > the yoke in youth,
> to sit alone in silence
> > when the Lord has imposed it,
> to put one's mouth to the dust
> > (there may yet be hope),
> to give one's cheek to the smiter,
> > and be filled with insults.
>
> When all the prisoners of the land
> > are crushed under foot,
> when human rights are perverted
> > in the presence of the Most High,
> when one's case is subverted
> > —does the Lord not see it?

Compare this to Jesus' words:

> But I say to you, Do not resist an evildoer. But if any one strikes you on
> the right cheek, turn the other also. (Matt. 5:39)

> If anyone strikes you on the cheek, offer the other also; and from anyone
> who takes away your coat do not withhold even your shirt. (Luke 6:29)[33]

The similarities go far beyond this brief reference. Jesus repeatedly
warns his followers to expect suffering. He urges them to patiently accept
life as it comes. He counsels them to allow injustice in some measure and
await God's retaliation at the end. Lamentations' presentation of trouble
comes from two perspectives—hope for divine reward and a sign of God's
disfavor. Jesus' teachings regarding persecution and hope seem to assume
this background.

One further example of poetry employed in the New Testament adds
another dimension to its use among early Christians. Hebrews 2:11–12
attributes the words of Psalm 22:22 to Jesus:

> For the one who sanctifies and those who are sanctified all have one
> Father. For this reason Jesus is not ashamed to call them brothers and
> sisters, saying,
> > "I will proclaim your name to my brothers and sisters,
> > in the midst of the congregation I will praise you."

The quotation comes directly from the Psalm. The author of Hebrews
seemingly puts these words in the mouth of the preexistent Christ. Perhaps
the association of Psalm 22 with the crucifixion (Mark 15:34) leads to such
an association. In Hebrews this represents a side issue. The heart of the
matter relates to Jesus' identification with humans. Hebrews 10:5–9 uses a
similar attribution of Psalm 40:6–8 to Jesus in support of another theological

---

33. The similarities between Lamentations 3:25–30 and Jesus' teaching to turn the other
cheek were suggested by Benedict de Spinoza in *A Theologico-Political Treatise and a Political Treatise*, trans. R.H.M. Elwes (N.Y.: Dover Publications, Inc., 1951), 105.

promise. *The author's knowledge that the passage existed long before the time of Jesus of Nazareth does not dim the conviction these are the words of Jesus.*

In each case, the use of poetry in the New Testament follows the practice of proof texting. The passages confirm the theological positions held by the writers. A sizable portion of their readers probably held these positions as well. Whether in messianic predictions or theological defense, the poetic nature of these texts seems of little consequence to the writers. They employ their content and show interest in their form only for the purposes of quotation. Perhaps poetic texts did offer more appealing units for preaching or public reading. The use of Scripture as proof text does not describe Jesus' use of Lamentations. Here, the general use of biblical teachings reveals a commitment to Scripture itself that informs Jesus' own theological positions. Many more quotations of Psalms and other poetry occur in the New Testament. Yet those cited constitute the typical varieties.

Poetry in Patristic Literature

Barnabas and 1 Clement

According to one author, Christians shortly after 100 C.E. viewed the Bible through the lenses of Greek literature and art. Because of their love for things Greek, they did not always affirm the Bible's own viewpoint of exclusive revelation. This resulted in the conception of the poets as prophets[34] and represented a shift from divine authority to human authority. This trend eventually led to a direct association of divine authority with human authorship. Biblical writers become individual muses on behalf of God. These few inspired individuals serve as the exclusive channels for God's message.

The Epistle of Barnabas (70–135 C.E.), and 1 Clement (95–96 C.E.), are two of the earliest sources with strong reliance on the Psalms. Barnabas illustrates the tendency to refer to scriptural "prophecy" through the authority of the poet. The Epistle of Barnabas introduces references to the Psalms by the formula "the prophet has said. . . ." This may represent simply a way of referring to remembered Scripture in general. It indicates that early interpreters thought of all Scripture as prophetic rather than as a collection of individual works. More likely, "the prophet" refers specifically to David. At times Barnabas specifically indicates this with the words "David said." David "becomes" a prophet due to the concept and use of the Psalms. Compare this to the rather bland introduction to psalm quotes in 1 Clement, "It says somewhere. . . ."

Both Barnabas and 1 Clement show interest in a specific theme from Psalms. Barnabas 9:1–4 appeals to Psalm 18:44 and 34:11 with reference to listening and ears in proof of the thesis that God "has circumcised our ears, so that we may hear the word and believe." First Clement 14:1–5 provides

---

34. James Kugel, *The Idea of Biblical Poetry: Parallelism and Its History* (New Haven: Yale University Press, 1981), 146.

an even fuller list of psalms containing references to deceitful speech to condemn hypocrisy in speech.[35] These uses of poetry reveal the reliance on Scripture as the medium for divine message. The "voice" of the psalms texts settles all issues as an incontrovertible authority. First Clement pursues such theological themes in other passages as well. Chapter 18:2–17 cites Psalm 51:1–17 and uses the verses to urge peaceful relations with one another in view of God's mercy on all. The argument finds its greatest support in the first verse of the psalm: "Have mercy on me, O God, according to your steadfast love; according to your abundant mercy blot out my transgressions" (Ps. 51:1). In 1 Clement 22:1–8, Psalm 34:11–17 provides support for the contention that God shows mercy toward the religious. First Clement 35:7–12 warns sinful Christians of divine punishment based on Psalm 50:16–23. First Clement 52:2 expresses the need to give thanks as indicated in Psalm 69:30–32. Clement's use of the Psalms to teach theology closely parallels some of the more valid approaches to Psalms in our situation. The writer shows thorough understanding of the content of the psalms. He does not apply the Psalms to overly specific situations. He does not use personal presuppositions to govern interpretations.

Irenaeus

Irenaeus exercised a less cautious approach in *Against Heresies* 32:9–12. He employed messianic psalms to describe Christ's suffering. He then claimed this suffering prefigured the suffering of the church.[36] The work dates to about 200 C.E. Its approach to the Psalms mirrors that of the New Testament in its preoccupation with messianic predictions.

Origen

Some of the earliest comments on the Song of Songs appear in Origen (184-251 C.E.). He termed the Song an "epithalamium" (a wedding song praising the bride or groom) and more specifically, a wedding song written as drama.[37] Origen interpreted its references to the parts of the body figuratively rather than literally.[38] All the same, Origen warned that the work held danger for the spiritually immature.[39] He astutely compared the title Song of Songs to the similar phrases, "holy of holies," "work of works," and "ages of ages."[40] His recognition of the Song's dramatic nature as well as its high poetic form show unusual sophistication.

---

35. Quotations from 1 Clement and Barnabas are from Edgar J. Goodspeed, *The Apostolic Fathers* (New York: Harper & Brothers, Publishers, 1950).

36. *The Apostolic Fathers with Justin Martyr and Irenaeus*, trans. A. Cleveland Cox, The Ante-Nicene Fathers, vol. 1 (Grand Rapids: Eerdmans, 1885).

37. "Prologue to the Commentary on the Song of Songs" in *Origen*, trans. Rowan A. Greer (New York: Paulist Press, 1979), 217.

38. Ibid., 222.

39. Ibid., 218.

40. Ibid., 236.

For Origen, the nature of the book as the greatest song dictates against its literal interpretation. Solomon's writings fall into three categories: ethics, physics, and enoptics. These categories name Proverbs, Ecclesiastes, and the Song of Songs, respectively. *Solomon taught these categories to the Greeks.* These three disciplines, by which humans understand the world, also bear the designations moral, natural, and contemplative. The canonical order of the three books (as arranged in the Septuagint) presents the proper sequence of the three.[41] Origen's assignment of the Song to the contemplative sphere of human thinking reveals his understanding of the abstract nature of the book. Origen probably feared that less philosophical minds would tend toward obsession with the literal meaning of the work. Origen's interpretation of the Song of Songs showed complete dependence on allegory.

His comments on Psalms tend to be prophetic in nature. In "On Prayer" he used Psalm 109:11a, 12a as a reference to Judas Iscariot. The lines read, "Let the extortioner seek out all that he hath, let him have no helper."[42] "On Prayer" also provides illustration of his allegorical reading of the Song of Songs. Origen interpreted "looking through the lattice" (Song of Songs 2:9) as viewing the world through temptation. To this the Savior answers, "Arise" (Song of Songs 2:10).[43] One can scarcely imagine a less literal rendering. In a similar vein he interpreted "winter is past" in Song of Songs 2:11 as referring to the necessary suffering of martyrs and other followers of Christ. "Winter is past" indicates the end of suffering in the peace of death.[44]

Cyprian

Once Origen identified the Song as allegory, all possibility of instruction for love and the family was displaced by abstract symbols. Such an approach to the Song appears about 250 C.E. in Cyprian's interpretation of Song of Songs 6:9, "My dove is but one." This passage, according to Cyprian, referred to the unity of the church. The church should not allow strangers to congregate with it.[45] Cyprian applied the metaphor consistently. If God's relationship with the church compares to man's relationship with his bride, then the church (bride) must remain pure. It seems Cyprian makes a comparison to the presence of unknown persons in the church with the presence of a mistress in the house of a married man. The interpretation reveals some understanding of the claim of exclusivity in the phrase "my dove is but one." When interpreters read the Song as an allegory of God's love for the church, this affirmation of the incomparable nature of its membership represents a logical conclusion.

---

41. Ibid., 231–32.
42. "On Prayer" in *Alexandrian Christianity*, trans. John Earnest Leonard Oulton and Henry Chadwick, LCC, vol. 2 (Philadelphia: Westminster, 1954), 288. In "On Prayer" and "Exhortation to Martyrdom" Origen quotes Psalms more than any other book of the Hebrew Bible.
43. *Alexandrian Christianity*, 314.
44. Ibid., 413.
45. Letter 69 and "The Unity of the Catholic Church" in *Early Latin Theology*, trans. and ed. Stanley L. Greenslade, LCC, vol. 5 (Philadelphia: Westminster, 1956), 151, 126.

Athanasius

Between 300 and 350 C.E. Athanasius offered some revealing comments regarding Psalms. According to Athanasius, "The Book of Psalms is like a garden containing things of all these kinds that is, [things common to other portions of Scripture], and it sets them to music."[46] This statement reflects his respect for the Psalms. The view seems unique to Athanasius. Another reference to the Psalms in the letter confirms Athanasius' view of the diversity of the Psalms. He encouraged the recital of psalms in contemporary situations matching those of the individual psalms themselves. So, when living among the poor, Psalm 41 appears appropriate: "Happy are those who consider the poor" (v. 1).[47] Such a program for reading the Psalms is timeless. Athanasius also read the Psalms prophetically. He believed "lift up your gates" in Psalm 24 foretold Christ's ascension.[48] The psalm also refers to ascending the hill of the LORD (v. 3) which Athanasius undoubtedly read literally.

Saint Basil

Saint Basil (320–379) also shows a broad respect for the Psalms. Basil believed that the diversity of the entire canon was present in the Psalms. This passage from his sermons reveals his fascination with Psalms:

> Now, the prophets teach one thing, historians another, the law something else, and the form of advice found in the proverbs something different still. But, the Book of Psalms has taken over what is profitable from all. It foretells coming events; it recalls history; it frames laws for life; it suggests what must be done; and, in general, it is the common treasury of good doctrine, carefully finding what is suitable for each one.[49]

The appeal of the Psalms apparently led Basil to use them frequently in preaching. He, like Athanasius, saw the Psalms as a compendium of the Old Testament as a whole. The nature of the collection makes them adaptable to various applications. This is less true of other books, poetic or not.

Cyril of Jerusalem

Such diversity enabled Cyril of Jerusalem (d. 386) to use the Psalms to support the view that the church replaced Israel as God's chosen.[50] Much of this free-wheeling interpretation arises from the seeming lack of context

---

46. "A Letter to Marcellinus" in *Athanasius: The Life of Antony and The Letter to Marcellinus*, trans. Robert C. Gregg (New York: Paulist, 1980), 102.
47. Ibid., 117.
48. Ibid., 105.
49. Saint Basil, *Exegetic Homilies*, trans. Agnes Clare Way, The Fathers of the Church, vol. 46 (Washington, D.C.: The Catholic University Press, 1963), 151.
50. Catechetical Lecture 18, "On the resurrection of the flesh, the Catholic Church, and eternal life" in *Cyril of Jerusalaem and Nemesius of Emesa*, trans. and ed. William Telfer, LCC, vol. 4 (Philadelphia: Westminster, 1955), 187.

from psalm to psalm. This invites prophetic or allegorical readings, since no specific context limits the interpreter. Cyril's allegorical reading of the Song of Songs displays poetic form of its own:

> Be of good courage, Jerusalem, the Lord will take away all thine iniqui-ties. The Lord shall wash away the filth of his sons and daughters. . . . Angels will circle round you, crying, "Who is this that cometh up in white apparel, leaning on her near of kin?" [LXX Song of Songs 8:5] [Jesus speaks in the following] "Behold thou art fair, my love: behold thou art fair; thy teeth are as flocks of shorn sheep" [SS 4:1–2] because she has made her profession with a good conscience, and "each of them bearing twins" because of the twofold grace (I mean that grace completed of water and the Spirit, or preached in the old covenant and the new).[51]

In accordance with this, he applies Song of Songs 5:3, "I have put off my coat; how shall I put it on?" to the former life, before baptism.[52] Again, poetry allows the kind of free association which enables the support of New Testament theology in a pre-Christian text.

Ambrose

Ambrose (339–397) used the Song of Songs to defend his decision not to rebuild a local synagogue destroyed by Christians. His defense reveals no logic, but plenty of passion: "The synagogue has no kiss. The Church has the kiss, the Church which waited for Christ, which loved him, which said: 'Let him kiss me with the kisses of his mouth' (Song of Sol. 1:2). Her long and ardent desire had grown with waiting for the Lord's coming."[53] This displays a thoroughgoing perspective tracing the account about the lovers as the church's longing (the bride) for the absent Christ (the groom). His advice to a parent about the raising of a daughter departs from the allegorical method of reading the Song. In the latter case, he used the Song of Songs to provide instruction to the parents. To protect the woman's chastity, he urged com-plete isolation from all contact with males, based on certain proof texts. [54]

In Letter 108, Ambrose returned to the allegorical method: "Rise up and come away" referred to Christ's call at death.[55] Ambrose's use of alle-gory presents an interesting play on the conventional mode of reading the Song. Instead of Christ's love for the church as the central theme, he under-stood the church's longing for Christ as the central theme. Actually, this offers closer accord with the content of the Song. The female spends much more time proclaiming her love for the male than vice versa.

---

51. "Catechetical Lecture 3, On Baptism," *Cyril*, 97–98.
52. Ibid., 98.
53. Letter 41 in *Early Latin Theology*, trans. and ed. Stanley L. Greenslade, LCC, vol. 5 (Phila-delphia: Westminster, 1956), 245.
54. Letter 107, *Early Latin*, 339.
55. *Early Latin*, 379.

Jerome

Jerome (390–415) left fifty-nine homilies on different Psalms. The homilies show an amazing independence of one another. Each homily contains themes all its own, without repetition of content. His approach resembles midrash in that statements drawn from the Psalms find explication in statements drawn from other portions of the Bible. He applies the approach sporadically. Midrash, by contrast, employs a programmatic approach. Jerome claimed that each psalm held its own "key." The First Psalm provides the key to all the Psalms. The contents of the Psalms apply to all believers. For example, the blessing of Psalm 1 does not speak prophetically of the righteousness of Jesus or Joseph, his father, as some believed. Instead, the blessing exists for all the righteous.[56]

In general, Jerome found moral lessons in the Psalms. He also used the Psalms in theological arguments. He used Jesus' statement of Matthew 22:43 (from Ps. 110) to challenge Jews, Arius, and others who diminished Jesus' divinity. Of the Jews, Jerome asked, "If Christ is Son of David, how, then, does David call his own son, Lord?"[57] Of Arius, he asked, "Does a craftsman call his work his son?"[58]

Theodore of Mopsuestia

Theodore of Mopsuestia (d. 428) expressed various attitudes toward the Psalms. On the one hand, he rejected all the psalm titles as added, connecting the Psalms with Zerubbabel and Hezekiah as most Jews did at the time.[59] In spite of his willingness to challenge the antiquity of titles and many other presuppositions of the times, he continued to refer to the Psalms as authored by David in their entirety. His division of the Psalms into types recalls Cyril of Jerusalem's view of their diversity.[60] Theodore accepted only a few psalms as christological (Pss. 2, 8, 45, 110).[61] He challenged current trends which considered the Psalms to be largely messianic. Instead, he understood later historical situations as analogous to David's historical situation. So, symbolism and not predictive intent led to their Christian application. This argument led him to refute the predictive intent of Psalm 22 which Jesus quoted (v. 1) from the cross.[62]

His own Christological interpretation owed more to allegory than prophetic interpretation. For example, the royal wedding song of Psalm 45 celebrated the marriage between Christ and his bride, the church.[63] Curiously,

---

56. *The Homilies of Saint Jerome*, vol. 1 (Homilies 1–59, *On the Psalms*), trans. Marie Liguori Ewald, The Fathers of the Church, vol. 48 (Washington, D.C.: The Catholic University of America Press, 1964), 3–4.

57. Ibid., 271.

58. Ibid., 273.

59. Dimitri Zaharopoulos, *Theodore of Mopsuestia on the Bible: A Study of His Old Testament Exegesis* (New York: Paulist, 1989), 48.

60. Ibid., 83–84.

61. Ibid., 149.

62. Ibid., 144–46.

63. Ibid., 150.

Theodore refused to read the Song of Songs allegorically. He saw it as an epithalamium celebrating Solomon's marriage to an Egyptian ("dark but beautiful," Song of Songs 1:5). According to his view the work presented Solomon's defense of an inappropriate marriage to one of a different race.[64] His distaste for the work led him to exclude it from his personal reckoning of Hebrew canon. His preference for Psalms makes his reaction understandable. The theological content of Psalms presents a strong contrast to the language of love in the Song of Songs.

Augustine

Augustine (354–426?) taps this theological content of the Psalms in support of Christian theology. The Psalms provide points of departure for figurative readings. His approach displays a derivative nature, that is, his interpretation is dependent on Christian theology rather than on the Hebrew setting. Like many other interpreters, he referred to the psalmist as prophet. He showed preference for christological interpretations.[65] Augustine quoted Psalm 45:2–10 and claimed even a "dull witted" person would recognize that the psalm speaks of Christ. Other psalms, in his view, required teachers to interpret the figurative meaning. Also in Psalm 45 he identified the female figure (vv. 11–17) as Zion. He spoke of Babylon as her demonic counterpart.[66] Augustine, like most other early interpreters, concentrated on supporting the work of the church rather than offering objective criticism of the Hebrew Bible.

Cassidorus

Cassiodorus left a good deal of information on his view of the Psalms in *Explanations of the Psalms* (about 550). He considered David the only author of the Psalms. Others mentioned in the titles performed the psalms rather than authoring them.[67] His discussion of each psalm began with the title of the Psalm. He then divided the psalm into portions. After his explanation, a conclusion indicated the message of the psalm for the church. The length of the work (3 vols.) and his descriptions of the Book of Psalms reveal the relish with which he searched the Psalter. He used Song of Songs 4:12 to describe the Psalms: "A garden enclosed and fountain sealed up, a paradise full of all fruits."[68]

Apparently his appreciation of Psalms included an appreciation of their musical nature, for he said, "A psalm is a sweet and tuneful melody issuing forth from a single musical instrument, the psalter."[69] For

---

64. Edward Gray, *Old Testament Criticism: Its Rise and Progress* (New York: Harper & Brothers, 1923), 43.

65. See *Nine Sermons of Saint Augustine on the Psalms*, trans. Edmund Hill (New York: J. J. Kenedy & Sons, 1958).

66. *City of God*, trans. Gerald G. Walsh, et. al., abridged (Garden City, N.J.: Doubleday, 1958), 386–87.

67. *Explanation of the Psalms*, vol. 1, trans. P. G. Walsh (New York: Paulist, 1990), 29.

68. Ibid., 24.

69. Ibid., 31.

Cassiodorus no biblical book offered more relevance than the Psalms. His methodical approach to their interpretation foreshadows the contemporary practice of separating the ancient context from the current message.

Pseudo-Dionysius

The writings of Pseudo-Dionysius (about 500) conclude this section on early Christian thinkers. The reader cannot take his response to the Song of Songs at face value. When he claimed "in the Song of Songs there are those passionate longings fit only for prostitutes,"[70] he understood that such views of God hide mysteries regarding his character. In other words, given that the song is Scripture, it cannot mean what it seems to mean. Its message must lie beneath the surface. The supposition of the authoritative nature of the work led Pseudo-Dionysius to the opposite conclusion to that of Theodore of Mopsuestia, who assumed the work was not inspired. Happily, current interpreters do not object to the explicit nature of the work. Consequently, some view the interaction of the lovers as a wholesome depiction of human love. It seems the early centuries after Christ presented no option for such a view. Indeed, allegorical interpretation continued through the reformation.

The Applicability of Hebrew Poetry to Christian Settings

Through the patristic period, allegorical views became polished and standardized. The view of the Song representing God's love for Israel or the church received wide acceptance. In subsequent centuries such views achieved the status of official interpretations for Jewish or Christian communities. They began, of course, as the individual readings of community leaders. The preoccupation of certain writers with the Psalms continues the preference for living liturgy, reflecting the Psalms' common use in liturgy. The connections between Christian theology and the content of the Psalms came as a natural result of this familiarity. Certain thinkers also expressed a personal interest in the Psalms, indicating their private use of Psalms in a devotional setting. Such interest looks forward to later use of Psalms in monastic communities. Only a few leaders who faced hardships found application for Lamentations. The themes of this work could not be adapted as readily as the images of the Song or the more varied emotions expressed in the Psalms. The understanding that such longings corresponded to the woes of the sinner or the plight of Jews without Christ offered the only options for allegorical readings. In general, throughout the period, the church emphasized its application of Hebrew poetry to distinctly Christian (especially christological) contexts. The Jewish community similarly found applications to support the current community or its special outlook on Israel's history.

---

70. Letter 9, 1105 B, *Pseudo-Dionysius: The Complete Works*, trans. Colm Luibheid (New York: Paulist, 1987), 282.

Poetry in Medieval Literature

Cassain's *Conferences* and "The Rule of Saint Benedict"

Interpreters in the Middle Ages continued the practice of interpreting the poetic books out of a preoccupation with the needs of the current church. Cassain, in the fifth century, used Lamentations 3:27–28 to commend the life of the hermit: "Blessed is the man that hath borne the yoke from his youth. He shall sit solitary and keep silent, because he hath taken it upon himself."[71] The rendering shows dependence on the Septuagint, rather than the Hebrew text. Throughout the *Conferences* Cassain wrote to hermits or to those considering this lifestyle. Only slightly later, "The Rule of Saint Benedict" (after 500) practically mandated the singing of the entire Book of Psalms each week. When the divine office did not include all the Psalms each week, he described it as a "mean devotion."[72] Although Cassain and Benedict made quite different use of the material, both resorted to Hebrew poetry for support of an alternative lifestyle—namely the hermit or the monk. The spirituality of the medieval period, including monasticism especially, owes much to biblical poetry.

Junilius Africanus

Attention to the content of Hebrew poetry appears frequently throughout the history of interpretation. Attention to poetic form occurs rarely. Kugel provides a couple of rare glimpses of early views of poetic meter in the Hebrew Bible. The first comes from Junilius Africanus before 600 C.E. The catechism, "*De Partibus Divinae Legis* " ["On the Divisions of Divine Law"] records the following dialogue:

Student:	How many are the types of discourse in the Scriptures?
Teacher:	Two; for they are either written in the Hebrew meters in that language or in prose.
Student:	What things are written in meter?
Teacher:	The Psalms, the story of Job, Ecclesiastes, and some parts of the Prophets.
Student:	What parts are written in prose?
Teacher:	All the rest.
Student:	Why are they not written in those meters in our (Latin) version?
Teacher:	Because no utterance is able to keep the meter in another language, unless it change the force of the words or their order.[73]

---

71. *Conferences in Western Asceticism*, trans. Owen Chadwick, LCC vol. 12 (Philadelphia: Westminster, 1958), 268 n. 7; 284.
72. "The Rule of Saint Benedict," *Western Asceticism*, 309.
73. James Kugel, *The Idea of Biblical Poetry: Parallelism and its History* (New Haven: Yale University Press, 1981) (trans. by Kugel from Patrilogae Latinae 68:20), 168.

The selection shows Africanus' distinction of Hebrew meter as unique. He does not force it into a Greek pattern.

Rabanus Maurus

Rabanus Maurus (after 600 C.E.) left several notes on prose/poetry in the Hebrew Bible. In an inventory of biblical literature, he noted that Job began and ended in prose. In addition, he noted various systems of Greek meter in Proverbs, the Song of Songs, and Ecclesiastes. He also observed that Lamentations, though ascribed to Jeremiah, showed poetic meter, unlike other prophetic works.[74] Jeremiah manifests such significant differences from the poetic form of Lamentations that Maurus' comment still applies. The comments on meter from Africanus and Maurus possibly indicate nothing more than a recognition of the lined form of certain Hebrew texts. Even if this is true, the consideration of Scriptures in two genres (poetry and prose) makes room for significant advances in literary interpretations.

Agobard of Lyons and Anselm of Canterbury

The allegorical reading of the Song of Songs constitutes one of the most frequently occurring phenomena of medieval interpretation. About 850 Agobard of Lyons understood "open to me, my sister, my lover" (Song of Songs 5:2) to voice Christ's request to the unbeliever.[75] Allegorical interpretations of the Song flourished around 1000 when participants at Jewish festivals sung them as hymns.[76] At about the same time Anselm of Canterbury used the Song of Songs to express devotion to Mary. He produced the document "A Prayer to Saint Mary," containing frequent use of the Song.[77]

Rabbi Solomon ben Judah Hababli

Rabbi Solomon ben Judah Hababli paraphrased the first five verses of the Song:

1 The Light and Saviour of the chosen people
Deserving protection,
He shall have from His beloved assembly
"A song of Songs."

2 The Graceful One, the object of all longing desires.
The Reviving Cordial of the fainting heart,
The Bountiul Source of abundant supply,
"He hath kissed me with kisses."

---

74. Kugel from *De Universo* Book 5 *Pl* 111:107.
75. "On the Truth of the Faith and the Establishment of All God—An Exhortatory Sermon to the People" in *Early Medieval Theology*, trans. and ed. George E. McCracken, LCC vol. 9 (Philadelphia: Westminster, 1957), 335.
76. Christian D. Ginsburg, *The Song of Songs and Coheleth* (New York: KTAV, 1970), 38.
77. "A Prayer to Saint Mary to Obtain Love for Her and for Christ" in *A Scholastic Miscellany: Anselm to Ockham*, ed. and trans. Eugene R. Fairweather, LCC vol. 10 (Philadelphia: Westminster, 1956).

3 The loved one above all nations,
   The keeper of the Law Thou has given,
   Her didst Thou perfume with Thy spices,
   "The odour of Thy sweet ointments."

4 The chosen of Thy house and nobles,
   Lo! we are surrounded with splendour,
   We press to the house of Thy glory,
   "Oh draw us after thee."

5 O Thou all majestic, yet mild,
   Thou hast crown'd me with grace above many,
   Though now with grief I am marred,
   "I am swarthy, but comely."[78]

Hababli supplied explanations of the last lines of verses 2–5. The "kisses" of verse 2 refer to God's face-to-face relaying of the Law. The "odor" of verse 3 speaks of the spreading of Israel's wisdom through the Law. "Swarthy" in verse 5 refers to the sin of the golden calf, while "comely" refers to the reception of the Law.[79] His mode of reading employed single nouns or adjectives to correspond to other nouns and adjectives. The giving of the Law displaces the literal meaning of the text. Many more examples of allegorical renderings of the Song could be cited.

Moshe ibn Ezra

During the same period Moshe ibn Ezra (1055–1140) left one of the more accurate descriptions of canonical material: "We find nothing [in the Bible] that departs from the category of prose, except for three books: Psalms, Job, and Proverbs. And even these, as you can see, do not employ [fixed] meter or rhyme as Arabic poetry does."[80] Ibn Ezra expressed the common view of the time that identified only these three books as poetry. Yet, Moshe ibn Ezra also claimed Solomon wrote both prose (Proverbs) and poetry (songs). So, he concluded, 1 Kings 4:32 indicated proverbs and songs as distinct types of literature.[81] He also identified tropes of Hebrew prose and poetry including metaphor, paranomasia, repetition, and inclusio.[82] These literary notations present some of the first recognitions of the importance of poetic form as we know it.

Bernard of Clairvaux

In the late medieval period, the allegorical rendering of the Song of Songs blossomed in enthusiasm and complexity. Bernard of Clairvaux (1090–1153) used passages from the Song in "Of the Three Ways in Which

---

78. Ginsburg, 39.
79. Ibid.
80. Chapter 4 of Kitāb al-Muḥāḍara wa-'l-Mudhākara, trans. by Adele Berlin, *Biblical Poetry Through Medieval Jewish Eyes* (Bloomington: Indiana University Press, 1991), 69.
81. Ibid.
82. Ibid., 73–80.

We Love God." The Song illustrated the nature and passion of human love for God. So, words which express the lovers' desire to be together and the strength of their love speak for the Christian.[83] In 1135 or later Bernard produced eighty-six sermons on the Song of Songs, most of them on the first two chapters of the Song. Throughout these sermons, he discussed the book as an allegory of Christ and the church. The love songs contained figurative rather than literal language, according to Bernard. His interpretations show amazing agility. The kiss of his mouth is the Holy Spirit.[84] The two breasts (4:5) represent Christ's patience and mercy.[85]

Bernard preached by quoting brief sentences from the book and expounding on the images. He made use of the visual quality of the language of the Song. His suggestions seem less a final word on the meaning of each image than a single meaning with the possibility of an endless number of interpretations. Bernard provided a hierarchy of significances which undergirded his hermeneutics. For this he used language from the Song. The garden indicated "simple history;" the storehouses, the "moral sense," and the chambers, the "mystical and inmost meaning." The sequence increases in intimacy as the significance of each level of understanding increases.[86]

In this hierarchy Bernard shows his preference for mystical truth as the ultimate understanding of Scripture. His search for these deep truths resulted in some inconsistency in the application of the roles to the bride and groom. At times the church assumes the groom's role. The Song also contains interpretation of other Scripture as Bernard understands it. For example, "I have likened thee, My love, to My horsemen among the chariots of Pharaoh" he discussed under the title, "The Spiritual Meaning of the Exodus."[87] He located three flowers in the Song: (1) the flower of the garden (virginity), (2) the flower of the field (martyrdom), and (3) the flower of the bridal couch (good works).[88] Throughout the book, sleep signified contemplation.[89] The "little foxes" of 2:15 stood for temptation.[90]

The contemporary reader can agree with this final interpretation, because the reference to the foxes presents no obvious literal meaning. A similar sort of hidden message lay beneath Psalm 108:2, according to Rupert of Deutz. In "On the Victory of God's Word" (1120–1130) the phrase, "Awake, O psaltery and lute!" provided the basis for a highly imaginative reading. The psaltery and lute were the body of Christ in the tomb.

83. In *Late Medieval Mysticism,* trans. and ed. Ray C. Petry, LCC, vol. 13 (Philadelphia: Westminster, 1957).
84. *Saint Bernard on the Song of Songs,* trans. and ed. by an unnamed member of monastic community (London: A. R. Mowbray & Co. Limited, 1952), 30.
85. Ibid., 33.
86. Ibid., 62.
87. Ibid., 115.
88. Ibid., 145.
89. Ibid., 166.
90. Ibid., 201.

The playing of the lute indicated Jesus' teaching, but his death made the sweeter music of the psaltery available.[91] The contemporary reader can imagine that those with such mystic interpretations sat contemplating or praying for hours on end. As a result of this meditation, such allegorical truths likely caused a deep sense of special divine revelation. The special interpretation probably came as an instantaneous idea. This suddenness added to the worshiper's understanding of the truth as divine gift. All this enthusiasm for spiritual renderings of the Song makes a contention offered by Roland Murphy more plausible. He claimed that the Middle Ages brought more attention to the Song of Songs than any other book of the Bible. Among other things, this involved the writing of more commentaries than for any other biblical book. The twelfth century alone produced at least thirty commentaries.[92]

Maimonides' *Guide to the Perplexed*

During this period Maimonides (1135–1204) produced his *Guide to the Perplexed.* In this work he used individual verses of the Song on a few occasions, but always in a most derivative manner. The issues connected with the Song never relate to the Song's own contents. Maimonides, like many other medieval interpreters, showed no interest in understanding the Song of Songs as poetry. He referred to Song of Songs 1:4, "Draw me, we will run after thee" as a reference to zeal for Torah. He drew this interpretation from a midrash on the Song which related the statement to Israel's promise of obedience at Sinai.[93]

Maimonides read the Song figuratively, referring to it as a "parable." Whatever else he meant by the term, *parable* indicated nonliteral interpretation. He, along with other medieval interpreters, found attraction in the Song because it provided multiple metaphors open to all sorts of didactic interpretations.

Maimonides' treatment of Lamentations followed a much more logical course. He related the loss of the prophetic message, "Her prophets find no vision from the Lord" (Lam. 2:9), to the exile. He anticipated the return of prophetic revelation at the dawn of the messianic age.[94] This Jewish viewpoint relates Lamentations to its proper historical context—the exile. He presented a more poetic rendering of Lamentations 5:19: "Thou, O LORD, sittest for all eternity/Thy throne is from generation to generation." For Maimonides, "throne" represented God's "sublimity and greatness." This sublimity and greatness made God's office (unlike offices which place humans in authority) "inseparable from Him."[95] In other words, God's

91. In *Early Medieval Theology*, trans. and ed. George E. McCracken, LCC vol. 9 (Philadelphia: Westminster, 1957), 279.
92. Roland Murphy, "Song of Songs, Book of," *ABD* 6:154.
93. Moses ben Maimonides, *The Guide to the Perplexed*, trans. Shlomo Pines (Chicago: University of Chicago Press, 1963), 532.
94. Ibid., 362, 373.
95. Ibid., 35.

eternal nature frees his authority from the limits of time. Time always limits human authority.

Maimonides referred to Psalms as a book of "prophecy."[96] He used the work theologically, describing the relationship between humans and God. "Commune with your own heart on your bed and be still" (Ps. 4:4), he applied to intellectual meditation. He explained that silence allows persons to learn from others.[97] He showed special interest in God's action in creating the world as depicted in the Psalms. A rather extended passage appeals to the "song on mishaps" (Ps. 91) to express the certainty of divine protection.[98]

The readings of Maimonides show increasingly less awareness of the poetic nature of the Song, Lamentations, and the Psalms: the first, he interpreted allegorically; the second, historically and symbolically; and the third, he read for theological content.

Thomas Aquinas

Similar to Maimonides' use of the Psalms, Aquinas (1225–1274) referred to Lamentations 5:21 to support a theological position. "Turn thou us unto thee, and we shall be turned" referred to predestination. This verse supported not simply the idea of predestination. For Aquinas, Lamentations 5:21 showed the benefit of predestination for humans.[99] Aquinas felt only the aid of God's grace allowed humans access to that grace.[100] The changeable nature of human minds made this necessary. This represents an unusual attitude toward Lamentations. Yet the interpretation remains consistent with the theology of Lamentations. The book understands tragedy and redemption as ultimately determined by God. Humans may bring on his wrath, but the timing for divine action is not controlled by humans.

Joseph ibn Kaspi

Toward the end of the Middle Ages, approaches to poetry developed which show more accord to contemporary notions. Joseph ibn Kaspi wrote a commentary on the Song of Songs before 1300. He described the three books attributed to Solomon in terms of their literal or nonliteral language. Ecclesiastes contained strictly literal language. The Song of Songs contained completely nonliteral language, using symbols and images. Proverbs contained a combination of literal and nonliteral language.[101] Kaspi used this scheme to warn against the confusing of literal and figurative language in expositions of all the Hebrew Bible. The contemporary student of the Bible should avoid the tendency to place scholars like Kaspi too far ahead of their times. Though we cannot discount Kaspi's depiction of the works,

96. Ibid., 36–37, 478.
97. Ibid., 112, 140, 260.
98. Ibid., 626–27.
99. *Summa Theologica* in *Nature and Grace: Selections from the Summa Theologica of Thomas Acquinas*, trans. and ed. A. M. Fairweather, LCC, vol. 2 (Philadelphia: Westminster, 1954), 110.
100. Ibid., 146.
101. Adele Berlin, *Biblical Poetry*, 5,105–6.

his observations do not guarantee that his reading of any specific text, literal or nonliteral, would accord with contemporary exegesis.

Summary: Scripture First, Poetry Second

Medieval interpreters and many of their Jewish predecessors showed little awareness of what we would call poetic form. Jewish interpreters identified poetry by its "falseness," that is, its metaphorical language. One noun stood for something else. Medieval interpreters scarcely recognized rhyme, meter, and other indications of poetic rhythm.[102] Early Jewish and Christian interpreters, in spite of their unyielding commitment to Scriptures (or perhaps because of it), failed to recognize the second parallel term as a repetition of the first. Instead, they interpreted successive lines independently, assuming each word communicated some divine mystery. This oversight of parallelism continued during the Middle Ages.[103] These trends continued the patristic tendency to read the Bible in support of the common theology of the church. Medieval interpreters did not connect Hebrew literature to the historical community which produced it. In this respect, their view of the Hebrew Bible as Scripture outweighed all other interpretive concerns. As Scripture, they expected the Hebrew Bible to confirm Christ's ascendancy even in the smallest detail. It does not surprise the student of this history that they found the theology they searched for. Similarly, the Jewish interpreter, Maimonides, found support for current intellectual views. We can expect the reformation emphasis on objective study of the Bible to pave the way for more careful exegesis.

Questions for Discussion

1. In what ways did early interpretation of poetry lead to meanings inconsistent with the original meanings of the biblical texts? What caused such interpretations?

2. What exegetical and theological lessons do you learn from early Jewish and Christian interpretation of poetry?

---

102. Solomon ibn Parhon in *Mahberet Hearuk* (1160–1161) considered rhyme and meter bad things since in his view the Bible didn't employ them. Parhon could not imagine that biblical writers wrote without an awareness of these techniques. In Berlin, *Biblical Poetry*, 84.
103. Robert Gordis, *Poets*, 61–62.

Chapter 12

History of Interpretation
Since the Reformation

Before the era of the reformation began, Dietrich of Niem wrote "Ways of Uniting and Reforming the Church" (1410). He opened his call to reform with a paragraph dependent on Lamentations 1:1–2. He applied the desolation of Israel to the impoverished state of the medieval church.[1] He intended such critique to lead to an internal reform. Apparently, he hoped the pitiful description of Jerusalem in Lamentations 1:1–2 would lead church leaders to remorse. Though reform of the church came slowly and painfully, those committed to Hebrew poetry show a remarkable transformation in the views of Hebrew poetry prior to and during the following centuries.

Precursors to the Reformation

Allemano and Don Isaac Abravenel

The period prior to the Reformation also produced advances in consideration of biblical poetry by Jewish interpreters. Allemano attributed the following quotation to Abraham ibn Ezra: "All Arabic poems are about love and desire, Latin poems about wars and vengeance, Greek poems about wisdom and craftiness, Hindu poems about proverbs and riddles, and Hebrew poems about songs and praise to the Lord of Hosts."[2] Allemano's quotation of ibn Ezra shows a willingness to consider biblical literature against the backdrop of world literature. A similar world perspective resulted in the typification of poetry by Don Isaac Abravanel (1437–1508) in his *Commentary on Exodus 15*. He described three types of poetry. First,

---

1. In *Advocates of Reform: From Wyclif to Erasmus,* trans. and ed. James Kerr Cameron, LCC, vol. 14 (Philadelphia: Westminster, 1953), 149.
2. Quoted in Yohanan ben Isaac Allemano (1435–1505), *Heseq Selomoh,* cited in Berlin, *Biblical Poetry,* 140.

some poetry exhibits a standard line length, meter, and rhyme. This type of poetry does not occur in the Hebrew Bible. Second, some poetry follows a melody, though without meter or rhyme. This type exists in certain psalms. Third, some poetry works through exaggeration, hyperbole, and metaphor. This type appears in some psalms, the Song of Songs, Solomon's songs, and the Song of the Sea.[3] In this last category he included prophetic speeches as the highest form of poetry.[4] While contemporary exegetes cannot afirm his precise categories, his effort to distinguish various types of poetry represents quite an advance.

Savonarola

Savonarola (d. 1498) presented various sensitive interpretations of the Psalms. He authored expositions of Psalm 51 and 31. He used the psalms as personal meditations, actually assuming the voice of the psalmist. The expositions exhibit a very simple writing style. They convey deep pathos. He presented Psalm 51 as a prayer of penance and Psalm 31 as a prayer of trust. These depictions approximate the designations common in current interpretation of the Psalms. He showed consummate skill in reproducing and amplifying the mood of the Psalms. He accomplished this by exaggerating each element through repetition and illustration.[5]

Erasmus

Other Reformation interpreters used poetic passages to support their philosophy or theology. Erasmus, advocating self-knowledge, cited Song of Songs 1:8 in *The Enchiridion* (1503): "If you do not know yourself, O beautiful among women, go forth and follow after the sheep of your flock." The word *yourself* does not appear in current translations. Rather, the statement of 1:8 appears an answer to the question directed to the male in 1:7: "Tell me . . . where you pasture your flock?" Erasmus used 1:8 to defend his belief in self-knowledge as a fundamental component of wisdom. He continued by explaining that no one presuming wisdom should understand self-knowledge as sufficient.[6]

The Reformers

Zwingli

Zwingli supported popular interpretation of Scripture by quoting Psalm 36:9. "In your light we see light" indicated that God's direct inspiration enabled any believer to understand the Bible.[7]

---

3. Berlin, *Biblical Poetry*, 121–23.
4. Ibid., 126–27.
5. *Meditations on Psalm 51 and Part of Psalm 31 in Latin with an English*, trans. E. H. Perowne (London: C. J. Clay and Sons, 1900).
6. In *Advocates of Reform*, 282.
7. Ulrich Zwingli, "Of the Clarity and Certainty of the Word of God" in *Zwingli and Bullinger*, trans. G. W. Bromiley, LCC vol. 24 (Philadelphia: Westminster, 1953), 78.

Melchior Hofmann

Melchior Hofmann used a different approach in "The Ordinance of God." He referred to images of the bride and bridegroom in the Song of Songs and the New Testament to underpin a more mystical interpretation of Christianity. The wilderness symbolized suffering and separation from the bridegroom, which he understood as a necessary part of the believer's pilgrimage.[8] The understanding of all three (bride, bridegroom, and wilderness) views employ the technique of proof text. Current interpretations receive support from Scripture texts with no background studies.

Luther

Martin Luther employed more wide-ranging uses of the Psalms. In his interpretations of Psalms he accepted the ascriptions in Psalms as literally naming the author. This person "prays" the content of the psalm. When the psalm named no individual, Luther assumed Davidic authorship. Psalms which Luther read as referring to the future, he ascribed to David as "prophet." In *Lectures on Romans* Luther referred to Psalms more than any other biblical book (including those of the New Testament). This preference for Psalms holds true for many of Luther's writings. The following Psalms appear most often in *Lectures on Romans:* (1) Psalm 1, especially verse 2 because of its emphasis on meditating on the Law, (2) Psalm 32, a thanksgiving song emphasizing forgiveness and confession, (3) Psalm 45, the royal wedding song which Luther read as a messianic psalm, (4) Psalm 51, introduced in the Psalter as a lament based on the Uriah-Bathsheba incident (this psalm appears especially frequently), and (5) Psalm 119, the lengthy Torah psalm.[9]

In his "Preface to the Psalter" Luther claimed the Psalms contain promises of Christ's death and resurrection. They also depict the kingdom of God and the church. Due to this anticipation of future realities, Luther considered the Psalms, "a little Bible."[10] In the Psalms Luther heard the actual words of the saints. He considered the personal communication of the saints through the Psalms both earnest and sincere.[11]

Luther's Works devotes three full volumes (12–14) to Luther's interpretations of Psalms. Yet Luther remained relatively unaware of the nature of the book as poetry. Instead, his interest lay in connecting the words of the psalmists to the gospel and the contemporary church. His recognition of the personal nature of psalm composition remains a legacy to the popular reading of Psalms. The devotional reader of the Psalms tends to understand them primarily as prayers. Yet Luther also used them as a theological bridge

8. In *Spiritual and Anabaptist Writers*, trans. Selina Gerhard Schultz, LCC, vol. 25 (Philadelphia: Westminster, 1957), 184–203.

9. *Luther: Lectures on Romans*, trans. and ed. William Pauck, LCC, vol. 15 (Philadelphia: Westminster, 1961).

10. *Luther's Works*, vol. 35, trans. E. Theodore Bachmann (Philadelphia: Fortress, 1960), 254.

11. Ibid., 255.

between the Hebrew Bible and the New Testament. The works of Luther contain only rare references to Lamentations. The following interpretation of Lamentations 2:14, though serious in intent, seems almost playful in style:

> This leads to something else: because such teachers do not bite, they do not chew and grind, i.e., they do not criticize and down their pupils; they do not lead them to repentance and do not pull them down and break them up. But being what they are, they swallow them down whole in their faithlessness as it says in Lam. 2:14: "Your prophets have not opened your eyes to your sins that would induce you to repentance." To reprove and chasten a sinner with words, means to bite him with one's teeth until he becomes very small and soft (i.e., humble and meek). But to flatter him, to extenuate his sins, and to grant him many liberties, means to gulp him down one's throat, i.e., to leave him whole and big and strong, i.e., proud and hardened against repentance and unable to take any treatment. Hence, the bride in The Song of Solomon is said to have "teeth like a flock of sheep that are shorn" (S. of Sol. 4:2), i.e., words of rebuke taken from the Scripture without the intent to accuse anyone by them.[12]

In this instance, instead of expounding on an image taken from scripture, Luther formed his own image and used Scripture to support it.

Luther devoted much time and attention to the Song of Songs. He described the Song of Songs as a "song of praise" which Solomon offered to God in thanks for his own obedience. In the Song God functioned as the head of a household. Obedience comes as God kisses his bride (the believer) with his word. Luther depicted this work as the third book of Solomon, since its joy characterized the one who lived according to the teaching of the first two (Proverbs and Ecclesiastes).[13] Luther does not interpret the Song as the account of the love between Solomon and the daughter of Pharaoh, nor does he accept Jewish or Christian allegories.[14] Specifically, the Song is "an encomium[15] of the political order, which in Solomon's day flourished in sublime peace."[16]

Luther capitalized on the idyllic pastoral tone of the Song, but ignored the dissatisfaction and dangers which connect the peaceful scenes. Luther does not soften references to body parts, but interprets them as metaphors of productiveness on a spiritual level. Similarly, the nakedness of the figures conveyed a message regarding the church:

> Therefore the church's entire praise in The Song of Solomon belongs to Christ who dwells in it through faith just as all this light of the earth does not come from the earth but from the sun that shines upon it. So,

---

12. *Lectures on Romans*, 95.
13. "Preface to the Books of Solomon" in *Works*, vol. 35, 260–61.
14. "Lectures on the Song of Solomon" in *Works*, vol. 15, trans. Ian Siggins, 194.
15. The word *encomium* basically designates a work of praise—a hymn.
16. "Lectures on the Song," 195.

in The Song of Solomon, the church often confesses herself to be naked, longing, so it is written, only for the bridegroom and saying: "Draw me after thee, we will run in the odor of thy ointments" (S. of Sol. 1:4). She always seeks, always desires, and always praises the bridegroom. Thus she shows clearly that she is inwardly empty and bare and that her fullness and righteousness are outside her.[17]

Luther also applied images from the Song to his doctrine of justification by faith:

So the people of faith spends its whole life in search of justification. And this is how it gives utterance to its quest: "Draw me, we will run after thee" (S. of Sol. 1:4). "In my bed I sought him; I sought him and found him not" (S. of Sol. 3:1); "I called him, and he did not answer me" (S. of Sol. 5:6); i.e., I never believed that I had attained, but I continually seek. This is why its utterance is at last called the voice of a turtledove (cf. S. of Sol. 2:12), because it sighs so longingly.[18]

He certainly captured the mood of desire communicated by the Song.

Luther's interpretation of Hebrew poetry introduced several different avenues for interpretation. Luther attempted to limit the fanciful or defensive extremes of interpretation. Yet such corrective interpretation does not limit his allegorical application from the Song and Psalms. The literature seems most often used in apology. Interpretations of poetic books as Scripture provide more free-ranging interpretations. The reader cannot easily connect such interpretations with the passages at hand. Perhaps this shows a special attitude toward poetry: While texts like Romans demand explanations, Psalms and other poetic texts simply encourage metaphorical connections with other texts. Reason provides the means for understanding a narrative like Romans. Spiritual discernment provides access to the meaning of the Psalms.

Calvin

Calvin exhibited a similar attitude toward the Psalter. He accepted titles without question. He related the content of each psalm directly to the historical situation named in the title. Calvin offered a French translation of the Psalms from Hebrew at the conclusion of the fifth volume of *Commentary on the Book of Psalms*.[19] He explicitly labeled Psalms as prophecy.[20] Calvin often used Psalms against opponents. He cited them as a last word on doctrinal issues, including the providence of God, the insufficiency of works, the hope of heaven, Christ's preeminence, and more. In the preface to his

---

17. *Lectures on Romans*, 134.
18. Ibid., 119.
19. Trans. James Anderson (Grand Rapids: Eerdmans, 1963).
20. *The Institutes of the Christian Religion*, trans. Ford Lewis, LCC, vols. 20–21 (Philadelphia: Westminster, 1960). Vol. 1 contains nearly six hundred references to the Psalms (far more than for any other biblical book). This compares to only three references to the Song of Songs in the same volume.

Commentary on the Book of Psalms, Calvin compared his enemies ("papists") to the enemies of David in the Psalms (for example, 61:3; 35:16; 120:7).[21] Like Luther, he tended to read the psalms as composed by individuals, especially David. Calvin provided his own superscriptions which set the historical or theological context for each psalm. He regularly related the message of the Psalms to Christ's love or salvation. Accordingly, David (or others) received the title "prophet." Theologically, most of the Psalms presented the ideas of praise, thanks, or God's faithfulness, according to Calvin. Calvin noted the special perspective of Psalms as compared to other biblical books. The Psalms presented "an anatomy of all the parts of the soul."[22]

Rather than an indirect message from God, Psalms contained the words of the people. Stated another way, "The Psalms speak for us rather than to us." This involves a recognition of the diverse sources for the independent psalms. In the introduction for the first Psalm, Calvin speculated that Ezra put the Psalms into a single volume. Whoever the editor, according to Calvin, he placed Psalm 1 first because its content encouraged reflection on the divine law.[23]   The strong allusion to Law also implies a connection with Ezra (see Neh. 8–10). Calvin's understanding of the Hebrew Bible as well as his familiarity with the Hebrew language enabled him to understand the Psalter's background and style quite well. When Calvin interpreted the message of psalms, he revealed less sophistication, as seen in the preceding paragraph.

Calvin held a traditional view of the authorship of Lamentations. He understood their connection with the exile, which led him to connect Lamentations with Jeremiah. Jeremiah wrote the book to offer hope in spite of the apparent hopelessness of the exile. He based this hope on the condition of repentance. Through the work, Jeremiah fulfilled his task of gathering the remnant amid the unfaithful.[24] What Calvin missed in his explication of Lamentations, many contemporary interpreters miss as well: the sense of disorientation and doubt which alternates with the encouragements and confessions. Calvin read the entire book as a pattern for the church's response to trouble from within and without. He unapologetically read Lamentations as espousing Christian theology, as shown in two examples. First, Lamentations 3:38, "Is it not from the mouth of the Most High that good and bad come?" taught against the Jewish idea that good or bad occurred apart from God's agency.[25] Second, Calvin gave a christological interpretation of Lamentations 4:20: "The LORD's anointed, the breath of our life, was taken in their pits—the one of whom we said, 'under his shadow we shall live among the nations.'" According to Calvin, the refer-

---

21. Vol. 1, xlvi–xlviii.
22. Ibid., xxxvii.
23. Ibid., 1.
24. *Commentaries on the Book of the Prophet Jeremiah and the Lamentations,* vol. 5, trans. John Owen (Grand Rapids: Eerdmans, 1950), 300–301.
25. *Institutes,* vol. 21, 221.

ence to the anointed showed that even in a pre-Christian era, people knew God through Christ.[26]

Calvin possessed a well-informed view of poetry, but like Luther, except for the note of the subjective nature of Psalms, he provided few comments on poetic form. Calvin displayed less interest in allegorical readings than other reformers. His preference for theological proof texts led him to practically ignore the Song of Songs.

Metrical Psalms

At the time of the Reformation, the production of metrical psalms (for singing) gained popularity. This trend continued through the 1600s. Philip Sidney (1554–1586) produced numerous lined psalms. Some examples of his work remain in the hymns of today's church. The following sample from a lament (Ps. 6:2–5) shows a strong sensitivity to the emotion of the psalmist:

2 But mercy, lord, let Mercy thyne descend
3 For I am weake, and in my weakness languish;
4 Lord help, for ev'n my bones their marrow spend
   With cruel anguish.

5 Nay ev'n my soul fell troubles do appall;
   Alas, how long, my God, wilt Thou delay me?
   Turne Thee, sweet lord, and from this Ougly fall
   My Deare God stay me.
6 Mercy, O Mercy lord, for Mercy's sake,
   For death doth kill the Witness of thy glory;
   Can of thy prayse the tongues entombed make
   A heavnly story? (lines 5–16)[27]

Comparison with the psalm text shows the relative freedom of the paraphrase:

2 Be gracious to me, O LORD, for I am languishing;
   O LORD, heal me, for my bones are shaking with terror.
3 My soul also is struck with terror,
   while you, O LORD—how long?
4 Turn, O LORD, save my life;
   deliver me for the sake of your steadfast love.
5 For in death there is no remembrance of you;
   in Sheol who can give you praise? (Ps. 6)

Sidney's sister, the Countess of Pembroke, also produced metrical psalms, such as the following example written around 1594:

---

26. Ibid., 344–45.
27. In Rivkah Zim, *English Metrical Psalms: Poetry as Praise and Prayer 1535–1601* (Cambridge: Cambridge University Press, 1987), 162. Zim's work presents an excellent overview of metrical psalms.

1   O all you landes, the treasures of your joy
    In mery shout upon the Lord bestow:
Your service cheerfully on him imploy,
    With triumph song into his presence goe.
2   Know first that he is God; and after know
    This God did us, not we our selves create:
We are his flock, for us his feedings grow:
    We are his folk, and he upholds our state.
3   With thankfullnesse O enter then his gate:
    Make through each porch of his your praises ring,
All good, all grace, of his high name relate,
4   He of all grace and goodnesse is the spring.
    Tyme in noe termes his mercy comprehends,
From age to age his truth it self extends (Psalm 100)[28]

Calvin and others could not accept the metrical psalms as proper hymns. They altered the words of Scripture. Although metrical psalms did not present official interpretations, their influence with the populace made them determinative for the theology of large portions of the church. The production of such works of poetry illustrates the progressive freedom subsequent biblical readers experienced. The reformers' willingness to disseminate Scriptures to the masses in popular language provided much of the impetus for enlightenment views. The popular use of Scriptures also laid the foundation for historical criticism.

Contributions of Reformation Interpretation

The progress of the Reformation did not result in the degree of objectivity present in the rise of historical criticism. A few thinkers, principally Jewish ones, showed strong interest in the literary forms of poetry in the Bible. Others, including most of those cited above, provide only brief recognitions of poetic form. While major thinkers such as Calvin and Luther changed the face of interpretation, others of the same period enjoyed little freedom of interpretation. Sebastian Castellio (1515–1563), a contemporary of Calvin, for example, was refused ordination in Geneva. This resulted from his insistence that the Song of Songs was a love song rather than a book of symbolic, spiritual significance.[29] Two advances indicative of Reformation interpretations stand out. First, the Reformation developed further allegorical interpretations of the Song of Songs.[30] Second, the Reformation fostered appealing insights into the special perspective of the Psalms. The

---

28. Ibid., 196–97.
29. S. L. Greenslade, ed., *The Cambridge History of the Bible*, vol. 3 (Cambridge: Cambridge University Press, 1963), 8, 71.
30. The resiliency of this view is illustrated in John Gill's 120 sermons on the Song of Songs as an allegory of Christ's love for the church. In *An Exposition of the Song of Solomon* (Marshallton, Del.: The National Foundation for Christian Education, 1854), 141, Gill's interpretation of 4:3, "By her lips may be meant the doctrines of the gospel delivered by her ministers . . . ," also recalls the Jewish understanding that the same passage indicated the Torah. So, all major religions and churches embracing the Hebrew canon applied allegorical readings to the Song.

Psalms held special importance for these early interpreters and their predecessors. Among the uses of the Psalms were the following:

- pointing out sin,
- pointing out God's sovereignty and love,
- prophesying Christ's atonement,
- comfort and assurance,
- evoking praise and joy, and
- direct praise.

In summary, the Psalms interpreters attempted to discern in the Psalms: (1) the voice of God, (2) confirmations of prophecy, or (3) support for Christian doctrine. The Psalms served as a multipurpose book uniting all the theology of the church. The Song of Songs, due to its less comprehensive nature, offered less support for this purpose. But what it lacked in content, it made up for with rich symbolism. Lamentations offered more limited usefulness. Its content forced its application to suffering of some sort. The difference between these viewpoints and our own concerns is the matter of genre recognition. The attempt to identify the perception of these materials in their ancient context (as in chapter 9 of this study) held no relevance for the reformers.

Post-Reformation Interpretation

Later interpreters reinforced the assumptions of traditional authorship. Strong associations of biblical poetry with human authors depends on notions of artistic production such as those presented in "On the Sublime": "Sublimity is the echo of a great soul." So, the sublimity of Genesis 1:3, "God said . . ." belonged to Moses, who was "no ordinary man."[31] The 1600s showed a pronounced commitment to the principle of the "great soul." Following this pattern, theorists about 1650 emphasized the creativity of a privileged human author as the key to poetic communication.

John Donne

In 1622 John Donne referred to an interpretation, apparently quite common, which read Psalms 90–100 as authored by Moses.[32] The title of Psalm 90 suggests the ascription to Moses: "A prayer of Moses, the man of God." No ascriptions appear in following psalms until Psalm 101. Donne held a similar strong view of Davidic authorship of other psalms. The following excerpt from a sermon in 1625 indicates this: "The Psalmes are the Manna of the Church. As Manna tasted to every man like that he liked best, so doe the Psalmes minister Instruction, and satisfaction, to every man, in every emergency and occasion. David was not onely a clear Prophet of

31. Longinus, "On the Sublime" in *Critical Theory Since Plato*, ed. Hazard Adams (San Diego: Harcourt, Brace, Jovanovich, 1971), 81–82.

32. "Preached at St. Paul's" (a sermon on Psalm 90:14) in *John Donne's Sermons on the Psalms and Gospels*, ed. Evelyn M. Simpson (Berkeley: University of California Press, 1963), 45.

Christ himselfe, but a Prophet of every particular Christian; He foretells what I, what any shall doe, and suffer, and say."[33] Donne's description of David as a prophet serves as example of his understanding of inspiration channeled through an individual.

Spinoza

In many respects Spinoza serves as an interesting bridge between more contemporary approaches and traditional views such as those of Donne. Spinoza cited three passages from Psalms (145:9; 145:18; 33:15) to support the view that God gave all persons an equal capacity for understanding and morality: "He fashioneth their hearts alike. (33:15)"[34] He contended that the Jews of the second temple period (after 515 B.C.E.) collected and edited the Psalms. Philo of Alexandria earlier expressed this view. Spinoza anticipated later rationalistic views of Scripture in his interpretation of Psalms 147:18; 104:4: "You make the winds your messengers, fire and flame your ministers." Such verses show that so-called "natural elements" appear as wonders of God.[35] Accordingly, all miracles have natural explanations. This represents a vast distinction from the traditionalism of his near contemporary, Donne.

Historical-Critical Interpretation

The dawn of a more critical approach to Scripture interpretation brought steady challenges to traditional views. Unfortunately, it brought few suggestions regarding the special form of poetry, except for the considerable contributions to the understanding of parallelism by Robert Lowth. Historical critics ceased to read the Song of Songs as allegory, challenged the Jeremianic authorship of Lamentations, and made an abortive attempt to interpret the Psalms historically. During the push for scientific evidence as a basis for biblical interpretation, the themes and forms of poetry provided little support. To this day, the subjectiveness (individualistic perspective) or the aesthetic nature of biblical poetry receives slight treatment. The mainstream categories promote interest in narrative criticism or, ironically, the (nonpoetic) interpretation of prophecy.

Herder's *Commentary on the Psalms*

Herder's intense romanticism carried on much of the spirit of precritical interpretation. He also helped introduce historical interpretations. He read Psalm titles as settings for texts and searched the Psalms for histori-

---

33. "2nd Prebend Sermon Preached at Saint Paul's (Psalm 63:7)," *Sermons*, 94. According to Donne, this psalm (63) summarized the message of the entire Psalter, 95.
34. Benedict de Spinoza, *A Theologico-Political Treatise* in *A Theologico-Political Treatise and a Political Treatise*, trans. R. H. M. Elwes (New York: Dover Publications, 1951), 49.
35. Ibid., 90.

cal allusions. He followed earlier christological readings as shown in his identification of the messiah in Psalm 2:2 with Christ.[36]

Ewald's Commentary on the Psalms

Ewald's later historical approach involved much more thoroughgoing studies of Hebrew contexts for the Psalms. He rearranged the Psalms according to date. The earliest Psalms belonged to the time of David (authentic Psalms of David). The latest belonged to the fifth century.[37] Ewald noted that the comparison of the themes of the David psalms led to the conclusion that they come from different authors. So, he concluded, the superscriptions did not come from the poets themselves. Ewald confirmed authorship on the basis of titles only when the content of the Psalm affirmed the association with the individual named.[38] The historical tenacity shown in Ewald's quest for evidence characterizes the movement. In his preface, he offered strong criticism of other commentators on the Psalms, naming Hengstenberg (1842), Delitzsch (1859), Hupfeld (1862), and Hitzig (1835). These commentators did not approach the Psalms "scientifically."[39]

Ewald gave more attention to generic form than the previous generation of interpreters. His discussion of Lamentations in his *Commentary on Psalms* provides evidence of his attention to genre. He considered the five laments as a sort of extension of Psalms. He described Jeremianic authorship as "impossible" to maintain due to the psalmlike style of the work.[40] Such critical scrutiny also challenged the allegorical interpretation of the Song of Songs.

Delitzsch's Interpretation of the Song as Drama

Shortly before 1900, practically all major thinkers rejected allegory. Instead, they showed preference for reading the Song as drama. Early interpreters suggested the dramatic nature of the Song of Songs. In historical criticism drama serves as the framework for virtually all points of interpretation. Franz Delitzsch understood the work as an account of a country girl who drew Solomon away from his harem to realize an exclusive relationship with a single wife. In 1877 he presented it as a drama with six two-part acts. The drama detailed the couples' love and courtship

---

36. Johann Gottfried von Herder, *Herder's Commentary on the Psalms*, trans. Bernard Fritz (Westminster, Md.: The Newman Preess, 1961; original, 1782), 7–9.

37. G. Heinrich A. von Ewald, *Commentary on the Psalms*, trans. E. Johnson (Edinburgh: Williams and Norgate, 1881). Bernhard Duhm represents the most extreme of these historical exegetes. He assigned seventy-four psalms to the time of Antiochus Epiphanes' persecution of the Jews in 167–164 B.C.E. He dated the final form of the edited Psalter no earlier than 70 B.C.E. D. Bernhard Duhm, *Die Psalmen*, Kurzer Hand-Commentar zum Alten Testament (Freiburg: J. C. B. Mohr [Paul Siebeck], 1899), xx, xxiii.

38. *Psalms*, 1881, 2:45–46.

39. *Psalms*, 1880, 1:ii–iv.

40. *Psalms*, 1881, 2:105.

from beginning to end.[41] The simplistic development he noted does not accord with the complex appearance of the book. Delitzsch would not read the Song of Songs allegorically.[42] (He even described it as "erotic."). He claimed, however, that the identification of Solomon as a type of Christ made a "spiritual" interpretation possible. On this level the Song of Songs relates to the mystery of Christ's love for the church.[43]

Pouget and Guitton interpreted the Song of Songs as a drama in twelve scenes. They identified three central characters: Solomon, the beloved, and the young woman.[44] In accordance with a careful reading of the Song, Pouget and Guitton reduced Solomon's role to a cameo appearance (only in 3:7 and 3:11, and there in the third person).

Driver's *Introduction to the Literature of the Old Testament*

Driver's *Introduction* represented an approach which surveyed the literature of the Bible in a comparative perspective. The popular but short-lived movement began in the early twentieth century. Driver's claims regarding Hebrew poetry reflect some of the concerns of these critics. He divided Western poetry into two types: epic and drama. Hebrew poetry represented the epic type. Hebrew poetry itself consisted of two forms: lyric (as in the Song of Songs) and gnomic (as in Job).[45] Driver recognized the speakers of the Song but named it a "poem" rather than drama.[46] He, too, rejected the traditional view that identified Solomon and his bride as the only speakers.[47]

The trend toward the consideration of the Bible as literature influenced later criticism, but at or near the time of Driver's writing, it reached an end as a distinctive movement. His work actually contained more traditional scholarship than comparative studies. This insured the acceptance and continued influence of the book. Current literary approaches to biblical poetry deal with the texts with less a sense of romanticism. They rely on rhetorical and linguistic data, and their findings typically show less subjectivism than the movement which influenced Driver's remarks on poetry.[48]

---

41. *Commentary on the Song of Solomon and Ecclesiastes*, trans. M. G. Easton (Grand Rapids: Eerdmans, 1950; German original, 1877).

42. Typology differs from allegory in that typology will not allow definitive interpretations of specific events and individuals. Instead, the "type" provides a basis for general associations and thematic interpretations (likenesses).

43. *Song of Solomon and Ecclesiastes*, 3. Unlike many historical critics, Delitzsch raised no challenge of Solomonic authorship (p. 11).

44. G. Pouget et J. Guitton, *Le Cantique Des Cantiqués*, Études Bibliques 9 (Paris: Librairie Lecoffre, 1948).

45. Samuel R. Driver, *An Introduction to the Literature of the Old Testament* (Cleveland: World Publishing Company, 1956; original edition, 1891, revised, 1913), 360–61.

46. Ibid., 436.

47. Ibid., 437.

48. The Psalms retains high importance for daily and weekly worship. Early monastic communities (for example, the Benedictines) emphasized the importance of Psalms for personal piety. In the middle of the twentieth century Thomas Merton approached the Psalms as the sustaining force of the monastic lifestyle. Hence the title, *Bread in the Wilderness* (New York: New Directions Books, 1953).

Confessional/Devotional Approaches

More recent developments in the interpretation of Hebrew poetry do not displace the value of more confessional approaches. These treatments have shaped the identity of Christianity. In such approaches interest centers on the Psalms. Committed to the spirituality of the Psalms, contemporary authors continue the flood of devotional works on the Psalms. Pastors or other ministers rather than Hebrew Bible specialists usually produce such works. The views presented in many of the works reflect the views of previous centuries of interpreters, and the claims which formed the mainline scholarly interpretations of earlier thinkers now often appear in devotional works. This phenomenon exerts influence adjacent to the influence of more critical interpretations.

Meanwhile, critical scholarship narrows into increasingly specialized considerations. Due to the nature of the Psalms themselves, crossover works are not infrequent. Yet these dual levels of interpretations bear special notice relative to Psalms, because both lines of pursuit remain vastly influential. Critical scholarship first explored three defining characteristics of Hebrew poetry: parallelism, meter, and form.

Parallelism

Robert Lowth offered the first full treatment of the poetic forms of the Hebrew Bible.[49] He also presented the first thorough discussion of parallelism as a distinct feature in Hebrew poetry. His categories of parallelism were synonymous, antithetic, and synthetic.[50] *Synonymous parallelism* repeats the idea of the first line in the second line:

Our inheritance has been turned over to strangers,
our homes to aliens. (Lam. 5:2)

This example presents a complete, easy-to-recognize correspondence. The subjects and objects of both lines nearly repeat the idea—our inheritance, our homes; strangers, aliens. This type of relationship follows the pattern A B A' B'. One should not carry the implications of the word *synonymous* too far. The two lines do not convey identical thoughts. The second qualifies and adds to the first.[51] The sample from Lamentation 5 does not provide indication of the complex relationships possible even in this subcategory. Similarities can be based on syntax, sound, images,

49. *Lectures on the Sacred Poetry of the Hebrew* (Andover: Crocker & Brewster, 1829; originally published, 1753). His coverage included the Prophets, Proverbs, the Song of Songs interpreted as drama, and Job as a partially dramatic form.

50. *Isaiah: A New Translation with a Preliminary Dissertation* (Boston: William Hilliard, 1834), ix. Since parallelism depends upon theme as well as vocabulary, English translations reveal parallelistic structures.

51. As noted below, Kugel challenged not only synonymity but also the common notion of parallelism itself on this basis. He emphasized the importance of contrast and complement in the second line. See James Kugel, *The Idea of Biblical Poetry: Parallelism and Its History* (New Haven: Yale University Press, 1981), 1–58.

allusion, theme, or other correspondences in addition to vocabulary, as in the example above.

Antithetic parallelism typically uses negation in the second line:

His enemies I will clothe with disgrace,
but on him, his crown will gleam. (Ps. 132:18)

The structure remains A B A' B' but A and A', and B and B' show a negative relationship. The idea of the two lines appears relatively the same (divine favor toward the Davidic king), but the lines express the idea negatively (line 1) and positively (line 2). Again, the content expresses no direct inference: The reader could not infer the exaltation of the ruler on the basis of the enemies' disgrace. The combination of the lines provides the key to understanding. So content goes hand in hand with form to determine meaning. Antithetic parallelism occurs frequently in *mešālîm* (proverbs). Special wisdom interests lead to a preference for this type of parallelism. Proverbs major on distinctions. The contrasts between the lazy and the industrious, the wicked and the righteous, the fool and the wise, and so forth find ready expression in parallelistic depictions of opposite behavior and fortunes. Antithetic parallelism appears less frequently, though is by no means rare, in the Psalms. The following verse contains a double set of antithetic lines:

For a day in your courts is better
    than a thousand elsewhere.
I would rather be a doorkeeper in the house of my God
    than live in the tents of wickedness. (Ps. 84:10)

Lowth and subsequent critics used *synthetic parallelism* as a catchall category for many forms which did not fit the synonymous and antithetic schemes. Lowth intended the designation "synthetic" to describe sets in which the second strophe further described or added narrative-like content to the first strophe. If not cast in lines, these units show little or no parallelism. Scholars soon recognized the vagueness of the category, which one scholar renamed "incomplete parallelism."[52] Other interpreters use additional designations. Due to its storylike content, the Song of Songs exhibits a great deal of synthetic parallelism, as in the following:

He brought me to the banqueting house,
    and his intention toward me was love. (Song of Songs 2:4)

Many current interpreters reject this category altogether on the basis that its purpose is to find a structural parallel in lines which contain none.

New Approaches. Serious challenges to traditional descriptions of parallelism appear from recent theorists. None of the systems proposed promise the kind of standardization for discussion which Lowth's achieved. However, the present level of dissatisfaction with the traditional concept of

---

52. George B. Gray, *The Forms of Hebrew Poetry* (Hoboken, N.J.: KTAV, 1972; originally published, 1915), 59.

parallelism indicates the eventual eclipse of Lowth's terminology. The following offers a simplified description of a few recent characterizations of "parallelism."

Watson added to the term *parallelism* two other descriptions of poetic form—symmetry and asymmetry.[53] According to Watson, classical parallelism accounted for only a fraction of Hebrew poetry. He divided the forms into several types: (1) gender-matched parallelism, (2) parallel word pair, (3) number parallelism, (4) staircase parallelism, and (5) a miscellany of four minor types.[54]

In contrast to this rather complicated series of divisions, James Kugel profered a description of parallelism as simply a second line supporting the first one.[55] According to Kugel, Lowth provided a sense of order to the study of the Hebrew Bible, a sense of order not present in the Hebrew Bible itself.[56] Lowth's misunderstanding related to a broader misunderstanding which Lowth inherited. The word *poetry* as originally applied to the Hebrew Bible relied on the imposition of Greek metrical patterns on the Hebrew text. Kugel understood the dialectic between prose and poetry did not exist for the ancient Hebrews.[57] Instead, "parallelism is the only meter of biblical poetry."[58] For Lowth, parallelism simply involved line form. For Kugel parallelism represented the nearest equivalent to a Hebrew understanding of poetry—even then, not very similar to contemporary notions.

Kugel rejected the notion of metrical balance as the essence of parallelism: The second line simply elaborated on the first. The Hebrew poet, according to Kugel, showed no interest in distinctions regarding the precise nature of the elaboration. The following types illustrate the possible relationships: (1) "incomplete B completed by reference to A," (2) "incomplete A completed by B," (3) repetition of portion of A in B, (4) word pairs, (5) sequence (implied subordination of B to A), and (6) "unusual word order, chiasmus, etc."[59]

Luis Alonso Schökel, like Kugel, noted the dependence of the second strophe on the first.[60] He related parallelism to the basic function of language rather than to artistic expression: In verbal communication we divide complex reality into parts and "reassemble" it. The pairing of lines in Hebrew poetry represents an extension of this.[61] He tentatively proposed classifying types in very general but straightforward categories: Parallelism

---

53. Wilfred G. E. Watson, *Classical Hebrew Poetry: A Guide to Its Techniques*, JSOTSup 26 (Sheffield: JSOT Press, 1984, 1986), 114–19.
54. Ibid., 123–59.
55. Kugel, *The Idea of Biblical Poetry*, 51–52.
56. Ibid., 57.
57. Ibid, 85.
58. Ibid, 301.
59. Ibid., 54–55.
60. Luis Alonso Schökel, *A Manual of Hebrew Poetics*, Subsidia Biblica 11 (Rome: Editrice Pontifico Instituto Biblico, 1988), 50.
61. Ibid., 51.

involves (1) the number of parallel lines, (2) the quantity of text, (3) the relationship of the contents, and (4) the correspondence of components.

Hrushovski closely correlated parallelism and meter. His description of parallelism deserves close examination:

> The system of this type of rhythm may be described as semantic-syntactic-accentual free parallelism. It is based on a cluster of shifting principles, the most prominent one being the semantic-rhetorical, the obviously restricted one being rhythmical. In late periods the rhythm of this poetry was taken to be basically accentual. Indeed, in biblical poetry the number of stresses per verset, though free, is clearly restricted—usually 2, 3, or 4, and quite often equal or similar in both versets of a pair (e.g., 3 + 2, the so-called "dirge meter"). The number of syllables between these stresses, though perceived from the point of view of later and more rigorous meters as entirely free, was sometimes very much regulated as well: two adjacent stresses in one clause were precluded, and if a word was too long it had a secondary stress, thus providing usually 1 or 2 unstressed syllables between adjacent stresses. As a result, scholars have often perceived syllabic regularity in biblical versets. No systematic rhyme is to be found in the Bible, but there is a very pervasive usage of alliteration, sporadic end-rhyme, puns, acrostics and formulas, either embellishing or reinforcing the major principles of parallelism.[62]

Adele Berlin noted that parallelism may occur on the level of half lines, words, or sounds in addition to its occurrence in double lines. Consequently, she broadened the definition of parallelism to account for these levels.[63] Further, parallelism involves the convergence of similar word class (morphology), similar syntax, similar lexical forms, similar semantics, and similar phonology.[64] The entire book follows these categories.

Terence Collins offered a further elaboration of parallelism as a more complex phenomenon. He found four basic types of sentences:

- noun phrase + verb,
- noun phrase + verb + modifier,
- noun phrase + verb + noun phrase, and
- noun phrase + verb + noun phrase + modifier.[65]

Collins felt he could answer objections to the claim that parallelism served as the central feature of Hebrew poetry "by an analysis of lines based on grammatical structures."[66] The interplay of the line types listed above dis-

---

62. Benjamin Hrushovski, "Notes on the Systems of Hebrew Versification" in *The Penguin Book of Hebrew Verse*, ed. T. Carmi (New York: Penguin Books, 1981), 58.

63. Adele Berlin, *The Dynamics of Biblical Parallelism* (Bloomington: Indiana University Press, 1985), 3; compare her "The Grammatical Aspect of Biblical Parallelism" in *Beyond Form Criticism*, ed. Paul R. House, Sources for Biblical and Theological Study 2 (Winona Lake, Ind.: Eisenbrauns, 1992), 311–48.

64. Ibid., 140.

65. Terence Collins, *Line-Forms in Hebrew Poetry* (Rome: Biblical Institute Press, 1978), 23.

66. Ibid., 7.

tinguishes poetry, according to Collins. No single interpreter carried forward Collins' suggestions. Based on the work of Collins and others, current interpreters rarely question the significance of parallelism.

Since the 1960s some scholars have suggested the key to understanding parallelism lies in the recognition of parallel word pairs. The pairs were clichés recognizable to the Hebrews. Parallel lines broke the words apart, though the reader continued to recognize the word pairs employed in the poetry. For example, in the following lines *ordinances* and *statutes* may be closely associated words broken apart in Psalm 18:22:

> For all his *ordinances* were before me,
> and his *statutes* I did not put away from me. (italics added)

Stanley Gevirtz compared such constructions with the stock phrases used in Homer and elsewhere.[67] Mitchell Dahood provided a list of word pairs shared by Ugaritic texts and the Psalms.[68] The recognition of word pairs highlights a feature of biblical poetry, perhaps obvious to the original readers or hearers, lost to the average English reader.

Meter

Eduard Sievers pioneered critical metrical studies. His *Metrische Studien* provided the groundwork for many subsequent claims regarding metrical patterns.[69] Sievers found metrical patterns consisting of light and heavy stresses in all Hebrew poetry. He also identified distinct forms of prose meter. Sievers represents a group of scholars who presume metrical patterns. They show a willingness to alter the masoretic indications of meter where necessary.[70]

Mowinckel supposed the Hebrew Bible presented two styles of poetic meter. The earlier form he designated, "sense rhythm."[71] The meaning of the words governed their arrangement rather than a rhythmic structure. Later poetry appeared in the format of light and heavy streses. Mowinckel, like his predecessors, would alter the metric indications of the Hebrew text, when helpful.

Frank Cross, along with many other more recent interpreters, identified rhythm or balance rather than formal metrical style.[72] His studies of

---

67. *Patterns in the Early Poetry of Israel*, Studies in Ancient Oriental Civilization no. 32 (Chicago: University of Chicago Press, 1963), 6–14.

68. See *Psalms III:101–150*, AB 17A (Garden City, N.J.: Doubleday, 1970), 445–56; and "Ugaritic-Hebrew Parallel Pairs" in *Ras Shamra Parallels: The Texts from Ugarit and the Hebrew Bible*, vol. 1 (Rome: Pontificum Institutum Biblicum 1972), 71–382. In the latter work, Dahood listed 624 word pairs shared in the Bible and Ugaritic texts. The second vol. (Loren R. Fisher, ed. 1975) added 78 additional pairs (pp. 1–39).

69. 3 vols. (Leipzig: G. G. Tebner, 1901).

70. Proponents include Briggs and Briggs, *Commentary on the Psalms* and Duhm, *Psalmen*.

71. Sigmund Mowinckel, *The Psalms in Israel's Worship*, vol. 2, trans. D. R. Ap-Thomas (Sheffield: Sheffield Academic Press, 1992; original Norwegian edition, 1951; English, 1962), 161.

72. Frank Moore Cross, Jr., "Studies in Ancient Yahwistic Poetry" (Ph.D. disst. Johns Hopkins University, 1950), 18–23; compare F. M. Cross and D. N. Freedman, *Studies in Ancient Yahwistic Poetry* (Missoula, Mont.: Scholars Press, 1975).

meter involved syllable counts which identified basic patterns in the number of syllables in half lines. Freedman promoted a similar approach. He counted syllables, scanning for a balance of lines and patterns in the number of syllables per strophe.[73] Robert Culley referred to this type of syllable reckoning as "descriptive."[74] Such work deals with the text in its existent form rather than relying on major emendations. This trend continues.

Michael O'Connor based his view of meter on syntax. Hebrew meter involved a balance of thought. Each half line contains a complete thought, so this individual segment functions as the basic unit of Hebrew poetry.[75] O'Connor recognized both half stops (at the end of half lines) and full stops (at the conclusion of a parallel unit) as essential to Hebrew poetry. Collin's *Line Forms in Hebrew Poetry* followed a similar syntactical outline, as seen in the previous discussion of parallelism. Collins drew a close correlation between meter and parallel form.

The Song of Moses (Exod. 15:1–5a) contains the indications of stress pattern identified by W. O . E. Oesterly:

I will síng to Yahwéh;	He is híghly exálted,
Hórse and its ríder;	He flúng into the séa.
My stréngth is Yáh;	Hé was my delíverer,
He alone is my Gód, I praíse him,	The Gód of my fáther, I extól him
Yahwéh is a wárrior,	Yahwéh is his náme;
The cháriots of Pháraoh;	He cást into the séa;
The chósen leáders;	Sánk into Yam-súph;
The deéps covered óver them,	They went dówn to the dépths
	like a stóne.[76]

Oesterly's translation of Exodus 15:1–5 makes the observation of Hebrew meter seem much simpler than the reality. Without some artificial indication of word division and stress, English translations give little indication of Hebrew meter. Connecting with a hyphen the single words of Hebrew rendered by more than one word in English offers some impression of the balance of the line:

1 Give-ear-to my-words O-Lord;
   give-heed-to my-sighing.
2 Listen to-the-sound-of my-cry,
   my-king and-my-God, for-to-you I-pray.
3 O-Lord, in-the-morning you-hear my-voice;
   in-the-morning I-plead-my-case-to-you, and-watch.
                    (Ps. 5)

73. David Noel Freedman, *Pottery, Poetry, and Prophecy: Studies in Early Hebrew Poetry* (Winona Lake, Ind.: Eisenbrauns, 1980), 7–11.
74. Robert C. Culley, *Oral Formulaic Language in the Biblical Psalms* (Toronto: University of Toronto Press, 1967).
75. Michael O'Connor, *Hebrew Verse Structure* (Winona Lake, Ind.: Eisenbrauns, 1980), 60–63.
76. Oesterly, *Ancient Hebrew Poems* (New York: The Macmillan company, 1938), 3. Oesterly saw meter as rhythmic with the stresses in each line corresponding in some way to the foot movements of dance. He described the rhythms with Greek terms, but his "metrical" translations include the extraneous words between stresses and provide a helpful portrait of meter based on accented syllables.

In this scheme, each hyphenated set of words represents a single stress. The pattern of the lines (number of stresses) is 3 + 2; 3 + 2 + 2; 3 + 3. A look at the entire poem indicates these lines present irregular expressions of a basic 3 + 2 "meter." Such word counts never reveal perfect symmetry. This lack of symmetry holds true for all other systems for reckoning meter as well. The *qinah*, or dirge, rhythm (3 + 2) presents the most consistent structure.[77]

Form Criticism

Among the developments of historical criticism, none offers more significance for poetry than the rise of form criticism. Hermann Gunkel first developed the method.[78] Gunkel proposed a perspective on the Psalms that accounted for their use in worship. At the time historical speculations comprised the bulk of scholarly Psalms studies. Form criticism also offered a radical advance over pre-critical exegesis. Patristic, medieval, and reformation interpreters quoted the Psalms almost exclusively on the level of the single verse (especially Luther) to support theological positions. The setting of these verses within the context of the psalm and within the context of the worship of Israel received little attention. By contrast, Gunkel's style of exposition allowed each line of a given psalm to play a role in the general temple performance. Through this approach Gunkel read the entire psalm as a unit constructed to suit a given purpose.

Gunkel's *formgeschichtliche* method (form-historical or form-critical method) connected various types (*Gattungen*, genres) of psalms with various types of temple performances.[79] The general categories included hymns, laments, songs of thanksgiving, and royal psalms. Gunkel recognized various subtypes and mixed types as well. Each psalm provided enough indications for a relatively certain identification of type. Beyond this each type of psalm conformed to a context in worship which Gunkel named its *Sitz im Leben* (life setting). Such interpretations apply to noncultic poetry (outside the Book of Psalms) as well.[80]

Gunkel's student, Sigmund Mowinckel, challenged some of Gunkel's basic assumptions. Gunkel remained reluctant to assign a temple origin to

---

77. The *qinah* occurs in Isaiah 1:21. The form typically indicates a lament, but the form also appears in Psalm 27 and other examples lacking the themes common to laments. The Book of Lamentations provides sure evidence of the recognition of this special meter in Israel.

78. See *The Psalms: A Form-Critical Introduction*, trans. Thomas M. Horner (Philadelphia: Fortress, 1967; German original, 1930).

79. Samples of these types appear on pages 210–214 of this work.

80. The reader interested in a more complete presentation of form criticism including detailed descriptions of the components of representative genres is referred to Klaus Koch, *The Growth of the Biblical Tradition: The Form-Critical Method* (New York: Charles Scribner's Sons, 1969). A less intense overview of each of the major genres of Psalms is available in Erhard Gerstenberger, "Psalms" in J. H. Hayes, ed., *Old Testament Form Criticism* (San Antonio: Trinity University Press, 1974); Gerstenberger, *Psalms Part 1 with an Introduction to Cultic Poetry*, FOTL 14 (Grand Rapids: Eerdmans, 1988); D. Brent Sandy and Ronald L. Giese, Jr., eds. *Cracking Old Testament Codes: A Guide to Interpreting Old Testament Literary Forms* (Nashville: Broadman & Holman Publishers, 1995).

some Psalms. Gunkel understood them as refashioned by or newly composed by individuals in their current forms. With such editing they took the shape of spiritual songs and prayers. Mowinckel charged that the reluctance to associate psalms' origins with cultic performance stemmed from a bias against ritual faith allied with a bias in favor of personal expression. Further, Mowinckel claimed even more-liturgically minded Roman Catholic interpreters committed the same error out of concern to protect the individual authorship of the Psalms.[81] *Mowinckel proposed cultic settings for all the Psalms.*[82] Mowinckel also sought an understanding of the way Israel viewed the effectiveness of cultic activity.[83] He understood his contribution as the addition of "cult-functional" criticism to Gunkel's "form-historical" criticism.[84]

Two related proposals of Mowinckel remained important for subsequent interpreters. First, he tended to read more of the psalms as corporate in nature due to his understanding of their comprehensive relation to worship. Second, he associated a number of psalms with an autumn festival of kingship. These he designated "enthronement psalms."[85]

Building on Mowinckel, Aubrey Johnson presented evidence for the festival of kingship through study of kingship psalms and royal psalms.[86] Gunkel identified only Psalms 2; 18; 20; 21; 45; 72; 89; 101; 110; 132; and 144 as royal in their origination. Johnson visualized the festival piece by piece. He described its importance for the religion and worship of monarchical Israel. [87]

Assuming the importance of an enthronement festival, J. H. Eaton expanded the category, identifying three to four times the number of royal psalms identified by Gunkel.[88] Eaton used vocabulary from psalms definitely identified as royal psalms to identify other psalms originally connected to a royal festival.

Claus Westermann expressed similar interest in the cultic functions of the Psalms, but placed all the psalms in the overarching category of praise.[89] This led to the identification of two basic types: praise and lament. As with Gunkel, Westermann distinguished group psalms from individual psalms. The thanksgiving song Westermann renamed a "declarative song of praise." The hymn he renamed a "descriptive song of praise."[90]

The form-critical investigations of Gunkel and his successors apply not only to Psalms, but also to all biblical poetry. For most of the twentieth century, scholars refined and applied the suggestions of Gunkel. Most of these

---

81. *Psalms*, vol. 1, 13.
82. *Psalmenstudien*, 6 vols. (Amsterdam: Schippers, 1961; original publication 1921–1924).
83. *Psalms*, vol. 2, 15–22.
84. *Psalms*, vol. 1, 34.
85. Ibid., 106.
86. *Sacral Kingship in Ancient Israel* (Cardiff: University of Wales Press, 1967).
87. Ibid., 23.
88. *Kingship and the Psalms* (London: SCM Press, 1976). The book contains a thorough study of issues relating to kingship and the Psalms.
89. *Praise and Lament in the Psalms*, trans. Keith R. Crim and Richard N. Soulen (Atlanta: John Knox Press, 1965, 1981; German original 1961, revised, 1977).
90. Ibid., 31.

filtered their comments through the lenses of Mowinckel. In 1969 James Muilenburg proposed methodologies intended to advance form critical findings without displacing them.[91] He advocated the study of figures of speech, formal structures, and other literary features to complement form-criticism. The proposals form the basis for a distinct approach to biblical poetry known as rhetorical criticism.[92]

Rhetorical criticism paved the way for many recent approaches to biblical poetry. Current literary theory, linguistic theory, and speech act theory exerted simultaneous influence. Most of these approaches, for reasons clarified in the following discussion, fall under the designation, "reader-oriented strategies."

Latest Trends in Interpretation

Reader-Oriented Strategies

The wide proliferation of reader approaches to poetry makes a general assessment of the movement difficult. The shift in emphasis broadens the concept "poetry" to include genres of biblical literature not previously included under the rubric "poetry." Northrop Frye presented an overview of the use of language in the Bible under the categories of myth, metaphor, and typology. According to his presentation, much of the imagery of the Hebrew Bible follows broad patterns. From this perspective, explications involve standard "types" (referring to typology rather than form criticism) and levels subsumed under each of the three categories (myth, metaphor, and typology). Such an overview shows a preoccupation with the nature of the entirety of the Hebrew Bible as the canon of Scripture. This broad perspective opens much of the biblical revelation to consideration as poetry. The Bible "is as literary as it can well be without actually being literature."[93] Simply put, the special religious nature of the Bible places it in a special category between literary and nonliterary language. The implication is that apart from its high seriousness as "the word of God," the Bible possesses features common to all literature. The prophets acted primarily as prophets, that is, expressions of God's own voice; but they were incidentally poets. The psalmists primarily engaged in worship, but they incidentally practiced literary art.

---

91. "Form Criticism and Beyond," *JBL* 88 (1969), 1–18.

92. For a review of the development of the rhetorical approach and a sample application, see Donald K. Berry, *The Psalms and Their Readers: Interpretative Strategies for Psalm 18* (Sheffield: Sheffield Academic Press, 1993), 15–17, 81–103; recent review of biblical studies "beyond form criticism" appears in Paul R. House, ed., *Beyond Form Criticism: Essays in Old Testament Literary Criticism*, Sources for Biblical and Theological Study 2 (Winona Lake, Ind.: Eisenbrauns, 1992), especially Mona West, "Looking for the Poem: Reflections on the Current and Future Status of the Study of Biblical Hebrew Poetry," 423–31.

93. *The Great Code: The Bible and Literature* (New York: Harcourt, Brace, Jovanovich, 1982), 62.

Harold Fisch presented a slightly different viewpoint. He described Hebrew poetry (poetic expression in the broad sense) as "anti-literature." According to Fisch, the Bible repeatedly expresses contempt for artistic language for its own sake. Instead, the value of literary design lay in its accomplishment of higher purposes.[94] Biblical poetry (in either sense) existed as the medium for a more important divine communication. Fisch included in his corpus of biblical poetry any work which involved artistic language. He added Hosea and Esther to the poetic canon. This broadening of the concept of poetry presents one means of bypassing problematic issues relating to poetic form. If, in fact, the biblical authors and their audiences gave no consideration to the designation of prose and poetry, why should the distinction provide the basis for current interpretations? Instead, interpreters can recognize poetic form throughout the Bible. This may include styles of parallelism, meter, and life settings formerly set aside as "narrative."[95] The distinction between prose and poetry in the Bible assumes much less importance now that theorists recognize the distinction as a convention shared by interpreters rather than a distinction integral to the biblical literature.

Prophets as Poetry

The prophets represent the most incontestable portion of the new additions to the poetic canon. "Poetry and prophecy in the biblical tradition share so many of the same features and overlap to such an extent that one cannot be understood except in terms of the other."[96] The association of prophecy with poetry continued in apocalyptic, a later form of prophecy (for example, Daniel). Due to his reliance on apocalyptic and other prophecy, Jesus himself could be considered a poet-prophet.[97]

The broadening of the concept of poetry originates in the larger definition of poetry as literary craft. All artful use of language constitutes poetry. This involves a good deal of subjectiveness on the part of the interpreter. Such a reader's perspective may evolve into the sort of self-interested analysis which Buber termed "existential exegesis."[98] Buber's analysis is more psychological than historical-scientific, but serves as an example of extremely subjective analyses among biblical critics. At the heart of the operation of Hebrew poetry, according to Robert Alter, is the intensification of language and image which builds from line to line. This heightening occurs on every level—linguistics, structure, sound, employment of parallel-

---

94. H. Fisch, *Poetry with a Purpose: Biblical Poetry and Interpretation* (Bloomington: Indiana University Press, 1988), 2–7.

95. Accordingly, William van der Meer and Johannes C. deMoor, eds. *The Structural Analysis of Biblical and Canaanite Poetry* (Sheffield: Sheffield Academic Press, 1988) included Joshua, Jonah, and Job in their sample.

96. David Noel Freedman, "Pottery, Poetry, and Prophecy: An Essay on Biblical Poetry" in J. R. Maier and V. L. Tollers eds., *The Bible in Its Literary Milieu* (Grand Rapids: Eerdmans, 1979), 92.

97. Ibid., 95–96.

98. Martin Buber, *Right and Wrong: An Interpretation of Some Psalms*, trans. Ronald Gregor Smith (London: SCM Press Ltd, 1952), 9; also published in *Good and Evil* (New York: Charles Scribner's Sons, 1953).

ism, theme, etc.—so that structure and sense combined enable Hebrew poetry to carry the most penetrating and haunting images of the Hebrew Bible.[99] Analysis of this artful use of language assumes central importance in the interpretations of the Song of Songs in the following paragraphs.

Recent Approaches Applied to the Song of Songs

The Song of Songs provides a convenient model for these analyses because it so often presents images, symbols, or metaphors rather than narrative descriptions. Some suggest the identification of the Song of Songs as an allegory in a broader sense than that indicated by early interpreters: "We are talking about a poetic language that, when it reaches a certain pitch of intensity, becomes foregrounded as pure image, pure gesture, pure sign."[100] The thing signified blurs within the imagery of seeking, desiring, longing. Fisch understood the song as a dream, yet a dream without a literal meaning.[101] Another interpreter identified the "dominant image pattern" as "enclosure," including both the danger of exclusion and the safety of inclusion. This theme ultimately expressed the opening of the individual to a full experience of life.[102] Again, the emphasis of the interpreter rests in the use of language.

Raymond Tournay suggested the language of love songs involved covenant language. Consequently, the love songs appeared as tributes to divine love. He designated this multilayered use of language "double-entendre."[103] Tournay did not reject the literal sense of the Song, but proposed reading it on both levels.

Others read the Song purely as a poetic expression of human desire and love. Falk identified five themes which occur throughout with some variations:

- beckoning the beloved,
- banishing the beloved,
- searching for the beloved,
- the self in a hostile world, and
- praise of love itself.[104]

The centrality of the female speaker contrasts with other biblical books. The Song presents a "balance between the sexes."[105] The strong symbols of the book represent the universal experiences of human companionship and its opposite, isolation. Francis Landy offered a more abstract

---

99. Robert Alter, *The Art of Biblical Poetry* (New York: Basic Books, Inc., Publishers, 1985), 62–84.

100. Fisch, *Poetry*, 88.

101. Ibid., 89.

102. Kenneth R. R. Gros Louis, "The Song of Songs" in *Literary Interpretations of Biblical Narratives*, vol. 2, ed. Kenneth Gros Louis with James Ackerman (Nashville: Abingdon, 1982), 257.

103. Raymond Jacques Tournay, *Word of God, Song of Love*, trans. J. Edward Crowley (New York: Paulist Press, 1988), 1, 148.

104. Marcia Falk, *The Song of Songs: A New Translation and Interpretation* (San Francisco: Harper and Row, 1990), 143.

105. Ibid., 115–18.

reading along similar lines. The Song of Songs concerns juncture and separation as the couple experiences both union and separation throughout. Landy distilled a single basic truth from the Song: "Our individuality is at odds with our identity."[106] The couple found meaning in togetherness, and driven to isolation, they felt compelled to seek union. Employing comtemporary literary theory and metaphorical interpretation, Landy found the nature of the book in its lack of a single conclusive theme. His approach, like that of other literary critics, shows indebtedness to a dialectic framework. The Song offers special opportunities for this approach due to its dual voices and radical shifts in mood.

Examining Poetic Language from the Bible's Own Perspective

These contemporary reader-oriented approaches represent a strong move away from precise measurements of meter and parallelistic structure. Instead, a poetic sensibility leads to the recognition of poetry or prose and further interpretive findings. In the current milieu, specialists interpret even statistical studies in the light of the critic's own survey of biblical materials. This assumes more importance for biblical poetry than other divisions of biblical literature, since poetry generally designates material according to its formal features. This emphasis on formal features makes comparisons with other types of biblical literature even more important. Within this broad perspective of canonical materials, distinctions between literary and nonliterary language and between religious and nonreligious language assume importance. In the end, formal structure takes second place to the primary desire of the poet to convey sense. When Freedman recommended the employment of statistical data to support the identification of poetry, he proposed a third type of literature: prophetic discourse.[107] The new category combined the features of prose and poetry. His suggestions show the limitations of the categories "prose" and "poetry." They also illustrate the tendency to expand our model of the Bible's language as understanding increases.

David Clines' discussion of parallelism reveals a similar sensitivity to the Bible's own manner of expression. Clines applied the concept of "parallelism of greater precision" (a following line clarifies or explains a preceding line) to passages from Isaiah 40. Clines concluded even the broad concept of parallelism of greater precision could not account for all the operations of parallelism. The reader's inability to predict the relationship among lines comprises the central characteristic of parallelism (semantically). This feature places a higher degree of responsibility on the reader than more predictable semantic orders (particularly prose). This diminishes the role of the author or text in the process of reading or interpretation, and it heightens the role of the reader.[108]

---

106. Francis Landy, *Paradoxes of Paradise: Identity and Difference in the Song of Songs* (Sheffield: The Almond Press, 1983), 272.

107. David Noel Freedman, "Another Look at Biblical Hebrew Poetry" in *Directions in Biblical Poetry*, ed. Elaine R. Follis (Sheffield: Sheffield Academic Press, 1987), 12–18.

108. David J. A. Clines, "The Parallelism of Greater Precision" in *Directions in Biblical Poetry*, 94–95.

The same intent towards an understanding of parallelism consonant with the Bible's own language appears in Berlin's discussion of parallelism. Berlin offered a reminder that parallelism existed as a pervasive idea that went beyond the levels of lines and word pairs to include all "aspects and levels" of language.[109] She proposed "grammatical parallelism" divided into morphology (pairing of differing forms on the level of parts of speech) and syntax (pairing of lines with differing syntax).[110] On the level of parts of speech, word pairs communicate through differences in (1) morphological class, (2) tense, (3) conjugation, (4) gender, and (5) number. Syntactic parallelism shows variations reflected in (1) the positive or negative nature of the word group, (2) changes in mood, (3) appearance as subject or object, and (4) nominal or verbal character.[111]

Berlin highlighted the contrasting or complementary nature of parallelism so that differences in "repetition" contain the sense of poetry. The value of Berlin's study resides in its dependence upon parallelism as it occurs in the Hebrew Bible. The investigations rely on deductive study of the biblical materials rather than speculative reasoning.

Date of Poetry Books

Few contemporary scholars would affirm the late date for the Psalms proposed by Duhm and others. Discoveries relating to the development of the Hebrew language (so-called "late vocabulary") and cultic practices lend support to ancient dates for some of the psalms.[112] The superscription, "to David" in some cases introduces a psalm which dates to the time of David.[113] Artur Weiser reminded the reader that some psalms dedicated to David contain references to the temple or other features not yet present in David's day. Mowinckel claimed the reference to the speaker of royal psalms in the first person, "I" indicated the presence of a reigning monarch.[114] Mowinckel raised a similar issue regarding Psalm 2:7—"today I have begotten you." This presumes a current participant in the liturgy and dates to the monarchy.[115]

Dahood favored an eighth-century date for most of the Psalms with a few psalms dating to the time of David.[116] Weiser warned that late linguistic

---

109. Adele Berlin, "Grammatical Aspects of Biblical Parallelism" in *Hebrew Union College Annual*, vol. L (1979), ed. Sheldon Blank (Cincinnati: Hebrew Union College, 1980), 19.

110. Ibid., 19–21.

111. Ibid., 21–42. Berlin, p. 42, also called for study of the techniques involved in parallelism: (1) omission or addition of terms, (2) change of word order, (3) assonance, (4) rhythm and meter, (5) lexical semantic practices, and (6) the use of similar surface level structure with reordering of terms.

112. See Mitchell Dahood, *Psalms 1*, AB (Garden City, N.Y.: 1966), xxix; he cited the Ras Shamra texts as indication that the syntax common to the Psalms existed long before the time of the prophets, xxx.

113. Artur Weiser, *The Psalms: A Commentary* (Philadelphia: Westminster, 1962), 95.

114. Sigmund Mowinckel, *The Psalms in Israel's Worship*, tran. D. R. Ap-Thomas, 2 vols. (Sheffield: JSOT Press, 1991), vol. 2, 86.

115. Ibid., vol. 1, 47.

116. Dahood, xxx.

forms or deuteronomic themes do not necessarily indicate late origins for a psalm. These features could appear long after the original construction of a psalm. He assigned the majority of the psalms to the preexilic period.[117] In spite of uncertainties regarding the date of the final compilation of the Psalter, most contemporary interpreters would place the majority of the psalms during the monarchy, between the time of David and Josiah (late 600s). Certainly, a few of the psalms (for example, 137) are postexilic in their current form.

Although the Book of Lamentations contains no explicit reference to datable events, the circumstantial evidence for a date near the time of the fall of Jerusalem (586 B.C.E.) could hardly be stronger. The tremendous sense of horror and defeatism reflected in the book indicates a date near the event. There seem to be no vestiges of hope in the current situation which indicates distance from the events of 539–538 B.C.E. when the Babylonian empire ended and Persia allowed the Jews to return to Palestine. Scholars share a firm consensus on a date within a few years of the nation's fall. Most interpreters would not identify the work as a prophecy uttered by Jeremiah. Even fewer interpreters would date the poetry to later periods of Israel's history.[118]

The dating of the Song of Songs involves far less consensus. The first verse indicates Solomonic authorship. As will be seen, many of those who date the Song to the time of Solomon doubt his authorship. Mentions of Solomon in the work appear more literary than historical. Murphy claims most recent interpreters assign the book to the postexilic period.[119] Pope, on the other hand, cited numerous interpreters who associated the Song with the time of Solomon.[120] In spite of its age, Pope's discussion of the date of the Song offers the best discussion available. Among the views Pope considers are the attribution of the Song to Hezekiah or Isaiah.[121] The mention of Tirzah in 6:4 indicates a date before 700 B.C.E., since after the Assyrian invasion, the town was certainly not "beautiful." Others would claim an earlier date (up to the time of Solomon) based on the mention of the town.

Uncertainty has led to a wide range of suggestions. On the basis of theme or likeness to Egyptian literature, some date it to the time of Solomon (but not to Solomon as the author).[122] Those connecting the work with fertility rituals assign it an early date (seventh century or much earlier; Pope, 24). One interpreter viewed the collection of materials in the Song as spanning from the time of Solomon to the Persian era.[123] Pope himself favors the view of Chaim Rabin, who compared the content of the Song to

---

117. Weiser, 92–93.
118. This consensus is reflected by the closely similar treatments of the date of Lamentations in two resources: Delbert R. Hillers, *Lamentations*, AB (Garden City, N.Y.: Doubleday, 1972), xviii–xix; and F. B. Huey, Jr., *Jeremiah/Lamentations*, NAC (Nashville: Broadman, 1993), 444.
119. "Song of Songs" ABD 6:150
120. Marvin H. Pope, *Song of Songs* AB, 1977, 22–33; compare Garrett, NAC 14, 348–352.
121. Ibid., 22.
122. Ibid., 23–24.
123. Robert Gordis, as discussed in Pope, 25–26.

Tamil love poetry from India. This places the poem in the time period of Solomon or another king of Israel under whom trade flourished. The writer encountered the love poetry of India and wrote this sample as an allegory of individual Israelites longing for God. In this way the author sacralized a secular art form. [124]

The Theology of Poetry

As mentioned, recent studies of biblical poetry concentrate on thematic and formal issues. This makes the "canonicity" (identity as Scripture) of the documents the central concern. An even broader canonical approach often shows itself in interpretation of the theology of poetry. Brueggemann suggested the grouping of psalms according to three theological categories. Psalms of *orientation* contain hopefulness and affirmation. Psalms of *disorientation* reveal alienation and pain. Psalms of *new orientation* show unanticipated transformation to hope out of pain and disillusionment. The three correspond to hymns, laments, and thanksgiving songs, but Brueggemann patterned his categories after the death and resurrection of Christ.[125]

Such interpretations rely neither on allegorical nor prophetic readings. The reader remains conscious of the historical distance between the ancient and contemporary communities. Yet the existence of the biblical text provides connections between the theology of the Psalms and the Christian church. The preeminence of the work of Christ leads the church to interpret in this light. The dynamic resembles the feature that literary theorists name "intertextuality." Previous critics called it typology—the suffering and celebration of the psalmist appears "like" that of Christ. The Christian reader subsequently experiences the text under Christ's influence.

Political interpretations of biblical texts concentrate on the political influence on the writer, reader, or interpreter. For instance, Luis Stadelmann saw the Song of Songs as coded language that could be deciphered by the right key. Like the message of apocalyptic, the message escaped the writer's enemies. He interpreted this theme (and thus, the "key") as the restoration of the Davidic kingship.[126] The thesis emphasizes the incidental themes of the song and diminishes some of the major themes. Brueggemann applied his political exegesis to the Psalms. He presumed the use of the Psalms to undergird and exert "social power."[127] Secondarily, he recognized the current use of liturgy by ministers to consolidate the Christian community around socio-political ideas.[128]

124. Pope, 27–32.
125. Walter Brueggemann, *The Message of the Psalms* (Minneapolis: Augsburg, 1984), 19–27.
126. Luis Stadelmann, *Love and Politics: A New Commentary on the Song of Songs* (New York: Paulist, 1992), 1–2.
127. Walter Brueggemann, *Israel's Praise: Doxology against Idolatry and Ideology* (Philadelphia: Fortess, 1988), ix.
128. Ibid., x.

Royal interests in Israel sponsored a mutation of Israel's praise involving: (1) removal of God's specific activities, (2) the granting of privilege to the social order permitting no questions or dissent, (3) the molding of adherents into inept conformists without moral sensibilities, and (4) the guarantee within the design of the liturgy itself that no issues of justice would be raised.[129]

The removal of remembered and present suffering from worship constituted an important side effect of this approach. In this and other ways formality replaced human concerns. The voice of authority replaced the popular voice. Brueggemann used this discussion as background for suggestions regarding the conception of the pastor's role.

New Approaches to Translation

A few recent translations follow the contemporary practice of making the Hebrew Bible understandable in terms familiar to present readers. The recasting of biblical narrative and poetry into English by Everett Fox follows concepts helpful in a review of the forms of poetry in the Hebrew Bible.[130] Fox took care to preserve repetitions, allusions, alliteration, wordplay and other features. He mentioned some difficulties encountered in the translation: (1) the Hebrew Bible provides no regular meter or rhyme; (2) it mixes oral and written forms; (3) its dates and origins are difficult to identify, and (4) the difference between the times and cultures of the Hebrews and their translators affects the text's re-creation for our times and culture.[131]

Fox attempts a reproduction of the style of biblical literature as an oral form. His translation recasts the Bible as speech. This involves the reproduction of Hebrew word play and the reproduction of the meanings inherent in proper names, among many other principles. He emphasizes the sound of the words and the balance of the lines rather than literal renderings of words. Few translations since the King James Version (1611) give attention to sound. The KJV continues its strong appeal for English readers who value its formality and oracular style. Until recently most translators expressed more interest in accurate word-for-word representations than in the aesthetic quality of the whole. The features Fox listed are particularly important to Hebrew narrative (rather than poetry). Yet the concerns for oral origins and rhythm and sound apply more to our concept of poetry than prose. In addition to Fox, other examples of such translation include Marcia Falk and Stephen Mitchell.[132]

---

129. Ibid., 105–117.

130. Everett Fox, *In the Beginning: A New English Rendition of the Book of Genesis* (New York: Schocken, 1983) and Fox, *These Are the Names: A New English Rendition of the Book of Exodus* (New York: Schocken, 1986).

131. Fox, *Genesis*, xii.

132. Marcia Falk, *The Song of Songs*; Stephen Mitchell, *The Book of Job* (New York: HarperCollins Publishers, 1992), and Mitchell, *A Book of Psalms: Selected and Adapted from the Hebrew* (New York: HarperCollins Publishers, 1994).

Distinctives of Hebrew Poetry

The differences between ancient and contemporary poetry can be discussed in two categories: differences in the use and concept of poetry and differences in form. Much of the distinctiveness of Hebrew poetry from today's perspective centers on (1) its association with song, (2) its presentation as speech, and (3) its oral origins. The Hebrew categories arise from perceptions of the setting and use of the poetry. Hebrew poetry exhibits these general characteristics in nearly all its examples. The settings for Hebrew poetry determined these traits. Hebrew poetry falls into two broad categories: cultic poetry (psalms and prophecy) and secular poetry (work songs and love songs). "Secular poetry" designates songs used in contexts other than temple liturgy. All these manifestations of poetry show chanted or sung forms, and thus, oral composition. Such forms as prophecy presume an authoritative individual who voices divine expectations or expresses the community's prayers.

Hebrew and Contemporary Poetry

These differences in use and concept between Hebrew and contemporary poetry do not represent absolute differences. Contemporary society also associates poetry with song, speech, and oral origins. Contemporary poetry shows the characteristics only by careful design. Western characterizations of poetry presume written forms and concentrate on the concept of poetry rather than its use. One common depiction of the categories of Western poetry describes poetry as narrative, didactic, or lyric. Narrative poetry includes historical accounts (whether actual or fictional) in the form of epics (for example, *The Iliad*) or ballads (for example, *The Rime of the Ancient Mariner*). Didactic poetry deals with a moral or theological theme or in some other way presents a philosophical argument or behavioral dictum (for example, Pope's "Essay on Criticism"). Lyric poetry, the modern category most akin to biblical poetry, involves brief subjective poems expressing human experience rather than a unified story or message (for example, Blake's "The Lamb" or "The Tiger"). The categories themselves show a more literary approach to poetry. They could easily apply to certain genres of biblical poetry, but interest in poetry of the Hebrew centers on usage rather than the concepts of poetry. This emphasis stems from the early introduction of form criticism as the means of interpreting Hebrew poetry.

Much of the difference in classification relates to the rather broad use of poetry in Hebrew society. By contrast, current poetry (as conventionally understood) almost always asumes a textual form. We apply "poetry" to a narrow scope of texts intended for aesthetic pleasure or recreation. Nursery rhymes, musical texts, and poetry anthologies include most of our contact with poetry. The anthologies contain poems admired for their artistry of expression. For the ancient Hebrews, poetry existed as a world-organizing medium including the most solemn religious texts.[133]

Poetic accounts of creation, victories, divine decrees, and cultural history indicate poetry comprised the preferred medium for more serious forms of communication. The genres of epic poem, creation story, war song, taunt song, wedding song, parable, hymn, song of thanksgiving, song of praise, lament, prophecy, and prayer show scant representation in current poetry. On the other hand oral/tribal cultures exhibit many similar forms. A few of the subcultures in American society share similar interests, but these represent very small numbers.

Poetry and Prose

Scholars remain divided on the question of the usefulness of the term *poetry* to describe content in the Hebrew Bible. David Freedman discussed the mixture of poetry and prose under three headings in the article "Pottery, Poetry, and Prophecy: An Essay on Biblical Poetry": (1) reading narrative as poetry, (2) positing a foundational epic text upon which Hebrew authors based the prose, and (3) seeing the Hebrew authors or editors as artistically combining the coexisting prose and poetry. Freedman showed special interest in the Hebrews' use of poetry to highlight the speech of a key character.[134] Freedman clearly assumed the legitimacy of the prose-poetry distinction. James Kugel claimed the Hebrew Bible does not contain two types of writing (prose and poetry). Instead, multiple features such as balance, parallelism, and metaphorical language provide various styles of language. Greek concepts impose the strong distinction between poetry and prose noted by students of Hebrew literature. Kugel recommends abandonment of the categories.[135]

Obviously, the viewpoint of this study lends credit to Freedman's ready use of the terms *prose* and *poetry*. When poetry receives its definition in terms of the degree to which features such as parallelism appear, then commonly accepted classifications (for example, "poetry") become important tools in the description of the literature. Poetry presents more a question of what something "looks like" from our perspective, than a question of how something functioned in its original perspective. This justifies the

---

133. Today people still compose poetry to capture personal responses to a particular event that brought them joy or caused stress. Such poets experience much of the seriousness common to ancient poetry. The contemporary poet cannot experience the religious effect attached to ancient poetry, due to differences in cultures. With this in mind, the less than sublime phenomenon of rap music approaches the seriousness of poetry in the Hebrew setting. Like the Hebrew poet, the performer captures life's experience in an oral, musical expression presented as speech. The relevance of the poem to a sizeable group among the population serves as the coordinating feature. While the genre does not generally express religious themes, it serves as an outlet for ultimate concerns (for example, injustice, celebration, etc.). A huge gap exists between this lively phenomenon (rap music) and the popular perception of poetic literature as bookish and uninteresting.
134. In J. R. Maier and V. L. Tollers, eds., *The Bible in Its Literary Milieu* (Grand Rapids: Eerdmans, 1979), 88–89.
135. James Kugel, *The Idea of Biblical Poetry*, 85.

practice of studying all forms and features of ancient poetry in comparison with and in contrast to current conventions. Kugel's refusal of the term *poetry* does serve as a reminder of the nondistinct nature of Hebrew poetry. Its forms and features do not differ in specifics from prose.

Among the indicators of poetry in the Hebrew Bible, Wilfred Watson gives the following:

- lineation formulas, meter, or rhythm,

- ellipsis,

- unsual or archaic vocabulary,

- conciseness,

- unusual word order,

- regularity and symmetry,

- parallelism,

- word pairs,

- chiastic patterns and envelope structure,

- broken stereotyped phrases, and

- sound patterns.[136]

Hebrew prose exhibits all these features. The concentration of many of the features in certain texts constitutes poetry. Certain obvious features need little explanation. Among these are acrostic formats found in Psalms 9–10; 25; 34; 37; 111; 119; and 145. Acrostic structures also appear in Lamentations 1–4 and Proverbs 31:10–31. Acrostic organization always signals identification of a unit as poetic to some degree. Yet one of the most common indicators of poetry in our culture almost never appears in the Hebrew Bible. Rhyme schemes occur in very few Hebrew texts. These include 1 Samuel 18:7; 21:11; and 29:5 (repetitions of the "Saul has killed his thousands" proverb), for example. In such a small sample, the possibility exists that the similarity of sounds occurred incidentally rather than intentionally. These examples tend to appear in "poetic" texts, but repetition of sounds represents the greater principle. This repetition occasionally produces rhyme. The absence of rhyme is one of the many differences between Hebrew and Western poetry. Most of these differences relate to the vastly different conceptions of poetic form.

Features of Hebrew Poetry

Three features prominently appear in the poetic forms of the Hebrew Bible: parallelism, meter, and strophic structure.[137] None of these conform in a significant way to similar forms in modern poetry.

---

136. Watson, *Classical Poetry*, 46–47.
137. See extensive discussion on pages 275–281.

Parallelism is more than a poetic device. It comprises the heart of Hebrew poetry—its organizing principle. Hebrew prose also employs parallelism, but not in such a determinative fashion. This study favors common sense descriptions of Hebrew poetic art like those of Kugel, Schökel, and Hrushovski rather than complex taxonomies like Watson's or descriptions burdened by special linguistic terminology.[138]

It is especially important to keep in mind that biblical parallelism does not come from poets seeking to apply a critical device. Parallelism arises from the special discourse of a community of faith. We cannot expect its forms to display absolute consistency or mathematical precision. In many respects, the nuances of each example of parallelism (that is, meanings) assume more importance than an understanding of how it works. The interpretations of Hebrew poetry in this study follow this emphasis.

As Hrushovski suggested, *meter* works in coordination with parallelism. Yet the description of meter offers much more difficulty, since interpreters cannot reconstruct its rules (in as much as they existed). The views of Robert Gordis offer a representative approach. According to his perspective, the meter of Hebrew poetry depends on the number of important words. Each unit of thought received a single accent. This differs greatly from the Western concept of meter as the relative stress of measured syllables.[139] Lines contain between two and five stresses with the first line almost always receiving more than or an equal number of stresses than its following parallel.[140] Most lines receive three or four stresses.

The uncertainty of Hebrew meter leads to multiple proposals for the recovery of metrical patterns. Since only knowledge of the Hebrew language can make these accessible, a simple overview will suffice. Watson listed six means for calculating the meter:

- counts of heavy stresses (accents),

- alternating patterns of single beats (either light-heavy or heavy-light sequences),

- word count (not necessarily single words only),

- counts of thought units,

- syllable count, and

- letter count.[141]

The reason for the uncertainty stems not so much from our lack of understanding, but from the seemingly inconsistent attention to meter in Hebrew texts. Our concept of poetry leads us to scan for lyric regularity. Instead, the Hebrew performance of poetry seems more a chant than a

---

138. See, for example, O'Connor, *Hebrew Verse Structure.*
139. Robert Gordis, *Poets, Prophets, and Sages: Essays in Biblical Interpretation* (Bloomington: Indiana University Press, 1971), 64–65.
140. Ibid., 66–67.
141. Watson, *Classical Poetry*, 97–106.

song. Perhaps the adding of extraneous beats or other variations occurred as part of the art of performance.[142]

The secret to understanding Hebrew meter lies in understanding the types of oral perfomance which gave rise to it. This remains true even though some of the poetry of the Hebrew Bible shows reworking to fit a more literary scheme. The poetic texts retain their ties to oral performance as indicated by their irregular meter. Masoretes (copyists of texts) or editors (collectors and arrangers of scriptural literature about 500 B.C.E.) could certainly preserve or make texts conform to a regular metrical system, if it existed, rather than complicating it![143]

With respect to *strophic structure*, the Hebrew art appears much clearer than for parallelism and meter. Unfortunately, strophic structure does not play as important a role in the composition of Hebrew poetry as these other features. Strophic structures occur frequently. Their recognition presents little difficulty. The Hebrew techniques for indicating larger structures are so similar to current practices, they give little sense of the unique artistry of Hebrew poetry. Aside from the obvious manners of indicating units by themes and type (as in form criticism), a few central devices appear. *Inclusio* serves as the most important feature to indicate beginnings and endings of units. The repetition of lines, words, or phrases identifies the outline. The repetition does not always exactly reproduce the line or phrase. It can even occur by subtle allusions or wordplay based on opening lines. One rather clear example appears in Isaiah 43:1–7:

1 But now thus says the LORD,
    he who *created* you, O Jacob,
    he who *formed* you, O Israel:
7 everyone who is called by my name,
    whom I *created* for my glory,
    whom I *formed* and made. (italics added)

At times the occurrence of key words (*Leitwörter*) or the absence of key words already given can show the unity of a passage. Hebrew poetry employs key words frequently, but they do not always provide a clear sense of strophic structure. Staircase parallelism provides the clearest sense of a passage's unity and isolation. Psalm 122 exhibits this special structure:

Lines of the psalm correspond to those at the same space in the left margin. Chapter division also isolates the psalm, of course, but staircase parallelism or ring composition occurs frequently in texts where chapters are divided or spanned by the unit.

---

142. Gordis, *Poets, Prophets, and Sages*, 70–71, suggested units were lengthened by concluding with extra lines, extra syllables, using a longer pattern in the last doublet or line, and combinations of these.

143. The systems of accents provide little support for the view that more literate editors homogenized the biblical books: The accentuation of Psalms, Proverbs, and Job shows a simpler system than in other biblical books. Less indication was needed perhaps because the books already contained indications of lines. This attention to versification likely extends to the original oral forms as well.

A   I was glad when they said to me,
            "Let us go to the house of the LORD!"
B   Our feet are standing
                    within your gates, O Jerusalem.
C   Jerusalem—built as a city
                        that is bound firmly together.
D   To it the tribes go up, the tribes of the LORD,
                            as was decreed for Israel, to give thanks to the name
                            of the LORD
E   For there the thrones for judgment were set up,
                                the thrones of the house of David.
D   Pray for the peace of Jerusalem:
                            "May they prosper who love you.
C   Peace be within your walls,
                        and security within your towers."
B   For the sake of my relatives and friends
                    I will say, "Peace be within you."
A   For the sake of the house of the LORD our God,
            I will seek your good.

At times recurring stanzas indicate units. In Psalms 42 and 43 the refrain, "Why are you cast down, O my soul, and why are you disquieted in me? Hope in God; for I shall again praise him, my help and my God" recurs in 42:5, 11; and 43:5 indicating that the two chapters form a single composition. Acrostic organization appears in Psalms and Lamentations to indicate incontestable units. Less commonly, numerical patterns indicate units. Numerical proverbs like 6:16–19 provide examples of this type of organization.

Poetry serves as a quite eclectic body of literature in current culture, encompassing everything from tribal songs to hip hop. Its forms range from the irregular cadences of Gertrude Stein to the immaculate measure of hymn texts. In comparison with contemporary authors and readers, ancient Israel possessed a rather limited notion of poetry (though they did not recognize it as such). One might expect the sameness of Hebrew verse to lead to stagnance. However, the following survey of poetic literature will show biblical poetry revels in the variations possible within the narrower conception of poetry. The variations involve:

- theme and subject

- sound

- tone

- structure

- rhythm

Within the confines of parallelism, meter, and strophic structure we find love poetry, prayer and ritual, prophecy, wisdom, and law. Each possesses not only its own content, but also its own poetic expression.

Summary: The Shape of the Canonical Text

The above review illustrates a shift in focus from early historical-critical interpretation of poetry (especially Psalms) to the current trends. Followers of Gunkel tended to investigate the history of the cultus, the identification of the enemies, the relationship of the Psalms to kingship, and other such concerns. These issues remain relevant, but current studies emphasize poetic communication rather than historical background. The interest in how language works leads to a new appreciation of poetic forms. This encourages attempts to make the forms of Hebrew poetry understandable by means of popularizing translations. Current trends represent a rebirth of interest in the study of the Bible on its own merits. Hermeneutics offers the recognition that communities (or religions) choose certain books for special reverence.

A more objective and logical approach recognizes the relative equality of inspired materials. This canonical perspective allows no privilege to the study of law, or narrative, or prophecy. On the critical level, each interpreter works under the presumption of the ultimate significance of the book or books under study. In this and other respects, scientific-historical criticism assumes a less "scientific" shape. Interpreters invest more interest in the canonical value of the biblical book. They read it in light of community conventions (theirs and others). They recognize the subjective element and equip themselves to account for these biases. Historical questions carry no less significance. Yet these represent raw data rather than final conclusions. Interpreters place emphasis upon the shape of the text as communities experienced it. This deemphasizes supposed original forms on the one hand and complicated reconstructions of Hebrew originals on the other hand.

Questions for Discussion

1. What special views of Psalms, Song of Songs, and Proverbs arise with the advent of historical critical interpretation?

2. What distinguishes Hebrew poetry from prose?

3. Why are three basic features of Hebrew poetry so difficult to define and identify? Give a brief description of each feature.

Chapter Thirteen

Poetry Outside the Poetic Canon

Poetry in the Torah

Genesis

In the early chapters of Genesis, all speech appears poetic, though some lines contain no indication of such in the current Hebrew text. In the creation account of Genesis 1, the measured style of description indicates poetry though the passage reveals little poetic form according to typical recognition. Adam's pronouncement, "This is at last bone of my bones and flesh of my flesh; this one shall be called Woman, for out of Man this one was taken" (Gen. 2:23), provides a better sample of the type and use of poetic lines throughout Genesis. Poetry (speech) comes as strong personal responses made by either God or humans. Here, Adam enthusiastically welcomes the woman, his corresponding other, for whom he had searched without success (vv. 18–20). In a similar way, the birth announcement of Ishmael carries deep emotional overtones:

> "Now you have conceived and shall bear a son;
> you shall call him Ishmael,
> for the LORD has given heed to your affliction.
> He shall be a wild ass of a man,
> with his hand against everyone, and everyone's hand against him;
> and he shall live at odds with all his kin."
> (Gen. 16:11–12)

The angel brings the climax of the action, conveyed, most fittingly from the standpoint of Hebrew narrative, in speech. The message supplies the hope which Hagar needed to play her role in the patriarchal history.

These communications come, directly or indirectly, from God. In more explicit fashion, God himself utters the two announcements in Genesis 8:22; 9:6. The first statement comes after the animal sacrifices of Noah:

299

"As long as the earth endures, seedtime and harvest, cold and heat, summer and winter, day and night, shall not cease" (Gen. 8:22). God's pleasure at the smell of the offerings led him to make the announcement. The unit follows the trend of poetry, conveying strong emotional responses.

After the promise that no further catastrophe will occur, God proclaims the sanctity of blood, expecially human blood: "Whoever sheds the blood of a human, by a human shall that person's blood be shed; for in his own image God made humankind" (Gen. 9:6). With these words God reinstitutes the creation by emphasizing the special nature of human life. Both Genesis 9:6 and 8:22 base their claims on nothing less than creation itself. With the first of these imperatives God binds himself to the nurture of his creation. The second binds humans to protect God-given life.

This approaches the concern of the most common form of poetry in Genesis—the blessing, with its companion form, the curse. One would expect the curse form to appear in equal measure in Genesis, but at least six blessings appear in contrast to only four curses (in 3:14–19; 9:25). The curses of Genesis 3:14–19 limit the pleasure of the serpent, the woman, and man due to their collaboration in taking the forbidden fruit. In 9:25, the curse of Canaan (Ham's son), the words appear at the climax of the story. They chronicle the subservice of the Canaanites to the Hebrews through the person of their ancestor.

The blessings generally show a more specific nature, that is, they are directed toward individuals or specific groups. The curses of Eve, Adam, and the serpent describe the condition of all humans. The blessings of Genesis appear in the table below.

Table 11
Blessings in Genesis

CHAPTER/ VERSE	RECIPIENT	SPEAKER
9:26–27	Shem and Japheth	Noah
14:19–20	Abram	Melchizedek
24:60	Rebekah	Milcah and Laban
27:27–29	Jacob	Isaac
27:39–40	Esau	Isaac
48:15–16	[Joseph]	Jacob (Israel)
48:20	Ephraim and Manasseh	Jacob

Two of the units above need explanation. First, the blessing of Esau in 27:39–40 comprises at best a weak blessing, "promising" lesser status to

Esau. It presents the promise that Esau will eventually break free of his brother's control as its only positive prospect. These dynamics find their explanation in the prior narratives of the brothers' rivalry. Second, the blessing supposedly conferred on Joseph (Gen. 48:15) actually falls upon Ephraim and Manasseh. Joseph remains the only major figure of the patriarchal narratives who receives no blessing, except of course, through his children. We should probably think of the blessings as essential confirmations of the divine choice. Those who confer them speak in God's stead, supporting the divine destiny of those blessed. No less than other poetic units of speech, the blessings occur at the climax of the patriarchs' personal histories.[1]

Genesis describes its only lengthy unit of poetry as a blessing when Jacob describes the fortunes of his sons (49:25–26, 28). This "blessing" title does not fit the document. It includes a statement of the personality of each son (tribe). It takes on some appearance of prophecy. Since it occurs before the formation of the tribes, the context directs its reading as allegory-riddle. The unit encourages the later reader to find the qualities in the tribe in their corresponding histories. For example, in the "blessing on Dan"— "Dan shall judge his people as one of the tribes of Israel. Dan shall be a snake by the roadside, a viper along the path, that bites the horses' heels so that its rider falls backward"—some of the content communicates straightforwardly (for example, the image of the judge). The image of the snake remains enigmatic. Current readers of the Bible may not possess sufficient information to understand these references fully.

David N. Freedman includes the testimony of Jacob in a list of ten poems originating in the early Iron age (1200–900 B.C.E.):

Table 12
Earliest Hebrew Poetry According to Freedman[a]

Testimony of Jacob	Genesis 49	11th century
Blessing of Moses	Deuteronomy 33	11th century
Song of Deborah	Judges 5	12th century
Song of the Sea	Exodus 15	10th century
Oracles of Balaam	Numbers 23–24	11th century

1. Between the blessings of chapter 27 and chapter 48 almost no poetry appears. This coincides with the stories of Jacob and Joseph. Their narratives contain a more storylike form than previous patriarchal histories.

Table 12 (Continued)
Earliest Hebrew Poetry According to Freedman[a]

Song of Moses	Deuteronomy 32	12th century
David's Lament for Saul and Jonathan	2 Samuel 1	10th century
Lament for Abner	2 Samuel 3	10th century
Testimony of David	2 Samuel 23	10th century

a. "Pottery, Poetry, and Prophecy." In his catalog of the earliest poetry, Peter Craigie, *Psalms 1–50*, WBC 19 (Waco: Word, 1983), 25; included Exodus 15:1–8; Numbers 10:35–36; Numbers 23–24; Deuteronomy 32–33; Judges 5; and 1 Samuel 2:1–10.

The first three of these reveal interest in tribal groups. The Blessing of Moses in Deuteronomy 33:1–29 contains a list of tribes with a lengthy statement of blessing for each. An incomplete list of tribes appears in Judges 5:14–18: The characteristics of each tribe arise from their willingness to or refusal to engage in the battle. These early examples of poetry underscore the emphatic nature of poetic language in the Hebrew Bible. In deepest sorrow, highest praise, or in consummate description, poetry prevails.

Exodus and Leviticus

The poetic units of Exodus show the same characteristic of speech as those in Genesis. They also show similar placement as the climactic content of the narrative. Aside from a single triplet spoken by Moses (32:18), all of the poetry of Exodus deals with the identity of Yahweh. Exodus 3:14–15; 34:6–7 presents God's name and personality, respectively. The Song of the Sea (15:1–18, 21) emphasizes his identity as the deliverer of the Hebrews. Exodus 20:1–23:33 convey his expectations to his people in the form of the Decalogue and other legislation.

In Exodus 3:14–15, poetry conveys the divine name "Yahweh" in answer to Moses' request for his title. The answer comes in the densest poetic language: *ʾehyeh ʾăšer ʾehyeh* (אֶהְיֶה אֲשֶׁר אֶהְיֶה) means "I will be what I will be." This presents several possible meanings. It could refer to God's self-determination (God is whatever he chooses to be). It may indicate that he causes all life and events. If taken as a future, it may indicate God as the one who decides all destinies. These words offer explanation of the divine name Yahweh (יְהוָה) which literally means, "He is." The phrase presents an enigmatic portrait, but further identification is clearer: Yahweh identifies himself as the God of Israel's ancestors (Exod. 3:16).[2] Later, when Moses ascended the mountain to make the second copy of the tablets, God elaborated on his name with the following proclamation:

6 The LORD, the LORD [LORD translates the name, Yahweh],
   a God merciful and gracious,
   slow to anger,
   and abounding in steadfast love and faithfulness,
7 keeping steadfast love for the thousandth generation,
   forgiving iniquity and transgression and sin,
   yet by no means clearing the guilty,
   but visiting the iniquity of the parents
   upon the children
   and the children's children,
   to the third and the fourth generation. (Exod. 34)

This presents two aspects of God's character: mercy and justice. Perhaps this offers explanation of just what God "is" or "causes to be" (as in Exod. 3:14–15). God orchestrates events to play out his mercy and justice. All or a portion of the content of the sixth verse reoccurs in Numbers 14:18; Nehemiah 9:17; Psalms 103:8; 145:8; and Jonah 4:2. Psalm 145 seems to illustrate the qualities of Yahweh identified in verse 6, providing a commentary on this confession and detailing the divine qualities latent in the name, "Yahweh."

Moses' speech in the Song of the Sea (Exod. 15:1–18) illustrates God's mercy in the deliverance of his people. The song displays remarkable action such as in this three-line unit: "At the blast of your nostrils the waters piled up, the floods stood up in a heap; the deeps congealed in the heart of the sea" (Exod. 15:8). The song exhibits only synonymous parallelism; the repetition lends weight to the wonder of divine deliverance. This account presents God as a warrior on behalf of his people in verses 1–12. In verses 13–17 the focus shifts to his people themselves as the sign of his greatness and love. The two halves turn on verses 11–12 which express the central theme running through both pieces: "Who is like you, O LORD, among the gods? Who is like you, majestic in holiness, awesome in splendor, doing wonders? You stretched out your right hand, the earth swallowed them" (Exod. 15:11–12). In most respects the song conforms to the form of the hymns of thanks in Psalms.

The most prominent revelation of God's identity occurs in the giving of the Law in Exodus 20:1–23:33. Such literature cannot conform to accepted standards for poetry. The units, whether small or large, show attention to form common to all rhythmic sayings. The patterned format made memorization easier.

The laws reveal God's expectations. Their form reveals that they developed as sayings—oral poetry. The narrative assumes direct transmission

---

2. For a fuller discussion of the meaning of the divine name, see the discussion of Exodus 3:14 in Brevard Childs, *The Book of Exodus*, OTL (Philadelphia: Westminster, 1974), 60–64.

from God to Moses throughout, whether voiced in that precise format or not. The section conveys a pronounced "I . . . you" tone. God's identity serves as foundation and continued basis for the demands (Exod. 20:1–11). The people find their identity in that of the deity. The smaller pieces of legislation show independent form. Lines such as, "You shall not murder; You shall not commit adultery; You shall not steal; and You shall not bear false witness against your neighbor" (Exod. 20:13–16), reveal the stacatto nature of all the sayings. They existed as isolated wholes even though set within the greater context. At times units consist of a family of laws rather than a single law (for example, 21:28–32 has laws relating to an ox who gores persons to death). This design allowed Israel to apply individual laws or small bodies of laws in independent situations.

The law code of Exodus 20–23 lacks parallelism, but includes rhythmic expression (meter) and clear strophic structure. The appearance of the commands as measured speech gives the section its poetic identity.

It remains unclear whether the attention to divine identity in the poetry of Exodus occurs incidentally or intentionally. It may simply appear as a product of the theme of the Exodus narratives—divine deliverance. Genesis emphasized the beginnings of human society and consequently emphasized the theme of blessing.

The divine identity theme recurs in the only poetic passage in Leviticus: "Through those who are near me I will show myself holy, and before all the people I will be glorified" (Lev. 10:3). Moses mouthed these words of God after fire consumed the sons of Aaron (for offering "unholy fire," Lev. 10:1). We expect similar content to manifest itself in Numbers and Deuteronomy, since these books continue the epic of God's deliverance.

Numbers

Numbers shows less consistency in its presentation of God's character. Only the poetry of Numbers 14:18 identifies God. Numbers repeats much of the content of Exodus 34:6–7, at times verbatim. These repetitions show less elaborate form than the Exodus version. Much of the emphasis upon God in Genesis and Exodus shifts to God's people in Numbers. Numbers 6:24–27 prescribes the exact manner for Aaron's blessing of the congregation:

> Thus you shall bless the Israelites: You shall say to them,
>> The LORD bless you and keep you;
>> the LORD make his face to shine upon you and be gracious to you;
>> the LORD lift up his countenance upon you, and give you peace.
> So they shall put my name on the Israelites, and I will bless them.

God speaks in this unit. The blessing serves to attach God's name (including his identity) to the people. This identification of the people with God leads him to protect them as a part of himself. When Israel recited this passage, the recurring name, "Yahweh" ("the LORD") must have left the strongest impression on the hearer, giving effect to the blessing. The power of the name guaranteed the people would experience each blessing. This represents far more than a magic formula, for the name assumes significance in the context of God's active holiness. The blessing fits between two independent units: the first describing the Nazirite vow (Num. 6:1–21), and the second describing the completion of the tabernacle.

Aaron's blessing clearly illustrates the shift in focus from God to his community. The transition does not end here. A more significant shift makes Moses the divine representative. When Miriam and Aaron challenge Moses' authority, God responds adamantly: "When there are prophets among you, I the LORD make myself known to them in visions; I speak to them in dreams. Not so with my servant Moses; he is entrusted with all my house. With him I speak face to face—clearly, not in riddles; and he beholds the form of the LORD" (Num. 12:6–8). Moses received unparalleled authority. To "be entrusted with all my house" calls to mind Joseph's coregency in Egypt.

Moses' identification with God appears most clearly in passages which chronicle challenges to his leadership. A relatively lengthy poetic passage records his conflict with Korah and followers (Num. 16:3–30).[3] The Levites objected to the higher cultic status of Aaron and Moses. The presentation appears as a mini-drama reproducing the rebellion (especially its end). Such a retelling reinforced the authority of legitimate leaders and warned of the perils of rebellion. Another disputation (Num. 20:3–5) repeats these emphases. All Israelites join the rebellion; they state their preference for Egypt over the journey with Moses; and they challenge Moses' authority and competence. Moses falls on his face in prayer. God intervenes to show his leadership of Moses, not with words, but with the sign of water from the rock. This "satisfies" the congregation, dealing with both their thirst and their doubt. Interestingly, only the speech of the rebels reveals explicit poetic form.

Other poetic passages relate less directly to God's identity, though the connection remains evident. Numbers 10:35-36 presents invocations Moses uttered when the ark was taken up at the beginning of a march and set down after the march: "Arise, O LORD, let your enemies be scattered, and your foes flee before you. . . . Return, O LORD of the ten thousand thousands of Israel." Neither Moses nor the people represent God. Instead, the symbol of God's presence conveys his power. The attention of the first phrase centers on warfare, but this could also refer to general protection.

The taunt song against Moab in Numbers 21:27–30 lacks any mention of Yahweh. This unit arises in the context of Israel's settlement of Heshbon, a former Moabite stronghold. The taunt opens with mention of "ballad singers" who perform it. Apparently, these challenges to enemies existed as

---

3. The prominence of speech in this and other disputation passages leads to the unusual identification of Numbers 16:3–30 as poetry. The characters speak with fluid syllables unlike the surrounding narrative.

popular poetic forms. Such texts served as propaganda to reinforce a people's sense of superiority and intimidate their enemies.

The final series of poetic passages display the most sustained and distinct poetry of Numbers: The oracles of Balaam return attention to the person of God and his people. There are four oracles. The first records Balaam's inability to curse a people so upright and favored as Israel (Num. 23:7–10). The second serves notice of God's presence with Israel, resulting in their triumph over all enemies (Num. 23:18–24). The third oracle (Num. 24:3–9) contains an idyllic description of Israel the elect with a brief blessing attached:

5 How fair are your tents, O Jacob,
   your encampments, O Israel!
6 Like palm-groves that stretch far away,
   like gardens beside a river,
 like aloes that the LORD has planted,
   like cedar trees beside the waters.
7 Water shall flow from his buckets,
   and his seed shall have abundant water,
 his king shall be higher than Agag,
   and his kingdom shall be exalted.
8 God who brings him out of Egypt,
   is like the horns of a wild ox for him;
 he shall devour the nations that are his foes
   and break their bones.
 He shall strike with his arrows.
9 He crouched, he lay down like a lion,
   and like a lioness; who will rouse him up?
 Blessed is everyone who blesses you,
   and cursed is everyone who curses you.

The fourth oracle (Num. 24:15–24) predicts the fate of Moab (Balak's kingdom), Edom, Amalek, and the Kenites at the hands of Israel.

All four oracles, the earliest prophetic oracles of the Bible, present virtually complete parallel form. They present a most idealistic portrait of Israel as Yahweh's community, without any mention of hardship or rebellion. The lengthy story of Balak and Balaam (Num. 22–24) consolidated Israel by presenting their enemies as powerless buffoons. Yet the poetic portions of the story maintain a serious tone in contrast to the antics of Balak, Balaam, and the ass (all in prose). When Israel describes its divine identity, poetry serves as the medium. The message of the poetry allows no intrusion of humor or skepticism.

Deuteronomy

Poetry in Deuteronomy[4] offers a striking contrast to that in the other books of the Torah. Deuteronomy offers a second copy of the Decalogue

---

4. Duane L. Christensen, WBC 6A, argues for poetic form of all of Deuteronomy.

(5:6–21) and laws (19:1–25:16) similar to those in Exodus, but the format of much of the material differs. The Decalogue's poetic form shows little difference, but the laws appear as a re-presentation. Words of warning and recollection follow the Ten Words, before additional legislation appears (5:22–33). These lines contain commentary rather than speech and hence are not poetry. Such transitions occur frequently in Deuteronomy. They carry much of the special directive force of the book. Following a lengthy list of narrative warnings (chaps. 6–18), legal materials in poetic form appear again in 19:1–25:16. The special tenor of Deuteronomy marks prose as well as poetry.

The most notable difference between poetic legislation in Deuteronomy 19–25 and that of Exodus 20–23 involves the suppositional form of many deuteronomistic codes. Similar case laws in Exodus do not reveal poetic form, nor do they investigate as many possible offenses as counterparts in Deuteronomy.

The Shema and its afterword (6:4–25) fall under consideration as poetry as well as wisdom. Moses speaks, but as in other cases, he speaks for God. The encouragement to remain faithful to the laws is a confession including a pledge of exclusive devotion to God and his statutes. It also rehearses the history of his deliverance (vv. 10–13). Again, God's identity and attributes take center stage in poetry.

A related passage similarly places a brief confession in a larger explanatory context. On the day the people harvest the first fruits of the promised land, they must accompany their offerings with a confession:

5 A wandering Aramean was my ancestor;
  he went down into Egypt
  and lived there as an alien
  and there he became a great nation, mighty and populous.
6 When the Egyptians treated us harshly and afflicted us;
  by imposing hard labor on us,
7 We cried to the LORD, the God of our ancestors;
  the LORD heard our voice
  and saw our affliction, our toil, and our oppression.
8 The LORD brought us out of Egypt
  with a mighty hand and an outstretched arm,
  with a terrifying display of power, and with signs and wonders;
9 And he brought us into this place
  and gave us this land,
  a land flowing with milk and honey.
10 So now I bring the first of the fruit of the ground
  that you, O LORD have given me.[5] (Deut. 26)

5. Here and elsewhere the division into lines, when the NRSV is not lined, is provided by this author.

The poem attributes Israel's survival and prosperity to God's mercy (v. 7). The confession reduces the history of the Exodus to its barest elements. Verses 9 and 10 conjoin the gift of the land and the gift of the worshiper's offering. The issue of identity carries over from Yahweh's nature to the identity of the one receiving identity from him.

In both the above examples the reminiscent tone of the book emerges. The poetry follows the overall theme of (1) looking back at what the people have gained and (2) contemplating what they have to lose by disobedience or neglect. Poetic units like these two remind the worshiper of these truths.

A dialectic of blessing and curse pervades Deuteronomy (including its poetry). Five sections contain poetic curses or blessings. Deuteronomy 27:15–26 contains a series of twelve curses pronounced in conformity to the contents of the Pentateuch. For example, "'Cursed be anyone who dishonors father or mother.' All the people shall say, 'Amen!'" (27:16).[6] Some of the tribes assumed responsibility for responding to the blessing (27:12). Deuteronomy lacks a parallel set of blessings.

Four blessings unrelated to this appear in the following verses (28:1–6). The list of blessings includes (1) the worshiper in city and field, (2) children, crops, and livestock, (3) basket and kneading bowl, and (4) the worshiper in all "coming and going." These blessings depend upon the person's obedience. Following the phrase, "but if you will not obey the LORD" (28:15), a series of four opposing curses appear (28:16–19). They contain curses of person and property identical to those listed in the previous blessing.

Deuteronomy 32:1–43 contains a more polished composition which recounts the history of God's intervention for his people. The Deuteronomist laces this fine poetic form with threat. It contains three thematic divisions: (1) God chose and protected his people (1–14); (2) they rebelled, and he contemplated lashing out at them (15–27); and (3) instead, God resolved to destroy the enemies of his foolish people (28-43). The following segments portray God as the divine warrior:

22 For a fire is kindled by my anger,
    and burns to the depths of Sheol;
  it devours the earth and its increase,
    and sets on fire the foundations of the mountains.
23 I will heap disasters upon them,
    spend my arrows against them:
24 wasting hunger,
    burning pestilence.
  The teeth of beasts I will send against them,
    with venom of things crawling in the dust.
25 In the street the sword shall bereave,
    and in the chambers terror,

6. According to Deuteronomy 27:12–14, the Levites pronounced curses, and the people uttered the "Amen."

for young man and woman alike,
nursing child and old gray head.

39 See now that I, even I, am he;
    there is no god beside me.
I kill and I make alive;
    I wound and I heal;
    and no one can deliver from my hand.
40 For I lift up my hand to heaven,
    and swear: As I live forever,
41 when I whet my flashing sword,
    and my hand takes hold on judgment;
I will take vengeance on my adversaries,
    and will repay those who hate me.
42 I will make my arrows drunk with blood,
    and my sword shall devour flesh—
with the blood of the slain and the captives,
    from the long-haired enemy.

In the former example God vents his anger toward his people. In the latter example their enemies receive his wrath.

The following chapter departs from the threatening speech and synonymous parallelism of chapter 32, displaying more of a narrative style. God confers blessing on the tribes. In contrast to Jacob's words in Genesis 49:2–27, Moses' deathbed sayings offer blessing only, no predictions of disaster. Parallelism in most lines is synthetic or incomplete. The content of the blessings take precedence over their purity of form.

In summary, poetic materials in Deuteronomy show reminiscent attitude and reflective tone. In Deuteronomy poetry takes a step away from the conferring of law in Exodus and Numbers to encourage obedience as well as providing the law codes.[7] The book is structured as three lengthy discourses delivered by Moses. Given the Hebrew identification of speech and poetry, we may ask, "Why not read Deuteronomy as poetic throughout?"[8] The answer comes from the book's narrative technique. Moses' voice operates as a narrative device. The nature of the book as a rehearsal of former events leads away from the more dynamic poetry which unfolds current acts of Yahweh. Somewhat like an indirect quote ("remember what God said"), the contents appear literary rather than oral.

This second-hand "retelling" leads the Deuteronomist to employ poetic materials in ways not encountered in other books of the Torah (that is, confessions, lengthy blessing-and-curse formulas, reflective case laws). Laws, blessings, and basic confessions show an immediacy not present in the elaborate ritual of the Psalms. Poetry serves a more philosophical or aes-

7. Gerhard von Rad, *Studies in Deuteronomy*, SBT 9 (London: SCM Press, 1953; German original, 1948), 15 noted that "Deuteronomy is not divine law in codified form, but preaching about the commandments."
8. See Christensen, WBC 6A.

thetic role. Through the laws and other features of the Torah's poetry, the relationship between humans and God became explicit. Poetry encountered in subsequent books of the canon bases its content on these rudimentary components: blessing, law, and remembrance.

Poetry in the Former Prophets

Joshua

The lengthy historical span of the former prophets provides a wide variety of types of poetry. Joshua includes only two brief pieces of poetry. Joshua 6:26 contains a curse uttered by Joshua: "Cursed before the LORD be anyone who tries to build this city—this Jericho! At cost of his firstborn he shall lay its foundation, and at the cost of his youngest he shall set up its gates!" This curse acts emblematically to cover all the conquered towns of Canaan. A play on words based on similar sound provides the substance of the curse: The word *Jericho* (*yĕrîḥo*, יְרִיחוֹ) sounds something like, "his firstborn son" (*bibkōrô*, בִּבְכֹרוֹ).

Joshua also utters the other brief poetic saying: "Sun, stand still at Gibeon, and Moon, in the valley of Aijalon" (10:12b). The narrator then comments that never before or since has the LORD "heeded a human voice" (v. 14). The words could involve an incantation, but Yahweh's authority typically rests on the character of the speaker as one called by him. In this case too, as alliterative as the formula is, it is the person of Joshua who merits God's intervention. In an incantation, the words alone would carry the effect.

Judges

Judges contains considerably more poetry than Joshua. The Song of Deborah (5:2–31) commands as much attention as any poem in the Bible.[9] In contrast to the celebrational and psalmic Song of Deborah stands the rough fable which Jotham satirically chants from atop Mount Gerizim. The fable mocks the illegitimate way Jotham's brother Abimelech achieved the crown:

> 8 The trees once went out
> to anoint a king over themselves.
> So they said to the olive tree,
> "Reign over us."
> 9 The olive tree answered them,
> "Shall I stop producing my rich oil
> by which gods and mortals are honored,
> and go to sway over the trees?"
> 10 Then the trees said to the fig tree,
> "You come and reign over us."

---

9. Pages 179–181 offers a discussion of this work.

11 But the fig tree answered them,
"Shall I stop producing my sweetness
and my delicious fruit,
and go to sway over the trees?"
12 Then the trees said to the vine,
"You come and reign over us."
13 But the vine said to them,
"Shall I stop producing my wine
that cheers gods and mortals,
and go to sway over the trees?"
14 So all the trees said to the bramble,
"You come and reign over us."
15 And the bramble said to the trees,
"If in good faith you are anointing me king over you,
then come and take refuge in my shade;
but if not, let fire come out of the bramble
and devour the cedars of Lebanon."
(Judg. 9:8–15)

Jotham used the last lines of the story to place doubt in the minds of the lords of Shechem regarding their choice of Abimelech. The words drip with irony. How can a choice be made "in good faith" when the person concerned represents the last choice and the least qualified? The saying functions as a unit of wisdom which Jotham employs craftily. He makes sure that all hear it and disappears, leaving them to brood over it. When Abimelech receives his recompense, the narrator cites this unit as "the curse of Jotham" (9:57) which fell on Shechem. When Jotham proclaimed the parable, he followed it with clear narrative explanation of its import (9:16–20). The message coupled with the poetry scarcely allowed misunderstanding. Throughout the former prophets, narrative explanations proceed and follow most units of poetry. The Deuteronomist provides the reader not only with the divine word (poetry), but also with a deep sense of the responsibility to heed it.

Samson's riddle presents an entirely different dynamic. The riddle "Out of the eater came something to eat. Out of the strong came something sweet" (14:14), and its solution "What is sweeter than honey? What is stronger than a lion?" (14:18) offer no moral to be pondered. They comprise parts of a word game, harmless in other contexts, but terrible in the life of Samson. The line contains no rhythmic or sound patterns distinct from other lines of Hebrew poetry.[10] Samson's reply to their solution offers a less straightforward *double entendre*. "If you had not plowed with my heifer, you would not have found out my riddle"[11] (Judg. 14:18). The weight falls upon the tiny pronoun "my." The Philistines invaded Samson's most private

---

10. The rhyme of verse 14 in English does not occur in the Hebrew text.
11. The reader should not confuse English conventions on the association of persons with livestock with Hebrew conventions. "Heifer" does not indicate any displeasure with his wife's appearance. To the contrary, such terms (like the sheep and goats of the Song of Songs) were offered as flattering endearments.

domain, entering into "negotiations" with his wife. The metaphor shows a lot of sophistication, especially for one who, like Samson, elsewhere appears a boorish person.

The historical boast of 15:16 shows less sophistication: "With the jaw-bone of a donkey heaps upon heaps, with the jawbone of a donkey I have slain a thousand men." Samson's braggadocio works on two levels. The feat of strength lends fascination, but the ignoble weapon detracts from the wonder by introducing a humorous element. The strange weapon makes Samson's victory no less believable. Rather, the instrument does not fit the valor of the hero.

Poetry relating to Samson's exploits continues with a poetic dialogue. It relates his verbal sparring with Delilah. Repetition abounds. Delilah pleads, "Tell me how you could be bound." Samson explains if so and so were done, "I shall become weak, and be like anyone else." Likewise, the words, "The Philistines are upon you, Samson" recur three times. Slight variations in the fourth repetition show the characteristics of prose rather than poetry. Otherwise, the measure of the line and the careful alliteration of words reveal the character of dramatic poetry.

Samuel

First Samuel 2 opens with a conventional psalm. The Song of Hannah expresses her joy at the gift of a son. In historical context, the song of thanks would concentrate on Samuel's service as priest: Hannah sings it not at the time of birth, but when she offers Samuel to Eli at the temple. The special theme of the song makes antithetic parallelism the expression of choice:

4 The bows of the mighty are broken,
   but the feeble gird on strength.
5 Those who were full have hired themselves out for bread,
   but those who were hungry are fat with spoil.
   The barren has borne seven,
   but she who has many children is forlorn.
8 He raises up the poor from the dust;
   he lifts the needy from the ash heap,
9 He will guard the feet of his faithful ones,
   but the wicked shall be cut off in darkness;
   for not by might does one prevail.

A poetic unit seemingly based on a proverb of the "better than . . ." variety appears in 1 Samuel 15:22–23. The phrase "surely to obey is better than sacrifice, and to heed than the fat of rams" (v. 22b) supplies the central idea by which Yahweh deposes Saul. Similar condemnations of empty sacrifices occur in Hosea 6:6 and Isaiah 1:11–20, but neither of these relate to a *māšāl*. Samuel condemned Saul's failure to destroy all the property of the Amalekites as instructed. Saul explained that he saved the best for sacrifice, which led to Samuel's proverb. These words actually effect Saul's dethronement, in the same way the words, "I now pronounce you husband and wife" constitute marriage. Discussion of the issues appears in prose, but the word from God comes through poetry.

Like the Samson-Delilah dialogue, the story of David's defeat of Goliath forms a poetic account (1 Sam. 17:24–47). Perhaps the telling and retelling of such compelling accounts led to poetic language. Troubadours polished the accounts in their repeated performances. This narrative poetry exhibits little parallelism, but contains a steady, predictable rhythm, as though the character (and narrator) speak in verse. The direct encounter of the hero and villain especially exhibits this poetic nature:

42 When the Philistine looked and saw David, he disdained him, for he
   was only a youth, ruddy and handsome in appearance.
43 The Philistine said to David, "Am I a dog, that you come to me with
   sticks?"
   And the Philistine cursed David by his gods.
44 The Philistine said to David,
   "Come to me and I will give your flesh,
   to the birds of the air and to the wild animals of the field."
45 But David said to the Philistine,
   "You come to me with sword and spear and javelin;
   but I come to you in the name of the LORD of hosts,
   the God of the armies of Israel, whom you have defied.
46 This very day the LORD will deliver you into my hand,
   and I will strike you down and cut off your head
   and I will give the dead bodies of the Philistine army this very day
   to the birds of the air and to the wild animals of the earth,
   so that all the earth may know
   that there is a God in Israel,
47 And that all this assembly may know
   that the LORD does not save by sword and spear;
   for the battle is the LORD's
   and he will give you into our hand. (1 Sam. 17:42–47)

This account displays a more poetic nature than the legal material of Exodus and Deuteronomy designated "measured prose," and may be designated "narrative poetry" (more specifically, dramatic poetry).

The last bit of poetry in 1 Samuel exudes little sense of high drama. The saying "Saul has killed his killed his thousands, and David his ten thousands" (18:7) carries the force of a political cartoon. The military boast appears in 21:11 and 29:5 as well. According to the context in 18:7, this insult to Saul's military prowess began before David engaged in a military campaign. The killing of Goliath formed its sole basis. Merry-making women sang for Saul's army when they returned after David killed Goliath. Saul took it serously (vv. 8–9). This military boast also circulated among the Philistines (21:11; 29:5), making the Philistines suspicious of David as an ally.

The first poetic units of 2 Samuel are not "about" but "by" David. David sings a lament (chap. 1) and makes a brief statement of lament (chap. 3). The lament in 1:17–27 does not conform to the psalmic variety evident in the Book of Psalms and Lamentations. This lament expresses grief at the loss of an individual. The promises of divine intervention and statements of hope which punctuate other biblical laments fail to appear. The unit functions as pessimistic commemoration of loss.

> 17 David intoned this lamentation over Saul and his son Jonathan.
> 18 (He ordered that The Song of the Bow be taught to the people of
>   Judah; it is written in the Book of Jashar.) He said:
> 19 Your glory, O Israel, lies slain upon your high places!
>   How the mighty have fallen!
> 20 Tell it not in Gath,
>   proclaim it not in the streets of Ashkelon;
>   or the daughters of the Philistines will rejoice,
>   the daughters of the uncircumcised will exult.
> 21 You mountains of Gilboa,
>   let there be no dew or rain upon you,
>   nor bounteous fields!
>   For there the shield of the mighty was defiled,
>   the shield of Saul, anointed with oil no more.
> 22 From the blood of the slain,
>   from the fat of the mighty,
>   the bow of Jonathan did not turn back,
>   nor the sword of Saul return empty.
> 23 Saul and Jonathan, beloved and lovely!
>   In life and in death they were not divided;
>   they were swifter than eagles,
>   they were stronger than lions.
> 24 O daughters of Israel, weep over Saul,
>   who clothed you with crimson, in luxury,
>   who put ornaments of gold on your apparel.
> 25 How the mighty have fallen
>   in the midst of the battle!
>   Jonathan lies slain upon your high places.
> 26 I am distressed for you, my brother Jonathan;
>   greatly beloved were you to me;
>   your love to me was wonderful,
>   passing the love of women.
> 27 How the mighty have fallen,
>   and the weapons of war perished! (2 Sam. 1)

The title, "The Song of the Bow," seems unusual in view of the Hebrew Bible's usual lack of titles. The poem apparently bore this title in the venerable Book of Jashar. Three interwoven themes hold the lament together. First, it expresses geographic interest. Among the vocabulary related to geography it includes "high places," "Gath," "Ashkelon," and "Gilboa." Second, it voices love for the dead heroes (vv. 23, 26). Third, and most significantly, it describes the loss in terms of the warriors' weapons. During battle their weapons did not "turn back" or "return empty" (v. 22). At their deaths, these weapons returned without them. In verse 21, the shield of Saul represents his kingship. Its "anointing" refers not only to the regular maintenance of leather shields, but also to Saul's special office as king anointed by Yahweh. The killer desecrated this office (see 2 Sam. 1:14–16). The bow of Jonathan which provides the title for the song appears in verse 22 along with the sword of Saul. The association of these dead men with their material possessions appeals to a universal facet of human grief. Implements which remain after the death of a loved one remind the survivors of their bereavement.

Certain structures reinforce the effect of the poem. One line recurs: "How the mighty have fallen!" This *non sequitur* communicates David's shock: "Here are the noblest warriors of Israel, and they have died in humiliation." Clearly, David remembered Saul and Jonathan as *gibbōrîm* (גִּבּוֹרִים), the word translated, "the mighty." "Mighty ones" carries the connotation of prowess in war and could be rendered "soldiers," but here the intent is "heroes." The word occurs five times in the song in identical form. This concept gives the song movement from high to low thoughout. It opens with a reference to "high places" and ends with introspective suffering. The song shows some of the most careful design of the Hebrew Bible, both in terms of its linguistic structure and the psychology of grief.

David's lament for Abner evokes a brief statement of the nature of his death: "Should Abner die as a fool dies? Your hands were not bound, Your feet were not fettered; as one falls before the wicked you have fallen" (2 Sam. 3:33–34). An appropriately simple structure marks the statement. The word for fool (*nābāl*, נָבָל) occurs early in the first line. It sounds much like the word translated "you have fallen" (*nāpāltâ*, נָפָלְתָּ) in the last line. Accentual markings indicate that the last word should be read in a line by itself. The starkness of the one-word line creates a bluntness, emphasizing the word and encouraging the comparison with "fool." The sudden stop indicates finality, most appropriate to the epitaph. The coarse or vulgar wordpair *nābāl/nāpāltâ*, "You have died a fool" may have provided the basis of the poetic unit. A sudden death in circumstances where the victim was unwary (that is, almost any act of violence other than warfare) was understood as a horrid end. The reference to Abner as a fool may also refer to his opposition to David. He had recanted, but he had no time to atone for his treason before he was murdered.

Further intrigue against official rule provides the background for the summons to withdraw in 20:1: "We have no portion in David, no share in the son of Jesse! Everyone to your tents, O Israel!" This public announcement reminds one of Jotham's fable in Judges 9, but here the proclamation is of a less poetic nature. The accents of the lines show three independent phrases. Only the parallelism of the first two lines reveals poetic form. It functions in the opposite effect of a call to assembly. Households return to their private dwellings, showing extreme disinterest in David as ruler.

David's words in 2 Samuel 22 fit less neatly in their context. This psalm follows a rather anticlimactic account of nondescript conflicts with the Philistines (21:15–22). The psalm combines the features of victory song and thanksgiving song.[12] Interest lies not so much in its poetic form, as its place in the context of the history of the king: "David spoke to the LORD the words of this song on the day when the LORD delivered him from the hand of all his enemies, and from the hand of Saul" (22:1). The deliverance from Saul refers to events in 1 Samuel. If it refers to Saul's defeat, a strong contradiction appears to exist between this high praise and the lament for Saul and Jonathan in the first chapter of 2 Samuel. Perhaps the priority of The Song of the Bow prevented the court historian or collector from placing the psalm there, or perhaps the two poems form a contrasting type of inclusio for the larger literary unit. Canonically, the psalm is a fit conclusion, describing David's attitude at the end of his life. The closing line surely offered special appeal to the historian: "He [Yahweh] is a tower of salvation for his king, and shows steadfast love to his anointed, to David and his descendants forever" (22:51).

This final summary of David's life prior to the death account opening 1 Kings also includes words introduced as the oracle of David:

1 The spirit of the LORD speaks through me,
   his word is upon my tongue.
2 The God of Israel has spoken,
   the Rock of Israel has said to me:
3 One who rules over people justly,
   ruling in the fear of God,
4 is like the light of morning,
   like the sun rising on a cloudless morning,
   gleaming from the rain on the grassy land.
5 Is not my house like this with God?
   For he has made with me an everlasting covenant,
   ordered in all things and secure.
   Will he not cause to prosper
   all my help and my desire?
6 But the godless are all like thorns that are thrown away;
   for they cannot be picked up with the hand;
7 to touch them one uses an iron bar
   or the shaft of a spear.
   And they are entirely consumed in fire on the spot.
           (2 Sam. 23)

The word translated "oracle" (*nĕʾum*, אֻם) in the introduction (v. 1) often applies to prophetic speeches. The unit involves some prophetic intent, but the "oracle" more clearly represents a royal psalm. "David" assumes dynastic proportions in this unit, which peers far into the future

---

12. The poem occurs also in Psalm 18.

(v. 5). Verses 6–7 offer an indirect curse on enemies of David, the ideally just representative of God.

Kings

Solomon's reign, recounted in 1 Kings, begins with the building of the temple. At the dedication, Solomon offers the longest prayer of the Hebrew Bible. Its formulaic nature reveals liturgical use. The prayer follows two briefer poetic units (1 Kings 8:12–13, 15). First, after the delivery of the ark of the covenant, Solomon relates the new idea of the temple as God's dwelling place to earlier traditions about the ark: "The LORD has said that he would dwell in thick darkness. I have built for you an exalted house, a place for you to dwell in forever" (8:12–13). Then Solomon briefly blesses God (v. 15) and retells the history of building the temple (vv. 16–21).

Although poetic form runs from verses 12–61, the prayer proper begins in verse 23. The prayer names various conditions in which Israel will need God's help. Solomon urges God to respond when prayer is offered from the new temple. Various petitions possess a form much like this one:

> 35 When heaven is shut up and there is no rain because they have
> sinned against you
> and then they pray toward this place, confess your name,
> and turn from their sin, because you punish them
> 36 then hear in heaven, and forgive the sins of your servants, your
> people Israel.
> when you teach them the good way in which they should walk;
> and grant rain on your land,
> which you have given to your people as an inheritance.
> (1 Kings 8)

All the contingencies mentioned call to mind the legislation of the Book of Deuteronomy with its compounding of hypothetical cases.

With respect to royal splendor as well as worship, Solomon's achievements merit poetic expression. First Kings 10 contains two such units. The Queen of Sheba offered this response to Solomon's wisdom and wealth:

> 6 So she said to the king,
> "The report was true
> that I heard in my own land
> of your accomplishments and of your wisdom,
> 7 but I did not believe the reports
> until I came and my own eyes had seen it.
> Not even half had been told me;
> your wisdom and prosperity
> far surpass the report that I heard.
> 8 Happy are your wives!
> Happy are these your servants,
> who continually attend to you
> and hear your wisdom!

9 Blessed be the LORD your God,
  who has delighted in you
  and set you on the throne of Israel!
  Because the LORD loved Israel forever,
  he has made you king
  to execute justice and righteousness."
10 Then she gave the king 120 talents of gold,
  a great quantity of spices, and precious stones;
  never again did spices come in such quantity
  as that which the queen of Sheba gave to King Solomon.
                    (1 Kings 12)

This passage expands the common form of accounts of the splendor of kings. First Kings 10:23–25 resembles the poem:

23 Thus King Solomon excelled
  all the kings of the earth
  in riches and in wisdom.
24 The whole earth
  sought the presence of Solomon
  to hear his wisdom,
  which God had put into his mind.
25 Every one of them brought a present,
  objects of silver and gold,
  garments, weapons, spices,
  horses, and mules,
  so much year by year.

The Queen of Sheba's praise takes the form of a blessing. Both the passages conform to the pattern of heightened speech—poetry.

The poetic unit associated with Rehoboam, Solomon's successor, records a dispute rather than praise. The poetic dialogue of 1 Kings 12:4–16 presents Rehoboam's error in judgment, which led to the division of the kingdom. The closing lines present a summons to withdraw, almost identical to the summons to withdraw given in 2 Samuel 20:1b, "To your tents, O Israel!" Previous to this, the account follows the pattern laid by the discussions of Samson and Delilah or the banter related to David's killing of Goliath. The representative passage below rests in the heart of the narrative:

8 But he disregarded the advice that the older men gave him,
  and consulted with the young men who had grown up with him
  and now attended him.
9 He said to them,
  "What do you advise
  that we answer this people
  who have said to me,
  'Lighten the yoke
  that your father put on us'?"

10 The young men who had grown up with him
Said to him,
"Thus you should say to this people
who spoke to you,
'Your father made our yoke heavy,
but you must lighten it for us';
thus you should say to them,
'My little finger is thicker than my father's loins.'"
(1 Kings 12:8–10)

The harsh reply, of course, leads to the separation. The event exhibits a ritualized form, suggesting its current form developed through years of dramatic presentation. The northern kingdom could especially enjoy this rehearsal in answer to the question, "How did Israel become two nations?"

The final poetic unit of 1 Kings expresses Elijah's frustration following his flight from Jezebel: "He answered, 'I have been very zealous for the LORD, the God of hosts; for the Israelites have forsaken your covenant, thrown down your altars, and killed your prophets with the sword. I alone am left, and they are seeking my life, to take it away'" (1 Kings 20:14). The brief poem carries the effect of a mini-lament. Elijah rehearses his own faithfulness, the wickedness of his enemies, and in attitude, at least, a charge against God for allowing the trouble. All these components appear in typical psalmic laments.

The first prophecy similar to the oracles of the latter prophets appears in 2 Kings 3:16–19:

16 And he said, "Thus says the LORD,
'I will make this wadi full of pools.'
17 For thus says the LORD,
'You shall see neither wind nor rain,
but the wadi shall be filled with water,
so that you shall drink, you, your cattle, and your animals.'
18 This is only a trifle in the sight of the LORD,
for he will also hand Moab over to you.
19 You shall conquer every fortified city and every choice city;
every good tree you shall fell,
all springs of water you shall stop up,
and every good piece of land you shall ruin with stones."

The oracle came to Elisha while a performer played a stringed instrument (2 Kings 3:15). The prophet himself requested the musician. Under the influence of the music "the power of the LORD" (3:15) came upon Elisha. The content of the oracle followed the rhythm or notes of the music. Later prophets sang their oracles accompanied by players at the temple or other worship centers.

The prophetic word itself employs the word *wadi* (*nahal*, נַחַל) as a play on the word, *naqal* (נְקַל, "little thing"). The miraculous filling of the wadi comprised a "little thing." This little miracle would foreshadow the great measure of help God would provide in their victory over Moab.

Warfare also provides the setting for the challenge to Jerusalem that Rabshakeh[13] uttered. Rabshakeh attempted to persuade the people of Jerusalem to avoid seige by capitulating to the Assyrians (2 Kings 18:19–35). His arguments carry a lot of persuasive content:

- Egypt, on whom they depend, is less than reliable.

- How can they say they will trust in God when Hezekiah has destroyed their local sanctuaries to consolidate worship in Jerusalem?

- They couldn't even use horses to fight if the Assyrian leader gave them to them.

- Rabshakeh claims to conquer at the command of Yahweh.

- Rabshakeh promises personal property and independence to those who surrender.

- The gods of other nations could not save their citizens from the Assyrians' armies.

All these words, along with mention of the hardship of seige, come in the Hebrew language of the populace rather than Aramaic (the language of diplomacy). This historical incident shows the careful wording of a dramatic account. Perhaps a historical drama recited the history of Jerusalem's fortunes through this and other incidents.

The prayer of Hezekiah (2 Kings 19:15–19) and Isaiah's oracle (19:21–28) combine to answer the Assyrian threat. The three pieces of poetry form a trilogy remarkable for the substantially different types of poetry involved. Hezekiah's prayer includes specific information on the trouble which does not occur in psalmic pleas for deliverance (laments):

15 and Hezekiah prayed before the LORD and said:
   O LORD the God of Israel, who are enthroned above the cherubim,
   you are God, you alone,
   of all the kingdoms of the earth;
   you have made
   heaven and earth.
16 Incline your ear, O LORD and hear;
   open your eyes, O LORD and see;
   hear the words of Sennacherib,
   which he has sent
   to mock the living God.
17 Truly, O LORD,
   the kings of Assyria have laid waste the nations and their lands,
18 and have hurled their gods into the fire,
   though they were no gods
   but the work of human hands—wood and stone—and so they were
      destroyed.

---

13. This is probably a title, "chief of officers," rather than a name.

19 So now, O LORD our God
   save us, I pray you, from his hand,
   so that all the kingdoms of the earth may know that you, O LORD,
   are God alone.

The first half of the prayer has a very slow, halting pace. The longer lines of explanation beginning with verse 17 show an increase in speed. The unit builds from orthodox confession of God's character to outright request for help in verse 19. The theme, Yahweh's unique identity as God, shows a relationship to Rabshakeh's challenge. As the centerpoint of Hebrew faith, radical monotheism offers the ultimate incentive for God's intervention.

God answers Hezekiah's prayer almost immediately through Isaiah's prophecy (2 Kings 19:21–28). Assyria's mockery of Jerusalem (v. 21) amounted to mockery of God himself. Assyria committed the crime of pride. God used the Assyrians to accomplish his purposes, but their arrogance meant they would again become a nation of little consequence (v. 28). The form of the oracle resembles other oracles against Assyria in the Book of Isaiah. Like many other psalms and oracles, it employs spatial metaphors of height and depth to indicate human experiences of pride and humiliation, respectively.

The final poetic units in the former prophets (2 Kings 22:13; 22:16–20) relate to the discovery of the book of the Law at the remodeling of the temple. Josiah sent for a prophet to determine the full significance of its contents: "Go, inquire of the LORD for me, for the people, and for all Judah concerning the words of this book that has been found; for great is the wrath of the LORD that is kindled against us, because our ancestors did not obey the words of this book, to do according to all that is written concerning us" (2 Kings 22:13). The request carries the weight of momentous speech phrased in frugal lines. It resembles the kind of proclamation we expect to hear from a public speaker behind a microphone when the effect of the address outweighs the content. The answer of Huldah the prophet constitutes a judgment oracle supported by Deuteronomic theology:

16 Thus says the LORD,
   I will indeed bring disaster on this place and on its inhabitants—
   all the words of the book
   that the king of Judah has read.
17 Because they have abandoned me
   and have made offerings to other gods,
   so that they have provoked me to anger
   with all the work of their hands,
   therefore my wrath will be kindled against this place and it will not
   be quenched.
18 But as to the king of Judah,
   who sent you to inquire of the LORD,
   thus you shall say to him,
   Thus says the LORD, the God of Israel:
   Regarding the words that you have heard.

19 Because your heart was penitent, and you humbled yourself before
   the LORD,
when you heard how I spoke aginst this place, and against its
   inhabitants,
that they should become a desolation and a curse,
and because you have torn your clothes,
and wept before me,
I also have heard you, says the LORD.
20 Therefore I will gather you to your ancestors,
and you shall be gathered to your grave in peace;
your eyes shall not see
all the disaster
that I will bring on this place.

Verses 16–17 seem to contain the oracle proper. Succeeding verses, though part of its content, actually limit its applicability. Verses 18–20 appear less poetic than the first two lines.

After the Book of Deuteronomy, the poetry of the Bible breaks into numerous forms. Forms important even to Deuteronomy (for example, blessing and curse) receive little representation in the poetry of the remaining Deuteronomistic literature. Other briefer units appear: (1) Joshua 10:12–13 presents a miracle formula; (2) 1 Samuel 15:33 proclaims a death sentence; (3) 2 Samuel 20:1*b* and 1 Kings 2 :16*b* issue summons to withdraw; (4) historical boasts flaunt the achievements of Israel's leaders (Judg. 15:16; 1 Sam. 18:17 and parallels; 1 Kings 10:23–25); (5) 2 Kings 10:19, by ruse, summons the prophets of Baal to a cultic festival; and (6) Josiah calls for a prophetic interpretation of events (2 Kings 22:13). The table on the following page illustrates the diversity of poetic materials in the former prophets.

Poetry in the Latter Prophets: Major Prophets

Prophetic oracles undoubtedly exhibit poetic form. Our discussion will concentrate on distinguishing the oracles from and comparing them to early poetry (that is, those units identified by Freedman and Craigie). Also, to some degree, the discussion compares the oracles of the prophets from book to book to gain a sense of the scope of their poetic literature.

Isaiah

Isaiah displays some of the most carefully crafted language of the Bible. By the time of Isaiah (740 to 700 B.C.E.) prophecy had become more of an art form than for previous figures like Balaam (Num. 23–24). In previous centuries prophets showed their link with the divine world by noisy frenzies, while in a later period the ability to compose beautiful and metrically correct lines indicated inspiration. Influenced by temple and royal

Table 13
Types of Poetic Units in the Former Prophets

TYPES OF POETRY	SUBTYPES	SCRIPTURE
Curses and Blessings	curse [blessing]	Josh. 6:26; 1 Kings 10:6–9
	miracle formula	Josh. 10:12–13
Brief Sayings	historical boasts	Judg. 15:16; 1 Sam. 18:7; 21:11; 29:5; 1Kings 10:23–25
	death sentence	1 Sam. 15:33
	summons to withdraw	2 Kings 10:19
	summons to festival	2 Kings 10:19
	request for prophecy	2 Kings 22:13
Psalms	victory song	Judg. 5:2–31
	thanksgiving hymn	1 Sam 2:1–10; 2 Sam. 22:2–51
	lament	2 Sam. 1:19–27; 3:33–34; 1 Kings 19:14
	royal psalm	2 Sam. 23:1–7
Proverbs and Riddles	riddle	Judg. 14:14
	proverb	Judg. 14:18; 1 Sam. 15:22–23
	satirical fable	Judg. 9:8–15
Prayers	liturgical prayer	1 Kings 8:12–61
	prayer for deliverance	2 Kings 19:15–19
Prophecy		2 Kings 3:16–19; 7:1; 19:21–28; 20:17–18; 22:16–20
Poetic Dialogue		Judg. 16:6–17, 27–30; 1 Sam. 17:24–27; 1 Kings 12:4–16; 2 Kings 18:19–35

institutions, prophets used literary skill to make their prophecy gain a hearing.[14] Isaiah's poetic skill showed his audience he had immediate contact with God.[15] Throughout all sixty-six chapters the Book of Isaiah presents a panoply of self-standing visions. Few of these enable us to determine the oracle's context within Israel's history or Isaiah's ministry.[16]

Chapter 1 offers a representative sample of the special concerns of Isaiah's poetry. Verse 1 introduces the work as a vision. The prophecy opens with an allusion to the first line of the Song of Moses: "Hear, O heavens, and listen, O earth" (compare Deut. 32:1). The threat so blatantly expressed in Deuteronomy 32 lies at the heart of Isaiah's discussion of the people's rebellion. The chapter also contains an allusion to Sodom and Gomorrah (v. 10; compare Deut. 32:32). The poem interprets the problem as one of understanding, in the sense of recognizing God's special favor: "I reared children and brought them up, but they have rebelled against me. The ox knows its owner, and the donkey its master's crib; but Israel does not know, my people do not understand" (Isa. 1:2b–3). Israel has already received punishment and currently courts further disaster. At the center of the oracle God directly pronounces his rejection of Israel's worship (vv. 11–17). The poem forecasts further warfare as punishment for their lack of justice. Beyond the judgment, the city (Jerusalem) will "be redeemed by justice." The oracle looks ahead to a city characterized by faithfulness and prosperity.

The chapter follows a pattern common to divine lawsuits which occur throughout the prophets: the call for witnesses (v. 2a), the charge (v. 23), the promise of retribution (throughout), and in this case, a look ahead to restoration. "I will turn my hand against you; I will smelt away your dross as with lye and remove all your alloy. And I will restore your judges as at the first, and your counselors as at the beginning. Afterward you shall be called the city of righteousness, the faithful city" (Isa. 1:25–26). At the time of the prophecy, the country stood in disarray, but the prophetic book opens by explaining why and beginning to look ahead. This chapter contains thematic elements common to all three of the major sections of the book. Already, the reader has experienced Israel's sin, judgment, and reshaping into an ideal community.

Jeremiah

In contrast to Isaiah's poetry, Jeremiah's distinction lies in the lengthy section of prose (chaps. 32–45). Chapters 1–31 contain approximately half poetry and half prose. Chapters 46–52 contain predominantly poetry. Some

---

14. For prophetic strategies in transforming public thought, see Gary V. Smith, *The Prophets as Preachers: An Introduction to the Hebrew Prophets* (Nashville: Broadman & Holman Publishers, 1994).

15. The three-part construction of Isaiah under the general themes of judgment (1–39), hope (40–55), and the people's responsibility to make a choice (56–66) was introduced on pages 199–200.

16. This unusual sense of context as well as Isaiah's high language provides a different complexion for this prophetic book. Trent C. Butler, *Isaiah*, Layman's Bible Book Commentary 10 (Nashville: Broadman Press, 1982) provides estimated dates and forms for each of the oracles. John D. W. Watts *Isaiah 1–33*, WBC 24 (Waco: Word, 1985) and *Isaiah 34–66*, WBC 25 (Waco: Word, 1987) suggested the work presented a drama in which the main characters were Yahweh, Heaven, and Earth.

oracles even appear in prose rather than poetry (for example, 7:1–20). At certain points this prose receives reinforcement by poetic lines. For example, a brief lament (7:29) occurs amid a prose oracle (7:21–30). This prose oracle continues into chapter 8, which contains mostly poetic form.

Where the book employs poetic form, the oracles directly reveal an effort to communicate with common citizens. They contain unusually strong images, most often employing humans or animals as their objects. The book reveals a less artistic form than does Isaiah, yet by no means unpolished. The presentation of simple images in everyday terms simply does not allow for the kind of subtle communication common in Isaiah's fantastic presentation. The second-person voice occurs quite frequently. The message to the hearers consists of logical arguments accusing Israel of sin. The following oracle understands Israel's political and military dependence on Egypt and Assyria as tantamount to dependence on their gods: "Has a nation changed its gods, even though they are no gods? But my people have changed their glory for something that does not profit" (2:11). The oracle compares Israel's reliance on these nations and their deities to sexual lust (2:23–25, 33; 3:1–3). Jeremiah's strong presentation apparently leaves his audience no room to argue their innocence. Israel's current deprivation and future woes are directly related to their sins. God thus takes on the character of either a punisher (2:30) or a rewarder; yet Jeremiah's oracles present hardly any examples of the latter.

Jeremiah's poetic oracles serve as medium for his special language of sorrow. His personal complaints (11:18–12:4; 15:10–21; 17:14–18; 18:19–23; 20:7–13; 20:14–18) reflect the prophet's unique ministry of suffering. The following illustrates the spirit of these laments:

> 15 O LORD, you know,
> > remember me and visit me,
> > and bring down retribution for me on my persecutors.
> > In your forbearance do not take me away;
> > know that on your account I suffer insult.
> 17 I did not sit in the company of merrymakers,
> > nor did I rejoice;
> > under the weight of your hand I sat alone,
> > for you had filled me with indignation.
> 18 Why is my pain unceasing,
> > my wound incurable,
> > refusing to be healed?
> > Truly, you are a deceitful brook,
> > like waters that fail. (Jer. 15)

In the laments (not to be equated with psalmic laments) Jeremiah blames God for his suffering and urges God to punish those who abused the prophet. In varying degrees, all six confessions deal with theodicy from the perspectives of the suffering of the righteous and the impunity of the persecutor. In contrast to his own sense of righteousness in suffering, Jeremiah considers Israel's troubles well deserved.

The book displays remarkable attention to suffering from beginning to end. Consider this depiction of famine:

2 Judah mourns
    and her gates languish;
 they lie in gloom on the ground,
    and the cry of Jerusalem goes up.
3 Her nobles send their servants for water;
    they come to the cisterns.
 they find no water,
    they return with their vessels empty.
 They are ashamed and dismayed and cover their heads,
4 because the ground is cracked.
    Because there has been no rain on the land
 the farmers are dismayed;
    they cover their heads.
5 Even the doe in the field forsakes her newborn fawn
    because there is no grass.
6 The wild asses stand on the bare heights,
    they pant for air like jackals;
 their eyes fail
    because there is no herbage. (Jer. 14)

The closing oracles against Egypt, Philistia, Moab, Ammon, Edom, Damascus, and Babylon (chaps. 46–51) present the suffering of these nations under God's judgment. As expected, the book presents their suffering less sympathetically.

Ezekiel

Ezekiel's prophecies replay deuteronomistic theology. Still, Ezekiel offers a wide variety of thought-provoking depictions of God's displeasure and the people's status. Taking little time to describe their sins, Ezekiel laid a blanket charge of disobedience against Judah (especially Jerusalem).

Ezekiel's oracles against the nations take the form of lamentations. Several oracles follow allegorical images as in 15:1–5:

1 The word of the LORD came to me:
2 O mortal, how does the wood of the vine surpass all other wood—
    the vine branch that is among the trees of the forest?
3 Is wood taken from it to make anything?
    Does one take a peg from it on which to hang an object?
4 It is put in the fire for fuel;
    when the fire has consumed both ends of it
    and the middle of it is charred,
    is it useful for anything?
5 When it was whole it was used for nothing;
    how much less—when the fire has consumed it,
    and it is charred—
    can it ever be used for anything! (Ezek. 15)

Verses 6–8 provide a brief interpretation of the allegory. The unit reflects the spirit of most of Ezekiel's oracles.

Most of Ezekiel's poetry announces disaster. However, Gog's battle against Israel signals the end of punishment (Ezek. 38–39), and, thereafter, the book centers attention on Israel's hopes for restoration. The account of divine punishment through Gog reveals the cadences of measured prose. Ezekiel's vision of the new temple in 40–48 assumes the same style. The account of the temple begins with simple measurement, yet builds to the spectacular river flowing from the temple:

> 3 Going on eastward with a cord in his hand, the man measured one
>   thousand cubits,
>   and then he led me through the water; and it was ankle-deep.
> 4 Again he measured one thousand,
>   and he led me through the water; and it was knee-deep.
>   Again he measured one thousand,
>   and led me through the water; and it was up to the waist.
> 5 Again he measured one thousand,
>   and it was a river that I could not cross,
>   for the water had risen; it was deep enough to swim in,
>   a river that could not be crossed. (Ezek. 47)

The passage provides no clear explanation of the symbolism, but the river seems to indicate God's life-giving presence. The renewed temple provides the backdrop for a new division of the land, closing with a description of the limits of the city (Jerusalem), to be renamed: "Yahweh Is There" (yĕhwâ šammâ, יְהוָה שָׁמָּה). Though these closing passages (that is, the division of the land and the limits of the city) do not exhibit lineation or poetic meter, they reveal a formal cast in the overall construction of the book. They add closure to the cycle of judgment and restoration.

All three of the major prophets employed poetry to communicate God's judgment. Isaiah especially used older poetic forms and concepts to convey the message. Isaiah's oracles appear more psalmic, at times, especially in chapters 40–55, resembling the hymn. Jeremiah and Ezekiel show less familiarity with earlier poetry and less similarity to the psalms. They do reflect some of the more negative sections of the individual and group laments from Psalms. The books also display varying degrees of hope for the future, mostly presented in poetic forms. Isaiah, of course, contains the strongest commitment to the restoration, with sixteen chapters (40–55) devoted to little else, along with many more oracles of hope in other sections. Ezekiel ends with a hopeful look to a distant utopian future, but elsewhere the book's overwhelming concern is to warn Judah of impending judgment. Outside chapters 30–33, Jeremiah contains only scattered oracles and small sections expecting restoration. Consistent with earlier findings, poetry most often provides the medium for speech and especially divine speech.

Poetry in the Latter Prophets: Minor Prophets

The minor prophets, like the major prophets, present far too much poetry for interpretation or even summary in this review. The following discussions offer a few examples and a simple characterization of each prophet's use of poetry.

Hosea

Hosea's poetry consists of images using the language of family and divorce:

1 Say to your brother, Ammi, and to your sister, Ruhamah.
2 Plead with your mother, plead—
       for she is not my wife,
       and I am not her husband—
   that she put away her whoring from her face,
       and her adultery from between her breasts,
3 or I will strip her naked
       and expose her as in the day she was born,
   and make her like a wilderness,
       and turn her into a parched land,
       and kill her with thirst. (Hos. 2:1–3)

Much of the description of Hosea's marriage (chaps. 1–3) appears in prose. After chapter 3 the work consists entirely of poetry. Other than its principal interest in divine judgment, much of the language of chapters 4–14 concerns treachery among family members. This symbolically describes God's disappointment with Israel. The kinship of God and his people recurs as a constant image. The peoples' rebellion created a relationship more like that betweeen criminal and judge. "For they are kindled like an oven, their heart burns within them; all night their anger smolders; in the morning it blazes like a flaming fire. All of them are hot as an oven, and they devour their rulers. All their kings have fallen; none of them calls upon me" (Hos. 7:6–7). Many similar strong images convey the people's rebellion. Occasionally, Yahweh's love becomes the subject:

1 When Israel was a child, I loved him,
       and out of Egypt I called my son.
2 The more I called them,
       the more they went from me;
   they kept sacrificing to the Baals,
       and offering incense to idols.
3 Yet it was I who taught Ephraim to walk,
       I took them up in my arms;
       but they did not know that I healed them.
4 I led them with cords of human kindness,
       with bands of love.

> I was to them like those
> who lift infants to their cheeks.
> I bent down to them and fed them. (Hos. 11)

The entire book presents a summons to return to faithfulness.

Joel

All the poetry of Joel shows connection with psalmic poetry. The lines do not appear as recognizable cultic genres, but provide a clear example of cultic prophecy. Chapters 1 and 2 present God's judgment upon his people:

> 3 Fire devours in front of them,
>   and behind them a flame burns.
>   Before them the land is like the garden of Eden,
>   but after them a desolate wilderness,
>   and nothing escapes them.
> 4 They have the appearance of horses,
>   and like war-horses they charge.
> 5 As with the rumbling of chariots,
>   they leap on the tops of the mountains,
>   like the crackling of a flame of fire
>   devouring the stubble,
>   like a powerful army
>   drawn up for battle. (Joel 2)

This locust plague may symbolize utter destruction at the hands of an army. The prose of Joel 3:1–3 provides a transition from judgment to hope. God's attention begins to focus on Israel's enemies. The warfare oracle (3:9–21) presents Israel as the victor over all competing nations in somewhat apocalyptic terms.

Amos

Like his contemporary Hosea, Amos issued well-formed oracles warning of punishment. Yet the poetic units of Amos possess an entirely different tone than Hosea. Amos warns of certain doom, with little or no emphasis on the Northern Kingdom's former relationship with God. God's intent to act should spread terror among the nation, according to 3:3–8:

> 3 Do two walk together
>   unless they have made an appointment?
> 4 Does a lion roar in the forest,
>   when it has no prey?
>   Does a young lion cry out from its den,
>   if it has caught nothing?
> 5 Does a bird fall into a snare on the earth,
>   when there is no trap for it?
>   Does a snare spring up from the ground,
>   when it has taken nothing?

6 Is a trumpet blown in a city,
   and the people are not afraid?
   Does disaster befall a city,
   unless the LORD has done it?
7 Surely the Lord GOD does nothing,
   without revealing his secret
   to his servants the prophets.
8 The lion has roared;
   who will not fear?
   The Lord GOD has spoken;
   who can but prophesy?

The prophet's words (God's words) compare to the roar of a lion. Similar images of threat include the lion, bear, and poisonous snake of 5:18–20.

Amos offers some of the most interesting poetic forms of the Bible. Two of the three visions in 7:1–9 present a stereotyped response: "O Lord GOD, cease, I beg you! How can Jacob stand? He is so small!" (7:5a, slight variations from 7:2b). The Book of Amos also contains a good deal of word-play as in the vision of 8:1–3: "He said, 'Amos, what do you see?' And I said, 'A basket of summer fruit.' Then the LORD said to me, The end has come upon my people Israel; I will never again pass them by" (Amos 8:2). The word for "basket of summer fruit" (qāyiṣ, קַיִץ) and the word for "end" (qēṣ, קֵץ) sound very much alike in Hebrew. These similar sounds guide the interpretation of the vision. Such understated proclamations of doom and pessimistic portraits of destruction with no chance of escape give the poetry of Amos an air of fatalistic doom.

Obadiah

The brief prophecy of Obadiah directs the message of doom to Edom:

1 The vision of Obadiah.
   Thus says the Lord GOD concerning Edom:
   We have heard a report from the LORD,
   and a messenger has been sent among the nations;
   "Rise up! Let us rise against it for battle!"
2 I will surely make you least among the nations:
   you shall be utterly despised.
3 Your proud heart has deceived you,
   you that live in the clefts of the rock,
   whose dwelling is in the heights.
   You say in your heart,
   "Who will bring me down to the ground?"
4 Though you soar aloft like the eagle,
   though your nest is set among the stars,
   from there I will bring you down, says the LORD.

A most unusual series of verses lists Edom's mistreatment of Israel in the repeated framework, "You should not have _____ on the day of ____" (vv. 12–14). The mention of injustices Edom committed leads not only to the forecast of their doom, but to that of other nations as well. The "day of the LORD" (v. 15) in Obadiah consists of Israel's successful battle against surrounding nations. "For the day of the LORD is near against all the nations. As you have done, it shall be done to you; your deeds shall return on your own head" (v. 15).

Jonah

The only poetic unit in Jonah appears in the prophet's song of thanks sung from the belly of the fish.

1 Then Jonah prayed to the LORD his God from the belly of the fish, saying,

2 "I called to the LORD out of my distress,
    and he answered me;
out of the belly of Sheol I cried,
    and you heard my voice.

3 You cast me into the deep
    into the heart of the seas,
    and the flood surrounded me;
all your waves and your billows passed over me.

4 Then I said, 'I am driven away
    from your sight;
how shall I look again
    upon your holy temple?'

5 The waters closed in over me;
    the deep surrounded me;
weeds were wrapped around my head
    at the roots of the mountains.

6 I went down to the land
    whose bars closed upon me forever;
yet you brought up my life from the Pit,
    O LORD my God.

7 As my life was ebbing away,
    I remembered the LORD;
and my prayer came to you,
    into your holy temple.

8 Those who worship vain idols
    forsake their true loyalty.

9 But I with the voice of thanksgiving
    will sacrifice to you;
what I have vowed I will pay.
    Deliverance belongs to the LORD." (Jon. 2:1–9)

In every respect, Jonah's prayer constitutes a typical thanksgiving song, but Jonah sings the prayer from Sheol (that is, the belly of the fish representing the abode of the dead) rather than after deliverance. Images that are otherwise strictly symbolic take on physical characteristics (for example, *Sheol,* threatening waters). In addition, the otherwise generic mention of the vow can be read as Jonah's renewed commitment to his prophetic calling. Apart from the special context of Jonah's psalm, Psalm 116 appears very similar.

Micah

Micah announces the appearance of God in language similar to the theophanies of the Psalms: "For lo, the LORD is coming out of his place, and will come down and tread upon the high places of the earth. Then the mountains will melt under him and the valleys will burst open, like wax near the fire, like waters poured down a steep place" (Mic. 1:3–4). His announcement of judgment shows itself in various poetic forms: lament (1:8–16), taunt song (2:4), oracle of hope (4:1–8), divine lawsuit (6:1–16), and hymn of praise (7:14–20). The tone of judgment turns to the language of restoration and hope beginning in chapter 4:

> 1 In the days to come
>> the mountain of the LORD's house
> shall be established as the highest of the mountains,
>> and shall be raised up above the hills.
> Peoples shall stream to it,
> 2   and many nations shall come and say:
> "Come, let us go up to the mountain of the LORD,
>> to the house of the God of Jacob;
> that he may teach us his ways
>> and that we may walk in his paths."
> For out of Zion shall go forth instruction,
>> and the word of the LORD from Jerusalem.
> 3 He shall judge between many peoples,
>> and shall arbitrate between strong nations far away;
> they shall beat their swords into plowshares,
>> and their spears into pruning hooks;
> nation shall not lift up sword against nation,
>> neither shall they learn war any more;
> 4 but they shall all sit under their own vines and
>> under their own fig trees,
> and no one shall make them afraid;
> for the mouth of the LORD of hosts has spoken.

In Micah's vision the mountain of the LORD's house replaces the illicit high places used to worship Canaanite deities (1:3). This figure resembles the more elaborate new temple of Ezekiel.

Nahum

Nahum presents a battle curse similar to Obadiah's oracle against Edom. Both more properly comprise prophetic oracles than curses. Nahum contains vivid portrayals of the chaos of defeat (2:1–13; 3:1–3):

> 1 Ah! City of bloodshed,
>   utterly deceitful, full of booty—
>   no end to the plunder!
> 2 The crack of whip and rumble of wheel
>   galloping horse and bounding chariot!
> 3 Horsemen charging,
>   flashing sword and glittering spear,
>   piles of dead,
>   heaps of corpses,
>   dead bodies without end—
>   they stumble over the bodies! (Nah. 3)

The poetry of the book shows uniformity in that all judgment targets Nineveh, and the book contains no oracles of hope. It closes with observations regarding the suffering of Nineveh, whereas most prophetic books end with hopeful looks into the future.

Habakkuk

The poetry of Habakkuk expresses the prophet's frustration at God's slowness to respond to the suffering of the righteous.

> 2 O LORD, how long shall I cry for help,
>   and you will not listen?
>   Or cry to you "Violence!"
>   and you will not save?
> 3 Why do you make me see wrong-doing
>   and look at trouble?
>   Destruction and violence are before me;
>   strife and contention arise.
> 4 So the law becomes slack
>   and justice never prevails.
>   The wicked surround the righteous—
>   therefore judgment comes forth perverted.
>   (Hab. 1:2–4)

The series of taunt songs (four woe oracles) in Habakkuk 2:6–17 describe the eventual downfall of the unjust in terms indicated by the following unit: "'Alas for you who heap up what is not your own!' How long will you load yourselves with goods taken in pledge?" (Hab. 2:6b). The third chapter of Habakkuk contains a unit described as a prayer. It exhibits the form of a hymn with a few elements common to individual laments. Directions both at the beginning ("according to Shigionoth") and the end ("to the choirmaster: with stringed instruments") confirm its psalmic nature.

The poem lauds the victory won by God's intervention. It includes the divine warrior imagery (compare Deut. 32:39–42) which characterizes God "fighting" in a fashion consonant with his power and glory:

> 3 God came from Teman,
>   the Holy One from Mount Paran.
>   His glory covered the heavens,
>   and the earth was full of his praise.
> 4 The brightness was like the sun;
>   rays came forth from his hand,
>   where his power lay hidden.
> 5 Before him went pestilence,
>   and plague followed close behind.
> 6 He stopped and shook the earth;
>   he looked and made the nations tremble.
>   The eternal mountains were shattered;
>   along his ancient pathways
>   the everlasting hills sank low. (Hab. 3:3–6)

This spectacular statement of hope ends with the worshiper stating trust in God. This joins the poem to the earlier question (1:2).

Zephaniah

Zephaniah does not include the questioning of God's lack of intervention, but responds to a similar mood of despair. The poetry of Zephaniah considers the end of the world:

> 2 I will utterly sweep away everything
>   from the face of the earth, says the LORD.
> 3 I will sweep away humans and animals;
>   I will sweep away the birds of the air
>   and the fish of the sea.
>   I will make the wicked stumble.
>   I will cut off humanity
>   from the face of the earth, says the LORD.
>   (Zeph. 1:2–3)

The book anticipates the day of the LORD, brought on by the sin of God's people as well as the nations. Repeated references to "that day" or "that time" introduce description after description of the punishment to come. The phrase serves as the basis for a series of anaphoric lines in Zephaniah 1:14–16:

> 14 The great day of the LORD is near,
>   near and hastening fast;
>   the sound of the day of the LORD is bitter,
>   the warrior cries aloud there.
> 15 That day will be a day of wrath,
>   a day of distress and anguish,

> a day of ruin and devastation,
>   a day of darkness and gloom,
>   a day of clouds and thick darkness,
> 16 a day of trumpet blast and battle cry
>   against the fortified cities
>   and against the lofty battlements.

Anaphoric lines also advise the reader to prepare:

> 1 Gather together, gather,
>   O shameless nation,
> 2 before you are driven away
>   like the drifting chaff,
>   before there comes upon you
>   the fierce anger of the LORD,
>   before there comes upon you
>   the day of the LORD's wrath.
> 3 Seek the LORD, all you humble of the land,
>   who do his commands;
>   seek righteousness, seek humility;
>   perhaps you may be hidden
>   on the day of the LORD's wrath. (Zeph. 2:1–3)

Zephaniah contains one of the most stinging rebukes of Jerusalem in the Bible: "Ah, soiled, defiled, oppressing city! It has listened to no voice; it has accepted no correction. It has not trusted in the LORD; it has not drawn near to its God" (Zeph. 3:1–2). The book is so entirely negative that the introduction of hope in 3:9 appears out of place. Even more so, the joy expressed in 3:14–15a: "Sing aloud, O daughter Zion; shout, O Israel! Rejoice and exult with all your heart, O daughter Jerusalem! The LORD has taken away the judgments against you, he has turned away your enemies." The oracle of hope extends from 3:14 to the end of the book (3:20).

Haggai

Haggai contains only brief portions of poetry. The opening oracle (1:3–11) conveys God's disappointment with the settlers who had returned to Palestine:

> 4 Is it a time for you yourselves
>   to live in your paneled houses,
>   while this house lies in ruins?
> 5 Now therefore thus says the LORD of hosts:
>   Consider how you have fared.
> 6 You have sown much, and harvested little;
>   you eat, but you never have enough;
>   you drink, but you never have your fill;
>   you clothe yourselves, but no one is warm;
>   and you that earn wages earn wages
>   to put them into a bag of holes. (Hag. 1)

Two other oracles (2:3–9,14–19) show similar concern that Israel's poor fortunes relate to the poor state of the temple. The final oracle promises God's impending establishment of world rule through Zerubbabel (2:20–23). This represents a decided shift from the more physical concern of rebuilding the temple. On the other hand, this utopian look ahead seems characteristic of prophetic poetry before and after the Babylonian exile.

Zechariah

Chapters 1 through 7 of Zechariah contain only brief units of poetry in the form of oracles. Their brevity makes them unusual. They record communications from God to the prophet which interpret the visions Zechariah encounters. Chapter 8 contains an oracle promising better days for Jerusalem. It offers a more restrained image of hope than the closing oracles of other prophets (for example, Haggai). The anticipation of security receives expression in verse 12: "For there shall be a sowing of peace; the vine shall yield its fruit, the ground shall give its produce, and the skies shall give their dew; and I will cause the remnant of this people to possess all these things" (Zech. 8:12). Chapters 9–14 are entirely poetic. Each of two units bears the title, "an oracle." The first oracle contains judgments of Syria, Philistia, and Lebanon along with promises of peace to Jerusalem:

> 9 Rejoice greatly, O daughter Zion!
>   Shout aloud, O Daughter Jerusalem!
>   Lo, your king comes to you;
>   triumphant and victorious is he,
>   humble and riding on a donkey,
>   on a colt, the foal of a donkey.
> 10 He will cut off the chariot from Ephraim
>   and the war horse from Jerusalem;
>   and the battle bow shall be cut off,
>   and he shall command peace to the nations;
>   his dominion shall be from sea to sea,
>   and from the River to the ends of the earth.
>   (Zech. 9)

The second oracle (chaps. 12–14) encourages Jerusalem even further: God's people will enact God's judgment against the nations. Finally, God will set up universal rule through a Davidite. All worship of idols will cease, and the people be purified (13:1–2). "On that day . . . all who survive of the nations that have come against Jerusalem shall go up year after year to worship the King, the Lord of hosts" (Zech. 14:9, 16).

Malachi

Malachi's poetry reveals less careful measuring but possesses a captivating, rational style.

A son honors his father,
  and servants their master.
If then I am a father,
  Where is the honor due me?
And if I am a master,
  Where is the respect due me?
Says the LORD of hosts
  to you, O priests, who despise my name.
    (Mal. 1:6)

The first two chapters of Malachi use measured prose to express God's dissatisfaction, with special emphasis on the priests. Chapters 3 and 4 turn to the future and announce God's appearance for judgment. His appearance introduces deliverance for the righteous:

1 See, the day is coming,
  burning like an oven,
  when all the arrogant and all evildoers will be stubble;
  the day that comes to burn them up,
  says the LORD of hosts,
  so that it will leave them neither root nor branch.
2 But for you who revere my name
  the sun of righteousness shall rise,
  with healing in its wings.
You shall go out leaping like calves from the stall.
    (Mal. 4 [Heb. 3:19–20])

In other portions of the book, Malachi employs rhetorical questions. Answers or misanswers fill lines following the questions. The answers provide introductions for more lengthy statements of problems and judgment.

Prophecy as Poetic Speech

As in other poetic literature, the prophets provide expression of emotional human experience. Their similarities in style do not obscure the differences in degree. The pronounced passion of select psalms appears endemic to the speech of prophets. The canon presents the prophets as skillful oral poets able to use widely varied forms to complement and develop the oracular form. These creative agents transmitted the divine message through traditional and innovative media. The prophetic employment of images stands out as extreme in its art with more vivid form and stronger meanings than any other biblical poetry. The poetry of the prophets seems more diverse as a whole than the sum of all the poetry of the Hebrew Bible outside the prophetic books.

Prophets also proved to be masters at conveying sound in poetry. Much of the repetition of words does not escape the notice of the English reader. Much more than this, the measured beats of lines and half lines lend rhythm to an already impressive tone. The language often appears extremely concise, providing a simplicity and, when needed, a brutality that forces the message home.

The role of the prophet in Hebrew society gave poetic power. Prophetic speeches contain direct accounts of God's intent, a sort of heavenly perspective, accompanied by real or imagined ritual actions. These actions serve not to satisfy the deity, but to convince the hearer of the truth of the prophetic word. The nature of prophecy as speech assumes central importance. This involves related dynamics, including: (1) the original delivery of prophecy for the hearing of an audience rather than performance in a ritual context, (2) the agent of prophecy as an inspired individual, therefore a bearer of unique truth, and (3) the form of prophecy as vehicle for a beautiful aural expression.

These prophetic poetic distinctives produce important prophetic perspectives:

(1)   Prophecy expected a *reaction from the audience*, whether repentance, hope, or bracing for a harsh future. This identifies intent to persuade its recipients as its aim.

(2)   Prophecy emphasized the *human operations involved in religion*. The prophets issued innumerable requests for response. This represents a reorientation from poetry as communication *to* the deity to poetry as communication *from* the deity.

(3)   With rare exception, poetic truth finds expression in the *voice of a single speaker*. This "prophet" serves as the voice of authority, an exclusive intercessor and as such, the ultimate "priest."

Each of these emphases occurs in varying degrees throughout biblical poetry, but their prominence gives peculiar identity to prophetic poetry.

Poetry in the Wisdom Books

Proverbs

Is Proverbs poetry? Modern readers have difficulty here because we see poetry as a series of lines. Two lines (half lines from the Hebrew perspective) seem insufficient to exist as a "poem." From the biblical perspective, the two lines form a set of parallel lines—the basic unit of Hebrew poetry.[17] The longer *mešālîm* of Proverbs 1–9 and 30:1–31:31 comprise units more recognizable as "poems."

Two further factors relate to the discussion of proverbs as poetry. First, prophetic speeches like Amos 3:3–8 consist of a series of proverbs. Many of the prophets' brief sayings are proverbs. This connection of prophecy with the proverb reinforces the proverbs' connection with poetry. Second, the

---

17. The inclusion of these double lines as poetry also stretches the Hebraic measures of poetic form. The smallest proverbs can scarcely present strophic structure, though they do contain parallelism and meter.

transmission of proverbs may well have involved singing. Several options for performance exist: (1) a steady repetition of a single proverb, (2) a proverb placed within a song, and (3) a proverb sung with its own interpretation. Related forms, like the riddle of Samson (Judg. 14:14) or the boast of David's warrior skills (1 Sam. 18:7 and elsewhere) lend themselves to music. The latter bears the name, "song." Proverbs may well then represent Hebrew poetry in its simplest presentation.

Ecclesiastes

The first eleven verses of Ecclesiastes represent a sort of vanity song. The discourse regarding time in 3:1–8 exhibits an even more convincing lined structure. Elsewhere, Ecclesiastes contains numerous proverbs. The content of the book shows careful design. This presumes a very deliberate presentation of the content. These features make it difficult to imagine its presentation as straight prose. Even an English reading calls for calculated pauses and various rhythms. These factors do not lead to the identification of the bulk of Ecclesiastes as poetry. Still, the prose presents a rhythmic structure unlike other books. The book may contain a medial form with enough balance to qualify as poetry, but possessing thematic development more common to prose.

Job

Job, like Ecclesiastes, exhibits the high themes and language common in poetry. Job's dialogues (3:1–42:6) contain no prose. Job displays numerous poetic forms. The hymn to wisdom (28:1–28) shows verse structure similar to that of the hymns in Psalms:

> 23 "God understands the way to it,
> and he knows its place.
> 24 For he looks to the ends of the earth,
> and sees everything under the heavens.
> 25 When he gave to the wind its weight,
> and apportioned out the waters by measure;
> 26 when he made a decree for the rain,
> and a way for the thunderbolt;
> 27 then he saw it and declared it;
> he established it, and searched it out.
> 28 And he said to humankind,
> 'Truly, the fear of the Lord, that is wisdom;
> and to depart from evil is understanding.'"

The dialogues (actually speeches) show signs of careful crafting, with recurring letimotifs. Each speech contains more or less clear divisions which appear as stanzas. Such divisions typically begin with statements which provide content for elaboration within the stanza. For example, in Job 8:11 Bildad's speech begins with a proverb: "Can papyrus grow where there is no marsh? Can reeds flourish where there is no water?" The interpretation of the proverb relates it to divine retribution on the one who forgets God.

The creation challenge (chaps. 38–41) presents a second form of poetry in Job. The genre consists of questions: "Have you entered into the springs of the sea, or walked in the recesses of the deep? Have the gates of death been revealed to you, or have you seen the gates of deep darkness? Have you comprehended the expanse of the earth? Declare, if you know all this" (Job 38:16–18). Elaborations which illustrate the wonder of the cosmos often follow the questions. This mysterious poetry underscores the limits of human power and understanding. The descriptions of Behemoth and Leviathan command special attention. These supernatural creatures assume the forms of the hippopotamus and the crocodile, respectively. Yet both clearly represent cosmic forces which only God can control. Such creatures commonly appeared in the creation stories of many ancient cultures. The Book of Job uses the allusion to these creatures to elaborate on the theophany's central idea: No person can do what God can do.

Wisdom as Didactic

The wisdom books as a whole show special poetic forms related to their common interests. Poetry serves as medium for the communication of these highest truths or self-evident maxims. These definitive expressions of truth make poetic forms the ideal (even the expected) means of communication. Proverbs offer ultimate truths on a wide variety of very specific issues. Job and Ecclesiastes approach more narrowly focused experiences. Wisdom displays poetic qualities which add to the canonical definition of poetry. Among these, the isolation of two-line thematic units assumes prominence. Parallelism appears commonly throughout Hebrew poetry, but proverbs accent the individuated reading of two-line units. The content of the wisdom books appears to reflect assumed truth. The emphasis falls on teaching rather than persuasion based on special revelation as in the prophets. Also, distinct from psalms and prophecy, wisdom consists more of human-to-human communication than divine communication and appeals to the deity. It locates authority in the presumed maturity or common sense of the reader rather than making overt claims to divine inspiration. This accounts, in part, for its nature as assumed truth.

Several of the wisdom books contain styles of florid narrative which convey the didactic tone. This involves an emphasis on speech, though the sage presumes less authority in these readings than the prophet or other spokespersons presume in non-wisdom poetry. Perhaps because of this, in wisdom, lineation almost always appears more important than semantic parallelism or meter. This implies a less poetic form for wisdom than for the prophets. More significantly, this implies that wisdom materials issued mostly from speech rather than singing. This distinctive, as well as others reviewed above, calls for a different designation of wisdom poetry as didactic poetry (rather than oracular or liturgical poetry).

Poetry in Other Books of the Writings

Nehemiah

Nehemiah includes a single salvation history hymn (9:5–37):

6 You are the LORD,
   you alone;
   you have made heaven,
   the heaven of heavens, with all their host,
   the earth and all that is on it,
   the seas and all that is in them.
   To all of them you give life,
   and the host of heaven worships you.
7 You are the LORD, the God
   who chose Abram
   and brought him out of Ur of the Chaldeans
   and gave him the name Abraham;

The long psalm traces Israel's history from Abraham to the judges with reference to the then current situation. Psalm 106 shows similar preoccupation with Israel's rebellion, though it relates only the Exodus period.

Chronicles

First Chronicles places a somewhat similar unit on the lips of David:

8 O give thanks to the LORD, call on his name,
   make known his deeds among the peoples.
9 Sing to him, sing praises to him,
   tell of all his wonderful works.
10 Glory in his holy name;
   let the hearts of those who seek the LORD rejoice.
11 Seek the LORD and his strength,
   seek his presence continually.
12 Remember the wonderful works he has done,
   his miracles, and the judgments he uttered,
13 O offspring of his servant Israel,
   children of Jacob, his chosen ones.
14 He is the LORD our God;
   his judgments are in all the earth.
15 Remember his covenant forever,
   the word that he commanded, for a thousand generations,
16 the covenant that he made with Abraham,
   his sworn promise to Isaac,
17 which he confirmed to Jacob as a statute,
   to Israel as an everlasting covenant,
18 saying, "To you I will give the land of Canaan
   as your portion for an inheritance."

19 When they were few in number,
    of little account, and strangers in the land,
20 wandering from nation to nation,
    from one kingdom to another people,
21 he allowed no one to oppress them;
    he rebuked kings on their account,
22 saying, "Do not touch my anointed ones;
    do my prophets no harm."

23 Sing to the LORD, all the earth.
    Tell of his salvation from day to day.
24 Declare his glory among the nations,
    his marvelous works among all the peoples.
25 For great is the LORD, and greatly to be praised;
    he is to be revered above all gods.
26 For all the gods of the peoples are idols,
    but the LORD made the heavens.
27 Honor and majesty are before him;
    strength and joy are in his place.

28 Ascribe to the LORD, O families of the peoples,
    ascribe to the LORD glory and strength.
29 Ascribe to the LORD the glory due his name;
    bring an offering, and come before him.
    Worship the LORD in holy splendor;
30 tremble before him, all the earth.
    The world is firmly established; it shall never be moved.
31 Let the heavens be glad, and let the earth rejoice,
    and let them say among the nations, "The LORD is king!"
32 Let the sea roar, and all that fills it;
    let the field exult, and everything in it.
33 Then shall the trees of the forest sing for joy
    before the LORD, for he comes to judge the earth.
34 O give thanks to the LORD, for he is good;
    for his steadfast love endures forever.

35 Say also:
"Save us, O God of our salvation,
    and gather and rescue us from among the nations,
that we may give thanks to your holy name,
    and glory in your praise.
36 Blessed be the LORD, the God of Israel,
    from everlasting to everlasting."
Then all the people said "Amen!" and praised the LORD.
        (1 Chron. 16:8–36)

The work exhibits a compound structure, mixing elements of several types of psalms. It opens as a song of thanks (vv. 8–9); shows interests common to salvation history hymns (vv. 15–22); contains praise like a general hymn (vv. 27–34); and ends with an appeal for deliverance (vv. 35–36). The passage does not present a single psalm, but a mixture of portions from three different psalms (105; 96; 106). In addition to adding this collection of Psalm pieces, the Chronicler has also omitted much of the poetic material from 1 and 2 Samuel: the thanksgiving hymns (1 Sam. 2:1–10; 2 Sam. 2:2–51) and David's laments (2 Sam. 1:19–27; 3:33–34).

Second Chronicles reproduces Solomon's prayer at the dedication of the temple without omissions (2 Chron. 6:4–40). The Chronicler's version adds a formula, closely resembling Psalm 132:8–10, invoking God to inhabit the temple: "'Now rise up, O LORD God, and go to your resting place, you and the ark of your might. Let your priests, O LORD God, be clothed with salvation, and let your faithful rejoice in your goodness. O LORD God, do not reject your anointed one. Remember your steadfast love for your servant David'" (2 Chron. 6:41–42). Chapter 7 shows God's answer as fire falls to consume the sacrifices (v. 1). This spectacle is not recorded in 1 Kings. The summons to withdraw appears in 2 Chronicles 10:16 and follows the same form as its counterparts in 2 Samuel 20:1 and elsewhere. Second Chronicles 16:7–9 introduces Hanani, the seer or prophet, and his oracle:

7 Because you relied on the king of Aram
   and did not rely on the LORD your God,
   the army of the king of Aram has escaped you.
8 Were not the Ethiopians and Libyans a huge army
   with exceedingly many chariots and cavalry?
   Yet because you relied on the LORD,
   he gave them into your hand.
9 For the eyes of the LORD range throughout the entire earth
   to strengthen those whose heart is true to him.
   You have done foolishly in this;
   for from now on you will have wars.
   (2 Chron. 16)

In general, both 1 and 2 Chronicles contain fewer and less impressive units of poetry than comparable passages in the former prophets. This suggests that such poetry waned in importance in later Israel. Liturgical poetry flourished during the period of the Chronicler. At the same time, unlike the Former Prophets, writers of narrative showed less interest in the support of narrative accounts with striking examples of poetry.

Daniel

Daniel offers some of the latest examples of Hebrew poetry. The Babylonian king speaks poetically, as well as Daniel. The herald's proclamation commanding worship when instruments sound out comes through poetry (3:4–6). Other dreams in Daniel show no poetic structure.

Daniel's first poetic unit involves thanks to God for the interpretation of a dream:

20 Blessed be the name of God from age to age,
   for wisdom and power are his.

21 He changes times and seasons,
    deposes kings and sets up kings;
  he gives wisdom to the wise
    and knowledge to those who have understanding.
22 He reveals deep and hidden things;
    he knows what is in the darkness,
    and light dwells with him.
23 To you, O God of my ancestors,
    I give thanks and praise,
  for you have given me wisdom and power,
    and have now revealed to me what we asked of you,
    for you have revealed to us what the king ordered."
               (Dan. 2)

The unit mixes wisdom concerns with the language of hymns, but most appropriately fits the category of song of thanks. The unit resembles some very old poetry, since it occurs in conjunction with prose (similar to the Song of Deborah in the context of Judg. 4–5).

Nebuchadnezzar's dream in 4:10–17 (Heb. 4:7–14) differs from dream accounts like Jacob's dream (Gen. 28:10–22) or prophetic visions (for example, Ezek. 1:1–3:15 or 37:1–14). Not only the speech of the holy watcher (4:14–17), but also Nebuchadnezzar's description of his dream (vv. 10–12) appears in poetic lines. Daniel's interpretation, however, assumes a prose form. This stands opposed to what the prophetic books have led us to expect. In the prophets, mention of a divine word like this would normally introduce a poetic prophetic oracle. (Daniel's similar interpretation in 5:17–28 is poetic.)

Nebuchadnezzar reported:

10 "upon my bed this is what I saw;
    there was a tree at the center of the earth,
    and its height was great.
11 The tree grew great and strong,
    its top reached to heaven,
    and it was visible to the ends of the whole earth.
12 Its foliage was beautiful,
    its fruit abundant,
    and it provided food for all.
The animals of the field found shade under it,
    the birds of the air nested in its branches,
    and from it all living beings were fed.
13 I continued looking, in the visions of my head as I lay in bed, and
    there was a holy watcher, coming down from heaven.
14 He cried aloud and said:
'Cut down the tree and chop off its branches,
    strip off its foliage and scatter its fruit.
Let the animals flee from beneath it
    and the birds from its branches.

15 But leave its stump and roots in the ground,
   with a band of iron and bronze,
   in the tender grass of the field.
   Let him be bathed with the dew of heaven
   and let his lot be with the animals of the field
   in the grass of the earth.
16 Let his mind be changed from that of a human,
   and let the mind of an animal be given to him.
   And let seven times pass over him.
17 The sentence is rendered by decree of the watchers,
   the decision is given by order of the holy ones,
   in order that all who live may know that the Most High
   is sovereign over the kingdom of mortals; he gives it to whom
   he will and sets over it the lowliest of human beings.'"

Even though the passage shows clear poetic form, its construction reflects few of the poetic features common to much Hebrew poetry. Its parallel lines follow the synthetic pattern, closer to prose style. It contains little alliteration, wordplay, or repetitive structures. We cannot liken it to free verse, because its semantic development appears so similar to prose. The account breaks its content into phrases which comprise independent units with subject, verb, and object. If written in English prose, the lines would provide little notice of poetic style or form. In Daniel 4:34–35 and 4:37 (Heb. 4:31–32, 34), Nebuchadnezzar again speaks in poetic form. The hymnic language indicates a much more poetic style than in the previous example. Not surprisingly, the content of the lines concerns God's sovereignty and the corresponding humility of humans. The lines do not comprise a complete hymn, but appear very much like lines of praise common to the Psalms.

In Daniel 5:17–28 Daniel interpreted the inscription Belshazzar (Nebuchadnezzar's son) saw on the wall: *mĕnēʾ mĕnēʾ tĕqēl ûparsîn* (מְנֵא מְנֵא תְּקֵל וּפַרְסִין). This involves wordplay. All three words (*minah, tekel,* and *parsin*) describe units of weight. In addition, the words offer the meanings "counted, counted, weighed, divided" to indicate the downfall and subsequent division of Belshazzar's kingdom.

Chapter 7 signals a turning point in the book. Chapters 7–12 relay Daniel's four visions of the future. The visions employ humans and animals as the vehicles for allegorical pictures of the future. The last vision dispenses with metaphorical language to reveal God's triumph and the end of the world. Daniel's visions represent a poetic form otherwise unknown to the Hebrew Bible. The nearest corollary appears in the night visions of Zechariah 1–6. Daniel's dreams and visions communicate ultimate truth regarding events expected to close the current era of human history. Daniel's poetry creates (or polishes) new genres. By contrast, the Chronicler distills poetry from existing psalms and so adds little to the development of poetry. Daniel opens a fresh horizon. The visions and dreams of Daniel stem from original revelation. Daniel's poetry offers dynamic communication from

God. This involves poetry so unlike traditional forms that its detailed study belongs to interpreters of apocalyptic form rather than a general study of poetry.

Poetry in the Deuterocanon

The poetry of the Deuterocanon offers some helpful comparisons with poetry of the Hebrew Bible. Much of the poetry in Tobit, The Wisdom of Solomon, Sirach, Baruch, The Prayer of Azariah and the Song of the three Jews, the Prayer of Manasseh, and Psalm 151 derive from the poetry in the Hebrew Bible.

Tobit

In Tobit's first bit of poetry a man prays after bird droppings blind him. The unit compares more to narrative in its content than to biblical laments. Unlike the Psalms, it ends with a request for death. In this respect it recalls Job's despair of living (Job 3). Tobit's prayer (Tobit 3:2–6) does contain phrases common to lament psalms. It connects suffering with sin (compare Ps. 51). Yet the prayer of Tobit lacks references to God as deliverer as well as statements of hope, both characteristic of psalmic laments. The personal nature of the prayer also distinguishes it from the Psalms. Even the individual laments of the Psalms reveal a liturgical shape that makes them applicable to all worshipers. Personal references in Tobit's prayer limit its application to the one situation. In addition, private prayers do not occur in the Psalms and rarely occur in the poetry of the Bible (only in 1 Kings 8:12–61 and its parallel in 2 Chron. 6:4–41, plus 2 Kings 19:15–19).

A second prayer occurs in Tobit 3:11–15. Sarah offers this prayer after her loss of seven husbands to a demon. Like Tobit's prayer, Sarah's includes a request for death: "'I am my father's only child; he has no other child to be his heir; and he has no close relative or other kindred for whom I should keep myself as wife. Already seven husbands of mine have died. Why should I still live? But if it is not pleasing to you, O Lord, to take my life, hear me in my disgrace.'" Her prayer, though much like Tobit's, exhibits even less similarity to the psalms. Her unique situation provides most of the basis for the prayer. A statement of innocence in verse 14 (like those in Ps. 18:20–26) offers the only exception. In Sarah's case, innocence describes her sexual morality. Sarah and Tobit speak their prayers simultaneously, and God guarantees their healing.

Tobit sings a hymn after his healing (13:1–17). It contains several elements common to psalmic hymns: "'Blessed be God who lives forever, because his kingdom lasts throughout all ages. For he afflicts, and he shows mercy; he leads down to Hades in the lowest regions of the earth, and he brings up from the great abyss, and there is nothing that can escape his hands.'" The general praise of the hymn possesses liturgical features, unlike other poetry in Tobit. The praise relates not so much to Tobit's healing, but to God's retribution, which brought punishment for sins and reward for repentance. This involves a national interpretation of God's action. Israel bore his blessing. During the time of national struggle, Tobit's suffering and deliverance represented the suffering of the nation and the deliverance of the righteous. Israel's response to their treatment at the hands of others likewise determined their standing with God.

The hymn also incorporates the language of Zion songs:

9 O Jerusalem, the holy city,
    he afflicted you for the deeds of your hands,
    but will again have mercy on the children of the righteous.
16   For Jerusalem will be built as his house for all ages.
    How happy I will be if a remnant of my descendants should survive
      to see your glory and acknowledge the King of heaven.
    The gates of Jerusalem will be built with sapphire and emerald,
      and all your walls with precious stones,
    The towers of Jerusalem will be built with gold,
      and their battlements with pure gold.
    The streets of Jerusalem will be paved
      with ruby and with stones of Ophir.
17 The gates of Jerusalem will sing hymns of joy,
    and all her houses will cry, 'Hallelujah!
    Blessed be the God of Israel!'
    and the blessed will bless the holy name forever and ever.
    (Tobit 13)

Other units of poetry in Tobit (8:5–7, 15–17; 11:14–15) add little to this overview.

Wisdom of Solomon

The Wisdom of Solomon presents a flowing verse style.[18] Most of the parallel units of the book show a synthetic relationship. Communication of information drives the poetry of the book rather than literary devices. The entire work, though divided into many sections, displays a remarkable unity of epic style:

1 Wisdom prospered their works by the hand of a holy prophet.
2 They journeyed through an uninhabited wilderness,
    and pitched their tents in untrodden places.
3 They withstood their enemies and fought off their foes.
4 When they were thirsty, they called upon you,
    and water was given them out of flinty rock,
    and from hard stone a remedy for their thirst.
    (Wisdom 11:1–4)

---

18. Pages 111–113 of this study review the content of the book.

The poetry of Wisdom shows closest similarity to the salvation history psalms. Reading from this perspective alone, however, severely limits the impact of the book.

Sirach[19]

Sirach's poetry differs completely from the flowing epic style of The Wisdom of Solomon. The styles of poetry in Sirach vary more than in any other wisdom book. Sirach contains numerous poetic units:

Table 14
Poetic Units in Sirach

LOCATION	DESCRIPTION
1:1–10	hymn to wisdom
1:11–30	fear of the Lord poem
2:1–17	call to faithfulness during testing
3:1–14:19	collections of proverbs
14:20–15:10	blessings of wisdom poem
16:26–17:14	creation hymn
18:1–14	creation hymn
18:15–39:1	collections of proverbs
39:12–35	creation hymn
40:1–42:14	collections of proverbs
42:15–43:33	creation hymn
44:1–50:24	historical hymn
51:1–12	prayer of Sirach
51:13–30	acrostic wisdom poem

The historical hymn of 44:1–50:24 resembles the salvation history hymns of Psalms with an important difference. This hymn emphasizes human accomplishments more than divine accomplishments. Its subjects appear as heroes of Israel.

The creation hymns attract special attention. Sirach 39:16–21 illustrates Sirach's employment of poetic units to convey wisdom:

16 "All the works of the Lord are very good,
        and whatever he commands will be done at the appointed time.

---

19. Sirach's contents are reviewed on pages 113–115.

17 No one can say, 'What is this?' or 'Why is that?'—
    for at the appointed time all such questions will be answered.
  At his word the waters stood in a heap,
    and the reservoirs of water at the word of his mouth.
18 When he commands, his every purpose is fulfilled,
    and none can limit his saving power.
19 The works of all are before him,
    and nothing can be hidden from his eyes.
20 From the beginning to the end of time he can see everything,
    and nothing is too marvelous for him.
21 No one can say, 'What is this?' or 'Why is that?'—
    for everything has been created for its own purpose.

When hymns occur, they present wisdom theology. The single exception to this tendency appears in chapter 51.[20] The first twelve verses present a song of thanks identical to those found in the Psalms:

1 I give you thanks, O Lord and King,
    and praise you, O God my Savior.
  I give thanks to your name,
2   for you have been my protector and helper
  and have delivered me from destruction
    and from the trap laid by a slanderous tongue,
    from lips that fabricate lies.
3 In the face of my adversaries
    you have been my helper and delivered me,
    in the greatness of your mercy and of your name,
  from grinding teeth about to devour me,
    from the hand of those seeking my life,
    from the many troubles I endured,
4 from choking fire on every side,
    and from the midst of fire that I had not kindled,
5 from the deep belly of Hades,
    from an unclean tongue and lying words—
6   the slander of an unrighteous tongue to the king.
  My soul drew near to death,
    and my life was on the brink of Hades below.
7 They surrounded me on every side,
    and there was no one to help me;
  I looked for human assistance,
    and there was none.
8 Then I remembered your mercy, O Lord,
    and your kindness from of old,
  for you rescue those who wait for you
    and save them from the hand of their enemies.
9 And I sent up my prayer from the earth,
    and begged for rescue from death.

---

20. The differentiation of these verses from the remainder of the book makes many scholars regard this as an added section.

10 I cried out, "Lord, you are my Father;
   do not forsake me in the days of trouble,
   when there is no help agaisnt the proud.
11 I will praise your name continually,
   and will sing hymns of thanksgiving."
   My prayer was heard,
12   for you saved me from destruction
   and rescued me in time of trouble.
For this reason I thank you and praise you,
   and I bless the name of the Lord.[21]

The book ends with an epilogue (51:13–30) encouraging attention to wisdom. Even though the hymn does not finally conclude the work, the presence of the hymns at the opening and at the conclusion of Sirach frames the book's wisdom with orthodox worship.

Baruch

The last half of the Book of Baruch consists of two poems. Baruch 3:9–4:4 blames Israel's rejection of wisdom (identified with Torah) for the exile. The search for wisdom resembles that of Job 28. Yet Job emphasized rulers and other successful persons whom wisdom eluded. The poem in Baruch ends with a description of God's "house," emphasizing his ascendancy above human abilities. This leads to a final identification of wisdom as equivalent to obedience to the commandments. Effectively, Job's question, "Where can wisdom be found?" receives the answer, "In the Torah."

1 She is the book of the commandments of God,
   the law that endures forever.
   All who hold her fast will live,
   and those who forsake her will die.
2 Turn, O Jacob, and take her;
   walk toward the shining of her light.
3 Do not give your glory to another,
   or your advantages to an alien people.
4 Happy are we, O Israel,
   for we know what is pleasing to God. (Baruch 4)

The second poem (4:5–5:9) includes four stanzas of varying length, each introduced with the phrase, "Take courage. . . . " The spirit of the poem and some of its phrases come from Isaiah 45–66 (also to a lesser extent portions of Jeremiah and Ezekiel). A widow whose plight is blamed on the sins of her children (rebellion against the Torah) serves as the speaker in much of the poem. The widow (Jerusalem) also represents the people themselves, who stand powerless against their captors. The poem

---

21. The Hebrew text adds responsive material between verses 12 and 13 not in the Greek copy of the work. These responses follow a construction similar to the formula in Psalm 136: "Give thanks to _____, for his mercy endures forever."

encourages the children to wait for God's certain vindication. Joy at the reunion of scattered Israel concludes the passage:

> 5 Arise, O Jerusalem, stand upon the height;
>   look toward the east,
>   and see your children gathered from west and east
>   at the word of the Holy One,
>   rejoicing that God has remembered them.
> 6 For they went out from you on foot,
>   led away by their enemies;
>   but God will bring them back to you,
>   carried in glory, as on a royal throne. (Baruch 5)

Overall, the poem presents a rather tidy summary of Israel's circumstances, including the cause of Israel's current struggles. The presentation follows a three-part format: (1) neglect of Torah, (2) lament, and (3) promise of future joy. This historical review probably functioned as a teaching unit which presented the later portion of Israel's history from an authoritative source (Baruch—the prophet Jeremiah's scribe—Jer. 36:32). The unit encouraged the current community to remain devoted to Scripture (that is, Torah) and to maintain hope for God's eventual intervention.

The Book of Baruch spells out the prescriptions for the ceremony of public confession of sin in prose (1:14–3:8) rather than incorporating the direction into the poetry. The ceremony would correspond to the form of psalm known as community lament, but little evidence of such a psalm exists in Baruch. The prose unit reveals a historical orientation emphasizing the people's sin. Psalmic laments, by contrast, raise an appeal to the deity. According to 1:10–14, Baruch produced a scroll which he sent to Jerusalem along with money for sacrifices. Among other requests, Baruch asked the residents of Jerusalem to pray for Nebuchadnezzar. Given this background, one would expect the book to depend heavily on the Psalms. It shows preference for Job and the latter prophets instead. The lack of dependence on psalmic material implies the unit served as a public reading (1:3–4) rather than a liturgy. The poetry[22] hints at the desire to place the work in a more liturgical setting.

The Prayer of Azariah and the Song of the Three Jews

The Septuagint (Greek Version of the Hebrew Bible) adds The Prayer of Azariah and the Song of the Three Jews to the Book of Daniel. The lengthy title refers to one entirely poetic work which includes the texts of both the prayer and the song. The text appears between Daniel 3:23 and 3:24. Azariah's prayer comes from within the furnace. His presence "in the fire" provides a powerful image of Israel's second temple era. Israel faces death. Azariah's prayer remains oblivious to the fire surrounding him. Only the prose introduction (v. 1) and the concluding summary (vv. 23–27) mention

---

22. Many scholars regard the poetry as an addition to the original work.

the furnace. Azariah acknowledges Israel's plight (exile) as brought on by inattention to the commandments. As such, Israel deserved the punishment. Still, Azariah pled for remembrance lest the nation dissolve. He asked that their contrition be accepted as atonement. He alluded to a psalm.

> 16 For you have no delight in sacrifice;
>   if I were to give a burnt offering, you would not be pleased.
> 17 The sacrifice acceptable to God is a broken spirit;
>   a broken and contrite heart, O God, you will not despise.
>   (Ps. 51:16–17)

> Yet with a contrite heart and a humble spirit may we be accepted,
> as though it were with burnt offering of rams and bulls,
> or with tens of thousands of fat lambs;
> such may our sacrifice be in your sight today,
> and may we unreservedly follow you,
> for no shame will come to those who trust in you.
>   (Azariah 16–17)

The entire unit reflects the structure of Psalm 51 (an individual lament), both admitting guilt and seeking repentance. The Prayer of Azariah appears quite liturgical throughout, displaying much of the tone and form of community laments. The reader can trace the lament form through the psalm (1) address to God and praise (vv. 3–5), (2) admission of guilt (vv. 5–8), (3) statement of difficulty (vv. 9–10), (4) plea for mercy (vv. 11–15), (5) request for God to accept repentance (vv. 16–19) (6) request for deliverance (vv. 20–21) and (7) concluding praise (v. 22). The content for the psalm reflects passages collected from throughout the Hebrew canon plus Baruch.

The Song of the Three Jews also comes "from the furnace." It follows a narrative description of the incredible heat of the fire and a description of the control of the heat by the angel present with them. The first thirty-eight double lines begin with "bless" or "blessed." Thirty-one of these pairs start the second line with "sing praise to him and highly exalt him forever." Most of the poem calls on the natural elements and animals to bless the Lord. The final seven calls to bless God summon humans of all stations to join the praise. The three men receive the last mention:

> 66 Bless the Lord, Hananiah, Azariah, and Mishael;
>   sing praise to him and highly exalt him forever.
> For he has rescued us from Hades and saved us from the power of
>   death,
> and delivered us from the midst of the burning fiery furnace;
>   from the midst of the fire he has delivered us.
> 67 Give thanks to the Lord, for he is good,
>   for his mercy endures forever.
> 68 All who worship the Lord, bless the God of gods,
>   sing praise to him and give thanks to him,
>   for his mercy endures forever.

Other than this unit, only verses 29–34 contain substantive praise. Other verses simply call on different parts of creation to voice praise. The formulaic repetition seems tailored for antiphonal performance. Thematically, the lack of development draws emphasis to the entities addressed. Is there some attempt to present a comprehensive list of all things, animal, vegetable, and mineral, which owe praise to God? Perhaps the song attempts to provide a likeness to the Hellenistic lists of all portions of creation. God's willingness to harness the malevolent force of the fire reinforces such an intent. All nature, by comparison, falls subject to his direct control. Nature presents its response to the divine will through its own poetic praise. This involves a creative literary interpretation of Psalm 148. Its high degree of repetitiveness and the corresponding lack of substantial praise make the Song of the Three Jews very much unlike most hymns.

The Prayer of Manasseh

Manasseh was remembered in the Deuteronomic History as the most wicked king of Judah (2 Kings 21:1–18; compare 2 Chron. 33:1–9). The Chronicler recorded Manasseh's repentance: "While he was in distress he entreated the favor of the LORD his God and humbled himself greatly before the God of his ancestors. He prayed to him, and God received his entreaty, heard his plea, and restored him again to Jerusalem and to his kingdom. Then Manasseh knew that the LORD indeed was God" (2 Chron. 33:12–13). The Chronicler then recorded Manasseh's reform of his own abuses and mentioned the record of his prayer of repentance (2 Chron. 33:14–20). The Prayer of Manasseh appears a later production, supplying the words of Manasseh's prayer. The author probably intended it more as a statement on the breadth of God's mercy than as a forgery of an actual document. The prayer appears much more of an original and artistic creation than other deuterocanonical poems. The unit shows subtle dependence rather than direct dependence upon the Hebrew Bible, without extended quotations. This leads the reader to consider the theme in its original terms. Otherwise, interest would center on the explicit concerns of the Torah, history, and the current status of Israel. Indirectly, the author applied the theme of forgiveness to the then current community. In this way the prayer encouraged hearers to ponder the prospects of each individual's restoration of standing with God. If God would forgive Manasseh, whom could he not forgive?

In form Manasseh begins with an opening address and praise which accents God's mercy in anticipation of a favorable hearing (vv. 1–7). It continues with an admission of guilt and repentance (vv. 8–10). A direct request for forgiveness follows (vv. 11–14). The request for mercy displays a heavy emotional timbre with strong dramatic effect:

> 12 I have sinned, O Lord, I have sinned,
>   and I acknowledge my transgressions.

13 I earnestly implore you,
  forgive me, O Lord, forgive me!
  Do not destroy me with my transgressions!
  Do not be angry with me forever or store up evil for me;
  do not condemn me to the depths of the earth.
  For you, O Lord, are the God of those who repent,
14 and in me you will manifest your goodness; for, unworthy as I am,
  you will save me according to your great mercy,
15 and I will praise you continually all the days of my life.
  For all the host of heaven sings your praise,
  and yours is the glory forever. Amen.

It concludes with a promise of praise after forgiveness and an "Amen" (v. 15). The prayer conforms to the individual lament. It seems carefully modeled after songs of penitence such as Psalm 51. Yet in almost every case, individual laments in the Psalms offer responses to trouble caused by enemies rather than self.

Psalm 151[23]

Psalm 151 assumes the form of a historical poem. The poem offers the election of David as incentive for the praise of God, but attention to David far outweighs hymnic elements. The poem contains only two lines of praise: "For who can proclaim and who can bespeak and who can recount the deeds of the Lord? Everything has God seen, everything has he heard and he has heeded" (v. 4 of Qumran version, NRSV). The Septuagint version of Psalm 151 devotes attention solely to David, with no praise. The psalm characterizes David as a harper whom God selected in spite of his unimpressive size and appearance. The Septuagint version connects David's anointing by Samuel with his victory over Goliath. In this way his defeat of Goliath comes as a result of his choice as anointed one. This version (Septuagint) may contain the compilation of two once distinct units: one represented by the Qumran text, and the other detailing the conquest of Goliath. Since Psalm 151 exhibits a character and structure so unlike canonical psalms, scholars consider it an addition to the older collection. Psalm 151 attested to the Davidic authorship of Psalms by appending a personal note from David himself. In addition, 151 offers testimony to the pervasiveness of stories about David. Writers relived David's history by recreating his poetry. The intent of the unit shares more with the titles of the Psalms than their contents.

Summary: Poetry Outside the Poetic Canon

Poetic units of varying forms and varying degrees of poetic structure and power abound throughout the canon and Deuterocanon. Torah intro-

23. Page 242 gives the text of Ps. 151.

duces poetry to make explicit the relationship between God and people. Its basic elements of blessing, law, and remembrance reappear in other parts of canon. These parts employ a plethora of poetic forms emphasizing heightened speech. Narrative explanations often bracket poetic elements. Poetry shows various types of word plays and sounds, creating tense emotional feelings in various degrees. The greatest poetic skill appears in the Latter Prophets who developed innovative media to announce God's message in oral form displaying divine authority. Wisdom reveals poetry in its smallest form: two lines. Wisdom poetry is didactic, teaching assumed truth without explicit divine authority. Wisdom differs in that it appears to have minimal connections with singing and performance so vital to most other poetry.

Writings center on reusing liturgical forms and content. Except in Daniel, creative poetry seldom appears. Daniel does create new apocalyptic genres. In the Deuterocanon, poetry becomes more personal and often more human-centered and more interested in communicating information. Wisdom poetry here adopts many forms which are used to teach theology. Such poetry is removed from liturgy.

Questions for Discussion

1. In what ways do poetic units outside the poetic canon use and modify forms from the Psalms?

2. What different functions does poetry perform outside the poetic canon?

3. How does poetry relate to the authority of the poetic materials?

Chapter Fourteen

Poetry in the Psalms

Introduction to Psalms

Divisions

Thematically, Psalms presents no beginning, middle, and end. It contains one hundred fifty (more in some collections) individual units.[1] Some depict the Psalms as the hymnbook of the second temple—referring to the temple rebuilt and rededicated between 520 and 515 B.C.E. Only by analogy can the word *hymns* describe psalms. [2] More properly, the Psalms served as temple liturgies which through prayer, penitence, or requests for deliverance offered praise to Yahweh. The Hebrew title of the book, *těhillîm* (תְּהִלִּים), most literally means, "praises." For the current reader, these praises exist independent of the set forms of worship they comprised in ancient Israel. We tend to read them thematically rather than formally. It remains helpful to recall their connection to temple worship. For this reason, basic form-critical findings (see pages 210–214, 281–283) provide an essential foundation for Psalms study. The contemporary encounter of psalms as poetry builds on this foundation.

The special vocabulary of the Psalms proves important to other poetic books as well. The word for praise, *hālāl* (הָלָל), occurs almost exclusively in the intensive forms, *hillēl* (הִלֵּל) and *hullāl* (הוּלָל). The latter form combines with a shortened form of the divine name to form the often occurring

---

1. The discussion of Psalms in this chapter, while accurate in detail, cannot provide a full introduction to the Psalms due to length. Bernhard W. Anderson, *Out of the Depths* (Philadelphia: Westminster, 1983) provides the best basic-level introduction to the Psalms for laypersons, undergraduates, and Master students without background in Psalms studies. The advantages of the work include its clear, creative style; its commitment to widely accepted standards; and its confessional stance. *Out of the Depths* should be placed in the hands of all those who resist form-critical studies on the basis they are too complex and too far removed from the needs of the current church.

2. This study considers them poems with the caveat that this twentieth-century perspective implies a notion of poetry distinct from the views of ancient temple worshipers.

"hallelujah" (הַלְלוּיָה), "praise Yah." The word which names the Book of Psalms originates with the same verb for praise. The plural *tĕhillīm* (תְּהִלִּים) from the singular *tĕhillâ* (תְּהִלָּה) introduces the entire collection as "praises." The Greek title *psalmois* (ψαλμοῖς) originally indicated songs accompanied by the harp. The content of Psalm 150 and to a lesser degree the content of Psalms 146–149 reveals the importance of the conception of psalms as "praise."

The term *mizmōr* (מִזְמוֹר) more specifically designates a song. It typically introduces and describes individual psalms. It commonly occurs in psalm titles as in the description "a song of David" (for example Ps. 4). The term *šīr* (שִׁיר), also translated "song," does not carry the connotation of hymnic music. The term most often designates songs outside the Book of Psalms, for instance, in prophecy, in the work of the Chronicler, and in the Song of Songs (note the title). The term applies to psalms as well but not as frequently as *mizmōr*.

Discussions of the genres of Psalm 36 introduce more specialized vocabulary. Several directions or designations in the Book of Psalms remain mysterious. For example, the term *miktām* (מִכְתָּם) which introduces Psalms 16 and 56–60 remains completely unknown. The meaning of *selâ* (סֶלָה), a very common word, often interpreted as a pause or congregational response, remains far from certain. English versions of the Psalms transliterate a few other words as well because of their disputed meanings.

Before considering the poetic nature of individual psalms, several of the general divisions and titles of Psalms demand attention. At some point in their history the preservers of the Psalms divided them into five collections (or joined five collections to form the whole). A closing statement of general praise (or doxology) marks the end of each collection.[3]

Table 15
Major Divisions of Psalms

COLLECTION	CHAPTERS	CLOSING STATEMENT (DOXOLOGY)
Book 1	1–41	Blessed be the LORD, the God of Israel from everlasting to everlasting. Amen and Amen. (41:13)
Book 2	42–72	Blessed be the LORD, the God of Israel who alone does wondrous things. Blessed be his glorious name forever; may his glory fill the whole earth. Amen and Amen. (72:18–19) The prayers of David son of Jesse are ended. (72:20)
Book 3	73–89	Blessed be the LORD forever. Amen and Amen. (89:52)

---

3. See table on page 185.

Table 15 (Continued)
Major Divisions of Psalms

Book 4	90–106	Blessed be the LORD, the God of Israel from everlasting to everlasting. And let all the people say, "Amen." Praise the LORD! (106:48)
Book 5	107–150	Let everything that breathes praise the LORD. Praise the LORD! (150:6)

The collections do not comprise independent works. Instead, the finished Psalter was divided into five units, perhaps to corrrespond to the five books of the Torah. Some of these units possibly existed in whole or in part prior to the finished form of the book, but the identification of precise units remains tenuous. The five-part division does not indicate a special relationship between Book 1 and Genesis, Book 2 and Exodus, and so forth.[4]

Headings

In addition to the labeling of the five books, 116 psalms also include headings which indicate the origin, manner of performance, or type of the psalm. These descriptive phrases appear in the Hebrew texts of the Psalms as part of the first verse. In English translations they appear above the body of the psalm, apart from the numbered verses. Lengthier headings equal a full verse in length. For this reason, the verse numbering of the Hebrew will often differ from the English by the addition of one. This work employs the verse numbers of English only to avoid the confusion of numerous double references.

The titles appear for the purposes of identification (of a historic figure connected with the psalm and/or the psalm's type) and directions for various sorts of performance. A few examples illustrate both the variety of headings and their enigmatic nature. The persons and officials named in the headings include David (the most common), the Korahites, Asaph, Moses (only Ps. 90), Solomon (only Ps. 72), Heman the Ezrahite (only Ps. 88), and Ethan the Ezrahite (only Ps. 89). Psalms receive further designations as "a prayer" (Pss. 86; 90), "a psalm of thanksgiving" (100), songs "of ascent" (none prior to 120), and "praise." Various psalms also provide a descriptive phrase which places the poem in a precise context, such as "A Psalm of David, when the prophet Nathan came to him, after he had gone in to Bathsheba" (51). Directional clues involve the designation, "to the leader (often rendered, "choirmaster")." Other directions seem to indicate melody or meter, for example, "according to the Lilies." The titles name instruments as well: for example, "with flutes" or "with stringed instruments." A few psalms designate their usage: "for the memorial offering" or "for the Sabbath day."

---

4. Book 2 actually ends with the notation, "The prayers of David son of Jesse are ended" (72:20). Yet the content of the collection and lack of such clues elsewhere militate against the use of this concluding phrase to name or definitively describe Book 2.

The Five Books

A look at the five books of the Psalter in terms of these headings, especially the persons and officials, provides much of the informaton for a loose
depiction of the book's makeup. Book 1 (1–41) contains mostly David
psalms. Missing titles in Psalms 10 and 33 probably indicated Psalms 9–10
and 32–33 originally appeared under the single David heading. With these
accounted for, only the introductory chapters (Pss. 1–2) display no David
heading. *These two psalms display the fundamental themes of wisdom: Torah and
kingship. They are intended to introduce the entire collection rather than simply Book
1.*[5] Most of the psalms within the first book assume a second-person-singular
perspective, so belonging to the type described below as "individual" rather
than "corporate."

Book 2 (42–72) exhibits few characteristics which unify the collection.
Chapters 42–49 name the "sons of Korah," or Korahites. Most of the remaining psalms in this group begin with a David heading (51-65; 68–70), but contain no other obvious identifying features. Preference for the divine name,
Elohim (rather than Yahweh) connects Book 2 with Book 3. Chapters 42–83
display this characteristic. The predominance of Korah, David, and Asaph
psalms in these books hints at a historical connection between the use of the
divine name Elohim and these figures or their times.

Book 3 (73–89) contains mostly psalms of Asaph which assume the
form of corporate laments (that is, complaints of distress issuing from the
entire community).[6] Book 4 (90–106) shows fewer titles, thus fewer connections to figures such as David. Special interests include hymns to God as
king (93; 95–99). The book concludes with four hymns (103–106). Book 5
(107–150) constitutes the largest collection. Like Book 3, it contains numerous hymns. For undetermined reasons, laments tend to appear early in the
Psalms, and hymns appear mostly in the final third of the book.

The Problems of Authorship

The translation of the preposition *lě* לְ holds special importance for
the deciphering of the titles. Psalms introduced with the phrase "of David"
contain this preposition as do those associated with Korah, Asaph, and others. What can *lědāvid* (לְדָוִד) mean? The most common translation of לְ is
"to" or "for."[7] Among the possible ranges of meaning are possession, relation, purpose, or approach. The possible interpretations include: (1) "dedicated to," (2) "belonging to," (3) "about," (4) "by," (5) "for," (6) "of," or

---

5. Psalms 1 and 2 possibly formed a single unit. Evidence for this includes: (1) the "blessed
is" formula which begins Psalm 1 and ends Psalm 2 (an inclusio?) and (2) the quotation from
some manuscripts of Acts 13:33, "As also it is written in the first psalm" when the citation actually comes from Psalm 2. These suggestions are offered by James Limburg, "Psalms, Book of"
ABD vol. 5 (New York: Doubleday, 1992), 526.
6. The center of Psalms in terms of Books (Book 3) and chapters (73–83) offer mostly corporate laments, adding confirmation to the view that the Psalms were redacted during exile.
7. *BDB*, 510, suggested a basic indication of direction towards (but not motion) and in the
sense of reference to.

(7) "for use by." The list could go on. Authorship remains a disinct possibility; however, another grammatical feature typically ascribes authorship. The construct state (used, for example, in the phrase "the Book of Moses") most commonly names an author. The preposition may present intentional ambiguity. If so, it describes the psalm as having one or more of the following relations to the person mentioned—collected by him, performed in his honor, relating to his position, originating from those close to his office, or reinforcing his authority. Of course, the identity and function of the person—David, Korah, or Asaph—influences the understanding of the references. David's identification with the kingship makes it appealing to consider Davidic psalms as psalms relating to kingship or used by the king. The title introduces psalms linked to his life or authored by him. If interpreted as a looser connection, the titles simply dedicate the psalm "to David."[8]

Psalms introduced by "to Korah" or "to Asaph" were related to these priestly families by their authorship and usage. They tend to be corporate psalms which include more praise and less complaint than David psalms. The Book of Chronicles provides some information relating to these psalm titles.[9] First Chronicles 16:4–7 associates Asaph with the music accompanying the ark. This seems to specifically relate to the singing of psalms (v. 9). The Korahites appear among a list of Levitical families in Numbers 26:58. They also offered praise in worship as Jehoshaphat prepared for battle with the Ammonites (2 Chron. 20:19). Both David and the others are connected with later temple worship by the Chronicler. The superscriptions probably do not predate the time of the exile (586–539 B.C.E.). Perhaps the headings themselves originated at the time of the Chronicler (450-400 B.C.E.). Most interpreters believe the Psalms congealed into a single volume at that time.

Form Criticism and the Psalms

The work of Hermann Gunkel[10] determined the course for most study of the Psalms. Gunkel's genres remain the most helpful way to classify the Psalms. A brief overview of some of the basic types of psalms sets the stage for the review of select psalms which follow. This overview concentrates upon only six types of psalms: the individual lament, the corporate lament, the thanksgiving song, the hymn, royal psalms, and wisdom psalms.

8. Likewise, the title introduces the Song of Solomon as "the Song of Songs which [is] to Solomon" šir hašširim ʾasher lišlomōh (שִׁיר הַשִּׁירִים אֲשֶׁר לִשְׁלֹמֹה). Here the intent appears slightly clearer. The Song "belongs to" or "is about" Solomon. Yet the English translation offers little more clarity than the Hebrew expression.
9. A rather exhaustive study of the special vocabulary of the headings and the Psalms in general is available in Hans-Joachim Kraus, *Psalms 1-59: A Commentary*, trans. Hilton C. Oswald (Minneapolis: Augsburg, 1988), 21–31.
10. See above pages 281–283.

Laments

Many personal laments, though by no means all of them, open with a formal statement of praise. Others, like Psalm 13, open with a question or sentence alerting the deity of the speaker's distress: "How long, O LORD? Will you forget me forever? How long will you hide your face from me? How long must I bear pain in my soul, and have sorrow in my heart all day long? How long shall my enemy be exalted over me?" (vv. 1–2). The following line expresses the sufferer's desire that God hear the request: "Consider and answer, O LORD my God!" (v. 3a) In this particular psalm the quest for a hearing attaches to and combines with two other elements of the individual lament. The line, "Give light to my eyes, or I will sleep the sleep of death (v. 3b)" rather indirectly calls for a definite intervention by Yahweh while implying the nature of the distress. The psalmist fears annihilation at the hands of an unnamed enemy (or enemies). Accordingly, the psalmist asks for help to defeat the adversary.

Verse 4 contains a typical rationale for God's intervention: "And my enemy will say, 'I have prevailed'; my foes will rejoice because I am shaken." Such lines recall Moses' insistence that if God failed to protect Israel in the wilderness, it would be for the surrounding nations a sign of his impotency (Num. 14:13–16). Yet the Psalms themselves never ultimately doubt God's ability and willingness to deliver the devout: "But I trusted in your steadfast love; my heart shall rejoice in your salvation" (13:5). It seems odd that such utter confidence would follow the attempt to persuade in verse 4. This reveals the tendency to muster all possible arguments and reasonings for intervention. Such tactics help convey the depth of the suffering. Verse 5 combines the statement of trust with an expression of the certainty of salvation (line two). The psalm closes with an a confident vow, promising to praise God when victory comes. To sum up, these elements commonly appear in individual laments: (1) an opening statement of praise and/or an address to the deity, (2) some expression of the nature of the difficulty, (3) a request for God's hearing, (4) a request for specific help, at times incorporating reasons God should intervene, (5) an expression of confidence in God's deliverance, and (6) a promise to thank or praise God on account of his aid.

The enemies alluded to in Psalm 13 play an important role in many individual laments. The text does not fully identify these foes. They may embody threats such as illness which do not involve human agents. When these enemies are not human attackers of the psalmist, they may represent evil deities, opponents who would rejoice at the speaker's ultimate calamity, rival groups of Israelites, or simply any threat by way of poetic description. It seems best to avoid the pitfall of limiting the identity of the enemies to a single individual or group. If the psalmists intended simple associations like these, they left mysterious indications.

Although no psalm of any type fits an ideal pattern, Psalm 13 serves as a fine example. It contains traces of each characteristic element, yet combines and uses these in its own way. Novice interpreters of the Psalms must recognize the fluidity and imperfection of the construction of the genres. The characteristic parts of the lament or other genres appear as random components. They unite and blend to form a unique pattern in each psalm. Various components may typically appear at the beginning, middle, or end of a psalm or immediately following some other component. Yet expressions, or themes derived from them, may appear at any juncture in a given psalm. To consider the Psalms as somehow built out of the combination of such elements represents the height of arrogance. Instead, the components prove themselves useful in the exposition of individual psalms. The original design of a psalm consitutes a much more intricate and spontaneous process. Producers of psalms did not begin with choices of various form-critical components: Form-critical analysis merely serves as one way to recognize and describe the artistic pattern and the life-setting of the psalm.

The form-critical approach to the Psalms appeals to the ancient Near Eastern specialist because it seeks a connection between the written form of the psalm and its use in the temple or elsewhere.[11] The life setting[12] of individual laments involved a single worshiper's private or public ceremony to induce God's intervention. Personal laments often express penitence for the sin of the psalmist, as seen in Psalm 51. Some of the psalms which appear to be individual laments in form show design for the community with each worshiper thinking of self as the "I."[13]

One possible context for an individual lament appears in 1 Samuel 1:1–18. Hannah visited the sanctuary to petition God for a child. Her barrenness provided the basis for her plea. The text contains no lament as such, but the circumstances called for one. Whether she performed an already existing psalm or voiced her own prayer, the movement of her lips, which Eli confused with drunkenness, likely involved the expression of some sort of private lament. Childlessness, bitter curse that it represented, occasioned many such prayers. We cannot suggest that all settings for laments compare to Hannah's. In some cases, the performance involved ceremony—including the priests and congregation. Also, such a circumstance as Hannah's could involve her husband in the lament as well. Myriads of possibilities for precise settings called for laments.

The corporate lament differs from the individual lament in that its settings involve the community rather than the individual. Slight differences in form relate to the community orientation of the public lament. Otherwise, its form matches that of the individual lament. Psalm 74 opens with an address to God in question form: "O God, why do you cast us off forever?"

---

11. Psalms and other liturgical poetry accompanied ritual performance. Gunkel compared this to the combined word and act of the Lord's Supper. See *The Psalms: A Form-Critical Introduction,* trans. Thomas M. Horner (Philadelphia: Westminster, 1967), 6.

12. See page 281 for a full explanation.

13. Gunkel defended the view that the "I" of the Psalms identified the author unless the context demanded a communal reading, *Psalms,* 15. Current scholars would question the communal nature of the "I" of individual laments. This accords with the earlier findings of Rudolf Smend, "Über das Ich des Psalmen," ZAW 8 (1888): 49–147.

Notice the plural "us" rather than the singular "me" of the individual laments. Verse 2 urges the deity to "remember" his earlier intentions toward Israel. This conforms to the request for a hearing. A rather elaborate description of the trouble begins in verse 3: The "enemy" possessed the temple (compare 74:3–9). A further plea for intervention appears in verses 10–11. The statement of confidence in God follows (vv. 12–17). It uses the theme of creation to argue God's intent to save. The closing verses (20–23) again urge God's intercession with two arguments for his involvement. The first argument encourages God's covenantal protection of his people. The second involves the derision which God's enemies continue to express toward him and his people as long as deliverance waits. The psalm seems barely aware of its own voice, expressing the need of help more in terms of reason than ritual: It bases its request for God's response on his commitment to his people.

Of the six elements mentioned in connection with individual laments, this psalm lacks only a promise of thanks or praise to be offered after deliverance.[14] Corporate laments tend to lack the request for hearing and the voicing of praise common to individual laments. Perhaps the emphasis on the community as God's elect lessens the need for pleas for attention. These belong to the individual worshiper (in personal laments). The absence of the vow to praise allows no easy explanation. Most of these psalms leave the impression the downbeaten community possesses little energy for praise.

The settings for these psalms involve wide-reaching crises for the community at large: war or defeat, persecution, famine, plague, or any of a number of deep losses.[15] Psalm 74 presents an almost uniquely detailed specific setting. It portrays the loss of the temple to invaders (vv. 3–9). Other corporate laments contain few clues to their settings. As a recurring ceremony, the content of the psalm suggests ties to the loss of the temple (perhaps composed in Babylon). The most notable example of the setting for community laments appears in Lamentations. In every way Lamentations conforms to the pattern outlined for laments. At the same time, the five psalms present unusually detailed descriptions of the tragedy. Laments probably involved performances in special assemblies at the temple (when available). The congregation or its representatives surely took a direct role in the performance of the psalm. The lament enacted the depth of suffering before God and provoked his mercy.[16]

Hymn

As the lament directs an appeal to the deity for deliverance, the hymn directs praise to Yahweh for his providence. The hymn differs from the song

---

14. As noted above the request for God's hearing appears only as exaggerated calls for his "remembrance" of his designs for his people (v. 2).

15. The Book of Joel calls for community fasting (1:14; 2:15–16) providing a typical setting for the group lament. 1 Kings 8:33–40 discusses Yahweh's role in responding to laments.

16. More information on laments can be gained in Paul Wayne Ferris, Jr., *The Genre of Communal Lament in the Bible and the Ancient Near East*, SBLDS 127 (Atlanta: Scholars Press, 1992).

of thanks in that the song of thanks tends to target specific acts of grace. The hymn generally expresses appreciation for God's timeless greatness and mercy. In public worship hymns occurred more commonly than other forms. They fit all occasions and reinforced orthodox notions of God's sovereignty. In accord with their interests, their forms are simplistic and their content repetitive. Psalm 100 exhibits the essential features:

1 Make a joyful noise to the LORD, all the earth.
2 Worship the LORD with gladness;
   come into his presence with singing.
3 Know that the LORD is God.
   It is he that made us, and we are his;
   we are his people, and the sheep of his pasture.
4 Enter his gates with thanksgiving,
   and his courts with praise.
   Give thanks to him, bless his name.
5 For the Lord is good;
   his steadfast love endures forever,
   and his faithfulness to all generations.

Hymns typically open with a call to praise; continue by citing reasons God is worthy of praise; and conclude with a restatement of the call to praise. In Psalm 100, verses 3 and 5 elaborate reasons for praise—here, God's creation and his dependability. The mention of thanksgiving (v. 4) does not indicate its nature as a song of thanks, since it mentions no specific immediate benefit. At times the hymns cite God's historical activity in protection of Israel (for example, Ps. 111) as proof of his worthiness of praise. Creation (as in v. 3 above) appears quite commonly.

The life settings of most hymns remain unclear. They fit a limitless band of community celebrations. In Sabbath worship, the hymn could set the tone for the entire service. Festivals set a most appropriate atmosphere for hymns which could express the community's satisfaction or thanks. The separate components of a hymn like Psalm 100 lend themselves to performance by different personnel in temple worship. Priest, congregant, or king may each perform entire psalms or assigned portions. Other psalms prescribe such practice (for example, Ps. 118:2–3, a song of thanks). The deep involvement of the entire community marks the hymn as distinct from other types.

Song of Thanks

The song of thanks, both corporate and individual, is actually a specialized type of hymn. The individual song of thanks relates closely to the individual lament and may represent the carrying out of the vow made in the lament. Like laments, individual songs of thanks could result from a number of situations. Anything an individual could give thanks for occasioned such songs. Most frequently the psalmist expresses thanks for healing or deliverance from enemies. Songs such as Psalm 30 issue from a personal setting of worship in response to divine blessing. In this case, the worshiper sought and found personal healing from a life-threatening disease.

Individual songs of thanks make use of many common images. Psalm 30 provides examples of some of these: The opening address and statement of praise (vv. 1–2) lead to a reference to "Sheol" and "the pit" (v. 3). These references express the chaos of the sufferer at the height of distress. Sheol represents the parabolic hopeless situation which requires an act of God for rescue. The psalmist often expressed the difficulty in terms of the deity's favor toward the worshiper. God's "anger" (v. 5) or "absence" (v. 7) represents a theological interpretation of extreme distress. The sufferer recounts the appeal for help (vv. 8–10) to which God faithfully responded. Songs of thanks play on the irony that one so disfavored as to come near death should later be so favored as to prosper once more (v. 11). The promise of continual thanks concludes this song (v. 12). Often the worshiper promises a vow of thanks or a thanksgiving offering as a result of deliverance. A clear expression of this occurs in Psalm 116:17–19.

In contrast to this personal basis for thanks, corporate songs express the thanks of the community in concert. Psalm 65, for instance, voices the people's appreciation for the year's harvest. In spring or fall the entire community would gather to ceremonially thank Yahweh for the harvest. The celebration served as an inducement for God to repeat his generosity. Interestingly, even this corporate mercy relates to the forgiveness of sin and moral integrity (vv. 2–3). The opening praise (vv. 1–2) also includes the mention of payment of vows. Mentions of God's general power and beneficence (vv. 5–8) set the stage for praise related directly to the bounty of the crops. The simple structure of this corporate song of thanks mirrors the simplicity of the hymn. Individual songs of thanks share many features with the individual laments while corporate songs of thanks look more like hymns.[17]

Several examples of songs of thanks outside the Psalms provide indication of the range of situations involved. Such songs typically offered thanks after deliverance, but from the belly of the fish Jonah prayed an unexpected song of thanks (Jonah 2:1–9). Jonah's less-than-certain deliverance from danger makes the thanks unusual. One would expect an individual lament rather than a song of thanks. In spite of its untimeliness, Jonah's song fits the book very well, since Jonah eventually emerges from the fish's belly. The song of thanks in 1 Kings 8:1–66 celebrates the dedication of the temple. Worship expressing praise always accompanied such public occasions. Victory songs offered corporate thanks based on God's deliverance of Israel in battle. Psalm 18 (duplicated in 2 Sam. 22:2–51) opens with the

---

17. The tone of praise common to all songs of thanks indicates the affinity of all songs of thanks with hymns. See page 282 for the contributions of Claus Westermann, *Praise and Lament in the Psalms*. The broader category of hymn or descriptive praise praises God for his personal traits and the smaller category of thanksgiving or declarative praise praises God for specific favors to the worshiper.

words: "David spoke to the LORD the words of this song on the day when the LORD delivered him from the hand of all his enemies, and from the hand of Saul." Similar songs appear with similar indications of contexts in Judges 5:1–31 (the Song of Deborah) and Exodus 15:1–18 (the Song of the Sea). The account of Jehoshaphat's victory song sung before his battle with the Ammonites (2 Chron. 20:13–18) indicates that such songs were used before battle to encourage troops by celebration of a sure victory.

Royal Psalms

The victory song of Jehoshaphat along with many other related psalms falls under the rubric of royal psalms. This genre, as well as the genre of wisdom psalms in later discussion, serves as a broader thematic grouping. The psalms named royal psalms typically exhibit the characteristics of other genres (laments, hymn, songs of thanks). They also provide clues of some direct tie to the monarchy. The two examples above (2 Sam. 22:2–51/Ps. 18 and 2 Chron. 20:13–18) comprise victory songs. Others incorporate the features of the lament (Ps. 144:1–15) and hymns (Ps. 45:1–17). The royal settings for these psalms most often relate to requests for victory in battle and dominance over other kingdoms. Some of these psalms seem connected with the coronation ceremony (especially Pss. 2; 110). Psalm 45 appears designed for a royal wedding. All the royal psalms show a common interest in the connection of the king's authority to Yahweh. The king regularly receives the title, Yahweh's "anointed."[18] The king acts in Yahweh's stead, or, more directly, Yahweh works in the person of his regent. Consequently, much of the dignified description normally reserved for Yahweh applies to the king in these psalms.

The temple offers the most likely setting for kingship psalms. In this context, the king assumed authority as Yahweh's agent, providing mercy and deliverance for his people. Mowinckel connected the royal psalms to an annual enthronement festival in which Israel ceremonially reinstalled Yahweh (and so, his king) as king of Israel.[19] This coronation ritual paralleled Mesopotamian kingship ideas to some degree. Psalm 47 possibly incorporates some of its specifics. The reenthronement occurred during the feast of booths. Although Mowinckel stretched the evidence in his depiction of the ceremony, his idea finds wide acceptance among Psalms scholars. With or without this specific ritual, the royal psalms specify some sort of community worship in which the king assumed his role as God's representative to his people.

Wisdom Psalms

The wisdom psalms display a special approach to the human response to God. They emphasize disgression and righteousness in personal lifestyles. Psalm 1 serves as a prologue to the entire Psalter. It contrasts the

---

18. This Hebrew term becomes "Messiah" when transliterated in English.
19. See pages 279, 281 above.

happy estate of the righteous with the instability of the wicked. The central idea expressed in verse 2 guides the discussion: "Their delight is in the law of the LORD, and on his law they meditate day and night." The emphasis on torah (law) as the body of knowledge which enables the righteous to excel leads to the designation of a few wisdom psalms as torah psalms. Psalm 119 presents the strongest example (compare Ps. 19). Wisdom psalms show common interest in the "two ways." Psalm 1 reveals this approach to life very clearly. Psalm 73 addresses philosophical questions and thus presents a unique example of a wisdom psalm. The major philosophical issue is theodicy in relation to the prosperity of the wicked (vv. 10–14). This theme appears commonly in wisdom literature but rarely in the Psalms. More commonly in Psalms, the speaker assumes that God intends to intervene for the righteous. Psalm 73 ends on this note as well.

The life setting of the wisdom psalms presents difficulties. The wisdom psalms convey simple truths at a most basic level. Such ideals proved fundamental to a well-ordered religious community. The psalms seem to originate from private reflection on the religious lifestyle. In their current form and context they likely served as public affirmations of the benefit of faithfulness to torah. Psalm 119 stands as a strong example. The lengthy psalm contains twenty-two stanzas going through the Hebrew alphabet, each line of a stanza beginning with the same Hebrew letter. The attempt at comprehensiveness hints at the importance of meticulous attention to religious duty. The repetition of such a psalm could have a profound effect on the religious development of children and young adults. It also served to solidify the community, reinforcing its commitment to torah, not unlike the Shema (Deut. 6:4–9). Rather than a connection with some specific festival, such a basic document calls for regular repeated rehearsals. All the wisdom psalms give the same indication.

The review of the genres cannot do justice to the variety of the Psalms. Other genres and subgenres include narrative psalms (78), songs of trust (23), songs of Zion (84), and songs of ascent (122). Still the categories above account for the majority of the Psalms as will appear clearly in the following discussion. The following list assigns each psalm to a form-critical category and notes unique features and the relationships to surrounding psalms (if any).

Characteristics of Individual Psalms

Form-critical observations help us understand the purpose and structure of individual psalms. By adding thematic observations, we can briefly characterize each of the canon's 150 Psalms.

Psalm 1, a wisdom psalm, depicts the righteous as trees and the wicked as chaff—one of the more colorful contrasts in Psalms.

Psalm 2 is a royal psalm with probable association with a coronation ceremony. It presents the futility of challenges against Yahweh's "anointed." Reasons for reading Psalms 1 and 2 as a single unit were noted above.[20]

---

20. See page 360, note 5.

Psalm 3, the Psalter's first lament, is individual in nature, complaining of numerous enemies. The psalmist's placid fearlessness is remarkable (vv. 5–6).

Psalm 4, a personal lament on account of enemies, encourages constant devotion to God in the midst of such trials (vv. 4–5).

Psalm 5, a third lament based on similar complaints, goes beyond a call for constancy. The psalmist calls God himself to action based on his commitment to punish the wicked (enemies) and reward the righteous (psalmist).

Psalm 6 expresses a sick person's complaint. The psalmist's pronounced description of grief emphasizes the distress (vv. 6–7) which erodes the sufferer's religious confidence (vv. 1–3).

Psalm 7, a more formal complaint based on the threat of enemies, repeatedly voices the speaker's innocence (vv. 3–4, 8, 10). Accordingly, deliverance is attributed to God's righteousness (v. 17).

Psalm 8, a hymn emphasizing creation, celebrates the high status God grants humans in the world's scheme. The first line praising God's majesty is repeated in the last line. Psalm 7's closing line vowing to thank God for his righteousness may have led to the placing of the hymn at this juncture.

Psalm 9 combines elements of individual thanksgiving and lament. Yahweh receives praise for already accomplished deliverance and yet is asked to intervene at present as well (vv. 13, 19).

Psalm 10, a corporate lament, carefully depicts the wicked while showing a striking interest in God as deliverer of the helpless (vv. 12, 14, 17–18). Psalm 9 shares this preoccupation. These two psalms occur as a single psalm in the Greek translation. Together, Psalms 9 and 10 form an acrostic.

Psalm 11, a song of trust, describes the worshiper's security in the temple and the refusal to forsake it in spite of threats.

Psalm 12, a complaint of an individual faced with enemies, contrasts boastful human speech (vv. 2–4) with Yahweh's trustworthy speech (promises, v. 6).

Psalm 13, an individual lament, focuses on God's absence in the face of enemy domination. It stresses the psalmist's trust in God's love.

Psalm 14 comprises a corporate lament. It emphasizes the categories of the fool and the wise, lamenting the rarity of wisdom.

Psalm 15, an entrance liturgy, continues wisdom themes from Psalm 14, now emphasizing the demeanor essential for communion with God rather than 14's absence of wisdom. See Psalm 24 below.

Psalm 16, a song of trust in Yahweh, probably had connections with some kind of sacrificial ritual (note the drink offering of v. 4 and the cup in v. 5).

Psalm 17, an individual lament for deliverance from enemies, claims total innocence (vv. 1, 3–5) and requests violence against those planning violence, wanting God to deal with them as they would deal with others.

Psalm 18 begins with the language of lament, but quickly transforms into a song of thanks, more specifically a victory song. The same unit appears in 2 Samuel 22. Yahweh fights like a warrior for the psalmist (vv. 7–15).

Psalm 19 opens with a hymn (vv. 1–6) describing God's power as revealed in creation. This natural revelation yields to the special revelation of the Torah (vv. 7–14) in a Torah hymn.

Psalm 20, a blessing for the king (vv. 1–5), expresses confidence that God will help the king (vv. 6-8), before a concluding prayer for victory or deliverance (v. 9).

Psalm 21 follows 20's prayer for victory with a song of thanks for the king's victory. The king's successful reign is tied closely with divine defeat of his enemies.

Psalm 22, an excellent example of an individual lament, pairs the awful suffering of a sick person with the joy of divine deliverance.

Psalm 23 uses the metaphor of shepherd to dress a song of trust. The psalm ends with the tranformation of the image from sheep to the human subject of God's honor (vv. 5–6).

Psalm 24 combines praise and wisdom in an entrance liturgy used as worshipers process into the temple. (Compare Ps. 15.)Verses 7–10 portray God's entrance into the sanctuary with the repeated phrase, "Lift up your head, O gates and be lifted up, O ancient doors that the King of glory may come in!"

Psalm 25 appears to be a song of trust incorporating the worshiper's request for forgiveness. Closer examination reveals an individual lament. Verse 22 refers to all Israel, leading to a communal reading of the "I." The acrostic psalm holds together thematically without the alphabetic organization.

Psalm 26 contains an individual lament. The speaker boasts of devoted service and righteousness which motivate Yahweh's deliverance.

Psalm 27, an individual lament punctuated by frequent calls for intervention (vv. 7, 9, 11, 12), lays the early accent on the nature of Yahweh's help.

Psalm 28, an individual lament, calls for help and voices thanks for it.

Psalm 29, a nature hymn, picturesquely uses a thunderstorm to attest to God's greatness. Anaphoric lines and repetition appear throughout. (Note the opening, "ascribe to . . ."; the final "the LORD sits . . ." [v. 10] and "the LORD"; and the sevenfold, "the voice of the LORD . . ." [vv. 3–5, 7–9].)

Psalm 30, a thanksgiving song of one recovered from a life-threatening illness, sums up the experience as the turning of mourning into dancing (v. 11).

Psalm 31 begins as a typical lament but incorporates thanks for deliverance. It combines threats of enemies (v. 8) and of personal illness (vv. 9–10).

Psalm 32, containing elements of wisdom and personal lament, appeals to the reader to offer penitence to God. It encourages trust in God rather than self-sufficiency.

Psalm 33, a creation hymn, depicts God's effortless control of the vast world as an encouragement to trust him.

Psalm 34, an acrostic song of individual thanks (vv. 1–10) coupled with a wisdom psalm (vv. 11–22), advises righteous conduct.

Psalm 35, an individual lament displaying unusual preoccupation with God's punishment of enemies, calls on God to intervene. It provides a clear portrait of the types of affliction expected from a lamenter's "enemies."

Psalm 36 unites the descriptions of what the wicked expected in wisdom psalms (vv. 1–4) with descriptions of God's steadfast love (vv. 5–10). The tone changes dramatically at the conclusion with mention of the wicked suspended until the two closing verses.

Psalm 37, combining elements of a song of trust and a wisdom psalm, repeatedly urges the reader to "wait" for God's intervention. Trust centers on God's eventual punishment of the wicked and rescue of the righteous. A four-line "better . . . than" proverb (vv. 16–17) serves a pivotal role in communicating the theme.

Psalm 38, a lament expressing physical complaints of illness, opens by describing suffering in terms of God's wrath and his "arrows." A single set of parallel lines (v. 18) offers the worshiper's repentance. Verses 11–19 concentrate on abuse suffered at the hands of friends and foes.

Psalm 39, a lament without a formal opening, continues the request for mercy, in narrative form: "I said, 'I will guard my ways that I may not sin with my tongue . . .'" This unit emphasizes God's role in the speaker's troubles. Silence proved impossible, leading to what the psalmist apparently considered impious outspokenness (vv. 3–13).

Psalm 40, with elements of thanks and lament, expresses appreciation for God's deliverance, but the nature of the trouble remains unclear. Concern shifts at verse 11 to future help with urgings that God not withhold his deliverance. Verses 1–10 and 11–17 comprise two independent units.

Psalm 41, an unusual lament, begins with an *ʾăshrê* (blessing) formula at home in wisdom materials. It switches from confessional statements of God's protection (vv. 1–3), to report of previous lament (v. 4), to present lament over enemies (vv. 5–9), to petition (v. 10), to confession of trust (vv. 11–12). Perhaps the psalmist expects the reader to characterize the psalmist as one who "consider[s] the poor" and thereby deserves deliverance.

Psalms 42 and 43, a single community lament, has its life setting in a pilgrimage to the temple (43:3–4). A formal refrain (42:5; 42:11; 43:5) unifies the psalm. The worshiper repeatedly encourages self to maintain hope in spite of trouble.

Psalm 44, a community lament after defeat in battle (vv. 10–11), unites narrative description of God's former help (vv. 1–8), narrative of his present rejection of his people (vv. 9–16), and a plea for intervention based on the people's faithfulness (vv. 17–26). The argument that the nation remained loyal to the covenant (v. 17) is most unusual.

Psalm 45, a royal wedding song with hymnic elements, praises the royal bridegroom (vv. 1–7) and advises the bride to offer the king the proper allegiance (vv. 10–12).

Psalm 46, a hymn, emphasizes Jerusalem as God's special city (vv. 4–5). God's "help" (vv. 1–2) is his defeat of military foes (vv. 6–10).

Psalm 47, a hymn, urges the congregation to praise God for choosing Israel and emphasizes God's ascendancy over other nations.

Psalm 48, a hymn, celebrates God's defeat of Israel's enemies, repeatedly mentioning Mount Zion with one reference to the temple (v. 9).

Psalm 49, a wisdom psalm, draws lessons from human mortality, using a proverb (vv. 8–9) to teach that riches cannot buy eternal life. The psalmist is confident personal integrity brings deliverance (vv. 14–15).

Psalm 50, a prophetic psalm, uses divine speech to encourage "a sacrifice of thanksgiving" (vv. 14, 23) rather than animal offerings.

Psalm 51, a personal lament, confesses sin and penitence. The request for forgiveness is global, encompassing all the psalmist's faults (vv. 1–2).

Psalm 52, prophetic instruction, combines invective against the powerful evildoer (vv. 1–7) with personal confession of confidence and vow to praise (vv. 8–9). The comparative ends of doom and favor show a wisdom influence. The psalm ends with thanks for God's goodness.[21]

Psalm 53, a wisdom psalm virtually identical with Psalm 14, uses the divine name "Elohim," while Psalm 14 uses "Yahweh" and has a different reading in verse 5 (compare 14:5–6).

Psalm 54, an individual lament in the face of enemies, promises a thank offering at the time of deliverance (vv. 6–7).

Psalm 55, a lament, sensitively and picturesquely describes betrayal by a friend who did not honor a covenant (vv. 20–21) and urges the strongest punishment for misusing the relationship.

Psalm 56, an individual lament, confesses trust in God for deliverance from numerous foes and vows to give thanks for deliverance.

Psalm 57, a lament seeking mercy from enemies, confidently sings of faith in God's help. The abrupt transition from the enemies' trap (v. 6) to rejoicing (v. 7) reveals the contrasting emotions common to anxiety.

Psalm 58, a community lament, describes the injustice of unnamed "lords" (v. 1) and urges God to deprive them of power to show his justice.

Psalm 59, a lament, characterizes the psalmist's enemies as "howling . . . dogs" abusing people each evening (vv. 6, 14) and leaves no doubt that God will destroy the bloodthirsty enemies.

Psalm 60, a community lament following defeat in battle, urges God to intervene. It depicts the defeat as an earthquake (v. 2), attributing it to God's momentary rejection (v. 10).

Psalm 61, a royal lament, arose on occasion of fear or lack of confidence. It requested divine favor and thanked God for his election and help.

---

21. See Gerstenberger, *Psalms*, FOTL 14:215–18 on the complex structure, setting, and purpose of this psalm.

Psalm 62, an individual lament with didactic tone, encourages trust in God alone. False hopes in violence and wealth contrast to this.

Psalm 63, an individual lament over enemies intending to kill the psalmist, exudes an unusually hopeful tenor with more praise than complaint.

Psalm 64, a lament, proclaims that God's arrow (v. 7) will find those who persecute the psalmist and hope to hide from retribution.

Psalm 65, a lavish hymn of community thanksgiving for a bountiful harvest, mentions God's forgiveness, deliverance, creation (vv. 3–8), and providence (vv. 9–13). The thanksgiving motif appears in the promise to perform vows and in the mention of answered prayer (vv. 1–2).

Psalm 66, a song of thanks, connects personal deliverance to God's deeds in Israel's history (vv. 5–6) where testing preceded the awarding of land (vv. 10–12).

Psalm 67, a hymn wih elements of the song of thanks, praises the God of harvest (v. 6).

Psalm 68, an ancient communal liturgy with a hymnic tone, fosters intense nationalism by praising God for establishing and maintaining Israel. Its performance included a procession of tribal leaders (vv. 26–27).

Psalm 69, the most extreme and emotional lament, deals with personal humiliation but turns to thanksgiving in verses 30–36.

Psalm 70, the personal lament of one facing death from enemies, reveals the criticial emergency by its brief urgent appeal.

Psalm 71, a lament, uses God's constant protection in the past as leverage for present deliverance (vv. 17–18). It concludes with profuse promise of praise (vv. 22–24).

Psalm 72, a royal blessing, includes pronouncements of justice, long life, and prosperity and easily assumes a messianic interpretation.

Psalm 73, a classic wisdom psalm, emphasizes the fates of righteous and wicked. Depression at the impunity of the wicked gives way to recognition of their imminent end.

Psalm 74, a community lament over the destruction of the temple, still maintains trust in God based on his power in creation (vv. 12–17) and appeals to God to act against the scoffers.

Psalm 75, a liturgy, uses the image of a foaming cup of wine (v. 8) to promise God's ultimate judgment on the wicked. The people's thanks introduces God's own statement regarding the fate of his adversaries.

Psalm 76, a song of Zion, praises God for deliverance in battle. The psalm begins with praise originating in Judah and Israel and closes with recognition that all nations fear him.

Psalm 77, a lament, meditates on God's rejection (vv. 3–9) and then on God's greatness in the Red Sea crossing and other Exodus images to assure the sufferer that God can intervene.

Psalm 78, a wisdom psalm, concentrates on the rebellion in the wilderness to recount the Northern Kingdom's sins and God's choice of David and Judah (vv. 67–70).

Psalm 79, a lament of a community controlled by a foreign power, urges God to act to silence the taunts and blasphemy of the conquerors.

Psalm 80, a community lament, pictures Israel as God's vine, contrasting its former lushness to its latter state as fodder for wild boars (v. 13) and fuel for fire (v. 16). The psalmist requests restoration for God's choice vine (vv. 14–17).

Psalm 81, a prophetic psalm, opens with a call to joyous celebration at a harvest festival, but concentrates on Israel's rebellion, especially worship of other gods (v. 9), that has impeded God's plans for blessing.

Psalm 82, a prophetic psalm explaining life's injustice as the work of lesser divine beings, pictures Yahweh berating the Divine Council (other heavenly beings) for preferring the wicked. Their unjust administration leads him to promise they will die like mortals (v. 6).

Psalm 83, an unusual community lament with no mention of sorrow, concentrates on punishment God should enact against those who attempt to wipe out his people.

Psalm 84, a hymnic song of Zion expressing intense desire to visit the temple, rejoices in memory of experiences of God in the temple and celebrates the happiness of those who trust in God.

Psalm 85, a community lament requesting God's mercy and restoration following his judgment, majors on the love and faithfulness of the restored community and their desire for a good harvest.

Psalm 86, a lament in persecution (v. 14), offers a broad range of complaint, praise, trust, and thanks.

Psalm 87, a song of Zion, praises Zion (Jerusalem) as the hometown of persons scattered throughout the world. A single line (and variations) recurs: "This one was born there."

Psalm 88, a lament lacking any expression of confidence, presents an individual sufferer already in Sheol (that is, experiencing death).

Psalm 89, a royal psalm, opens as a song celebrating God's faithfulness to his people and then turns (vv. 38–51) to a community lament urging God to act according to the best intentions for his people.

Psalm 90, a community lament, concentrates on God's wrath against his people (vv. 5–12), framing the theme with statements regarding his trustworthiness (vv. 1–2) and a call for compassion (vv. 13–17).

Psalm 91, a song of trust like Psalm 23, employs numerous images to illustrate God's care.

Psalm 92, an individual song of thanksgiving abounding with hope, thanks God for deliverance from trouble.

Psalm 93, a brief hymn, uses natural wonders to indicate God's greatness and praise Yahweh as king.

Psalm 94, a community lament, deals with the general social abuses rather than specific foes. It requests God's intervention, but also calls fellow worshipers to unite against the wicked (v. 16).

Psalm 95, a hymn encouraging worship of God as king, ends with an appeal not to rebel as those delivered from Egyptian exile did.

Psalm 96, a hymn portraying God enthroned as ruler of the world, praises God without mentioning his historical acts.

Psalm 97, a hymn, emphasizes God's mystery and transcendence. His power causes Zion to rejoice because he represents the righteous.

Psalm 98, a hymn, presents the creation (sea, floods, and hills) as joining in the praise of God and looks forward to God's righteous rule.

Psalm 99, a hymn to God as king, praises God for his historical work through the priests, Moses, Aaron, and Samuel.

Psalm 100, a hymnic call to worship, invites all the earth to praise God.

Psalm 101, a wisdom psalm emphasizing the righteous and wicked, expresses a leader's commitment to enforce justice.

Psalm 102, an individual lament combined with or functioning as a community lament, uses metaphors to describe the pain of an individual during illness and of Zion's fortunes (vv. 12–28).

Psalm 103, a hymn, concentrates on God's forgiveness and justice to bless God for generic benefits.

Psalm 104, a hymn with a lengthy description of the wonders of creation, praises God's providence that sustains all creatures (vv. 24-30).

Psalm 105, a community thanksgiving recounting God's blessing of the patriarchs and the community of the Exodus, explicates the covenant promise of the land and motivates hearers to remain faithful to God.

Psalm 106, a liturgy functioning as a community lament, recounts Israel's rebellion at each stage of its early history along with God's lenient punishment to ask God to save his exiled people.

Psalm 107, a community thanksgiving, recites a series of circumstances from which God delivered his faithful and then draws a wisdomlike conclusion.

Psalm 108, a prophetic liturgy, combines portions of two laments: 57:7–11 (vv. 1–5) and 60:5–12 (vv. 6–13) to promise victory.

Psalm 109, an individual lament, lists curses which enemies uttered and asks God to bring the curses back on the enemies.

Psalm 110, a royal liturgy, confers on the king authority to rule and serve as priest. Divine election assures the king's success.

Psalm 111, a hymn concluding with a proverb teaching the "fear of the LORD," praises God's acts of justice, creation, and redemption.

Psalm 112, a wisdom psalm, opens with "happy are those who fear the LORD" and portrays the fates of wicked and righteous.

Psalm 113, a hymn, emphasizes God's special deference to the poor and needy as the basis for praise.

Psalm 114, a theophanic hymn featuring the Red Sea crossing, dramatizes God's control of the earth by depicting the sea and the mountains as fleeing like sheep at God's appearance.

Psalm 115, a hymn, shows scant formal organization with its mockery of idols, its appeals to trust in God, and its blessings.

Psalm 116, a classic song of thanksgiving, uniquely features humility and a direct tone.

Psalm 117, the shortest psalm, has the opening and closing verses of a hymn without the normal hynmic body.

Psalm 118, a thanksgiving liturgy sung perhaps upon entry into the temple, looks like a responsive reading. Verses 2–4 mention three groups of respondents—Jews, priests, and converts. It expresses the community's thanks for God's acts of deliverance.

Psalm 119, the longest psalm, is a wisdom meditation on Torah,[22] the acrostic format attracting a variety of formal elements in praise of God's law.

Psalm 120, a lament over verbal abuse suffered in alien territory, shows unusual thematic uniformity, giving constant attention to "speech."

Psalm 121, an individual lament encouraging trust in God to deliver and protect, briefly mentions difficulties (vv. 1–2) before concentrating on God's trustworthiness.

Psalm 122, a Zion song beginning and ending with references to the temple, recounts a pilgrimage to Jerusalem and the worshiper's joy at arriving.

Psalm 123, a rather incomplete individual lament in oppression, requests God's mercy.

Psalm 124, a corporate thanksgiving alluding to the Red Sea crossing, incorporates a direction to the congregation to recite the psalm together ("let Israel now say").

Psalm 125, a Zion song, expresses trust in God who protects Zion and rules from the city with righteousness.

Psalm 126, a community lament, remembers the joy when God helped previously and then pleads for the restored fortunes of Zion.

Psalm 127, a wisdom psalm using three proverbs with no obvious unifying design, discusses what God provides.

Psalm 128, a wisdom psalm based on an ʾăshrê (blessing) saying, attests to God's blessing of those who fear the LORD.

Psalm 129, a community lament over abuse from enemies, contains another appeal for congregational recitation (as in 123).

Psalm 130, a lament, voices the patient confidence of an individual sufferer. God's steadfast love motivates the prayer.

Psalm 131, a song of trust, confesses the worshiper's absence of pride and so preparedness for God's visit.

Psalm 132, a Zion song, contains both an appeal for God's help for the king (vv. 8–10) and reminders of God's choice of Zion.

Psalm 133, a Zion song, celebrates the joy of unity with two images—the anointing oil used on Aaron and the dew on Mount Hermon.

Psalm 134, a hymn, urges God's priests to praise God, expecting God to bless them from his residence on Zion.

Psalm 135, a hymn, invites priests to bless God for his work in Egypt and Israel's early history in Canaan. Depictions of dumb idols (vv. 15–18) provide a contrast to his worthiness of blessing.

---

22. See page 368 above.

Psalm 136, a hymn with a unique structure (the phrase "for his stead-fast love endures forever" recurs in each verse), relates God's work in creation, his deliverance of Israel from Egypt, and his gift of the land.

Psalm 137, a community lament of the exiles in Babylon, requests violent revenge on Israel's captors and encourages memory of Jerusalem.

Psalm 138, a royal thanksgiving for deliverance, presents strong contrasts: the king's humility and exaltation, God's highness and regard for the lowly, and the king's safety though he walks amid trouble.

Psalm 139, song of trust transformed into a personal lament by verses 19–24, expresses a worshiper's awe at God's knowledge and providence and then calls for the destruction of the wicked.

Psalm 140, a personal lament, pleads for God's protection from violent enemies. Statements of confidence in God alternate with statements describing the enemies' cruel abuse.

Psalm 141, a lament, appeals to God to prevent the speaker from falling into the hands of enemies and asks that prayer be accepted as incense or sacrifice.

Psalm 142, a lament of a sufferer who has no other friend than God, expresses desperation in face of tormentors in simple, honest terms.

Psalm 143, a lament of one fleeing from enemies by fleeing to God (v. 9), voices the fear that God may hide from the psalmist (v. 7).

Psalm 144, a lament with only limited pleas for help, blesses God for his warfare for the psalmist and also blesses God's people (vv. 12–14).

Psalm 145, a hymn emphasizing God's kindness and the divine "name," praises God's goodness. His mercy extends beyond the righteous person or the Israelite to all persons.

Psalm 146, a hymn, encourages trust in God rather than humans. His mercy toward the needy supports his reliability.

Psalm 147, a hymn, lists numerous activities of God which make him worthy of praise. Some of these depend on creation (vv. 4–9), and some stem from his activity in behalf of Israel (vv. 12–14).

Psalm 148, a hymn, calls on the natural elements to join in praise of God.

Psalm 149, a hymn, contains nationally-oriented praise. Israel sings expecting God's victory, vengeance, and judgment.

Psalm 150, a hymn with little else but calls to praise, contains four sections: (1) the place for praise (v. 1); (2) the reason for praise (v. 2); (3) the instruments of praise (vv. 3–5); and (4) the offerers of praise (v. 6). It exemplifies the disinterested praise common to the genre.

The Canonical Context of the Psalms

The Psalms assume primary significance as the determinative category for biblical poetry. Four major factors contribute to the Psalms' central role in this regard. First, the massive size of the collection adds to its influence. Second, the placement of the collection in biblical texts alters its impact.

Third, both general readers as well as historians recognize that the Psalms assumed a key function in the worship and faith of Israel. Fourth, the Psalms have assumed a predominant position in the liturgical and devotional activities of the current worshiping community.

The size and location of the Psalms in the canon exercises a strong influence on their acceptance, giving the reader the impression of an unlimited supply of forms. The steady repetition of key phrases enforces the significance and effect of the sacred words and provides repeated evidences of Israel's sometimes wavering commitment and Yahweh's unwavering willingness to deliver. The sheer number of the psalms makes it possible to learn much about Israel's special devotion to God from their contents.

The placement of the Psalms reflects and enforces the preferential attitude toward the collection. Placement varies in two major printed editions (the Greek and the Hebrew Bible). In the Septuagint, whose order is followed by English translations, the Psalms appear in the center of the entire bilbical collection, Old and New Testaments. Whether this has exercised a direct influence or not, it is at least symbolic of the centrality of the Psalms for Christian worship and praxis. To stretch this symbolism further, Psalms also occurs near the center of the number of Old Testament books and in the middle of the so-called poetical books. The lengthy Job precedes it as the first work of the segment, and the shorter books of Proverbs, Ecclesiates, and the Song of Solomon follow it. The Hebrew canon grants the Psalms even more primacy. The book appears as the first work of the third division of the canon, the Writings (Ketubim). As such it follows the prophets and precedes Job. Thus, for the Hebrew canon, the Psalms also exercise some influence over the reading of all the Writings.

The ordering provides evidence of the cultural consensus which made the Psalms the central type of literature in Israel's worship. As expressions of praise, Psalms could be associated with almost any notable event. They expressed celebration and grief, to name only two extremes of their wide application. They were especially employed in temple worship, yet they did not rely on the worship space of the temple. For this reason, Psalms use survived the loss of the temple. These "verbal offerings" assumed even more importance during the hardship of the exile and restoration. These special contexts serve as mere examples of the limitless application of Psalms texts.

In a more literary fashion, the use of Psalms as key texts in today's worship molds the reader's perspective. Their contents encompass practically all the theological themes of the Scriptures. Even in secular circles, writers show a profound influence from the Psalms. As a normative form of poetry, the Psalms continue to exercise influence over much creative literature. The encounters with Psalms, whether directly through Bible readings or indirectly through other literature, leads to their centrality for the recognition of biblical poetry. It is no wonder that our experience of the Psalms prescribes our perception of all biblical poetry. In short, the way we look at the Psalms determines in large measure the way we look at biblical poetry in general.

Summary: The Role of the Psalms in the Community

We showed above[23] that poetry functioned four ways in Israel's life and worship: poetry as *personal confession*, poetry as a *means toward unity and stability* in the community, poetry as a *medium for instruction*, and poetry as a *means to reconstitute reality*. Instead, intervention depended upon the choice of the sovereign, dependable God.[24] As sacred literature the Psalms may be appropriated by the contemporary reader following similar patterns.

Now we relate the Book of Psalms to these categories. Some psalms take on the nature of prayer and relate private thoughts, while others take on the nature of song and relate public attitudes. Private psalms often utilize personal confession. Personal laments contain intimate descriptions of the psalmists' suffering, voicing the sufferers' private fears of pain and death. Such open confession offers therapeutic benefit, as does the occasional confession of sin which appears in various types of psalms.

Personal Confession

The laments provide a format for the expression of "improper" reactions to suffering and struggle. Psalmists, like Job, frequently overstep the limits of propriety based on Israel's standards as well as our own. In the framework of a lament the worshiper can voice strong expressions of God's unfairness or capriciousness. The worshiper does not fear reprisal, since the questionable attitudes remain incidental to the greater purpose of the lament. The lament achieves its purpose by fostering confidence in God's eventual deliverance. Within this context, most negative portrayals of God assume only historical importance, since the psalm concludes with faith. Whether the worshiper intends to describe suffering, to obtain forgiveness, or to release pent-up anger, the psalmist always directs the confessions of the psalms to God.

Community Unity and Stability

The use of psalms to relase detrimental emotions also relates the place of the Psalms in maintaining the unity and stability of the community. The Psalms absorb tensions including: (1) contrasting feelings (in a single person), (2) attitudes and words unacceptable in other contexts, and (3) God's disposition toward his people. The community gained solidarity when

---

23. See pages 217–219.
24. If contemporary lyric poetry contains similar uses of language, it expresses them much more subtly. Assuming that the psychological benefit of music or poetry contains all the basic religious functions ascribed above to Psalms constitutes a reckless claim. Yet certain parallels do exist in the use of language. The high-flying language of hymns approximates the contemporary aesthetic understanding of poetry. Contemporary poetry paints word pictures similar to those in Hebrew hymnic language.

psalms served as acceptable outlets for potentially damaging attitudes. Psalms provided an outlet for the individual's admixture of joy and grief, depression and confidence. They allowed that person to voice the deepest emotions in the strongest terms even when the emotions and their expression were not socially acceptable (for example, the claim in Ps. 44 that God had wrongly punished his obedient people, or the desire to wreak vengeance on innocent babes in Ps. 137). These psalms gave voice to the "deep tension" between Israel's "slave memory" and the reckless optimism of the enthronement psalms.[25] These psalms present a hopefulness out of character with the later history of Israel (700–500 B.C.E.) which collected and produced the Psalms. Yet the tension between the community's dejection and hope for the future finds expression in them.

Aside from the release valve for tension, the Psalms also added to the stability of the community by identifying common foes and suggesting common goals. Common goals relate these two tasks. The identification of the type of behavior acceptable to God differentiated the community of Israel from the wicked or proud. Certain psalms project such negative attitudes onto the Edomites. Yet the tension rather than the unanimity of Psalms appears most prominently. The psalms present widely varied portraits of God, Israel, the ideal community, and the goodness of the world. The extremes run from God as cruel judge to God as loving shepherd; from Israel as holy community to Israel as a collection of rebellious sinners; from the ideal community as a nationalistic consolidation of the nation to the ideal community as a peaceful conglomeration of all peoples; and from the world as the setting for incessant pain to the world as the medium for God's lavish blessing. These perspectives added to the unity and stability of second temple Judaism due to their eclecticism. The Psalms as a whole show eclecticism rather than exclusivism. They tend to promote the broadest range of response to history rather than limiting the worshiper to a narrow band of propriety.

Medium of Instruction

When the Psalms serve as a medium for instruction, traits of both eclecticism and exclusivity become important. The tension between God as avenger and God as the redeemer of Israel remains. Each aspect provides insight into important dimensions of theology. Several characteristics of God receive emphasis. The Psalms depict God as the avenger of the righteous (at times this term offers an equivalent to "Israelite"). Several psalms carefully portray his attitude and action toward Israel in terms of ḥesed (חֶסֶד)—"covenant love." This special characterization of God often sees all of his activity motivated by intense care for his people. The Book of Psalms

---

25. See Walter Brueggemann, *Israel's Praise: Doxology against Idolatry and Ideology* (Philadelphia: Fortress, 1988), 55–56. According to Brueggemann, the enthronement psalms represent a Jerusalem liturgy employed to reinforce the claims of the current priest or king. They presented the Jerusalem temple as the focus of Yahweh's (and thus, the king's) authority.

also teaches about God's acts as *creator* and *elector.* The presentation of God's work in history instills a sense of identity as well as providing theological insight for the individual believer and the community.

The wisdom psalms (the most notable tools for instruction in the Psalter) reveal this same dual identity. Torah psalms such as 1; 19; 119 encourage devotion to God and draw attention to religious duty. The reflection they engender compares to that recommended by the Shema (Deut. 6:4–9). Maintaining a relationship with God and fellow worshipers of God involves constant meditation on the meanings and ramifications of the commitment. The wisdom psalms, including torah psalms and others, concentrate on a single dynamic in this relationship. The wisdom psalms describe this dynamic simply in terms of the "righteous" and the "wicked." To the contemporary ethicist these designations represent a radical over-simplification of complex moral decision making. On the other hand, their usefulness as basic resources for moral instruction appears clearly. All moral responsibility depends on the primary categories, "good" and "bad." This provides a foundation for the more sophisticated reflections urged in the torah psalms.

Reconstituting Reality

In contrast to the earthy concerns of the wisdom psalms, the laments especially express the aim of reconstituting reality. This involves a denial of current negative experiences and a reimagining of the present. Laments base these attitudes on trust in Yahweh's activity in the future. From this perspective, the poetry of the Psalms aims to reconstitute present experience. As ritual documents, the psalms enable hope amid hopelessness and justice amid injustice. A similar phenomenon occurs in the hymns (especially Zion songs) in their anticipation of an era under God's complete control. Such psalms provided opportunity for worshipers whose current experience offered no encouragement to live in the future. They understand the goals of faith as achieved in spite of situations to the contrary in the here and now.

This special philosophy of time occurs when words serve as the medium for faith. The psalms attempt to express transcendent experience with finite communication. This process necessarily either diminishes the grandness of hope in God or stretches the human language. The Hebrew psalmists continually stretch language out of a constant preference for God's sovereignty. Since these poems actually made God present, they also worked as effective agents to bring change in the worshiper's experience. The laments often called God to earth, which makes anything possible. So, this poetry actually changed the face of God, linking its effect directly to his identity. As mentioned, the Psalms did not effect magic.

Questions for Discussion

1. What do you learn from the arrangement and headings of the Psalms?

2. How do form critical categories help you interpret the Psalms?

3. What roles do psalms play in your individual life and in your life as part of a religious community?

Chapter Fifteen

Poetry in the Song of Songs

Introduction to the Song of Songs

The Song of Songs shows an uncertain connection with wisdom literature at best. When considered in connection with poetry, the uncertainty disappears. According to all standards included in this study, the Song definitely contains poetry.[1] According to three important measures (theme, form, and height of expression), it exhibits the most poetic features of any book of the Hebrew Bible. The thematic measure accords with contemporary notions of poetry more than ancient Hebrew notions. Love is the most commonly expected theme for poetry for current readers. The formal measure includes the three elements which identify Hebrew poetry: parallelism, meter, and strophic organization. Most of the parallelism revolves around simple repetition:

> My beloved is to me a bag of myrrh
> that lies between my breasts.
> My beloved is to me a cluster of henna blossoms
> in the vineyard of En-gedi.
> (Song of Songs 1:13–14)

The repetition provides for haunting alliteration. This repetition of sound deepens the significance of the 3 + 3 meter of the two double lines.

The strophic structure of the book evades simplistic classification. The units vary in size and uniformity. They also lack clear transitions from unit to unit in some cases. For this reason interpreters differ widely on the precise beginnings and endings of some sections. For example, verses 1–4 of chapter 3 either continue the previous unit begun in 2:8 or comprise a stro-

---

1. As observed by Roland Murphy, *The Song of Songs* (Minneapolis: Fortress, 1990), 5; the only uncertainty regarding the identification of the Song as poetry relates to the nature of its poetry: Is the Song simply folk poetry or a refined artistic production?

phe of their own. Despite these uncertianties, the Song displays a number of clear units which mark unquestionable strophic organization.

In some ways, the measure of height of expression presents the strongest evidence for poetic identity. The language of the Song stretches communication to its metaphorical limits. Garden imagery provides a series of symbolic descriptions of the individuals' passion as well as their bodies. Some associations remain loose and fluid, such as the repeated reference to gazelles or the references to vineyard and flock. Seemingly, the language sacrifices what we know as historical description for emotional expression. Many of the references use expressions that remain completely unclear. Yet the emotion (longing, devotion, adoration) leaves an indelible impression. In spite of the unclear use of language (perhaps because of it), the passionate tone of the Song carries a strong effect. Such an aim toward influence or persuasion appears basic to poetic discourse. So, by all these measures, the Song definitely conforms to the model of poetry, especially according to modern standards.

The Structure of the Drama

The general description "dramatic poem" best accounts for the literary form. The Song cannot comprise a drama in the proper sense, due to the lack of plot. Other features associated with drama (characters, scenes, settings, action) occur frequently. Without the indications given by a plot and a climax (also lacking in the Song), the identification of the basic theme of the dramatic poem remains tentative. On the basis of vocabulary and the content of images, the sentiment expressed in 8:6 identifies the theme: "Love is strong as death." Emphasis throughout the work is on the exclusive devotion of the couple to one another. Love remains in spite of interference (2:7), separation (5:6), and beating (5:7). Not only does it endure, but its intensity never diminishes. Instead, its depth may actually increase from beginning to end. This tenous development offers the nearest thing to plot, making the drama something of a dramatic illustration of the moral expressed in 8:6.

Identification of Characters

To achieve a deeper understanding of the drama, the first stage involves the separation of characters in the dialogue.

Literary Units

The separation of speakers does not provide the clearest divisions of the literary units.[2] A few poems (or lines) employ speech from two characters.

---

2. Murphy suggested changes and halts in dialogue as the most basic evidence for the divisions of poetic units. On this basis, he identified ten units ranging in size from five verses to units equal to chapters in size. He included dialogues between the two as single units. Murphy's choices are clear and well chosen: 1:2–6; 1:7–2:7; 2:8–17; 3:1–5; 3:6–11; 4:1–5:1; 5:2–6:4; 6:5–12; 7:1–8:4; 8:5–14 (these last verses not an integrated unit). Roland Murphy, "Song of Songs, Book of," ABD, vol. 6 (New York: Doubleday, 1992), 152–53.

Table 16
Speakers in the Song of Songs

1:1	[introduction]
1:2–4	woman
1:5–7	woman
1:8	chorus
1:9–11	man
1:12–14	woman
1:15	man
1:16	woman
1:17	man
2:1	woman
2:2	man
2:3–7	woman
2:8–17	woman
3:1–5	woman
3:6–11	woman
4:1–15	man
4:16	woman
5:1	man
5:2–8	woman
5:9	chorus
5:10–16	woman
6:1	chorus
6:2–3	woman
6:4–10	man
6:11–12	woman
6:13 (Heb. 7:1)	chorus
7:1–9 (Heb. 7:2–10)	man
7:10–8:4 (Heb. 7:11–8:4)	woman
8:5a	chorus
8:5b–7	woman
8:8–10	woman
8:11–13	man
8:14	woman[a]

a. These divisions are based on those of the Revised English Bible. Departures from REB designations present this author's view.

More often, a single speaker utters two or more distinct poems in succession. The following presentation of the units of the Song identifies the poetic units on the basis of theme rather than the presumed speaker.

Table 17
Thematic or Formal Units in the Song of Songs

1:2–4	love
1:5–8	pastoral images
1:9–17	royal luxury
2:1–7	pastoral images
2:8–17	pastoral images
3:1–5	night/sleep
3:6–11	royal references
4:1–5:1	pastoral/garden imagery
5:2–8	report of events (linked to 5:9–6:3 by question in 5:9)
5:9–6:3	questions (5:9; 6:1)
6:4–10	pastoral images (linked to 5:9–6:3 by question in 6:10
6:11–13 (Heb. 6:11–7:1)	pastoral images, "looking"
7:1–9 (Heb. 7:2–10)	pastoral images, beauty
7:10–8:4 (Heb. 7:11–8:4)	pastoral images
8:5	(isolated question)
8:6–7	strength of love
8:8–10	breasts/building imagery
8:11–12	vineyard/Solomon
8:13	(isolated statement)
8:14	(isolated statement)

A review of the larger units provides a sense of both their random order and their surprising similiarities. The opening profession of love (1:2–4) sets the stage for the book. The general tone fits the remainder of the book, yet the specific statements reveal a special setting. The pronouns "him" and "you" presumably refer to Solomon (the "king" mentioned in v. 4). These words issue from a new member of the king's harem. Her joy at inclusion among the women results in the profession of love. Her extreme devotion calls forth images related to all five senses (taste—wine; touch—kisses and "drawing"; smell—perfume and anointing oils; sight—chambers; and sound—"extolling love").

Following this first mention of love, the autobiographical statement (1:5–7) shows little relation to the passage. The scene changes from the palace to pastoral images of vineyard and flock. Some interpreters connected the two units by supposing the second passage describes the humble origins of an Egyptian wife.[3] The description itself relates her dark skin (vv. 5–6) to her work in family vineyards. This dark-skinned woman expresses her longing to openly associate with a neighboring shepherd she admires (v. 7). She states concerns for her complexion to her peers ("daughters of Jerusalem"), but this concern certainly implies insecurity about the reaction of the man she admires. The descriptions of her beauty (v. 5) interpret her dark skin as a unique part of her distinct attractiveness. Within this unit, the expression "my own vineyard I have not kept," offers the most compelling statement, involving some sort of self-neglect. In addition to physical appearance, this neglect likely relates to the suppression of her love for the shepherd and perhaps to her discovery of her sexual nature. In the course of the Song, the sexual identity of the male and female assumes primary importance. Images of the "vineyard" help develop the theme of sexual awareness. Other references to vineyard offer similar connotations of sexual love and intimacy (2:15; 8:12).

The biographical statement of Song of Songs 1:5–7 ends with the woman's question, "Where [do] you pasture your flock?" Verse 8 offers an answer to this search for a place of liaison: "If you do not know . . . follow . . . the flock." The encouragement to seek her beloved seems unusual in a culture that sheltered the woman and gave males the prerogative to initiate relationships. The male head of the clan typically arranged marriage. Prior to such an arrangement, daughters avoided contact with adult males. Perhaps the suggested place of meeting indicates love's vineyard or pasture rather than a physical location. In this case, the encouragement urges the woman to yield to her impulses and fall under the influence of love. Other brief statements by the chorus urge similar actions (5:9; 6:1; 6:13 [Heb. 7:1]; 8:5a). Each of the remaining statements of the chorus includes a question which provides opportunity for male or female to pursue their affection. The following list presents all five of the chorus's parts.

Table 18
Dialogue from the Chorus in the Song of Songs

Chorus	Interpretation
If you do not know, O fairest among women, follow the tracks of the flock, and pasture your kids beside the shepherds' tents. (1:8)	Answers the woman's request to know the place the beloved pastures his flock. Precedes series of interchanges between male and female (1:9–2:2).
What is your beloved more than another beloved, O fairest among women? What is your beloved more than another beloved, that you thus adjure us. (5:9)	Follows woman's request to daughters of Jerusalem to tell beloved she is faint with love, if they find him. Precedes woman's elaboration on superb appearance of man.

3. For example, Theodore of Mopsuestia as cited in Edward M. Gray, *Old Testament Criticism: Its Rise and Progress* (New York: Harper & Brothers, 1923), 43.

Table 18 (Continued)
Dialogue from the Chorus in the Song of Songs

Where has your beloved gone, O fairest among women? Which way has your beloved turned, that we may seek him with you? (6:1)	Follows elaboration on superb appearance of man (5:10–16). A continuation of search begun in 5:8–9. Precedes woman's explanation that he has gone to pasture his flock in the gardens.
Return, return, O Shulammite! Return, return, that we may look upon you. Why should you look upon the Shulammite, as upon a dance between two armies? (6:13 [Heb. 7:1])	(connection with context uncertain)
Who is that coming up from the wilderness, leaning upon her beloved? (8:5a)	Follows request to daughters of Jerusalem not to awaken love until it is ready. Precedes woman's account of awakening man under the apple tree where he was born.

In various ways the chorus recommends the woman's pursuit of her partner and an examination of the relationship of the pair. The chorus' recommendation for the woman to pursue her partner stands as a transition between the opening of the book and the beginning of more typical themes. Actually, the woman's request to know where he pastures his flock ends the preface and gives a first glimpse of the tone of the drama. The lover's praise (1:2–4) does not match the more lavish descriptions to follow. The woman's self-description in 1:5–6 finds a parallel only in 8:8, where the lack of development of the "sister" serves as a similar concern. The seeking and finding which characterize the dialogue begins with 1:7–9. The previous passages form a preface introducing some general concerns of the woman. These concerns form a loose introduction to the intense descriptions of love in following passages.

The woman begins her search for the beloved at the urging of the chorus. Instantly, the male speaks with words of adoration for the female. Though the woman speaks prior to this, the unit includes no physical description of the male. This marks an important distinction between the roles of male and female in the Song. The male's speech involves descriptions of the female's body almost exclusively. [4] The female's speech involves similar descriptions of the male's body only in 1:13–14; and 5:10–16. The thought and speech of the woman develops the storyline much more than the thought and speech of the male. The female's dialogue sets the tone for the encounter by describing settings and voicing the devotion of each for the other. Descriptions of the garden and the sheepfold come from the woman. The man uses such pastoral imagery only in the description of the lover's body (with the exception of 8:11–12). So, while the male concen-

---

4. The descriptions of 2:10–15 seem an exception, but closer examination reveals this unit as indirect speech offered by the female.

trates on the description of the female, the female concentrates on the nature of love itself. This contrast in the roles of the major speakers shows the work's emphasis on the female's perspective. The male plays a more passive role. He adores the woman, but expends few words of dialogue on the subject of love itself.

The Lovers' Descriptions of One Another

The beginning of the male's dialogue (1:9–11) opens the exchange between the lovers. Most of the interchange involves their descriptions of one another. Five special references stand out. He compares her to Pharaoh's horses (1:9). She provides a narrative referring to the king sitting on his couch (1:12). Another reference to the couch they possess introduces a brief description of their house (1:16–17). In 2:1–2 they exchange lines describing the woman as a flower. The five previous place references set the stage for the action. The mentions of settings provide the only clues to the context of this dialogue. The references to Pharaoh and the king imply a royal context. Such references provide support for the view that the woman of the Song comes from Egyptian royalty to become the wife of Solomon. The references to couch and house suggest a domestic setting which seems unusual for a royal couple (compare 1 Kings 7:8). Solomon and his wives lived in the palace rather than independent dwellings. The word translated "house" (bāyit, בַּיִת) could refer to a dwelling within the palace complex, though this constitutes an unusual use of the word.

The closing exchange (2:1–2) opens the following unit (2:1–7). These verses add no evidence to the discussion of setting. They contain simple affirmations of the woman's beauty by both lovers:

Woman: I am a rose [crocus] of Sharon,
        a lily of the valleys.
Man: As a lily among brambles,
        so is my love among maidens.

The woman continues with a corresponding comparison of the male to an apple tree. As the woman's beauty distinguishes her like a crocus among weeds, the man's appeal compares to that of an apple tree in a natural forest. The images operate within the same field of reference. Something valued by persons (crocus and apple tree) compares to something with little or no value (weeds and wild trees). The description says little about the relative value of other men or women, despite the implication of their lack of value. Instead, the description presents the emotional commitment of the lovers. This commitment distinguishes the admired individual. The lack of interest in other males/females reflects the devotion of the couple to each other. To the lovesick, the one loved always appears most lovely. This accords with the superlative title of the book. In the Song of Songs both passion and commitment stretch to the highest levels imaginable. It concerns the most compelling love and involves the most attractive lovers.

Beyond their similarity, the images of lily and apple tree bring out different types of responses. The lily serves as an object of sight. The woman's comparison of the man to an apple tree leads to images of taste. She "tastes" the apples (2:3). He entertains her in the banqueting house (2:4). She asks for raisins and apples (2:5). The following verse (2:6) uses literal language to describe a reclining embrace. The language appears less poetic, but the situation approximates the situation alluded to by the tasting metaphor.

Verse 7 concludes the unit. Its relation to the heady expressions in verses 3–6 remains unclear. What does the woman mean by the request, "Do not awaken love until it is ready"? Several options exist. First, perhaps this primarily warns against external interference. This presents love as a matter reserved for the two individuals. Matchmaking or other encouragements encroach into private territory. Second, emphasis may fall on the phrase "until it is ready" so that one cannot rush or force love. The racing passions of the couple demand extra time to moderate their responses. Third, the reference may simply offer advice to young females (the daughters of Jerusalem) to exercise patience rather than rushing into romantic relationships. The uncontrollable yearnings which the woman experiences lead to her warning that love's pressures are best avoided as long as possible. In spite of the logic of all three possibilities, the second suggestion best fits the poem as a whole. The Song illustrates the ups and downs of the couple's experience. Their passion ebbs and flows at its own pace. The entire book represents an attempt to savor the relationship by taking full account of each encounter. Love assumes a life of its own, as though love acted as the central character of the drama and the players simply responded to its demands. Love follows its own timing. The lovers' proximity and absence become tools which provoke irresistable passions. This romantic understanding of love influences the character of the entire book. Human choice and human will take virtually no role in the destinies of the lovers. They travel on the winds of passion.

The Quest for a Rendezvous

In the following unit (2:8–17) this passion brings the male to the scene. He bounds over the hills like an antelope. He crosses the distance between them swiftly and confidently. He suddenly appears, standing outside and peeking through the window (2:9b). His speech to the woman (quoted by her vv. 10–15) shows no attempt to hide his intentions: "Arise, my love, my fair one, and come away." He invites her to leave the house for a liaison in the countryside (v. 14). He persuades her with the argument that the end of the rainy winter season means spring has arrived. Their meeting place "in the clefts of the rock, in the covert of the cliff" appears a cool, secluded place. There, they can avoid distractions and concentrate on their interest in one another. The mysterious ending of the quotation (2:15) may focus on this need for privacy: "Catch us the foxes, the little foxes, that ruin the vineyards—for our vineyards are in blossom." "Foxes" represent impediments to love (the vineyard) and catching them ends the interference.[5] This supports the previous intent to get away from all others. The couple can then pursue their relationship without hindrance. The general theme of meeting apart from all other concerns occurs repeatedly in the Song.

Verse 17 indicates the meeting took place before dawn. Presumably the shepherd attends to the flock during daylight hours. He remains free to meet with the woman before daylight, perhaps all night. The closing of the unit with the depiction of the man as a leaping antelope parallels the opening (2:8–9). The Hebrew poet employed such repetition, known as inclusio or envelope structure, to mark poetic units. Well-designed poems often began and ended with the same words. For example, Psalm 113 and many similar hymns open and close with statements of praise. The inclusio stresses the importance of the liaison by offering a repeated call to union. This reflects the tendency of young lovers to spend every available moment together.

The following passage (3:1–5) shows the longing of the woman when they remain apart. She rises from bed to find him. After a diligent search through the city, she finds him (3:4). She attaches herself to him and brings him to her mother's room. The woman's perspective involves seeking and finding. In previous lines, the role of the male involved the aggressive provision for a rendezvous. The sense of deprivation belongs to the female alone. She expresses an attitude of being without the one she needs. She closes the unit with another request to the daughters of Jerusalem not to awaken love until it is ready (v. 5).

Solomon's Palanquin

Next, a spectacle is introduced unlike any other passage of the book (3:6–11). The event matches none of the material immediately preceding and following. The narrative describes the passage of the litter of Solomon. The material appears unusual in theme. The previous section describes the female's search for her lover. The following unit presents one of several lists detailing the incomparable form of the female's body. The king's arrival stands out as a historical report placed between a dream sequence (3:1–5) and an expression of devotion (4:1–5:1). Presuming at least a loose narrative sequence, how can this historical event fit into the storyline? Some interpreters would elevate the status of the simple description of the king's visit to make it the controlling historical reference. According to this reading, all the expressions of love contained in the Song are presumed to belong to a royal setting related to this one.[6] Such a view depends upon the

5. Michael Fox, *The Song of Songs and the Ancient Egyptian Love Songs* (Madison: University of Wisconsin Press, 1985) offered three common interpretations of the "foxes": (1) the passage expresses a wish that nothing harm the woman; (2) the passage expresses a wish that nothing damage the lovers' relationship (as above); and (3) the "vineyards" are young women chased by young men (the "foxes"). Fox opted for the third interpretation, p. 114. In *Poetry with a Purpose* (Bloomington: Indiana University Press, 1988), 81, Harold Fisch interpreted the "foxes" as a symbol of "jealousy."

6. For example, Franz Delitzsch, *Commentary on the Song of Solomon and Ecclesiastes*, trans. M. G. Easton (Grand Rapids: Eerdmans, 1950; German original, 1875).

phrase, "On the day of his wedding" in 3:11. When this verse assumes precedence, the entire scene takes on the identity of a wedding procession. It requires only a brief jump in logic to connect this procession to a wedding as the supposed context for the entire book.

From an alternate perspective, perhaps the appearance of Solomon's litter should not be privileged in this way. The above interpretation grants a special authority to the historical language of Song of Songs 3:6–11. In this case, the contemporary priority granted to history may impose a bias which does not reflect the intent of the Song. Special weight in determining context need not be accorded this unit. It could simply serve as another scene in the collage of the Song, conveying strong impressions through simple images. The images of the unit fit within a range of masculine roles which make the male attractive to the female. References and allusions include: (1) wilderness (v. 6), (2) trade (v. 6), (3) warriors (vv. 7–8), (4) craftmanship (vv. 9–10), and (5) dominion (v. 11). Throughout the book, Solomon serves as the embodiment of such masculine roles. He represents the extreme fulfilment of the traits admired by the female voice of the Song. Metaphorically, every woman who admired her husband married a "Solomon" just as every husband who admired his wife married the uniquely beautiful shepherd of 1:5–6. Enthusiasm for the burgeoning relationship which begins with marriage calls for the portrayal of each wedding as a royal wedding. Accordingly, the "arrival" of Solomon heightens the romance associated with every marriage celebrated through the use of the Song. The unit also heightens the experiences of 3:1–5 and 4:1–5:1 by imagining the fulfilment of unresolved love in a wedding of splendid proportions. This alternate view of 3:1–5 depends on the simple exercise of reading 3:1–5 as imagery (like other portions of the Song) rather than history.

Wasfs

The following unit (4:1–5:1) forces no such choice between historical and figurative language. It contains figurative descriptions of the female's body. The Arabic name for these descriptions of the body is *wasf*.[7] The *wasf* describes the beauty of the spouse's (or lover's) body. It typically surveys the subject's appearance from feet to head or head to feet. Verses 1–5 review the appearance of her upper torso involving images listed in the following chart (Table 19).

The images predominantly employ visual imagery, but in 4:10–5:1 the images relate to smell and taste. The order of the entire passage appears sequential. First, the man admires her appearance (4:1–5). Second, he urges her to share a repose with him (4:6–8). Third, the visual images give way to taste and touch as the male imagines the lovers meeting (4:9–15). Fourth, the woman announces her assent to the proposed meeting (4:16). Fifth, the

---

7. Marcia Falk, *The Song of Songs: A New Translation and Interpretation* (HarperSanFrancisco, 1990), 127–35 presents a rather thorough treatment of the descriptions as *wasfs*.

Table 19
Description of the Woman's Body in Song of Songs 4:1–5

verse 1	eyes	doves
verse 1	hair	flock of goats
verse 2	teeth	twins of washed sheep
verse 3	lips	crimson thread
verse 3	cheeks	pomegranate halves
verse 4	neck	tower of David
verse 5	breasts	twin fawns

male, either actually or imaginatively, enjoys her favors (5:1). Sixth, the chorus responds by encouraging the uninhibited pursuit of love (5:1). The sequence conforms to the pattern expected of wedding poetry which symbolically represents the consummation of the couple's relationship.

Such a concept—historical construction of the narrative from 4:10–5:1—cannot account for the following scene. Chapter 5, verses 2–8 presents a dream sequence depicting deprivation rather than consummation. In a dream, the woman heard her lover knocking, but illogically hesitated to open her room to him. When she does open the bedroom door, he has disappeared. As her nightmare continues, she searches for him in the city streets, but her quest for love ends in a beating at the hands of the night watchmen. She ends with a pitiful appeal (5:8) to the daughters of Jerusalem: "I adjure you, O daughters of Jerusalem, if you find my beloved, tell him this: I am faint with love." The fitful sequence reflects all the implausibility, terror, and nondescript longing common to dreams. The complete unit serves as a forceful iteration of the complaint expressed in the final line of verse 8. Her emotional longing robs her of sleep.

The following unit (5:9–6:3) begins (v. 9) with the chorus' response to her request: "What is your beloved more than another beloved, O fairest among women? What is your beloved more than another beloved, that you thus adjure us?" The question appears less serious than formal. It provides the woman an opportunity to describe the one whose absence leaves her sick. Her description shares many features with the similar unit in 4:1–5.

Differences in style show that this description possesses its own identity. It does not provide a masculine copy of images matching those in 4:1–5. First, the description includes more lavish references to gold and jewels. Second, the second line of each description displays an "adding" style which compounds the image. This distinguishes it from chapter 4 in which the

Table 20
Description of the Man's Body in Song of Songs 5:10–15

verse 11	head	gold
verse 11	hair	raven
verse 12	eyes	doves bathed in milk
verse 13	cheeks	beds of spices
verse 13	lips	lilies
verse 14	arms	gold with jewels
verse 14	body	ivory with sapphires
verse 15	legs	alabaster columns
verse 15	feet	gold

second line continues with a more specific description of each image. Third, the list of body parts involves the entire body from head to feet, and the list aims at comprehensiveness rather than careful description. Fourth, in addition to its comprehensiveness, the list in chapter 5 also shows careful metrical measure. Its construction suits a tune with regularly recurring rhythmic patterns, while the song of 4:1-5 demands a loose meter due to its irregular pattern of accents. The brevity and terseness of 5:10–16 in its English translation provide evidence of this. All these differences reveal the nature of 4:1–5 and 5:10–16 as independent units. In spite of differences, similarities show that the two poems are separate examples of the same literary form. The two examples of *wasfs* in Song of Songs 4 and 5 exhibit several common features. Both comprise freestanding poetic units which can be treated within or apart from the surrounding context. Both open with a general description of the loved one's attractiveness. This holds true for the units beginning in 6:4 and 7:6 as well, but not for the *wasf* in 7:1–5, which begins with the description of the woman's feet. Both examples, and all such forms, employ metaphorical images (especially in the form of similes) rather than literal descriptions. Apparently, such units were preexistent forms which the work incorporated into the immediate situations of the Song. Unlike many other portions of the book, the interpreter can easily imagine these *wasfs* as independent units which developed in isolation from surrounding passages.

Following the *wasf* of 5:10–16, the chorus asks another question of the woman. Their request to know the location of the woman's beloved is reminiscent of the search outlined in the dream scene (5:2–8).[8] In this occasion, the question offers a further convenient setting for a speech by the woman (compare 5:9 and response). The unit began in 5:9 concludes with the woman's report of the male's presence in the garden with his flock. Even though the units show independence, this suggests some resolution to the frantic search of the dream. On the other hand, what location is specifically

---

8. This passage also presents a reversal of 1:7–8 in which the woman asks the chorus where to find the man, and the chorus provides directions.

designated? The woman's reply may indicate little more than that her lover resides in "the place of love" (that is, a nondescript pastoral location).

Another *wasf* offered by the man (6:4–10) follows the woman's speech. The technique of inclusio marks the unit. It begins with a description of the woman as "terrible as an army with banners" and concludes with the same phrase. Two emotional comments frame the description of her body. First, arising from the army imagery, the man exclaims (6:5a): "Turn away your eyes from me, for they overwhelm me!" Second, the conclusion attaches several observations regarding her superlative appearance:

> 8 There are sixty queens and eighty concubines,
>   and maidens without number.
> 9 My dove, my perfect one, is the only one,
>   the darling of her mother,
>   flawless to her that bare her.
>   The maidens saw her and called her happy;
>   the queens and concubines also, and they praised her.
> 10 "Who is this that looks forth like the dawn,
>   fair as the moon, bright as the sun,
>   terrible as an army with banners?"

The mention of queens and concubines again suggests a connection with Solomon's court. This passage could indeed celebrate the arrival of a new addition to the king's harem, but one need not read the entire book accordingly. The woman receives the admiration of the other members of the harem, expressed in the closing verse (6:10). The comparison of the woman to sun and moon occurs only here in the Song. Perhaps it relates the woman's ascendancy over her peers, similar to the use of sun, moon, and stars in Joseph's dream (Gen. 37:9–10). There, the heavenly bodies represent the authority of Joseph's father, mother, and brothers whom Joseph will supercede. The king's preference for a single maiden in Song of Songs 6:8–9 would create envy among the other wives, except for their recognition that the new beauty clearly outshines them! If this appears implausible, such a flawed perspective commonly clouds the reason of individuals in love.

The woman resumes her search for the male in verses 11–12. She walked to the orchard to look at the blooms and check on the growth of the garden (v. 11). Verses 2 and 3 alert the reader that the male himself also visits the garden. Again, the "blooms" and "buds" seem to refer to awakening love rather than literal gardens. While she "checks the fruit," the male appears and places her beside him in his chariot (v. 12).[9] The responding voice of the chorus (6:13; Heb. 7:1) implies the woman (named the "Shulammite" in this verse) has gone. They call for her return in a set of double lines which appear as a sung refrain: "Return, return, O Shulammite!

---

9. The Hebrew of this verse remains uncertain. According to an alternate reading, the male rather than the female speaks in verses 11 and 12. So, in the Revised English Bible, "my fancy set me in a chariot beside my prince." NRSV reads instead, "She made me a prince chosen from myriads of my people."

Return, return, that we may look upon you. Why should you look upon the Shulammite, as upon a dance before two armies?" In spite of the obscurity of the last half line, the general context shows the obvious intent of the passage. It concentrates on the woman as a subject for admiration. In this way, the refrain echoes the *wasfs* of 6:4–10 and combines the counterposed themes of description of the one loved and unfulfilled longing. When the appearance of one so desired shows such careful detail, the reader assumes a meeting between the couple. On the contrary, the two meet only briefly at irregular intervals so that their drive for togetherness remains unsatisfied. This implies that such physical descriptions as verses 4–7 occur while one of the pair imagines the presence of the other. At times of separation the physical characteristics of the other come distinctly into focus. Such a reading of the book arises from the attempt to reconcile themes of seeking and possession. While not explicitly presented in the course of the Song, extended sections which begin and end with seeking (like chap. 6) encourage the reader to interpret the absence and presence (in the descriptions) of the lovers as a metaphor for the craving and fulfilment involved in romance.

When the reader considers 7:1–9 (Heb. 7:2–10) a continuation of the previous passage, the description of the woman comes during her absence. The interpreter should not press this metaphorical interpretation, because these descriptions refer to the one described as if she were present ("you"). In all the *wasfs* and similar material, the male addresses the woman in second person speech—"you." The female always speaks of the male in the third person ("he") as though speaking to companions. From such a perspective, the *wasfs* become instruments for praise intended to convince the subject of the speaker's love or bolster the listener's confidence in her allure. Such an interpretation introduces the possiblity that such lavish praise involved manipulation. Whether offered by male or female, the flattery could represent an attempt to seduce the other. This does not necessarily involve wicked intent, nor would it necessarily express an overtly sexual desire. Instead, its encouragement urges the one loved to yield to mutual desire rather than be intimidated by it.

The content of 7:1–5 (Heb. 7:2–6) offers three distinct features. First, it catalogues the woman's beauty by progressing step by step from feet to head. The list includes feet, thighs, navel, belly, breasts, neck, eyes, nose, head, and hair. Second, the section begins and ends with allusions to royalty ("queenly maiden" in v. 1 and "a king is held captive in the tresses" in v. 5). Third, the list involves a progression of images as well. The size and type of metaphor used shows increased scale and grandeur proceeding from beginning to end.

The description begins without a metaphor ("graceful") and ends with a similarly nondescript reference to her hair as purple (rich?). Between these, a logical development exists from jewelry, to agricultural/pastoral images (wine; fawns), to images of building construction, and finally to the legendary beauty of the fields of (and perhaps the view from) Mount Carmel. Succeeding images tend to be larger and more spectacular.

Table 21
Description of the Woman in Song of Songs 7:1–5

verse 1	feet	[graceful in sandals]
verse 1	thighs	jewelry
verse 2	navel	bowl of mixed wine
verse 2	belly	heap of wheat
verse 3	breasts	twin fawns
verse 4	neck	ivory tower
verse 4	eyes	pools in Heshbon (a reservoir?)
verse 4	nose	tower of Lebanon
verse 5	head	Carmel
verse 5	hair	purple [fabric]

The following verses (7:6–9; Heb. 7:7–10) attach themselves to the *wasf.* The metaphors concentrate on the male's enjoyment of the female's body. Palm tree, grape vine, apples, and wine represent the taste, touch, and smell of the woman. This description of beauty culminates in the experience of a kiss, involving enigmatic images. The change in language, from passive description (vv. 6–8) to direct sensory experience (v. 9), may account for the semantic difficulties involved in the translation of verse 9 (Heb. 7:10). "And your palate like good wine which goes down for my beloved smoothly, Flowing over the lips of those who fall asleep." The NRSV adjustment makes this literal translation more understandable: "And your kisses like the best wine that goes down smoothly, gliding over lips and teeth." No matter what the precise form of the verse, it describes a more intimate physical encounter than previous verses. It serves as the climax and ending of the unit.

The following section (7:10–8:4; Heb. 7:11–8:4) includes another visit to the garden (compare 5:1; 6:11–12). Perhaps the controlling metaphor appears in 4:12–15, where the woman herself becomes the garden. The pastoral locations provide opportunity for intimate encounters, so that in some respects, the garden represents love itself. Amid the blossoms of the grapes and pomegranates, the female promises, "I will give you my love" (7:12). The mention of mandrakes in the following verse reinforces the sensual overtones of the offer. Mandrake roots were valued for their supposed properties to induce fertility.[10] This faint allusion to pregnancy and childbearing leads to the references to mother, brother, and nursing child in 8:1. Such references could lead the contemporary reader to a mistaken perception of incest: The description of lover as "brother" involves maternal and filial connotations, rather than sexual connotations. The first line of 5:1 indicates that the Hebrews used the term "sister" to apply to fiancé or spouse. In 8:1–2, the woman wishes for the same sort of relationship—an affection tran-

---

10. Rachel's efforts to obtain the mandrakes found by Esau in Genesis 30:14–16 involve an attempt to end her barrenness.

scending sexual interest. The desire for a brother-sister relationship also appears something of a ruse. It would offer opportunity for them to express their affection in embraces (8:3). Still, no explicit sexual references occur, and the woman's intent seems symbolic rather than literal. Mainly, she wishes they could express their interest in one another without stigma or impediment. The request not to stir up love until it is ready (v. 4) mediates the strong emotions invoked by the idea of their presence in the same household. The woman makes the same request in 2:7; 3:5; and 5:8. Especially in the context of 7:10–8:4, the command occurs at the point that her fantasies approach impropriety. Part of the attraction of love unexperienced arises from excitement based on the danger involved. She needs no matchmaker or other forms of encouragement. Instead, she remains content to allow love to take its own course, growing naturally.

Possible Resolution: Song of Songs 8:5–14

The remainder of the Song (8:5–14) possesses no sequential scheme or single unifying theme. In 5a the chorus observes: "Who is that coming up from the wilderness, leaning upon her beloved?" The question implies a loose resolution of the themes of the book. In previous observations, the chorus noted the appearance or absence of the lovers. Here, both male and female walk together. Perhaps the couple realized their goal of meeting without interference. The depiction of a leisurely stroll involves less pressure and longing than appear elsewhere. In subsequent verses, only verse 14 indicates the lovers' separation. In fact, the warning regarding awakening love (v. 4) finds some fulfillment in 5b: "Under the apple tree I awakened you. There your mother was in labor with you; there she who bore you was in labor." Several themes of this chapter unite loosely in the content of this verse. First, the lovers achieve the rendezvous wished for in 8:1–3. Second, love awakens in answer to verse 4. Third, the mention of mother and birth apply to the male's family as well as the female's (8:1–2).

The familial themes presented in 8:5b again (as in 8:2–3) introduce an emphasis upon a more passionate love. In verses 6–7, however, the force of love serves as an issue for objective reflection. Previously, love controlled the actors' emotions and found expression in terms of their desire for one another. Following the first double line of verse six, the comments describe the nature of love itself. The descriptions match the tempest of emotions expressed by the couple (especially the woman) throughout the book. The attachment of the woman to the man (the seal on his arm/heart) calls forth the strongest of images—death, fire, flood, and wealth.

> 6 Set me as a seal upon your heart,
>   as a seal upon your arm;
>   for love is strong as death,
>   passion fierce as the grave.
>   Its flashes are flashes of fire,
>   a raging flame.

7   Many waters cannot quench love,
        neither can floods drown it.
    If one offered for love
        all the wealth of his house,
        it would be utterly scorned.

These descriptions capture the tone of the Song but cannot fully account for subtle content of all its meticulous scenes. We can affirm the book's emphasis on the strength of love. It also concerns the personal effects of love on one controlled by its drives. Admittedly, reading the fire, and so forth of verses 6 and 7 as images of the turmoil love brings offers the same result. Still, the book shows a more complex structure than any simple summary of theme can present. In spite of its strong images, this objective description of love remains too one-dimensional to account for the multiple perspectives, scenes, and emotions of the Song.

Verses 8–10 bear a negative relation to 6–7. They express the plight of one too immature to enjoy love. Some scholars read the first-person statement of verse 10 as the reply of the younger sister herself, presumed to be the narrator's voice (the female) throughout the Song. This author prefers to consider the speaker of verse 10 as one of the siblings of the little sister. According to this view the speaker of verse 10 narrates the female statements throughout the book, but is not the little sister of verse 8.[11] This passage cannot be related to the other speakers of the text with certainty, since it is so brief and so independent of its context. The siblings of the underdeveloped young woman anticipate her betrothal. In verse 9, references to building a silver battlement and enclosing a door with cedar may indicate her eventual physical development. References to the speaker's breasts as towers lead to this interpretation. The "I" of the passage seems to be the woman of the Song. The elements of contruction employed involve connotations of beauty (silver, cedar) and threat (battlement, tower). Yet the threat of love (the intimidation caused by extreme beauty?) finds its resolution in peace (v. 10) at the close of the unit. In a rather free-flowing narrative the little sister's lack of feminine features leads her siblings to think of her future marriage and development. In turn, the feminine voice of the Song remembers her own attractiveness. Apparently, the successful outcome (peace) of her allure resulted in reassurance regarding the sister's ability to find pleasure in her eventual marriage.

As with other units at the conclusion of the Song, slight connections exist with the previous and subsequent contexts. Verses 11–12 show a loose connection through the theme of devotion to spouse. This brief statement comes from the male. He compares his vineyard to Solomon's. On the literal level, references to Solomon and his keepers show the value and care which Solomon gave to his vineyard. When the precise ideas are applied to

---

11. For an overview of the several views of this unit, see Marvin H. Pope, *Song of Songs: A New Translation with Introduction and Commentary*, AB 7C (New York: Doubleday, 1977), 678–86. Compare Garrett, NAC 14:427–30.

Solomon's harem, they lose their literal signification. We cannot imagine a situation by which Solomon's wives received sponsorship from others. These images of the worth Solomon placed on his wives provide opportunity for the male to illustrate his uncompromising commitment to the female. He has found one woman whom he values so much that he wants only her. His vineyard is his lover/bride whom he admires above any of all other women.

Verses 13 and 14 offer concluding statements by each of the couple. The male speaks first (13) and then the female (14). In conformity with much of the content of the book, each expresses a desire to be with the other. The man wishes to hear her voice. In the course of the Song, the male offers direct speech to the female, inviting her to meet him and share love with him. Perhaps now he awaits her answer to all invitations. The woman likewise imagines her beloved answering her longing by leaping like a gazelle to her side. The invitations appear provocative, but in accord with most of the speech in the book they involve more imagination than description. The couple rarely kiss or engage in other shows of affection. Their words describe these actions, but as yearnings rather than actual behavior.

The Song as Poetry and Wisdom

The contents of the book reveal no convincing connection with wisdom literature. The closest parallels, passages relating to love and marriage in Proverbs 1–9, show a primary interest in warning and instruction. By contrast, the Song of Songs explores the relationship of the two lovers without mentions of propriety or morality. It is difficult to imagine the community associated with Proverbs approving the unstructured love poetry in the Song. The book belongs under the looser designation "poetry," since even in terms of its applicability to everyday life (a basic trait of wisdom) it approaches the subject of love through categories and behaviors not appropriate to wisdom.[12]

Assuming the basic nature of the Song as poetry rather than wisdom does not solve issues regarding the unity of the book. Even the assumption of the description "dramatic poem" leaves uncertainty as to its unity. Is it primarily a single work or a compilation of poems? Two features of the book comprise the problem. First, the Song employs numerous single units with separate origins. The clearest example appears in the similar yet dissimilar *wasf* forms. A single author would not produce several examples of the same type of list, but a collector of such lists would include multiple examples of the form. Second, the author/editor conceived the separate units as a single entity. As it now exists the Song contains a beginning, middle, and end. Considering the work as an anthology runs counter to the develop-

---

12. Roland Murphy presented a brief but significant overview of the wisdom connections of the Song of Songs in *The Tree of Life: An Exploration of Biblical Wisdom Literature*, Anchor Bible Reference Library (New York: Doubleday, 1990), 106–7.

ment and repetition which mark the finished product. Psalms and Lamentations follow an anthological organization distinguished from the Song in terms of clear division into units and unpredictable arrangement. Following the arrangement and development of the Song proves difficult at times, but the points of contact relating the units suggest an ongoing composition. The reader's inability to unite related images and themes into a definite shape arises from the nondescriptive language of the poem rather than its disunity. Communication through such hints and intuitions provide much of the distinct flavor of poetic discourse as distinguished from prose.

Four Possible Genres

The precise character of the poetic whole of the Song evades simple description. In spite of the previous suggestion that the Song assumes the form of a dramatic poem, other options need some investigation. The four following depictions apply especially to the contemporary reader. They provide a means of making sense of the Song's diversity, loose associations, and recurring images. Optional forms include: (1) a dream or dreams, (2) a collage not unlike the organization of a music video, (3) love notes (in a figurative sense), or (4) an elaborate, if loosely organized, royal wedding.

Harold Fisch described the dreamlike quality of the Song.[13] Many previous scholars noted this feature. The presence of dream/sleep sequences in 3:1–5 and 5:2–8 supports this view. The use of nonliteral language in the metaphorical descriptions of the bodies reminds the reader of the supposed symbolism common to dreams. The fantasy-like depiction of the couple's adoration and romance lends further support.

The comparison of the Song to a video collage in many ways provides the most straightforward explanation for its multi-faceted scenes. All the action can be subsumed under the single theme of a couple's devotion for one another. The collation of the many scenes of the Song compel the reader to associate actions with love. These same actions in other contexts carry no connotation of romance. The portraits of garden and pasture assume significance for the topic because they appear in close connection with the numerous affirmations of love. For example, in 5:1 the man comes to his garden, mixes myrrh and spice, eats honey and honeycomb, and drinks milk and wine. The closing line, "Eat, friends, drink, and be drunk with love," encourages an association between his eating and his courtship of the woman. Such associations remain common as in the popular song which relates a man's taste for "bread and butter, toast and jam" with his devotion to his lover. The types of scenes employed in the Song vary widely, yet all presume a similar context in the union of the pair. The term *collage* describes this relationship of units far more accurately than the term *anthology*. Though the themes differ, such collages also appear in prophetic works. There, divergent visions, oracles, and historical actions find commonality in their communication of God's message of love (Hosea),

---

13. *Poetry with a Purpose*, 88–90.

judgment (Amos), or mixed themes (Isaiah and Ezekiel). Similarly, Ecclesiastes shows no formal order, but otherwise unrelated observations find their union in the skeptical perspective of the speaker. Such collages apparently appeared commonly in the love poetry of the ancient Near East.[14]

The independence of the units in the book may suggest separate origins for these units. Like love notes or independently composed odes, their contents suit the mood or intent of the author at the time of their creation. Whether the enactment of the Song was dramatic or liturgical, the individuals' responses to one another on given occasions determine the nature of the individual compositions. We may assume such elaborate praise occurred in select circumstances rather than in public discourse. The "sweet nothings" of intimate discourse present a contemporary equivalent to the lavish commitments and descriptions which comprise the Song's love notes. Presuming the Song belonged to a public ceremony, the open declaration of these words of adoration would have a moving effect on the hearers. Perhaps they were offered to seal the emotional commitment of bride and groom through the open delaration of their passion.

Related to this view, some understood the Song as a royal wedding ceremony.[15] Alternatively, the Song offers the "historical account" of Solomon's marriage to an Egyptian woman. Equal doubt exists for both options. As a royal wedding ceremony, the book lacks the formal structure expected. The wedding would be a free-for-all affair with much emotion but little decorum. A royal wedding probably involved public statements linking the marriage with the prosperity of the kingdom and the office of the king. As a historical account, the Song lacks any definite historical setting. The woman does not speak as the Shulammite (or another single identity) throughout. In spite of mentions of Solomon, he does not act as the central character. The recital of such poetry as part of a wedding (whether royal or not) offers the most logical connection to the wedding context. It remains appropriate to describe the work as "wedding poetry" in spite of uncertainty regarding the precise use of the poetry.

As a written unit the Song retains the character of a dramatic poem, but of course, the preceding suggestions involve far more specific settings. No amount of discussion can exhaust the possiblities. Due to the complex, near chaotic organization of the work and its uncompromising emotional tone, the interpreter can only guess its precise setting in life. This should not devastate the contemporary interpreter, since the ambiguous character of the Song arises from its own language and organization. The document shows a construction that, apart from its unquestionable commitment to human love, belongs to no specific situation. Though it originally possessed a quite precise setting, the work does not mention that setting or reveal it in its narrative.

---

14. See the examples in pages 224–231 of this work and in the work of Michael B. Fox, *The Song of Songs and the Ancient Egyptian Love Songs.*
15. See preceding discussion, 391–392

Rhetorical Questions in the Song

Whatever the original setting of the work, its prominent literary features reveal much about the nature of the existing document. Among the larger structures which add to the Song's effectiveness are: (1) the use of rhetorical questions, (2) the use of images relating to royalty, shepherding, gardens, and construction, (3) the *leitmotifs* (key words or phrases) of sleep and awakening, (4) inclusio, and (5) refrains. The following table lists the rhetorical questions of the Song:

Table 22
Rhetorical Questions in the Song of Songs

1. 1:7	Where do you pasture your flock?	woman
2. 3:3	Have you seen him?	woman
3. 3:6	What is coming? [Solomon's litter]	woman
4. 5:9	What is your beloved more than another?	chorus
5. 6:1	Where has your beloved gone?	chorus
6. 6:10	Who is this? [woman]	man
7. 6:13	Why do you look at the Shulammite?	chorus
8. 8:5	Who is coming? [woman]	chorus
9. 8:8	What shall we do for our sister?	woman

Questions 1, 2, 4, and 5 relate to the location and appearance of the man. Of these, 1, 2, and 5 involve the woman's search for the man. Question 3 concerns the litter of Solomon and presents the only remaining masculine image in the list. Questions 6, 7, and 8 relate to the woman, and all include some reference to her appearance. The same is true for 9, in which the young woman's lack of development causes concern. All of the rhetorical questions share a preoccupation with sight expressed in spectacle (3, 6, 7, 8, and 9) or a request for location (1, 2, and 5) or a request for description (4 and 7). The queries of the chorus present notable encouragements for the pursuit of love (4, 5, 7, and 8). The questions present an accurate overview of the nondescript passions and longings presented in the book, even though they add little or no details to the physical descriptions. The questions, "Where is he?" and "Who is this?" as well as encouragements to describe the uniqueness of the individuals (4 and 7) reveal much of the special tone of the Song.

Metathemes

The uniqueness of the Song relates more closely to the major themes (known as metathemes). Practically all the images presented find affiliation with royal, shepherding, garden, and construction motifs. The royal vocabulary includes the words: pharaoh, queen, Solomon, king, litter, palanquin, sword, war, crown, banqueting house, jewels (of various kinds), and precious metals. Major passages dealing with this set of images include 1:1–4; 1:9–12; 3:7–11; 7:1–5; and 8:11–12. The references typically appear as nondistinct allusions to wealth, sovereignty, or grandeur. They lend seriousness to the text by elevating common love to royal status. They appear literal when referring to the king's appearance, but these contexts do not occur frequently enough to ensure the connection of the Song with a royal wedding or palace setting. Instead, the lavish setting of the palace, the "eligibility" of Solomon, and the legendary beauty of his brides provide images specially suited to the overwhelming passion and devotion of the couple. For him, her beauty compares to the most exotic of Solomon's brides, or the wealth of his jewels, or the structural perfection of his buildings. For her, his exploits and value rival those of the most wealthy and wise king. Her delight at his appearance and her joy in his presence could be no greater, if she were the favorite bride of Solomon himself. This interpretation of the royal vocabulary enables the reader to place these passages in accord with other metathemes which contrast sharply with the nobility of the regal venues.

Shepherd

The portrait of the male as a shepherd presents the strongest contrast. References to shepherding occur in 1:7–8; 2:16; 4:1–2; 6:2–3; and 6:5–6. Reference to gazelles may also relate to shepherding due to associations with rough terrain and desolate regions (2:7–9; 2:17; 3:5; and 8:14). However, only the reference to gazelles in 2:17 occurs in the same context as shepherding images. Images of shepherd and flock appear in a wide range of contexts. In 1:7–8 the woman searches for the man by asking him where he rests his flock at noon. In 2:16 and 6:2–3 she simply asserts that her beloved "pastures his flock among the lilies." The Hebrew word šôšan (שׁוֹשָׁן) probably designates a waterlily (by taxonomy, a type of crocus) indicating a pasture near a water source. Both the reference to water and to the lily carry connotations of love as well, especially since the lily occurs on several occasions in the *wasfs*. Such references serve as nonliteral images of the man's inclination toward romance. Direct references to sheep also serve as descriptive terms in the *wasfs*. In both 4:1–2 and 6:5–6 references to sheep and goats describe the appearance of the woman's hair and teeth.

> How beautiful you are, my love, how very beautiful!
> Your eyes are doves behind your veil.
> Your hair is like a flock of goats, moving down the slopes of Gilead.

Your teeth are like a flock of shorn ewes that have come up from the
   washing,
all of which bear twins, and not one of them is bereaved.
   (4:1–2)
Turn away your eyes from me, for they overwhelm me!
Your hair is like a flock of goats, moving down the slopes of Gilead.
Your teeth are like a flock of ewes, that have come up from the
   washing;
all of them bear twins, and not one of them is bereaved.
   (6:4–5)

The lines containing references to flocks show strong resemblance. The units also share the description of her cheeks as pomegranate halves (4:3; 6:7). The *wasf* devoted to the male (5:10–16) contains no metaphors related to sheep. Looking at the metatheme as a whole, domesticated herding animals symbolize the woman. Masculine images refer to the "shepherd" of such animals or to the gazelle (a wild animal). The stereotypes behind these sets of images relate the passivity, beauty, and dependence of the sheep to the female. Another set of stereotypes relate the isolation, ruggedness, and freedom of the gazelle to the male. The roles of the characters in the drama fit this scheme. The woman appears lost without the male (like sheep with no tender) and the male bounds into and out of the scenes in spite of the female's coaxing (like an untamed animal). A good example occurs in 1:8–15 where the "gazelle" leaps in, appearing as if from nowhere in the woman's window (v. 9).

Garden

The metatheme of the garden unites with shepherding metaphors to comprise the "pastoral" imagery of the Song. In this sense, "pastoral" indicates isolated settings. At times these settings are rural. They always involve plants, animals, or natural features such as rocks and pools. More important than the rural atmosphere, the pastoral scenes set the lovers apart to pursue their affections without any human interference (for example, the insidious foxes which spoil the vineyard, 2:15). Pastoral settings predominate in all love poetry. Recent interpreters such as Northrop Frye[16] and Harold Fisch[17] discussed such themes in connection with the Song and other biblical literature. Garden images, not surprisingly, make up the most common and most striking units of the Song. The table on the following page lists the garden images.

The table illustrates the wide variety of pastoral themes. More than any other set of images, pastoral images serve as the language of love in the Song. Subgroups within this collection of themes include: food, drink, vine-

---

16. Northrop Frye, *The Great Code: The Bible and Literature* (New York: Harcourt Brace Jovanovich, 1982). Frye suggested the garden and the wasteland as one set of competing images common throughout the Hebrew Bible.

17. One chapter in *Poetry with a Purpose* titled "The Song of Moses: Pastoral in Reverse" presents Deuteronomy 32 as an anti-pastoral, linking deprivation to covenant rebellion (pp. 55–79).

Table 23
Garden Images in the Song of Songs

1. 1:2–4	wine
2. 1:5–6	vineyard
3. 1:12–12	fragrances
4. 1:15	doves
5. 2:1–2	flowers
6. 2:3–5	apple tree, raisins
7. 2:10–15	wilderness, flowers, birds, blossoms, fragrances, foxes, vineyard
8. 2:16	flowers
9. 3:6	fragrances
10. 4:1–8	birds, fruit, flowers, wilderness, fragrance, beasts
11. 4:10–5:1	fragrances, food wine, nectar, fruit, spices, water
12. 5:12–13	birds, springs, food, fragrances, flowers
13. 5:15	trees
14. 6:2–3	spices, lilies
15. 6:7	fruit
16. 6:10	sun and moon
17. 6:11	blossoms
18. 7:2–9 (Heb. 7:3–10)	wine, food, flowers, grain, pools, wilderness, tree, fruit, wine
19. 7:11–13 (Heb. 7:12–14)	fields, villages, vineyards, blossoms, fruit, mandrakes
20. 8:2	wine
21. 8:5	wilderness, apple tree
22. 8:11–12	vineyard
23. 8:13	garden
24. 8:14	spices

yard, animals, plants, wilderness, fragrances, spices, water, agricultural products, and wine. The units of the Song mix these groups randomly. The images may appear in passages with several loosely related themes or appear separately as distinct metaphors. Single broad themes relate the images in only a few cases. The example in 7:6–8 compares the woman's body to a palm tree, using two related thoughts: "You are stately as a palm tree, and your breasts are like its clusters. I say I will climb the palm tree and lay hold of its branches." Elsewhere, consecutive verses describe the woman under a loosely constructed garden metaphor (4:12–15).

Other units present a riot of pastoral images like those in 2:10–15. The scene shifts from bounding gazelle, to visiting lover, to a wilderness rendezvous incorporating references to flowers, birds, figs, and blooms. It concludes with the enigmatic mention of the foxes which spoil the vineyard. While this unit shows a greater diversity than most, its radical shifts and compilation of varied images illustrates the type of structure characteristic of most passages. Successive images simply add description to description. The relation of the images to the subject described (that is, the male or the female) provides the only unity. The descriptions of 4:10–11 reveal an organization based on the interlacing of taste and smell. The larger unit (4:10–5:1) within which these verses fit comprises the most extensive use of garden imagery in a single section. The comparison of the woman to a garden presents a broad image which can unite all the pastoral images relating to the woman. With a few exceptions, every description of the woman belongs to the larger theme of the woman as garden or vineyard. Pastoral imagery related to the man tends to reflect shepherding, but shows less consistency than feminine imagery when viewed in light of a single theme. An overview of the sets of images used in the *wasfs* and similar material reveal thematic trends.

Table 24
Thematic Subgroups in the Wasfs of the Song of Songs

1:9–10	royal jewels, horses
1:13–14	fragrance, plants
1:15	birds
4:1–7	birds, sheep, fruit, construction, fragrance
4:11–15	food, fragrance, fruit, spices, water
5:10–16	precious metal, birds, water, food, spices, flowers, jewels, construction, plants
6:4–7	army, goats, fruit
7:1–9	jewels, agricultural products, deer, construction, water, flowers

Wasfs

Apart from the preference for garden images, the *wasf* combines all available images in the most elaborate description possible. Apparently, poets intentionally gave them their loose order. The entire book resembles the *wasf* in that various diverse metaphors combine without a sequential structure.

This loose organization applies especially to the building and construction images of the Song. They occur in 1:17; 3:9–10; 4:4; 5:15; 7:4; and 8:9–10. In 1:17, the house of the lovers serves as the theme. 3:9–10 describes Solomon's litter. In the individual verses 4:4; 5:15; and 7:4 various portions of buildings represent breasts, legs, neck, eyes, and nose in the *wasfs*. The most curious example of construction imagery appears in 8:9–11:

> We have a little sister,
>   and she has no breasts.
> What shall we do for our sister,
>   on the day when she is spoken for?
> If she is a wall,
>   we will build for her a battlement of silver;
> but if she is a door,
>   we will enclose her with boards of cedar.
> I was a wall,
>   and my breasts were like towers.

Fittingly, battlements and paneling adorn the young woman. Similarly, such construction features describe the man and woman in the passages listed at the beginning of this paragraph.

Sleep and Awakening

The themes of sleep and awakening serve as *leitmotifs* rather than metaphors. As such, they provide a good deal of cohesion for the book. Perhaps, as suggested previously, they give the entire book the quality of a series of dreams. Attention to sleep and awakening occurs in seven passages: 2:7, 9–10; 3:1–5; 5:2–7; 8:4, 5. Three of these (2:7; 3:5; and 8:4) are adjurations from the chorus: "I adjure you, O daughters of Jerusalem, by the gazelles or the wild does: do not stir up or awaken love until it is ready" (2:7 and 3:5).

The three statements carry the same content except for the omission of the second line in 8:4. Verses 9–10 of chapter 2 contain an allusion to sleep. The lover peers through the lattice and says, "Arise, my love, my fair one, and come away" (2:10b). The following pastoral scene culminates in their meeting "in the clefts of the rock." This constitutes an awakening scene. As previously mentioned, "awakening" represents the sexual awareness of the couple. The theme occurs both early and late in the book—an indication of its pervasiveness. Following the adjuration of 8:4 comes a mention of the man's awakening the woman: "Under the apple tree I awakened you. There your mother was in labor with you; there she who bore you was in labor" (8:5).

The mention of family and childbirth offers sexual connotations unmistakably set within the wholesome context of home and parents. This single passage contains the only direct reference to the awakening of one of the pair by the other. It provides a union for the couple anticipated in all previous references to their meeting. The testimony to love (8:6–7) and the statement of ownership of the "vineyard" (8:12, probably a reference to the woman) lend weight to the interpretation that the meeting sought throughout the book is achieved here. The concluding comments indicate separation (8:13–14), but in weaker fashion than other indications of frustrated desire.

The sleep scenes in 3:1–4 and 5:2–7 convey the motif of sleep/awakening even more strongly. The units convey much of the passion underlying other scenes of searching and longing. They carry an unusually strong impact, leaving an impression on the reader which influences the response to the book as a whole. In the first sleep scene, she engages in a successful nighttime search for the lover. This seems to mirror the message of the Song: The lovers, though threatened by outside interference and the overwhelming danger of their own emotions, find union. Yet the second sleep scene better reflects the nature of most of the book. Her search ends unsuccessfully. They come close to uniting, but the woman ends up mistreated and deprived of her lover. Her physical abuse at the hands of the sentinels (5:7) emphasizes the sense of deprivation common in most of the Song.

Summary: The Canonical Context of the Song of Songs

The foregoing discussions of the themes and movement in the Song account for its language as "poetry." A more difficult issue remains: What is the place of the expressions of the Song in the biblical canon? The themes which shape the book also present the problem of canonical identity. In terms of poetic form or linguistics the book solidly conforms to usages common in the Hebrew Bible. Nowhere else, however, do we find such free treatment of human love. Consciously or unconciously, readers expend a great deal of energy in attempts to "make room" in the biblical canon for the Song of Songs.

A study of its placement in the two major arrangements of the canon provides no solution to such canonical questions. In the Hebrew canon the Song appears after Ruth and before Ecclesiastes. The Song as much as any writing in the Hebrew scriptures adds to the description of the Writings as miscellaneous or anthological works. Yet its appearance at the relative center of the Writings gives no indication of preference or neglect. Under the influence of the Septuagint, current English editions provide slightly more order. In these texts, all three works attributed to Solomon appear at the conclusion of the so-called poetical books. The three books, Proverbs, Ecclesiastes, and Song of Songs, precede the major prophets. Such an arrangement hints that the attributions to Solomon played a central role in canonical considerations. They also share some association with wisdom, but they are separated from Job by Psalms in the Septuagint order. The three books show little else in common, which highlights the concern for authorship over content.

Authorship provides one avenue to make room for the Song in biblical canon. Solomonic authorship enabled the rabbis at Jamnia to give it official approval. Perhaps the association with Solomon also led to the tendency to read the book allegorically. This has been the most common strategy for dealing with the unique themes of the book. When linked with Solomon, the book assumes an aura of mystery. If authored by such an intellectual, perhaps the book conceals some deeper meanings. It takes on the identity of a vast proverb which says one thing and teaches another.

The combined influence of the book's wisdom associations and its connection with Solomon make space for the Song in the biblical canon. Without these associations, the book is normative in no sense. As a wisdom book, however, the book in fact addresses pragmatic concerns which comprise a major portion of a healthy person's self-consciousness. Companionship and its opposite, isolation, appear so integral to the human condition that the book can account for relationships beyond the level of individuals. So the book speaks to family relationships, friendship, even to the relationship of God to Israel, the church, and the world. All these concerns share an interest in another facet of wisdom integral to the Song of Songs: human experience. No person exists without the feelings related in the Song. No other biblical book accounts for human love in this way. Such a book not only belongs to canon, but its presence among the Writings is inevitable. Its attribution to Solomon appears equally inevitable, since he knew love and other forms of relationship better than any other figure of Hebrew history. The Song of Songs provides a pattern for passion which is both grandiose and recognizable in common experience.

Questions for Discussion

1. Who are the characters in the Song of Songs? Describe their relationship and feelings toward one another.

2. What do you learn from reading Song of Songs? How is this the Word of God to you?

Chapter Sixteen

The Poetry of Lamentations

Introduction to Lamentations

Psalms shows the clearest similarities to the Book of Lamentations. In fact, Lamentations contains five or more psalms, conforming to the patterns followed in the Psalter. Appropriate to the title of the work, the entire book consists of psalms of distress. The Book of Lamentations, like the Torah and Psalms, neatly divides into five units corresponding to the chapter divisions. Within each of the first four chapters, succeeding lines begin with successive letters of the Hebrew alphabet. Chapter 5 does not reflect this pattern, although it contains the number of double lines equaling the number of letters of the Hebrew alphabet—twenty-two. Chapter 3 emphasized the acrostic pattern by beginning three successive double lines with the same letter of the alphabet. In other chapters, each double line corresponds to one verse in English translation. One additional feature distinguishes Lamentations: *All the poems relate in theme to the fall of Jerusalem in 586 B.C.E. and the subsequent Babylonian exile.*

In almost every respect the poetry of Lamentations exhibits the features of psalms of lament.[1] Yet the extremity of its mood far exceeds that of most examples of psalms of lament. Lamentations launches direct accusations toward God for the trouble it describes. This feaure of the lament receives prominence while the hope of deliverance is deemphasized. Such challenges of God resemble the contents of Job's accusations (for example, Job 7:11–21). In structure, the book contains songs of lament. In mood, the work exhibits skepticism or ambivalence regarding God's providence.

Qînâ ("lamentation", קִינָה) describes the six or more units of the work, though the title in the Hebrew text, as usual in the Bible, comes from the first word of the first acrostic poem, *'êkâ* ("how" אֵיכָה). The Greek title

---

1. Heinrich Ewald included Lamentations in his classic *Commentary on the Psalms*, vol. 2, trans. E. Johnson (Edinburgh: Williams and Norgate, 1881; German third ed., 1866), 99–124.

threnoi(θρῆνοι, pl) and Latin *threni* translate the Hebrew *qînâ* to provide the basis for the English title. The Hebrew term refers to a special rhythm, probably associated with a limping dance. Worshipers sang these laments. The regularity of the meter shows the special attention to form expected of musical texts. The *qînâ* meter usually contained three heavy accents in the first half of the line and two heavy accents in the second half of the line. Such laments occur throughout the Hebrew Bible.[2]

Association with Jeremiah

At the death of Josiah, Chronicles records: "Jeremiah also uttered a lament for Josiah, and all the singing men and singing women have spoken of Josiah in their laments to this day. They made these a custom in Israel; they are recorded in the Laments" (2 Chron. 35:25). The occurence of the word *qînâ* in Jeremiah and mention of Jeremiah's laments in 2 Chronicles led to the association with Jeremiah indicated in the traditional title, the Lamentations of Jeremiah. The similarity of laments in Jeremiah to those in Lamentations offers more convincing evidence for the claim of Jeremianic authorship:

> 10 Take up weeping and wailing for the mountains
>   and a lamentation for the pastures of the wilderness,
>   because they are laid waste so that no one passes through,
>   and the lowing of cattle is not heard;
>   both the birds of the air and the animals
>   have fled and are gone.
> 11 I will make Jerusalem a heap of ruins,
>   a lair of jackals;
>   and I will make the towns of Judah a desolation,
>   without inhabitant.)
>
> •   •   •   •   •
>
> 17 Thus says the LORD of hosts:
>   Consider, and call for the mourning women to come;
>   send for the skilled women to come;
> 18 let them quickly raise a dirge over us,
>   so that our eyelids flow with water.
> 19 For a sound of wailing is heard from Zion:
>   "How we are ruined!
>   We are utterly shamed,
>   because we have left the land,
>   because they have cast down our dwellings."
> 20 Hear, O women, the word of the LORD,
>   and let your ears receive the word of his mouth;
>   teach to your daughters a dirge,
>   and each to her neighbor a lament.

2. See Amos 5:2; Ezekiel 19:1–14; Jeremiah 7:29.

21 "Death has come up into our windows,
    it has entered our palaces,
to cut off the children from the streets
    and the young men from the squares."
22 Speak! Thus says the LORD:
"Human corpses shall fall
    like dung upon the open field,
like sheaves behind the reaper,
    and no one shall gather them."
    (Jer. 9)

In spite of similarities, several factors argue against the acceptance of Jeremiah's authorship. First, the laments in Jeremiah 9 forecast disaster rather than responding to it after the fact. Second, the Lamentations show an eyewitness perspective, yet Jeremiah the prophet ended up in Egypt (Jer. 43–44). Third, it is unthinkable that a book such as Lamentations could come from Jeremiah without once mentioning his authorship. This evidence notwithstanding, the attribution of the book to Jeremiah extends to the time of the Septuagint and receives mention in other ancient sources.[3]

Acrostic Structure

Lamentations contains a series of five acrostic psalms of lament. Several features make the series unique. First, Lamentations concentrates on a single disaster—the fall of Jerusalem in 586 B.C.E. along with subsequent hardships. Second, the book views the disaster from at least three perspectives, including complaints from individuals, the community as a whole, and Jerusalem itself. Third, Lamentations shows signs of thematic development from poem to poem. Fourth, the acrostic structure of the units show four variations in type in the five chapters. All these unique features combine to indicate that Lamentations, unlike the Psalms, comprises a single carefully constructed unit.

The acrostic structure presents obvious evidence of the book's careful design. All five of the poems contain a number of lines divisible by twenty-two (the number of letters in the Hebrew alphabet).

Table 25
Acrostic Form in Lamentations

Chapter	No. of Verses	Acrostic Structure
1	66	first letter of first line of triple lines forms acrostic
2	66	first letter of first line of triple lines forms acrostic

---

3. See page 288 of this study along with F. B. Huey, Jr., *Jeremiah, Lamentations*, NAC 16 (Nashville: Broadman Press, 1993), 441–46.

Table 25 (Continued)
Acrostic Form in Lamentations

3	66	first letters of all three triple lines form acrostic
4	44	first letter of first line of double lines forms acrostic
5	22	no acrostic form

The lines of chapters 1 and 2 follow an AXX, BXX pattern. Chapter 3 follows an AAA, BBB pattern. Chapter 4 follows an AX, BX pattern. Chapter 5 can be designated X,X with no acrostic pattern. Of course, English translations indicate none of these patterns. Two features of this acrostic organization reveal a concern for the development of the book as a whole. First, the numbers of lines per chapter decrease from beginning to end. Such a design may mimic the 3 + 2 pattern of *qînâ* rhythm. Second, the acrostic pattern reaches its climax with chapter 3. Chapter 3 possesses three lines in succession beginning with each letter of the Hebrew alphabet. Only chapter 3 exhibits this threefold acrostic structure. This represents the apex of the exiles' complaint. The third chapter deserves special attention for this reason.

The thematic structure of Lamentations complements the acrostic structure in many ways. Chapters 1 and 2 express complaint for Jerusalem. Both chapters are community laments. The personification of the city in 1:16 and 1:19 enables Jerusalem itself to speak of its suffering. Chapter 3 stands out because it contains an individual lament. Only chapter 3 contains the perspective of an individual. Chapter 3 also presents an unusually strong orientation toward God as the initiator of the suffering. Ironically, the same chapter emphasizes the role of enemies in the psalmist's suffering. Chapters 4 and 5 are both community laments. Chapter 4 rehearses the suffering experienced under seige and in exile. Chapter 5 concentrates on the suffering of the exiles.

Types of Units in Lamentations

The preceding brief overview makes Lamentations look much less complex than further study indicates. A view of the types of units the book contains provides a sense of the varieties of combinations employed in the chapters.

Reports of suffering and grief occur in each chapter. The verbal expression of unthinkable suffering seems the general purpose of the work. Inevitably, the worshipers looked for the cause of the trouble in their own conduct. This gives rise to the confessions of sin in laments—these commonly serve as incentives for Yahweh to act in the worshipers' behalf. It is surprising that Lamentations directs so much attention to the fall as a divine operation. From this perspective, the disaster becomes an act of judgment.

Table 26
Types of Units in Lamentations

1. report of suffering and grief	(throughout)
2. corporate confessions of sin	3:40–42
3. account of the fall as a divine operation	2:1–9
4. call for help	1:22; 2:20
5. call for lamentation	2:18–19
6. statement of trust	3:22–39
7. remembrance of better fortunes	4:7
8. imprecations against enemies	4:21–22

Otherwise these acts of God are random and as such, meaningless. As indicated in following discussions, such skepticism does appear in the Book of Lamentations. The book mixes multiple calls for help with this skepticism. These appeals to Yahweh's mercy seem to be at the center of the genre of the lament. The narrator does not direct all speech to Yahweh. An occasional call for lamentation urges the companions of the lamenter(s) to wail with them. This universal summons for additional mourners underscores the depth and pervasiveness of the struggles. In spite of the degree of suffering, sporadic statements of trust in Yahweh appear. Such units commonly appear in both individual and group laments. Remembrances of better fortunes occur rarely as do imprecations against enemies, though both commonly appear in literature of this type. In addition to these eight general genres, a number of briefer, less easily classified units occur. All the various speech types show an integral relationship with the special interest of the book in the fall of Judah, the exile, and associated events.

Sensory Imagery

The sensory imagery of Lamentations, as well, matches its special theme. References to hearing and sound record groans, crys, insults, and taunt songs. By contrast, silence (chap. 3) and whispers appear more prominently than in other books. References to seeing and to eyes occur frequently. Some of these references describe God (1:9, 11; 2:20; 3:50, 59–60; 5:1). The lamenter repeatedly asks God to "look" at the trials of the people. Another use of visual imagery refers to the lack of prophetic visions (2:9, 14). A similar emphasis on deprivation appears in 3:6; 4:14, 17. All three refer to the physical blindness of various exiles. The theme of deprivation reaches its climax when mentions of eating emphasize starvation (2:12; 4:4) and cannibalism (2:20; 4:10). In 2:16 Israel's enemies behave as predators celebrating after devouring the nation. Some of the strongest images of suffering come in the tactile imagery of chapter 4. Ruddy princes suffering from malnutrition have withered miserably (4:7–8). The violence and injustice of priests and prophets brought on the bloodshed of war, which defiled all the people through their contact with blood (4:13–15). The sensory imagery of Lamentations enables the reader indirectly to experience the horrors and ignominy of Israel's defeat.

The Structure of Lamentations

Chapter 1

In some measure, the entire work expresses an intent to lead the reader to experience the horrors and ignominty of Israel's defeat, as a review of the five chapters shows. Chapter 1 begins with mention of Jerusalem's isolation and desolation. The chapter contains elaboration on the city's change in fortunes. Comparisons between the city's previous wealth and honor and its current disgrace magnify the tragedy. Beneath the obvious forms of the lament, a linguistic substructure exists. A simplistic formula presents the contrast between former glory and present shame in a "once . . . now" format.[4] The following table lists the major examples from chapter 1.

Table 27
"Once . . . Now" Formula in Lamentations 1

Once	Now	Verse
full of people	a widow	1
princess	vassal	1
many lovers	no comforter	2
many friends	all enemies	2
festivals	mourning	4
foes	masters	5
majesty	rulers displaced	6
precious things	affliction and wandering	7
pure sanctuary	filled with Gentiles	10
treasures	starving	11
lovers	liars	19

4. The "once . . . now" scheme also appears in 4:1–2 and 5:1–18.

The description begins with a third-person account of the city's fate. Beginning with verse 13, attention turns to God's part in the disaster and his interest in the aftermath. So, what begins as a report of suffering and grief turns into a combined account of (1) the fall as a divine operation and (2) a call for God's help.

Chapter 2

Chapter 2 puts heavy emphasis upon God's role in the destruction (vv. 1–8). The text presents him as the active agent who fought and killed his people, destroying people, dwellings, and temple. With verse 13, attention turns to the city itself addressed as "you." The remainder of the chapter follows this perspective consistently. It recurs several times in verses 13–19 alone. The chapter reaches an emotional climax in verses 18–19:

> Cry aloud to the Lord! O wall of daughter Zion!
> Let tears stream down like a torrent day and night!
> Give yourself no rest, your eyes no respite!
> Arise, cry out in the night, at the beginning of the watches!
> Pour out your heart like water before the presence of the Lord!
> Lift your hands to him for the lives of your children,
> Who faint for hunger at the head of every street.

Through such statements, the inhabitants purge themselves of incomprehensible grief. Verses 20–22 follow by urging God to consider what he has done. Verses 1, 22 mention God's anger, the central concern of this psalm.

Chapter 3

Chapter 3 serves as the formal center of the book. It opens with an individual perspective and consistently portrays the suffering of an individual. The more elaborate acrostic form (three lines rather than one) helps to draw attention to chapter 3. The chapter contains some of the strongest images of the book. Its private perspective provides the deepest pathos of the book as well. The chapter conforms to the traditional laments of the Psalms more closely than other chapters. An individual presents his distress to God and affirms God's salvation. Prior to this conclusion, the psalmist describes his disaster in the harshest terms: God imprisons him (vv. 7–9); preys on him (vv. 10–11); and hunts him (vv. 12–13). In spite of these events the worshiper remembers God's steadfast love (vv. 21–33). A call to repentance follows (vv. 39–40). Yet, God's mercy is delayed as the speaker laments: "We have transgressed and rebelled, and you have not forgiven" (v. 42). God has not yet acted out of his love. Beginning with verse 55, God intervenes on behalf of the sufferer. The lamenter includes God's retribution against their enemies as a part of God's vindication (vv. 59–66).

Lamentations 3 and other portions of the book share with Job concerns regarding God's role in the sufferer's misery. The similarites involve little or no direct borrowing. The language of lament issues a challenge to the deity that, at least for the current reader, stands in marked contrast to expressions of hope. Such challenges occur most often where suffering is most extreme. This feature, like many others in the book, emphasizes the depth of pain. The experiences constituted nothing less than maltreatment at the hands of the deity. Some of the strongest challenges appear below:

1 I am one who has seen affliction
   under the rod of God's wrath;
2 he has driven and brought me
   into darkness without any light;
3 against me alone he turns his hand,
   again and again, all day long.
4 He has made my flesh and skin waste away,
   and broken my bones;
5 he has besieged and enveloped me
   with bitterness and tribulation;
6 he has made me sit in darkness
   like the dead of long ago.

10 He is a bear lying in wait for me,
   a lion in hiding;
11 he led me off my way and tore me to pieces;
   he has made me desolate;
12 he bent his bow and set me
   as a mark for his arrow.

43 You have wrapped yourself with anger and pursued us,
   killing without pity;
44 you have wrapped yourself with a cloud
   so that no prayer can pass through.
45 You have made us filth and rubbish
   among the peoples.

It is not so much the presence of these statements as their prevalence which makes Lamentations a "philosophical" work. By accusing God of levying judgment, the book emphasizes theodicy. Amid the negative passages printed above, confidence in God's mercy represents the ultimate resolution of the matters.

21 But this I call to mind,
   and therefore I have hope:
22 The steadfast love of the LORD never ceases,
   his mercies never come to an end;
23 they are new every morning;
   great is your faithfulness.
24 "The LORD is my portion," says my soul,
   "therefore I will hope in him."
25 The LORD is good to those who wait for him,
   to the soul that seeks him.

The sufferer affirms God's choice to vindicate self and others. According to this statement, the evils seem such because the worshiper remains impatient. Over the longer span of time God confirms his justice.

Chapter 4

Chapter 4 presents a panorama of the suffering the people have endured and do endure. The deprivation belongs both to the initial siege and subsequent years of bare subsistence. Various strong images communicate the bleakness of the situation: (1) valuable metals and jewels are now worthless (v. 1); (2) even children are no longer valuable (v. 2); (3) people allow infants to starve (vv. 3–4); (4) the rich starve (v. 5); (5) the punishment was greater than Sodom's (v. 6); (6) the appearance of nobles has changed from cleanliness and health to filth and emaciation (vv. 7–8); (7) those killed outright were fortunate (v. 9); (8) compassionate women have boiled their own children (v. 10); (9) God's anger allowed overthrow of the city due to the sins of the prophets and priests (vv. 11–13); (10) all his people are defiled with blood and so condemned to exile by God's own action (vv. 14–16); (11) the citizens waited vainly for help and instead watched the attackers fall on them (vv. 17–19); (12) their enemies imprisoned the king who assured their future (v. 20); and (13) the destruction will also eventually extend to Edom (vv. 21–22). Again, the events comprise the direct work of God. As in verses 6, 11, 13, and 16, the closing lines (v. 22) interpret the suffering as punishment from God: "The punishment of your iniquity, O daughter of Zion, is accomplished, he will keep you in exile no longer; but your iniquity, O daughter Edom, he will punish, he will uncover your sins." This conclusion interprets the retribution as thorough and complete, except that Edom will yet receive its due. The realism of this chapter marks it as special. It recounts much of the horrendous experience, consistently presenting it as God's punishment. The chapter contains no mention of mercy or repentance. Instead, it matter-of-factly reports the execution of justice. The announcement of the end of exile above recalls Isaiah 40:2: "Speak tenderly to Jerusalem, and cry to her that she has served her term, that her penalty is paid, that she has received from the Lord's hand double for all her sins." Yet Lamentations 4 falls short of the comfort and hope in Isaiah 40. It offers only bleak announcement of the end of punishment.

Chapter 5

The opening verse of chapter 5 introduces the unit as an appeal to God for mercy. The cry for help serves as a natural conclusion to the four previous chapters. This last chapter leads to the interpretation of the entire book as an extended psalm of lament. As such, it closes with the appeal for help. However, this chapter does not include the expected statement of trust in God. This compounds the accounting of Israel's woes. In this case, the complaints involve current status rather than past suffering. Verses 1–18 all refer to conditions which illustrate Israel's loss of autonomy and reliance on others for its fate: famine, rape, loss of leaders, and slavery. Verses 17–18 closely associate all of these ills with Jerusalem's ruin: "Because of this our hearts are sick, because of these things our eyes have grown dim: because of Mount Zion, which lies desolate; jackals prowl over it." The cry for help in verses 19–22 appears unusually desperate. It admits the possibility that God has spurned his elect forever:

> 19 But you, O LORD, reign forever;
>   your throne endures to all generations.
> 20 Why have you forgotten us completely?
>   Why have you forsaken us these many days?
> 21 Restore us to yourself, O LORD, that we may be restored;
>   renew our days as of old—
> 22 unless you have utterly rejected us,
>   and are angry with us beyond measure.

This rather pitiful plea falls short of the confident trust of most psalms of lament. Rather than urging God to action, it admits defeat. The worshiper expresses complete reliance on God's unpredictable (unexpected?) restoration.

Summary:
Differences and Similarities with the Psalms

In spite of the similarity to psalms of lament in form, the structure and content of Lamentations appear unique. It relays history though poetry in an unfamiliar manner. Historical psalms also convey history in poetic form, but the psalms report victories as well as suffering. Historical psalms tend to present Israel's experience against the backdrop of God's election and ongoing efforts to sustain the nation (for example, Ps. 78). The "history" of Lamentations employs the language of complaint. In psalms of lament the worshiper commonly provided a brief presentation of the nature of the trouble (for example, Ps. 7:2, 14). Yet in these cases, the trouble receives a stereotypical description rather than a realistic one (for example, "enemies" and "Sheol"). Metaphors convey the strong sense of threat without historical detail, such as the following description of mistreatment at the hands of enemies: "See how they conceive evil, and are pregnant with mischief, and bring forth lies" (Ps. 7:14). The scenes in Lamentations remind the reader more of Job's comparison of his former prominence to his latter disgrace (Job 29–30). Like Job the voice (or voices) of Lamentations recount experiences too awful to remain unexpressed. Only chapter 3 resembles Psalms more closely than Job in this respect. Only chapter 3 contains statements of trust in God (an important feature of laments). Only chapter 3 offers the first-person perspective.[5] This feature does not neces-

---

5. In this respect, chapter 3 resembles Job. Also, many of the positive statements in Lamentations 3 parallel the positive statements of Job. Yet these positive statements do not reflect the general character of the Book of Job. Job spends most of his speeches on complaint.

sarily reflect the psalms, but it shows the special character of this central poem. Chapter 3 also contains the more metaphorical language expected in lament. The other chapters in Lamentations show preference for "historical" reports of suffering.

The historical nature of Lamentations stems from the manner in which the poems developed and were preserved. The content of the book relates to an annual commemoration of the fall of Jerusalem. The present day of fasting known as the Ninth of Ab may have originated in such responses during the exile. These laments evolved into the current text which is more a record of the depth of suffering than a conventional lament. Perhaps these chapters represent a wide body of literature produced as lamentation during exile. These chapters survive as reminders to future generations of the absolute desperation of the times. Some comparisons exist between this genre and epic poetry. Yet the constant skepticism of the period does not match the broad range of emotions encountered in epics. This leads to the conclusion that Lamentations exists as a genre to itself, matched only by comparable literature in companion cultures (see chap. 10) and a few biblical psalms.

Conclusion:
A Canonical Portrait of Poetry

The poetry of the Hebrew Bible reveals a broad range of purposes in the life of Israel. Proverbs and the Song of Songs supported the family structure. Psalms and Lamentations provide outlets for varied religious expression. The prophets interpret Israel's history with a special emphasis on God's message to the current community. When contemporary notions of poetry provide the perspective for an overview, the range is no less broad. The Song expresses the height of human joy, and it conveys the hope of youth. Lamentations chronicles the experience of incredible suffering. The Psalms reach in both the direction of joy and the direction of misery. According to unexamined opinions, the Bible simply contains religious poetry, offering bland devotion to God. Such notions cannot account for the skepticism of Lamentations or the eroticism of the Song of Songs. Biblical poetry evades simple categorization. Only the context of life itself stretches wide enough to encompass its themes. If this is true of the extremes in Lamentations and the Song, it is no less true of the extremes within the Psalter. Poetry offers communication to and from the divine. Because of the pervasiveness of Hebrew belief in God, this context includes all the experiences of life. The record of such experience allowed only the most carefully styled speech available to humans. This accounts for the artistry of Hebrew poetry.

Questions for Discussion

1. How did Lamentations function for Israel in exile? How can it function for you?

2. What does Lamentations teach about God and human suffering?

3. How does Hebrew poetry offer a unique emotional, instructional, and theological quality to Scripture?

Glossary of Terms

ʾašrê: Literally, "happy" or "fortunate"; type of Hebrew blessing on which the Beatitudes are based: "Happy is the one who . . . "

Allegory: Literally, "saying something other than what one seems to say"; a method of interpreting texts that looks for a mystical, deeper meaning rather than for a literal one.

Anagogy: Deriving meanings from portions of Scripture by comparisons with other portions of Scripture.

Anaphora: Identical words or phrases repeated at the beginning of successive poetic lines.

Anthropomorphic: Presenting God as appearing or acting like a human.

Apodictic: Literally "from God"; laws directly from God (for example, the Decalogue) as distinguished from laws regarding the everyday maintenance of a community (that is, casuistic or case laws).

Biblia Hebraica Stuttgartensia: The current edition of the Hebrew Bible most widely used by contemporary biblical interpreters.

Bloodguilt: The curse automatically falling on one responsible for the death of another person.

Book of Jashar: Lost book of poetry whose date cannot be determined. It is referred to in Joshua 10:13 and 2 Samuel 1:18 and possibly in Septuagint translation of 1 Kings 8:12–13. It apparently includes archaic popular poetry.

Canon: A body of writings accepted as authoritative by a given community; examples include the Hebrew canon, Deuterocanon, New Testament canon.

Catechesis: A document or oral presentation specifically designed for the training of children or converts.

Christology: The study of views relating to Jesus' identity as Messiah or Christ.

Clan Wisdom: Type of wisdom enforced by and passed on to the next generation by tribal leaders, especially heads of extended families and judges.

Construct State: Indication of the possessive or genitive relationship in Hebrew language; for example, the construct state of "sons" yields, "sons of."

Cosmology: A culture's beliefs regarding the nature of the universe; modern science reflects a heliocentric cosmology (earth revolves around the sun). Ancient Israel spoke of a firmament above and Sheol below.

Creation Theology: Theology which emphasizes the created order and God as creator, marked by a universal rather than a nationalistic perspective.

Cult: The entire system of worship of a people; Israel's cult or cultus included the temple, its priests, temple servants, the system of festivals and sacrifices, and everything else used in national worship.

Dead Sea Scrolls: Materials found in the caves at Qumran, including copies or portions of every biblical text except Esther, dated as early as 200 B.C.E.

Defiled with Blood: Contact with blood made one ritually unclean, because contact with blood was contact with God-given life; the unclean could not participate in temple worship until rites of purification were complete.

Deuterocanon: Literally, "second canon"; religious writings included in the Septuagint, but not in the Hebrew canon and not in most Prostestant Bibles; in this study Sirach, The Wisdom of Solomon, Tobit, Baruch, The Prayer of Azariah and The Song of the Three Jews, and The Prayer of Manasseh; sometimes these and other works are known as Apocrypha.

Deuteronomist: The name scholars assign to the supposed editor (or editors) of the history from Deuteronomy through Kings (omitting Ruth); also known as the Deuteronomistic Historian.

Deuteronomistic History: Name recent sholars have applied to the Former Prophets with the understanding that these books reflect the theology of the Book of Deuteronomy.

Diaspora: Literally "dispersion" or "scattering"; the displacement of a people by war or persecution, as the Jews under Asssyria and Babylon.

Divine Council: The heavenly beings God consults as a king would consult his cabinet, also known as "sons of God" (see Job 1: 6).

Encomium: A document expressing praise for the deeds or characteristics of persons (for example, Sirach 44:1–50:24) or movements all told to express praise for the final person mentioned.

Epithalamium: A wedding song in which the bride or bridegroom praises the other.

Etiology: A narrative (for example the story of the building and destruction of the tower of Babel in Gen. 11) to explain the origins of a natural phenomenon or social practice such as differing languages and cultures; use of the term *etiology* does not make any judgment about the historicity of the event narrated.

First temple/Second temple: These terms divide Israel's history into the time of Solomon's temple (about 966 to 586 B.C.E.) and postexilic temple (515 B.C.E. to 70 C.E.)

Former Prophets: Jewish designation for the books of Joshua, Judges, Samuel, and Kings in Hebrew canon; Septuagint and most modern translations place these books among the "historical books."

Formgeschichtliche: Literally, "form historical" or "form critical," the study of biblical materials in terms of their usage in the daily life of the ancient community.

Gattung: A literary type or genre identified by form criticism on the basis of features common in several examples (for example, a victory song or a lament).

Gîbôrîm: Literally, "mighty men," heroes with exceptional fighting abilities.

Hellenization: The introduction of Greek culture among peoples not of Greek descent.

Hermeneutics: The science of interpretation as distinguished from the results; method(s) used to interpret a text for a contemporary audience.

High Place: Hilltops or groves on which Baal and other fertility deities were worshiped.

Hypostasis: The identification of wisdom or some other entity as an integral part of the Godhead.

Hesed: Hebrew word for steadfast love, also known as "covenant love"; the special attitude of mercy which God exercises toward his people and expects them to return to him.

Implied Author: The "author" the text presents; documents give an impression of the producer, a figure who is often more literary than historical according to much contemporary literary theory.

Imprecation: A wish of evil on one's enemies; Psalms occasionally calls for merciless violence against the psalmist's persecutors or national enemies (see Ps. 137:9).

Inclusio: Indication of a *strophe* through the repetition of identical words or phrases at beginning and end.

Intertextuality: Literary similarities, indicated by themes and other features, shared between two or more documents without direct influence (for example, the flood stories of many remote cultures share features with others).

J material: The name critical scholars use for units belonging to one of the four sources identified in the Documentary Hypothesis; the name is based on the German spelling of the divine name, Jahweh.

Latter Prophets: Jewish designation for the classical or writing prophets; in the Hebrew canon this includes Isaiah, Jeremiah, Ezekiel, and the twelve minor prophets.

Maccabean Age (167 B.C.E.–63 B.C.E.): Period of Jewish rebellion against Seleucids sparked by forced worship of Zeus under Antiochus Epiphanes; named after the nickname Maccabeus (the Hammerer) of Judas Maccabeus.

Marcionite: Named after heretic Marcion who denied the canonicity of the Hebrew Bible; so, any view devaluing the inspired character of the Old Testament. A more stringent definition would include only those persons who held Marcion's entire theological system.

Masoretes (Masoretic): Jewish experts in the Hebrew Bible text who set its current written form and pronunciation before 1000 C.E.

Metatheme: Recurring ideas which find expression in numerous specific themes.

Metonym: A portion of a thing or sphere of influence substituted for the whole; for example, "David's sword" meaning "David's fighting ability," generally a stronger association than a metaphor.

Midrash: Literally, "inquiry." Jewish method of biblical interpretation and the resulting collection of biblical commentary. Such interpretations usually sought a deeper meaning of a biblical text applied to a contemporary situation.

Mishnah: Jewish legal and procedural oral materials collected shortly after 200 C.E. by Judah ha-Nasi; these materials are the foundation for the Talmud.

Mnemonic Device: A literary unit specially designed as an aid to memory (for example, an acrostic or a numerical pattern).

Nazirite: An Israelite holy person who fulfills a vow to abstain from wine, avoid touching corpses, and allow no cutting of hair (Num. 6:1–21).

Onomasticon: Ancient list of persons or things, often alphabetized.

Onomatopoeia: The reproduction of sounds through poetic language (for example, "tick tock" to represent a clock's sound).

Palanquin: A litter, or covered carriage, transported by two or more persons; Solomon built one as described in Song of Songs 3:9.

Parenesis: A unit containing rules or suggestions for daily conduct.

Patristics: The study of the history and teachings of the church fathers; in this study from about 100 to 800 C.E.

Pentateuch: Literally "five books"; the Greek name for Genesis— Deuteronomy, also known as Torah, Law, and Books of Moses.

Proof Text: The use of select Scripture verses to support and defend presuppositions; contrasts with "scientific" approach of *hermeneutics.*

Prophetic Oracle: Speech from God voiced by a prophet, often with the introduction, "Thus says Yahweh."

Pseudepigrapha: Literally, "falsely ascribed"; the name designates works like Enoch which have obviously been written long after the death of the author to whom the work is ascribed. In this study Pseudepigrapha refers to religious writings similar to Deuterocanon but not a part of the canon of existing Jewish or Christian communities.

Restoration Period: Stage in Israel's history beginning with freedom from Babylon in 539/538 B.C.E. and ending with the work of Nehemiah and Ezra around 400 B.C.E.

Retribution/Retributive Theology: View that life's fortunes match the person's lifestyle; that is, God rewards the righteous and punishes the wicked.

Rhetorical Criticism: The study of structural features such as repetition and figures of speech in order to discern the artistry employed in the design of a literary unit.

Salvation History: (Based on the German, *Heilsgeschichte*) Israel's history presented as the account of God's election, judgment, and providence.

Sapiential: Expressing themes or interests common to wisdom or wisdom literature.

Septuagint: Literally "seventy"; the earliest (about 250 B.C.E.) Greek translation of the Hebrew Bible along with the Deuterocanon apparently produced in Alexandria, Egypt; its name is based on traditions recorded in the Letter of Aristeas regarding its authorship; these traditions say that seventy translators produced the work.

Shema: Literally, "hear," since it transliterates the Hebrew word meaning "hear"; used to refer to Deuteronomy 6:4–9 (especially v. 4), an important confession of Israel's commitment to Yahweh beginning, "Hear O Israel, Yahweh is God, Yahweh alone."

Sitz im Leben: Life setting; in form criticism the specific context in life (including worship) to which a literary *Gattung* belongs.

Speech Act Theory: The study of the way speech is employed in communication processes, including literature.

Strophic Structure: The division of lengthy literary materials into smaller units, often based on subtle clues.

Succession Narrative: Second Samuel 9 through 1 Kings 2, a special segment and perhaps source of the Deuteronomistic History detailing events relating to David's kingship and the struggles to name David's successor.

Synagogue: Jewish house of worship; in *second temple* Judaism it served as a local house of prayer; sacrifices were offered only in the temple.

Talmud: Jewish interpretation of Scriptures, collected and produced around the time of Jesus of Nazareth in both a Jerusalem and a Babylonian form.

Thank Offering: A specific type of thanksgiving song or the simple sacrifice that accompanied it, expressing gratitude to God for a specific act on behalf of the worshiper.

Theocentric: Showing special interest in the divine perspective, usually opposed to the human perspective (anthropocentric).

Theodicy: Any attempt to defend God's justice in light of evil or suffering in his world.

Theophany: An appearance of God usually characterized by fantastic displays of divine power.

Torah: Literally, "teaching or instruction"; the first five books of the Bible (Genesis, Exodus, Leviticus, Numbers, Deuteronomy), most often designated, "Law."

Tropology: Deriving figurative meanings from Scripture; tropes are figures of speech like puns, metaphors, etc.

Typology: Study of biblical themes in terms of likenesses in which a later truth is seen as foreshadowed by an ancient symbol (see Rom. 5:14 and 1 Pet. 3:21).

Bibliography—Wisdom

Bauer-Kayatz, Christa. *Studien zu Proverbian 1–9.* Wissenschafttliche Monographien zum Alten und Neun Testament 22. Neukirchen-Vluyn: Neukirchener Verlag, 1966.

Blenkinsopp, Joseph. *Wisdom and Law in the Old Testament.* Oxford: Oxford University Press, 1983.

Borg, Marcus J. *Jesus, A New Vision: Spirit, Culture, and the Life of Discipleship.* HarperSanFrancisco, 1987.

Brown, Teresa. "Ben Sira's 'In Praise of Israel's Ancestors': An Example of Intra-Biblical Midrash." M.A. Thesis, Mobile College, 1992.

Bryce, Glendon E. *A Legacy of Wisdom.* Lewisburg, Pa.: Bucknell University Press, 1979.

Camp, Claudia. "The Wise Women of 2 Samuel: A Role Model for Women in Early Israel." *CBQ* 43 (1981), 14–29.

Childs, Brevard. *Introduction to the Old Testament as Scripture.* Philadelphia: Fortress, 1979.

Clements, R. E. *Wisdom in Theology.* Grand Rapids: Eerdmans, 1992.

Crenshaw, James L. *Ecclesiastes: A Commentary.* OTL. Philadelphia: Westminster, 1987.

———. *Old Testament Wisdom: An Introduction.* Atlanta: John Knox, 1981.

———. "The Wisdom Literature." *The Hebrew Bible and Its Modern Interpreters.* Ed. Douglas A. Kinght and Gene M. Tucker. Chico; Calif.: Scholars Press, 1985, 380.

Eichrodt, Walther. *Theology of the Old Testament.* 2 vols. Trans. J. A. Baker. Philadelphia: Westminster, 1967.

Eissfeldt, Otto. *The Old Testament: An Introduction.* Trans. Peter Ackroyd. New York: Harper & Row, 1965.

Emerton, John A. "Wisdom." *Tradition and Interpretation.* Ed. George W. Anderson. Oxford: Clarendon Press, 1979.

Fichtner, Johannes. *Die altorientalische Weisheit in ihrer israelitisch-jüdischen Ausprägung: Eine Studie zur Nationalisierung der Weisheit in Israel.* BZAW 62. Giessen: Topelmann, 1933.

Gese, Hartmut. *Lehre und Wirklichkeit in der alten Weisheit.* Tubingen: J. C. B. Mohr (Paul Siebeck), 1958.

Gesenius, William. *A Hebrew and English Lexicon of the Old Testament.* Rev. Brown, Driver, Briggs. Oxford: Clarendon, 1953.

Gerstenberger, Erhard. "Covenant and Commandent." JBL 84 (1965), 50–51.

Gordis, Robert. *Koheleth—The Man and His World: A Study of Ecclesiastes.* 3rd ed. New York: Schocken, 1968.

Gottwald, Norman. *The Tribes of Yahweh.* Maryknoll, N.Y.: Orbis, 1979.

Köhler, Ludwig. *Hebrew Man.* Trans. Peter Ackroyd. Nashville: Abingdon, 1957.

McKane, William. *Prophets and Wise Men.* SBT 44. Napierville, Ind.: Alec R. Allenson, 1965.

———. *Proverbs: A New Approach.* OTL. Philadelphia: Westminster, 1970.

Meade, David G. *Pseudonymity and Canon: An Investigation of the Relationship of Authorship and Authority in Jewish and Earliest Christian Tradition.* Grand Rapids: Eerdmans, 1986.

Morgan, Donn. *Wisdom in the Old Testament Traditions.* Atlanta: John Knox, 1981.

Murphy, Roland. *The Tree of Life: An Exploration of Biblical Wisdom Literature.* New York: Doubleday, 1990.

Noth, Martin, and Thomas, D. Winton, eds. *Wisdom in Israel and in the Ancient Near East: Presented to Professor Harold Henry Rowley.* VTSup 3. Leiden: Brill, 1955.

Perdue, Leo. *Wisdom and Cult.* SBLDS 30. Missoula, Mont.: Scholars Press, 1977.

———. *Wisdom in Revolt: A Metaphorical Theology in the Book of Job.* JSOTSup 112. Sheffield: Almond Press, 1991.

Rad, Gerhard von. *Old Testament Theology.* 2 vols. Trans. D. M. G. Stalker. OTL. New York: Harper & Row, 1962.

———. *The Problem of the Hexateuch and Other Essays.* Trans. E. W. Trueman Dicken. London: SCM Press, 1966.

———. *Wisdom in Israel.* Nashville: Abingdon, 1972.

Rylaarsdam, John Coert. *Revelation in Jewish Wisdom Literature.* Chicago: University of Chicago Press, 1946.

Scott, R. B. Y. *The Way of Wisdom in the Old Testament.* New York: Collier Books, Macmillan Publishing Co., 1971.

Sheppard, Gerald T. *Wisdom as a Hermeneutical Construct: A Study in the Sapientializing of the Old Testament.* BZAW 151. Berlin: Walter deGruyter, 1980.

Skehan, Patrick. *Studies in Israelite Poetry and Wisdom.* CBQMS 1. Washington, D.C.: The Catholic Biblical Association of America, 1971.

Stamm, J. J. *The Ten Commandments in Recent Research.* Trans. M. E. Andrew. SBT. 2d Series, 7. London: SCM Press, 1967.

Talmon, Shemaryahu. "Wisdom in the Book of Esther." VT 13 (1963), 419–55.

Terrien, Samuel. "The Play of Wisdom: Turning Point in Biblical Theology." *Horizons in Biblical Theology* 3 (1981), 134–37.

Ulrich, Eugene, et al., eds. *Priests, Prophets and Scribes: Essays on the Formation and Heritage of Second Temple Judaism in Honour of Joseph Blenkinsopp.* JSOTSup 112. Sheffield: Sheffield Academic Press, 1992.

Whybray, R. N. *The Composition of the Book of Proverbs.* JSOTSup 168. Sheffield: Sheffield Academic Press, 1994.

———. *The Intellectual Tradition in the Old Testament.* BZAW 135. New York: Walter deGruyter, 1974.

———. "The Social World of the Wisdom Writers." *The World of Ancient Israel.* Ed. R. E. Clements. New York: Cambridge University Press, 1989, 227–50.

———. *The Succession Narrative: A Study of 2 Samuel 9–20; 1 Kings 1 and 2.* In SBT 2d Series, 9. London: SCM Press, 1968.

Wolff, Hans Walter. *Amos the Prophet: The Man and His Background.* Trans. Foster R. McCurley. Philadelphia: Fortress, 1973.

———. *Joel and Amos.* Her. Trans. Waldemar Janzen, et al. Philadelphia: Fortress, 1977.

Zimmerli, Walther and Helmut Ringgren. *Sprüche/Prediger.* Das Alte Testament Deutsch xvi/I. Gottingen: Vandenhoeck und Ruprecht, 1980.

Zimmerman, Frank. *The Inner World of Qohelet.* New York: KTAV Publishing House, Inc., 1973.

Bibliography—Poetry

Adams, Hazard, ed. *Critical Theory Since Plato*. San Diego: Harcourt, Brace, Jovanovich, 1971.

Alter, Robert. *The Art of Biblical Poetry*. New York: Basic Books, Inc., Publishers. 1985.

Anderson, Bernhard W. *Out of the Depths: The Psalms Speak for Us Today*. Philadelphia: Westminster, 1983.

Berlin, Adele. *The Dynamics of Biblical Parallelism*. Bloomington: Indiana University Press, 1985.

Berry, Donald K. *The Psalms and Their Readers: Interpretive Strategies for Psalm 18*. Sheffield: Sheffield Academic Press, 1993.

Blank, Sheldon, ed. *Hebrew Union College Annual 50* (1979). Cincinnati: Hebrew Union College, 1980.

Briggs, C. A. and E. G. *A Critical and Exegetical Commentary on the Book of Psalms*. International Critical Commentary. Edinburgh: T&T Clark, 1901.

Brueggemann, Walter. *Israel's Praise: Doxology against Idolatry and Ideology*. Philadelphia: Fortress, 1988.

————. *The Message of the Psalms*. Minneapolis: Augsburg, 1984.

Buber, Martin. *Right and Wrong: The Interpretation of Some Psalms*. Trans. Ronald Gregor Smith. London: SCM Press, Ltd., 1952.

Carmi, T., ed. *The Penguin Book of Hebrew Verse*. New York: Penguin Books, 1981.

Childs, Brevard. *The Book of Exodus*. OTL. Philadelphia: Westminster, 1974.

Collins, Terence. *Line-Forms in Hebrew Poetry*. Rome: Biblical Institute Press, 1978.

Cross, Frank Moore, Jr. "Studies in Ancient Yahwistic Poetry." Ph.D. diss. Johns Hopkins University, 1950.

Culley, Robert C. *Oral Formulaic Language in the Biblical Psalms*. Toronto: University of Toronto Press, 1967.

Dahood, Mitchell. *Psalms III: 101–150*. AB 17A. Garden City, N.J.: Doubleday, 1963.

Delitzsch, Franz. *Commentary on the Song of Solomon and Ecclesiastes*. Trans. M. G. Easton. Grand Rapids: Eerdmans, 1950.

Driver, Samuel R. *An Introduction to the Literature of the Old Testament*. Cleveland: World Publishing Company, 1956.

Duhm, D. Bernhard. *Die Psalmen*. Kurzer Hand-Commentar zum Alten Testament. Freiburg: J. C. B. Mohr (Paul Siebeck), 1899.

Eaton, J. H. *Kingship and the Psalms*. SBT 2nd Series, 32. London: SCM Press, 1976.

Ewald, Heinrich A. von. *Commentary on the Psalms*. Trans. E. Johnson. Edinburgh: Williams and Norgate, 1881.

Falk, Marcia. *The Song of Songs: A New Translation and Interpretation.* HarperSanFrancisco, 1990.

Ferris, Paul Wayne, Jr. *The Genre of Communal Lament in the Bible and the Ancient Near East.* SBLDS 127. Atlanta: Scholars Press, 1992.

Fisch, Harold. *Poetry with a Purpose: Biblical Poetry and Interpretation.* Bloomington: Indiana University Press, 1988.

Follis, Elaine R. *Directions in Biblical Poetry.* Sheffield: Sheffield Academic Press, 1987.

Fox, Everett. *In the Beginning: A New English Rendition of the Book of Genesis.* New York: Schocken, 1983.

————. *These Are the Names: A New English Rendition of the Book of Exodus.* New York: Schocken, 1986.

Fritz, Bernard, trans. *Herder's Commentary on the Psalms.* Westminster, Md.: The Newman Press, 1961.

Frye, Northrop. *The Great Code: The Bible and Literature.* New York: Harcourt, Brace, Jovanovich, 1982.

Gevirtz, Stanley. *Patterns in the Early Poetry of Israel.* Studies in Ancient Oriental Civilization, No. 32. Chicago: University of Chicago Press, 1963.

Ginsburg, Christian D. *The Song of Songs and Coheleth.* New York: KTAV, 1970.

Gordis, Robert. *Poets, Prophets, and Sages.* Bloomington: Indiana University Press, 1971.

Gros Lonis, Kenneth, and James Ackerman, eds. *Literary Interpretations of Biblical Narratives.* Vol. 2. Nashville: Abingdon, 1982.

Gray, George B. *The Forms of Hebrew Poetry.* Hoboken, N.J.: KTAV, 1972.

Gunkel, Hermann. *The Psalms: A Form-Critical Introduction.* Trans. Thomas M. Horner. Philadelphia: Fortress, 1967.

Hay, David M. *Glory at the Right Hand: Psalm 110 in Early Christianity.* Nashville: Abingdon, 1973.

Hayes, John H., ed. *Old Testament Form Criticism.* San Antonio: Trinity University Press, 1974.

Hrushovski, Benjamin. "Prosody, Hebrew." *Encyclopedia Judaica.* Jerusalem: Keter Publishing House Jerusalem Ltd., 1972.

Johnson, Aubrey. *Sacral Kingship in Ancient Israel.* Cardiff: University of Wales Press, 1967.

Knight, Douglas A., and Gene Tucker, eds. *The Hebrew Bible and its Modern Interpreters.* Chico, Calif.: Scholars Press, 1985.

Koch, Klaus. *The Growth of the Biblical Tradition: The Form-Critical Method.* New York: Charles Scribner's Sons, 1969.

————. *The Prophets: The Assyrian Period.* Philadelphia: Fortress, 1982.

————. *The Prophets: The Babylonian and Persian Periods.* Philadelphia: Fortress, 1982.

Kraus, Hans-Joachim. *Psalms: A Commentary.* 3 vols.Trans. Hilton C. Oswald. Minneapolis: Augsburg, 1988.

Kugel, James. *The Idea of Biblical Poetry: Parallelism and Its History.* New Haven: Yale University Press, 1981.

Landy, Francis. *Paradoxes of Paradise: Identity and Difference in the Song of Songs.* Sheffield: The Almond Press, 1983.

Lowth, Robert. *Isaiah: A New Translation with a Preliminary Dissertation.* Boston: William Hilliard. 1834.

————. *Lectures on the Sacred Poetry of the Hebrews.* Andover: Crocker and Brewster, 1829.

Maier, J. R., and B. L. Tollers, eds. *The Bible in Its Literary Milieu.* Grand Rapids: Eerdmans, 1979.

Meer, William van der, and Johannes C. deMoor, *The Structural Analysis of Biblical and Canaanite Poetry.* Sheffield: Sheffield Academic Press, 1988.

Merton, Thomas. *Bread in the Wilderness.* New York: New Directions Books, 1953.

Mitchell, Stephen. *The Book of Job.* New York: HarperCollins Publishers, 1992.

————. *A Book of Psalms—Selected and Adapted from the Hebrew.* New York: HarperCollins Publishers, 1994.

Mowinckel, Sigmund. *Psalmen Studien.* 6 vols. Amsterdam: Schippers, 1961.

————. *The Psalms in Israel's Worship.* 2 vols. in 1. Trans. D. R. Ap-Thomas. Sheffield: Sheffield Academic Press, 1992.

Muilenburg, James. "Form Criticism and Beyond." *JBL* 88 (1969), 1–18.

Murphy, Roland. *Ecclesiastes.* WBC. Dallas: Word, 1992.

————. *The Song of Songs.* Her. Minneapolis: Fortress, 1990.

————. "Song of Songs, Book of." ABD. New York: Doubleday, 1992.

O'Connor, Michael P. *Hebrew Verse Structure.* Winona Lake, Ind.: Eisenbrauns, 1980.

Oesterly, W. O. E. *Ancient Hebrew Poems.* New York: The Macmillan Company, 1938.

Perrine, Laurence. *Sound and Sense: An Introduction to Poetry.* 7th ed. San Diego: Harcourt, Brace, Jovanovich, 1987.

Pope, Marvin. *Song of Songs.* AB. New York: Doubleday, 1977.

Pouget, G. et Guitton J. *Le Cantique Des Cantiqués.* Études Bibliques 9. Paris: Librarie Lecoffre, 1948.

Schökel, Luis Alonso. *A Manual of Hebrew Poetics.* Subsidia Biblica 11. Rome: Editrice Pontifico Instituto Biblico. 1988.

Sievers, Eduard. *Metrische Studien.* 3 vols. Leipzig: G. G. Tebner, 1901.

Smend, Rudolf. "Ueber das Ich des Psalmen." ZAW 8 (1888), 49–147.

Stadelmann, Luis. *Love and Politics: A New Commentary on the Song of Songs.* New York: Paulist, 1992.

Tournay, Raymond Jacques. *Word of God, Song of Love.* Trans. J. Edward Crowley. New York: Paulist, 1988.

Watson, Wilfred G. *Classical Hebrew Poetry: A Guide to Its Techniques.* JSOTSup 25. Sheffield: University of Sheffield Press, 1986.

Watts, John D. W. *Isaiah 1–33.* WBC. Waco: Word, 1985.

Westermann, Claus. *Basic Forms of Prophetic Speech.* Louisville: Westminster/John Knox, 1991.

————. *Praise and Lament in the Psalms.* Trans. Keith R. Crim. Atlanta: John Knox, 1981.

Bibliography—History of Interpretation

Altmann, Alexander, ed. *Biblical Motifs: Origins and Transformations.* Cambridge: Harvard University Press, 1966.

Anderson, George W. A., ed. *Tradition and Interpretation.* Oxford: Clarendon, 1979.

Armstrong, Regis J., and Ignatius C. Brady, trans. *Francis and Clare: The Complete Works.* New York: Paulist, 1982.

Bachmann, E. Theodore, trans. *Luther's Works.* Vol. 35. Philadelphia: Fortress, 1960.

Basser, Herbert, and Barry D. Walfish, eds. *Commentary on the Book of Job* by Moses Kimhi. Atlanta: Scholars Press, 1992.

Berlin, Adele, trans. *Biblical Poetry Through Medieval Jewish Eyes.* Bloomington: Indiana University Press, 1991.

Bokser, Ben Zion, trans. *The Talmud: Selected Writings.* New York: Paulist, 1989.

Bowker, John, ed. *The Targums of Rabbinic Literature: An Introduction to Jewish Interpretations of Scripture.* Cambridge: Cambridge University Press, 1969.

Braude, William G., trans. *The Midrash on Psalms.* Vol. 1. New Haven: Yale University Press, 1959.

Bromiley, G. W., trans. *Zwingli and Bullinger.* Vol. 24 LCC. Philadelphia: Westminster, 1953.

Calvin, John. *Commentaries on the Book of the Prophet Jeremiah and Lamentations.* Trans. John Owen. Grand Rapids: Eerdmans, 1950.

———. *Commentary on the Book of Psalms.* Trans. James Anderson. Grand Rapids: Eerdmans, 1963.

———. *The Institutes of the Christian Religion.* 2 vols. Trans. Ford L. Battles. Vols. 20–21 LCC. Philadelphia: Westminster, 1960.

Cameron, James Kerr, ed. and trans. *Advocates of Reform: From Wyclif to Erasmus.* Vol. 14 LCC. Philadelphia: Westminster, 1953.

Chadwick, Owen, trans. *Western Asceticism.* Vol. 12 LCC. Philadelphia: Westminster, 1958.

Charlesworth, James. *The Old Testament Pseudepigrapha.* 2 vols. Garden City, N.J.: Doubleday & Company, 1983.

Clements, Ronald. *100 Years of Old Testment Interpretation.* Philadelphia: Westminster, 1976.

Cohen, A., trans. "Lamentation." *Midrash Rabbah.* Eds. H. Freedman and Maurice Simon. London: Soncino, 1961.,

———. trans. *Midrash Rabbah Ecclesiastes.* Vol. 8. London: Soncino, 1939.

Cox, A. Cleveland, trans. *The Apostolic Fathers with Justin Martyr.* Vol. 1 of The Anti-Nicene Fathers. Grand Rapids: Eerdmans, 1885.

Defarrari, Roy J., trans. *Saint Cyprian: Treatises.* Vol. 36 of The Fathers of the Church. New York: The Fathers of the Church Press, 1958.

Elwes, R. H. M., trans. *A Theologico-Political Treatise and a Political Treatise.* New York: Dover Publications, 1951.

Epstein, I., trans. *The Babylonian Talmud.* Seder Nezikin. London: Soncino, 1935.

Ewald, Marie Liguori, trans. *The Homilies of Saint Jerome.* Vol. 1. Vol. 48 of The Fathers of the Church. Washington, D.C.: The Catholic University of America Press, 1964.

Fairweather, A. M., trans. and ed. *Nature and Grace: Selections from the Summa Theologica of Thomas Acquinas.* Vol. 2 LCC. Philadelphia: Westminster, 1954.

Fairweather, Eugene R., trans. and ed. *A Scholastic Miscellany: Anselm to Ockham.* Vol. 10 LCC. Philadelphia: Westminster, 1956.

Falls, Thomas B., trans. *Saint Justin Martyr.* Vol. 6 of The Fathers of the Church. New York: Christian Heritage, Inc., 1948.

Farrar, Frederic W. *History of Interpretation.* New York: E. P. Dutton, 1886.

Fishbane, Michael, and Emmanuel Tov, eds. *"Sha'arei Talmon": Studies in the Bible, Qumran, and the Ancient Near East Presented to Shemaryahu Talmon.* Winona Lake, Ind.: Eisenbrauns, 1992.

Freer, Coburn. *Music for a King: George Herbert's Style and the Metrical Psalms.* Baltimore: Johns Hopkins University Press, 1972.

Gill, John. *An Exposition of the Song of Solomon.* Marshallton, Del.: The National Foundation for Christian Education, 1854.

Goldman, Edward A., trans. *The Talmud of the Land of Israel.* Chicago: University of Chicago Press, 1988.

Goodspeed, Edgar J. *The Apostolic Fathers.* New York: Harper & Brothers. Publishers, 1950.

Gray, Edward M. *Old Testament Criticism: Its Rise and Progress.* New York: Harper & Brothers, 1923.

Greenslade, Stanley L., ed. and trans. *Early Latin Theology.* Vol. 5 LCC. Philadelphia: Westminster, 1956.

Greer, Rowan A., trans. *Origen.* New York: Paulist, 1979.

Gregg, Robert C., trans. *Athanasius: The Life of Antony and the Letter to Marcellinus.* New York: Paulist, 1980.

Hayes, John, and Frederick Prussner. *Old Testament Theology: Its History and Development.* Atlanta: John Knox, 1985.

Hill, Edmund, trans. *Nine Sermons of Saint Augustine on the Psalms.* New York: J. J. Kenedy & Sons, 1958.

Hinke, William J., ed. and trans. *Zwingli: on Providence and Other Essays.* Durham, N.C.: The Labyrinth Press, 1922.

Hobbes, Thomas. *Leviathan.* Book Three, "Of a Christian Commonwealth." Vol. 23 in Great Books of the Western World. Chicago: Encyclopedia Britannica. Inc., 1952.

Holmes, Peter, and Robert Wallis, trans. *A Select Library of Nicene and Post-Nicene Fathers of the Christian Church.* Vol. 5. Grand Rapids: Eerdmans, 1887.

Jackson, Samuel M., and Clarence N. Heller, eds. *Commentary on the True and False Religion,* by Ulrich Zwingli. Durham, N.C.: The Labyrinth Press, 1981.

Jardine, William, ed. *Shepherd of Hermas: The Gentle Apocalypse.* Redwood City, Calif.: Proteus Publishing, 1992.

Jarick, John, trans. *Gregory Thaumaturgos' Paraphrase of Ecclesiastes.* Atlanta: Scholars Press, 1990.

Luibheid, Colm, trans. *Pseudo-Dionysius: The Complete Works.* New York: Paulist, 1987.

McCracken, George E., trans. and ed. *Early Medieval Theology.* Vol. 9 LCC. Philadelphia: Westminster, 1957.

Metzger, Bruce. *Introduction to the Apocrypha.* Oxford: Oxford University Press, 1957.

Migne, Jacques P., ed. *Patrologiae Graecae.* Vol. 66. Turnholt: Brepols, 1967.

———, ed. *Patrologia Latina.* Vols. 75–79. Paris: Apud Garnier Fratres Editores, 1849–1878.

Mulder, Martin Jan, ed. *Mikra: Text, Translation, Reading and Interpretation of the Hebrew Bible in Ancient Judaism and Early Christianity.* Philadelphia: Fortress, 1988.

Neusner, Jacob, trans. *The Mishnah: A New Translation.* New Haven: Yale University Press, 1988.

Olofsson, Staffan. *God Is My Rock: A Study of Translation Technique and Theological Exegesis in the Septuagint.* Vol. 31 of Coniectanea Biblica Old Testament Series. Stockholm: Almqvist & Wiksell International, 1990.

Oulton, John E. L., and Henry Chadwick, trans. *Alexandrian Christianity.* Vol. 2 LCC. Philadelphia: Westminster, 1954.

Pelikan, Jaroslav, ed. and trans. *Luther's Works.* Vol. 1. Saint Louis: Concordia, 1972.

Perowne, E. H., trans. *Meditations on Psalm 51 and Part of Psalm 31 in Latin with an English Translation.* Savonarola. London: C. J. Clay and Sons, 1900.

Petry, Ray C., ed. and trans. *Late Medieval Mysticism.* Vol. 13 LCC. Philadelphia: Westminster, 1957.

Pines, Shlomo, trans. *The Guide to the Perplexed,* by Maimonides. Chicago: Chicago University Press, 1963.

Pauck, William, trans. and ed. *Luther: Lectures on Romans.* Vol. 15 LCC. Philadelphia: Westminster, 1961.

Rambaut, W. H., trans. *The Writings of Irenaeus.* Vol. 1. Edinburgh: T&T Clark, 1868.

Rosenblatt, Samuel, trans. *The Book of Beliefs and Opinions,* by Saadia Gaon New Haven: Yale University Press, 1948.

Saint Bernard on the Song of Songs (trans. and ed. by an unnamed member of monastic community). London: A. R. Mowbray & Co. Limited, 1952.

The Septuagint Version of the Old Testament and Apocrypha with an English Translation. London: Samuel Bagster and Sons Limited, 1870.

Siggins, Ian, trans. *Luther's Works.* Vol. 15. Philadelphia: Fortress, 1961.

Simpson, Evelyn, ed. *John Donne's Sermons on the Psalms and Gospels.* Berkeley: University of California Press, 1963.

Swete, Henry B. *An Introduction to the Old Testament in Greek.* New York: KTAV, 1968 (Original 2d ed. Cambridge University Press, 1902).

Tappert, Theodore G., ed. and trans. *Luther's Works.* Vol. 54. Philadelphia: Fortress, 1967.

Telfer, William, ed. and trans. *Cyril of Jerusalem and Nemesius of Emesa.* Vol. 4 LCC. Philadelphia: Westminster, 1955.

Verduin, Leonard, trans. *The Complete Writings of Meno Simons 1496–1561.* Scottdale, Pa.: Herald Press, 1956.

Visotzky, Burton L., trans. *The Midrash on Proverbs.* New Haven: Yale University Press, 1992.

Walsh, Gerald G., et. al., trans. *City of God,* by Augustine. Abridged. Garden City, N.J.: Doubleday, 1958.

Walsh, P. G., trans. Cassiodorus. *Explanation of the Psalms.* Vol. 1. New York: Paulist, 1990.

Way, Agnes Clare. *Exegetic Homilies,* by Saint Basil. Vol. 46 of The Fathers of the Church. Washington, D.C.: The Catholic University Press, 1963.

Wenger, John C., trans. *Conrad Grebel's Programmatic Letters of 1524.* Scottdale, Pa.: Herald Press, 1970.

Whiston, William, trans. *Josephus' Complete Works.* Grand Rapids: Kregel Publications, 1960.

Williams, George H., and Angel M. Mergal, eds. *Spiritual and Anabaptist Writers.* Vol. 25 LCC. Philadelphia: Westminster, 1957.

Williamson, Ronald, trans. *Jews in the Hellenistic World: Philo.* New York: Cambridge, 1989.

Winston, David, trans. *Philo of Alexandria: The Contemplative Life, The Giants, and Selections.* New York: Paulist, 1981.

Wright, D. F., trans. and ed. *Common Places of Martin Bucer.* Appleford, Eng.: The Sutton Courtenay Press, 1972.

Zaharopoulos, Dimitri Z. *Theodore of Mopsuestia on the Bible: A Study of His Old Testament Exegesis.* New York: Paulist, 1989.

Zim, Rivkah. *English Metrical Psalms: Poetry as Praise and Prayer 1535–1601.* Cambridge: Cambridge University Press, 1987.

Bibliography—Ancient Near Eastern Literature

Beyerlin, Walter, ed. *Ancient Near Eastern Texts Relating to The Old Testament*. Philadelphia: Westminster, 1978.

Dahood, Mitchell. *Ras Shamra Parallels: The Texts from Ugarit and the Hebrew Bible*. Vol. 1. Rome: Pontificum Institutum Biblicum, 1972.

Erman, Adolf, ed. *The Ancient Egyptians: A Sourcebook of Their Writings*. Trans. Aylward Blackman. New York: Harper & Row, Publishers, 1966.

———. "Eine Ägyptische Quelle der Sprüche Salomos." *Sitzungsberichte der preussischen Akadamie der Wissenschaften*, 15, 16 (May 1924).

Fisher, Loren R., ed. *Ras Shamra Parallels: The Texts from Ugarit and the Hebrew Bible*. Vol. 2. Rome: Pontificum Institutum Biblicum, 1975.

Fox, Michael B. *The Song of Songs and the Ancient Egyptian Love Songs*. Madison: University of Wisconsin Press, 1985.

Gammie, John C., and Leo G. Perdue, eds. *The Sage in Israel and the Ancient Near East*. Winona Lake, Ind.: Eisenbrauns, 1991.

Gardener, A. H. *Ancient Egyptian Onomastica*. 2 vols. Oxford: Oxford University Press, 1947.

Lambert, W. G. *Babylonian Wisdom Literature*. London: Oxford University Press, 1960.

Lichtheim, Miriam. *Ancient Egyptian Literature: A Book of Readings*. 3 vols. Berkeley: University of California Press, 1973.

Matthews, Victor H., and Don C. Benjamin. *Old Testament Parallels: Laws and Stories from the Ancient Near East*. New York: Paulist Press, 1991.

Nougayroul, Jean, et. al. *Ugaritica V*. Mission de Ras Shamra 16. Paris: Imprimerie Nationale, 1968.

Pritchard, James B., ed. *Ancient Near Eastern Texts Relating to the Old Testament*. 3rd ed. with supplement. Princeton: Princeton University Press. 1969.

Sanders, James A. *The Dead Sea Psalms Scroll*. Ithaca: Cornell University Press, 1967.

Vermes, Geza. *The Dead Sea Scrolls in English*. 3rd ed. London: Penguin Books, 1987.

Name Index

A

Abravanel, Don Isaac   263
Adams, Hazard   179
Africanus   256
Agobard of Lyons   256
Albright, William F.   87
Alden, Robert L.   95, 155
Allemano   263
Allen, Leslie C.   185
Alt, Albrecht   89
Alter, Robert   284
Ambrose   69, 251
Amemar   54
Andersen, Francis I.   150
Anderson, A. A.   241
Anderson, Bernhard W.   357
Andrew, M. E.   99
Anselm of Canterbury   256
Aquinas, Thomas   71, 260
Aristotle   5
Arius   68
Athanasius   68, 250
Augustine   70, 79, 253

B

Barnabas   247
Basil, Saint   250
Bauer-Kayatz, Christa   90
Benedict, Saint   255
Benjamin, Don C.   32, 33, 34
Berlin, Adele   257, 263, 278, 287
Bernard of Clairvaux   257
Berry, Donald K.   283
Beyerlin, Walter   228, 230
Blenkinsopp, Joseph   5, 15, 43, 88, 94
Borg, Marcus J.   58
Briggs, C. A.   241, 279
Briggs, E. G.   241, 279
Brown, Teresa   114
Brueggemann, Walter   25, 101, 289, 290, 380
Bryce, Glendon E.   25, 121
Buber, Martin   284
Bucer, Martin   79
Bullock, C. Hassell   199
Burchard, C.   236, 237
Butler, Trent C.   202, 324

C

Calvin, John   81, 267, 268, 269, 270
Camp, Claudia V.   93, 106
Carlstadt   77
Cassain   255
Cassiodorus   253, 254
Castellio, Sebastian   270
Charlesworth, James H.   48, 49, 238, 240
Childs, Brevard   143, 303
Christensen, Duane L.   196, 306, 309
Chrysostom, John   70
Clement   248
Clements, Ronald E.   37, 91
Clines, David J. A.   286
Collins, John J.   214
Collins, Terrence   278, 279, 280
Countess of Pembroke   269
Craigie, Peter   302, 322
Crenshaw, James L.   8, 64, 90, 92, 94, 95
Cross, Jr., Frank Moore   279
Culley, Robert   280
Cyprian   68, 249
Cyril of Jerusalem   69, 70, 250, 252

D

Dahood, Mitchell   279, 287
Darnell, D. R.   239
Delitzsch, Franz   273, 274, 391
deMoor, Johannes C.   284
Dietrich of Niem   263
Donne, John   271, 272
Driver, Samuel R.   274
Duhm, Bernhard   273, 279, 287

E

Eaton, J. H.   282
Eck, John   79
Eichrodt, Walther   85
Eissfeldt, Otto   88
Ellis, E. Earle   46
Emerton, John A.   90
Erasmus   78, 264
Erman, Adolf   32, 227
Ewald, G. Heinrich A. von   273, 411

F

Falk, Marcia   285, 290, 392
Farrar,   74
Ferris, Jr., Paul Wayne   364
Fichtner, Johannes   84
Fiensy, D. A.   67, 239
Fisch, Harold   284, 285, 391, 401, 405
Fishbane, Michael   50, 109
Fisher, Loren R.   229, 279
Fontaine, Carole R.   40
Fox, Everett   290
Fox, Michael B.   224, 391, 402
Francis of Assisi   74
Freedman, David Noel   176, 177, 179, 199, 279, 280, 284, 286, 292, 301, 322
Frye, Northrop   283, 405
Frymer-Kensky, Tikva   97

G

Gammie, John G.   37, 41
Gardiner, A. H.   32
Garrett, Duane A.   37, 95, 121, 160, 161, 222, 288
Gerstenberger, Erhard   89, 209, 281, 372
Gese, Hartmut   88
Gevirtz, Stanley   279
Giese, Jr., Ronald L.   182, 199, 209, 281
Gill, John   270
Ginsberg, H. L.   35, 228
Ginsburg, Christian D.   256
Glatzer, Nahum   71
Goodspeed, Edgar J.   248
Gordis, Robert   13, 175, 288, 294
Gottwald, Norman   91
Gowan, D. E.   106
Gray, Edward   71, 253, 387
Gray, George B.   276
Grebel, Conrad   80
Greenslade, S. L.   270
Gregory Thaumaturgos   68
Gregory the Great   71
Gros Louis, Kenneth R.   285
Guitton, J.   274

441

Gunkel, Hermann 84, 85, 88, 182, 209, 281, 282, 297, 361, 363

H

Hals, Ronald M. 199, 214
Harris, Rivkah 132
Hartley, John E. 150, 152, 155
Hayes, John 85
Hengstenberg 273
Herder, Johann Gottfried von 272, 273
Hermisson, H.-J. 100
Hillers, Delbert R. 288
Hitzig 273
Hobbes, Thomas 83
Hofmann, Melchior 265
Horbury, William 50, 56
Hrushovski, Benjamin 179, 278, 294
Huey, Jr., F. B. 288, 413
Hupfeld 273

I

ibn Ezra, Abraham 263
ibn Ezra, Moshe 257
ibn Kaspi, Joseph 260
Irenaeus 66, 248
Isaac, E. 48, 239

J

Jardine, William 50
Jerome 3, 69, 77, 79, 252
Johnson, Aubrey 282
Josephus 242
Judah, Rabbi 243
Junilius Africanus 255
Justin Martyr 66

K

Kimhi, 73
Koch, Klaus 199, 281
Köhler, Ludwig 86
Kramer, Samuel N. 229, 231
Kramer, Samuel Noah 34
Kraus, Hans-Joachim 186, 361
Kugel, James 247, 255, 275, 277, 292, 294

L

Lambert, W. G. 34, 36
Landy, Francis 285
Laroche, Emmanuel 33
Lemaire, Andre 37
Lichtheim, Miriam 31, 32, 33, 222, 223, 227
Limburg, James 241, 360
Lindblom, Johannes 17, 86
Longinus 271
Longland, Bishop 74
Lowth, Robert 272, 275, 276, 277
Lunt, H. G. 240
Luther, Martin 4, 79, 265, 266, 268, 270, 281

M

Mack-Fisher, Loren R. 36
Maimonides, Moses 71, 73, 259, 261
Matthews, Victor H. 32, 33, 34
Maurus, Rabanus 256
McCann, Jr., J. Clinton 187
McCarter, Jr., P. Kyle 100
McKane, William 90, 92, 183
Mead, David 93
Meer, William van der 284
Merton, Thomas 274
Metzger, Bruce 62, 82
Miller, Patrick D. 99
Mitchell, Stephen 290
Morgan, Donn F. 14, 89, 110, 123
Moses 82
Mowinckel, Sigmund 107, 221, 279, 281, 283, 287, 367
Muilenburg, James 283
Murphy, Roland 8, 131, 166, 214, 259, 288, 383, 400

N

Neusner, Jacob 53
Nougayrol, Jean 33

O

O'Connor, Michael 280, 294
Oesterly, W. O . E. 280
Olofsson, Staffan 241
Origen 68, 69, 248, 249

P

Perdue, Leo G. 7, 26, 33, 37, 93, 107, 132, 148, 158
Pfeiffer, R. H. 34
Philo of Alexandria 44, 50, 52, 272
Plato 6, 69
Pope, Marvin H. 288
Pouget, G. 274
Prussner, Frederick 85
Pseudo-Chrysostom 71
Pseudo-Dionysius 254

R

Rabin. Chaim 288
Rad, Gerhard von 5, 15, 20, 86, 87, 89, 90, 118, 125, 158, 309
Ringren, Helmut 85
Rinkart, Martin 82
Rubinkiewicz, R. 237, 238
Rupert of Deutz 258
Rylaarsdam, J. Coert 44, 85

S

Saadia Gaon 71, 72
Sachs, A. 231
Sanders, James A. 234, 235
Sandy, D. Brent 182, 199, 209, 281
Savonarola 264
Schaeffer, C. F. A. 33
Schmid, 88
Schökel, Luis Alonso 277, 294
Scott, R. B. Y. 7, 16, 121

Sellin, Ernst 85
Seow, C. L. 105
Sheppard, Gerald T. 84, 88, 186
Sidney, Philip 269
Sievers, Eduard 279
Simeon ben Laish 243
Simons, Meno 80
Skehan, Patrick 120
Smend, Rudolf 363
Smith, Gary V. 182, 199, 324
Solomon 7
Solomon ben Judah Hababli, Rabbi 256
Speiser, E. A. 34
Spinoza, Benedict de 81, 82, 272
Stadelmann, Luis 289
Stamm, J. J. 5, 7, 99
Stephens, Ferris J. 231
Stuart, Douglas 202
Sweet, Ronald F. G. 35
Swete, Henry Barclay 241

T

Talmon, Shemaryahu 90
Terrien, Samuel 91
Theodore of Mopsuestia 70, 71, 252, 253, 254, 387
Toorn, Karel van der 130
Tournay, Raymond 285
Tov, Emmanuel 51
Tuttle, G. A. 106

V

Van Leeuwen, Raymond C. 86, 101, 103
Vangemeren, Willem A. 199
Vermes, Geza 233, 234, 235
Virolleaud, Charles 33

W

Watson, Wilfred G. E. 176, 277, 293, 294
Watts, John D. W. 324
Weinfeld, Moshe 99
Weiser, Artur 287
Westermann, Claus 87, 199, 223, 231, 282
Whallon, William 177
Whedbee, J. W. 101
Whybray, Roger N. 5, 22, 37, 39, 89, 90, 91, 92, 95, 100
Williams, Ronald J. 31
Wilson, Gerald H. 185
Wilson, John A. 32, 33, 221, 222, 224
Wolff, Hans Walter 90, 106
Wright, G. Ernest 87
Wyclif, John 77

Z

Zaharopoulos, Dimitri Z. 70, 252
Zim, Rivkah 269
Zimmerli, Walther 85
Zwingli, Ulrich 79, 264

Subject Index

A

Aaron 304–305, 375–376
Aaron's blessing 305
Ab, feast of 243
Abaddon 139
Abigail 23, 99–100
Abimelech 310–311
Abner 315
Abraham 30, 52, 55, 112, 218, 237,
    300, 341
Absalom 100
absurdity 166
accents 207, 294, 315, 394, 412
Account of Prophetic Suffering 212
account of the fall as a divine opera-
    tion 415
acrostic 109, 115, 192–193, 235, 242–
    243, 278, 293, 296, 348, 369–371,
    376, 411, 413–414, 417
acrostic wisdom poem 348
Adam 112, 239, 299–300
adding syle 393
admonitions 13, 23, 40, 169
Admonitions of Ipuwer 33
adultery 98, 124, 129–130, 133
advice 23, 27, 101, 113, 126, 131, 133,
    135, 137, 157, 159, 198
advisors 39
Affirmation of Leadership 210
affirmations 368
afterlife 51, 68, 111
agnosticism 145
agricultural 219
Agur 95, 127
Ahiqar 29, 35
Aijalon 310
Akkadian 33–34, 228, 232
Akkadian invocation to an anony-
    mous god 230
alcohol 20
Alexander 43
allegory 2, 27, 43, 50, 52–53, 63, 65,
    71, 73–74, 77, 79, 86, 104–105,
    118, 174, 201, 204, 207, 212, 216,
    244, 249, 251–254, 256–257,
    259–260, 266–267, 269–270,
    272–274, 285, 289, 301, 326–327,
    345, 410
alliteration 179, 205, 207, 278, 290,
    310, 312, 345, 383

allusion 174, 276, 290, 295
Amalekites 306, 312
ambiguity of life 165
Amen-em-opet 29, 31, 91, 121, 222
Amenhotep III 223
Amenope 33
Ammon 326
Ammonites 361, 367
Amon 223
Amon-Re 222
Amorites 30
Amos 4, 86, 90, 106, 202, 229, 329,
    402
Amun 232
anagogy 74
analogy 252
anaphora 334–335
Anaphoric 370
Anat 229
Ancient Near East 7, 17, 19, 25, 29,
    36, 83, 87, 93–94, 167, 174, 176,
    201, 221, 229, 232, 363, 402
angels 4
anger 20, 136, 145–146, 151, 154,
    156, 160, 187–188, 193, 309, 366,
    379
Ani 32
annihilation 163
announcement of judgment 332
anointed 315–316, 367–368, 376
anonymity 111
anthologies 224, 291, 400–401, 409
anthropomorphic 187, 241
anti-literature 284
Antiochus Epiphanes 273
antiphon 115, 229
antiphonal 353
anti-theme 155
antithetic 118, 135, 205, 222, 275–
    276, 312
anti-wisdom 97
Anu 229
Anum 231
aphorism 88, 118, 128, 140, 163, 195,
    197
Apocalypse of Abraham 236–237,
    239
apocalyptic 48, 78, 87, 110–111, 115,
    202–203, 205, 215, 284, 289, 329,
    346

Apocalyptic Oracle 212, 236
Apocrypha 3–4, 44
apocryphal 78
apocryphon 235
apodictic 89
apologetics 70
Apostle's Doctrine 50
Apostolic Church Ordinances 65
Apostolic Constitutions 67, 236, 239
apparition 212
appeal for deliverance 342
appeal for help 366
appeals 192–194
appetite 34, 158, 164
Arabic 263
Aram 198
Aramaic 320
Arians 66
Aristotle 125
Arius 252
ark of the covenant 305, 317
arrogance 109, 146, 321
art 283
artisan 2, 22, 99
Asa 204
Asaph 359–361
ascension 250
Aseneth 236–237
Ashkelon 314
assimilation 44
assonance 287
assumed truth 340
assurance 271
Assyria 29–30, 33, 35, 37–38, 101, 198,
    320, 325
asymmetry 277
atheism 125
atonement 143, 218, 271, 352
authenticity 94
authority 41, 49, 60–61, 73, 77, 94,
    107, 139, 146, 152–154, 163, 169,
    177, 219, 247–248, 254, 259,
    290–291, 305, 310, 338, 340, 351,
    367, 375, 380
authorship 94, 235, 247, 253, 257,
    265, 268, 271–273, 282, 288, 354,
    360–361, 410, 413
autobiographic 119–120
Azariah 205, 351

443

B

Baal 198, 229, 232, 322
Baal myths 228
Baba Bathra 70
Babylon 33–34, 230, 237, 253, 326,
   377
Babylonia 30, 38, 94–95, 231–232,
   288
bad 381
Balaam 30, 117, 301, 306, 322
Balak 306
balance 277, 292
balance of thought 280
ballad singers 117, 305
ballads 291
baptism 251
Barak 179, 197
Barnabas, Epistle of 50, 65, 247
Baruch 205, 237, 346, 350, 352
Bathsheba 265
battle 361, 366, 371, 373
Battle Blessing 210
Battle Boast 214
battle cries 215
battle curse 333
Beatitudes 107, 165
beauty 150, 389, 397, 399, 404–405
behavior 64–65, 67–68, 70, 83, 88,
   92–93, 96, 98, 100, 105, 107–108,
   113, 122, 126, 128–129, 140, 151,
   162–163, 165, 167, 234, 276, 291,
   400
Behemoth 340
Bel 230
belief 124–125
belief system 175
believer 111, 247, 381
Beloved 229, 231
Belshazzar 205, 345
benevolence 59
betrayal 372
better . . . than 371
Bezalel 99
Biblia hebraica stuttgartensia 207
Bildad 145, 148, 152, 339
biographical statement 387
birth announcement 299
Birth Oracle 212
blasphemy 148, 374
blessing 8, 15–17, 30, 98–100, 107,
   110, 122–123, 164, 191, 195–197,
   206, 210, 219, 223, 229, 236,
   300–302, 304–306, 308–310,
   318, 323, 347, 352, 366, 371,
   374–376
blessing and curse 196, 206, 215, 219,
   236, 308, 322–323
blessing for the king 370
Blessing of Moses 301–302
blessings of wisdom poem 348
blood 300, 416
bloodguilt 99
boast 369
Boaz 204
Book of Jashar 314
book of the Law 321
bow 228
braggadocio 312
breath of life 223
bride 249
brother 229, 397
building 35, 99
business 4, 38–39

C

Cain 112

calendar 215
call for help 415
call for lamentation 415
call to assembly 315
call to faithfulness during testing 348
Call to fidelity 210
Call to justice 212
call to praise 223, 365
call to repentance 417
call to worship 189, 210, 375
Canaan 26, 29–30, 33, 112, 124, 228–
   229, 300, 332
canon 2, 4, 13–14, 19, 31, 39, 45, 53,
   56, 65, 73, 77–78, 80–82, 85, 91,
   93–94, 120, 124, 140, 142, 155,
   166, 169–170, 176, 205, 207, 209,
   216, 219, 233–235, 237, 240, 242,
   249–250, 253, 257, 270, 283–284,
   289, 297, 316, 337, 340, 352, 354,
   377–378, 409–410
canonical approach 2–3, 25
canonical criticism 3
Carmel, Mount 396
case law 214, 217
catechesis 56
catechism 109
celebration 289, 374
Ceremonial Naming 210
ceremony 363–364
change of mood 181
chant 294
chaos 93, 366
character 384, 390
chasing after wind 159
chaste 129
Chester Beatty I papyrus 232
chiasmus 277
chiastic 293
children 4, 37, 40, 80, 88, 113, 120–
   121, 126, 129, 136, 163
choirmaster 333, 359
chorus 387–388, 393–395, 408
Christ 56, 61, 63–66, 68–70, 74, 78–
   79, 81, 132, 239, 248–254, 256,
   258, 261, 265, 268–269, 272–274,
   289
Christ's preeminence 267
Christian 218
christological 52, 65, 79, 252–254,
   268, 273
christology 61, 66, 83
Chronicler 23, 204, 206–207, 343,
   345, 358, 361
Chronicles 101, 204, 341, 343, 361
church 46, 48, 52, 57, 59, 64, 66, 68,
   74, 78, 83, 113, 248–254, 258,
   261, 263, 265–266, 270, 274, 410
city gate 39, 86, 141, 148
clan 60, 89, 98, 387
clan wisdom 38, 90–91, 93, 96, 106,
   141, 148
collage 401
collections 120, 185, 192, 233, 235,
   358–359
collections of proverbs 348
comedy 147, 163
comfort 200, 271, 419
commandment 89, 99, 109
commentary 307
commitment 389, 402
common sense 128
communal liturgy 373
community 2, 4, 13, 18, 25, 31, 40, 46,
   48, 53, 57, 63–64, 68, 77, 92, 94,
   150, 175, 181–182, 187–188,
   190–191, 195, 206, 217–218, 233,
   235, 237, 242, 244, 254, 289, 294,
   297, 305–306, 324, 351, 360,
   363–365, 367–368, 379–380,

   400, 421
community lament 351, 371–377,
   414
community meetings 175
community thanksgiving 375
comparative 274
comparative proverbs 139
comparison 91, 117, 119, 135
compassion 26
complaint 108, 142, 147, 149–150,
   182, 193, 237, 325, 360–361, 369,
   374, 420
conduct 53, 60, 68, 70, 72, 74, 97, 99–
   100, 102, 108, 111, 117, 122,
   125–126, 130, 136–137, 147–
   148, 157, 169, 371, 414
confession 193, 206, 217, 237, 265,
   307, 321, 372, 379
confession of confidence 372
confession of sin 204, 351, 379, 414–
   415
confession of trust 371
Confessional 275
confessions of belief 206
confidence 186, 376–377, 379–380
congregation of Israel 108
connotation 174
contemplation 223, 249, 258
content 101, 128, 276, 309
contradiction 104, 158, 160, 167, 191
contrition 154
control 188–191
conversion 80
cooperation 159
coronation 367–368
corporate laments 361, 363–364, 369
corporate song of thanks 366
corporate thanksgiving 376
correction 23, 122, 136
corrective literature 12
corrective to Torah 7
correspondence of components 278
cosmic 84, 188
cosmos 31, 67, 93, 153, 340
council 39
counsel 22–23, 39
counselor 15, 100
Counsels of Wisdom 34
court 7–8, 22, 24–25, 29, 32, 35, 37–
   38, 40, 98–99, 101, 121, 316, 322,
   389, 391, 395, 404
court history 240
court history of David 4
covenant 89, 251, 285, 364, 371–372,
   375, 405
covenant lawsuit 202
covenant love 380
crafty 24
creation 4, 8, 18–19, 24, 30–31, 64,
   66–68, 72, 79, 86–88, 93, 98,
   103–104, 106, 108, 112, 131–132,
   151–153, 155, 190–191, 194, 222,
   239–240, 260, 292, 300, 340, 353,
   365, 369–370, 373, 375, 377
creation challenge 213
creation hymn 348, 371
creation story 292
Creator 35, 70, 102, 223, 381
crocodile 224
crucifixion 61
cry for help 420
cult 18, 65, 86, 107, 177, 192, 196,
   205–206, 209, 215, 217–218, 282,
   287, 297, 305, 322, 329
cult-functional criticism 282
cultic chants 195, 206
cultic disputation 210, 215
cultic poetry 210, 214–215, 291
cultic prophecy 329

cultural settings 84
cunning 27
curse 15–17, 30, 144, 151, 206, 210, 229, 300, 306, 308, 310, 317, 323, 333, 375
cynical 163
cynicism 135

D

dā‘āt 22
daily conduct 30
daily living 4
Damascus 326
dame wisdom 48
Dan 301
dance 175
Daniel 37, 110, 204, 207, 216, 284, 343, 345, 351
David 7, 69, 89, 99–100, 176, 197–198, 204, 234–235, 239, 241, 247, 252–253, 265, 268, 271, 273, 287, 302, 313, 315, 339, 359–361, 373
David's Lament for Saul and Jonathan 302
day of the Lord 202, 331, 334
dead 332
Dead Sea Scrolls 233, 235
death 23, 33, 51, 66, 68, 109, 111, 114, 122, 130, 132–133, 135, 137, 145, 149, 152, 159, 162–164, 168, 182, 186, 194, 249, 251, 265, 289, 315, 346, 366, 373, 379, 384
death sentence 322–323
debate 216
Deborah 179, 197, 301
Decalogue 5, 50, 89, 99, 196, 206, 302, 306–307
decision 6–7, 18, 100, 168, 182
declarative song of praise 282, 366
defeat 187, 219, 371–372
dejection 380
Delilah 197, 312
deliverance 195, 366, 372–373
denotation 174
depression 373, 380
deprivation 415, 419
descriptive song of praise 223, 230, 282, 366
despair 334
desperation 161
determinism 127
Deuterocanon 2–6, 11, 17, 29, 44, 50, 77–78, 82, 97, 111, 113, 115, 181, 205, 207, 346, 353
Deuteronomic 288, 321
Deuteronomic history 8, 100, 123, 173, 240, 353
Deuteronomist 4, 206, 311
Deuteronomistic 26, 99, 121, 142, 144, 170, 193, 204, 307, 322, 326
Deuteronomistic literature 123
Deuteronomy 5, 8, 15–18, 23, 27, 99, 175, 196, 306–309, 313, 317, 322
devil 97
devotion 11, 72, 143, 191, 194, 255, 265, 307, 351, 369, 381, 384, 388–389, 391, 399, 401, 404
devotional 254, 275
dialectic 160
dialogue 142, 155, 198, 213, 216, 236, 318, 339
Diaspora 43–44
diatribes 216
Didache 50, 65
didactic 27, 31–33, 35–36, 41, 46, 84, 86, 107–109, 113, 117–118, 127, 209, 216, 222, 237, 259, 291, 340,

373
didactic poetry 340
didactic questions 91
didacticism 128, 139, 142
diligence 23, 39
directive 107, 125
dirge 281
dirge meter 278
disadvantaged 59
disappointments 217
discernment 15, 22, 24
disciple 59–60
discipline 23, 26, 30, 64–66, 73, 109, 126, 136
discord 136
discouragement 191
discretion 5–6, 22, 36, 56, 101, 127, 131, 165
disobedience 7, 16, 136, 326
disorientation 289
disputation 305
dispute 318
dispute over suicide 33, 221
distress 191–192
divination 34
divine comfort 219
divine commissioning 200
Divine Council 374
divine council 143
divine decrees 292
divine deliverance 193, 304
divine demands 205
divine determinism 136
divine displeasure 200
divine favor 217
divine freedom 81, 85
divine gift 38
divine help 186
divine identity 304
divine intervention 123, 193, 314
divine judgment 112, 201–202, 328
divine knowledge 102
divine lawsuit 212, 324, 332
divine mercy 109
divine message 175
Divine Name 215
divine name 210
divine plan 100
divine power 218
divine protection. 260
divine punishment 193–194, 248
divine reward 27
divine speech 327
divine vindication 193
divine warrior 228, 334
308
Divine Warrior Hymn 210
divine will 21–22, 30, 127, 137, 143–144, 151, 166, 218, 353
divine wisdom 103
divine word 311, 344
divine wrath 151, 189
divinity 78, 110
divorce 218, 328
Doctrina Apostolorum 50, 65
doctrine 18, 238, 250, 267, 271
dogma 59
double entendre 285, 311
doubt 81, 115, 126, 156, 168–170, 188, 244, 268, 305, 311
doxology 185, 358
drama 198, 209, 216, 218, 232, 248, 273–275, 320, 324, 384, 400, 402, 405
dramatic dialogue 214
dramatic poetry 313
dramatic ridicule of idols 212
dramatization 212
dream 15, 31, 34, 110, 204–205, 240,

285, 305, 343–345, 391, 393–394, 401, 408
dream account 212
drinkers 119
dualism 122

E

ēsâ. 22
ēhillīm 358
Ea 34
earth 324
earthquake 372
ecclecticism 380
Ecclesiastes 2–8, 11–15, 17, 21, 25–26, 29, 33–35, 45–46, 54–56, 58–59, 61, 64, 68, 70, 72–73, 79–81, 83, 85, 87, 95, 100, 102, 106, 114, 119–120, 122, 126, 140, 142, 150, 157–158, 161, 163–164, 166–170, 203, 249, 256, 260, 340, 378, 402, 409
Ecclesiasticus 44, 113
economics 163
Edom 29, 33, 51, 104, 187, 202, 306, 326, 330–331, 333, 380, 419
education 5, 8, 12, 36–38, 78, 115, 129
Egypt 7–8, 15, 25, 29–33, 39, 46, 87–88, 94–95, 98–99, 112, 121, 124, 207, 221–224, 227, 231–232, 236, 288, 305, 320, 325–326, 376–377, 389, 402, 413
elders 39, 66, 86, 141, 148
election 18, 45, 98, 105, 181, 187, 190, 197, 215, 250, 301, 306, 364, 372–373, 375–376, 420
election of David 354
elector 381
elevated speech 177
Eli 312, 363
Elihu 71, 145, 147, 152
Elijah 142, 319
Eliphaz 145, 148, 152
Elisha 198
ellipsis 293
Elohim 108, 360, 372
emotions 191, 209, 243, 254, 372, 379, 398–399, 409, 421
emotion 402
emotional 192, 194, 198, 206, 300, 384, 389, 393, 395, 417
emotional distress 186
emotional expression 182
emptiness 161
empty 13–14, 51, 157–158, 160–161, 165
enclosure 285
encomium 114, 266
encounter 153
end of the world 334, 345
end-rhyme 278
enemies 108, 186, 219, 223, 229, 232, 240, 268, 276, 289, 297, 305–306, 308–309, 317, 319, 329, 362, 364, 369–373, 375–377, 414–415, 417, 420
enjoyment 13–14, 33, 159, 161, 163, 165, 167–168
Enlil 229
Enoch 114
enoptics 249
enthronement 229
enthronement festival 367
enthronement psalms 282, 380
entrance liturgy 370
Enuma Elish 34

envelope structure 293, 391
Ephraim 300–301
epic 12, 274
Epic of Gilgamesh 30
epic poetry 236, 291–292, 421
epicurean 164
Epistle of Barnabas 247
epitaph 315
epithalamium 248, 253
equity 24
erotic 274
eroticism 421
Esarhaddon 35
Esau 219, 300–301
eschatology 240
essentialism 158
essentialist 164
Esther 90, 204, 284
eternal life 372
Eternal Wisdom 63
Ethan the Ezrahite 359
ethics 5, 7, 26, 53, 61, 88, 108, 110,
    117, 122, 124–125, 188, 249
etiology 210, 215
Eve 300
evil 21, 68, 80–81, 88, 108, 119, 137,
    143, 148, 154, 161, 163, 189, 219,
    362, 372, 419
exaggeration 264
excess 122
exclusion 285
exclusivism 380
exhortations 50, 120
exile 38, 41, 200, 215, 219, 259, 268,
    336, 350, 352, 411, 414, 419, 421
exodus, the 31, 258, 308, 373, 375
Exodus, the Book of 99, 175, 195,
    302, 304, 307, 313
experience 160, 168, 174
experiential 223
Ezekiel 17, 104–105, 201–202, 209,
    326–327, 332, 350, 402
Ezra 50, 204, 268

F

fable 197, 207, 213, 310
faith 5, 7, 18, 30, 59, 62, 68, 86–87,
    145, 161, 170, 232, 267, 372,
    378–379, 381
faithful 114, 129, 375
faithfulness 206, 319, 324, 329, 368,
    371, 374
family 8–9, 26, 29–30, 36–38, 40, 61,
    66, 89, 100, 113, 129–130, 132–
    133, 136, 143, 150, 158, 215, 249,
    328, 389, 398, 409–410, 421
famine 326, 364
fantasy 398, 401
fatalism 163, 166, 168, 330
father 32, 219
Fealty Oath 214
fear of the Lord 3, 13, 15, 20–21, 30,
    35, 65, 81, 99, 103, 109, 111, 113,
    115, 123–124, 128, 150, 157–158,
    164–166, 169–170, 375–376
fear of the Lord poem 348
feast of booths 367
female 388, 392, 396–400, 405, 407
fertility 288
fertility religion 31, 229
festivals 175, 190, 215, 322, 365
Fides Nicaena 65
figurative language 174, 253, 258
figures 191
first fruits 307
folk songs 175
folly 24, 59, 62, 99, 101, 103, 112,

122–123, 126, 129–133, 137–
    138, 158, 160, 162, 164, 167
food 20, 113, 159, 165
fool 5–6, 19, 22, 51, 62, 100, 122–123,
    125–127, 130–131, 133, 136, 138,
    164–167, 315
foolish 15, 58, 100, 112, 128, 130, 137,
    139
forgiveness 234, 237, 265, 353, 366,
    370, 372–373, 375, 379, 417
form 27, 94, 105, 107–108, 114, 117,
    119, 128, 173, 181, 191–192, 194,
    203–205, 207, 216–217, 232–
    233, 236–238, 244, 255–257, 261,
    269, 273, 275–276, 284, 286, 289,
    299, 303–307, 309, 315–317, 319,
    321–322, 325, 327, 333, 338, 340,
    345–346, 352, 357, 368, 383–384,
    394, 400, 402, 412
form criticism 83–84, 110, 176, 209,
    214, 232, 281–283, 291, 357, 361,
    363
Former Prophets 16, 99, 196, 198,
    209, 310–311, 321, 323, 343
formgeschichtliche method 281
forms 8, 17, 27, 30–31, 43, 50, 52, 84–
    86, 88, 101, 104–105, 113, 115,
    121, 123, 127, 132, 137, 142, 167,
    196, 203, 206, 209, 215, 217–218,
    221, 223, 232, 235, 242, 270, 272,
    275–276, 290, 292, 294, 297, 306,
    322, 330, 332, 337, 339–340, 365
formulas 278
foxes 391, 405, 407
free verse 345
free will 70
friendship 135–136, 158, 410
frustration 146, 216, 244, 333
future 18, 126, 134, 159, 162, 164,
    182, 201–202, 216, 223–224, 265,
    333, 337, 345, 351, 381

G

garden 404–405, 407
Gath 314
Gattungen 281
gazelle 224
gender-matched parallelism 277
General Psalm 236
Genesis 97, 115, 173, 195, 222–223,
    299–301
genre 43, 83–84, 209, 214, 216, 232,
    239, 256, 271, 273, 281, 283,
    291–292, 329, 340, 345, 358, 361,
    363, 367–368, 401, 415, 421
Gerizim, Mount 310
gibbōrîm 315
Gibeon 310
Gilboa 314
Gilgamesh 30
Gladness 137
glory 334
gnomic 274
gnomic sayings 197
gnosticism 238
God 6–8, 11–13, 15–16, 62, 66, 69, 71,
    73, 79, 84, 88, 92, 103–104, 114,
    122, 127, 132, 137, 141, 147–149,
    151–154, 157–160, 162, 166–
    168, 177, 179, 186–188, 191–194,
    218, 223, 238–241, 243–244, 254,
    259, 272, 302–304, 306, 308,
    324–326, 334, 340, 346, 350, 353,
    360, 369, 373, 380, 410, 415, 417,
    419, 421
God as king 374–375
God's anger 193, 417, 419

God's deeds 190
God's deliverance 186, 371
God's displeasure 201
God's faithfulness 268, 374
God's goodness 372, 377
God's grace 260
God's hearing 187
God's help 317
God's identity 303–305, 307, 321
God's intervention 194, 308, 321,
    334, 351, 362–363, 368, 371–372,
    374, 417
God's judgment 326–327, 329
God's kindness 377
God's kingdom 375
God's kingship 189
God's knowledge 377
God's love 105, 108, 202, 249, 254,
    328
God's majesty 369
God's mercy 308, 353, 364, 374, 376,
    415, 417–418
God's mystery 375
God's nature 106
God's plan 182, 374
God's presence 191, 240, 306, 327,
    381
God's punishment 371, 419
God's purpose 162, 321, 338
God's righteousness 369
God's spirit 161
God's steadfast love 371, 376, 417
God's trustworthiness 206, 376
God's vindication 351
God's will 162
God's wrath 186, 371, 374
Godhead 47–48
Gog 327
golden calf 257
Goliath 198, 313, 354
good 6, 8, 13, 15, 17, 20, 53, 68, 80, 88,
    108, 158, 163, 165, 167, 191, 268,
    381
good and evil 5, 21, 35, 98, 122, 144,
    146
good life 146
good works 258
goodness 148, 380
goods 167–168
gospel 60–61
Gospels 57
government 37
grace 70, 80, 86, 100, 251, 260
grammatical parallelism 287
grandeur 404
Great Hymn to Khnum 222
great soul 271
greed 135
Greek 35, 37, 43, 46–48, 52, 56–57,
    61, 65, 67, 70, 77, 94–95, 111,
    114, 174, 179, 236, 242, 247, 256,
    263, 277, 292, 358, 369, 378
Greek culture 6, 29
Greek Orthodox 78
grief 160, 186–187, 191, 193, 195,
    314–315, 369, 380, 414, 417
guilt 142, 244, 352

H

Hokmâ 22
Habakkuk 17, 106, 202–203, 223, 333
Hagar 299
Haggai 202, 335–336
hallelujah 358
Ham 300
Hammurabi 30
Hammurabi, code of 30

Hanani 204, 343
Hannah 197, 217, 239, 312, 363
happiness 108, 168
Hardjedef 29, 31
harp 358
Harper 33
harvest 307, 366, 373–374
harvest festival 374
hate 163
headings 120
healing 114, 219, 234, 346, 365–366
health 135
heaven 122, 267, 324
heavenly court 142
hebel 13, 161
hedonism 158, 160
hedonist 164
hell 4, 70, 80, 122
Hellenism 44, 78
Hellenistic 95, 114, 353
Heman the Ezrahite 359
hermeneutics 111, 143, 175, 258, 297
Hermon, Mount 376
heroes 315
hesed 380
Heshbon 305
hexameter 242
Hezekiah 25, 54, 95, 99, 121, 198, 252, 288, 320
hieroglyphic 31
high places 314, 332
Hindu 263
historians 31, 250
historical 186–187, 191, 218
historical boasts 322–323
historical criticism 270, 273, 281
historical hymn 348
historical poem 354
historical revelation 88
historical-criticism 272, 297
historiography 114
history 74, 88–89, 94, 100, 124, 173, 175, 201, 204, 206, 215, 218–219, 223, 231, 239, 258, 260, 272, 307, 324, 345, 353, 380–381, 384, 392–393, 401–402, 420–421
history of Israel 18
hōkmâ 35
holiness 305
Holiness Pronouncement 210
holy 380
Holy Spirit 56, 67, 85, 101, 111, 132, 258
home 132, 409
Homer 279
honesty 136, 154, 188
honor 123, 131, 159
hope 126, 158–159, 166, 182, 186, 191, 193, 200, 207, 215, 217, 237, 240, 268, 299, 314, 324, 327, 329, 332–336, 338, 346, 351, 371, 374, 380–381, 411, 418–419
hopelessness 188
horse 224
Hosea 4, 105, 202, 207, 229, 284, 328, 401
house of the Lord 190
hubris 109
Huldah 321
human conduct 22, 45, 53, 88
humanism 100
humanistic 157
humans 148, 161–163, 167, 223, 240, 260, 272, 300, 345, 372, 390
humiliation 321, 373
humility 123, 126–127, 131, 137, 139, 159, 345, 375, 377
humor 306, 312
Hushai 100–101

hymn 18, 30, 65, 108, 110, 113, 131, 142, 149–150, 182, 190, 197, 203, 210, 222, 229, 231–233, 236–237, 239, 256, 266, 270, 281, 289, 292, 303, 327, 332–333, 339, 342, 344–346, 348–350, 353, 357, 360–361, 364–367, 369–370, 372–377, 381, 391
hymn in praise of Israel's ancestors 114
hymn of community thanksgiving 373
Hymn to Amon as Creator 223
Hymn to Amon-Re 222
Hymn to Ishtar 231
Hymn to Khnum 223
hymn to the ancestors 205
Hymn to Wisdom 205, 213, 339, 348
hymnic 107
hyperbole 186, 264
hypocrisy 248
hypostatization 29, 37, 46–48, 60, 67, 72, 84, 87–88, 111, 132

I

I Will Praise the Lord of Wisdom 34
idea 174
Ideal Wife 133
idealism 40
idealistic 154
identity 188, 190, 193, 206, 215, 218, 286, 302, 304, 306, 308, 381
identity building 182
idolatry 46, 62, 103, 112
idols 103, 336, 375–376
illness 186, 362, 370–371, 375
imagery 86, 118, 137, 161, 174, 186–188, 190–191, 195, 200–202, 216, 224, 228–229, 231–233, 244, 254, 258, 260, 266, 275, 283–285, 325, 328, 330, 332, 334, 336–337, 351, 366, 373–374, 376, 384, 386, 388–389, 392–393, 395–396, 398–401, 403, 405, 407–408, 415–417, 419
immortality 81, 111, 149, 205
imperative 223
imprecations against enemies 192, 224, 232, 415
incantation 34, 205, 310
incarnation 57, 62
inclusio 178, 181, 257, 295, 316, 391, 395, 403
inclusion 285
incomplete 277
incomplete parallelism 276
individual lament 361, 363–365, 369–373, 375–376, 414
individual song of thanksgiving 369, 374
individuality 286
industrious 121–122, 133, 137
inevitabilities 164, 166
inevitability of death 159
infinitude 104
injustice 33, 104, 109, 119, 124, 149, 151, 161–163, 331, 372, 374, 381, 416
innocence 142, 346, 369
inscrutability 153–154
insightfulness 99
inspiration 2, 4, 37, 70–71, 175–176, 247, 254, 264, 272, 297, 322, 338, 340
instruction 8, 12, 23, 29–31, 36, 38, 45, 53, 56–57, 60, 64–65, 68, 107–108, 112–114, 121, 128, 136,

145, 155–157, 169, 175, 187, 217–218, 244, 251, 379–381, 400
instruction of Amen-em-opet 29, 32, 222
Instruction of Ani 32
Instruction of Kagemni 31
Instruction of Prince Hardjedef 29, 31
Instruction of Ptahhotep 29, 31
Instruction to King Merikare 29, 32
instructional 113, 129
instruments 333, 343, 359
integrity 151, 164, 372
intellectual 16, 22, 63, 80, 100, 168, 223
intelligence 16, 59, 132, 163
Intertestamental Literature 94
intertextuality 289
intervention 188, 370
intimacy 387
intolerance 99
introspection 51
invective 372
Investment with Divine Authority 210
Invitation to Wisdom 131
invocations 219, 305
Ipuwer 33
irony 14, 34, 62, 97, 104, 112, 117, 128, 130, 135, 149, 157, 163–164, 170, 174, 180, 311, 366, 414
Isaac 300
Isaiah 4, 17, 101, 198–201, 288, 320–322, 324–325, 327, 402
Ishtar 231
isolation 285–286

J

Jabin 179
Jacob 112, 195, 240, 300–301, 309, 344
Jael 180
James 56, 63–64
Jamnia 410
Japheth 300
Jashar 197, 314
jealousy 391
Jehoshaphat 361, 367
Jehu 198
Jeremiah 4, 17, 40, 86, 103–104, 106, 200–201, 217, 242, 256, 268, 272–273, 288, 324, 327, 350, 412–413
Jericho 310
Jerusalem 110, 190–191, 235, 237, 243, 263, 288, 320, 327, 335, 350, 372, 411, 413
Jesus 50, 56–61, 64–67, 70, 78, 81, 110, 193, 252, 259, 284
Jesus ben Sira 113
Jesus' divinity 252
Jethro 27, 38, 98
Jewish interpretations 50
Jezebel 319
Job 3–8, 11–17, 21–24, 26, 33–36, 39, 44–46, 50–51, 54–55, 58–59, 61, 63–65, 68–71, 73, 78–83, 86–87, 93, 95, 102, 106, 114, 122, 126, 140–143, 147–149, 152–153, 155, 157, 166, 168, 170, 203, 207, 209, 216, 256–257, 274–275, 284, 295, 339–340, 346, 350–351, 378–379, 410–411, 417, 420
Jobab 51
Joel 202, 329, 364
John 65
John the Baptizer 59

John, Gospel of 238
Jonah 203, 207, 284, 331–332, 366
Jonathan 197, 302, 316
Joseph 4, 15, 31, 37–38, 86, 90, 98,
    112, 252, 300–301, 305, 395
Joseph and Aseneth 236–237
Joshua 16, 196, 284, 310
Josiah 99, 288, 321–322
Jotham 310–311, 315
joy 20, 34, 158–159, 189, 191–192,
    271, 312, 335, 351, 370, 374, 376,
    380, 404, 421
Jubilees 236
Judaism 18, 77–78, 83, 94
Judas Iscariot 249
judge 15–16, 24, 27, 37–38, 101, 341
Judges 142, 197, 310
judgment 152, 160, 189, 200–201,
    228, 233, 324, 327, 329, 332–333,
    336–337, 373–374, 377, 402, 414
judgment oracle 202, 212, 321
justice 39, 59, 103, 106, 108–109, 115,
    124, 131, 137, 141, 144–146, 149,
    152, 155, 157–158, 163, 168,
    188–189, 202, 215, 290, 303, 324,
    372–373, 375, 419
justification 267
juxtapositions 119

K

Kagemni 31
Kenites 306
key words 295
Khnum 222–223
kindness 44, 66, 126, 193
king 2, 7, 9, 12, 16, 18, 22, 24–27, 35,
    37–38, 41, 54, 59, 66, 87, 99–100,
    105, 111, 121, 137, 157, 161,
    163–165, 188, 197, 219, 223, 231,
    243, 276, 315–316, 353, 365, 367,
    370, 372, 375–376, 380, 395, 402,
    419
kingdom 57, 59–60, 149, 189
kingdom of God 265
Kings, Book of 141, 197, 317
kingship 215, 289, 297, 315, 360–361
kingship psalm 210, 215, 223, 239,
    282
kingship, festival of 282
knowledge 6, 22, 34, 46, 52, 71, 81,
    131, 141, 159, 164
knowledge of God 103, 109
Korah 305, 360–361
Korahites 359–360

L

Laban 300
Ladder of Jacob 236, 240
lament 109, 115, 142, 149, 158, 182,
    191, 197, 209, 211, 215, 230–232,
    237, 239, 265, 269, 273, 281–282,
    289, 292, 302, 313–316, 319–320,
    323, 325–327, 332–333, 343, 346,
    351–352, 354, 360, 362–363, 367,
    369–377, 379, 381, 412, 417
Lament for Abner 302
lamentation 182, 201, 235
Lamentation over the Destruction of
    Sumer and Ur 229
Lamentation over the Destruction of
    Ur 229
Lamentations 173, 175, 177, 182–
    183, 192–194, 197, 201, 229, 232,
    235, 240, 242–244, 254, 256,
    259–260, 266, 268, 271–273, 281,
    288, 296, 314, 364, 401, 411, 418,

421
Latin 263
Latter Prophets 17, 101, 199, 202,
    207, 322, 328, 351
laughter 159
law 31, 43, 45, 47, 50, 52, 54–55, 60–
    61, 84–86, 88–90, 96, 124, 169,
    250, 257, 265, 268, 296–297, 303,
    310, 368
lawsuit 202, 324
laziness 121–122, 133, 137–138
lĕdāvid 360
leadership 305
Lebanon 336
legal 196, 215, 218, 307, 313
legal forms 206
Legal Prohibition 211
legalism 7
legalistic 45, 125
leitmotifs 339, 403, 408
Leitwörter 295
Lemuel 95, 133
Leviathan 340
Levites 305, 308
Levitical families 361
Leviticus 195, 304
libraries 30–31
lies 24
life 135, 137, 159, 164, 373
Life Change 218
Life of Schnudi 65
life setting 281, 284, 363, 365, 368,
    371
Lilies 359
line 264
lineation 174, 205–206, 293, 327, 340
lined prose 201
lined psalms 269
linguistic structure 315
linguistics 284
litany 190
literary 286
liturgical enactment 181
liturgical poetry 235, 340, 343
liturgical prayer 323
liturgical summons 198
liturgy 109, 117, 150, 175, 179, 187,
    189–190, 193, 196–197, 199,
    204–207, 209, 215, 218, 229, 254,
    287, 290–291, 317, 346, 351–352,
    357, 373, 375, 380, 402
Logos 52, 63, 132
Lord of Hosts 263
Lot 112
love 4, 136, 163, 182, 194–195, 231–
    232, 240, 244, 249, 254, 258, 268,
    271, 274, 285, 303, 374, 383–384,
    386, 388, 390–391, 393, 398–402,
    404–405, 409–410
love notes 401–402
love poetry 2, 4, 117, 182, 206–207,
    209, 213, 216, 224, 229, 232, 289,
    296, 400, 402
love song 199, 213, 228, 270, 285, 291
Love Song/Oracle 213
Lovers' Descriptions 389
loyalty 12, 30, 59, 151
Luke 58–60
lyric poetry 274, 291

M

ma'at 88
ma'at 31, 88
madness 158–159
Magicians 31
majesty 189, 238
Major Prophets 199, 322

Malachi 59, 202, 336
male 388, 392, 396–399, 404–405,
    407
Man and His God 34
Manasseh 187, 198, 300
mandrakes 397
Marcionite 65
Marduk 230
marriage 4, 30, 40, 131, 133, 136, 202,
    218, 244, 249, 253, 313, 328, 387,
    392, 399–400, 402
marriage poems 231
martyrs 249
Mary 256
masculine 393
Masoretes 181, 295
Masoretic 207, 234, 241–242, 279
Masoretic text 177
Matthew 58–59
maturity 129
meaning 153, 157–158, 162–163,
    165–166, 168, 174
meaning of life 126, 167, 170
measured prose 201, 208–209, 313,
    327, 337
measured speech 304
mediator 240
medieval 261, 281
Medieval Literature 71, 255
mediocrity 22
meditation 23, 124, 259–260, 381
megatheme 123
Melchizedek 300
melody 217, 264, 359
mercy 112, 193, 248, 258, 303, 377,
    419
Mercy Song 211
Merikare 29, 32
Merodach-baladan II 35
Mesopotamia 25, 29–30, 34, 124, 132,
    229, 231–232, 367
messiah 61, 65, 252, 273, 367, 373
messianic age 259
Messianic Oracle 212
messianic psalm 248, 265
metaphor 35, 135, 139, 174, 191–192,
    194–195, 241, 249, 257, 259, 261,
    264, 266, 283, 285, 292, 312, 321,
    345, 370, 375, 384, 390, 392, 394,
    396–397, 401, 405, 407–408,
    420–421
metatheme 122, 404
meter 174, 178–180, 182, 196, 204–
    205, 207, 241, 255–257, 261, 264,
    275, 277–281, 284, 286–287, 290,
    293–296, 304, 322, 327, 338, 359,
    383, 394, 412
metonymy 174, 189
metrical 118
metrical psalms 269–270
metrical structure 174
Micah 202, 332
midrash 44, 54, 71–72, 114, 243–244,
    252, 259
Midrash Rabbah 243
Midrashim 243
Mikra 44
miktām 358
Milcah 300
military boast 313
mind 126
Minor Prophets 202, 328
miracle formula 211, 322–323
miracles 60, 112, 272, 319
Miriam 305
Mishnah 53
mnemonic device 134
Moab 187, 305–306, 319, 326
Moabites 30

mockery 321
moderation 135
monastic 74, 79–80
money 125, 164, 167
monotheism 30–31, 36, 85, 132, 231–232, 321
mood 264, 267, 334, 402, 411
moral 24, 60, 65–66, 99, 101–102, 105, 107–109, 122, 124, 126, 128, 135, 142–143, 145, 156, 158, 188, 249, 252, 258, 291, 366, 381
moral instruction 51, 62, 213
moral order 45
moral responsibility 16, 62
morality 5, 30, 41, 108, 125, 164, 400
morals 53, 200
morphology 278, 287
Moses 27, 29, 38, 54, 70, 98, 176, 195–197, 242–243, 271, 301–305, 309, 359, 362, 375
mourning 243
music 174, 198, 203, 217, 253, 259, 291, 319, 333, 339, 358, 361, 412
mystery 150, 254, 261, 274
mystical 124, 258–259, 265
myth 283

N

Nabal 99–100
nagging wife 122
Nahum 202, 223, 333
name 223, 232, 305, 377
naming ceremonies 215
naming rituals 215
narrative 46, 196, 199, 204, 284, 290–291, 297, 309
narrative criticism 272
narrative parallelism 205–206
narrative poetry 313
narrative psalms 368
Nathan 55
nationalism 373
natural 249
natural ability 38
natural law 45
natural order 31
natural principles 45
natural revelation 12, 62, 85, 370
natural world 188, 190
nature 33, 86, 106, 353
nature hymn 370
Nazirite 305
Nebuchadnezzar 204, 344–345
needy 375
Nehemiah 204, 341
New Testament 56, 78, 94, 248, 251, 265–266
nihilism 160–161
Nineveh 202, 333
Ninth of Ab 421
Nisaba 132
Noah 112, 299–300
non sequitur 315
nonbeing 168
nondirective 107
number parallelism 277
Numbers 195–196, 304, 306
numerical formula 119
numerical patterns 296
numerical sayings 91
Nursery rhymes 291

O

Oath Pledging Loyalty to King 212
Obadiah 202, 223, 330–331, 333
obedience 7, 15–16, 18, 26, 109, 124–

125, 137, 308–309, 350
ode 112
Odes of Solomon 65, 238
Oholah 201
Oholiab 99
Oholibah 201
omnipotence 127, 148
omniscience 34, 66
Once . . . Now 416
onomastica 32–33
onomatopoeia 179, 181
oppression 159, 163
optimism 142, 164
oracle 30, 118, 134, 175, 182, 198–202, 204, 207, 209, 215, 306, 316, 319–322, 324–325, 336–337, 343, 401
Oracle Against False Prophets/Priests 212
oracle of David 316
oracle of hope 212, 216, 332
Oracle Prophesying Defeat of Enemies 212
oracles against the nations 326
Oracles of Balaam 301
oracles of judgment 215
oracular poetry 340
oral 30, 36, 38, 41, 43, 134, 175, 205, 207, 290–292, 295, 303, 309, 337
oral composition 176
oral instruction 8
order 26, 45, 53, 64, 73, 88, 97–98, 103, 123, 131, 163–164, 191
orientation 289
orthodox 51, 77, 81, 83, 141, 147, 154, 350
overstatement 174

P

Palanquin 391
Papyrus Chester Beatty I 224
Papyrus Harris 227
parable 60, 73, 86, 110, 117, 207, 213, 259, 292
paradigm 87
paradox 174
parallel 118, 124, 127, 136, 190–191, 193, 195, 201, 222–223, 239, 261, 278, 306, 338, 345, 347, 371
parallel word pair 277
parallelism 33, 118–119, 127–128, 178–181, 183, 195, 203–207, 221–222, 228, 230–231, 237–239, 261, 272, 275–280, 284, 286–287, 292–296, 303–304, 309, 312–313, 315, 338, 340, 383
paranomasia 257
parenesis 57, 129, 169
parenetic 114, 117
parent 40, 113, 124, 126, 136, 251, 409
parousia 59
passion 61, 389–390, 402, 404, 409–410
past 159, 162, 164, 182
pastoral images 405
pathos 109, 192, 202, 264, 417
patience 34, 63, 65, 69, 145, 156, 165, 258, 390
patriarch 219, 375
patriarchal history 299
patristic 254, 281
patristic literature 64, 247
pattern 174
Paul 56, 61–63
peace 190–191, 202, 336, 399
Pelagians 70

Penalty Decree 211
penance 230, 232, 264
penitence 243, 357, 363, 370, 372
pentameters 242
Pentateuch 44, 51, 53
performance 186, 190, 192, 195, 203, 217–218, 253, 281–282, 294–295, 305, 313, 319, 338–339, 353, 359, 363–365, 373
performance of poetry 175, 182
Persia 288
personal confession 217, 379
personal lament 369–370, 372–373, 377
personal prayer 236
personification 46, 49, 52, 56, 72, 78, 81, 131–133, 174, 414
perspective 181
persuasion 338, 340
pessimism 35, 79, 141–142, 146, 160, 163, 168, 186, 314
pessimistic literature 33
petition 108, 231, 234, 371
pharaohs 38, 98, 111, 389
Pharisees 60
Philistia 187, 326, 336
Philistines 311, 313, 316
Philo of Alexandria 52
philosophy of living 6
phonology 278
physicians 114
physics 249
piety 44, 152
pilgrim 190
pilgrimage 371, 376
pit 366
plague 364
plagues 112
pleas for deliverance 320
pleasing God 159
pleasure 22, 158–159, 161, 163
poem 12
Poem of the Righteous Sufferer 33–34
Poetic Dialogue 323
Poetic Features 178
Poetic Speech 337
poetry 169, 173–174, 176–177, 179, 181, 183, 185, 187, 191–206, 209, 214, 217–218, 221–222, 228–229, 231–233, 235–237, 239–244, 251, 255–257, 259–261, 263–265, 267, 269–272, 274–275, 277–279, 282–284, 286, 289–293, 299, 301–307, 309, 311–313, 318, 320, 322, 324–325, 327, 329–330, 333–341, 343, 345–348, 351, 357, 377, 381, 383–384, 400, 409, 411, 420–421
poetry, definition of 284, 340
poets 199, 247
political cartoon 313
politics 128
polytheism 30, 57
poor 26, 44, 59, 61, 102, 108, 124, 159, 219, 250, 371, 375, 377
positivism 21
postexilic 38, 88, 90, 95, 121
Post-Reformation 271
Potiphar's wife 98
potter 223
poverty 74, 119, 135, 137
power 104, 319, 334, 366, 370
practical skill 11
pragmatic 83, 86
pragmatism 59
praise 109, 175, 186, 189–192, 194, 197, 204, 217, 219, 222–223, 229, 231, 233, 236, 240, 263, 268, 271,

282, 290, 318, 332, 342, 345–346, 353, 357–359, 361–362, 364, 366, 369–370, 372, 374–375, 377, 396
Praise Song to King 214
prayer 67, 69, 108, 114–115, 186, 188, 190, 197–198, 203, 207, 236–238, 240, 264–265, 291–292, 296, 305, 317, 321, 323, 331, 333, 343, 346, 353, 357, 359, 363, 373, 379
prayer for deliverance 323
prayer for victory 370
prayer of Azariah 346, 351
prayer of Hezekiah 320
prayer of Manasseh 205, 346, 353
prayer of Sirach 348
precepts 89
predestination 81, 166, 260
predetermined 163
predictive 252
pre-existence 48, 66, 78
prescience 98
presecution 364
presumption 103
pride 73, 80, 126, 137, 139, 188–189, 201, 321, 376
priest 39–40, 60, 84, 215, 219, 233, 240, 337–338, 363, 365, 375–376, 380, 416, 419
priorities 19, 119
procession 373
proclamation 204
profession 207
profession of Divine Love 213
professional 16, 23, 26, 30, 37, 39, 84, 86, 89, 96, 99, 114, 121
profit 163
prohibitions 89, 99
promise 187, 200
promise of thanks 364
pronouncement of tribal status 211, 215
pronouncement of wisdom/prosperity 213
proof text 265, 269
property 132
prophecy 30–31, 39–40, 46, 48, 52, 54, 60, 83–84, 86–87, 89, 91, 96, 100, 102, 104–105, 115, 117, 123–124, 134, 173, 175–176, 179, 182, 198–199, 204, 206–207, 214–215, 218–219, 223, 229, 235, 240, 244, 247, 249–253, 256, 259–260, 264–265, 267–268, 271–272, 275, 283–284, 288–289, 291–292, 296–297, 301, 305, 316, 319, 321, 323–325, 333, 336–338, 340, 343–344, 358, 378, 401, 415–416, 419
Prophecy of Dynastic Doom 213
prophetic calling 332
prophetic discourse 286
prophetic forms 15
prophetic instruction 372
prophetic interpretation of events 322
prophetic literature 17
prophetic liturgy 375
prophetic oracle 198–199, 306, 322, 333
prophetic poetry 212, 215
prophetic psalm 372, 374
prophetic vision 120
prophetic wisdom 96
propriety 20
prose 217, 256–257, 277, 284, 286, 292–294, 312–313, 324–325, 328–329, 339, 344–345, 351, 401
prosperity 21, 23, 26, 31, 38, 166, 168, 190, 219, 324, 368, 373

prostitute 130
protection 187, 228, 237, 305, 364, 371, 373, 377
proud 380
provenance 41, 84
proverb 4, 7, 11, 13, 17, 25, 27, 30–35, 40, 44, 46, 61, 84, 86, 92, 95, 100, 103–105, 110, 113–114, 117–118, 128, 135–139, 157–158, 167, 196, 203, 209, 213, 216, 236, 263, 276, 312, 323, 338–340, 348, 371–372, 375–376, 410
Proverbs 1–8, 11–15, 17, 23–26, 29, 32, 34, 36, 45, 48–49, 51, 53–54, 56, 58–59, 61, 64–65, 67, 70, 72–73, 81, 83, 87–88, 90, 92, 95, 100, 111, 113–114, 117–124, 126, 131, 134–135, 139, 141–142, 154, 157, 163, 167, 169–170, 173, 176–177, 182, 203, 205, 222, 249, 256–257, 260, 275, 295, 323, 338, 340, 378, 400, 409, 421
providence 30, 67, 79, 218, 267, 364, 373, 375, 377, 411
prudence 23, 131
psalm 107, 115, 117, 142, 182, 204–207, 224, 230–231, 233, 237, 253, 264, 291, 314, 316, 319–320, 325, 327, 329, 333, 337, 340, 342, 346, 354, 411
Psalm 151 354
psalm of lament 419
Psalms 1, 17, 26, 53, 69, 102, 107, 120, 142, 173, 175–177, 182–183, 185–186, 191, 197, 207, 209, 221–223, 230–244, 247–250, 252–255, 257, 260, 264–265, 267–268, 270, 272–273, 275–276, 281–282, 287, 289, 295–297, 303, 309, 314, 323, 332, 339, 345–346, 348, 351, 357, 362, 368, 377–381, 401, 411, 420–421
Psalms of Solomon 49, 236, 239
Psalms of Thanksgiving 236
Pseudepigrapha 3, 44, 47, 235–240
pseudonymity 93, 111
Pseudo-Philo 239
Ptahhotep 29, 31–32
public reading 351
pun 145, 278
punishment 23, 26, 34, 112, 122, 126, 136, 138, 144, 150, 154, 189, 192–194, 201–202, 240, 324, 327, 329, 334, 347, 352, 369, 371–372, 374–375, 380, 419
punishment or reward 16
purposes of God 139

Q

Qeren Happuk 70
qinah 281
Qoheleth 157–162, 164–169, 217
quantity of text 278
Queen of Sheba 101, 317
questioning 119, 141–142, 146, 153, 186, 188, 334, 340
Qumran 233–235, 354

R

rabbis 38, 48, 52–56, 67, 72, 78, 81, 243–244, 410
Rabshakeh 320–321
rap music 292
Ras Shamra 287
rationalism 100
rationality 125

Re 88
reader 286
Reader-Oriented Strategies 283
realism 188, 216, 419
realistic 154
realities 188
reality 187, 218
reason 22, 53, 86, 100, 126, 154–155, 364
Rebekah 300
rebellion 105, 206, 219, 328, 341, 350, 373–375, 405
rebellious 114
rebukes 335
reconciliation 104
reconstitute reality 379, 381
Red Sea 373, 375
crossing 376
redeemer 81, 152, 188, 380
redemption 8, 86, 204, 223, 260, 324, 375
reductionistic 158
redundancy 190
reflection 5, 18, 23, 36, 54, 60, 118, 125–126, 129, 140, 160–161, 170, 191, 368, 398
reflective 141, 201
Reformation 71, 74, 77, 80, 233, 261, 263, 270, 281
refrain 204, 371, 395, 403
regularity 293
Rehoboam 27, 101, 198, 318
rejection 187–188, 192
rejoicing 189
religion 40, 124, 137, 168, 182, 338
religiosity 36
religious 31, 166, 217, 248, 283, 286, 292, 368–369, 381
religious demands 124
religious devotion 3, 20, 31
religious discernment 12
religious impulse 165
religious instruction 128
religious obligation 99
remembrance 181, 192–193, 197, 206, 218, 307, 310, 364
remembrance of better fortunes 415
remnant 268
repentance 80, 152–154, 194, 268, 338, 347, 352, 419
repetition 180–181, 190–191, 195–196, 198, 204, 207, 218, 229–230, 237–238, 257, 261, 277, 287, 290, 293, 295, 312, 337, 345, 353, 370, 383, 391, 401
report of suffering and grief 415
reputation 130
request for God's hearing 364
request for prophecy 323
requests for deliverance 357
resignation 155
responsibility 123, 215, 311, 324, 381
restoration 223, 327, 332, 374
resurrection 63, 66, 81, 149, 265, 289
retribution 17, 21, 27, 34, 36, 39, 58, 61, 68, 80–81, 83, 85, 92, 99–100, 102, 105, 109, 112, 114–115, 122–123, 135–136, 141, 144–148, 150, 154–159, 161, 163, 165, 169–170, 189, 197, 202, 340, 347, 373, 417, 419
revelation 43–45, 48, 54, 59, 62, 65, 74, 85, 88, 110, 152–153, 176, 216, 247, 259, 283, 303, 345
revelation in history 87
revenge 100
reward 4, 34, 44, 51, 80, 108, 110, 123, 131, 136, 140, 142, 144, 154, 156, 169, 347, 369

reward and punishment 7, 21, 26, 83, 92, 115, 156, 163, 170, 189
rhetoric 106, 134, 148, 150, 274
rhetorical criticism 283
rhetorical patterns 138
rhetorical questions 17, 27, 106, 337, 403
rhetorical units 120
rhyme 257, 261, 264, 290, 293
rhythm 174, 179, 196, 198, 203–205, 207, 261, 278, 280–281, 287, 290, 293, 296, 303–304, 311, 313, 319, 337, 339, 394, 412, 414
riches 23, 98, 101, 104, 109, 125, 163, 372
riddle 27, 104–105, 111, 119, 139, 147, 197, 213, 263, 301, 311, 323, 339
riddles 5
right 24, 163
right and wrong 16, 126
righteous 15, 17, 21, 24, 59, 69–70, 80, 102–103, 107, 110–111, 119, 122–123, 136–137, 139, 143, 148, 164, 166, 189, 233, 325, 333, 337, 347, 368–369, 371, 373, 375, 380–381
righteousness 16, 24, 26, 36, 44, 49, 103, 119, 126, 131, 143, 151, 153–154, 252, 325, 367, 370, 376
righteous-wicked dichotomy 109
ring composition 178, 295
ritual 18, 44, 49, 59, 124, 181, 206, 215, 217–218, 282, 296, 319, 338, 364, 367, 369, 381
ritual actions 175
Ritual Invocation 211
ritual poetry 180
rock 241
roles 389, 405
Roman Catholic Church 77
romance 396, 401, 404
Romans 62, 267
romanticism 272, 274
Rome 239
royal 175, 404
royal blessing 373
royal ceremonies 175
royal decree 214
royal lament 372
royal liturgy 375
royal psalm 239, 281–282, 287, 316, 323, 361, 367–368, 374
royal songs 197
royal thanksgiving 377
royal wedding 367, 401–402, 404
royal wedding song 252, 265, 372
Ruth 173, 204

S

śākal 23
Sabbath 241, 365
sacred history 114
sacrifice 312, 372
sage 4, 7, 15, 21, 30, 36, 38–39, 48, 54, 56, 58, 60–62, 84, 86, 89, 91, 93, 98, 107, 110, 114, 119, 124–125, 127, 131, 141, 155, 166, 221, 340
salvation 158, 215, 268, 316, 417
salvation history 100, 215, 218
salvation history hymn 211, 215, 341–342, 348
salvation history song 196
Salvation Oracle 213
Samson 197–198, 311, 339
Samuel 141, 175, 197, 239, 312, 354, 375

Sarah 52, 346
Sargon 35
Satan 69, 73–74, 143–144
satirical fable 323
Saul 101, 197, 302, 312, 316
savior 188, 249
Sayings of the Wise 32, 121
school 8, 31, 36–37, 39, 88, 91, 115
scorners 123
scribe 31, 35–36, 41, 45–46, 48, 50, 52, 60, 99, 107, 114, 132
Scripture 4, 64, 74, 77, 83, 94, 140, 233, 247–248, 250, 254, 256, 258, 261, 264, 267, 270, 283, 289, 351
secular poetry 291
seer 343
sela 358
self-control 64
self-determination 21, 80, 302
self-determinism 154
self-discipline 23
self-neglect 387
semantics 118, 278, 286–287, 340
Sennacherib 35
sense rhythm 279
sentence literature 183
sentences 36, 278
Septuagint 2, 17, 50–51, 63, 69, 234–235, 241–242, 249, 255, 351, 354, 378, 409, 413
Sermon on the Mount 58
serpent 97–98, 300
Servant Song 213
servants 136
Sethos I 227
setting 364, 367
setting in life 209, 402
setting of wisdom 25
sex 40, 118, 120, 129–130, 203, 219, 229, 244, 346, 387, 396–397, 408–409
sexes 285
shame 114, 123, 180
Sheba 197
Shechem 311
Shem 300
Shema 15, 109, 124, 196, 307, 368, 381
Sheol 106, 138–139, 331–332, 366, 374, 420
shepherd 370, 404
Shepherd of Hermes 50
shepherding 404
Shigionoth 333
shrewd 24
Shulammite 395, 402
Shunammite 69
sick 369–370
silence 415
similes 394
Simon 114
sin 68, 70, 81, 101, 104, 111–112, 124, 145, 147–148, 151–152, 159, 182, 218–219, 237, 240, 243–244, 254, 257, 271, 324–325, 334, 346–347, 350–351, 372–373, 380, 419
Sinaiticus 241
sinfulness 79
singing 175, 182, 199, 205, 255, 269, 339–340, 346, 372
Sira 113
Sirach 2, 4–6, 8, 11, 14, 16–18, 21, 26, 29, 35, 40, 44–48, 57, 61, 77–78, 80, 97, 110, 113–115, 205–206, 346, 348
Sisera 180
sister 131, 224, 388, 397, 399
Sitz im Leben 84, 281
skepticism 3, 13, 21, 35, 57, 79, 106,

127, 158, 161–162, 164, 169, 306, 402, 411, 415, 421
skill 5, 16, 22, 35, 38, 96, 99, 102, 104, 129, 163, 339
skill to rule 16
sleep and awakening 408
social power 289
social setting 24, 26, 39–41, 48, 141, 209
social settings 209
social standing 91
Society 26
Sodom 112
Sodom and Gomorrah 324
solitude 74
Solomon 4, 6–7, 16, 22, 24–25, 35, 37–38, 44, 46, 49, 56, 59–60, 65, 72, 79–80, 83, 87, 93–95, 100–101, 110–111, 113, 117, 121, 128, 157, 170, 176, 197–198, 238, 249, 253, 257, 260, 266, 273–274, 288, 317, 343, 359, 386, 389, 391–392, 395, 399, 402, 404, 409–410
son 32
Son of God 61, 69
song 25, 237, 257, 291, 295, 339, 358, 364, 379, 394
song of ascent 110
Song of Deborah 182, 196, 206, 218, 224, 301, 310, 344, 367
Song of Hannah 312
Song of Hannah in Pseudo Philo 236
song of individual thanks 371
Song of Moses 27, 280, 302
song of praise 292
Song of Solomon 83, 267, 378
Song of Songs 2, 4–7, 11, 14, 65, 173, 175, 177, 182–183, 194–195, 207, 209, 216, 224, 229, 231–232, 240, 243–244, 248–249, 251, 253–254, 256–257, 259–260, 264–267, 269–276, 285–286, 288–289, 311, 358, 361, 383, 389, 400, 402, 409, 421
song of thanks 312, 331, 342, 344, 349, 365, 370, 373
song of thanksgiving 292, 375
Song of the Bow 314, 316
Song of the Harper 33
Song of the Sea 195, 218, 242, 264, 301–303, 367
Song of the Three Jews 205, 346, 351
song of trust 211, 369–371, 374, 376–377
song of Zion 368, 373–374
songs in praise of God and his wisdom 113
songs of ascent 359, 368
songs of penitence 354
songs of thanksgiving 281, 366–367
songs of trust 215, 368
songs of victory 182
sorrow 137
sound 174, 179, 186, 196–198, 201, 204–205, 207, 275, 284, 290, 293, 296, 311, 337, 383
sound patterns 181
sovereignty 12, 18–19, 21, 35, 64, 68, 80–81, 88, 142, 203, 271, 345, 365, 379, 381, 404
special possession 187
special revelation 12, 81, 85, 340, 370
speculative theology 80
speech 64, 122, 124, 126, 130, 136, 138–139, 177, 179, 186, 190, 195, 198, 204–205, 248, 290–291, 299, 301, 305, 307, 309, 327, 338, 340, 376
Spirit of God 15, 48

spiritual 274
spiritual songs 282
spirituality 275
stability 217, 380
staircase parallelism 277, 295
stanzas 178, 296, 339, 350
statement of trust 362, 415
status 188
steadfast love 103, 316
Stela of Amenhotep III 223
stereotyped phrases 293
Stoicism 35
storm god 232
stress 294
stress pattern 280
strophes 181
strophic structure 32, 178, 181, 293, 295–296, 304, 338, 383
structure 153, 155, 284, 296
stubborn 125, 136
student 140
style 90, 127, 150, 192, 207, 232, 238, 290, 336–337, 345
styles 84, 215, 221
stylized lines 209
stylized prose 201, 204
stylized speech 196
submission 168
success 2, 6, 38, 41, 92, 98, 101, 107, 137, 158, 164, 167, 219, 370, 375
succession narrative 5, 87, 89–90, 100
suffering 21, 33–34, 44, 61, 68–69, 73, 103, 123, 142–149, 151–152, 154, 163, 182, 186, 189, 192–193, 201, 217, 229, 240, 243–244, 248–249, 265, 271, 289, 315, 325–326, 333, 346–347, 362, 364, 366, 369–371, 373–374, 376–377, 379, 414–421
suffering servant 61, 103
suicide 33, 221
Sumer 33–34, 94
Sumerian 229–231
Summary of Doctrine 65
summary psalms 234
summons to festival 323
summons to withdraw 315, 318, 322–323, 343
Sun 310
superscriptions 268
Sybilline Oracles 236
syllable counts 280
symbolism 173–174, 191, 252, 260, 270–271, 285, 327, 332, 384, 398, 401
symmetry 277, 293
synagogal prayers. 239
synagogue 38, 41, 67, 251
Synod of Jerusalem 78
synonymous 124, 127–128, 205, 222, 275–276, 303, 309
syntax 179, 275, 278, 280, 287
synthetic 127–128, 222, 275–276, 309, 345, 347
Syria 33, 336
Syriac 234

T

tabernacle 305
Talmud 3, 50, 54–56, 73, 243
Tamil 289
Targums 71–72
taunt song 292, 305, 332–333
těhillim 357
teacher 23, 27, 39–40, 45–46, 84, 89, 91, 117, 167–168, 218, 340, 351, 375
Teacher of Righteousness 233

tears 187
Tekoa 106
temperance 20, 22, 164
temple 18, 35, 40–41, 49, 100, 103, 120, 190–191, 197, 199, 201, 206, 215, 217, 239, 243, 281, 287, 312, 317, 319, 321–322, 327, 332, 336, 343, 357, 363–367, 369–374, 376, 378, 380, 417
temple singer 199
Temple, second 215
temptation 249, 258
tensions 379
Terah 30
terror 186–187
Testament of the Twelve Patriarchs 46
Testimony of David 302
Testimony of Jacob 301
thank offering 372
thanks 109, 182, 188–189, 191–192, 197, 203–204, 215, 217, 223–224, 231, 233, 237, 239, 248, 265, 268, 281–282, 289, 303, 312, 331, 343, 359, 365, 370–374
thanksgiving hymn 323, 343
thanksgiving liturgy 376
thanksgiving offering 366
thanksgiving song 316, 361
Thanksgiving/Victory Song 211
themes 27, 50, 52, 66, 84, 90, 93–94, 97, 105–107, 109, 111, 114–115, 118, 120–122, 124, 127–128, 133, 135–137, 141, 155, 158, 161, 170, 173, 179, 181, 185, 188–194, 201–203, 206–207, 209, 214, 216, 222, 224, 232, 240, 247, 251, 254, 272–273, 275–276, 285–286, 288–289, 291, 295–296, 304, 314, 339, 353, 357, 371, 376, 383–384, 386, 388, 391, 398–399, 401, 404–405, 407–410, 413–415
theodicy 17, 34, 106–107, 109, 141, 325, 368, 418
theology 41, 84–85, 87, 91, 93–94, 102, 144, 147–151, 153–154, 158, 160, 168, 188, 193, 216, 218, 221, 223, 230–231, 233, 238–240, 248, 251–254, 260–261, 264–265, 268–271, 281, 289, 291, 326, 349, 366, 378, 380
theophany 27, 71, 147, 152–153, 155, 332, 337, 340, 375–376
thought rhyme 118, 128
threat 187, 308, 399
threefold sense of Scripture 69
thrones for judgment 190
thunder and lightning 228
time 3, 150, 159, 162, 164, 182, 203, 260, 339, 381
Tirzah 288
titles 234–235, 241–242, 252–253, 265, 267, 271–273, 287, 314, 333, 354, 358–359, 361
Tobit 44, 77–78, 205, 346
tone 174, 186, 188, 197, 223–224, 229, 231, 237–238, 296, 304, 306, 308–309, 329, 332, 337, 340, 352, 371, 373, 384, 386, 388, 399, 402
Torah 7–8, 15–18, 30, 41, 43, 45–50, 52–56, 60, 63, 66, 72–74, 82–84, 89, 91, 97, 101–102, 108–109, 117, 124, 128, 176, 195, 207, 209, 234, 243–244, 259, 270, 299, 306, 309–310, 350–351, 353, 359–360, 368, 370, 376, 411
torah 368
Torah hymn 211, 215, 370
Torah psalm 265, 381

trade guilds 39
traditional wisdom 165
traditions 154, 218, 221
tragedy 260
training 31–32, 37–41, 91, 169, 234
training for children 8
training for leaders 6
transcendence 18, 21, 47, 66, 106, 112, 124, 153–154, 375, 381
transition 180–181
translations 290
tree of knowledge 98
tree of life 98
Trent, Council of 77
tribe 8, 36, 38–40, 90–91, 98, 196, 215, 217, 292, 301–302, 308–309
trimeters 242
Trinity 79
tropes 257
tropologically 145
tropology 74
Troubadours 313
trouble 187
trust 104, 106, 108–110, 158, 187–188, 191, 193, 206, 237, 264, 320, 334, 370–377, 381, 415, 419–420
trustworthiness 369, 374
truth 14, 24, 73, 125, 127, 131, 138, 140, 154, 157–158, 160, 195, 259, 338, 340, 345
two ways 50, 53, 58–59, 61, 65, 122, 135, 368
typology 274, 283, 289, 295, 342
Tyre 104

U

Ugaritic 33, 36, 87, 228–229, 232, 279, 287
unbelief 125
understanding 23–24, 102, 105, 126, 131, 133, 155, 159, 161, 170, 324
understatement 174
unfairness 159
unity 217
unity and stability in the community 379
universities 71
unrighteous 5
Upper Class 37
upright 24
Ur 229
Uriah 265
utilitarianism 4
Uz 29–30, 34, 70, 73

V

values 119, 244, 389, 400
vandalism 138
vanity 13–14, 51, 72, 79, 159, 161, 163–165, 167
vanity song 213, 339
Vaticanus 241
vengeance 215, 377
Vengeance Song 211
verse 339
verse structure 179
vice 20
victory 187–188, 197–198, 219, 292, 375, 377, 420
victory psalms 232
victory song 239, 316, 323, 366–367, 370
vindication 111, 142, 193
violence 369, 373
virgin 236
virtue 20, 48, 69, 74, 158

Vision Account 213
visions 201, 205, 207, 216, 305, 324,
    330, 332, 336, 344–345, 401, 415
vocabulary 22–24, 27, 33, 35, 39, 86–
    87, 90, 97, 101, 105, 111–112,
    117, 150, 157, 201, 238, 275–276,
    282, 287, 293, 357–358, 384, 404
vocation 2, 11, 41, 48, 99
vow 197, 332, 364–366, 373
vow of praise. 231
vow of thanks 366
vow to praise 372
Vulgate 77, 79

W

war 191, 228, 364, 416
war song 292
warfare 187, 305, 320, 324
warfare oracle 329
warning 218
warrior 303
wars 263
wasf 231, 394, 396–397, 400, 404–405,
    407–408
water 189
wealth 22, 103–104, 130–131, 135,
    137, 139, 143, 150, 164, 167, 197,
    373, 404, 416
weather 228
wedding 175, 392–393, 402
wedding poetry 402
wedding song 213, 216, 292
Western Poetry 174
whispers 415
wicked 15, 17, 21, 23–24, 102, 107–
    109, 111, 122, 137, 139, 148–150,
    158, 163–164, 166, 189, 233, 319,
    353, 368–369, 371, 373–375, 377,
    380–381, 396
wife 67, 130–131, 133, 136, 273
wisdom 1–9, 11–18, 20–24, 27, 31,
    34–35, 37–38, 41, 43, 46–49, 52–
    53, 56–57, 59–64, 67–68, 72, 74,
    77, 79, 81, 83–84, 86–91, 93, 96–
    97, 99, 102–104, 110–112, 115,

117, 119, 121, 123–125, 127–133,
    140–141, 145, 148–150, 153, 155,
    157–160, 162–167, 169–170,
    173, 197, 203, 205, 209, 216, 218,
    221, 234, 236, 257, 263–264, 276,
    296, 307, 311, 338–340, 344,
    348–350, 360, 370–372, 375, 410
wisdom forms 17, 26
wisdom literature 4, 6, 8, 12, 14, 16,
    18, 22, 27, 30, 36, 43, 50, 57, 70–
    71, 74, 78, 80, 85, 87–88, 158,
    203, 207, 368, 383, 400
wisdom meditation 376
Wisdom of Solomon 2, 4–8, 11, 14,
    17–18, 21, 26, 29, 35, 37, 40, 46,
    62, 65–66, 71, 74, 77–78, 80, 85,
    97, 110–111, 205, 346–347
Wisdom Poetry 213
wisdom psalm 23, 107, 211, 215, 233,
    239, 361, 367–368, 371–373,
    375–376, 381
wisdom sayings 106–107, 117
wisdom tale 155–156, 169
wisdom themes 17, 19
wisdom traditions 17, 44, 59, 61, 64,
    83, 87, 96, 99, 111
wisdom, definition of 5, 9, 11, 14, 19,
    37, 91, 96, 170
wise 5–6, 11, 15–16, 19, 21–22, 24, 31,
    34–35, 37–38, 51, 54, 58–59, 62,
    98, 100, 103, 105, 110–111, 122–
    123, 126–127, 129, 132, 136–138,
    150, 160, 163, 165–167
wise sayings 103, 118, 169
wise women 93
woe oracle 196, 202, 213, 215, 232,
    333
Woes 236
woman 129–130, 133, 136, 162, 251,
    300
wonders 60
word of God 283
word order 287, 293
word pairs 33, 87, 137, 201, 228, 232,
    279, 287, 293, 315
word play 72–73, 179, 290, 295, 310,
    315, 319, 330, 345

wordplay 345
work 40, 61, 114, 158–159, 161, 163–
    165, 168, 175
work of God 160
work songs 291
works 267
world 6
worldview 91
worship 7, 31, 34, 44, 107, 175, 177,
    182, 190, 204, 206, 209, 217, 233,
    235, 244, 281–283, 290, 317, 319,
    324, 332, 336, 343, 350, 357, 361,
    365–367, 374, 378
worshiper 46, 182, 186–187, 190–192,
    217, 219, 308, 334, 346, 363,
    369–370, 374, 412, 419
wrath 34, 80, 104, 106, 194, 260
Writings 51, 107, 173, 204, 242, 341,
    378, 409
wrong 24

Y

Yahweh 18, 21, 30, 36, 45, 88, 90, 99,
    103, 108, 115, 123, 159, 166, 168,
    189, 199, 202, 206, 219, 223, 228,
    231, 302–305, 308, 312, 320, 324,
    360, 364, 367, 369, 372, 374, 380
    attribute of 48
Yam 228
youth 163, 165

Z

Zechariah 203, 216, 336, 345
Zephaniah 202, 216, 334
Zerubbabel 114, 252, 336
Zeus 70
Zion 191, 253, 372, 374–376
Zion Song 211, 215, 347, 376, 381
Zion song 376
Zophar 145, 147–148, 152

Scripture Index

Genesis

Genesis 30, 87, 299
1 8
1:1 72
1:1–5 177
1:3 271
1:31 13
2:7 . . . . 161, 223
2:18–20 299
2:23 . . . . 27, 210
3 98
3:1 24
3:1–7 . . . . 27, 97
3:14–19 . . . . 27, 210, 300
4:23–24 . . . . 27, 211
8:22 . . . . 27, 210, 299, 300
9:6 . . . . 211, 299, 300
9:6–7, 25–27 27
9:25 . . . . 210, 300
9:26–27 . . . . 210, 300
12–50 141
14:19–20 . . . . 27, 210, 300
16:1–12 210
16:11–12 . . . . 27, 299
18:11–15 52
21:2–12 52
24:60 . . . . 27, 210, 300
25:23 . . . . 27, 212
27:27–29 . . . . 210, 300
27:27–29, 39–40 27
27:39–40 . . . . 210, 300
28:10–22 344
28:12–15 240
36:33–34 51
37:5–11 98
37:9–10 395
37–50 . . . . 15, 27, 98
39:2–6 38
41:8 . . . . 15, 31
41:38 15
41:38–39 15
41:45 236
41:50 236
42:18 15
48:15 31
48:15–16 300
48:15–16, 20 . . . . 27, 210
48:20 300
49 . . . . 31, 195
49:2–27 . . . . 27, 39, 211

49:22 98
49:25–26, 28 31

Exodus

Exodus 98
1:8–2:14 . . . . 27, 98
2:23 299
3:14–15 . . . . 27, 32, 33, 210
3:16 33
7:11 27
15 . . . . 195, 31
15:1–5 280
15:1–8 32
15:1–12 33
15:1–18 . . . . 33, 367, 218, 242
15:1–18, 21 . . . . 27, 32, 211
15:8 33
15:11–12 33
15:13–17 33
18:13–27 . . . . 27, 38, 98
20 196
20–23 . . . . 34, 37
20:1–11 34
20:1–23:22 . . . . 195, 27
20:1–23:33 . . . . 32, 33, 244
20:1–26 211
20:13–16 34
21:1–23:22 214
21:28–32 34
28:3 . . . . 22, 27
31:3 27
32:18 . . . . 27, 32, 213
34 33
34:6–7 . . . . 27, 32, 34, 210
35:25 5
35:31–39:31 . . . . 27, 99

Leviticus

10:1 34
10:3 . . . . 27, 210

Numbers

6:1–21 35
6:24–26 . . . . 27, 210
6:24–27 34
10:35–36 . . . . 27, 211, 32

12: 3–5 196
12:6–8 . . . . 27, 35, 210
14:13–16 362
14:18 . . . . 27, 33, 34, 196, 210
16:3–30 . . . . 27, 35, 210
20:3–5 . . . . 27, 35, 196, 210
21:14–15 233
21:17–18 210
21:17–18, 27–30 27
21:27 117
21:27–30 . . . . 35, 196, 213
22–24 . . . . 30, 36
23–24 . . . . 31, 32, 117, 322
23:7–10 36
23:7–10, 18–24 . . . . 27, 210
23:18–24 36
24:3–9 . . . . 36, 210
24:3–9, 15–24 27
24:15–24 . . . . 36, 212
26:58 361

Deuteronomy

Deuteronomy 99
1:13,15 27
4:6 16
5:6–21 . . . . 27, 37, 196, 211
5:22–33 37
6–18 37
6:1–25 . . . . 27, 19,99
6:3 99
6:4–5 . . . . 15, 37
6:4–9 . . . . 124, 368, 381
6:4–25 . . . . 27, 196, 210
6:10–13 37
11:8–17 15
11:8–21 99
19–25 37
19:1–21:23 214
19:1–25:16 37
19:1–26:11 . . . . 27, 196
21:20 54
22:1–12 211
22:13–26:11 214
26:5–10 37
26:9–10 38
27:12 38
27:12–14 38
27:15–26 . . . . 27, 38, 196, 210
28:1–6 . . . . 38, 196, 210

28:1–6, 15–19. 27
28:15. 38
28:16–19. . . . . 38, 196, 210
29:29. 43
32 . . . . 27, 196, 197, 228, 32
32–33 32
32:1. 324
32:1–43. . . . . 27, 38, 211
32:1–47. 27
32:32. 324
32:39–42. 334
27, 33 . . . . 31, 196, 197
33:1–29. . . . . 32, 211
33:2–29. 27

Joshua

1:8. 27
5 196
6:26. . . . . 28, 210, 310, 323
10:10–13. 233
10:12. 310
10:12–13. . . . . 28, 211, 322, 323
10:14. 310
15:16. 197
16:17. 197
24:14–15. 30
23:14–16. 16
24:2. 30

Judges

4 . . . . 179, 180, 181
4–5 344
4:3. 181
4:3, 12, 24. 181
4:10. 181
4:11. 181
4:16. 181
4:18. 180
4:18–20. 179
4:21. 180
4:22. 181
4:24. 181
5 . . . . . 26, 31, 32, 179, 180, 181, 182
5:1. 179
5:1–31. . . . . 211, 218, 367
5:2–31. . . . . 310, 323
5:2. 181
5:2–9. 181
5:2,9 180
5:2–31. 28
5:3. 181
5:4. 181
5:6–9. 181
5:9. 180
5:10, 12, 23. 179
5:11. 180
5:14–18. 32
5:15–18. 180
5:22. 181
5:26–27. 180
5:27. 180
9 315
9:8–15. . . . . .197, 28, 213,
         311, 323
9:16–20. 311
9:57. 311
14:14. . . . . 311, 323, 339
14:14, 18. . . . . 28, 213
14:18. . . . . 311, 323
15:15. 214
15:16. . . . . 28, 312, 322, 323
16 197
16:6–17. 214
16:6–17, 23–24. 28
16:6–17, 27–30. 323
16:23–24. 211

29:5 28

Ruth

1:16–17 . . . . .24, 214
1:16–17, 20–21 28
1:20–21 211
1:20–21 .24

1 Samuel

1 Samuel 99
1:1–18 .363
2 . . . . .197, 312
2:1–10 . . . . . . 32, 28, 211–212, 217,
         323, 343
15:22–23 . . . . .312, 323
15:22–23, 33 28
15:33 . . . . .210, 322, 323
17. 197
17:24–27 323
17:24–47 . . . . .28, 214, 313
17:45–47 197
18:7 . . . . 28, 197, 214, 293, 313,
         323, 339
18:17 322
21:11 . . . . 28, 214, 293, 313, 323
25:2–42 . . . . .27, 99
25:3 23
29:5 . . . . .214, 293, 313, 323

2 Samuel

2 Samuel 93
1. 32
1:1 243
1:14–16 315
1:17–27 314
1:18 197
1:19–27 . . . . . .28, 197, 211, 323, 343
1:21–26 314
2:2–51 .343
3. 32
3:33–34 . . . . . .28, 211, 315, 323, 343
7:18 243
9. 87
9–20. . . . . .5, 28, 89, 100
12:1–6 55
14:2 16
17. 100
20:1 . . . .28, 214, 315, 318, 322, 343
21:15–22 316
22. . . . . .197, 198, 316, 370
22:1 316
22:2–51 . . . . . .28, 211, 323, 366, 367
22:51 316
23. 32
23:1–7 . . . . 28, 197,
         210, 234, 316, 317, 323
63:7 272

1 Kings

1 Kings. 100
1–2. . . . . .5, 28, 89, 100
1:1–4 69
2:16 322
3–10. 11
3–12. 100
3:1–12:15. 28
3:5–12 .100
3:5–14 11
3:16–28 . . . . .38, 100
3:23–38 .22
4. 16
4:20–28 .11
4:29–31 100

4:29–(Heb. 5:11–14) 16
4:29–34. 25
4:32. 257
4:32–33. . . . . 16, 100
4:33 (Heb. 5:13) 33
5 16
5–8 100
7:8. 389
8:1–66. 366
8:12–13. 197
8:12–13, 15. 317
8:12–61. . . . . . . 28, 211, 317, 323, 346
8:16–21. 317
8: 22–53 27
8:33–40. 364
10 16
10:1–3. 11
10:4–5. 11
10:6–9. . . . . 197, 214, 323
10:6–9, 23–25. 28
10:6–29. 11
10:23–25. . . . 197, 213, 318, 322, 323
11 11
11:26–39. 11
12 . . . . 11, 198
12:1–15. 27
12:4–15. 210
12:4–16. 28
         318, 323
12:6–10. 318
12:8–10. 319
12:16. . . . . 198, 214
19:14. . . . . 28, 211, 323
20:14. 319

2 Kings

3:15. 319
3:16–17. 213
3:16–19. . . . . 28, 198, 319, 323
3:18–19. 212
7:1. . . . . 28, 213, 323
10 210
10:19. . . . . 28, 198, 322, 323
13:17. 198
18:19–35. . . . . 28, 198, 214, 320, 323
19 210
19:15–19. . . . . .198, 211, 320,
         323, 346
19:15–19, 21–28. 28
19:21–28. . . . . 198, 213, 320,
         321, 323
20:17–18. . . . . . . 198, 28, 213, 323
21:1–18. 353
21:11–15. 198
22:13. . . . . 214, 323
22:13,16–20 . . . . 28, 321
22:16–20. . . . . 212, 322, 323

1 Chronicles

12:18. . . . . 24, 29, 212
16:4–7. 361
16:7. 24
16:8–36. . . . . 24, 29, 210, 342

21:1. 143

2 Chronicles

1–9 11
1:7–12. 16
1:10–12. 28
5:13. . . . . 24, 29, 211
6 24
6:1–42. 29
6:4–40. 343

6:4–41 346
6:41–42 343
7 343
7:3 . . . . 24, 29, 211
9:1–9,22–23 28
10 24
10:4–14 210
10:4–14, 16 29
10:16 . . . . 214, 343
16:7–9 . . . . 24, 343
20:13–18 367
20:19 361
20:21 . . . . 24, 29, 211
33:1–9 353
33:12–13 353
33:14–20 353
35:25 412

Ezra

3:11 . . . . 24, 28, 211

Nehemiah

8–10 268
9:5–37 341
9:6–37 . . . . 24, 29, 211
9:17 33

Esther

1:13–20 28

Job

Job 14, 28, 211, 213
1 146
1–2 . . . . 11, 142, 360
1:1 . . . . 11, 29, 34, 146
1:1–2 143
1:2–11 14
1:3 55
1:6–12 . . . . 12, 143
1:6–2:7 142
1:9 . . . . 143, 144
1:10 145
1:20–22 144
1:21 145
2:1–7 12
2:2 55
2:4–5 144
2:10 . . . . 21, 145
2:13 . . . . 145, 147
2:22–24 14
3 . . . . 33, 144, 346
3–41 . . . . 12, 142
3:1–42:6 339
3:1–4 144
3:1–8 14
3:2–42:6 . . . . 28, 148
3:20 145
3:23 145
4–5 . . . . 145, 148
5:17 17
5:17–26 66
6:1–4 145
6:24–30 145
6:28–30 146
7:1 78
7:3 55
7:17–18 146
8:2 148
8:7 148
8:11 339
8:15 55
9:1–20 150
9:5–13 152

9:8 70
10:2–13 151
10:8 55
10:11 222
11 . . . . 145, 149
11:1–6 145
11:2–3 148
12:1–8 14
12:2–3 149
12:13 55
12:20 53
13 149
13:1–7 149
13:13–18 151
13:20–24 149
13:24 55
14 149
14:4 79
14:14–17 149
15 148
15:4 124
15:13 62
16:2 . . . . 147, 149
18:13 148
19:7 149
19:25–27 81
20 149
21:7–34 . . . . 7, 150
23 148
23:1–7 142
24:21–22 150
24:24–25 150
25 148
26:2–4 149
26:12 24
26:14 81
27 . . . . 118, 150
27:1–6 151
27:6 70
28:1–28 . . . . 213, 339,
28:12 24
28 . . . . 19, 23, 66, 150, 155, 350
28:28 . . . . 5, 20, 81, 150
29 150
29–30 420
29–31 148
29:7 148
29:9–10 148
29:21 22
30:3–10 150
31 151
31:40 151
31:5–6 21
32–37 152
32:2 152
32:6–37:24 147
33:12–28 152
33:23 152
33:26–27 152
35:3–8 152
36:15–23 152
36:24–37:24 152
38 153
38–39 33
38–41 . . 12, 13, 16, 17, 27, 142, 147,
152, 213, 340
38–42 12
38:1 153
38:1–41:34 . . . . 147, 152
38:4 70
38:16–18 340
38:17 70
38:39–39:30 153
39:26 24
40:3–5 . . . . 147, 153
40:6 153
40:10–14 153
42 . . . . 142, 147
42:3–4 153

42:5 153
42:6 154
42:7 . . . . 11, 154
42:7–9 152
42:7–17 11
42:10–11 144
42:10–17 . . . . 143, 154
42:14 70

Psalms

Psalms 14, 17, 28, 250
1 . . . . 17, 98, 99, 211, 252, 265,
268, 367, 368, 381
1–41 . . . . 185, 358, 360
1:1 36
2 . . . . 210, 252, 282, 367, 368
2:2 273
2:7 287
3 . . . . 211, 369
4 . . . . 211, 358, 369
4:4 260
5 . . . . 211, 369
6 . . . . 186, 211, 230, 369
6:2–5 269
7 . . . . 211, 369
7:2, 14 420
7:14 420
8 . . . . 210, 252, 369
9 . . . . 211, 369
9–10 . . . . 241, 293, 360
9:1–10:18 . . . . 18, 28
10 . . . . 211, 360, 369
11 . . . . . 211, 230, 271, 282, 369, 375
12 . . . . 211, 369
12:12 53
13 . . . . 211, 211, 362, 369,
375
13:8 33
14 . . . . 28, 18, 210, 211, 234,
369, 375
14:1 125
14:4 272
15 . . . . . 210, 211, 343, 369, 370, 375
15:27–137:6 241
16 . . . . 211, 341, 343, 358,
369, 375
16:48 . . . . 185, 359
17 . . . . 211, 369, 375
17–150 . . . . 185, 359, 360
18 . . . . 197, 198, 211, 282,
316, 366, 367, 370, 375
18:2 258
18:20–26 346
18:22 279
18:31, 46 241
18:44 247
19 . . . . 17, 210, 211, 368, 370,
375 381
19:1–6 18
19:7–10 18
19:7–13 . . . . 28, 18
19:11–12 249
19:11–13 18
20 . . . . 210, 282, 370
21 . . . . 211, 282, 370
22 . . . . 211, 252, 370
23 . . . . 177, 211, 368, 370, 374
24 . . . . 210, 250, 370
24:3 250
25 . . . . 211, 293, 370
26 . . . . 211, 370
27 . . . . 211, 281, 370
28 . . . . 211, 370
28:1 241
29 . . . . 210, 370
30 . . . . 211, 365, 366, 370
31 . . . . 211, 264, 370

31:3...................... 241
32............... 230, 265, 370
32–33................... 360
33............ 210, 360, 371
33:15.................. 272
34............. 211, 293, 371
34:11................. 247
34:11–17............. 248
35............... 211, 371
35:16................ 268
36........... 28, 18, 211, 371
36:9................. 264
37......... 28, 211, 233, 293, 371
37:32–33............. 233
38....... 211, 230, 241, 371
39.................. 211, 371
40.................. 211, 371
41............. 211, 250, 371
41:13................ 185, 358
42............. 211, 296, 371
42–72........ 185, 358, 360
42–83............... 360
42:5, 11.............. 296
43............. 211, 296, 371
43:5................. 296
44............ 211, 371, 380
45..........213, 216, 252, 265,
        282, 367, 372
45:1–17............. 367
45:2–10............. 253
45:11–17............. 253
46................. 211, 372
47............. 210, 367, 372
48................. 211, 372
49........... 23, 28, 19, 211, 372
49:20–79:13............. 241
50................. 211, 372
50:16–23.............. 248
51..........211, 230, 264, 265,
        346, 354, 359, 363, 372
51–65............... 360
51:1................ 248
51:1–17.............. 248
52................. 211, 372
53........... 18, 28, 211, 372
54................. 211, 372
55................. 211, 372
56................. 211, 372
56–60............... 358
57................. 211, 372
57:7–11.............. 375
58............. 210, 372
59................. 211, 372
60............. 187, 211, 372
60:5–12............... 375
61................. 211, 372
61:2................ 241
61:3................ 268
62................. 211, 373
63................. 211, 373
64................. 211, 373
65............. 211, 366
66............. 210, 373
67............. 211, 373
68............. 210, 373
68–70............... 360
69................. 373
69:30–32.............. 248
70............. 211, 373
71............. 211, 241, 373
72........... 210, 282, 359, 373
72:18–19.............. 358
72:18–20.............. 185
72:20............. 358, 359
73........ 17, 28, 19, 211, 368, 373
73:27................ 17
73–83............... 360
73–89.......... 185, 358, 360
74............ 211, 363, 364, 373

74:3–9 364
75.................188, 211, 373
76....................211, 373
77....................211, 373
78.........211, 218, 368, 373, 420
79....................211, 374
80....................211, 374
81....................211, 374
82....................211, 374
83....................211, 374
84.................211, 368, 374
84:10......................276
85....................211, 374
86.................211, 359, 374
87....................211, 374
88.................211, 359, 374
89.............210, 282, 359, 374
89:52..................185, 358
90.............211, 271, 359, 374
90–16.............185, 359, 360
90–100....................271
90:20......................54
91.................211, 260, 374
92....................211, 374
93...........189, 210, 360, 374
94....................211, 374
95....................210, 374
95–99.....................360
96.................210, 343, 375
97....................210, 375
98....................210, 375
99.......................375
100...........210, 359, 365, 375
110.......210, 252, 282, 367, 375
111.........210, 293, 365, 375
111:10....................20
112............19, 28, 211, 375
112:1......................17
113.......................375
114.......................375
114–115...................241
115................210, 375
116.........211, 241, 332, 375
116:17–19.................366
117................210, 376
118.............24, 211, 376
118:2–3...................365
119........17, 18, 19, 28, 211, 265,
       293, 368, 376, 381
119:1–2...................17
120.............211, 359, 376
120:7....................268
121....................211, 376
122.......190, 210, 295, 368, 376
123.............211, 234, 376
124................211, 376
125................211, 376
126................211, 376
127..........28, 110, 211, 376
127:5.....................17
128.........28, 110, 211, 376
128:1.....................17
129................211, 376
130................211, 376
131................211, 376
132............210, 282, 376
132:8–10..................343
132:18...................276
133.............211, 234, 376
134................210, 376
135................210, 376
136.........115, 211, 350, 377
137.........211, 288, 377, 380
138................211, 377
139................211, 377
140................211, 377
141................211, 377
142................211, 377
143.............211, 230, 377

144........211, 234, 235, 282, 377
144:1–15..................367
144:3–4....................28
145................33, 210, 293,
145:6......................33
145:8......................33
145:9....................272
145:18...................272
146................210, 377
146–149..................358
147.........210, 241, 377
147:18...................272
148............210, 353, 377
149................210, 377
150.......... 185, 210, 358, 377
150:6....................359
151........ 25, 234, 242, 346, 354
152......................234
152–155..................234
153......................234
154................49, 234
155......................234

Proverbs

Proverbs............. 28, 28, 213
1–9 ..... 37, 40, 52, 87, 95, 98, 99,
   111, 113, 117, 118, 120, 127, 128,
   129, 133, 135, 139, 213, 338, 400
1–24 95
1:1............. 25, 118, 120
1:2–6....................124
1:2–6........ 40, 128, 129, 131, 140
1:5.......................23
1:6.......................15
1:7............. 20, 72, 124
1:10–19..................128
1:16......................61
1:20–33..................131
1:23–33...................66
1:24–26..................131
1:32–36..................131
2–7......................120
2:3.......................24
2:5......................124
2:16–19.............129, 130
2:31–33...................15
3:3–4.....................63
3:3–18...................131
3:7................64, 124
3:12......................73
3:19......................24
3:27.....................127
3:27–30...................89
4:2.......................53
4:5–9...............69, 131
5:3–20.............129, 130
5:15–17..................130
5:23......................23
6:6–11...................133
6:12–15..................134
6:16–19.............134, 296
6:23–35.............129, 130
6:27.....................130
6:27–28...................17
6:32.....................130
7:4......................131
7:6–21....................73
7:6–27.............129, 130
7:22......................72
8 ....66, 67, 132
8:1–21....................46
8:1–21, 22–31, 32–36.........131
8:1–31...................131
8:1–36............66, 131, 23
8:13.....................124
8:22..........52, 61, 68, 69, 72

8:22–23, 29–30 46
8:22–30 68
8:22–31 . . . . 63, 64, 88, 131, 132
8:22–36 79
8:30–31 132
8:32–36 132
8:34 17
9 128
9:1 . . . . 68, 120
9:1–6 . . . . 131, 133
9:1–12 133
9:13–18 . . . . 129, 130, 133
9:10 . . . . 20, 124
10–29 . . . . 87, 113, 114, 134
10–31 . . 95, 127, 128, 129, 135, 136,
137, 138
10:1 136
10:1–17 123
10:1–22:16 120
10:2 . . . . 44, 123
10:5 23
10:12 64
10:13 126
10:14 22
10:17 136
10:23 126
10:27 124
10:31 126
11:1 . . . . 118, 124
11:2 126
11:4 44
13:1 136
13:10 . . . . 51, 126
13:15 51
13:22 136
13:24 136
14:1 136
14:2, 27 124
14:8 126
14:12 122
14:28 137
14:33 126
14:35 137
15:9 122
15:10 136
15:11 139
15:20 136
15:21 137
15:33 . . . . 20, 72, 126
16:1–4 139
16:7 123
16:8 119
16:10 137
16:11 124
16:12 137
16:13 137
16:14, 15 137
16:16 . . . . 1, 125
16:32 53
17:2 . . . . 123, 136, 138
17:6 136
17:8 . . . . 122, 137
17:14 137
17:19 138
17:21, 25 136
17:22 135
17:24 126
18:4 138
18:6 138
18:6–8 139
18:10–12 139
18:11 . . . . 122, 137
18:13 138
19:2 138
19:4 135
19:8 126
19:12 137
19:13 136
19:14 136

19:23 . . . . 123, 124
19:25 136
19:26 136
20:2 137
20:3 117
20:5 126
20:7 . . . . 17, 136
20:8 137
20:11 136
20:12 138
20:14 128
20:18 23
20:20 136
20:26 137
20:27 138
20:28 137
20:30 136
21:1 . . . . 137, 139
21:3 124
21:5 138
21:19 136
21:23 138
21:30 127
22:11 137
22:15 136
22:17–18 222
22:17–24:22 . . . . 32, 120, 121
22:17–24:34 29
22:6 136
22:9,22 124
22:20 69
22:22–27, ... 139
23:9 127
23:13–14 136
23:20 54
23:22–25 136
23:23 125
23:29–30 119
24:1, 15, 17, 19, 28–29 125
24:3–4 125
24:14 . . . . 119, 126
24:19–20 118
24:21–22 137
24:23–34 120
24:25 136
24:28–29 125
24:30–34 119
24:7 127
25 121
25–29 . . . . 120, 121
25:1 . . . . 25, 95
25:1–15 7
25:1–29:27 54
25:6–7 . . . . 58, 137
25:11–14 139
25:12 136
25:15 137
25:18–20 139
25:21–22 62
25:24 136
26:17 138
26: 20–22 139
26:3 136
26:4 55
26:5 55
26:8 138
26:9 135
26:27 123
27:10 138
27:15–16 136
27:19–21 139
28:2 137
28:3 137
28:4 136
28:5 137
28:6 125
28:15 137
28:16 137
28:19 139

28:23 136
29:1 136
29:3 136
29:4 137
29:12 137
29:14 137
29:15 . . . . 126, 136
29:17 136
29:19 136
29:23 58
29:26 137
30 120
30–31 . . . . 117, 118
30:1–31:31 . . . . 213, 338
30:3 126
30:15b–16 138
30:17 136
30:18–19 138
30:21–23 119
31 . . . . 67, 120
31:1 . . . . 30, 133
31:10–31 . . . . 115, 293
31:10–41 133
31:14 54
31:20 124
31:30 124

Ecclesiastes

Ecclesiastes 28, 28, 213
1:1 . . . . 25, 157
1:1–11 . . . . 161, 213, 339
1:2–11 157
1:3 163
1:4–11 161
1:12 24
1:12–13 158
1:12–14 8
1:12–18 167
1:13 159
1:14 161
1:15 53
1:15, 18 158
1:16–17 158
1:18 . . . . 160, 164
1:25 159
1:26 159
2:1, 4–10 158
2:2 . . . . 159, 163
2:9 24
2:9–12 54
2:11 163
2:12 . . . . 157, 158
2:13–14 167
2:14 . . . . 158, 159
2:14–23 164
2:14b–17 167
2:15 51
2:24–25 . . . . 158, 167
2:26 . . . . 160, 165
3 161
3:1 159
3:1–8 . . . . 160, 161, 213, 339
3:1–9 23
3:1–15 159
3:2–8 162
3:11 . . . . 159, 162
3:11, 15 164
3:12–13. 22 167
3:14 163
3:14–15 162
3:15 159
3:16 163
3:16–17 158
3:18–21 162
3:19–20 159
3:20 163
4:1 . . . . 159, 163

4:2-3 163-164
4:4 164
4:5-6 158
4:9-12 .... 159, 165
4:13 .... 24, 165
4:13-14 7
4:13-15 164
5:1 165
5:1-9 8
5:5 165
5:10 164
5:11 164
5:12 164
5:13-17 163
5:18-20 168
6:9 165
6:10-12 162
6:11-12 165
7 23
7:1-5 165
7:8 165
7:11-12 167
7:14 168
7:15 21
7:15-18 22
7:16-18 164
7:18 166
7:19 167
7:23-24 160
7:23-29 162
8:2-5 .... 7, 25
8:3 163
8:6 3
8:6-8 159
8:7-8 162
8:9 163
8:10 164
8:11-13 163
8:12-13 165
8:14 164
8:15 167
8:16-9:1 162
8:17 160
9:1 .... 79, 162, 163
9:2-3 163
9:4 165
9:4-5 159
9:7-10 168
9:11-12 163
9:13-15 24
9:15 163
9:15-16 159
9:16-18 167
10 23
10:4 165
10:5-7 164
10:6-7 159
10:10 167
10:19 168
11 23
11:1-4, 6 168
11:5 162
11:9 51
11:9-12:7 .... 163, 165
12 32
12:1 40
12:8 161
12:9-12 167
12:9-14 166
12:12 37
12:13 50
12:13-14 166

Song of Songs

Song of Songs 28, 213
1:1 385
1:1-4 44

1:1-5 256
1:2 .... 243, 251, 258
1:2-4 .... 385, 386, 388
1:4 .... 259, 267
1:5 .... 244, 253
1:5-6 .... 46, 392, 388
1:5-7 .... 385, 386, 387
1:5-8 386
1:7 .... 43, 264
1:7-8 44
1:7-9 388
1:8 .... 264, 385, 387
1:9 258
1:9-1 386
1:9-10 47
1:9-11 .... 385, 389
1:9-12 44
1:9-2:2 387
1:12 389
1:12-12 46
1:12-14 385
1:13-14 .... 47, 383, 388
1:15 .... 46, 47, 385
1:16 385
1:16-17 389
1:17 .... 48, 385
2:1 385
2:1-2 .... 46, 389
2:1-7 .... 386, 389
2:2 385
2:3 390
2:3-5 46
2:3-7 385
2:4 .... 276, 390
2:5 .... 227, 390
2:6 390
2:7 384
2:7-9 44
2:7-10 48
2:8-9 .... 227, 391
2:8-17 .... 385-386, 390
2:8-3:4 383
2:9 .... 249, 390
2:10 249
2:10-15 .... 46, 390
2:12 267
2:14 390
2:15 .... 45, 258, 387, 390
2:16 .... 44, 46
2:17 44
3:1 267
3:1-4 49
3:1-5 .... 385-386, 391,
    392, 48
3:3 43
3:5 44
3:6 .... 43, 46
3:6-11 ...... 385-386, 391, 392
3:7 274
3:7-11 44
3:11 .... 274, 392
3:9-10 48
4:1-2 .... 44, 45, 251
4:1-5 .... 392, 393
4:1-7 47
4:1-8 46
4:1-15 385
4:1-5:1 .... 386, 391, 392
4:2 266
4:5 258
4:3 45
4:4 48
4:6-8 392
4:9-12 131
4:9-15 392
4:10-5:1 .... 46, 392, 393
4:11-15 47
4:12 253
4:12-15 227

4:16 .... 385, 392
5:1 .... 385, 393, 397
5:2 256
5:2-7 .... 48, 49
5:2-8 .... 385-386, 394
5:3 251
5:6 .... 267, 384
5:7 .... 49, 384
5:9 .... 43, 178, 194, 385, 387,
    394
5:9-6:3 .... 386, 393
5:10 194
5:10-16 .... 45, 47, 228,
    385, 388, 394,
5:12-13 46
5:15 .... 43, 46, 48
6:1 .... 385, 387
6:2-3 .... 44, 46, 385
6:4 288
6:4-5 45
6:4-7 47
6:4-10 385-386,395-396
6:5 395
6:5-6 44
6:7 .... 45, 46
6:9 249
6:10 .... 395, 43, 46
6:11 46
6:11-12 .... 385, 397
6:11-13 386
6:13 .... 43, 395
6:13(Heb. 7:1) 385, 387
7:1-5 .... 44, 394, 396, 397
7:1-9 .... 47, 386, 396
7:1-9 (Heb. 7:2-10) 385
7:2-9 46
7:4 48
7:6-9 397
7:10-8:4 ...... 386, 397, 398
7:10-8:4 (Heb. 7:11-8:4) 385
7:11-13 46
7:12 397
8:1-3 398
8:2 46
8:3 398
8:4-5 48
8:5 .... 43, 46, 49, 251,
    386-387
8:5a 385
8:5b-7 385
8:5-14 398
8:6 .... 194, 384
8:6-7 .... 49, 386
8:6-10 399
8:8 .... 43, 388
8:8-10 385-386
8:9-11 48
8:11-12 ...... 44, 46, 386, 388
8:11-13 385
8:12 387
8:13 .... 46, 386
8:13-14 .... 49, 400
8:14 .... 44, 46, 385, 386

Isaiah

Isaiah 11, 28
1 324
1:2-3, 26 28
1:2-31 212
1:10-17 212
1:11-20 312
1:21 281
1-39 .... 12, 17, 200, 324
2:2-4 212
3:2-3 28
5:1-10 199
5:1-2 182

5:1-5 ... 27
5:1-7 ... 213, 216
5:20-21, 24 ... 28
6:2 ... 240
6:9-13 ... 200
8:9-10 ... 28
10 ... 12
10:1-16 ... 28
10:13-15 ... 12, 13, 28
10:13-19 ... 198
12:1-4 ... 28
13:2-22 ... 212
19:11-15 ... 17, 28
22:1-14 ... 212
23:1-7 ... 211
25:6-10 ... 212
26 ... 28
26:7-15 ... 12
28:23-29 ... 17, 28, 213
29:13-16 ... 28
29:16 ... 62
32:5-8 ... 12, 28
40 ... 286
40:1-29 ... 212
40:1-31 ... 212
40:12-41:1 ... 28, 13
40:13-14 ... 17
40:18-20 ... 212
40-55 ... 13, 14, 61, 200, 324, 327
40-66 ... 240
42:1-4 ... 200, 213
42:5 ... 28
43:1-7 ... 295
44:24-26 ... 28
44:9-20 ... 13, 28
45-66 ... 350
45:9 ... 62
45:9-23 ... 28
46 ... 28
46:1-4 ... 212
47:1-15 ... 211
48:13 ... 28
49:1-6 ... 213
50:4-11 ... 213
52:13-53:12 ... 213
53:11 ... 13, 28
54:1-17 ... 212
56-66 ... 13, 200, 324
59:1-19 ... 212
61:1-3 ... 199
61:1-11 ... 212
61:11 ... 28
64:8 ... 62
65:6-7 ... 28
66:1 ... 13

Jeremiah

Jeremiah ... 13, 28
1-31 ... 324
1:2-10 ... 212
2:1-3 ... 213, 216
2:2-37 ... 212
2:11 ... 325
2:30 ... 325
2:23-25, 33 ... 325
3:1-3 ... 325
4:22 ... 28
5:3, 20-29 ... 28
5:20-29 ... 14
5:26-27 ... 27
7:1-20 ... 325
7:21-30 ... 325
7:28 ... 28
7:29 ... 211, 325, 412
8 ... 325
8:4-9 ... 28
8:8-9 ... 17

9 ... 413
9:12 ... 17
9:12, 23-24 ... 28
9:23-24 ... 13
10:1-16 ... 14
10:2-16 ... 212
11:18-12:4 ... 212, 325
13:12-14 ... 28
14:2-6 ... 326
14:2-10,17-22 ... 211
15:2-21 ... 212
15:10-21 ... 325
17:5-11 ... 14
17:5-11,23 ... 28
17:14-18 ... 212, 325
18:1-11 ... 62
18:18 ... 39
18:18-23 ... 28
18:19-23 ... 212, 325
20:7-13 ... 325
20:7-13, 14-18 ... 212
20:7-18 ... 28
20:14-18 ... 325
23:18-22 ... 28
23:9-15 ... 212
24:1-10 ... 213
25:9-11 ... 110
30-33 ... 327
31:35-37 ... 28, 14
32-35 ... 28
32-44 ... 200
32-45 ... 324
33:14-26 ... 212
36:32 ... 351
43-44 ... 413
46-51 ... 212, 326
46-52 ... 324
49:7 ... 28, 29, 34, 14
50:35-36 ... 28

Lamentations

Lamentations ... 28
1-4 ... 293
1-5 ... 211
1:1 ... 192, 235
1:1-2 ... 263
1:8 ... 192
1:9, 11 ... 415
1:12 ... 192
1:16 ... 414
1:19 ... 414
1:22 ... 415
2 ... 417
2:1-9 ... 415
2:5 ... 193
2:9 ... 259
2:9, 14 ... 415
2:12 ... 415
2:14 ... 266
2:16 ... 415
2:18-19 ... 415
2:20 ... 193, 415
3 ... 193, 417
3:1-6 ... 418
3:6 ... 415
3:10-12 ... 418
3:21-25 ... 418
3:22-39 ... 415
3:27-28 ... 255
3:37-45 ... 28
3:38 ... 268
3:40-42 ... 193, 415
3:43-45 ... 418
3:50, 59-60 ... 415
4 ... 419
4:1-2 ... 416
4:4 ... 415

4:7 ... 415
4:7-8 ... 416
4:10 ... 415
4:13-15 ... 416
4:14, 17 ... 415
4:20 ... 268
4:21-22 ... 415
5 ... 419
5:1 ... 415
5:1-18 ... 416
5:2 ... 275
5:17-22 ... 420
5:19 ... 259
5:21 ... 260

Ezekiel

Ezekiel ... 14, 28
1:1-3:15 ... 344
1:4-28 ... 213
4:1-17 ... 212
5:1-12 ... 212
6:1-7 ... 212
6:3-4 ... 21
7:26 ... 39
8:2-10:22 ... 213
12:1-20 ... 212
12:21-25 ... 28, 14
13:1-23 ... 212
15:1-5 ... 326
15:1-8 ... 21, 212
15:2-8 ... 15, 27, 28
15:6-8 ... 327
16:44 ... 17
16:44-63 ... 15, 28
17:1 ... 118
17:2-10 ... 15, 27, 28
17:3-10 ... 118
18:1-11 ... 212
18:2 ... 17
18:2-30 ... 28, 14
19:1-14 ... 21, 211, 212, 412
20:49 ... 27, 28
23:1-49 ... 21, 212
27:1-36 ... 211
28:2-19 ... 14, 28
31:2-18 ... 21
32:2-16 ... 211
32:2-18 ... 212
36-48 ... 21
37:1-14 ... 344
37:1-14 ... 213
38-39 ... 327
40-48 ... 327
40:2-44:8 ... 213
46:19-47:12 ... 213
47:3-5 ... 327
47:13-48:35 ... 212

Daniel

Daniel ... 110
1:3-5,17,20 ... 28
1:4 ... 37
2:12,20-23,25-30 ... 28
2:20-23 ... 24, 110, 211, 344
3:4-6 ... 24, 29, 214, 343
3:23-24 ... 351
4:10-12 ... 344
4:10-17 ... 212
4:10-17 (Heb. 4:7-14) . 24, 29, 344
4:14-17 ... 344
4:20 (4:17-24) ... 29, 212
4:20 (Heb. 4:17-24) ... 25
4:3 (3:33) ... 210
4:3 (Heb. 3:33) ... 29
4:34 (4:31-32) ... 210
4:34 (Heb. 4:31-32) ... 29

4:34–35, (Heb. 4:31–32, 34) . 25, 345
4:37 (4:34) 210
4:37 (Heb. 4:34) 29
5 25
5–12 25
5:11, 14 87
5:17–28 . . . . .25, 29, 212,
    344, 345
6:26 (6:27–28) 210
6:26 (Heb. 27–28) 29
7 345
7–12 . . . . 25, 29, 212, 345
9–12 110
9:2 110
9:22 28
11:1–9, 10–16 212
12:3 28
12:3–4 110
23:1–8 212

Hosea

Hosea 15, 28
1–3 . . . . 28, 212, 328
2:1–3 328
4:1–6 22
4:1–11 212
4:11 27
4:11, 14 . . . . 15, 28
4–14 328
6:6 312
7:6–7 328
9:7 28
11:1–4 329
11:1–4, 8–9 213
12:1 161
14:9 27
14:9 (14:10 Hebrew) 28
14:9 (Heb. 14:10) 15

Joel

Joel 28
1:2–2:2 211
1:14 364
2:3–5 329
2:15–16 364
2:30–3:8 28
3:1–3 329
3:9–21 329

Amos

Amos 16, 28
1–2 119
1:1 16
3:3–8 . . . . .17, 27–28, 16, 213,
    329, 338
5:2 412
5:8–9 14
5:8–15 . . . . 17, 28
5:14–15 212
5:18–20 330
7 22
7:1–9 . . . . 213, 330
8 22
8:1–3 . . . . 213, 330
9:2–6 . . . . 17, 27, 16
9:2–6 28

Obadiah

Obadiah 34, 28
1:1–4 330
1:12–14 331
1:15 331
8 . . . . 14. 28, 29

Jonah

2 23
2:1–9 . . . . .27, 331, 366
2:2–9 211
4:2 33

Micah

Micah 28
1:3 332
1:3–4 332
1:8–16 332
2:4 332
4 22
4:1–8 332
6:1–16 332
7:14–20 332

Nahum

Nahum 28
2 333
3:1–3 333

Habakkuk

Habakkuk 16, 28
1:1–2:5 28
1:2 334
1:2–4 333
1:1–2:5 16
1:2–2:5 211
2:6–17 . . . . .213, 333
3 . . . . .16, 27–28, 228
3:19 .23
3:2–19 210
3:3–60 334

Zephaniah

Zephaniah 28
1:2–3 334
1:2–18 212
1:14–16 334
2:1–3 335
3:1–2 335
3:6–20 212
3:9 335
3:14–15 335
3:20 .335

Haggai

1:3–11 335
1:4–11 28
2:3–9,14–19 336
2:3–9, 14–19, 21–23 28
2:20–23 336

Zechariah

Zechariah 28
1–6 .345
1–7 .336
1:8–6:15 212
3:1–2 143
8 336
8:12 .336
9–14 . . . . .23, 336
11:4–14:21 212
12–14 336
13:1–2 336
14:9, 16 336

Malachi

Malachi 28
1–2 337
1:6 . . . . 28, 337
1:6–2:9 212
2:6–9 28
3–4 337
4 (Heb. 3:19–20) 337
4:5–6 59
9:9–10 336

Matthew

5:3–12 . . . . 17, 165
6:24–33 61
7:13–14 58
7:24–27 58
10:16 58
11:19 58
11:25 59
11:28–30 57
12:42 59
13:54 59
22:43 252
23:12 58
24:45 59
25:1–13 59

Luke

1:17 59
2:40, 52 60
6:20–23 17
6:46–49 58
7:35 58
10:21 59
11:49 60
12:13–21 60
12:16–21 58
12:22–31 61
12:42 59
13:23–24 58
14:8–10 58
16:1–9 60
21:15 60
42:1–6 147

John

1 . . . . 52, 132
6:35 57

Acts

13:33 360

Romans

1 62
1:20–31 62
3:15–17 61
7:18–19 14
9:21 61
12:20 62

1 Corinthians

1:24 61
3:18–21 62
3:19 62

Colossians

1:15–18 63

Hebrews

6:11–7:1 386
7:1 395
7:2–6 396
7:2–10 . . . . 386, 396
7:3–10 46
7:7–10 397
7:10 397
7:11–8:4 . . . . 386, 397
7:12–14 46
12:5–6 64

James

3 64
3:13–18 64
4:6 63
5:11 63

1 Peter

4:8 64
5:5 63

Revelation

Revelation 110
3:14 64

QUMRAN MANUSCRIPTS

1QH 233
4Q171 233
4Q179 235
11QPs 234

DEUTEROCANONICAL WORKS

Azariah

16–17 352

Book of Baruch

2 Baruch 236, 237
1:10–14 351
1:14–3:8 351
3:9–4:4 350
4:5–5:9 350

1 Clement

1 Clement 65, 66, 247

1 Enoch

1 Enoch 47, 48, 236, 239
42:1–2 47–48
42:1–3 48
83:3 47
94:5 47

The Prayer of Manasseh

1–15 354

Sirach

Sirach 28, 113
1:1–10 . . . . 113, 348
1:11–21 113
1:11–30 348
1:13 80
1:22–30 113
2:1–17 348
3:1–4:10 113
3:1–14:19 348
4:1–50:24 348
11:18–19 58
14:20–15:10 348
18:1–14 348
18:15–39:1 348
24:1–8 47
24:1–22 27
24:3–22 113
24:21 57
24:23 . . . . 18, 47
24:28–29 47
30:1–13 113
30:18–25 113
35:13–26 114
36:1–22 115
36:23–37:31 113
37:3 114
38:1–15 114
38:16–23 113
38:24–39:11 . . . . 46, 114
39:1–8 45
39:12–35 . . . . 113, 348
39:16–21 348
40:1–13 114
40:1–42:14 348
41:14–42:1 114
42:1b–8 114
42:15–43:33 . . . . 113, 348
43 33
43:27 113
44:1–50:21 114
44:1–50:24 348
44–50 . . . . 18, 25
50 114

50:22–24 82
50:27–29 115
51:1–12 . . . . 115, 348–349
51:13–30 . . . . 348, 350
51:23 . . . . 37, 115
51:23–27 57

Song of the Three Jews

29–34 353
66–68 352

Tobit

3:2–6 346
3:11–15 346
4:10 44
8:5–7, 15–17 347
11:14–15 347
13:1–17 346

Wisdom of Solomon

Wisdom of Solomon 28, 111
1:1 111
1–5 . . . . 111, 25
1:6–7 111
1–9 111
4:16–5:13 111
6:1–11 18
6:1–11, 21 111
6–9 . . . . 37, 111, 112
6:16 111
6–19 26
6:22 112
7–8 48
7:1–4 111
7:18, 21, 27 46
7:21–27; 8:1 47
7:30 78
10:1–11:1 112
10–19 112
11:1–4 347
11:2–20 112
11:16 112
12 . . . . 80, 112
13:1 112
13–15 112
15:7 61
15:14 112
16 112
17 112
18 112
19:1–12 112
19:6 112
19:13–17 112
19:22 112